W9-AXC-184

MILITARY
SMALL ARMS
OF THE 20TH CENTURY

MILITARY

SMALL ARMS

OF THE 20TH CENTURY

A Comprehensive Illustrated Encyclopaedia
of the World's Small-Calibre Firearms

NEW 6TH EDITION FULLY REVISED

Ian V. Hogg
and
John Weeks

DBI BOOKS, INC.

Copyright © Ian V. Hogg and John Weeks. All rights reserved. No part of this publication may be reproduced, stored in a retrieval system or transmitted in any form by any means electrical, mechanical or otherwise without first seeking the written permission of the copyright owner and publisher.

Published in the United States by DBI Books, Inc., 4092 Commercial Ave., Northbrook, IL 60062. Printed in the United States of America.

ISBN 0-87349-120-3   Library of Congress Catalog Card Number 73-83466

Contents

Preface

Twenty-one years have now passed since the late John Weeks and I began to put together the first edition of this book, and in that time a great deal of weaponry has appeared – and disappeared. The past five years, since the last edition was published, have also seen weapons being introduced and retired, re-introduced and modified. In view of this, the opportunity has been taken of completely overhauling the text and checking it thoroughly, adding the newest weapons and discarding some which were included largely for their novelty. For this edition I have had to be more rigorous and, with one or two exceptions, exclude those weapons which never entered military service, otherwise the sheer bulk would have defeated me. The exceptions are a few weapons which, for historical reasons, must be mentioned since they were instrumental in introducing some new technical feature or tactical concept.

One of the most difficult decisions was whether to include the scores of weapons which have been put forward by hopeful inventors for possible military adoption. Experience tells me that only a few of these will ever be adopted; in the past I have included the latest designs, only to drop them out of the next edition when it has become clear that, in spite of glowing brochures from the manufacturers, only a couple of handmade tool-room prototypes ever existed. In this edition I have been very selective over the many current offerings and have included only those which appear to have some chance of survival or which are indicative of a trend and may, in modified form, become a successful weapon in due course; the latter class, for example, includes the various entrants in the American Advanced Combat Rifle programme, since although none of them may be chosen as they stand, there is every chance that one or two may see service in some slightly different form in the next century.

Looked at from the point of view of successful military adoptions, the past five years have hardly been exciting. The US Army have taken the M16A2, which is little more than the M16A1 with some improvements and a three-round burst facility instead of full automatic fire; evolution rather than revolution as one American commentator put it. The US forces finally settled upon the Beretta 92F as their service pistol, but the subsequent course of events has been strewn with lawsuits, countersuits, complaints, denials, fresh Congressional investigations, more tests . . . and the reaffirmation of the Beretta as the final choice. Nothing new has come out of Soviet Russia. The British have formally adopted the Enfield L85 rifle and L86 light support weapon and had the adoption followed by the most blood-curdling tales of defective weapons, poor quality control, and lost confidence that have been heard since the arrival of the Short Lee-Enfield back in 1903. A lot of this, it has to be said, had some substance to it, but with the move of the Royal Small Arms Factory from Enfield Lock to Nottingham opportunity has been taken to set up a completely new rifle-making facility with the latest machine tools and metrology equipment, and slowly but surely the quality has been creeping back. Unfortunately, 'A reputation once broken may possibly be repaired, but the world will always keep their eyes on the spot where the crack was,' as Josh Billings once said; it will take ten years of flawless production to live down the past five.

The assault rifle has now become a fairly standardised product, no matter from where it appears; a gas-operated, rotating bolt in bolt carrier weapon with an M16-pattern magazine interface, plastic furniture and possibly a folding metal butt. Carbine versions are generally available though they seem not to be so well liked. Perhaps the most interesting variation on the assault rifle theme is the adaptation of the basic designs to 9mm Parabellum calibre so that they function as a submachine-gun. Steyr had a head start in this because of the modular design of the AUG, which made changing barrels and other components very simple, but they have been followed by others, and perhaps the Colt, based as it is on the M16 design, stands the best chance of survival.

Submachine-guns as such seem to be going through a dull patch, though there have been occasional signs of life. One of the greatest problems here is not the matter of designing a weapon but of persuading a military force to adopt it. At least three good designs have appeared in the USA over the past five years, but in the absence of any encouragement from the military all have been, if not abandoned, at least placed in suspended animation. The big question at the moment is whether the new Uzi design, known as the Gal-Tech and to be manufactured by Sturm Ruger & Co in the USA, will attract a military following.

However, if conventional submachine-guns (whatever they may be) are not prospering, the new subdivision called 'Personal Defence Weapons' has gained ground. This area was pioneered by FN Herstal with their introduction, late in 1988, of the P-90 Personal Weapon. Here we have a futuristic design firing an entirely new calibre, and while the weapon may look peculiar and the calibre sound odd, as soon as you pick it up and start firing, the whole idea makes sense. The P-90 uses an entirely new design of 5.7mm cartridge, firing a slender, jacketed bullet at high velocity to give far better range and accuracy than the average submachine-gun and startlingly better penetration. The standard ball bullet is capable of piercing 30 layers of Kevlar armour at 100 metres' range, and a sub-calibre bullet will defeat NATO steel plate at 250 metres, which is a novelty for a hand-held weapon.

This was followed by Steyr-Mannlicher with their Tactical Machine Pistol, though this is more in the mould of the conventional submachine-gun, using normal 9mm Parabellum ammunition. It is, though, a one-hand weapon, with a folding front grip for those who require it, and it has the possibility of being modified to fire 10mm ammunition, a calibre which has been struggling for recognition for many years and which got a considerable boost when the FBI officially adopted it as their handgun calibre in late 1989. Not everyone agrees with the FBI's choice, and time will tell whether they have made the right move or merely succumbed to a fashionable whim; there are several critics who aver they would have been better off looking more closely at the .41 Action Express calibre, which has the advantage of using a cartridge case with the same rim diameter as the 9mm Parabellum, so requiring the minimum modification of a weapon to convert it.

The most recent entrant in the Personal Defence Weapon field is British, the 9mm Bushman 'Individual Defence Weapon'. This is a very compact submachine-gun which incorporates a revolutionary system of rate control, keeping the rate of fire to 450 rounds per minute instead of the 1,300+ which would be the natural cadence of the gun. This rate has been carefully selected to match the weight, balance and dynamic forces of the gun so that it merely rocks about its centre of gravity when firing and the muzzle does not rise at all. Less than eleven inches long, it can be comfortably fired at full automatic with one hand and will place all its shots in a cluster at the target, without wild rounds going into the air at the end of each burst.

The Bushman, together with some other weapons, also displays what might be called a 'new generation' system of manufacture. Ever since the demands of World War Two, gunmakers have been seeking ways to make weapons more quickly and easily, which has resulted in some remarkable applications of pressed steel, welding and synthetic materials. This system of manufacture has been due, as much as anything else, to the limitations imposed by the old-fashioned method of manufacture in which a skilled mechanic milled and carved away at a piece of steel until he had a recognisable receiver or bolt or other component. Pressing and casting cut down the time needed by this form of manufacture and, more importantly in many cases, it cut down the demand for skilled machine operators, always a scarce commodity in wartime.

In the past decade, however, the computer-controlled machine tool has become common-place, and computer-controlled automatic systems of measurement have been perfected. The degree of skill demanded from the machine operator is negligible, and is replaced by a far higher degree of skill in the man who programmes the machines. Once the machine has been programmed correctly it is simply fed with blanks and proceeds to cut, mill, plane and grind until the final article is produced, after which it is automatically measured to within a tolerance of five microns. Should any measurement indicate that the tool is blunt or out of adjustment, the measuring apparatus will automatically shut down the machine and call for a skilled tool-setter to come and adjust it.

Using this technology it becomes possible to make weapons the way they were made before 1939, out of solid steel, but at prices comparable with the pressed-metal and plastic technique. This produces a better weapon, and one which will last a good deal longer and stand up to the rough and tumble of military life. It is currently fashionable to say that the economic life of a military firearm is 25 years, but this must be seen as a comment upon the durability of the pressed-steel type of construction; Lee-Enfields, Mausers and Springfields were capable of lasting fifty or more years without serious degradation, and given that the weapon still fires reliably and accurately there is no immutable law which says it needs replacement after 25 years.

Although the 5.56mm cartridge is well on the way to replacing the 7.62mm NATO as the general non-Soviet standard round (and the Soviet 5.45mm is performing the same take-over within the Communist-armed world), there is still the same urge to discover an even smaller micro-calibre for use in assault rifles. The recent American Advanced

Combat Rifle Program has led to the revival of flechettes and multiple bullet rounds, both of which have been tried in the past and rejected. But each re-appearance brings some improvement, due to improved technology. For example, the flechette rounds of the 1960s suffered from problems with the sabots, which were necessary to fit the bore and drag the thin flechette to the muzzle. In the new designs from AAI and Steyr the sabots are made from liquid crystal polymer and apparently grip satisfactorily and discard cleanly, so improving the consistency and accuracy of the performance.

However, voices have been raised by wound ballistics experts who claim that the reduction from 7.62mm to 5.56mm to 1.5mm flechettes is merely reducing the wounding capacity of the ammunition and that while the present-day ammunition is less capable of producing disabling wounds than that of fifty or more years ago, the predicted 4.7mm bullets of the caseless family and the 1.5mm flechettes will be an even further reduction.

The whole object behind this reduction in calibre is to make the rifle more controllable by delivering a lesser recoil impulse; this improves the soldier's shooting and makes the weapon more comfortable to fire. But if this were the only consideration there would be a good argument for issuing the armies of the world with air rifles. There is a tendency today to make everything as easy as possible so that everyone can achieve excellence without having to try too hard. Unfortunately, all this does is lower the standard of excellence. Applying this concept to military rifle firing has resulted in a general level of mediocrity, since the rifle, in the endeavour to make it easy to shoot, is no longer capable of shooting excellently in the right hands. Most people can take a modern 5.56mm assault rifle and make good practise at 300 meters, but when the occasion arises for shot at 500 metres, the chances of it succeeding are remote, since the rifles and ammunition are rarely capable of consistently accurate fire at that range.

There is no easy path to military excellence; making the rifle easy to shoot does not make it more effective, and there can be no substitute for careful and rigorous training in shooting. There are, no doubt, many areas of military endeavour in which short cuts can be taken, but rifle training is not one of them, and sooner or later the decision has to be taken as to whether or not the terminal effect of the bullet is more important than the comfort of the individual firing the rifle. The object of the infantryman's rifle is to cause casualties among the enemy, and to give the soldier a less than effective weapon in order to cosset him is not doing him any service at all.

Apropos of this attitude, it is interesting to recall that one reason for turning down flechettes in the 1960s was the generation of glass-fibre dust, which constituted a health hazard, and that an objection to the present-day flechette designs, voiced by one of the US testing authorities, is the danger to the soldier from the flying sabot segments. One wonders if the people who raise these objections have the faintest conception of the conditions in which soldiers fight; being struck in the face by a tiny piece of polymer is a minor consideration when you contemplate what other missiles one is likely to be struck with during a firefight.

The section of this book covering anti-tank rifles is generally considered to be the only section which, if you like, has a measurable start and finish and is complete in itself. As John Weeks once pointed out, it would be possible to make a collection of all the world's anti-tank rifles inside quite a small room, and the entire history was over within thirty years. But the past decade has seen a sudden rivival of interest in this type of weapon, though not in the anti-tank role. Steyr-Mannlicher sum it up neatly in the title of their newest design, the 'Anti-Matériel Rifle', a weapon designed for long-range sniping not against individuals but against 'soft' and highly vulnerable high-technology targets, the loss of which can have significant effects upon the battle. Imagine, for example, a small squad of men with one of these rifles inserted into enemy territory and taking up a position a mile away from a forward fighter strip. With the contents of one magazine they can effectively disable every aircraft on the strip, abandon the gun and make their escape; the cost of the abandoned weapon is negligible in comparison to the value of the damage done, both monetary and logistic. The weapon could also be used against surveillance radars, fuel stores, computer-equipped headquarters and similar targets which can be easily and fatally disrupted by a heavy non-explosive bullet. Modern ammunition developments and modern weapon technology could take some of these elderly designs and turn them into highly effective weapons, and there seems little doubt that this is going to happen over the next few years. One interesting suggestion which has been made is that these weapons, with suitable ammunition, should be able to explode the reactive armour on modern tanks and so leave the basic tank vulnerable to attack by missiles and other heavy weapons. This development could bear watching.

I would like to thank the representatives of the various weapon manufacturers who have been good enough to provide information and photographs and, in many cases, have allowed me to examine and fire the weapons. Thanks, also, to the museums and collections which have permitted me to photograph older weapons and examine them, even though firing them has been out of the question. My hope for the future is that with the easing of tension between West and East, we shall firstly begin to learn a little more about the historical development of many Soviet weapons; and that, secondly, when the next edition is due there will perhaps be fewer additions required. Whilst my primary interest in weapons is technological, my military background ensures that I am never likely to lose sight of their primary function, and if the world becomes an easier place to live in, and the weapons designers turn to the manufacture of bicycles and garden hoes, I will still be quite happy to study the historical aspects and rejoice at the absence of new weapons.

Acknowledgements

In the course of preparing this book, the authors have sought the assistance of many individuals, manufacturers, museums and official agencies. Most responded handsomely, sending literature, photographs and information concerning the various weapons. It is with gratitude, therefore, that we record our thanks to the following:

AAI Corporation, Baltimore, USA
Accuracy International, Portsmouth, England
Mr. John Adler
Sr. Gaetano Paolo Agnini
Mr. John A. Anderson
Armi Benelli SpA, Urbino, Italy
Armscor, Pretoria, South Africa
Mr. Per Arvidsson
Astra-Unceta y Cia, Guernica, Spain
Barrett Firearms Mfg. Inc., Murfreesboro, USA
Pietro Beretta SpA, Gardone VT, Italy
V. Bernadelli SpA, Gardone VT, Italy
Breda Meccanica Bresciana SpA, Brescia, Italy
Browning SA, Liège, Belgium
M. Raymond Caranta
Ceska Zbrojovka, Uhersky Brod, Czechoslovakia
Chartered Firearms Industries, Singapore
China North Industries Corp., Beijing, China
Colt Firearms, Hartford, USA
Daewoo Precision Industries, Inchon, South Korea
Diemaco Inc., Kitchener, Ontario, Canada
Dr. Edward C. Ezell
Firearms Department, West Midlands Constabulary, Birmingham, England
Fabrica Militar de Armas Portatiles 'Domingo Matheu', Rosario, Argentine
FAMAE, Santiago, Chile
Federal Directorate of Supply & Procurement, Belgrade, Yugoslavia
FEG Arms & Gas Appliances Factory, Budapest, Hungary

FFV Ordnance, Eskilstuna, Sweden
Mr. Abraham Flateau
FN Herstal SA, Liège, Belgium
Luigi Franchi SpA, Fornaci, Italy
Col (Retd). Uzi Gal
GE Aerospace, Burlington, USA
GIAT, Versailles-Satory, France
Glock GmbH, Deutsche-Wagram, Austria
Heckler & Koch GmbH, Oberndorf/Neckar, Germany
Heckler & Koch Inc., Sterling, USA
Hellenic Arms Industry (EBO) SA, Athens, Greece
Howa Machinery Co., Aichi, Japan
IMBEL, Sao Paulo, Brazil
INDEP, Lisbon, Portugal
Indian State Arms Factory, Kanpur, India
Israel Military Industries, Ramat Hasharon, Israel
ITM AG, Solothurn, Switzerland
Llama-Gabilondo y Cia SA, Vitoria, Spain
Lyttleton Engineering Works, Lyttleton, South Africa
McDonnell-Douglas Helicopter Co., Mesa, USA
M/Sgt J. W. Maddock, USMC
Makina ve Kimya Endustrisi Kurumo, Ankara, Turkey
Dott. Ing. Franco Manassero
Mauser-Werke AG, Oberndorf/Neckar, Germany
Mekanika Industrio e Comercio Lda, Rio de Janeiro, Brazil
Productos Mendoza SA, Mexico
Mr. James Mongello
Mme. Monique Navarra
Mr. Tom Nelson
Norsk Forsvarsteknologi AS, Kongsberg, Norway
Omori Factory, Minebea Co., Tokyo, Japan
Parker-Hale Ltd, Birmingham, England
Pindad PT, Jakarta, Indonesia
Herr Walter Puhringer
Ramo Inc, Nashville, USA

ACKNOWLEDGEMENTS

Mme. Chantal Regibeaux
Remington Arms, Bridgeport, USA
Rheinmetall GmbH, Düsseldorf, Germany
Royal Military College of Science, Shrivenham, England
Royal Ordnance plc, Guns & Vehicles Division, Nottingham, England
Saco Defense Inc., Saco, USA
Sako Ltd., Jyvaskyla, Finland
Empresa Nacional Santa Barbara, Madrid, Spain
School of Infantry Museum, Warminster, England
SIG, Neuhausen-Rheinfalls, Switzerland
Sima-Cifar, Callao, Peru
SITES SpA, Turin, Italy
Mr. John Slough
Smith & Wesson Inc., Springfield, USA
Socimi SpA, Milan, Italy
Herr Wolfgang Stadler
Star-Bonifacio Echeverria y Cia, Eibar, Spain
Steyr-Mannlicher GmbH, Steyr, Austria
Mr. Eugene Stoner
Sturm, Ruger & Co., Prescott, USA
Sumitomo Heavy Industries, Tokyo, Japan
Tampeeren Asepaja Oy, Tampere, Finland
Fratelli Tanfoglio SpA, Gardone VT, Italy
Sr. Lino Tanfoglio

Dr. Martin Tuma
US Infantry Museum, Fort Benning, USA
US Marine Corps Museum, Quantico, USA
Vapensmia AS, Dokka, Norway
Mr. Stephen K. Vogel
Mr. John Walter
Carl Walther Waffenfabrik, Ulm a.d. Donau, Germany
Dr. Ingo Weise
Mr. H. J. Woodend, Curator of the MoD Pattern Room, ROF Nottingham, England
Zastava Arms, Belgrade, Yugoslavia
Dipl.Ing Fritz Zeyher

The majority of the photographs from the collections of the Pattern Room, the School of Infantry Museum and the Royal Military College of Science were photographed by the authors, who greatly value the permission granted by the various governing bodies to photograph the weapons in their care, and especial thanks are due to Mr. H. J. Woodend for his assistance in this respect. Other photographs have been provided by the various manufacturers, and our thanks are extended to them for their co-operation.

Pistols

ARGENTINA

The standard Argentine pistol in the early years of the century was the Mannlicher M1905, but in 1916 the Colt M1911 was adopted as the 'Pistola Automatica Modelo 1916' and this was later augmented by adoption of the M1911A1 as the Modelo 1927. Production of the M1927 took place in Argentina for many years. It was then decided to develop a local variation of the Colt design, which eventually appeared as the Ballester Molina (sometimes known as the 'Hafdasa' from the manufacturer's initials) in the late 1930s. It closely resembles the M1911A1, differing in the form of the hammer, the absence of a grip safety, the notching of the grips and slide, and the pivoting of the trigger instead of using a sliding action. The dimensions are slightly different, the pistol seeming to fit a small hand rather better than the Colt, and the finish is not up to Colt standards, though the pistol is reliable enough. A number of these pistols were purchased by the British in the 1940s, and were principally used to arm clandestine units.

.45in Ballester Molina

Hispano Argentino Fabrica de Automoviles SA

.45in ACP

Operation	Short recoil
Length overall	228mm (9.0in)
Weight empty	1,130g (2.49lb)
Barrel	127mm (5.0in), 6 grooves, rh twist
Magazine	7-shot detachable box
Muzzle velocity	262m/sec (860ft/sec)

AUSTRIA–HUNGARY/AUSTRIA

Like all the Mannlicher designs made by Steyr, the Model 1900 is a weapon of excellent workmanship, balance and finish which deserved a better success than it attained. The operation is unique; it is a delayed blowback pistol in which the delay is imposed by a heavy spring and cam bearing against the recoiling slide, so that the initial movement of the slide has to overcome the spring's resistance, so producing sufficient delay for the bullet to leave the muzzle. The magazine, like several other Steyr designs of the time, was a fixed unit inside the pistol grip and was loaded by pulling back the slide and inserting a charger of cartridges, then pressing them down into the magazine. A release catch on the side of the frame allowed the magazine to be emptied without having to operate the slide more than once. These pistols exhibit minor differences due to small modifications and improvements being added from time to time. Early models were made by Von Dreyse at Sommerda and carry the Von Dreyse marks but manufacture at Steyr began in 1901 and the pistols are so marked. Early models have the rear sight on the barrel, above the chamber, while later models mounted it on the rear of the slide so as to give a longer sight radius. Final production took place in 1905 and large numbers of this model were adopted by the Argentine Army, marked with the Argentine crest and 'Md 1905'. It is believed that just over 10,000 of the 1901 model, in its various forms, were made.

7.63mm Mannlicher M1901, M1905

Waffenfabrik Steyr
7.63 × 21mm Mannlicher

Operation	Delayed blowback
Length overall	246mm (9.68in)
Weight empty	910g (2lb)
Barrel	157mm (6.18in), 4 grooves, rh
Magazine	8-shot integral box (M1901) 10-shot (M1905)
Muzzle velocity	312m/sec (1,024ft/sec)

MANNLICHER M1901

BALLESTER MOLINA

8mm Roth Steyr M1907

Waffenfabrik Steyr; Femaru Fegyver es Gepgyar Rezvenytarsasag	
8 × 18.5mm Roth-Steyr	
Operation	Short recoil
Length overall	233mm (9.18in)
Weight empty	1,020g (2.25lb)
Barrel	131mm (5.18in), 4 grooves, rh
Magazine	10-round integral box
Muzzle velocity	332m/sec (1,090ft/sec)

The Roth-Steyr holds the distinction of being the first self-loading pistol ever to be adopted by a major army, having been taken into service by the Austro–Hungarian cavalry in 1908. It was later used to some extent by early Austro–Hungarian aviators, from which it became known as the 'Flieger-Pistole'. Although long obsolete it continued to be used by elements of the Italian Army until the early 1940s and some are still in use in obscure corners of the Balkans to this day, though where they get their ammunition from is a moot question. This pistol uses a most involved system of locking based upon a rotating barrel. The bolt undoubtedly qualifies as the original 'telescoped bolt' since the front portion is hollow and surrounds the entire length of the barrel inside the tubular frame. On firing, bolt and barrel move back together for about 12mm, during which time cam grooves on the bolt rotate the barrel through 90 degrees. The barrel is then halted and the bolt is free to recoil, ejecting the spent case and reloading on its return stroke. As the bolt closes up so it revolves the barrel to lock the breech and then barrel and bolt run forward into the firing position. The second unusual thing is the firing system. The operation of the bolt, either by hand or by firing, part-cocks the striker, and the cocking movement is completed by pulling the trigger, which first draws back the firing pin to full-cock and then releases it. Add to this a fixed integral box magazine which has to be loaded through the open action by means of a 10-round charger, and you have a somewhat idiosyncratic pistol. Nevertheless, some 90,000 were made before production stopped in the middle 1920s, and although odd in appearance they were well-made and reliable weapons.

9mm Steyr M1912

Osterreichische Waffenfabrik Steyr	
9 × 23mm Steyr	
Operation	Short recoil
Length overall	216mm (8.5in)
Weight empty	990g (2.19lb)
Barrel	128mm (5.1in)
Magazine	8-round integral box
Muzzle velocity	335m/sec (1,100ft/sec)

This became the Austro–Hungarian sidearm for elements other than cavalry in 1912. Like the Roth-Steyr, it used a rotating barrel to lock the breech, but the system was much simpler, using a conventional type of slide. Barrel and slide recoiled together for a short distance, during which lugs on the barrel engaged in cam grooves on the frame to turn the barrel through 20 degrees. This disengaged an upper lug from a groove in the slide, so that the barrel halted and the slide was free to recoil. The motion was reversed on the return of the slide. As with other Steyr designs the magazine is an integral box, loaded by means of a charger, and the cartridge is a unique and powerful 9mm cartridge. The 'Steyr-Hahn' (Steyr with a hammer – since it used an external hammer instead of the striker of the earlier design) was made in considerable numbers between 1911 and 1918, and was adopted in Roumania and Chile as well as being sold commercially. It remained the standard Austrian pistol after 1918, and when the Austrian Army was absorbed into the Wehrmacht in 1938 some 200,000 or so were re-barrelled to 9mm Parabellum so as to standardise with the German Army ammunition system. These are marked 'P-08' on the left side of the slide. Although the grip is somewhat square to the frame, the Model 1912 is an excellent pistol, strong and reliable, and it is possible that had it been made originally in a more common calibre it would have achieved greater success.

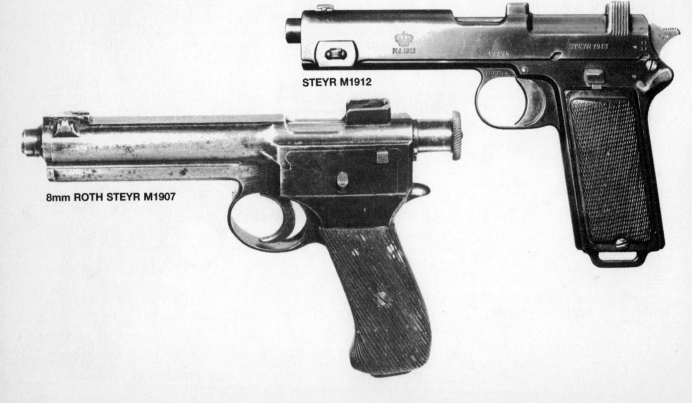

STEYR M1912

8mm ROTH STEYR M1907

This pistol was adopted by the Austrian Army in 1983, 25,000 being ordered. Thereafter it was adopted by India, Jordan, Norway, the Philippines and Thailand and has been widely sold to police forces around the world. It is a recoil-operated self-loader, using a cam-controlled dropping barrel which locks to the slide by means of a squared-off section around the breech fitting into the ejection port on the slide. Firing is by means of a striker controlled by the trigger; the first 5mm of trigger movement cocks the striker and releases the firing pin lock, and the next 2.5mm of travel releases the striker. The trigger pressure can be regulated. There is no manual safety, since the automatic firing pin lock prevents the pistol firing unless the trigger is properly operated. The Glock is of simple design, there being only 32 components, and much of the frame is of plastic material. This gave rise to much ill-informed speculation about its possible use by terrorists, but there is sufficient steel in the weapon to ensure that it can be detected by any airport X-ray machine.

The Glock 18 was developed from the Model 17 by the addition of a fire selector mechanism and enlarging the magazine capacity, turning the weapon into a machine pistol capable of automatic fire. In order to prevent unauthorised conversions, the main components of the Models 17 and 18 are not interchangeable. The basic mechanism remains the same, but the result is a somewhat larger pistol.

9mm Glock Model 17

Glock Ges.mbH	
9 × 19mm Parabellum	
Operation	Short recoil
Length overall	188mm (7.40in)
Weight empty	650g (1.44lb)
Barrel	114mm (4.49in), 6 grooves, rh
Magazine	17-shot detachable box
Muzzle velocity	350m/sec (1,148ft/sec)

9mm Glock Model 18

Glock Ges.mbH	
9 × 19mm Parabellum	
Operation	Short recoil
Length overall	223mm (8.78in)
Weight empty	636kg (1.40lb)
Barrel	114mm (4.49in), hexagonal, rh
Magazine	17-, 19-, or 33-shot detachable box
Muzzle velocity	350m/sec (1,148ft/sec)

GLOCK MODEL 17

BELGIUM

7.65mm Browning M1900

Fabrique Nationale d'Armes de Guerre

7.65 × 17mm (.32 ACP)	
Operation	Blowback
Length overall	170mm (6.75in)
Weight empty	620g (1.375lb)
Barrel	101mm (4.0in), 6 grooves, rh
Magazine	7-shot detachable box
Muzzle velocity	290m/sec (950ft/sec)

The Model 1900 was the first Browning automatic to be made by Fabrique Nationale of Herstal, the result of experimental models of 1898 and 1899, and the start of a long association between the inventor and the company. The mechanism is unusual, having a long recoil spring in a tube above the barrel, connected to the reciprocating breech-block by a lever in such a manner as to double as both a recoil spring and a firing pin spring, an elegant engineering solution which also kept the parts to a minimum. The barrel is fixed to the frame; the slide and breech-block are driven back on firing, pulling on the recoil spring. As the slide returns the striker is kept cocked by the sear, placing the recoil spring under additional compression to give the necessary motive power to the striker. Although produced in vast numbers, the Model 1900 was little used as a military weapon, since most armies, at that time, were a little suspicious of the self-loading pistol and somewhat contemptuous of such a small calibre. Some guns are known to have been used by the armies of Russia, Belgium, and possibly Holland. In addition to Fabrique Nationale's production, reputed to run into almost a million, untold numbers of cheap Chinese copies were made.

9mm Browning M1903

Fabrique Nationale d'Armes de Guerre

9 × 20SR (9mm Browning Long)	
Operation	Blowback
Length overall	203mm (8.0in)
Weight empty	910g (2lb)
Barrel	127mm (5.0in), 6 grooves, rh
Magazine	7-shot detachable box
Muzzle velocity	320m/sec (1,050ft/sec)

This is the Belgian-made version of the Browning design which was also produced as the Colt .32 and .380 pistols. Blowback operation is used, which is generally felt unwise in this calibre, but the 9mm Long Browning cartridge, though slightly longer than the 9mm Parabellum, is a weaker load and about as strong as a simple blowback will stand. A robust and accurate pistol, the Model 1903 was widely adopted throughout Europe as a police and military pistol and large numbers are still in use; the Swedish Army brought it back into service in the early 1980s when their Lahti pistols began to fail. It is also the weapon responsible for the fact that the word 'Browning' is synonymous with 'automatic pistol' in French common parlance, since the 1903 and millions of unlicensed Spanish copies flooded the commercial market in the first quarter of this century. A licensed copy was manufactured by Husqvarna Vapenfabrik in Sweden for the Swedish Army, where it is known as the Pistole M1907.

BROWNING M1903

BROWNING M1900

This model is referred to as the 1910, having been designed and marketed in that year. It was a considerable improvement upon the 1903 model, though it was less frequently copied since it demanded some rather more advanced methods of manufacture. The most important innovation was the mounting of the recoil spring around the barrel, giving the slide a tubular front end and the weapon a lighter and more handy appearance. The pistol is striker fired, and a grip safety is fitted. The Model 1910 was widely sold commercially and widely adopted in Europe as a police pistol. It was also frequently purchased by military officers as a personal weapon and was adopted in small numbers by several armies as a second-line weapon for service troops and staffs. Manufacture continued, in reduced numbers, as late as the 1960s.

7.65mm Browning M1910

Fabrique Nationale d'Armes de Guerre

7.65 × 17mm (.32 ACP) and 9 × 17mm (9mm Short)

Operation	Blowback
Length overall	152mm (6.0in)
Weight empty	600g (1.31lb)
Barrel	89mm (3.5in), 6 grooves, rh
Magazine	7-shot detachable box
Muzzle velocity	282m/sec (925ft/sec)

This is simply the Model 1910 with the barrel lengthened in order to improve velocity and accuracy and with the frame and slide similarly lengthened, and with a larger magazine capacity. The 1910 pattern slide was extended by attaching a nose-piece by means of a bayonet joint, so as to utilise existing machinery and stocks, a sensible measure which had been adopted by Walther some years before in similar circumstances. In either of its calibres, the 1910/22 was widely adopted by European police and military forces, and in 1940 it was adopted as a substitute standard weapon by the German Air Force as the Pistole 626(b). The weapon is striker fired and uses a grip safety in a similar manner to the 1910. The armies of Greece, Turkey, Holland, France and Yugoslavia were among those that adopted the 1910/22 as a service pistol.

7.65mm Browning M1910/22

Fabrique Nationale d'Armes de Guerre

7.65 × 17mm (.32 ACP) and 9 × 17mm (9mm Short/.380 ACP)

Operation	Blowback
Length overall	178mm (7.0in)
Weight empty	730g (1.56lb)
Barrel	114mm (4.50in), 6 grooves, rh
Magazine	9-shot detachable box
Muzzle velocity	266m/sec (875ft/sec) (9mm Short)

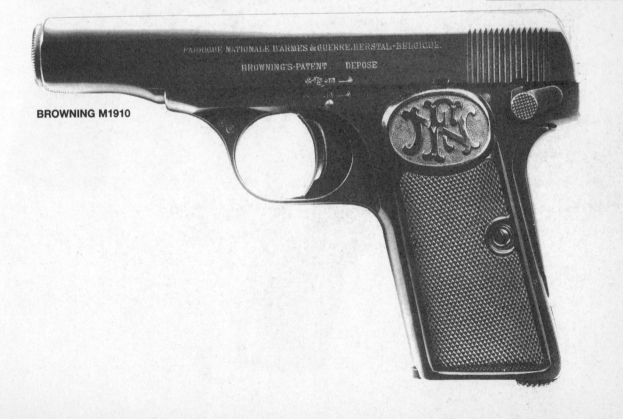

BROWNING M1910

9mm Browning GP35 (High Power)

Fabrique Nationale d'Armes de Guerre

9 × 19mm Parabellum

Operation	Short recoil
Length overall	197mm (7.75in)
Weight empty	990g (2.19lb)
Barrel	118mm (4.65in), 4 grooves, rh
Magazine	13-shot detachable box
Muzzle velocity	335m/sec (1,110ft/sec)

9mm Browning Mk 2

Fabrique Nationale d'Armes de Guerre

9 × 19mm Parabellum

Frequently called 'John Browning's last design', this pistol was originally developed by him between 1914 and 1926, when he died; after that it was taken over by Dieudonné Saive, FN's chief designer, who was responsible for turning it into a hammer fired weapon (instead of Browning's striker) and giving it a 13-shot double-row magazine. Due to the Depression, it was not put into production until 1935, whereupon it was adopted by Belgium, Latvia, Lithuania and China, but no more than about 35,000 were made before the outbreak of war. In 1940 the FN factory was commandeered by the Germans and the pistol was thereafter manufactured for the German Army as the Pistole 640(b). The design was smuggled to Britain and put into production in Canada for the Canadian and Chinese armies, and was also adopted by the British Army for Commando and Airborne forces. After the war FN went back into production and it was formally adopted by the British Army in 1954 to replace the .38 revolver. After this some 55 other countries adopted the pistol. The GP35 is the logical step from Browning's Colt M1911 design. He changed the trigger system to use a sear bar in the slide, and replaced the Colt's swinging link with a shaped cam, but the action, that of dropping the barrel out of engagement with the slide, is the same. Early models came in two forms; one with fixed sights, the other with an optimistic tangent sight marked to 500 metres and an attachable shoulder stock. This latter was favoured by the Chinese, but was not used to any extent elsewhere and was dropped shortly after production was resumed in 1947. It has proved a highly reliable and serviceable pistol in military hands; commercial models for target shooting were also made, but these were not widely adopted because the trigger mechanism did not lend itself to fine tuning.

This was a slightly improved version of the original GP35 pistol, introduced in the early 1980s. It adopted an ambidextrous safety catch, a new design of grip, wider sights and an anti-glare finish. It was purchased by a number of military forces, but in relatively small numbers and in the face of very strong competition from more modern designs. There were also complaints of failures from some quarters, which led FN to withdraw it in 1987 and set about retooling their production line and developing the Mark 3 (below). The dimensions and data are exactly the same as those for the GP35.

BROWNING 9mm HP

BROWNING 9mm Mk2

These pistols were introduced in January 1989 and are essentially the Browning Mk 2 but manufactured to a higher standard, using new computer-controlled machinery, and with new dimensions of the frame and slide and a re-dimensioned ejection port. The rear sight is now mounted in a dovetailed slot which is to the same dimensions as that of the Target GP35s so that owners wishing to improve the sights can easily have the target sights fitted. There are also recesses for the addition of Tritium night sighting spots alongside the rear sight and in the front sight blade. The safety catch is ambidextrous and the grips are newly designed to a better anatomical shape. The Mark 3 is the standard single-action weapon; the Mark 3S is a special version produced for police use and incorporates an automatic firing pin safety system in which the firing pin is positively locked against any movement except during the final pressure of the trigger. A mechanism linked to the sear bar then releases the firing pin in time for it to be struck by the falling hammer. The Mark 3S is produced under the Browning name, since in late 1988 the company was re-organised into two sections: FN Herstal SA deals with military business, while Browning SA attends to police and commercial sales. Within six months of its announcement, 25,000 of the Mark 3S had been sold to European police forces.

9mm Browning Mk 3 and 3S

FN Herstal SA (Mk 3)
Browning SA (Mk 3S)

9 × 19mm Parabellum

The BDA 9 is a further development of the High-Power and functions in the same way, differing in having a double-action trigger and a hammer de-cocking lever in place of the safety catch. The de-cocking lever is duplicated on both sides of the frame and can thus be used with either hand. The magazine release is normally fitted for right-hand use but can easily be removed and reversed to suit left-handed use. The pistol is loaded in the usual manner by pulling back and releasing the slide. It can then be fired or, by pressing the de-cocking lever, the hammer can be lowered. Operation of the lever inserts a safety device between the hammer and the firing pin, and a braking lever slows down the hammer's fall. There is also an automatic firing pin safety system which keeps the firing pin securely locked except during the final movement of the trigger when firing. Once the hammer has been lowered the pistol can be carried with a round in the chamber in perfect safety and can be instantly fired by simply pulling the trigger through.

9mm FN BDA 9

FN Herstal SA

9 × 19mm Parabellum

Operation	Short recoil
Length overall	200mm (7.87in)
Weight empty	905g (1.995lb)
Barrel	118mm (4.65in), 6 grooves, rh
Magazine	14-shot detachable box
Muzzle velocity	350m/sec (1,148ft/sec)

9mm FN BDA9

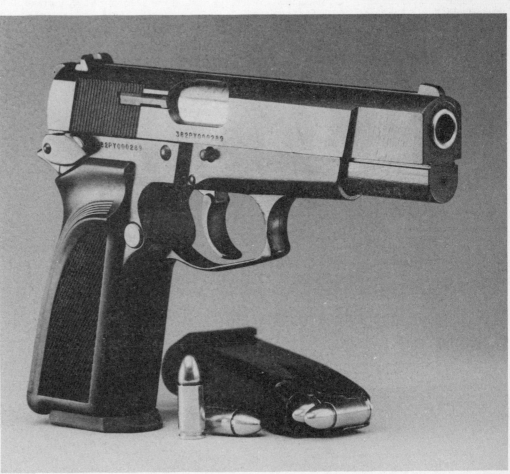

CHINA, PEOPLE'S REPUBLIC

7.62mm Type 51

State arsenals

7.62 × 25mm Soviet

This is simply a Chinese-manufactured copy of the Soviet Tokarev TT-33 pistol. The only observable difference, other than the markings in Chinese ideograms, lies in the external machining, the finger grip grooves on the slide being narrow and more numerous than those on the Soviet model.

7.65mm Type 64

State arsenals

7.62 × 17mm rimless	
Operation	Blowback
Length overall	222mm (8.74in)
Weight empty	1,810g (4.0lb)
Barrel	95mm (3.74in)
Magazine	9-shot detachable box
Muzzle velocity	205m/sec (672ft/sec)

This pistol is a most unusual design. Basically it is a simple blowback weapon but with the addition of a permanently attached Maxim-pattern silencer as part of the basic construction. The frame unit carries the bulbous silencer, formed of a wire mesh cylinder surrounded by perforated metal sleeves and containing a number of rubber discs through which the bullet passes. The result is to trap the gases emerging from the end of the short barrel and, by the internal baffling, reduce their eventual emergent velocity so that little or no noise results.

The rear section of the frame carries a short reciprocating slide which functions in the usual way to reload the pistol and carry the firing pin and extractor. However, this slide has a rotating-lug bolt head which, when maximum silence is required, can be turned by a manual catch so as to lock the slide to the receiver. Thus on firing there is no noisy movement of the slide, and after firing, at some convenient time and place when noise is no longer important, the slide can be unlocked and drawn back by hand to extract and eject the spent case and reload. When a lesser degree of silence is acceptable the manual catch can be pushed across to hold the bolt, lugs out of engagement, whereupon the slide functions in the normal blowback fashion.

It should be noted that the cartridge used with this pistol is unique; known as the 'Type 64', it is of the same appearance and dimensions as the common 7.65mm ACP round, but is in fact rimless rather than semi-rimmed and is loaded to a somewhat lower velocity. Normal 7.65mm ACP will not chamber in this pistol and cannot be used.

7.65mm Type 67

State arsenals

7.62 × 17mm rimless	
Operation	Blowback
Length overall	225mm (8.86in)
Weight empty	1,020g (2.25lb)
Barrel	89mm (3.5in)
Magazine	9-shot detachable box
Muzzle velocity	181m/sec (594ft/sec)

The Type 67 pistol is an improved version of the Type 64 described above. The improvement is simply a matter of making the silencer in a cylindrical form, more slender and lighter than that of the Type 64, which makes the pistol easier to carry in a holster and better balanced. The mechanism is exactly the same, and there are some minor changes in the assembly of the internal parts of the silencer though the system of operation remains the same.

TYPE 67

The design of this pistol is based upon that of the Mauser Model 712 (System Westinger) 'Schnellfeuerpistole' of 1932–36, several thousand of which were sold to China. The Type 80 uses the same basic mechanism, an internal reciprocating bolt which locks to the barrel extension by means of lugs and an external hammer striking a firing pin in the bolt. The magazine is ahead of the trigger guard in Mauser style but is removable and is noticeably sloped forward, probably to improve the feed. The grip angle has also been improved and there are minor changes in the external contours. A clip-on telescopic buttstock is provided, as is a bayonet, and with the stock attached the weapon is said to give good accuracy to a range of 150 metres.

Apart from small differences in weight and dimensions, the Type 59 pistol is a copy of the Soviet Makarov PM pistol, a blowback design with double action derived from the Walther PP. It is standard issue in the Chinese armed forces and is also offered for export.

7.62mm Machine Pistol Type 80

State arsenals	
7.62 × 25mm Soviet	
Operation	Short recoil, selective fire
Length overall	300mm (11.81in) (without stock)
Weight empty	1,100g (2.43lb)
Barrel	n/a
Magazine	10- or 20-shot detachable box
Cyclic rate	n/a
Muzzle velocity	470m/sec (1,542ft/sec)

9mm Pistol Type 59

State arsenals	
9 × 18mm Makarov	
Operation	Blowback
Length overall	162mm (6.37in)
Weight empty	730g (1.61lb)
Barrel	93.5mm (3.68in)
Magazine	8-shot detachable box
Muzzle velocity	314m/sec (1,030ft/sec)

TYPE 80

CZECHOSLOVAKIA

9mm VZ22, VZ24

Ceskoslovenska Zbrojovka, Brno Ceska Zbrojovka, Strakonice	
9 × 17mm Short	
Operation	Short recoil
Length overall	152mm (6.0in)
Weight empty	700g (1.5lb)
Barrel	91mm (3.55in), 6 grooves, rh
Magazine	80-shot detachable box
Muzzle velocity	295m/sec (970ft/sec)

This pistol was originally designed by Josef Nickl, an employee of Mauser, but the company decided not to develop the design. Nickl was then sent to Brno to assist in starting production of Mauser rifles for the Czech Army, and while there found that the Czechs were also seeking a pistol. He re-designed his pistol for 9mm Short cartridges and, after some testing, it was accepted as the VZ/22. About 15,000 were made, but production was slow and in 1924 the army shifted production to Strakonice, where mass production facilities were available. There another 20,000 were made before manufacture ceased in about 1926. The VZ/22 was unnecessarily complicated, using a rotating barrel to lock the breech. It was well made but otherwise had no particular virtues. The VZ/24 was a slight modification, largely due to the different manufacturing techniques employed at Strakonice. Assembly was slightly easier, a magazine safety was added, and, on later models, the wooden grips were replaced by hard rubber. Over 180,000 of these models were made, some of which were supplied to Lithuania, and it remained in production until the late 1930s.

7.65mm VZ27

Ceska Zbrojovka, Strakonice	
7.65 × 17mm	
Operation	Blowback
Length overall	158mm (6.25in)
Weight empty	700g (1.54lb)
Barrel	100mm (3.9in)
Magazine	8-shot detachable box
Muzzle velocity	280m/sec (918ft/sec)

In about 1926 Frantisek Myska set about changing the design of the VZ/24 to make it simpler. His principal change was to reduce the calibre to 7.65mm and do away with the rotating barrel breech lock so as to turn it into a simple blowback weapon. This became the VZ/27 and it was issued to Czech police and treasury guards and other official agencies as well as being exported. The principal visual differences between the VZ/22/24 and VZ/27 are that the locked breech design has the finger grip grooves on the slide vertical, while the blowback weapon has them slanted forward. The VZ/27 also has a longer barrel which protrudes some distance in front of the slide. Production of the VZ/27 continued after the German occupation of Czechoslovakia; original models are marked 'CESKA ZBROJOVKA AS V PRAZE' and have wooden butt grips, while those made after 1938 are marked 'BOHMISCHE WAFFENFABRIK PRAG' and have plastic grips. The German Armed forces took the VZ/27 into use as the Pistole 27(t). Production was resumed after the war, these later models being distinguished by the marking 'NARODNI PODNIK'.

CZ22

CZ27

In 1936 the Czech Ministry of National Defence directed the Armaments Department of the Military Technical Aviation Institute to begin the design of a completely new pistol to replace the VZ/24, demanding a weapon 'which will ensure maximum readiness and safety in the simplest possible way'. First models were tested early in 1937 and the design was approved for service as the VZ/38 in June 1938. A contract for 41,000 was placed, but no pistols were issued to Czech troops before the German occupation and the entire subsequent production of perhaps 12,000 pistols was taken by the German armed forces. The VZ/38 is not a good pistol; it is clumsy to hold and point, and the trigger mechanism is a self-cocking system demanding a heavy pull, so that accurate shooting is out of the question. Its sole virtue lies in its simple dismantling system. Releasing a catch allows the barrel and slide to hinge up at the muzzle so that the slide can be pulled from the barrel, making cleaning very easy. It is well-made, of good materials, but is otherwise an object lesson in designing a weapon with theoretical advantages in view but with practical operation kept as a secondary consideration.

The CZ50 is no more than a slightly modified copy of the Walther PP, developed on the orders of the Czech Ministry of the Interior for police and security force use. There are slight differences in the shape of the frame and trigger guard, the grip is slightly changed and the contour of the hammer is different from the original Walther. The biggest change is in the positioning of the safety catch on the left side of the frame instead of on the slide. In this position it works directly on the lockwork instead of demanding some rather complex machining and fitting of operating pins in the slide, which simplified manufacture. The double-action lockwork of the Walther was retained, and, in all, one feels that the changes were for change's sake rather than to add any improvement to the basic design. The CZ50 acquired a poor reputation for reliability and was reworked into the CZ70, which was issued in 1969. The differences are small, though important, matters of internal dimensions and improved materials, and the appearance of the pistol was unchanged except for the markings and the pattern on the grips. Production ceased in 1983.

9mm VZ38

Ceska Zbrojovka, Strakonice	
9 × 17mm Short	
Operation	Blowback
Length overall	206mm (8.1in)
Weight empty	940g (2.07lb)
Barrel	118mm (4.65in), 6 grooves, rh
Magazine	8-shot detachable box
Muzzle velocity	300m/sec (984ft/sec)

7.65mm CZ50 and CZ70

Ceska Zbrojovka, Strakonice	
7.65 × 17mm (.32 ACP)	
Operation	Blowback
Length overall	167mm (6.6in)
Weight empty	660g (1.45lb)
Barrel	94mm (3.75in), 6 grooves, rh
Magazine	8-shot detachable box
Muzzle velocity	280m/sec (920ft/sec)

CZ38

7.62mm VZ52

Ceska Zbrojovka, Strakonice	
7.62 × 25mm Soviet	
Operation	Short recoil
Length overall	209mm (8.23in)
Weight empty	960g (2.11lb)
Barrel	120mm (4.72in)
Magazine	8-shot detachable box
Muzzle velocity	457m/sec (1,500ft/sec)

9mm CZ75 and CZ85

Ceska Zbrojovka, Uhersky Brod	
9 × 19mm Parabellum	
Operation	Short recoil
Length overall	203mm (8.0in)
Weight empty	980g (2.16lb)
Barrel	120mm (4.72in), 6 grooves, rh
Magazine	15-shot detachable box
Muzzle velocity	338m/sec (1,110ft/sec)

Immediately after the war the Czech Army demanded a new pistol; the first solution was to revive the VZ/38, using the 7.62mm Soviet pistol cartridge, but this was hopeless, since it meant a total redesign in order to lock the breech. This idea was abandoned and after much discussion and testing the vz/52 was adopted. It was a considerable improvement over its predecessors, but over-complicated for what it had to do. The VZ/52 is a recoil-operated pistol with an unusual locking system which appears to be based upon a Mauser patent of 1910, modified along lines first explored in Poland and later incorporated into the MG42 machine-gun. Two rollers lock the barrel and slide together during a short recoil stroke and are then cammed out of engagement with the slide allowing the slide to recoil fully, extract, return, and chamber a fresh round. As the new round is chambered so the locking rollers are once again forced outwards into engagement.

This pistol, introduced in 1975, is rated by many authorities as one of the best combat pistols in current production. Chambered for the 9mm Parabellum cartridge it is obviously not for Czech military service, since they adhere to Warsaw Pact calibres, but it has been adopted by some elements of the Czech police and has been widely exported for police and military use. The CZ75 is a recoil operated weapon using the Colt-Browning dropping barrel, actuated by a shaped cam below the breech. The trigger mechanism is double-action, but the safety catch is positioned on the left side of the frame and locks the hammer linkage. The magazine is a double-column type holding 15 rounds, and a further round can be loaded into the chamber. The CZ85

CZ50

CZ52

is an updated version; in size, shape and general appearance it retains all the best features of the CZ75 but the manual safety catch and slide stop have been remodelled to permit ambidextrous operation. The top of the slide has been ribbed, to reduce reflection, and small internal mechanical changes have been made to improve the action.

CZ75

This is a conventional blowback pistol, with ambidextrous safety catch and magazine catch. The double action trigger mechanism includes an automatic safety system which blocks movement of the hammer until the trigger is fully pressed. The trigger guard is used for dismantling, in the Walther manner, but is interlocked with the magazine so that the pistol cannot be stripped unless the magazine has been removed and the magazine cannot be re-inserted unless the trigger guard is in the closed and locked position. The CZ83 has been issued to police and security forces in Czechoslovakia and also as a second-line armed forces weapon. It is also manufactured in 9mm Short and 9mm Makarov calibres.

7.65mm CZ83

Ceska Zbrojovka, Uhersky Brod

7.65 × 17mm (.32 ACP)	
Operation	Blowback
Length overall	173mm (6.81in)
Weight empty	650g (1.43lb)
Barrel	96mm (3.78in), 6 grooves, rh
Magazine	15-shot detachable box
Muzzle velocity	320m/sec (1,050ft/sec)

CZ83

DENMARK

9mm Bergmann-Bayard M1910, M1910/21

Anciens Etablissements Pieper, Liège
Haerens Tojhus, Copenhagen

9 × 23mm Bergmann-Bayard

Operation	Short recoil
Length overall	254mm (10.0in)
Weight empty	1,020g (2.25lb)
Barrel	101mm (4.0in), 6 grooves, lh
Magazine	10-shot detachable box
Muzzle velocity	395m/sec (1,300ft/sec)

This pistol was one of many designed by Theodor Bergmann in the early years of the century, although he only manufactured a small number – less than 2,000 – before, in 1907, the manufacturing rights were acquired by Pieper. Originally known as the Bergmann 'Mars', Pieper re-named it the 'Bayard Modèle 1908 (later, 1910)', but such was the influence of the designer's name that it is invariably called the Bergmann-Bayard. Bergmann had initially begun supplying the Spanish government in 1905, and this contract was fulfilled by Pieper, although some details of the pistol were changed; the barrel became slightly longer, forged integrally with the barrel extension, and the rifling was changed from the original 4-groove right-hand twist to 6-groove left-hand. The pistol was also adopted by the Greek Army at this time. After having been tested by various governments in a variety of calibres, the pistol was adopted in 1911 by the Danish Army as the Pistol M/10, made under contract by Pieper. The supply was terminated by World War One and in 1922 the Danes decided to make their own. This differed from the original Pieper issues by the use of large wooden or plastic grips and by having the lock cover-plate retained by a screw instead of by a spring catch. They were marked 'm 1910/21' with Danish inscriptions, and most of the original Pieper weapons were refurbished to 1922 standard by the addition of the larger grips and these were also marked 'm 1910/21' but still bore the original Belgian markings. The layout of the pistol, although vaguely reminiscent of the Mauser C/96, is a logical development of earlier Bergmann designs and owes nothing to Mauser. The great difference between this pistol and its forerunners is the use of a much more powerful cartridge and a positive breech locking system. The bolt is locked by a hollow locking block, which engages in slots in the bolt and is supported by a ramp in the frame. On firing, barrel and bolt recoil slightly until this block rides down the ramp and unlocks the bolt, which is then free to move back while the barrel is held. Another refinement absent from earlier Bergmann designs is a firing pin withdrawal spring which keeps the point of the pin inside the bolt during reloading.

9mm BERGMANN-BAYARD M1910

EGYPT

This is no more than a slightly improved copy of the Soviet TT33 Tokarev pistol, manufactured by FEG of Budapest and in 9mm Parabellum calibre, for use by the Egyptian armed forces. The changes to the original design are little more than skin deep: a better-shaped plastic one-piece butt grip, and a better quality of manufacture and finish than that usually found on the Soviet product. A safety catch has been added. The principal change is the adoption of a more common calibre, resulting in a very practical weapon. However, the Egyptian armed forces expressed dissatisfaction with the weapon and the contract was terminated before completion, those pistols delivered being used by the Egyptian police.

9mm Tokagypt 58

Femaru es Gazkeszuelekgyara NV, Budapest

9 × 19mm Parabellum	
Operation	Short recoil
Length overall	194mm (7.65in)
Weight empty	910g (2.01lb)
Barrel	114mm (4.5in), 6 grooves, rh
Magazine	7-shot detachable box
Muzzle velocity	350m/sec (1,150ft/sec)

FINLAND

This pistol takes its name from its designer, Aimo Lahti, and was officially adopted by the Finnish Army in 1935, replacing a Parabellum type. It was later adopted by Sweden as their m/40 pattern. The L/35 is exceptionally well-made and finished and is particularly well sealed against the ingress of dirt; as a result it has shown itself to be remarkably reliable in sub-zero conditions, even if a little heavy by today's standards. An unusual design feature of the Lahti is the provision of an accelerator, a device more usually found in machine guns, which is used to increase the rearward velocity of the bolt so as to ensure positive functioning in poor conditions. A drawback is the impossibility of stripping the gun completely for cleaning or repairs without the services of a trained armourer and access to a workshop, but against this it should be said that the likelihood of components breaking or wearing out is so remote that the Finns were prepared to take their chances. The Swedish weapon (which see) is less robust. Although it resembles the Parabellum, the action is more akin to a Mauser or Bergmann, with a bolt moving inside the barrel extension and locked by lugs beneath.

9mm Lahti L/35

Valtion Kivaaritehdas (VKT), Jyvaskyla

9 × 19mm Parabellum	
Operation	Short recoil
Length overall	245mm (9.68in)
Weight empty	1,220g (2.69lb)
Barrel	120mm (4.7in), 6 grooves, rh
Magazine	8-shot detachable box
Muzzle velocity	350m/sec (1,150ft/sec)

TOKAGYPT

LAHTI M35

FRANCE

8mm Modèle d'Ordonnance Mle 1892

Various state factories	
8 × 27.5mm Mle 92	
Operation	Six-shot revolver
Length overall	236mm (9.36in)
Weight empty	840g (1.85lb)
Barrel	117mm (4.6in), 6 grooves, rh
Magazine	6-shot cylinder
Muzzle velocity	228m/sec (750ft/sec)

The Modèle 1892 is generally referred to as the 'Lebel', though there is some doubt as to whether Nicolas Lebel really had much to do with the design which was developed at the State arsenal of St Etienne. It was introduced in 1893 and remained in use until 1945 due to the lack of sufficient replacements. The Mle 92 is a solid-frame, six-shot, side-opening revolver of fairly conventional form, one unusual feature being that the cylinder swings open to the right. It has a double-action lock, the workings of which can be examined by opening up the left-hand plate of the frame, which is hinged at its forward end. It appears to have a loading gate on the right-hand side of the frame, but this is actually a release lever for the cylinder locking system. The Mle 92 was a sound enough revolver, but its principal defect was the small cartridge it fired, selected, it seems, as a measure of standardisation since the French had recently adopted 8mm as their rifle calibre. It remained in police use for several years after being dropped by the Army.

7.65mm Modèle 1935A, 1935S

Manufacture d'Armes de Châtellerault (MAC); Manufacture d'Armes de St Etienne (MAS); Manufacture d'Armes de Tulle (MAT); Société Alsacienne de Construction Mécanique (SACM); Société d'Applications Générales, Electriques et Mécaniques (SAGEM)	
7.65 × 19.5mm Longue	
Operation	Short recoil
Length overall	189mm (7.45in)
Weight empty	730g (1.61lb)
Barrel	109mm (4.3in), 4 grooves, rh
Magazine	8-shot detachable box
Muzzle velocity	305m/sec (1,000ft/sec)

After World War One the St Etienne arsenal began exploring an automatic pistol and canvassed several makers for designs, finally selecting one developed by SACM. This was a design by Charles Petter, an enigmatic Swiss, and was little more than a modification of the existing Browning/Colt swinging link system, the principal difference being the construction of the firing lockwork in a removable module. Other differences include a somewhat different method of housing the recoil spring, provision of a magazine safety and a safety catch on the slide. A variant known as the 1935S changed the barrel locking system by forming a single lug on the barrel which locked into the ejection port. This version is recognisable by its straight butt and slightly protruding muzzle, whereas the 1935A has a curved butt and the muzzle flush with the front of the slide. The 1935S was developed in 1938 as being easier to mass produce and was made by all the four factories noted above; the 1935A was only made by SACM. Rarely seen outside France or French possessions, these are sound enough pistols but were chambered for a weak cartridge, the French 7.65mm Long, which was peculiar to the French Army.

8mm MODELE D'ORDONNANCE M1892

MODELE 1935A

The only real defect of the Mle 1935 pistol was its ammunition, and when, after World War Two, the French Army demanded a new pistol, St Etienne took the obvious course and re-designed the Mle 1935 to chamber the standard 9mm Parabellum cartridge. It retained the Petter-designed cross-bolt safety of the 1935A, since the users were familiar with it, and it also retained the magazine safety device, which is of dubious utility in a combat pistol. Introduced in 1951, the pistol can still be found in service in small numbers.

9mm Modèle 1950

Manufacture d'Armes de St Etienne Manufacture d'Armes de Châtellerault	
9 × 19mm Parabellum	
Operation	Short recoil
Length overall	192mm (7.6in)
Weight empty	680g (1.50lb)
Barrel	112mm (4.4in), 4 grooves, rh
Magazine	9-shot detachable box
Muzzle velocity	335m/sec (1,100ft/sec)

This French company had manufactured pistols since 1921, principally under the trade-name 'Unique', and the PA-15 was essentially a militarised version of their commercial 'Unique Modèle R Para'. In its original form the Modèle R fired the 7.65mm ACP cartridge, and upgrading it to handle 9mm Parabellum demanded some form of breech locking. In order to make as few manufacturing changes as possible it was decided to adopt a form of delayed blowback operation similar to that employed in the Savage pistol. The barrel is mounted in the frame so as to be free to rotate but not recoil; a cam on the barrel engages in a curved track in the slide. Recoil of the slide attempts to rotate the barrel by forcing the cam to conform to the curved track, but this is resisted by the initial gas pressure and the rotational torque of the bullet in the rifling. This is sufficient to hold the breech closed until the bullet is clear of the muzzle and the breech pressure has dropped, whereupon the barrel is free to rotate and the slide can move back in the usual manner. The standard PA-15 carries a 15-shot magazine in the butt; a small number of a variant known as the PA-8 exist, using an 8-shot magazine. This is, in fact, the commercial 'R Para' with military acceptance marks. A Modèle PAPF-1 also exists; this has the barrel and slide lengthened and is fitted with an adjustable

9mm Mab PA-15

Manufacture d'Armes de Bayonne	
9 × 19mm Parabellum	
Operation	Delayed blowback
Length overall	203mm (8.0in)
Weight empty	1,070g (2.36lb)
Barrel	114mm (4.49in), 6 grooves, rh
Magazine	15-shot box
Muzzle velocity	335m/sec (1,100ft/sec)

MAS MODELE 1950

rear sight. It is used solely as a target pistol. The Manufacture d'Armes de Bayonne went out of business in the middle 1980s and the PA-15 is no longer in production, though still in French service.

.357 Manurhin MR73

Manufacture des Machines du Haut-Rhin (Manurhin)	
.357 Magnum; .38 Special (9mm Parabellum with special cylinder)	
Operation	Double-action revolver
Length overall	195mm (7.67in)
Weight empty	880g (1.94lb)
Barrel	63.5mm (2.5in)
Magazine	6-shot cylinder
Muzzle velocity	Variable according to cartridge

The MR73 is a revolver which is intended to fulfil the requirements of a wide range of users. With a long target barrel it is a precision pistol for competitive shooting. With shorter barrels it becomes a military and police weapon. The design has been carefully thought out and incorporates some new features, particularly in regard to safety and trigger operation. In general terms the revolver is a solid-frame wing-cylinder type of double or single action. The outer contours are smoothed and the foresight is sloped to allow for easy drawing from pocket or holster. The barrel is cold-hammered – unusual in a pistol. There is the usual flat mainspring controlling the hammer, but the trigger is controlled by a separate flat spring which is strong enough to overcome the first one. This second spring works on a roller to decrease friction, and its main purpose is to move the trigger forward after firing and to move the safety block up to prevent the hammer from reaching the cartridge cap. The roller acts on this spring in such a way as to produce a practically constant pressure, so giving a steady pull on the trigger. By changing the cylinder 9mm rimless ammunition can be loaded, the change taking no more than a minute or two. In 1989 it was announced that the Manurhin pistol-making facility is to be taken over by FN Herstal SA, so it is probable that these pistols will in future appear under the Browning name. (Data table refers to the 63.5mm (2.5in) barrel model.)

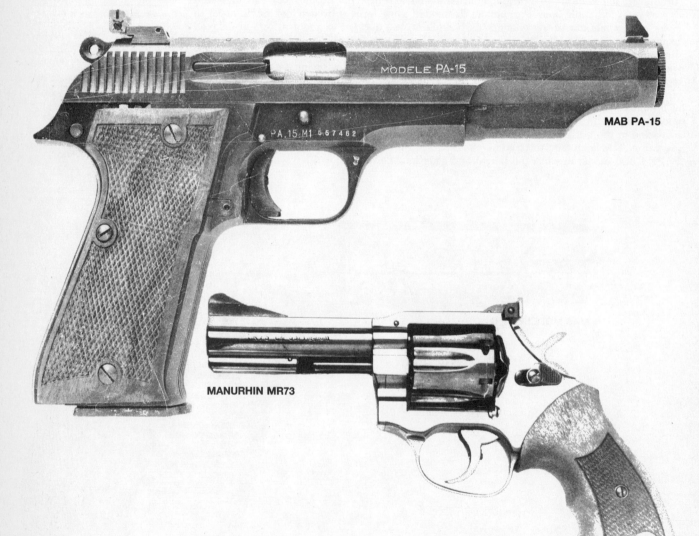

MAB PA-15

MANURHIN MR73

GERMANY (Pre-1945)

These revolvers are the designs approved by the various commissions which were charged, in the late 1870s, with providing new weapons for the German Army. In view of the number of advanced revolver designs available at that time the Reichs Revolver was remarkably conservative, reflecting the viewpoint of most contemporary military authorities. The two models differed principally in barrel length, the M79 (also known as the 'Trooper' or 'Cavalry' model) having a 178mm (7in) barrel and the M83 (also known as the 'Officers' or 'Infantry' model) having a 127mm (5in) barrel. Apart from that they were normally found as solid frame, single-action, non-ejecting six-shot revolvers of robust construction. Loading was done through a gate on the right side, the hammer being pulled back to half-cock to free the cylinder. Ejection of spent cases or unloading, was done by simply withdrawing the cylinder axis pin and removing the cylinder, then using the pin to punch out the cases or cartridges. Although superseded in 1908 by the Parabellum pistol, numbers of these revolvers remained in second-line service throughout World War One, and sufficient remained in private hands to make it worth one manufacturer's while to market ammunition commercially until 1939.

10.6mm Reichs Revolver

Various manufacturers including:
V. C. Schilling & Cie;
Spangenburg & Sauer;
C. G. Haenel & Cie;
Gebruder Mauser & Cie;
Königlich Gewehrfabrik, Erfurt

10.6 × 25mm Deutsche Ordonnance

Model 1879:

Operation	Single-action revolver
Length overall	310mm (12.2in)
Weight empty	1,040g (2.29lb)
Barrel	183mm (97.2in)
Magazine	6-shot cylinder
Muzzle velocity	205m/sec (670ft/sec)

Model 1883:

Operation	Single-action revolver
Length overall	260mm (10.25in)
Weight empty	940g (2.07lb)
Barrel	126mm (4.96in)
Magazine	6-shot cylinder
Muzzle velocity	195m/sec (640ft/sec)

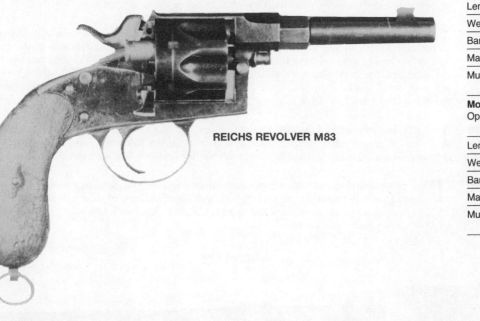

REICHS REVOLVER M83

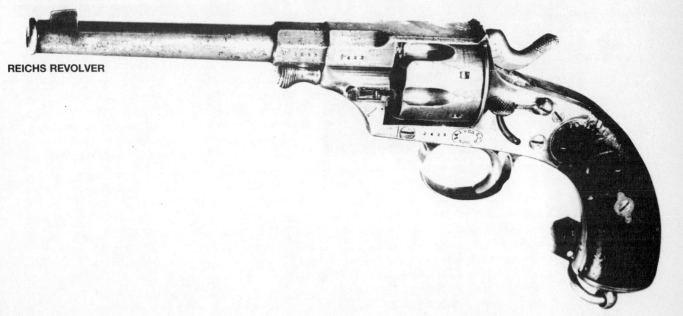

REICHS REVOLVER

7.63mm Mauser C/96

Waffenfabrik Mauser AG	
7.63 × 25mm Mauser	
Operation	Short recoil
Length overall	312mm (12.25in)
Weight empty	1,250g (2.75lb)
Barrel	139mm (5.5in), 4 or 6 grooves, rh
Magazine	10-shot integral box
Muzzle velocity	434m/sec (1,425ft/sec)

The Mauser Selbstladepistole C/96 was apparently invented by the three Feederle brothers, employees of Mauser, probably in 1894, and was patented in 1895 under Peter Paul Mauser's name. The prototype, chambered for the 7.65mm Borchardt cartridge, with a 10-shot magazine and a spur hammer, was made in the first months of 1895 and first fired on 15 March. The rest of 1895 was spent testing more prototypes in complete secrecy until in January 1896 Mauser began manufacture of 'pre-production' pistols, of which about 100 were made. These came in a variety of forms with magazines of various sizes, all of which were integral with the frame and clip-loaded through the top of the action. True production began in October 1896, when the design was finalised around the 7.63mm Mauser cartridge, which was really no more than the 7.65mm Borchardt with the bullet more securely anchored and a somewhat heavier loading. Assorted sizes of magazine – 6, 10 and 20 rounds – were provided, though the 20-round model was soon abandoned. At the start of 1897 a mechanical change was made when a supplementary locking lug was added to the underside of the bolt and several minor modifications were made to the mechanism. The C/96 failed to attract the favourable attention of the German military authorities and, with the emergence of the Parabellum, Mauser's chances receded. C/96 pistols were, however, supplied to the Regia Marina d'Italia and to Turkey, Persia and Russia. Almost all C/96 pistols were capable of being fitted to a hollowed wooden shoulder-stock/holster, with which they were often supplied.

Selbstladepistole C/96 mit Sicherung C/02

In 1902 Mauser attempted to improve the C/96 by patenting a revised form of safety device – the so-called 'hammer safety' – which consisted of a lever on the left side of the hammer. The safety lever could be used for single-handed cocking, which was virtually impossible with the standard hammer (designed for cocking against a horseman's saddle), and although the hammer could still be dropped in the 'safe' position, the lever blocked the hammer nose from the firing pin. Very few were made.

Selbstladepistole C/96 mit kurzer Auszieher

In 1905 Mauser modified the C/96 by the addition of a shorter extractor, a small hammer which no longer obscured the rear sight when resting on the firing pin, and a two-lug firing pin retainer. Some transitional models exist with similar features but with the older long hammer.

Selbstladepistole C/96 mit Sicherung neuer Art C/12

The 'new safety' could only be applied when the hammer was manually retracted from contact with the sear; those pistols with the older pattern of safety device could have it applied regardless of the position of the hammer. Pistols fitted with this safety had the entwined letters 'NS' on their rear surface.

MAUSER C/96

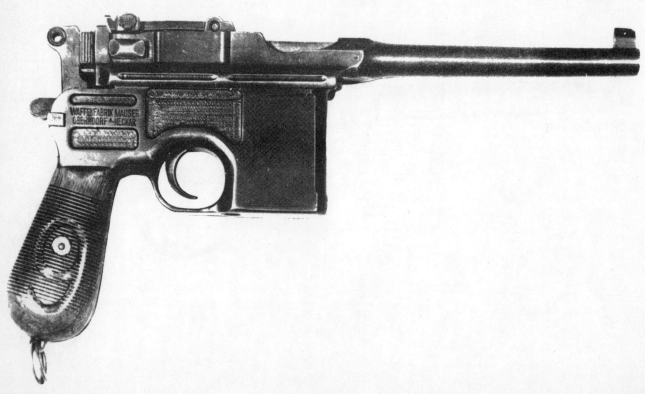

Mauser Selbstladepistole C/96, 9mm Parabellum

During World War One the German authorities soon realised they were faced with a grave shortage of small arms of every description, and that it would be most useful if a supply of Mauser C/96 pistols could be made available chambered for the 9mm Parabellum cartridge. As a result of investigations made in mid-1915, Mauser began the production of 150,000 C/96 pistols in the desired calibre; the weapons were marked on the grips by a large red-stained figure '9', though there are some in existence with black staining, and are often called the 'Model 1916'.

Bolo Model

The so-called 'Bolo' pistols were made in limited numbers in the early 1900s, and revived in 1920 and supplied in some numbers to Soviet Russia ('Bolo' being the contemporary slang term for Bolshevik). The principal difference was the fitting of a 7.63mm 99mm (3.38in) barrel in order to evade the prohibitions of the Treaty of Versailles, which forbade the manufacture of 9mm pistols except under very stringent conditions and of pistols with barrels longer than 100mm. The term is, however, frequently misapplied loosely to any short-barrelled Mauser C/96 pistol.

Model 1930 with Universal Safety

This was a 7.63mm 10-shot magazine version of the C/96, strengthened and fitted with a new type of safety similar in basic principle to that of 1902. The safety lever had three positions; in the rear position the pistol can be fired; in the uppermost position the hammer cannot reach the firing pin; and in the midway position everything – hammer, trigger and bolt – is locked. Pistols of this pattern were supplied to Norway and China and it remained in production until 1937, when the manufacture of the C/96 finally ended.

Schnellfeuerpistole M712, System Nickl

Sometimes known as the M1932, this 'rapid-fire pistol' is the M30 with the addition of a selective-fire mechanism designed by Josef Nickl. This design appeared after a number of Spanish makers had produced full-automatic imitations of the Mauser, notably for the South American and Far Eastern markets, and Mauser were virtually forced to compete. They developed the 712 with a simple bar lever on the left of the frame which, when pushed forward gave single shots and when pulled back gave automatic fire at a rate of about 850 rounds per minute. Removable 10- and 20-shot magazines were provided and could be reloaded either by removal or by a charger through the open action.

Schnellfeuerpistole M712, System Westinger

This appeared in 1936 and differed only in the selective fire mechanism, designed by Westinger, a Mauser engineer. It had a positive latch, unlike the Nickl design and can be recognised by the lozenge-shaped change switch on the left of the frame.

Numbers of the two 712 models were sold to China and Yugoslavia and in 1938 the remaining stock was taken by the German Army as the 'Reihenfeuerpistole Mauser' and issued to the Waffen SS.

MAUSER C/96 WITH SHOULDER STOCK

7.63mm Schwarzlose M1898

A. W. Schwarzlose GmbH	
7.63 × 25mm Mauser	
Operation	Short recoil
Length overall	273mm (10.75in)
Weight empty	940g (2.07lb)
Barrel	163mm (6.43in), 4 grooves, rh
Magazine	7-shot detachable box
Muzzle velocity	425m/sec (1,395ft/sec)

Parabellum Pistols 1898–1945

Deutsche Waffen- und Munitions-Fabrik (1900–1918);
Königliche Gewehrfabrik Erfurt (1911–1918);
Simson & Cie (1920–34);
Heinrich Krieghoff (1934–1940);
Mauser-Werke AG (1930–1943);
Mauser-Jagdwaffen GmbH (1970–);
Eidgenossische Waffenfabrik, Bern (1918–1947)

7.65 × 21.5mm Parabellum;
9 × 19mm Parabellum

Andreas Schwarzlose was an ingenious and versatile designer who patented a variety of weapons in the period 1892–1912. This pistol was the first of his many designs to be produced in quantity but unfortunately it arrived on the market shortly after the Mauser C/96 and fewer than 500 were ever made. It suffered by comparison with extant weapons and was not a commercial success. The remaining stocks were apparently sold by an enterprising Berlin salesman to the Russian revolutionary movement of 1905 but the shipment was intercepted by the Russian authorities; the pistols were then distributed to border police and similar official bodies, with the result that specimens are extremely scarce. The locking system is a rotating bolt operated by a stud in a fixed guide ring riding in a helical groove in the bolt. This rotates and unlocks the bolt during recoil, after which the bolt reciprocates in the usual way, ejecting on the rearward stroke and reloading on return. The Schwarzlose also ranks as one of the earliest designs to incorporate a bolt hold-open device. The pistol is well-balanced and fits the hand excellently, but the mechanism is complicated and proved to be unreliable unless meticulously maintained. In addition, the powerful cartridge gave rise to a violent action, resulting in rapid wear on many surfaces.

The history and development of the Parabellum pistol is an involved story – itself the subject of several specialised books – and much of it is only of marginal interest in these pages. As a result, what follows is confined to essential details of military pistols. The Parabellum was a direct descendant of the Borchardt pistol developed in 1893 by Hugo Borchardt and marketed in 1894 by Ludwig Loewe & Cie of Berlin. For its time, the strange-looking Borchardt was a revelation, but within three years better pistols began to appear, notably the Mauser C/96, and sales declined rapidly until in c. 1898–9 production ceased, about 3,000 pistols having been made. There were, though, sufficient good features about the pistol to make the design worth developing, though Hugo Borchardt appears to have lost interest and succeeding work was done by Georg Luger of the Deutsche Waffen- und Munitions-Fabrik, the new name of the Loewe company after 1896. Luger's first patents were granted in 1898 and covered a transitional pistol which appeared in 1900 and was adopted by the Swiss as the 'Parabellum Pistol, System Borchardt-Luger'.

The many variations which followed upon the success of the 1900 pistol made use of the same operating principle but with minor alterations. Luger was a champion of recoil operation and his pistol made use of the rearward-moving barrel to break open a toggle lock by moving the centre of the pivot above the axis of the bore. This allowed the lock to continue to break upwards while the breechblock moved directly rearward, compressing the mainspring (housed in the rear of the handgrip) as it did so. The compressed spring then returned the toggle to the closed position, driving the breech-block forward to close the breech, and as this happened so the entire barrel and barrel extension assembly returned to the firing position, locking the toggle by ensuring that the centre pivot now lay below the axis of the bore. The mechanism was well made from the finest materials then available, with the result that in the Parabellum DWM had one of the finest automatic pistols of its day. There were faults in the design, it is true – especially in the pattern of trigger mechanism (though it was perfectly adequate for

SCHWARZLOSE M1898

military purposes) and in the fact that the toggle system was particularly sensitive to variations in ammunition quality. Nevertheless, the Parabellum served the German and many other armies well through two World Wars, and although formally superseded after 1941 by the Walther P-38, it was never entirely displaced in German service. It remained in Swiss service until the 1950s, and, as a commercial venture, its manufacture in small numbers was revived by Mauser in 1970.

7.65mm Parabellum Model 1900

Operation	Short recoil
Length overall	211mm (8.33in)
Weight empty	840g (1.85lb)
Barrel	122mm (4.8in), 4 grooves, rh
Magazine	8-shot detachable box
Muzzle velocity	350m/sec (1,150ft/sec)

This was the original pistol adopted by the Swiss and extensively tested by various other countries; it was chambered for the 7.65mm Luger-designed bottle-necked cartridge. The pistol was fitted with a grip safety in the rear of the butt, which had to be depressed by the hand before the gun could fire, and a manual safety lever on the left side of the frame. A toggle lock was fitted into the right-hand toggle finger grip; this engaged with a rib on the frame and was intended to prevent the breech-block from bouncing open and causing misfires. A flat leaf-spring was fitted in the rear edge of the hand grip where it bore on the toggle mechanism by means of an intermediate crank; when this leaf spring was later replaced by a coil spring, the leaf-spring pistols were christened 'alter Art' (old pattern) or 'alterer Modell' (old model) as a means of distinguishing the two types.

9mm Parabellum Model 1902

The 1902 pattern was the first of Luger's pistols to use his 9mm Parabellum cartridge, which had been developed in 1901 by opening up the mouth of the 7.65mm case to accept the larger bullet; this was done in order to satisfy military demands for a cartridge with better stopping power than the 7.65mm bullet. By adopting this course, the base size of the cartridge remained the same, which meant that most of the existing machine facilities and spare parts could be used in the new weapons. Although few of the Model 1902 were produced, the pattern provided adequate scope for the subsequent development of the 1908 model. The gun was mechanically similar to the 1900 design (from which it can easily be distinguished by the heavier barrel) and had the same toggle lock and leaf-spring.

9mm Parabellum Marine Model 1904

Operation	Short recoil
Length overall	267mm (10.5in)
Weight empty	960g (2.12lb)
Barrel	152mm (6.0in), 4 grooves, rh
Magazine	8-shot detachable box
Muzzle velocity	365m/sec (1,200ft/sec)

The Model 1904 was the first Parabellum to be adopted by any branch of the German armed forces, in this case by the Imperial Navy. The original pistol was in 9mm calibre with a longer barrel than the standard army Pistol 08 of later years, and it can be easily recognised by the two-position rearsight protected by lateral 'wings'. It was also fitted with a lug at the bottom of the backstrap to which a shoulder-stock could be attached to give increased accuracy at longer ranges. Mechanically the Model 1904 was an interesting transitional variety which represents a mid-stage between the old and new models, since it married the leaf-spring and toggle lock to a new type of toggle finger grip which was flat-sided and completely knurled around its circumference. This design also introduced a combined extractor and loaded chamber indicator; with the breech closed on a loaded chamber the extractor rose from the breech-block to show the word 'Geladen' on its left side. The Model 1904 pistol is, today, extremely rare.

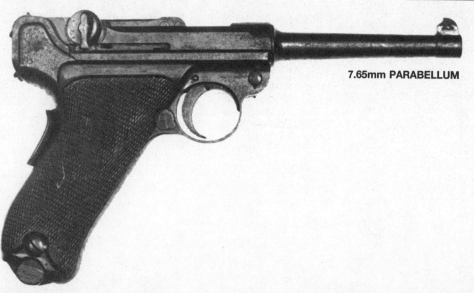

7.65mm PARABELLUM

9mm Parabellum Marine Model 1904/06

9mm Parabellum Marine Model 1904/08

7.65mm and 9mm Parabellum Model 1906 'neuer Art'

9mm Parabellum Model 1908

Operation	Short recoil
Length overall	223mm (8.75in)
Weight empty	870g (1.92lb)
Barrel	102mm (4.0in), 6 grooves, rh
Magazine	8-shot detachable box
Muzzle velocity	380m/sec (1,247ft/sec)

This was a modified version of the Model 1904 introduced in 1906; in accordance with the new patterns of that year, the leaf-spring was replaced by the coil spring and the toggle lock was discarded as being of no practical value.

The 1908 variation of the Model 1904 was the Naval equivalent of the Army Pistol '08, from which it differed only in the barrel length and sights.

The 1906 patterns replaced the leaf recoil spring with a coil spring and eliminated the toggle-lock. All guns produced to this modified pattern also adopted the combined extractor and chamber-loaded indicator and all adopted the grip safety. Two basic types were offered in this new range; the 7.65mm pistol was really the Model 1900 with the new features, while the 9mm pistol was a modified Model 1902.

The Model 1908, usually known simply as the 'Pistole '08' or 'P08' is undoubtedly the most famous of all the Luger-designed pistols. It was based upon the 9mm 'neuer Art' of 1906 with the elimination of the grip safety device and a revision of the manual safety catch which now moved down, instead of up, to the 'safe' position. The original issues came from the Deutsche Waffen- und Munitionsfabrik, but in 1911 manufacture got under way at the Erfurt Arsenal. In early 1914 the design was modified by adding a shoulder-stock lug and a hold-open device to the magazine follower and a number of earlier production pistols were retrospectively modified. The Pistole '08 had a long production life, surviving the restrictions of the Treaty of Versailles; with production continued by Simson & Cie (who acquired the Erfurt tooling) and DWM until the DWM tooling was moved to Mauser in 1928. Simson folded in 1934 and their production machinery was then taken over by Krieghoff, who produced 10,000 P08 for the German Air Force. By 1936 it was realised that the day of the P08 was over, and a replacement was sought, resulting in the adoption of the Walther P38 as being less expensive and easier to manufacture. In July 1941 Mauser turned to manufacture of the P38 and in June 1942 they made the last P08, the final batch of which was accepted by the German Army in November. In spite of its official replacement, the P08 remained in wide use until 1945, since production of the P38 was never sufficient to completely replace the old war-horse. According to the best estimates, a total of about 2,620,000 Pistole '08 were manufactured.

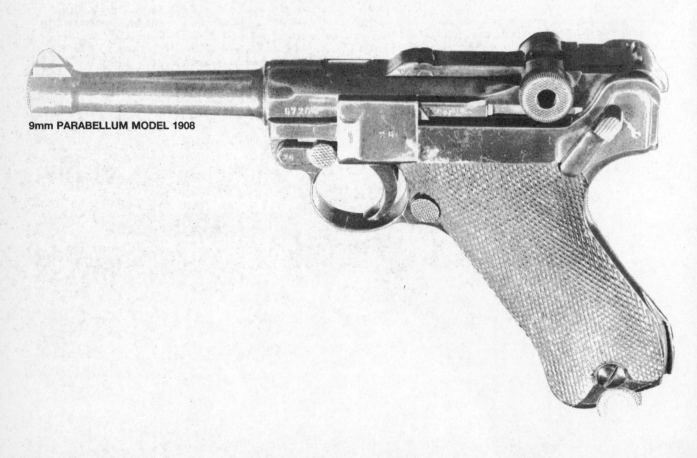

9mm PARABELLUM MODEL 1908

This is also variously known as the 'Artillery Model 1914', the 'Model 1917' and the 'Long '08'. Development began in 1911 and the weapon was intended to arm artillerymen, airmen and some fortress troops. Production began in February 1914 and orders for 144,000 were placed with DWM and Erfurt, though there is no record of exactly how many were actually produced. The Artillery Model 1908 was a standard Pistole '08 with a 190mm (7.5in) barrel carrying a tangent-leaf backsight. The fitting of this sight demanded that a lateral step had to be cut into the barrel ring at the front of the frame, and this modification was applied to all frames made in Erfurt, so that it also appears on Erfurt Pistole '08 production of the period. The sight was graduated, rather optimistically, to 800 metres' range. A drum or 'snail' magazine which held 32 rounds was introduced in 1917, though the standard box magazine could still be used. The provision of a flat board type of shoulder stock which could be fitted to the butt converted the weapon to a light carbine. Opinions as to the serviceability of the drum magazine vary, but it is certainly a fact that the standard flat-tipped conical 9mm bullet of the original Pistole '08 ammunition had a marked tendency to jam, as a result of which the ogival (round nosed) bullet became standard for military use and has continued to be up to the present day.

Walther had been making pistols since 1908, and in response to a 1915 request from the German Army for a 9mm pistol they produced this enlarged version of their commercial Model 4 as a military weapon. The Model 6 is therefore a blowback pistol, and since the cartridge is the 9mm Parabellum this meant using a very heavy slide and a very strong recoil spring in order to resist the opening of the breech against the heavier charge. The solution was far from ideal and not many Model 6 were made before production stopped in 1917.

9mm Parabellum Artillery Pistol Model 1908

Operation	Short recoil
Length overall	311mm (12.24in)
Weight empty	1,050g (2.31lb)
Barrel	190mm (7.5in), 6 grooves, rh
Magazine	8-shot box or 32-round 'snail' drum
Muzzle velocity	380m/sec (1,250ft/sec)

9mm Walther Model 6

Carl Walther Waffenfabrik AG	
9 × 19mm Parabellum	
Operation	Blowback
Length overall	210mm (8.25in)
Weight empty	960g (2.12lb)
Barrel	121mm (4.75in), 4 grooves, rh
Magazine	8-shot detachable box
Muzzle velocity	335m/sec (1,100ft/sec)

9mm PARABELLUM ARTILLERY MODEL

7.65mm Mauser Models 1914 and 1934

Waffenfabrik Mauser AG	
7.65 × 17mm (.32 ACP)	
Operation	Blowback
Length overall	159mm (6.25in)
Weight empty	600g (1.32lb)
Barrel	87mm (3.4in), 6 grooves, rh
Magazine	8-shot detachable box
Muzzle velocity	295m/sec (970ft/sec)

7.65mm Beholla

Becker & Hollander	
7.65 × 17mm (.32 ACP)	
Operation	Blowback
Length overall	140mm (5.5in)
Weight empty	640g (1.41lb)
Barrel	73mm (2.88in), 6 grooves, rh
Magazine	7-shot detachable box
Muzzle velocity	275m/sec (900ft/sec)

In 1910 Mauser produced a small blowback pistol in 6.35mm calibre. It was exceptionally well made and somewhat large for its calibre, but proved extremely popular. So much so that in 1914 they decided to introduce it in 7.65mm calibre, appropriately enlarged. This was widely adopted for police and second-line military use and stayed in production in post-war years until, in 1934, it was slightly revised and became the Model 1934. The design incorporates a removable barrel, very convenient for cleaning, and in the 1914 pattern this was locked in place by a long pin which slides in beneath the barrel and is retained by a somewhat complex spring catch. This model also had a removable side plate covering the lockwork. The 1934 model simplified the design by using a plain spring steel catch to retain the barrel locking pin and it had a more rounded wood or plastic butt grip. With the outbreak of war in 1939 the entire stock, and subsequent production, was taken into military service, largely being issued to the German Navy and Air Force; many of the examples found today carry the markings of one or other of these services. (Data refers to Model 1934.)

This simple and sturdy blowback was designed just prior to 1914 with a view to commercial sale, but the war intervened and in 1915 Becker was instructed to produce the Beholla as a pistol for officers and second-line troops. The design has one unusual feature: the barrel is retained in the frame by being slid into a dovetailed groove, and it is retained there by a cross pin. To dismantle the pistol it is necessary to remove the barrel first, and for this purpose there are two small holes in the slide which allow the pin to be driven out by a hammer and drift, after which the barrel can be driven forward out of its slot and the slide taken off. Due to military demand the Beholla was also made by three other companies; as the 'Menta' by August Menz, as the 'Leonhardt' by Gering & Cie, and as the 'Stenda' by Stendawerke. After the war Gering closed his pistol business down, but the other companies continued making the weapon, under licence from Becker & Hollander, in both 7.65mm and 6.35mm calibres for several years, so that it is relatively common in one form or another.

MAUSER MODEL 1914 IN 6.35mm CALIBRE

7.65mm BEHOLLA

The Rheinische company, later to become Rheinmetall, adopted the Dreyse name for their products in 1901 after purchasing the bankrupt Waffenfabrik Dreyse, and in 1907 developed a 7.65mm blowback pistol designed by Louis Schmeisser. It was an unusual design, with a cranked slide in which the major portion lay over the barrel and the lower section formed a breech-block within the frame sides and top. In 1911 Schmeisser decided to turn this into a 9mm pistol, and in order to resist the heavier recoil forces he fitted a very powerful recoil spring, so powerful that it was almost impossible to cock the pistol in the normal way by pulling back the slide. He therefore designed a system whereby the recoil spring was locked to the slide by an upper rib, which could be unhooked and lifted, freeing the slide from the spring, and thus allowed the slide to be very easily pulled back to cock the weapon. The slide was then pushed forward again and the rib reconnected, after which the pistol was ready to fire. Another unusual feature is that the striker was not fully cocked on recoil, additional cocking pressure being applied as the trigger was pulled. The design was not particularly successful, only about 1850 being made, but it was marketed commercially from 1912 to 1915 when manufacture stopped. Although not formally adopted by the German Army, numbers were carried by officers. It is uncommon today, and, due to wear in the locking surfaces of the rib, hazardous to fire since the recoil spring may be disconnected by the shock of firing, allowing the slide to fly back uncontrolled and jam the pistol.

Langenhan was a manufacturer of sporting arms and single-shot pistols, but in 1914 took out patents for this automatic pistol. Production began in 1915 and the entire production of some 50,000 was taken by the German Army as a substitute standard pistol and was never sold commercially. It is a blowback weapon, handy in use, but of peculiar construction. The breech-block is a separate unit held in the slide by a stirrup-lock which forms the rear sight and which is locked in place by a large screw at the rear of the block. The frame is cut away on the right side so that the breech-block is only supported on the left. Provided all the mating surfaces are unworn and the locking screw is secure, the pistol works well; but once wear takes place the locking screw and stirrup tend to loosen during firing and there is a considerable danger that, after twenty or thirty rounds, the breech-block might be blown into the firer's face.

9mm Dreyse Army

Rheinische Metallwaren und Maschinenfabrik AG	
9 × 19mm Parabellum	
Operation	Blowback
Length overall	206mm (8.16in)
Weight empty	1,050g (2.31lb)
Barrel	126mm (5.0in), 6 grooves, rh
Magazine	8-shot detachable box
Muzzle velocity	365m/sec (1,200ft/sec)

7.65mm Langenhan Army

Fritz Langenham & Cie	
7.65 × 17mm (.32 ACP)	
Operation	Blowback
Length overall	168mm (6.6in)
Weight empty	650g (1.43lb)
Barrel	105mm (4.15in), 4 grooves, rh
Magazine	8-shot detachable box
Muzzle velocity	280m/sec (925ft/sec)

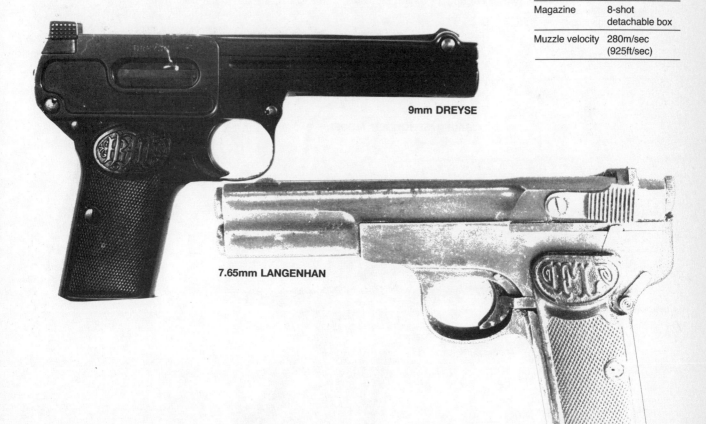

9mm DREYSE

7.65mm LANGENHAN

7.65mm Sauer Behorden Model

J. P. Sauer & Sohn	
7.65 × 17mm (.32 ACP)	
Operation	Blowback
Length overall	146mm (5.75in)
Weight empty	620g (1.36lb)
Barrel	77mm (3.03in), 6 grooves, rh
Magazine	7-shot detachable box
Muzzle velocity	275m/sec (900ft/sec)

7.65mm Sauer Model 38H

J. P. Sauer & Sohn	
7.65 × 17mm (.32 ACP)	
Operation	Blowback
Length overall	171mm (6.75in)
Weight empty	720g (1.58lb)
Barrel	83mm (3.27in), 4 grooves, rh
Magazine	8-shot detachable box
Muzzle velocity	275m/sec (900ft/sec)

Sauer developed a useful pocket 7.65mm pistol in 1913, for the personal defence and police market. It had a fixed barrel, coaxial recoil spring, a light tubular slide and a separate breech-block retained in the slide by a screwed cap at the rear end. This remained in production until 1930, an estimated 175,000 being made. In 1930 a new model was developed and put into production. This had the same general design but with detail improvements. The grip was more rounded, the bolt now carried a signal pin to show whether the chamber was loaded, and the trigger had a small catch which acted as a security lock; the trigger could only move if this catch was depressed, so that no external blow could fire the weapon. This model is frequently known as the 'Behorden' ('Authorities') model, since it was widely adopted by military and civil police throughout Germany and, in small numbers, was used by the Army as a staff officer's pistol. It remained in production until 1937.

This replaced the Sauer 'Behorden' Model in 1938 and, but for the war, might have been a considerable commercial success, since it was an innovative and extremely well-made pistol. As it was the entire production of some 200,000 went to the German armed forces and the design died in 1945; J. P. Sauer & Sohn returned to the firearms business in post-war years, but they never revived the Model 38H. In appearance the 38H (H for hammer) departed entirely from the tubular style of previous models and reverted to the more usual type of slide. The most important innovation was a thumb-catch at the top of the left grip which was connected to the internal hammer mechanism. If the hammer is down, the thumb-catch is depressed to raise it to the cocked position; if the hammer is cocked, pressure on the thumb-catch, followed by pressure on the trigger, allows the hammer to be lowered gently on to a loaded chamber. In addition, the firing lock is double action, so that the slide can be pulled back to cock in the normal way, or the trigger can be pulled through to raise and drop the hammer for the first shot. The combination of hammer control and double-action offers a variety of options to suit all tastes, and it was quite unique at that time.

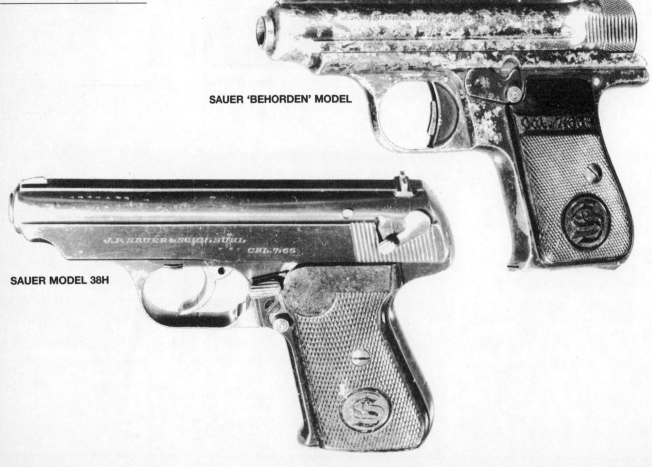

SAUER 'BEHORDEN' MODEL

SAUER MODEL 38H

This pistol, introduced in 1929, was a radical improvement on anything which had previously appeared. It was the first totally successful self-loader to incorporate a double-action trigger mechanism, and it exhibited a clean and modern appearance. It was originally introduced as a police weapon (PP for Polizei Pistole) for holster use by uniformed officers, and it was later widely adopted as an officers' pistol by the German armed forces. Originally developed in 7.65mm calibre, it was later produced also in 6.35mm (rare), .22 Long Rifle rimfire and 9mm Short calibres, all of which are almost identical in appearance. An uncomplicated blowback weapon, an interesting innovation found on the centre-fire models was the provision of a signal pin which floated in the slide and pressed on the rim of the chambered round so that the end of the pin protruded just above the hammer and gave visual and tactile indication that the weapon was loaded. Since the end of World War Two the PP has been copied, with or without benefit of licence, in a number of countries and is still being manufactured by Walther.

The PPK is a smaller edition of the Walther PP, intended for issue to plain-clothes police officers and hence easily concealable. In mechanism and construction it is almost identical to the PP, the only difference lying in the dimensions and in the construction of the butt. On the PP the butt is forged to shape, with two separate side-pieces of plastic. On the PPK the frame forging is a simple rectangle and the plastic grip is a one-piece wrap-around component which produces the final curved shape. Like the PP, the PPK can be found in .22LR, 6.35mm, 7.65mm and 9mm Short calibres, though the 7.65mm is by far the most common and only a few 6.35mm pistols appear to have been made.

7.65mm Walther Model PP

Carl Walther Waffenfabrik

7.65 × 17mm (.32 ACP)

Operation	Blowback
Length overall	162mm (6.38in)
Weight empty	710g (1.56lb)
Barrel	85mm (3.35in), 6 grooves, rh
Magazine	8-shot detachable box
Muzzle velocity	290m/sec (950ft/sec)

7.65mm Walther Model PPK

Carl Walther Waffenfabrik

7.65 × 17mm (.32 ACP)

Operation	Blowback
Length overall	148mm (5.38in)
Weight empty	590g (1.30lb)
Barrel	80mm (3.15in), 6 grooves, rh
Magazine	7-shot detachable box
Muzzle velocity	290m/sec (950ft/sec)

7.65mm WALTHER PP

7.65mm WALTHER PPK

7.65mm Mauser Model HSc

Waffenfabrik Mauser AG	
7.65 × 17mm (.32 ACP)	
Operation	Blowback
Length overall	152mm (6.0in)
Weight empty	600g (1.32lb)
Barrel	86mm (3.38in), 6 grooves, rh
Magazine	8-shot detachable box
Muzzle velocity	290m/sec (960ft/sec)

9mm Walther P38

Carl Walther Waffenfabrik; Waffenfabrik Mauser AG; Spreewerke GmbH	
9 × 19mm Parabellum	
Operation	Short recoil
Length overall	213mm (8.38in)
Weight empty	960g (2.11lb)
Barrel	127mm (5.0in), 6 grooves, rh
Magazine	8-shot detachable box
Muzzle velocity	350m/sec (1,150ft/sec)

The Mauser HSc (Hammerless, self-loading, Model C) was introduced in 1940, the design having been begun with commercial intent but, of course most wartime production being taken for the German armed forces. It represented a considerable advance in design upon previous Mauser models, being a double-action pistol of very modern appearance. The hammer is concealed within the slide, leaving only a small lip protruding sufficiently to allow thumb-cocking, and the safety catch in the slide was unusual for its period in that it lifted the entire firing pin into a recess and took it out of alignment with the hammer. A slightly improved version was put into production in post-war years until, in the mid-1970s, Mauser licensed production to an Italian company.

When the German Army made it known that they were contemplating retiring the Parabellum pistol, Walther produced a 9mm version of the PP which they called the MP (Militar Pistole). This was refused without much discussion, since the Army would not accept a blowback weapon in that calibre. Walther then developed a locked breech weapon with a concealed hammer, calling it the 'AP' (Armee Pistole) but this was refused on the grounds that with the hammer invisible it was impossible to see whether or not it was cocked. The design was changed to incorporate a visible hammer and now became the 'HP' (Heeres Pistole), and in this form it was finally approved and placed in production as the Pistole '38, or P38. Breech locking is performed by a wedge-shaped locking plate beneath the breech; when the pistol is fired, the barrel and slide recoil together for a short distance until the locking block is cammed down to disengage from the slide and halt the barrel. The P38 is fitted with a double-action trigger mechanism, derived from that on the PP and PPK, and a signal pin protrudes from the slide to indicate a loaded chamber. The safety catch, on the slide, locks the firing pin securely before dropping the hammer, allowing the pistol to be fired by simply releasing the safety catch and pulling through on the trigger.

The demands of wartime production ultimately proved to be more than Walther could handle, and various other firms became involved in production of the P38. Mauser and Spreewerke made complete pistols, and such diverse firms as Fabrique Nationale Herstal, Waffenwerke Brunn (Brno) and Ceska Zbrojovka were sub-contracted to manufacture component parts. Walther resumed production of the P38 in 1957 and it was again adopted as the official service pistol of the Bundeswehr under the new designation of Pistole 1 (P1). It has been used by a number of other armies in post-war years; the only pre-war foreign army to adopt it was the Swedish, where it was known as the Pistol Model 39.

WALTHER P38

7.65mm MAUSER HSc

GERMANY, FEDERAL REPUBLIC

The P9 pistol uses the same roller-locked delayed blowback system as is found in most other H&K weapons, including the G3 rifle and MP5 submachine-gun. It is a hammer-fired weapon, the hammer being concealed, and a thumb-operated hammer release and re-cocking lever is provided on the left side of the frame, a mechanism similar to that described above in the Sauer 38H pistol entry. However there is a difference in that the P9 offers single-action firing only, while the P9S model has a double-action lock. The barrel is unusual in having a polygonal rifled bore, in which the four grooves are merged into the bore diameter so that a cross-section of the bore resembles a flattened circle and the individual grooves of conventional rifling are absent. This system, it is claimed, reduces bullet deformity and improves muzzle velocity by reducing friction between bullet and barrel.

In addition to the standard 9mm calibre, a small number were made in 7.65mm Parabellum, and an export commercial version in .45 ACP. The P9S, in particular, has been widely adopted by police and military authorities around the world.

This is a blowback pistol with several unusual features. The magazine carries the unusual number of 18 rounds and the pistol can only be fired in the self-cocking mode, by means of a striker. Pulling the trigger first cocks and then releases the striker, and the trigger mechanism gives a distinct 'first pressure' as the cocking action takes place. Since this self-cocking system allows the pistol to be carried in a loaded condition quite safely, a safety catch is not normally fitted, though one can be provided as an optional extra. A holster-stock can also be fitted to the butt; once this is done an internal connection made by the butt allows for the firing of three-round bursts for a single trigger pressure. This burst facility removes the principal objection to the use of machine pistols: in most previous designs the rate of fire and the lightness of the weapon mean that while the first shot may hit the target, the subsequent climb of the recoiling weapon causes the remaining shots to miss. The Heckler & Koch burst fire facility ensures that the first three shots are the only shots of the burst, and there is a good chance that they will all land in the target area before the weapon climbs too high. The VP70 is also of interest because of the modern manufacturing procedures it introduced. The receiver is of plastic material with a moulded-in barrel support, a construction which is easy to make, resistant to damage, and demanding the minimum of field maintenance. The VP70 enjoyed commercial sales to African and Asian countries and has been adopted by a few military forces, but it was not the success the company had hoped and production ended in the mid-1980s.

9mm Heckler & Koch P9 and P9S

Heckler & Koch GmbH	
9 × 19mm Parabellum	
Operation	Delayed blowback
Length overall	192mm (7.56in)
Weight empty	880g (1.94lb)
Barrel	102mm (4.0in), polygonal, rh
Magazine	9-shot detachable box
Muzzle velocity	350m/sec (1,150ft/sec)

9mm Heckler & Koch VP70

Heckler & Koch GmbH	
9 × 19mm Parabellum	
Operation	Blowback
Length overall	204mm (8.03in)
Weight empty	820g (1.81lb)
Barrel	116mm (4.57in), 6 grooves, rh
Magazine	18-shot detachable box
Cyclic rate	2,200rds/min
Muzzle velocity	360m/sec (1,180ft/sec)

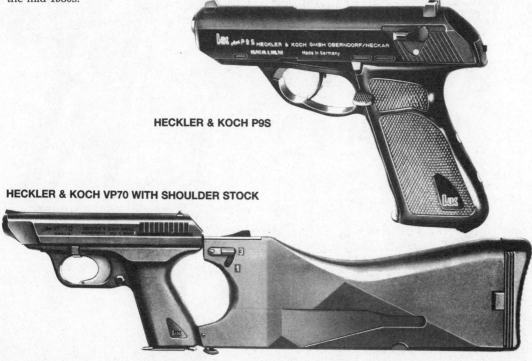

HECKLER & KOCH P9S

HECKLER & KOCH VP70 WITH SHOULDER STOCK

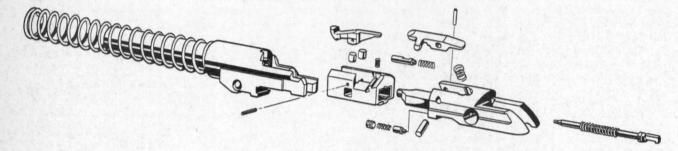

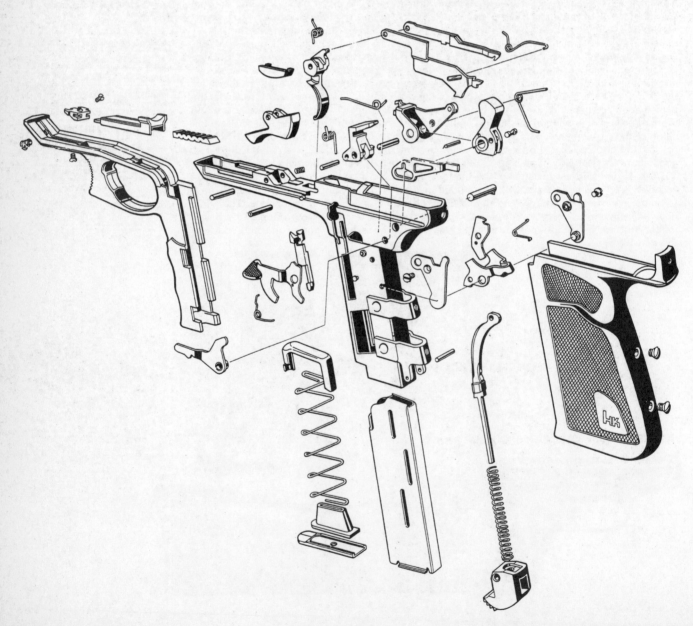

The P7 family was developed to satisfy a demand from the Federal German Police for a pistol which would be entirely safe to carry loaded but which could be brought into action with the minimum delay. This requirement has been satisfied by the adoption of a cocking lever which forms the front edge of the grip. Assuming the pistol to be empty, with the slide held open after the last shot, on inserting the magazine and squeezing the grip, the slide is released to run forward and chamber a round. Squeezing the grip will now cock the firing pin and pulling the trigger will release the firing pin and fire a shot. The action will cycle in the normal way and the pistol is re-cocked on recoil. As soon as the grip is released the firing pin is uncocked and the trigger is no longer connected to the firing pin, so that the pistol is entirely safe. As a result, there is no other safety device fitted. In order to fire the 9mm Parabellum cartridge safely, a gas-actuated delayed blowback system is used. Beneath the breech is a short cylinder connected to the barrel by a gas port. In the front end of this cylinder is a piston connected to the front end of the slide. There is a return spring around the barrel. On firing, some of the propellant gas passes into the cylinder at high pressure and forces against the piston, thus resisting the rearward movement of the piston and the slide. Once the bullet has left the barrel, the trapped gas can leak back into the barrel and the piston can move back freely, allowing the slide to move back and reload the pistol on its forward stroke.

There are four distinct members of the P7 family. The P7M8 and P7M13 are as described, differing only in their magazine capacities of 8 and 13 rounds respectively. The P7K3 is a simple blowback pistol chambered for the 9mm Short cartridge; there is no gas delay system employed, and there are conversion kits allowing it to be changed so as to fire .22LR or 7.65mm ACP cartridges. The P7M7 was a heavy pistol chambered for the .45 ACP cartridge; instead of a gas delay there was an oil buffer delay system using similar components but relying upon the piston forcing its way into a cylinder filled with oil to provide the desired delay. This also acted to soak up a good deal of the recoil energy, making the P7M7 a very pleasant pistol to shoot. (Data table refers to P7M13.)

Introduced in 1979 this is virtually an updated version of the P38, using the same breech locking system and double-action trigger. The safety arrangements have, however, been considerably altered. The safety catch is now on the left side of the frame and functions primarily as a de-cocking lever, providing safety as an adjunct. Safety is provided automatically by the firing pin having a degree of vertical movement within its housing. It is normally pressed down by a spring into a position where its forward movement is prevented by an abutment on the pin contacting a lug on the slide. In this position the exposed head of the firing pin is aligned with a recess in the face of the hammer, so that even should the hammer fall, it would not exert any pressure on the firing pin. Only when the trigger is pressed will a trip lever be actuated, first to lift the firing pin up in its housing to disengage it from the lock, and secondly to release the hammer so that it can fall and strike the pin. The P5 is also produced in 7.65mm Parabellum and 9 × 21mm IMI chambering to special order. It is in use by the Netherlands Police, by several German police forces and the Portuguese and Nigerian Armies among others.

9mm Heckler & Koch P7

Heckler & Koch GmbH	
9 × 19mm Parabellum	
Operation	Delayed blowback
Length overall	171mm (6.73in)
Weight empty	800g (1.76lb)
Barrel	105mm (4.13in), polygonal, rh
Magazine	13-shot detachable box
Muzzle velocity	350m/sec (1,150ft/sec)

9mm Walther P5

Carl Walther Waffenfabrik	
9 × 19mm Parabellum	
Operation	Short recoil
Length overall	180mm (7.10in)
Weight empty	795g (1.75lb)
Barrel	90mm (3.54in), 6 grooves, rh
Magazine	8-shot detachable box
Muzzle velocity	350m/sec (1,150ft/sec)

WALTHER P5

HECKLER & KOCH P7

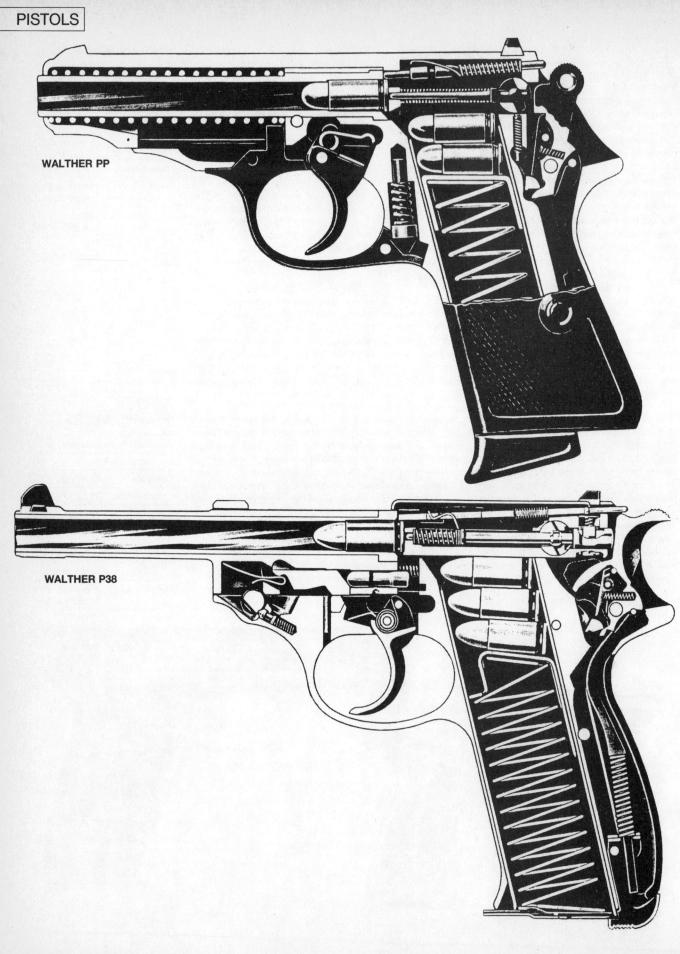

WALTHER PP

WALTHER P38

The P5 Compact is basically the same as the P5 described above except that it is shorter and lighter, the size and shape making it more convenient for concealment. A new lateral magazine release is fitted and the frame is of light alloy, in order to save weight.

9mm Walther P5 Compact

Carl Walther Waffenfabrik

9 × 19mm Parabellum

Operation	Short recoil
Length overall	169mm (6.65in)
Weight empty	780g (1.72lb)
Barrel	79mm (3.11in), 6 grooves, rh
Magazine	8-shot detachable box
Muzzle velocity	350m/sec (1,148ft/sec)

WALTHER P5 COMPACT

The P1A1 was announced in 1989 and is an improved version of the P5. The principal change is the adoption of a cross-bolt safety catch upon the slide which is pushed to the left for 'fire' and the right for 'safe'. This operates upon the firing pin; when pushed to safe the bolt forces the firing pin down, aligning it with a recess in the face of the hammer and locking against a lug in the slide. Should the hammer fall, the firing pin will not be struck. Except for being 1mm shorter in overall length, the dimensions, etc., of the P1A1 are the same as those of the P5.

9mm Walther P1A1

Carl Walther Waffenfabrik

9 × 19mm Parabellum

This appeared in 1988 and is a considerable departure from previous Walther practise, abandoning the wedge lock and adopting the familiar Colt/Browning dropping barrel controlled by a cam and locking into the slide by means of a squared section around the chamber fitting into the ejection port. It is a double-action hammer-fired weapon with an ambidextrous de-cocking lever which also functions as a slide release. There is an automatic firing pin safety system similar to that described for the P5 (above), and hence no manual safety catch.

The P88 is in current production and is undergoing evaluation by a number of military forces, including the British Army, at the time of writing.

9mm Walther P88

Carl Walther Waffenfabrik

9 × 19mm Parabellum

Operation	Short recoil
Length overall	187mm (7.36in)
Weight empty	900g (1.98lb)
Barrel	102mm (4.02in), 6 grooves, rh
Magazine	15-round box magazine
Muzzle velocity	350m/sec (1,150ft/sec)

WALTHER P88

GREAT BRITAIN

Pistol, Webley, Marks 1 to 6

Webley & Scott Ltd (see text)

.455in British service

During the years that this family of pistols was in production the manufacturer underwent three changes of name: the company operated as Philip Webley & Son until 1897, when the name changed to The Webley & Scott Revolver & Arms Co., changing again in 1906 to Webley & Scott Ltd. The company still exists, but no longer manufactures firearms. The titles used in this section are those of the Vocabulary of Ordnance Stores and the dates given are those of the formal approval for adoption as given in List of Changes of War Material and Stores.

It is worthy of note that while all these pistols are generally described as being of .455in (11.60mm) calibre, their actual bore calibre has always been .441in (11.20mm). The Webley pistol remained in use in British service until after World War Two and in use by Commonwealth forces even longer.

Pistol Webley, Mark 1
(8 November 1887)

Operation	Double-action revolver
Length overall	260mm (10.25in)
Weight empty	990g (2.18lb)
Barrel	101mm (4.0in), 6 grooves, rh
Magazine	6-shot cylinder
Muzzle velocity	183m/sec (600ft/sec)

This was a top-break six-shot revolver with hinged frame and automatic extraction. The butt was of the shape commonly called a 'Bird's Head', rounded and coming to a point, and a lanyard ring was fitted. The frame was locked by the familiar Webley stirrup mechanism.

Pistol, Webley, Mark 1*
(1 October 1894)

Upon repair or refurbishing of Mark 1 pistols, a hardened steel plate was added to the standing breech in order to approximate to the design of the Mark 2. The head of the butt grip was rounded off and the thumb-piece on the stirrup lock made smaller.

Pistol, Webley, Mark 2
(1 October 1894)

This model differed from the Mark 1 in the following details: a hardened steel plate was used in the breech to lessen erosion, the hammer was strengthened, the grip was a more rounded shape, slight changes were made in the extractor components, the hammer catch spring was spiral instead of V-shaped, and the stirrup-lock thumb-piece was smaller.

Pistol, Webley, Mark 3
(5 October 1897)

The Mark 3 was much the same as the Mark 2 but the attachment of cylinder to frame was improved, and a cam was fitted to unlock the cylinder for removal. In 1905 a number of revolvers of this pattern were fitted with 152mm (6in) barrels 'to meet the requirements of officers and cadets desiring to purchase such pistols from store'.

WEBLEY Mk 3

The Mark 4 differed from Mark 3 in that the steel was of different quality, the trigger stop was raised and the slots in the cylinder made wider, the ratchet teeth of the extractor were case-hardened, and the hammer was made lighter. As in the case of the Mark 3, a number were fitted with 6in barrels in 1905 for sale to officers.

Pistol, Webley, Mark 4 (21 July 1899)

This differed from Mark 4 in having a cylinder of larger diameter and rounded on the rear edge, and the frame modified to suit. Fitted as standard with a 101mm (4in) barrel it weighed 1,010g (2.23lb).

Pistol, Webley, Mark 5 (9 December 1913)

Intended for Naval service, this is the conversion, on repair, of the Mark 1 or 1* by fitting a Mark 4 barrel and a Mark 5 cylinder.

Pistol, Webley, Mark 1** (27 April 1915)

Not an officially approved nomenclature, this designation arose by virtue of a number of Mark 2 pistols being fitted with Mark 4 hammers and having a star stamped – erroneously – after the number on the barrel strap.

Pistol, Webley, Mark 2* (27 April 1915)

Similar to the Mark 1**, a conversion of the Mark 2 by fitting a Mark 4 barrel and a Mark 5 cylinder.

Pistol, Webley, Mark 2** (27 April 1915)

A fine example of how convoluted British nomenclature could get. This is another wartime Naval expedient in which, when undergoing repair, Mark 1 or 1* pistols had the 152mm (6in) barrels approved for Mark 4 or 5 pistols fitted, together with a removable foresight and a Mark 5 cylinder.

Pistol, Webley, 6in Barrel, Mark 1** (5 June 1915)

A similar Naval expedient to the previous model, in this case the repair of Mark 2 pistols by fitting the 6in barrel, removable foresight and Mark 5 cylinder.

Pistol Webley, 6in Barrel, Mark 2** (5 June 1915)

This is identical with the Mark 5 described above but with the original 4in barrel replaced by a 6in barrel carrying a removable foresight attached by a fixing screw. It weighed 1,070g (2.36lb).

Pistol, Webley, 6in Barrel, Mark 5 (24 May 1915)

This differed from the Mark 5 in having the 6in barrel with removable foresight, a different and more squarely cut grip, and a number of the component parts redesigned to facilitate faster production, thus making them special to this mark of pistol.

Pistol, Webley, 6in Barrel, Mark 6 (24 May 1915)

Length overall	286mm (11.25in)
Weight empty	1,090g (2.40lb)
Barrel	152mm (6in), 7 grooves, rh
Magazine	6-shot cylinder
Muzzle velocity	200m/sec (655ft/sec)

WEBLEY Mk 6

.455 Webley-Fosbery Automatic Revolver

Webley & Scott Revolver & Arms Co Ltd	
.455 British service	
Operation	Recoil
Length overall	280mm (11.0in)
Weight empty	1,240g (2.73lb)
Barrel	152mm (6.0in), 7 grooves, rh
Magazine	6-shot cylinder
Muzzle velocity	183m/sec (600ft/sec)

.455 Pistol, Self-Loading, Webley & Scott, Mark 1

Webley & Scott Ltd	
.455 W&S Auto	
Operation	Short recoil
Length overall	216mm (8.5in)
Weight empty	1,130g (2.49lb)
Barrel	127mm (5.0in), 6 grooves, rh
Magazine	7-shot detachable box
Muzzle velocity	228m/sec (750ft/sec)

This weapon, the design of which is based on the 1896 patents of G. V. Fosbery, is in a class of its own – an automatic revolver is which the force of recoil drives the barrel and cylinder unit back over the frame, cocks the hammer, and returns the unit by spring power to the firing position. During this movement a fixed stud on the frame is engaged in the grooves on the cylinder and the movement causes the cylinder to be rotated one-twelfth of a revolution during each stroke, thus completing one-sixth of a turn in the complete recoil cycle and hence indexing a fresh cartridge in front of the hammer. The Webley-Fosbery was never officially adopted for military service, but it was tolerated insofar as, prior to the approval of the .38in revolver, the British Army officer was permitted to purchase any pistol he liked so long as it accepted the service .455 cartridge. But on active service in 1914–15 the Webley-Fosbery was tried and found wanting, the recoil action being easily clogged and deranged by mud and dirt.

This pistol was introduced into the Royal Navy in 1913. It is a solid and reliable weapon with an ungainly appearance owing to the square angle of the butt, which makes instinctive shooting difficult, though deliberate shooting can be quite accurate. The cartridge is a semi-rimmed round of considerable power which will, unfortunately, chamber in the service .455in revolvers. This caused the sudden destruction of a number of revolvers during World War One before the difference was appreciated. The diameter of the automatic pistol bullet is .456in, and the revolver's calibre was .441, and this difference, coupled with a fast-burning powder, was sufficient to cause excessive pressure and blow out the revolvers' cylinders. The Webley automatic, in non-service patterns, was also produced in 9mm Browning Long and .38in ACP calibres.

The standard Mark 1 was fitted with a grip safety, but in April 1915 a modified version was approved for use by Royal Horse Artillery drivers. This differed in having a manual safety catch on the hammer, a rear sight adjustable to 200 yards and for windage, and by having the butt grooved for the attachment of a wooden stock. This model was known as the Number 2 Mark 1, and, upon its introduction, the original model became the Number 1 Mark 1. Although a small number of No 2 Mark 1 were issued to RHA units in France, it appears not to have been well received and did not become a general issue. The balance of those produced were re-allocated to the Royal Flying Corps.

The Webley is a locked breech design, locked by oblique machined ribs on the square rear end of the barrel which engage in recessed sections of the frame. In the firing position the barrel and slide are locked together by a lug on the barrel engaging with a shoulder in the slide. As barrel and slide recoil, the oblique ribs slide down the recesses in the frame and draw the barrel out of engagement with the slide, allowing the slide to recoil. The return spring is an unusual V-spring concealed under the left grip. Another unusual feature was the facility to withdraw partly the magazine and lock it in place so that the top round would not be loaded by the slide; in this position the gun could be fired as a single-shot weapon, hand-loading each round, with the magazine held in reserve.

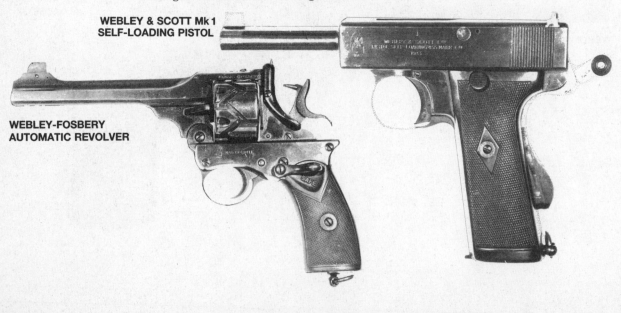

WEBLEY & SCOTT Mk 1 SELF-LOADING PISTOL

WEBLEY-FOSBERY AUTOMATIC REVOLVER

After World War One the British Army decided that the .455 bullet demanded too heavy a weapon and too great a degree of skill from the firer. Investigating possible replacements, they found that Webley & Scott were testing a .38in revolver for possible sale to police forces. With a 200 grain (12.97g) bullet this gave the required stopping power for a combat weapon and was yet sufficiently docile to be passably accurate in the hands of hastily trained wartime recruits. Specimens of the revolver were purchased, but the design project was taken over in 1926/27 by the Royal Small Arms Factory and changes were made in the lockwork and trigger mechanism, largely in the provision of a hammer safety lock and a separate cylinder lock. With this modification the pistol, no longer a Webley pattern, was designated the 'Enfield' revolver or, in accordance with the current system of nomenclature, the 'Pistol, Revolver, Number 2 Mark 1'. Eventually there were three models:

This was similar in appearance to the Webley Mark 6, which it replaced, but physically smaller. It was a double-action revolver, and the actual calibre was .352in. These pistols are now rare, since almost all were converted to Mark 1* when passing through ordnance factories for repair.

This differed from Mark 1 in that the hammer spur was removed so as to allow of self-cocking action only; it was no longer possible to thumb back the hammer and fire single-action. The mainspring was lightened to reduce the trigger pull, the grip sidepieces were reshaped to give a better grip, and a brass marking disc was recessed into the right side butt plate. The date of introduction is of interest since it disproves the widely held opinion that these self-cocking weapons were a wartime introduction for 'quick-draw' work by Commandos and other special troops. In fact the design was introduced at the request of the Royal Tank Corps, who found that the earlier model had a habit of snagging the hammer spur on various tank internal fittings.

This was a wartime dispensation, introduced to hasten production. It is the same as the Mark 1* but with the hammer safety stop removed and one or two minor manufacturing concessions granted. These weapons were all recalled after the war and, by the addition of the hammer safety stop, were reconverted to Mark 1* models, since without the safety stop they were notoriously unsafe if dropped.

.38 Pistol, Revolver, No 2 (Enfield)

Royal Small Arms Factory;
Albion Motor Co;
Singer Sewing Machine Co;

.38 British service

Pistol, Revolver, No 2, Mark 1 (2 June 1932)

Operation	Double-action revolver
Length overall	260mm (10.25in)
Weight empty	780g (1.72lb)
Barrel	127mm (5.0in), 7 grooves, rh
Magazine	6-shot cylinder
Muzzle velocity	198m/sec (650ft/sec)

Pistol, Revolver, No 2, Mark 1* (22 June 1938)

Pistol, Revolver, No 2, Mark 1** (29 July 1942)

ENFIELD No 2 Mk 1*

.38in Pistol, Revolver, Webley, Mark 4

Webley & Scott Ltd	
.38in British service	
Operation	Double-action revolver
Length overall	266mm (10.5in)
Weight empty	760g (1.69lb)
Barrel	127mm (5.0in), 7 grooves, rh
Magazine	6-shot cylinder
Muzzle velocity	183m/sec (600ft/sec)

This was the Webley design which had formed the basis of the Enfield No 2 pistol. Wartime demands were too much for the three factories making the Enfield revolver, and the Army therefore bought supplies of this model from Webley & Scott. This model was the final version of the design which began in 1923. Externally it shows differences from the Enfield model in the shape of the hammer and in cylinder details and, of course, it had the Webley name impressed into the grips. The only internal difference lies in the use of the original Webley lockwork instead of the Enfield modification. Although the official approval date is 20 September 1945, this is merely a matter of cleaning up the wartime paperwork; they were actually brought into service early in 1942 and remained until declared obsolete in June 1963.

.38 Pistol, Revolver, Smith & Wesson, No 2

Smith & Wesson Arms Co	
.38 British service	
Operation	Double-action revolver
Length overall	258mm (10.13in)
Weight empty	680g (1.50lb)
Barrel	4, 5 or 6in (102, 127 or 152mm), 5 grooves, rh
Magazine	6-shot cylinder
Muzzle velocity	200m/sec (650ft/sec)

Also known as the '.38/200' (from the combination of calibre and bullet weight), this is virtually the standard Smith & Wesson Military & Police Model with the chambers dimensioned to suit the British service cartridge. The design was developed to meet British contracts in 1940 and approximately 1,125,000 were eventually made for British and Commonwealth services. An accurate and handy weapon, its only defect was a tendency for the mainspring to age during long storage, leading to light hammer blows. This was accentuated by the fact that British service caps were harder than American and commercial caps, but an adjusting screw in the front of the grip allowed the mainspring tension to be adjusted so the problem was not serious. The finish on these pistols is a guide to their age. First production, from April 1940 to April 1942, were polished and blued and had 4, 5 or 6in barrels. Until January 1942 the grips were chequered walnut with a silver S&W monogram let into the top. After January 1942 the grips were of smooth walnut without the medallion, and after May 1942 the finish was sandblasted and only 5in barrels were fitted.

SMITH & WESSON .38 No 2

HUNGARY

These pistols represent a successful class of long-recoil operated automatics, a system of operation which demands that the barrel and bolt recoil locked together for a distance greater than the length of a cartridge. The bolt is then unlocked and held fast while the barrel is allowed to return to the forward position, during which movement the empty case is extracted and ejected. As the barrel reaches its firing position, the bolt is released and runs forward to chamber a new round and lock to the barrel. This system appears to have had a mesmeric attraction for the designers Rudolf Frommer, Georg Roth and Karel Krnka, who were, between them, responsible for a wide range of weapons employing this system. The Frommer Stop pistol is one of the few long recoil designs to ever prosper. It is open to question exactly why Frommer went to such lengths to lock the breech on a weapon firing the 7.65mm cartridge; a number were also made in 9mm Short calibre, but even this does not warrant the complexity of the design.

The pistol 12M was adopted by the Honved – the Hungarian element of the Austro–Hungarian reserve army – in 1912, chambered for the 7.65mm cartridge. In 1919 it was officially adopted as the pistol of the newly formed Hungarian Army, as the 19M, though it was precisely the same weapon. A third version, the 39M, was to be made in 9mm Short calibre in 1939 but this project appears to have foundered on the outbreak of war. The 19M remained in production until about 1930 and the pistol is relatively common; it was well-made from excellent materials, somewhat ugly, but not as awkward as it looks and, for all its complexity, had a good reputation for reliability.

In the late 1920s the Hungarian Army decided to adopt a simpler design than the Frommer Stop, and Frommer responded with the Model 29M. This was a simple and robust blowback weapon, somewhat angular, but serviceable and reliable and it went into service in 1930. The pistol used an external hammer, the barrel was retained in the frame by four lugs and a grip safety was fitted into the rear edge of the butt. In the middle 1930s the Army required more pistols and again Frommer came to the rescue with the 37M design. This was simply an improved 29M, the changes being largely cosmetic and resulting in a somewhat better-looking weapon. During World War Two a large number of 37M were made in 7.65mm calibre for the German Army, who adopted it as the Pistole 37(U). These can be distinguished by the German marking 'P MOD 37 KAL 7.65' on the slide and they were also provided with a thumb-operated safety catch on the rear of the frame in addition to the grip safety. (Data table refers to 37M).

7.65mm Pistol 12M and 19M (Frommer 'Stop')

Fegyvergyar es Gepgyar	
7.65 × 17mm (.32 ACP)	
Operation	Long recoil
Length overall	165mm (6.5in)
Weight empty	610g (1.34lb)
Barrel	95mm (3.8in), 4 grooves, rh
Magazine	7-shot detachable box
Muzzle velocity	280m/sec (920ft/sec)

9mm Pistols 29M and 37M

Fegyvergyar es Gepgyar	
9 × 17mm Short or 7.65 × 17mm (.32 ACP)	
Operation	Blowback
Length overall	182mm (7.17in)
Weight empty	770g (1.70lb)
Barrel	110mm (4.33in), 6 grooves, rh

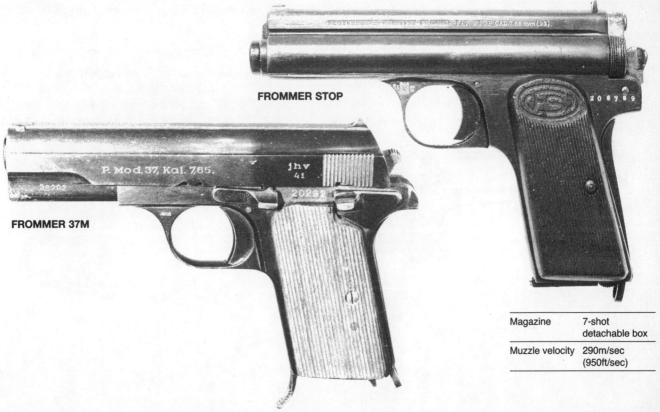

FROMMER STOP

FROMMER 37M

Magazine	7-shot detachable box
Muzzle velocity	290m/sec (950ft/sec)

9mm Pistol 48M (Walam)

Femaru es Szerszamgepgyar	
9 × 17mm Short	
Operation	Double-action, blowback
Length overall	175mm (6.89in)
Weight empty	700g (1.54lb)
Barrel	100mm (3.9in)
Magazine	8-shot detachable box
Muzzle velocity	295m/sec (965ft/sec)

9mm Pistol PA-63

State arsenals	
9 × 18mm Makarov	
Operation	Blowback
Length overall	175mm (6.89in)
Weight empty	595g (1.31lb)
Barrel	100mm (3.94in), 6 grooves, rh
Magazine	7-shot detachable box
Muzzle velocity	295m/sec (965ft/sec)

7.62mm Pistol Model 48

State arsenals	
7.62 × 25mm Soviet	

This pistol was manufactured in Hungary to meet an order from the Egyptian police in the early 1950s. For unknown reasons, the Egyptians abruptly terminated the contract and the balance of the order was completed and disposed of in the commercial market. The pistol is simply a copy of the Walther PP, though with a very slight difference in the chamber-loaded indicator. Early models have the name 'WALAM 48' on the slide; commercial models will have the company name and an ornate star and wreath badge on the grips. Later production was disposed of through a number of West German dealers and may be found with their trade names stamped on the frame.

This is another copy of the Walther PP, developed for the Hungarian Army in the late 1950s. The dimensions differ slightly, and the weapon is lighter than the Walther due to extensive use of light alloy in the construction. It is also manufactured in 7.65mm calibre, probably for police use.

This is simply the standard Soviet TT33 Tokarev pistol made under licence in Hungary. The Hungarian version can be distinguished by the crest on the grip (a star, wheatsheaf and hammer surrounded by a wreath) and by the vertical finger-grip cuts on the slide which are narrower and more uniform than those on Soviet weapons. Dimensions, etc., are exactly as for the Tokarev.

7.65mm WALAM

9mm PA-63

ITALY

The Glisenti pistol was actually designed by Capt. B. A. Revelli, who spent several years developing an automatic pistol through various designs before assigning his patents to the Siderurgica Glisenti in 1902 for further development. They eventually gained approval of their design from the Italian Army and in 1907 began producing a pistol chambered for a cartridge similar to the 7.65mm Parabellum though with a heavier bullet and shorter-necked case than the German standard. In 1907 the company decided to leave the firearms business and sold the patents to Metallurgica Brescia gia Tempini who continued to manufacture the 7.65mm model. In 1908 the Italian Army requested a 9mm pistol, and the design was suitably modified to accept a cartridge of the same dimensions as the 9mm Parabellum but, due to the construction of the pistol, of lesser power. This became the Glisenti Model 1910 and was taken into Italian service. In 1912 the design was slightly modified to simplify production, the external appearance being changed only by the removal of some cosmetic machining work and new grip plates bearing the initials 'MBT'. Internally there were a few minor production changes and the addition of a magazine safety in place of the grip safety used in the 1910 design. Both models bear some resemblance to the Parabellum, though their mechanism is more akin to that of the Mauser C/96, using a lug to lock the bolt. The strength of this lock is insufficient to permit the use of powerful cartridges, which is why the Glisenti round was loaded to a lower velocity. Another weakness is that the whole left side of the frame is a detachable plate which robs the frame of much-needed torsional strength. When used with the correct ammunition, both models are reliable enough, but it is notable that once the Beretta designs began to appear they were more popular with the users. Both the 1910 and 1912 models survived into the early part of World War Two.

When the demands of war outstripped the manufacturing speed of the Glisenti pistol, Beretta were asked to produce a new design. The Model 1915 was a simple blowback and was provided in either of the two quoted calibres. A small number were, however, given a stronger recoil spring and chambered for the 9mm Glisenti cartridge; although safe with this, they are, of course, not suitable for firing the similarly dimensioned 9mm Parabellum round. The pistol fires from a concealed hammer and, after the last round has been fired, the action is held open by the breech face striking the magazine follower. The 7.65mm model has no positive ejector; instead, the spent case is ejected by the firing pin protruding through the breech face at full recoil.

9mm Glisenti Model 10 and Brixia Model 12

Metallurgica Brescia gia Tempini
Societa Siderurgica Glisenti

9 × 19mm Glisenti

Operation	Short recoil
Length overall	207mm (8.22in)
Weight empty	820g (1.81lb)
Barrel	100mm (3.91in), 6 grooves, rh
Magazine	7-shot detachable box
Muzzle velocity	280m/sec (855ft/sec)

7.65mm or 9mm Beretta Model 1915

Pietro Beretta SpA

7.65 × 17mm or 9 × 17mm (.32 ACP or 9mm Short)

Operation	Blowback
Length overall	149mm (5.85in)

GLISENTI MODEL 10

7.65mm BERETTA MODEL 1915

Weight empty	570g (1.25lb)
Barrel	84mm (3.32in), 6 grooves, rh
Magazine	8-shot detachable box
Muzzle velocity	266m(875ft)/sec (7.65mm)

7.65 or 9mm Beretta Model 1915/19

Pietro Beretta SpA

7.65 × 17mm or 9 × 17mm
(.32 ACP or 9mm Short)

Operation	Blowback
Length overall	146mm (5.75in)
Weight empty	670g (1.48lb)
Barrel	87mm (3.43in)
Magazine	7-shot detachable box
Muzzle velocity	297m/sec (975ft/sec)

9mm Beretta Model 1923

Pietro Beretta SpA

9 × 19mm Glisenti

Operation	Blowback
Length overall	177mm (7.0in)
Weight empty	800g (1.76lb)
Barrel	87mm (3.43in)
Magazine	7-shot detachable box
Muzzle velocity	275m/sec (900ft/sec)

7.65mm Beretta Model 1931

Pietro Beretta SpA

7.65 × 17mm (.32 ACP)

After World War One the Model 1915 was redesigned and produced as a commercial model. The general appearance was slightly changed, largely by cutting away the top of the slide from the front sight to the breech face, a characteristic of Beretta pistols ever since. The principal internal change was a complete redesign of the lockwork, giving a much improved trigger pull. Small numbers were taken into military service as the 'Model 1922'.

Since the official Italian service pistol cartridge was still the 9mm Glisenti, it was decided to produce an enlarged Beretta pistol to accept it. This was the Model 1923 which was otherwise similar to the 1915/19 model. It was still a blowback, since although the Glisenti round was more powerful than the 9mm Short, it was still not sufficiently violent to require a locked breech. However, as noted above, since the powerful 9mm Parabellum cartridge will also fit and fire, there is an element of hazard if the user is careless. This may well have been the reason that this pistol did not last long in service, few being made after 1925. The total number placed in service was small and they are rare today.

The Model 1931 was a direct derivative of the preceding models of 1922 and 1923 but in 7.65mm calibre only. Although used only in small numbers by the Italian Army, it is frequently found with the wooden grips carrying a medallion bearing an 'R/anchor/M' device indicating service with the Italian Navy. The characteristics are essentially the same as those of the later Model 1934, for which this 1931 design served as a basis.

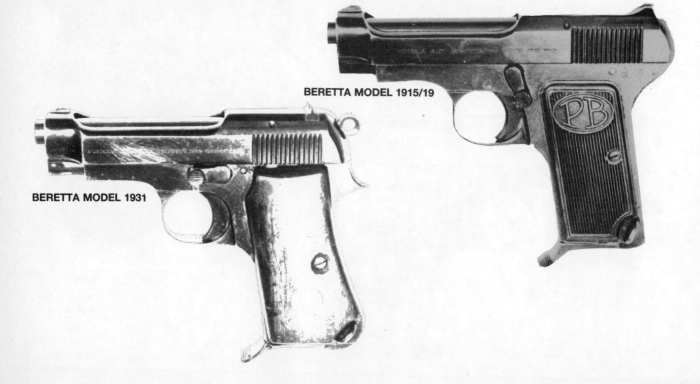

BERETTA MODEL 1915/19

BERETTA MODEL 1931

The 1934 model is, mechanically, an improved model 1915/19, with the addition of an external hammer similar to that of the 1923 and 1931 patterns and a general cleaner appearance. Well made and finished of first-rate material, they are excellent pistols though somewhat underpowered for military use. In common with previous models the magazine follower acts as a slide stop when the last shot has been fired, which is inconvenient in practical use since the slide must be pulled back to free the empty magazine, released forward, then pulled back again to load when the new magazine has been inserted.

A small number of these pistols were produced in 7.65mm calibre; they are somewhat rare today.

After World War Two the Italian Army decided to align themselves with the majority and adopt 9mm Parabellum as their service pistol cartridge. Beretta began the design of their new pistol, known in Italian service as the Model 951, in 1950 but had some difficulties and actual issues did not begin until 1957. This delay was due to the original intention to make the pistol with a light alloy frame, a praiseworthy attempt to keep the weight down, but the result was neither accurate nor pleasant to shoot, and the frame was re-designed in steel, giving a heavier but better weapon.

This is a locked-breech pistol using a locking wedge swinging in the vertical plane, a system very similar to that adopted in the Walther P38. Locking of barrel and breech is achieved by a pair of lugs engaging in recesses in the slide; unlocking is done by a floating plunger carried on the rear barrel lug, which releases the locking wedge to disengage the lugs from the slide on meeting a shoulder in the frame. Relocking is automatically achieved on the return stroke of the slide. An improvement on previous Beretta designs was the adoption of a slide stop which held the slide open after the last round and kept it open while magazines were changed; releasing the slide stop then allowed the slide to run forward and chamber the first round.

The Model 1951 was adopted by Italy, Israel and Egypt; during the 1960s a copy known as the 'Helwan' was made under licence in Egypt. A Model 951A was produced for the Italian Carabinieri. This was similar to the standard 951 but had a fire selector switch on the right side which allowed firing in full-automatic mode. A folding front grip was fitted to the front end of the frame and 10- or 20-shot magazines were available. In more recent years this design was revived as the **Model 951R**, the only difference being that this has a fixed, wooden, front grip and the 20-shot magazine was not provided. This version was issued to Italian Special Forces in small numbers and then went out of production.

9mm Beretta Model 1934

Pietro Beretta SpA	
9 × 17mm Short	
Operation	Blowback
Length overall	152mm (6.0in)
Weight empty	660g (1.46lb)
Barrel	94mm (3.70in)
Magazine	7-shot detachable box
Muzzle velocity	250m/sec (820ft/sec)

9mm Beretta Model 1951

Pietro Beretta SpA	
9 × 19mm Parabellum	
Operation	Short recoil
Length overall	203mm (8.0in)
Weight empty	890g (1.96lb)
Barrel	114mm (4.5in), 6 grooves, rh
Magazine	8-shot detachable box
Cyclic rate	750rds/min (951A and R)
Muzzle velocity	350m/sec (1,148ft/sec)

BERETTA MODEL 1934

BERETTA MODEL 1951

9mm Beretta Models 92, 92S

Pietro Beretta SpA	
9 × 19mm Parabellum	
Operation	Short recoil
Length overall	217mm (8.54in)
Weight empty	950g (2.09lb)
Barrel	125mm (4.92in)
Magazine	15-shot detachable box
Muzzle velocity	390m/sec (1,280ft/sec)

Introduced in 1976, this is really the Model 951 brought up to date and in line with contemporary thinking. The magazine capacity is increased and the trigger mechanism is now double-action, but the locking system and general appearance is still that of the Model 951. The Model 92S resembles the Model 92 but has an improved safety system. The safety catch is now on the slide (instead of the frame) and functions also as a de-cocking lever. When applied it deflects the firing pin away from the path of the hammer, releases the hammer, and breaks the connection between the trigger bar and the sear. Both models were adopted by the Italian and other armies and police forces in some considerable numbers. Production ceased in the middle 1980s.

9mm Beretta Model 92SB

Pietro Beretta SpA	
9 × 19mm Parabellum	
Operation	Short recoil
Length overall	197mm (7.75in)
Weight empty	980g (2.16lb)
Barrel	109mm (4.29in),
Magazine	13-shot detachable box
Muzzle velocity	385m/sec (1,263ft/sec)

In 1980 the US Army began trials to find a pistol to replace the Colt M1911A1, and Beretta modified their Model 92 to suit the US Army specification, resulting in the Model 92SB. It differed from the 92 in having a safety catch on both sides of the slide, a magazine catch behind the trigger guard, where it can be moved to either side as desired, and a new system of safeties including an automatic firing pin lock. The hammer was given a half-cock notch, and the butt is grooved at the rear to improve grip. The dimensions, etc., are exactly as for the Model 92. A 'compact' model, the 92SB-C was developed at the same time. This is similar and differs only in dimensions, which are set out in the data table.

9mm Beretta Model 92F

Pietro Beretta SpA	
9 × 19mm Parabellum	

The Model 92SB walked away with the US trials, but the Army required some minor changes before accepting it as the Pistol M9. The trigger guard was re-shaped to suit the two-handed grip, the magazine had its base extended to improve the grip and the butt front edge was curved at the toe, new grip plates and lanyard ring were fitted. The barrel is chromed internally and the external finish is 'Bruniton', a Teflon-type material. Since adoption by the US Army the Model 92F has been taken into use by the French Gendarmerie Nationale and by many military and police forces throughout the world. The dimensions, etc., are as for the Model 92.

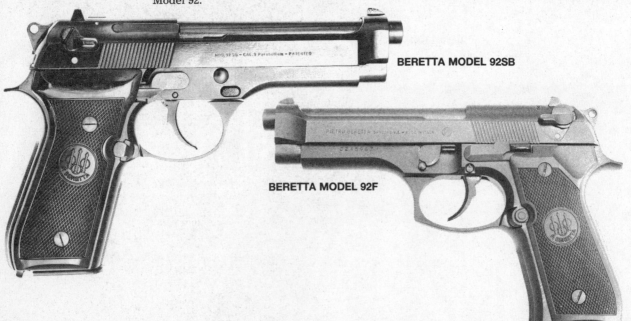

BERETTA MODEL 92SB

BERETTA MODEL 92F

This is really the 951R brought up-to-date, a selective-fire pistol with a three-round burst facility and several other refinements aimed at turning it into a passable machine pistol. The basic weapon is almost identical to the Model 92. There is a front grip which can be folded down to be grasped by the firer's free hand, giving better support than the fashionable two-handed grip usually used. For more deliberate work a folding stock can be attached to the butt. A fire selector lever on the left side of the frame allows selection of single shots or three-round bursts, and this facility is best used with the stock in place. Another accessory is an extended 20-shot magazine, useful when the burst-fire facility is used. A muzzle brake adds to the controllability of the weapon. The 93R has been adopted by Italian and other special forces.

9mm Beretta Model 93R

Pietro Beretta SpA	
9 × 19mm Parabellum	
Operation	Short recoil
Length overall	240mm (9.45in)
Weight empty	1,120g (2.47lb)
Barrel	156mm (6.14in)
Magazine	15- or 20-shot detachable box
Cyclic rate	1,100rds/min
Muzzle velocity	375m/sec (1,230ft/sec)

Beretta Variations

These are a number of variations upon the basic Beretta pistols which deserve recording, since they may turn up in military or police service, but are not sufficiently different to deserve full entries.

9mm Model SB-C Type M This is the Model SB-C but with an 8-shot single-column magazine with a shaped base providing a rest for the little finger.

7.65mm Model 98 The Model 98 is the SB-C chambered for the 7.65mm Parabellum cartridge, and is primarily intended for police use.

7.65mm Model 98F This is the same as the 92F but chambered for the 7.65mm Parabellum cartridge.

9mm Model 98F This is generally the same as the 92F but is a target pistol chambered for the 9 × 21mm cartridge, thus permitting it to be sold to countries in which 9mm Parabellum is legally a 'military' calibre and thus prohibited for commercial sale. It is also fitted with anatomical grips, target sights and a muzzle counterweight.

7.65mm Model 99 This is the same as the SB-C Type M but chambered for the 7.65mm Parabellum cartridge.

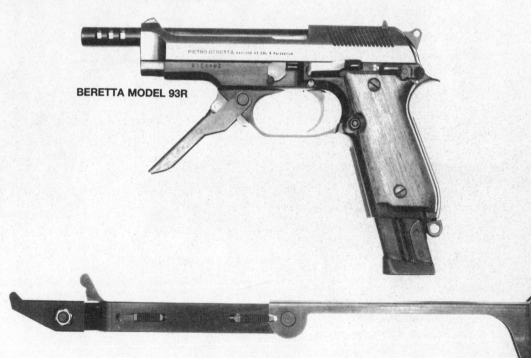

BERETTA MODEL 93R

9mm Bernadelli Model P-018

Vincenzo Bernadelli SpA	
9 × 19mm Parabellum	
Operation	Short recoil
Length overall	213mm (8.4in)
Weight empty	998g (2.20lb)
Barrel	122mm (4.8in), 6 grooves rh
Magazine	14-shot detachable box
Muzzle velocity	350m/sec (1,150ft/sec)

This is a double-action pistol, recoil operated and using a locking block system of breech locking. Somewhat square in outline it balances well and has a relatively soft recoil. A compact model is also manufactured, and both can be had in 7.65mm Parabellum calibre.

9mm Tanfoglio TA-90

Fratelli Tanfoglio SpA	
9 × 19mm Parabellum	
Operation	Short recoil
Length overall	202mm (7.95in)
Weight empty	1,015g (2.23lb)
Barrel	120mm (4.7in), 6 grooves, rh
Magazine	15-shot detachable box
Muzzle velocity	350m/sec (1,150ft/sec)

The TA-90 is a conventional double-action pistol, which appears to owe much of its inspiration to the Czech CZ75. However, the quality is exceptionally good, the barrel being rifled groove-by-groove in the traditional manner, and very accurate. There are a number of variant models chambered for the 7.65mm Parabellum, 9mm Police and 9 × 21mm cartridges, as well as a compact version. The pistol in its standard form appears to have a good commercial sale and lesser sales to police and security forces in various parts of the world.

TANFOGLIO TA-90

BERNADELLI MODEL P-018

JAPAN

Adopted in 1893 this is of local design insofar as it is an amalgam of features taken from various Western revolvers. The barrel latch and cylinder mechanism are from the contemporary Smith & Wesson design, the lock and trigger mechanism from European patterns, and the whole construction leans heavily on Nagant principles. It can be described as robust and serviceable, but little more. It is a self-cocking revolver, incapable of single action, uses a side-swinging cylinder and has a hinged cover plate in the frame which can be opened to expose the lockwork in much the same way as the French Mle 1892 revolver. The ammunition is unique to the weapon, and although some makes of commercial .380 might be persuaded to fit, it is not to be recommended.

9mm Type 26 Revolver

Koishikawa Arsenal, Tokyo

9 × 22R Japanese

Operation	Self-cocking revolver
Length overall	216mm (8.5in)
Weight empty	880g (1.94lb)
Barrel	120mm (4.7in), 6 grooves, lh
Magazine	6-shot cylinder
Muzzle velocity	230m/sec (755ft/sec)

Designed by Colonel Kirijo Nambu, this pistol was first made in 1906 for commercial sale and for sale to Japanese army officers; it was not formally adopted by the army, though the navy adopted it in 1909. The first production models were fitted for a wooden holster stock which attached to the butt, but this was abandoned after 1912. The Nambu is a locked breech design, the breech being locked by a floating locking block attached to the barrel extension. As the barrel unit moves forward, so this block is lifted by riding across the pistol frame, so forcing a lug upwards to lock into a recess in the bolt. There is no hold-open lock, the magazine follower holding the bolt back after the last shot has been fired, so that as soon as the empty magazine is withdrawn (with difficulty) the bolt closes. The striker spring is notoriously weak and spares were invariably carried in the holster. There is no manual safety, but a grip safety is fitted to the front of the butt. The Model 1904 exists in several variant versions. The first has a small cramped trigger-guard and the magazine bottom is of wood; the government of Siam (Thailand) acquired a number – perhaps 500 – of these in the 1920s. The latter versions have the magazine bottom of aluminium and a larger trigger-guard; there are also minor differences between pistols made by the two manufacturers.

8mm Nambu Model 1904

Koishikawa Arsenal (1906–27); Tokyo Gas & Electric Co (1915–30)

8 × 21.5mm Nambu

Operation	Short recoil
Length overall	228mm (8.97in)
Weight empty	880g (1.94lb)
Barrel	120mm (4.7in), 6 grooves, rh
Magazine	8-shot detachable box
Muzzle velocity	335m/sec (1,100ft/sec)

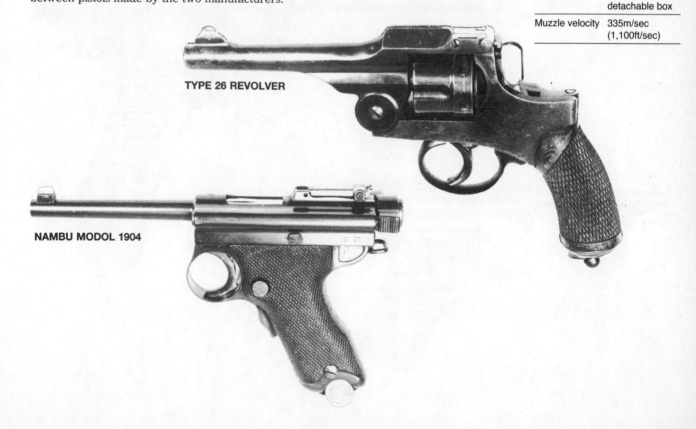

TYPE 26 REVOLVER

NAMBU MODOL 1904

8mm Nambu 14th Year

Nagoya Arsenal (1927–33; 1941–5);
Koishikawa Arsenal (1928–34);
Kokura Arsenal (1934–6);
Nambu Rifle Mfg Co (1936–44)

8 × 21.5mm Nambu

Operation	Short recoil
Length overall	227mm (8.93in)
Weight empty	900g (1.98lb)
Barrel	121mm (4.76in)
Magazine	8-shot detachable box
Muzzle velocity	335m/sec (1,100ft/sec)

7mm Small Nambu (Baby)

Koishikawa Arsenal (1911–27);
Tokyo Gas & Electric Co (1927–33)

7 × 19.5mm Nambu

Operation	Short recoil
Length overall	171mm (6.75in)
Weight empty	650g (1.43lb)
Barrel	83mm (3.25in), 6 grooves, rh
Magazine	7-shot detachable box
Muzzle velocity	290m/sec (950ft/sec)

The 14th Year Nambu is virtually an improved 4th Year and was introduced in 1925–6, the object of the improvements being to simplify manufacture and reduce the cost to a level at which the Japanese Army would be prepared formally to adopt the pistol. There are minor changes in the design to this end, but the basic weapon is the same. A safety catch was added, which can only be operated by the firer's free hand, to replace the grip safety, and the magazine-actuated hold-open was continued. The dual recoil springs and a magazine retaining spring (on later models) ensured that the chances of removing the magazine were only good when the weapon was well-maintained and the user's hands were dry. This led to the untimely demise of many Japanese soldiers. The 14th Year was officially adopted by the Army in 1927 as an issue pistol for NCOs and was available for purchase by officers. In the last quarter of 1939 the trigger guard was enlarged, as a result of experience in Manchuria, to allow the pistol to be used in a gloved hand. This version also has a magazine retaining spring let into the front edge of the grip. The model is sometimes referred to as the 'Kiska' model, since the first to be seen outside Japan were captured in the Aleutian Islands.

The Type 04 Nambu had disappointing sales, because most officers thought it too cumbersome, so in about 1910 Nambu developed this weapon, a three-quarters size version chambered for a new 7mm cartridge. Even so, it was still not widely liked since it cost about twice as much as contemporary Western designs. It remained in production until 1927 at Koishikawa Arsenal, and until the early 1930s at Tokyo Gas & Electric. It is doubtful if more than 6,000 or so were made.

NAMBU 14th YEAR

BABY NAMBU

Confronted by sales resistance to his designs, due principally to their bulk and price, Nambu set about designing a smaller and cheaper pistol in 1929. The first prototypes were submitted to the Army for their evaluation, whereupon the ordnance department began tinkering with the design, one result of which was the unprepossessing appearance and another a far higher price than even the 14th Year Nambu. Nevertheless, since the Army had approved the idea, the design was accepted and put into production in 1935. An estimated 70,000 or so were made before production ceased in 1945. Although prewar guns were well made and finished, the Type 94 rates as one of the world's worst automatic pistols. The design allows it to be fired before the breech is locked, and an exposed sear bar can be released to fire the pistol if clumsily handled. Breech locking is done by a very simple vertically sliding block which is cammed out of engagement during recoil. Guns manufactured in 1944–5 are generally crudely put together and finished.

The New Nambu revolver is a conventional solid-frame side-opening type. The grip is rather small by Western standards but the pistol is well made and robust, and is accurate. It has been the official Japanese police revolver since the early 1960s, being adopted in deference to American influence at that time. Since then two designs of automatic pistol, in 9mm and 7.65mm calibres, have been put forward but have not been accepted. The Model 60 is also used by the Japanese Maritime Safety Guard.

8mm Type 94

Nambu Rifle Mfg Co

8 × 21.5mm Nambu

Operation	Short recoil
Length overall	183mm (7.2in)
Weight empty	765g (1.68lb)
Barrel	96mm (3.77in), 6 grooves, rh
Magazine	6-shot detachable box
Muzzle velocity	305m/sec (1,000ft/sec)

.38mm Nambu Model 60 Revolver

Shin Chuo Kogyo, Tokyo

.38in Special

Operation	Double-action revolver
Length overall	197mm (7.75in)
Weight empty	680g (1.50lb)
Barrel	77mm (3.03in)
Magazine	5-shot cylinder
Muzzle velocity	220m/sec (725ft/sec)

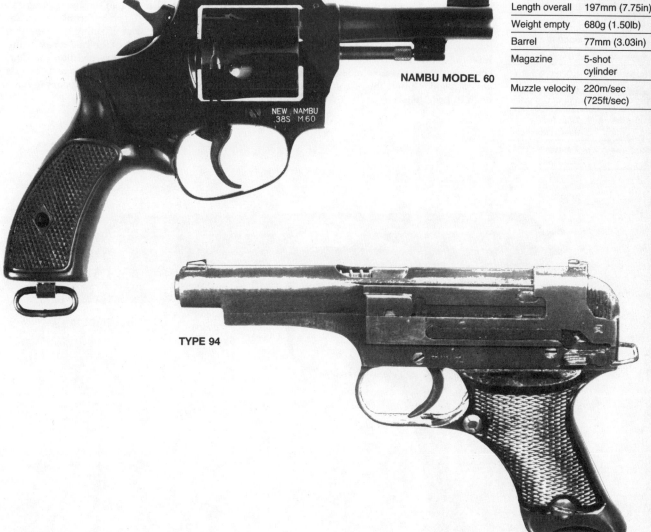

NAMBU MODEL 60

TYPE 94

KOREA, NORTH

7.62mm Type 68

State arsenals	
7.62 × 25mm Soviet	
Operation	Short recoil
Length overall	185mm (7.28in)
Weight empty	795g (1.75lb)
Barrel	108mm (4.25in), 4 grooves, rh
Magazine	8-shot box
Muzzle velocity	395m/sec (1,296ft/sec)

This is a much-modified Tokarev TT-33, shorter and more bulky than the original weapon or any other copies. It can be easily distinguished by the narrow oblique serrations at the rear of the slide. Internally the link system, which pulls the barrel in and out of engagement with the slide, has been replaced by a cam cut into a lug beneath the chamber; the magazine catch has been relocated to the heel of the butt; the slide stop pin has been strengthened, and the firing pin is retained by a plate instead of a cross-pin. The Tokarev magazine will work in this pistol, but the North Korean magazines have no cut-out for the Tokarev magazine catch and are thus unusable in that pistol.

MEXICO

.45in Obregon

Fabrica de Armas	
.45 ACP	
Operation	Short recoil
Length overall	210mm (8.25in)
Weight empty	1,020g (2.25lb)
Barrel	124mm (4.88in), 6 grooves, lh
Magazine	7-shot detachable box
Muzzle velocity	260m/sec (850ft/sec)

Outwardly this resembles the Colt M1911A1 except that there is a prominent safety catch/slide lock on the left side and the forward half of the slide is rounded. This is due to the adoption of a rotating barrel system of locking the breech. A helical cam on the barrel engages with a lug on the frame to rotate the barrel out of engagement with the slide during recoil. An unusual feature is that the designer adopted the Colt left-handed twist of rifling, making this the only rotating barrel design to operate right-handed, since the motion of the bullet resists the rotation of the barrel. Theoretically, the Obregon should shoot more accurately than the Colt, since the barrel remains axially stable; there are, though, no known comparative test records which might support this theory. The Obregon is well made and finished, and appears to have been in production from the mid-1940s to the mid-1950s.

wz/35 RADOM

POLAND

The Polish Model 35 pistol is variously known as the Radom, from its place of manufacture, or the VIS, from its designers Wilneiwczyc and Skrzypinski. Breech locking is performed by a cam-dropped barrel, similar to the Browning High-Power. On the slide is a catch which drops the hammer under control on to a loaded chamber, after first blocking the hammer's path to the firing pin, allowing subsequent thumb-cocking. On the frame is a switch which appears to be a safety catch but which is a slide lock to facilitate stripping. The only true safety device is a grip safety. During the course of the German occupation of Poland these weapons were made for the German Army as the Pistole 35(p) and may be found very roughly finished and without the hammer release or slide lock. The original Polish pistols are easily identified by the Polish eagle engraved on the slide, as well as by their excellent fit and finish. Heavier and larger than the general run of 9mm pistols, the Radom is among the best and certainly one of the most pleasant to shoot.

9mm wz/35 Radom

Fabryka Broni Radom	
9 × 19mm Parabellum	
Operation	Short recoil
Length overall	211mm (8.3in)
Weight empty	1,050g (2.31lb)
Barrel	115mm (4.53in), 6 grooves, rh
Magazine	8-shot detachable box
Muzzle velocity	350m/sec (1,150ft/sec)

This is the standard Polish service pistol and is an amalgam of features from the Soviet Makarov and German Walther PP patterns. Operation is blowback, and the trigger is a double-action mechanism similar to that of the Makarov, a simple and robust design. The safety catch is on the slide and when operated it rotates two lugs to protect the firing pin and then drops the hammer. A sound and simple design, it may not be very novel but is obviously serviceable and reliable.

9mm P-64

State arsenals	
9 × 18mm Makarov	
Operation	Blowback
Length overall	155mm (6.10in)
Weight empty	636g (1.40lb)
Barrel	84mm (3.31in), 4 grooves, rh
Magazine	6-shot detachable box
Muzzle velocity	314m/sec (1,030ft/sec)

SOUTH AFRICA

This pistol was developed in 1986 against a demand from the South African Defence Force, and went into production in 1989. It takes its title from the late T. D. Zeederberg, former general manager of Lyttleton Engineering, and from its year of approval. The design is that of the Beretta 92, although the precise connection is not known and it is unlikely that Beretta flouted the UN embargo on the supply of weapons technology to South Africa. Nevertheless, the appearance, functioning and dimensions are exactly the same as the Beretta. Perhaps 'imitation is the sincerest form of flattery'.

9mm Z-88

Lyttleton Engineering Works	
9 × 19mm Parabellum	

Z-88

SPAIN

9mm Campo-Giro Model 1913

Esperanza y Unceta Cia	
9 × 23mm Largo	
Operation	Blowback
Length overall	204mm (8.03in)
Weight empty	950g (2.09lb)
Barrel	165mm (6.49in), 6 grooves, rh
Magazine	7-shot detachable box
Muzzle velocity	355m/sec (1,165ft/sec)

9mm Astra Model 1921

Unceta y Compania	
9 × 23mm Largo	
Operation	Blowback
Length overall	235mm (9.25in)
Weight empty	1,080g (2.38lb)
Barrel	140mm (5.5in), 6 grooves, rh
Magazine	8-shot detachable box
Muzzle velocity	345m/sec (1,132ft/sec)

Designed by the Count of Campo-Giro, this was Unceta y Cia's first successful automatic design. Development began in 1900 and the pistol was adopted by the Spanish Army in 1913, rapidly replaced by a slightly modified model of 1916 which paved the way for the subsequent and successful Astra designs. Like the Astras which followed, the Campo-Giro is a blowback weapon designed around the 9mm Bergmann-Bayard cartridge, which, as the '9mm Largo', has been the standard Spanish service cartridge since their 1905 adoption of the Bergmann 'Mars' pistol. It should be noted, though, that the first Campo-Giro of 1904 was designed around a different and unique 9mm cartridge. Although of somewhat awkward appearance, the Campo-Giro was well made. A blowback, it relies entirely upon a powerful recoil spring to hold the breech closed during firing, and has a shock absorber in the frame to reduce the hammering of the slide during recoil and run-out. About 1,000 pistols were made, and then, in 1916, a change was made in the location of the magazine release, turning the pistol into the 'Model 13/16', and some 13,000 of these were made.

This, as is obvious from its appearance, is based on the Campo-Giro design and is simply an improved version. The improvements are largely in manufacturing techniques, the blowback mechanism being exactly the same. Early models had the Campo-Giro shock absorber but this was soon abandoned and the recoil and hammer springs take all the strain. The pistol was adopted by the Spanish Army in 1921 and remained their service pistol until the late 1940s. It was also sold commercially as the 'Astra 400'. A unique feature of this pistol is its ability to chamber and fire almost every 9mm cartridge and also the .38 Colt Auto round. This is due to careful dimensioning of the chamber and an unusually long firing pin which will reach sufficiently far to strike the primer of the shorter rounds. Nevertheless, this ability is only reliable in pistols which have seen little use; worn pistols are less likely to fire 9mm Parabellum or Glisenti cartridges since they frequently fail to feed cleanly into the chamber.

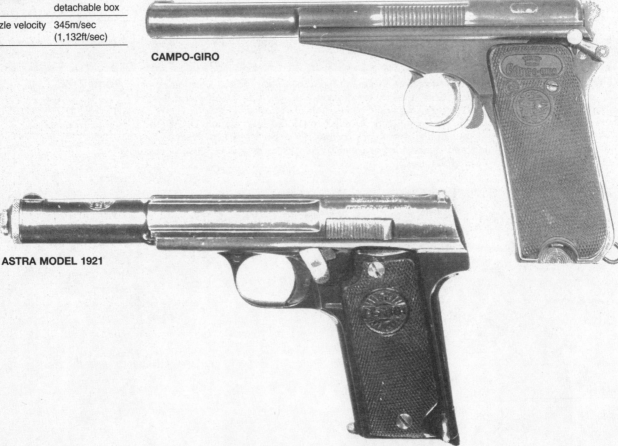

CAMPO-GIRO

ASTRA MODEL 1921

Outwardly this is a copy of the Mauser C/96 pistol; internally it is somewhat different from Mauser's mechanism. The left side of the frame is formed into a sliding plate which can be removed to give access to the lockwork, which is built into the frame and not, as in the Mauser, in a separate removable unit. The barrel is screwed and shrunk into the barrel extension not, as in the Mauser, an integral forging. The general design of the frame is different and the weapon is heavier and more solid, but all this modification has led to a heavy trigger pull, since the internal mechanism has been designed with an eye more to cost than to efficiency. While the weapon is an avowed copy of Mauser's design, the recoil of the barrel and bolt locked together is more than double the distance covered by the Mauser, a fact which defies rational explanation. The Model 900 began production in 1928, aimed largely at the Chinese and South American markets where the Mauser was a prestige weapon but where the genuine article was too expensive. Like the Mauser, it was also supplied with a wooden holster-stock. Production ended in the late 1930s, although some may have been assembled as late as the early 1950s.

This was an improved version of the Model 900, made by fitting a longer barrel, increasing the magazine capacity, and fitting a selector switch to permit full automatic fire. This, with the shoulder stock, turned the pistol into a rudimentary submachine-gun. The automatic fire selector is a short lever on the right side of the frame behind the trigger guard. Set vertically to the figure '1' it gives single shots; turned through 45° to the rear to the figure '20' it permits automatic fire. The pistol was only manufactured for two years, 1930 to 1931, and is uncommon today.

7.63mm Astra Model 900

Unceta y Cia	
7.63 × 25mm Mauser	
Operation	Short recoil
Length overall	317mm (12.5in)
Weight empty	1,300g (2.85lb)
Barrel	140mm (5.5in), 6 grooves, rh
Magazine	10-shot detachable box
Muzzle velocity	440m/sec (1,443ft/sec)

7.63mm Astra Model 902

Unceta y Cia	
7.63 × 25mm Mauser	
Operation	Short recoil, selective
Length overall	362mm (14.25in)
Weight empty	1,360g (3.0lb)
Barrel	183mm (7.2in), 6 grooves, rh
Magazine	20-shot integral box
Muzzle velocity	455m/sec (1,493ft/sec)

ASTRA MODEL 902

9mm Astra A-80 and A-90

Unceta y Cia	
9 × 19mm Parabellum	
Operation	Short recoil
Length overall	180mm (7.10in)
Weight empty	985g (2.17lb)
Barrel	96.5mm (3.80in)
Magazine	15-shot detachable box
Muzzle velocity	350m/sec (1,150ft/sec)

9mm Llama Model IX

Gabilondo y Cia	
9 × 23mm Largo	
Operation	Short recoil
Length overall	215mm (8.45in)
Weight empty	870g (1.92lb)
Barrel	127mm (5.0in), 6 grooves, rh
Magazine	8-shot detachable box
Muzzle velocity	435m/sec (1,427ft/sec)

9mm Llama M-82

Llama Gabilondo y Cia SA	
9 × 19mm Parabellum	
Operation	Short recoil
Length overall	209mm (8.23in)
Weight empty	1,110g (2.45lb)
Barrel	114mm (4.48in), 6 grooves, rh
Magazine	15-shot detachable box
Muzzle velocity	345m/sec (1,132ft/sec)

This pistol appears to have been influenced by the SIG P-220, having similar angular contours and a de-cocking lever which can lower the hammer safely. The firing pin is locked by a spring-loaded plunger which is engaged at all times except when the trigger is fully pulled back and is about to release the hammer. The breech is locked by a cam beneath the chamber which pulls the barrel from engagement with the slide. A safety catch is fitted on both sides of the pistol and the de-cocking lever can be removed from the left side, its normal place, and a special left-handed version fitted on the right side of the frame. The extractor functions as a loaded chamber indicator, and the sights have white inlays for use in poor light. The A-80 was introduced in 1980 and has been purchased by a number of military and security forces. In 1985 an improved design, the A-90 was introduced. This has an improved trigger mechanism and adjustable sights but is otherwise the same as the A-80.

The Llama series of pistols, produced in a variety of calibres to suit all customers, are simply copies of the Colt M1911A1 pistol, differing only in dimensions. The model chambered for the 9mm Largo cartridge was used in limited numbers by the Spanish Army for some years and also by Spanish police units. Specimens in 9mm Parabellum and 9mm Short were purchased by various combatant nations during World War Two. A few were also made for the .45 ACP cartridge.

This is a modern double-action pistol introduced in 1988 and adopted by the Spanish Army. Breech locking is performed by a dropping wedge, similar to the system used on the Walther P38. There is a slide-mounted safety catch which, when operated, conceals and locks the firing pin and disconnects the trigger bar. With the safety catch applied, loading the pistol will cause the hammer to fall safely, after which removing the safety and pulling the trigger fires the first shot.

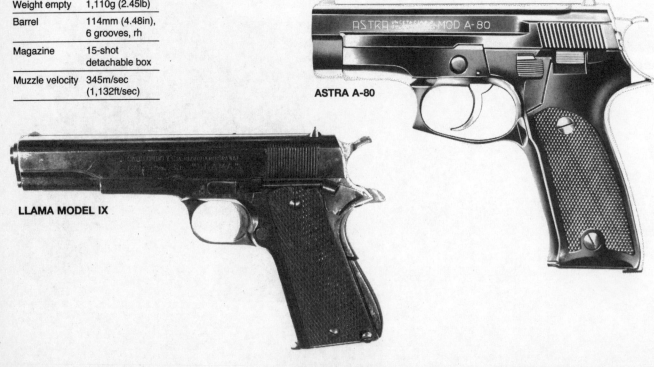

ASTRA A-80

LLAMA MODEL IX

The Star series of pistols are well distributed around the world in a variety of styles and calibres. The military models were generally based on the Colt M1911A1 pattern, though the smaller calibres are simple blowback weapons and the larger, although adhering to the Browning swinging link system of breech locking, show one or two simplifications such as the absence of a grip safety, intended to make their manufacture easier and cheaper. In addition to the 9mm Largo calibre for Spanish service use, the Model A could be supplied in .38 ACP and 7.63mm Mauser chambering, the latter being especially common. A minor aberration of the 1930s was the attempt to turn a reasonable pistol into a second-rate submachine-gun; Star duly made their run at this by modifying the Model A to achieve automatic fire, calling it the Model MD. Some were provided with the usual holster-stock and optimistic rear sight and with longer magazines holding 16 or 32 shots. Like all such conversions, and perhaps more so due to their powerful cartridge, they were quite impractical. The Model MD was manufactured in the early 1930s, just prior to the Spanish Civil War, and a number were supplied to the Nicaraguan Army; beyond that their military employment was rare.

The Super Star is little different from its predecessor the Model A. There are slight changes in the contours of the butt and there is a two-piece slide stop instead of a one-piece, and it is generally of a better quality and finish. The Spanish issue models were, of course, chambered for the 9mm Largo round, but commercially they were also available in 9mm Parabellum, .38 Super Auto and .45 ACP.

9mm Star Models A and MD

Star Bonifacio Echeverria SA

9 × 23mm Largo

Operation	Short recoil
Length overall	202mm (7.95in)
Weight empty	960g (2.12lb)
Barrel	127mm (5.0in), 4 grooves, rh
Magazine	8-shot box; 16 or 32 shot for Model M
Cyclic rate	800rds/min (Model M)
Muzzle velocity	365m/sec (1,200ft/sec)

9mm Star Super

Star Bonifacio Echeverria SA

9 × 23mm Largo

Operation	Short recoil
Length overall	204mm (8.03in)
Weight empty	1,020g (2.25lb)
Barrel	134mm (5.25in), 4 grooves, rh
Magazine	9-shot detachable box
Muzzle velocity	365m/sec (1,200ft/sec)

STAR SUPER

9mm Star Model 30M and 30PK

Star Bonifacio Echeverria SA	
9 × 19mm Parabellum	
Operation	Short recoil
Length overall	205mm (8.07in) (30M); 193mm (7.6in) (30PK)
Weight empty	1,140g (2.51lb) (30M); 860g (1.9lb) (30PK)
Barrel	119mm (30M); 98mm (30PK)
Magazine	15-shot detachable box
Muzzle velocity	380m/sec (1,250ft/sec)

A modern design introduced in 1988, the Model 30 uses the cam method of locking the breech and is somewhat unusual in having the slide running in internal frame rails; this gives excellent support throughout the slide movement and adds to accuracy. The trigger is double-action, and there is an automatic firing pin lock which only frees the firing pin during the last movement of the trigger. There is an ambidextrous safety catch on the slide which retracts the firing pin into its tunnel, out of reach of the hammer. The trigger and hammer action are not controlled by the safety catch and it is possible, after applying the safety, to pull the trigger and drop the hammer quite safely.

The Model 30M is made entirely of forged steel, while the Model 30PK has a light alloy frame. Both have been adopted by Spanish military and police forces and by police and security forces of Peru.

SWEDEN

9mm Pistol m/07

Fabrique Nationale Herstal; Husqvarna Vapenfabrik AB	
9mm Browning Long	

The Swedish Pistol m/07 is actually the Browning Model 1903 in 9mm Browning Long calibre. This was originally bought from Fabrique Nationale Herstal, but in 1908 Husqvarna Vapenfabrik began manufacture in Sweden, which continued until 1943, when the Pistol m/40 largely replaced it. In the middle 1980s the m/40 ran into trouble (see below) and the old m/07 models which had been put into reserve store were brought out and reissued. Dimensions, etc., are exactly as for the Model 1903 listed under Belgium.

9mm Pistol m/40

Husqvarna Vapenfabrik AB	
9 × 19mm Parabellum	
Operation	Short recoil
Length overall	272mm (10.7in)
Weight empty	1,100g (2.425lb)
Barrel	140mm (5.5in), 4 grooves, rh
Magazine	8-shot detachable box
Muzzle velocity	390m/sec (1,280ft/sec)

The Pistol m/40 is the Swedish-made version of the Finnish Lahti pistol (qv). In 1939 the Swedes had decided to adopt the Walther P38 but the outbreak of war stopped that; they therefore turned to Finland and obtained a licence for the Lahti. Production was to be done by Svenska Automatvapen AB but they went bankrupt before they were even tooled up, so Husqvarna took on the contract, the first pistols reaching the army in 1942. There are some differences in the Swedish version; it has a slightly longer barrel with a hexagonal at the breech reinforce, and the trigger guard is thicker and more oval. It does not have the Finnish loaded-chamber indicator and the foresight is higher, with a vertical rear edge. Some 83,950 pistols were made, the odd 950 being for the Danish Free Corps in Sweden, before production stopped in 1946. In general, the Swedish weapon was never as good as the original Finnish product, due to changes in the specification of the steels required in order to suit the wartime availability of steel in Sweden. This chicken came home to roost in the early 1980s when it was found that using the standard Swedish 9mm Parabellum round, which is hotted up for use in submachine-guns, in the m/40 pistols was leading to cracked frames; it was this which led to the resurrection of the m/07 pistol and the withdrawal of almost all the remaining m/40 weapons.

STAR MODEL 30

9mm PISTOL m/40

SWITZERLAND

The Swiss adopted the Parabellum pistol in 1901, followed by an improved version in 1906. These were precisely the same as the current German pistols of the day, though they were made under licence in Berne. In the 1920s the Swiss Army, dismayed at the cost of these pistols, asked Berne to try and devise modifications to reduce the price. Knurling on the toggles was eliminated, the front strap of the grip made straight, and plastic grip plates were fitted. This reduced the price somewhat but the pistol was still more expensive to make than to buy from Germany. Nevertheless, the Swiss Army adopted it, accepting the higher price as the cost of having control of their own pistol supply.

The 06/29 entered service in 1933 and some 27,900 were made before production ended in 1947; another 2,000 or so were made for commercial sale.

In 1937 SIG took up the Petter patents held by SACM (See France, Pistol 35A) and began to develop them for possible commercial use. The war put an end to that idea, but they continued work until in 1946, when the Swiss Army was looking for a replacement for the 06/29 Parabellum, they were able to put forward a finished design which was accepted as the Model 49. It was then put into commercial sale and attained great success since its accuracy and quality were unparalleled. The pistol was later adopted by the Danish Army, but its cost excluded it from consideration by other forces. The SIG P-210 is basically a Browning-locked pistol using a lug beneath the breech to move the barrel out of engagement with the slide. A notable feature, rarely copied elsewhere, is that the slide runs on rails inside the frame, rather than outside as is common. This gives the slide excellent support and contributes to the accuracy. There are several sub-models within the P-210 range; P-210-1 has a polished finish and wood grips; P-210-2 a sand-blasted finish and plastic grips; P-210-4 is a special production model for the West German Border Police; P-210-5 a target version with 150mm barrel; and P-210-6 a target model with 120mm barrel. The -1, -2 and -6 versions are produced in either 7.65mm or 9mm Parabellum chambering, and they can be converted to and from either calibre by substituting barrels and return springs. By changing barrels, springs, slide and magazine they can also be converted to .22 rimfire.

7.65mm Pistol 06/29

Waffenfabrik Berne

7.65 × 21mm Parabellum

Operation	Short recoil
Length overall	241mm (9.5in)
Weight empty	898g (1.98lb)
Barrel	120mm (4.7in)
Magazine	8-shot detachable box
Muzzle velocity	365m/sec (1,200ft/sec)

9mm Pistol M49 (SIG P-210)

Schweizerische Industrie Gesellschaft (SIG)

9 × 19mm Parabellum

Operation	Short recoil
Length overall	215mm (8.46in)
Weight empty	900g (1.98lb)
Barrel	120mm (4.7in), 6 grooves, rh
Magazine	8-shot detachable box
Muzzle velocity	335m/sec (1,100ft/sec)

7.65mm PISTOL 06/29

SIG P210

9mm Pistol 75 (SIG-Sauer P-220)

Schweizerische Industrie Gesellschaft (SIG); J. P. Sauer & Sohn	
9 × 19mm Parabellum	
Operation	Short recoil
Length overall	198mm (7.79in)
Weight empty	830g (1.83lb)
Barrel	112mm (4.40in), 6 grooves, rh
Magazine	9-shot detachable box
Muzzle velocity	345m/sec (1,132ft/sec)

9mm SIG-Sauer P-225

Schweizerische Industrie Gesellschaft (SIG); J. P. Sauer & Sohn	
9 × 19mm Parabellum	
Operation	Short recoil
Length overall	180mm (7.08in)
Weight empty	740g (1.63lb)
Barrel	98mm (3.85in), 6 grooves, rh
Magazine	8-shot detachable box
Muzzle velocity	340m/sec (1,115ft/sec)

SIG are in an invidious position; they produce some of the world's best firearms, but due to the Swiss government's political stance, find it difficult to export; as somebody said, they can only sell guns to people who don't want them. By associating with J. P. Sauer & Sohn of West Germany, their pistols can be made in Germany, whose export regulations are rather less restrictive, opening up a wider market. The designs are almost entirely SIG, though there are one or two features which may have been influenced by Sauer.

The P-220 is really the result of re-engineering the P-210 to make it easier and less expensive to produce. It retains the dropping barrel, but the method of locking into the slide is much simpler; a squared block around the chamber fits into the enlarged ejection port in the slide and does the locking. Instead of machining from slabs of steel, the new design makes use of investment castings which are then machined on computer-controlled tools. The trigger is double action and there is a de-cocking lever on the left side of the frame to permit the hammer to be lowered safely and then, if desired, cocked for single-action firing. There is an automatic firing pin lock which only allows the pin to move when the trigger is correctly pulled. In view of these features SIG see no reason to have a manual safety catch on the pistol. The P-220 was adopted by the Swiss Army as their Pistol 75; it is also used by the Japanese Self-Defence Force and by a number of Special Forces.

This is little more than a smaller and lighter version of the P-220 with an improved automatic firing pin locking system which quite positively prevents the pistol accidentally firing if dropped, even if the hammer is driven forward. The P-225 has been adopted by several Swiss and West German police forces (as the Pistole 6) and in other countries. It is believed that the US Secret Service have adopted it, and certainly a number of Special Forces use it.

SIG-SAUER P-220

SIG-SAUER P-225

This pistol was developed by SIG in response to specifications laid down by the US Army for their new 9mm pistol in 1980. Most of the parts are from the P-220 and P-225 and, like them, it is a double-action locked breech weapon with automatic firing pin safety and de-cocking lever. It differs principally in having a larger capacity magazine and an ambidextrous magazine catch. It failed to gain acceptance by the US Army on price grounds, it having performed exceptionally in all their tests. This has proved no drawback, however, and it has sold widely to security forces.

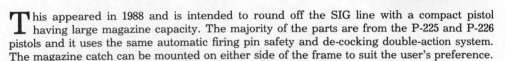

SIG-SAUER P-226

9mm SIG-Sauer P-226

Schweizerische Industrie Gesellschaft (SIG); J. P. Sauer & Sohn

9 × 19mm Parabellum

Operation	Short recoil
Length overall	196mm (7.72in)
Weight empty	750g (1.65lb)
Barrel	112mm (4.41in), 6 grooves, rh
Magazine	15-shot detachable box
Muzzle velocity	350m/sec (1,148ft/sec)

This appeared in 1988 and is intended to round off the SIG line with a compact pistol having large magazine capacity. The majority of the parts are from the P-225 and P-226 pistols and it uses the same automatic firing pin safety and de-cocking double-action system. The magazine catch can be mounted on either side of the frame to suit the user's preference.

SIG-SAUER P-228

9mm SIG-Sauer P-228

Schweizerische Industrie Gesellschaft (SIG); J. P. Sauer & Sohn

9 × 19mm Parabellum

Operation	Short recoil
Length overall	180mm (7.08in)
Weight empty	830g (1.83lb)
Barrel	98mm (3.86in), 6 grooves rh
Magazine	13-shot detachable box
Muzzle velocity	340m/sec (1,115ft/sec)

9mm ITM AT-88S

Industrial Technology & Machines AG	
9 × 19mm Parabellum	
Operation	Short recoil
Length overall	206mm (8.11in)
Weight empty	1,000g (2.2lb)
Barrel	120mm (4.7in), 6 grooves, rh
Magazine	15-shot detachable box
Muzzle velocity	352m/sec (1,155ft/sec)

This was originally the Czech CZ75 manufactured under licence, but now, after many improvements developed by the Swiss licensees, it can be considered a new and independent design. The tolerances and finish are improved, and several parts have been re-dimensioned so that they are no longer interchangeable with the CZ75. An automatic firing pin safety has been added, and the manual safety can be applied whether the pistol is cocked or uncocked. An ambidextrous safety catch is fitted and an ambidextrous slide stop is also available. As well as being made in 9mm chambering, it is also available in .41 Action Express calibre and a conversion kit is available to convert from one calibre to the other.

The AT-88S has been adopted by the British Army in Hong Kong and by several police forces.

TURKEY

7.65mm Kirrikale

Makina ve Kimya Endustrisi; Kirrikale Tufek FB	
7.65mm ACP	
Operation	Blowback
Length overall	168mm (6.65in)
Weight empty	700g (1.54lb)
Barrel	97mm (3.38in), 6 grooves, rh
Magazine	7-shot detachable box
Muzzle velocity	290m/sec (950ft/sec)

The Kirrikale is yet another copy of the Walther PP, the only changes from the original design being small modifications in machining in order to simplify production and a finger rest on the magazine bottom plate (although this was sometimes seen on Walther originals). Stripping, functioning and operation are exactly the same as the Walther PP.

9mm ITM AT84

KIRRIKALE

USA

This heading covers a number of revolver designs manufactured either by Colt or by Smith & Wesson for issue to US forces prior to the introduction of the M1911 automatic pistol.

US Revolvers 1889-1911

Colt's Patent Firearms Co; Smith & Wesson Arms Co

.38 Long Colt; .38 Special; .45 Colt

This pistol was the parent of all the subsequent small-calibre revolvers which entered military service. It lacks a separate cylinder bolt and was replaced on Colt's production lines by the New Army revolver of 1892. It is recorded that 5,000 of the M1889 were purchased for naval use.

US Revolver, Colt New Navy, M1889

.38 Long Colt

In 1890 the US Army decided that it must replace the revolvers then in its inventory with something more modern. After trials with the M1889 Navy revolver it was decided to adopt the weapon provided that a separate cylinder bolt could be incorporated into the design. This was done, and the pistol was adopted by the army in 1892. Like the M1889, this weapon was hampered by the anti-clockwise rotation of the cylinder (apparently insisted upon by naval experts) which tended to force the cylinder out of alignment with the barrel once wear took place.

US Revolver, Colt New Army, M1892

.38 Long Colt

Externally indistinguishable from the M1892, this incorporates an additional safety device in the form of Felton's trigger lock, which prevented operation of the trigger unless the cylinder was fully closed. Most of the 1892 weapons were converted to this pattern.

US Revolver, Colt New Army, M1894

.38 Long Colt

The Navy version of the Army M1894, this incorporates Felton's lock and has a five-grooved barrel, the Army pistols having six grooves.

US Revolver, Colt New Navy, M1895

.38 Long Colt

This is precisely the same as the M1894, the different nomenclature being given merely to distinguish between contracts.

US Revolver, Colt New Army, M1896

.38 Long Colt

A weapon of similar design to the various Colts, this was also provided with an anti-clockwise cylinder. It is easily recognised by the S&W monogram on the grips and the typically S&W cylinder release catch. Procurement of this pattern was relatively small, 1,000 for the Navy in 1900 and 1,000 for the Army in the following year.

US Revolver, Smith & Wesson Hand Ejector, M1899

.38 Long Colt

Another variation on the M1894, this one having a lanyard swivel on the butt and slimmer butt grips.

US Revolver, Colt New Army, M1901

.38 Long Colt

An improved version of the M1899, 1,000 of these being purchased in 1902 for the US Navy.

US Revolver, Smith & Wesson Hand Ejector, M1902

.38 Long Colt

The last of the line of official army issues of this type, the M1903 is of the same pattern as the M1901 but with a slightly reduced bore diameter.

US Revolver, Colt New Army, M1903

.38 Long Colt

US Revolver, Colt Double Action Marine Corps, M1905

.38 Special

US Revolver, Colt Army Special, M1908

.38 Special

Operation	Double-action revolver
Length overall	285mm (11.25in)
Weight empty	1,020g (2.25lb)
Barrel	152mm (6.0in), 6 grooves, lh
Magazine	6-shot cylinder
Muzzle velocity	263m/sec (865ft/sec)

US Revolver, Colt New Service, M1909

.45 Colt

Identical with the Army M1903 weapon, this has a rounded butt and is chambered for a different cartridge. Only 926 of these were ever manufactured.

This was the last .38 calibre service revolver to be adopted and had a service life of just one year. A reversion to clockwise cylinder rotation was made in this model, which was thus an improvement over the earlier designs. The frame of the M1908 is more robust than that of the New Army patterns and the cylinder latch is of a more rounded design. The reputation of the .38 revolvers suffered greatly in the 1898–1900 Philippines campaign, where they generally failed to stop fanatical Moros against whom they were used. One result of this was the hurried purchase of numbers of .45 revolvers, modified Colt DA Army M1878 pattern, and the other result was the abandonment of .38 calibre for .45 in US service.

The last service revolver to be adopted by the United States, with the exception of wartime emergency problems, slightly over 21,000 of the New Service model were supplied to the army, navy and Marine Corps between February 1909 and April 1911. It was then replaced by the M1911 automatic pistol. The revolvers incorporated Colt's positive lock of 1905, which they inherited from the Army Special model.

COLT ARMY SPECIAL, M1908

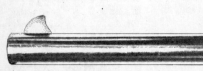

COLT NEW SERVICE

The Colt M1911 pistols are, among the classic designs, one of the most successful combat pistols ever invented. Incredibly robust, with more than enough lethality and stopping power from the 14.9g (230 grain) bullet, which delivers 474J (380ft/lb) of energy at the muzzle, the Colt armed the US forces and many others from 1911 until the 1980s. Numbers were also made in .455 Webley & Scott chambering during World War One for the Royal Navy and Royal Flying Corps, many of which were still in use in 1945. The original 1911 model developed from a series of improvements on Browning's 1900 design, and the first .45 model of 1905 competed in the US Government trial of 1907. This trial was convened in order to find a pistol of .45 calibre, firing a 230 grain bullet, to replace the existing .38 revolvers, and since automatic pistols were the innovation of the day, a variety were tested. The Board of Enquiry met in January 1907, tested nine pistols and reported back in April 1907 – an example of alacrity which is almost incredible by modern standards. As a result 200 Colt and 200 Savage pistols were acquired for extended troop trials, and after some user experience the Colt was selected, on the condition that Browning attended to one or two small points. This was done, and late in 1911 the pistol was formally adopted. During World War One the hammer spur was lengthened and in the 1920s, as a result of wartime experience, further changes were made: the spur of the grip safety was lengthened, the shape of the grip was altered, the trigger was shortened and chamfered, and the frame behind the trigger was also chamfered to give a better grip. With these changes the pistol became the M1911A1, formally adopted in June 1926, and it continued without further change until superseded by the Pistol M9 (Beretta 92F) in 1985.

While the pistol is always known as the Colt, other manufacturers' names will be found on them. The M1911 was made by Colt, by the government Springfield Arsenal and also by the Remington Arms-Union Metallic Cartridge Company of Bridgeport Conn., during World War One. Arrangements were also made for manufacture by the North American Arms Co of Canada, but the war ended before production got under way and only a few were made. During World War Two M1911A1 pistols were made by Colt, Remington, Union Switch & Signal, Ithaca Gun Company, and the Singer Sewing Machine Company. In addition to the military issues the pistols have been continuously manufactured by Colt for the commercial market, and these are easily distinguished by their more elegant finish and C-prefix serial numbers. Manufacture under licence has taken place in Norway (as the Pistol m/1914) and Argentina (as the Model 1927).

Locking of the breech is performed by having the top of the barrel ribbed and engaging in grooves in the inner surface of the slide top; the barrel has a link pinned beneath it, and the lower end of this link pivots about the slide stop pin. Thus as the slide recoils, it takes the barrel with it but, since the link is held at its foot, the barrel is made to move in a semi-circular path so that after a short amount of recoil the lugs are withdrawn from engagement, the barrel is held, and the slide is free to move back and complete the reloading cycle. On the return stroke it pushes on the breech as it chambers the new round, so causing the rear of the barrel to lift and re-engage in the slide. There is an external hammer, a manual safety catch, and a grip safety.

US Pistol, Automatic, Cal. 45in, M1911 and M1911A1

Colt's Patent Firearms Mfg Co;
Ithaca Gun Co;
Remington Rand Corp;
Remington Arms-Union Metallic
Cartridge Co;
Singer Mfg Co;
Springfield Armory;
Union Switch & Signal Co;
North American Arms Co;

.45 ACP

Operation	Short recoil
Length overall	216mm (8.5in)
Weight empty	1,130g (2.49lb)
Barrel	127mm (5.0in), 6 grooves, lh
Magazine	7-shot detachable box
Muzzle velocity	253m/sec (830ft/sec)

COLT M1911 AUTOMATICS

US Pistol, Automatic, General Officers' M15

Rock Island Arsenal	
.45 ACP	
Operation	Short recoil
Length overall	200mm (7.9in)
Weight empty	1,030g (2.27lb)
Barrel	106mm (4.17in), 6 grooves, lh
Magazine	7-shot detachable box
Muzzle velocity	245m/sec (800ft/sec)

US Pistol, Automatic, 9mm M9

Pietro Beretta Spa; Beretta Inc	
9 × 19mm Parabellum	

US Revolver, Cal. .45in, Smith & Wesson M1917

Smith & Wesson Arms Co	
.45 ACP	
Operation	Double-action revolver
Length overall	274mm (10.80in)
Weight empty	1,020g (2.25lb)
Barrel	140mm (5.5in), 6 grooves, rh
Magazine	6-shot cylinder
Muzzle velocity	265m/sec (870ft/sec)

The M15 was introduced in 1972 to replace the .380 Colt Pocket Automatic as the issue pistol for general officers. Designed by Rock Island Arsenal, it is a cut-down and rebuilt Colt M1911A1 pistol. Operation is precisely the same as that of the M1911A1; it is merely smaller in all dimensions. Due to the short barrel it produces more flash and blast than the issue pistol, but this is considered acceptable since it is only likely to be used in emergencies. It is finished in dark blue with 'General Officer Model RIA' engraved on the slide. Inset in the left grip is a brass plate which, on issue, has the individual officer's name engraved.

Adopted in January 1985, this is the Beretta Model 92F, which is described in the Italian section. The initial contract was for the supply of 315,390 weapons, the initial supply to be manufactured in Italy, with the Beretta factory in the USA taking over production in 1988. As might be imagined, the provision of a non-American weapon to the US forces raised a storm, but a second series of tests confirmed the Beretta as the selected weapon, and the company was awarded the contract for the second supply in 1989.

When the United States entered World War One in 1917 their standard pistol was the Colt M1911 automatic; supplies were short and it would obviously take time to gear up manufacture to the immense quantities needed by the expanded US Army. In view of this, numbers of Colt and Smith & Wesson revolvers were purchased, over 150,000 of the former and 153,000 of the latter. Since the standard pistol cartridge was the rimless .45 ACP, it meant that the revolver cylinders had to be shortened slightly and the rounds loaded in clips of three in order to stop them sliding inside the cylinder and to give the extractor something against which to push when unloading. As the Smith & Wesson revolvers had a step in the chamber at the position of the case mouth, it was unnecessary to use the clips for correct functioning, but without it the rounds would not eject. These pistols remained in service until well after World War Two, though large numbers were released to the commercial market in the 1920s. In order to simplify matters the Peters Cartridge Company developed a special rimmed .45 cartridge known as the '.45 Auto Rim'; this had a sufficiently thick extraction rim to take up the space behind the cylinder normally occupied by the clip and to position the cap so as to be properly struck by the hammer. The rim also gave the extractors something to push against. At the same time, Smith & Wesson produced replacement cylinders so that civilian owners could convert the pistols to fire standard .45 revolver ammunition.

.45in SMITH & WESSON M1917

This is the Colt equivalent to the Smith & Wesson revolver described above. It was originally the 'New Service' Model of 1897, a conventional double-action side-swinging cylinder model, made in a variety of calibres from .38 to .476. It was first used by the US Army as the M1909 (above) but was superseded by the M1911 automatic. When the need arose in 1917 it was reinstated, but chambered for the .45 ACP cartridge, as described for the Smith & Wesson. The first models of the Colt did not have the step in the chamber, so that the use of the clip was essential, though later production adopted the step. In addition to the US M1917 models, a quantity chambered for the .455 cartridge were supplied to the British Army in 1915–16.

US Revolver, Cal. .45in, Colt New Service, M1917

Colt's Patent Firearms Mfg Co

.45 ACP

Operation	Double-action revolver
Length overall	272mm (10.75in)
Weight empty	1,140g (2.51lb)
Barrel	140mm (5.5in), 6 grooves, lh
Magazine	6-shot cylinder
Muzzle velocity	265m/sec (870ft/sec)

This peculiar weapon was mass-produced in 1942 to the order of the Office of Strategic Services (OSS). The title 'Flare Projector' was simply a cover story; the pistol was a simple single-shot weapon intended to be dropped to Resistance and guerrilla forces in enemy territory. It was packed complete with ten rounds of .45 ACP and a comic-strip set of instructions which anyone, irrespective of nationality or language, could follow, all in a waterproof bag at a cost of $2, FOB Detroit. Manufacture is entirely of pressings and stampings and Guide Lamp made one million in three months; this works out at one every 7.5 seconds, probably the only pistol in history which could be manufactured faster than it can be loaded. They were distributed widely and still turn up from time to time. The pistol is a smooth-bore with a hand-operated breech-block. A sliding trap in the butt allows five rounds to be carried. To use, the striker is pulled back and turned, after which the breech plate is lifted and a cartridge inserted in the breech. The breech plate is dropped, to hold the cartridge in place, and the striker rotated to hold it cocked, aligned with the cartridge cap. The trigger is pulled to fire; after firing the striker is pulled back, the plate lifted, and the empy case punched out with a pencil or twig.

.45 'OSS' or 'Liberator' M1942 Flare Projector

Guide Lamp Div of General Motors Corp

.45 ACP

Operation	Single shot
Length overall	141mm (5.55in)
Weight empty	450g (1lb)
Barrel	101mm (3.97in), smoothbore
Muzzle velocity	250m/sec (820ft/sec)

The Deer Gun (the origin of the name is unknown) was a further development of the cheap and simple weapon pioneered by the OSS pistol and it was made under similar conditions of secrecy. It was the result of an idea by the CIA and was intended for dropping in Southeast Asia during the Vietnam War. The design was rather different from that of the OSS pistol; the butt was an aluminium casting, with a steel barrel screwed into the front and a self-cocking internal hammer. The barrel had to be unscrewed and a cartridge placed in the chamber, the barrel screwed back on and the gun was then ready to fire. Spare ammunition was carried in the hollow butt, together with a short stick to be used for poking the empty case out of the barrel for reloading. Again, there was a highly coloured and dramatic comic strip set of instructions. Several thousand were made in 1964, each packed in a polystyrene foam box ready for air-dropping. But a political decision prevented their use and all but a handful were destroyed.

9mm Deer Gun

Manufacturer unknown

9 × 19mm Parabellum

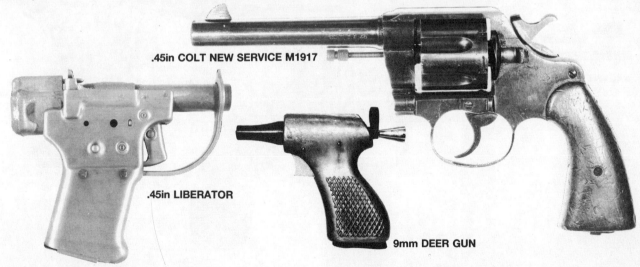

.45in COLT NEW SERVICE M1917

.45in LIBERATOR

9mm DEER GUN

USSR/RUSSIA

7.62mm Nagant Revolver M1895

Manufacture d'Armes Nagant Frères; Tula Arsenal	
7.62 × 38R Nagant	
Operation	Single- or double-action revolver
Length overall	229mm (9.06in)
Weight empty	790g (1.74lb)
Barrel	110mm (4.35in), 4 grooves, rh
Magazine	7-shot cylinder
Muzzle velocity	305m/sec (1,000ft/sec)

The Nagant revolver, adopted by the Russian Army in 1895, is similar in appearance to most revolvers of that period, but incorporates an unusual feature in the mechanism. In an endeavour to extract the maximum performance from the weapon, an attempt has been made to overcome one of the theoretical drawbacks of the revolver, the escape of gas between the front of the chamber and the rear of the barrel which, in theory at least, reduces the efficiency of the cartridge. The best revolver designs keep the clearance to a minimum, so that the gas loss is negligible, but Nagant was one of several designers who attempted to overcome this defect and perhaps the only one to produce a weapon which was a success.

The Russian M1895 was produced to Leon Nagant's 1894 patent, which was based upon earlier work by Nicolas Pieper. The trigger mechanism incorporates a cam which, on cocking the hammer, drives the cylinder forward so that the tapered rear end of the barrel enters the mouth of the aligned chamber. The cartridge is unusual in that the bullet is totally enclosed in the case and the case mouth is slightly reduced in diameter. Thus when the cylinder moves forward to enclose the barrel, the mouth of the case enters the rear end of the barrel. On firing the expansion of the case mouth spans any gap that might exist between the chamber and the barrel so that the bullet passes directly from the case into the barrel, followed by the propellant gas. As the action is operated for the next shot to be fired, so the cylinder is withdrawn, rotated, and thust forward once more to seal.

The revolver was produced in two forms, a single-action model for troops and a double-action model for officers. Production began in Liège, the revolvers being sent to Russia, but in 1900 the Russian Government bought the rights to the design and put it into production at Tula Arsenal, where it continued to be produced until the late 1930s.

7.62mm Tokarev TT-33

Tula Arsenal	
7.62 × 25mm Soviet	
Operation	Short recoil
Length overall	193mm (7.68in)
Weight empty	830g (1.83lb)
Barrel	116mm (4.57in), 4 grooves, rh
Magazine	8-shot detachable box
Muzzle velocity	415m/sec (1,362ft/sec)

This was designed by Feodor V Tokarev during the late 1920s and was approved for service in 1930, being called the TT-30 (Tula-Tokarev 30). Basically it was a Browning swinging-link breech lock with modifications to improve reliability and simplify manufacture and maintenance. The principal changes from, say, the Colt M1911 were a removable hammer and lockwork in a separate module which made initial assembly and subsequent repair much easier, the formation of the magazine feed lips in the pistol frame, thus making the manufacture of magazines much easier and their maintenance less critical, and the absence of any form of safety device other than a half-cock notch on the hammer.

In 1933 the design was slightly changed; the TT-30 had two ribs on top of the barrel which engaged in recesses in the slide, but in order to speed up production the TT-33 had these ribs formed as complete circles around the barrel. The operation of the breech lock remained the same but the cutting of the ribs could now be done during the shaping of the barrel exterior, and not as a separate machining operation. The new design completely replaced the TT-30, and specimens of the original weapon are rare. The pistol has been, and continues to be, manufactured under licence in various countries – Poland, Yugoslavia, Hungary, China and North Korea. Details of variations will be found under these countries.

NAGANT M1895

TOKAREV TT-33

This pistol was first heard of in the early 1960s and was a Soviet attempt to develop a machine pistol. The Stechkin is based broadly upon the Walther PP, though rather larger, and incorporates a selector mechanism which permits either semi- or full-automatic fire. It was supplied with a shoulder stock/holster which could be clipped to the butt to turn it into a submachine-gun. The cartridge used is slightly more powerful than the 9mm Short but not sufficiently powerful to demand a locked breech. Like all such modifications the Stechkin fell between two stools; as a pistol it was too big in relation to its cartridge, and as a submachine-gun it was too light to be controllable. Even the official Soviet manual recommended that it be fired two-handed from the prone position. It appears that the experiment was not a success and the Stechkin was withdrawn in the late 1970s. It was not exported in any numbers and is unlikely to be encountered.

The Makarov appeared in the early 1950s and is a slightly modified Walther PP; it is the standard sidearm for Soviet forces and for many Warsaw Pact armies and has been exported to several countries that use Soviet weapons. Like the Walther it is a double-action weapon, the slide-mounted safety catch locking the firing pin and dropping the hammer when applied. The shape is slightly changed from the Walther, and the grip is more bulky, making the pistol rather awkward to hold. The 9mm Makarov cartridge was introduced with this pistol; as previously noted, it is about as powerful a round as can be safely accommodated in a blowback pistol and it adheres to the Soviet policy of using ammunition that differs from the rest of the world.

This pistol was first known in the West in 1983 and is understood to be issued to security police and troops within the Soviet Union. Some are reputed to have been seen in Cuba and Grenada, but this is unconfirmed. It resembles the Walther PP in being a fixed-barrel double-action blowback but there are some small differences in the lock mechanism and the safety catch is fitted so as to protrude at the rear of the slide; this, it is claimed, has been done in order to reduce the width of the weapon and allow concealed carrying. The PSM (Pistolet Samozaryadniy Malogabaritniy – pistol, self-loading, small) fires an odd bottle-necked 5.45mm cartridge of low power. The available information suggests an excess of complication for what ought to be a fairly simple weapon.

9mm Stechkin

State Arsenals	
9 × 18mm Soviet	
Operation	Blowback, selective fire
Length overall	225mm (8.86in)
Weight empty	1,030g (2.27lb)
Barrel	127mm (5.0in), 4 grooves, rh
Magazine	20-shot detachable box
Muzzle velocity	340m/sec (1,115ft/sec)

9mm Makarov

State arsenals	
9 × 18mm Soviet	
Operation	Blowback
Length overall	160mm (6.30in)
Weight empty	663g (1.46lb)
Barrel	91mm (3.58in), 4 grooves, rh
Magazine	8-shot detachable box
Muzzle velocity	315m/sec (1,033ft/sec)

5.45mm PSM

State arsenals	
5.45 × 18mm	
Operation	Blowback
Length overall	160mm (6.30in)
Weight empty	460g (1.01lb)
Barrel	85mm (3.35in), 6 grooves, rh
Magazine	8-shot detachable box
Muzzle velocity	315m/sec (1,033ft/sec)

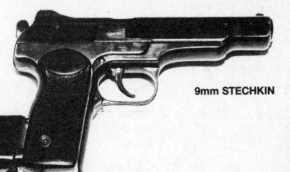

9mm STECHKIN

YUGOSLAVIA

7.62mm Model 57

Zavodi Crvena Zastava	
7.62 × 25mm Soviet	
Operation	Short recoil
Length overall	200mm (7.87in)
Weight empty	900g (1.98lb)
Barrel	116mm (4.57in), 4 grooves, rh
Magazine	9-shot detachable box
Muzzle velocity	450m/sec (1,476ft/sec)

This is the Yugoslav version of the Tokarev TT-33 and it differs only in the serrated finger-grips at the rear of the slide and the badge impressed into the plastic grips. Dimensions and data are slightly different from those of the Soviet weapon, doubtless a result of different manufacturing methods.

9mm Model 70 and 70A

Zavodi Crvena Zastava	
9 × 19mm Parabellum	

The Model 70 is the same as the Model 57 except that it is chambered for the 9mm Parabellum cartridge, which thus makes it rather more attractive on the export market and slightly more comfortable to shoot. The Model 70A is an improved model which has a slide-mounted safety catch which locks the firing pin when applied. Except for the change in calibre and the adoption of six-groove rifling there is no other difference and the dimensions, weight, etc., of the Model 70 are the same as those for the Model 57. In 9mm calibre the muzzle velocity is 330m/sec (1,082ft/sec).

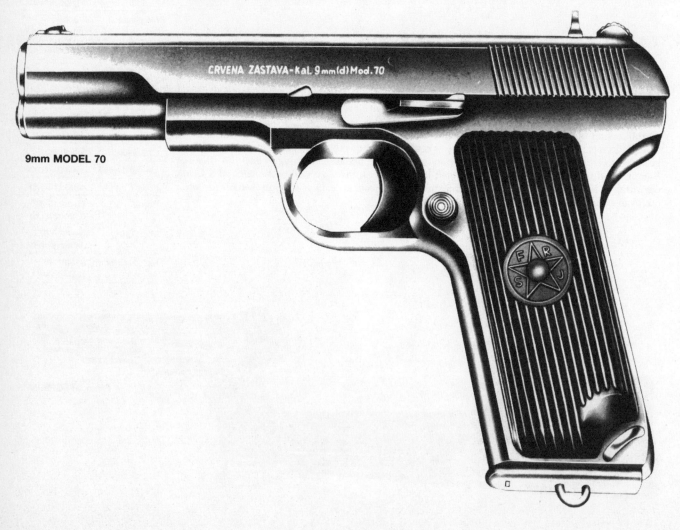

9mm MODEL 70

Confusingly known as the Model 70, this is a small pocket pistol designed for police use. It is a simple hammer-fired single-action blowback weapon chambered for the 7.65 ACP cartridge; a variant known as the M70(k) is chambered for the 9mm Short cartridge. Apart from the calibre change there is no dimensional difference between the two models.

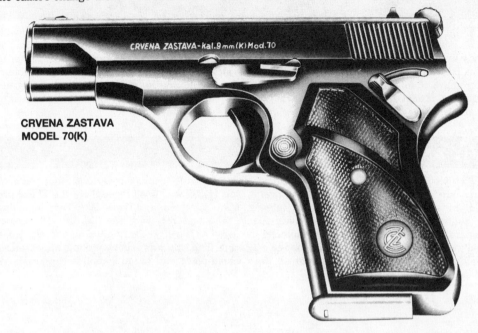

CRVENA ZASTAVA MODEL 70(K)

Crvena Zastava Model 70

Zavodi Crvena Zastava	
Various calibres	
Operation	Blowback
Length overall	200mm (7.80in)
Weight empty	740g (1.63lb) (M70): 720g (1.58lb) (M70(k))
Barrel	94mm (3.7in), 6 grooves, rh
Magazine	8-shot detachable box
Muzzle velocity	300m/sec (985ft/sec) (M70); 260m/sec (853.2ft/sec) (M70(k))

This was introduced in 1987 to complete the Crvena Zastava range of military weapons. It is a conventional double-action side-opening revolver chambered for the .357 Magnum cartridge; it can also fire the .38 Special round, and with a special cylinder it will also fire 9mm Parabellum ammunition. The standard military and police version has a 64mm barrel, but other barrel lengths, and special sights, are available for target and commercial use.

.357 Revolver Model 83

Zavodi Crvena Zastava	
.357 Magnum	
Operation	Double-action revolver
Length overall	188mm (7.40in)
Weight empty	900g (1.98lb)
Barrel	64mm (2.5in), 6 grooves, rh
Magazine	6-shot cylinder
Muzzle velocity	400m/sec (1,312ft/sec)

CRVENA ZASTAVA MODEL 83

Bolt-action Rifles

ARGENTINA

7.65mm Mauser Model 1891

Waffenfabrik Mauser AG

7.65 × 53mm Argentine Mauser

The Argentine Model of 1891 was little more than the Turkish Mauser Model of 1890 with some very small modifications. There were minor changes to the bolt and the extractor was strengthened. Apart from this they were virtually identical and the reader should refer to the Turkish Mauser for further information. **Cavalry Carbine Mauser Model 1891** was a short derivative of the rifle of the same year; the carbine could not be fitted with a bayonet. **Rifle, Mauser, Model 1891 modified 1909** was the 1891 pattern rifle with the sights re-graduated to conform to the ballistics of the 'Spitzer' pointed bullet adopted in 1909.

AUSTRIA–HUNGARY AND AUSTRIA

8mm Mannlicher Model 1895

Osterreichische Waffenfabrik Steyr

8 × 50R Austrian Mannlicher M1890

Length overall	1,270mm (50.0in)
Weight empty	3.78kg (8.31lb)
Barrel	765mm (30.12in), 4 grooves, rh
Magazine	5-shot integral box
Muzzle velocity	610m/sec (2,000ft/sec)

This became the official Austro–Hungarian service rifle, replacing various other patterns which were relegated to the Landwehr. The M1895 was used throughout the Habsburg Empire and was adopted, c. 1897, by Bulgaria. Many survived until World War Two, including a quantity in the hands of the Italian Army, who had received them in 1919–20 as war reparations. The 1895 rifle is mechanically the same as the 1890 carbine, using a straight-pull bolt with rotary locking, and a clip-loaded magazine. The rifle was of conventional appearance, recognisable by the prominent spur on the cocking-piece and the side-mounted piling hook alongside the exposed muzzle.

8mm Cavalry Carbine Model 1895

This was the carbine derivation of the basic rifle and existed in two forms, varying only in minor respects. The same rotary locking straight-pull action and clip-loaded magazine were used, and the carbine was fitted with sling swivels. One version was fitted for a bayonet; the other was not.

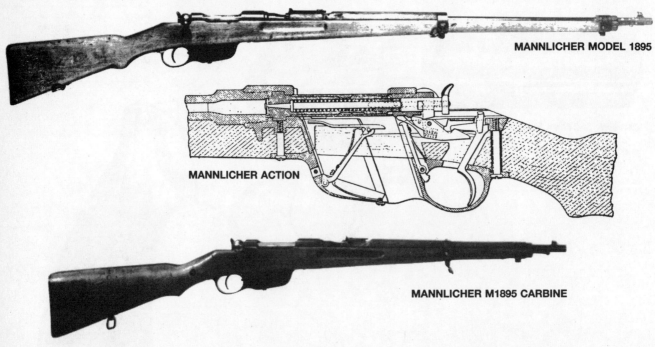

MANNLICHER MODEL 1895

MANNLICHER ACTION

MANNLICHER M1895 CARBINE

This was very similar to the cavalry carbine but was for issue to Engineers, Gunners and others to whom its handiness was an advantage. It was fitted with a special knife bayonet and had a secondary foresight on top of the muzzle ring which was designed to compensate for the alteration in trajectory as a result of firing the rifle with the bayonet fixed.

8mm Short Rifle Model 1895

Length overall	1,000mm (39.37in)
Weight empty	3.57kg (7.87lb)
Barrel	482mm (19.0in), 4 grooves, rh
Magazine	5-shot integral box
Muzzle velocity	533m/sec (1,750ft/sec)

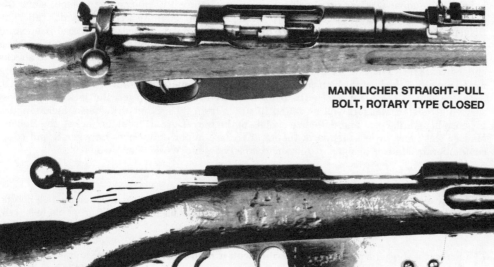

MANNLICHER STRAIGHT-PULL BOLT, ROTARY TYPE CLOSED

MANNLICHER STRAIGHT-PULL BOLT, ROTARY TYPE OPEN

Adopted for service in 1969, this is the Austrian Army's standard sniping rifle. It is well made and has a cold-hammered barrel which has an exceptionally long seating into the receiver, making for greater rigidity. The turnbolt is rigidly locked by six lugs. The stock is entirely of plastic material and is coloured dark green. The magazine is a rotary design, basically the Mannlicher-Schoenauer magazine developed in the late 1880s and brought up-to-date. The mechanism is of light metal and there is a clear plastic cover at the rear end, so that the user can drop it out of the rifle and make a quick check on the contents. It fits snugly into the stock and does not protrude at all. Alternatively a 10-shot removable box can be used. Simple iron sights are provided by the factory, but these are only for emergency and the rifle is meant to be used with a telescope sight, normally a 6k model graduated to 800 metres' range.

7.62mm SSG69 Sniping Rifle

Steyr-Mannlicher GmbH

7.62 × 51mm NATO

Length overall	1,140mm (44.88in)
Weight empty	3.9kg (8.60lb)
Barrel	650mm (25.60in), 4 grooves, rh
Magazine	5-shot rotary or 10-shot detachable box
Muzzle velocity	860m/sec (2,820ft/sec)

7.62mm SSG69 SNIPING RIFLE

BELGIUM

7.65mm Infantry Rifle Model 1889

Fabrique National d'Armes de Guerre	
7.65 × 53mm Belgian Mauser	
Length overall	1,295mm (50.5in)
Weight empty	4.01kg (8.82lb)
Barrel	780mm (30.6in), 4 grooves, rh
Magazine	5-round box
Muzzle velocity	610m/sec (2,000ft/sec)

This was the first bolt-action rifle adopted by Belgium, and instead of attempting a design of their own, the existing German Mauser was modified to suit Belgian requirements. Fabrique National was set up specifically to manufacture the rifle under licence, since the existing government arsenal could not produce them in quantity in the time desired. The Belgian Mauser differed from all others by virtue of its barrel jacket. The barrel is encased in a thin steel tube which isolates it from the furniture, the intention being to prevent warping woodwork from affecting the straightness of the barrel and to minimise the effect of shocks and blows. The sights are brazed to the jacket, so that heat generated during the brazing would not affect the barrel. Such care for the barrel is commendable, but brings disadvantages, one of which is the liability of rust to form between the barrel and the jacket, and most surviving Belgian Mausers will be found to suffer from this. Other drawbacks include extra expense in manufacture and defective cooling of the barrel. Apart from the jacket, the Belgian Mauser was more or less standard, though there are minor differences between it and other contemporary Mauser designs. It remained in service into World War Two.

7.65mm Civil Guard Rifle Model 1889

This was no more than a slight modification to the basic rifle pattern, in which the bolt handle was turned down. A different type of knife bayonet was used, with a different blade length, but the nosecap and bayonet bar were unchanged.

7.65mm Carbine, Foot Gendarmerie and Fortress Artillery, Model 1889

This was a shortened version of the rifle, with turned-down bolt handle, and issued with a long-bladed sword bayonet which had the same hilt as the infantry and Civil Guard types.

7.65mm Cavalry Carbine Model 1889

The cavalry carbine was a shortened rifle with an almost half-stocked appearance, a long section of the barrel jacket protruding beyond the stock. There was no provision for a bayonet.

7.65mm Mounted Gendarmerie Carbine Model 1889

This was similar to the Cavalry carbine but the stock was carried closer to the muzzle and an extra barrel band was used. A knife or sword bayonet could be attached.

7.65mm Rifles Models 1922 and 1924

The 1922 pattern rifles were basic 1889 models with the barrels slightly shortened, the barrel jacket omitted, and an integral box magazine fitted. It appears to have been a private venture by Fabrique National and relatively few were purchased by the Belgian Army. The Model 1924 was an entirely commercial product by Fabrique National for export, and it was very similar to the German Gew 98K, a short rifle with all the latest Mauser patented features.

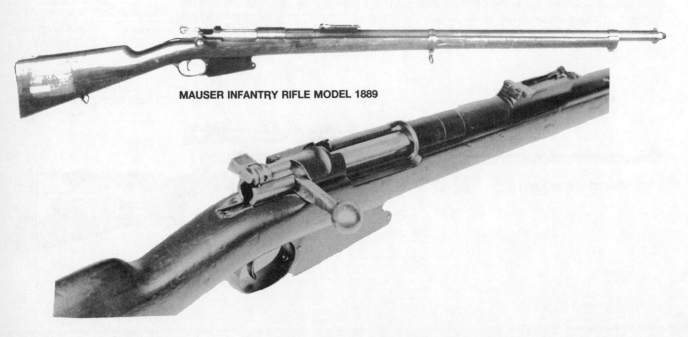

MAUSER INFANTRY RIFLE MODEL 1889

This was a modified version of the M1889 rifles incorporating the later Mauser improvements, such as a better bolt stop, changed bolt head and integral box magazine. Very few were made.

This was developed in the late 1970s to provide a precision weapon for military and police snipers. It uses a Mauser bolt action mounted into a heavy receiver and barrel, and the stock is fully adjustable for length and drop. The rifle is provided with Anschutz aperture sights but a telescope is more usual in this role. Accessories such as bipod, sling, butt extensions and inserts and carrying cases are available. Manufacture of the 30-11 ceased in 1986.

7.65mm Rifle Model 1936

7.62mm FN Model 30-11 Sniping Rifle

FN Herstal SA	
7.62 × 51mm NATO	
Length overall	1,117mm (43.98in)
Weight empty	4.85kg (10.69lb)
Barrel	502mm (19.76in), 4 grooves, rh
Magazine	10-shot detachable box
Muzzle velocity	850m/sec (2,788ft/sec)

CANADA

Sir Charles Ross designed his straight-pull action rifle in 1896 and patented it in the following year. After several sporting and target models had been produced between 1897 and 1902, the Ross Rifle was adopted in April 1902 by the Canadian Department of Militia and Defence as an official weapon of the Royal Northwest Mounted Police.

Ross's original design made use of an unusual locking system based upon the Mannlicher rifle, although undeniably using features of Ross's conception. The bolt locked on an interrupted thread in the original 1897 design, though in 1900 Ross changed this to a rotating lug system. A cam track was used to unlock the bolt when the handle was pulled straight to the rear. It is interesting to note that Ross reverted to a thread system on his 'perfected' 1910 design, though with inconspicuous results.

The Ross was extensively tested in Britain between 1900 and 1912, and on each occasion it was rejected for use as a service weapon. The Commandant of the Small Arms School at Hythe summed up military opinion in his 1910 report on the Ross Mark II**: 'It seems clear that this rifle is designed as a target rifle pure and simple, without regard to the requirements of active service or of the training of large bodies of men of average attainment.'

In spite of this opinion the Canadian Army of 1914 went to war with the Ross, but by 1915 the troops had lost confidence in it and were abandoning it in favour of Lee-Enfield rifles picked up on the battlefield. Official investigations revealed that the muddy conditions of trench warfare prevalent in Flanders were ill-suited to the bolt design, and there was insufficient

.303in Ross

Ross Rifle Co, Quebec	
.303in British	

FN30-11 SNIPING RIFLE

primary extraction, causing difficulties with cartridges of indifferent wartime manufacture. It was also found that much of the trouble arose because of the position of the bolt stop, which bore against the rearmost of the three bolt locking lugs, so that the lug battered the stop every time the rifle was fired, damaging the lug to the extent that it became almost impossible to force the bolt into the locked position. The Ross was consequently withdrawn from front-line use and relegated to a training role. It was revived for a short time during World War Two when numbers were sent from Canada to Britain and used to arm the Home Guard. Here it was discovered that careless assembly of the bolt after cleaning could result in it being blown backwards out of the receiver, and once more the Ross was withdrawn, this time for good.

There were innumerable minor variant models of the Ross rifles, mainly because Ross was constantly tinkering with the design in attempts to improve it; some Ross authorities recognise no less than 85 variations. The picture is further confused by periodic changes in the sights and magazine design and by bureaucratic changes of nomenclature. The following list is intended to clarify the more important of the variations.

Rifle, Ross, Mark I

This was the first service weapon, fitted with an unusual pattern of magazine known as the 'Harris Controlled Platform Magazine', in which the platform could be depressed by means of an external thumb lever. This allowed five loose rounds to be quickly dropped into the magazine, after which the lever was released and the magazine spring placed the cartridges under pressure. Various sights were used, giving rise to a bewildering number of sub-variants. It had originally been intended to use the Sight, Ross, Mark I, a large leaf sight, but this proved too fragile for service use and was replaced before the rifles were issued by the Sight, Ross, Mark II, a tangent sight based upon that of the Mauser Gew 98. It was later found necessary to modify this into the Mark III version.

Carbine, Ross, Mark I

This was a short version of the Mark I rifle, and could be recognised by the stock extending to the muzzle. It could not accept a bayonet.

Rifle, Ross, Mark II

As a result of defects in the Mark I, Ross designed an improved model in an attempt to stem the criticism. The Mark II had a slightly modified bolt mechanism which compressed the striker spring during the opening of the bolt, rather than the closing-stroke compression of the Mark I. The chamber dimensions were also changed to accept standard British service .303in ammunition.

Rifle, Short, Ross, Mark I

In April 1912 it was found necessary to change the nomenclature of the Ross rifles in an attempt to camouflage the number of modifications that had been made to the basic design. The Short Mark I was the new name for the Rifle, Ross, Mark II.

Rifle, Ross, Mark II*

The Mark II* was the same rifle as the Mark II with the substitution of the Mark III sight for the Mark II of the earlier rifle. Some changes were also made internally, both to rectify defects and simplify manufacture.

Rifle, Ross, Mark II**

This was similar to its predecessors but had a Sutherland rear sight rather than a Ross model.

ROSS Mk II

ROSS Mk III

These were minor variations of the Mark II*, using the Sutherland rear sight and incorporating other minor improvements. Neither saw much service. The barrels of these two models were 711mm (28.0in) long.

Rifle, Ross, Mark II* and Mark II*****

By the time five major modifications, to say nothing of innumerable minor ones, had been made to the Ross design, the Canadian authorities realised that something had to be done to further camouflage the amount of modifications, and so in April 1912 they re-named the rifles 'Short Mark II', even though they were still no more than variations upon the original Ross Mark II pattern. The Mark II***** was otherwise similar to its predecessors, with a Sutherland rear sight and changes to the shape of the wooden handguard over the chamber.

Rifle Ross, Mark II***

This was simply the Mark II***** re-christened in the 1912 re-naming programme.

Rifle, Short, Ross, Mark II

This designation arose out of the 1912 'adjustments' and was not the same thing as the original Mark II which had appeared in 1906. The '1912' Mark II was, in fact, the old Mark II**.

Rifle, Ross, Mark II

The Mark III was the first rifle to be made to Ross's improved 1910 design, in which the solid locking lugs of the earlier service weapons were replaced by a form of triple-thread interrupted screw system. A double-pressure trigger unit was fitted, and charger guides were added to the receiver so that the rifles could be loaded from the standard British 5-round charger. The standard model weighed 4.32kg (9.75lb), but a lighter version weighing 4.11kg (9.06lb) was made for trials in 1911.

Rifle, Ross, Mark III

This is thought to have been a modification of the basic Mark III in which alterations were made to the receiver and the bolt head so as to improve the efficiency of the bolt locking. A different foresight and muzzle band were apparently fitted, and the exact designation of this model is uncertain.

Rifle, Ross, Mark III*

This is the only Ross rifle to have been adopted by the British Army, in October 1915. It was the same as the standard Mark III, with the addition of a Lee-Enfield pattern magazine cut-off, so that the rifle could be used as a single-loader while keeping a full magazine in reserve. It was declared obsolete in November 1921; this should not be taken as evidence of long active service – the closing months of 1921 saw an immense clear-out of old equipment which had had its paperwork neglected during the war years.

Rifle, Magazine, Ross, .303in Mark IIIB

Length overall	1,285mm (50.56in)
Weight empty	4.48kg (9.87lb)
Barrel	765mm (30.15in), 4 grooves, lh
Magazine	5-shot detachable box
Muzzle velocity	790m/sec (2,600ft/sec)

ROSS Mk II*

ROSS Mk III 1910

Rifle, Ross, Mark III (Sniper's)

This was a standard Mark III fitted with a telescope sight made by Warner & Swasey of Cleveland, Ohio. The sight, which was offset to the left side so that the action could be charger-loaded, was a 5.2x type similar to the US Army's Telescopic Musket Sight M1913. The Ross sniper rifles were much-loved by those who used them, due to their undoubted accuracy (which was aided by the 775mm (30.5in) barrel), and many were retained after the standard service rifles had been withdrawn. The sniper weapons were, of course, better looked after by their owners and less liable to the severe conditions suffered by line rifles. Approximately 419,130 Ross rifles were manufactured between 1903 and 1915, 342,040 of which were delivered to the Canadian Army and 67,090 to Britain.

DENMARK

8mm Krag-Jorgensen Rifles

State Arsenals

8 × 58R Danish Krag

The Krag-Jorgensen system was developed in the late 1880s by Captain Ole Krag of the Royal Norwegian Artillery and Erik Jorgensen, an engineer at the Norwegian State Arsenal, of which Ole Krag later became superintendent. The rifles were first adopted in 1889 by Denmark and then in 1892, in a modified form, by the USA. After various improvements had been carried out to meet the demands of the Board of Officers supervising the US Army trials, Krag and Jorgensen patented an improved version of the rifle in 1893; this was later adopted by the Norwegian Army.

The turnbolt action makes use of a single locking lug at the front of the bolt, although the bolt handle turns down into a recess in the receiver to act as an auxiliary lock. This design has, in the past, been the subject of some criticism, but with the relatively low-powered cartridges for which it was designed the action is unquestionably safe. The most remarkable feature of the design is, though, the magazine, which loads laterally beneath the bolt through a hinged trapdoor. On the door's inner face is a magazine platform and leaf spring; with the trapdoor open, loose rounds are dropped into the magazine opening and the door is closed so that the spring and platform put the cartridges under pressure. The rounds are pushed across the rifle, beneath the bolt and up the left side of the action until the first round appears in a slot alongside the bolt. When the bolt is closed, its head strikes the protruding rim of this cartridge and pushes it forward until it reaches an enlarged section of the slot which allows the entire rim to pass through, so that the round can enter the feedway and the chamber.

The original Danish Krag-Jorgensen was given a loading trap vertically hinged at the front, so that it swung forward for loading; this meant that the rifle had to be canted over to the left when loading so that the rounds went into the magazine and did not fall out before the trap could be closed. The American and Norwegian patterns replaced this gate with a type having a horizontal hinge at the bottom of the door, so that the opened trap also acted as a loading platform.

KRAG-JORGENSEN

The pattern of 1889 was the first of a series of similar weapons: a long, somewhat clumsy, rifle, instantly recognisable by the barrel jacket, a feature possessed by few other rifles, and the side-loading gate which was hinged to the receiver at its front.

Rifle Model 1889

Length overall	1,330mm (52.35in)
Weight empty	4.42kg (9.75lb)
Barrel	832mm (32.75in), 6 grooves, rh
Magazine	5-shot internal tray
Muzzle velocity	600m/sec (1,968ft/sec)

In 1908 it was decided to modify the rifle design to incorporate a new type of safety catch designed by Barry, which appeared on the cocking piece.

Rifle Model 1889/08

In 1910 a second set of minor modifications was made, the most important being the re-graduation of the rear sight from 2,000m to 2,100m. Most of the earlier rifles then in service were altered to the new system, just as they had been in 1908, which means that original 1889-pattern rifles are now extremely rare.

Rifle Model 1889/10

This was the cavalry version of the 1889 rifle, a shortened and lightened arm with a wooden handguard and sling swivels on the left side of the stock and the left side of the top band. The original leaf sight was replaced by one of tangent pattern. The carbine was adopted in 1912, which leads to an alternative nomenclature 'Carbine m/89/12'.

Cavalry Carbine Model 1889

The basic cavalry carbine was modified in 1923 to accept the 1915 pattern of light sword bayonet, necessitating the addition of a suitable bayonet bar to the muzzle. All cavalry carbines then in service were altered.

Cavalry Carbine Model 1889/23

This carbine variation was for engineers and pioneers and differed from the cavalry model by having sling swivels under the butt, the barrel band and the nosecap. A bayonet bar was fitted beneath the muzzle and a wooden handguard over the barrel.

Engineer Carbine Model 1889/24

This was basically a short 1889 rifle, even to the fitting of a barrel jacket. There was no handguard and the stock was made with a grasping groove on each side below the rear sight. A bayonet bar was fitted to the barrel jacket at the muzzle.

Infantry Carbine Model 1889/24

This was essentially similar to the infantry carbine except that the bolt handle was turned downwards towards the stock.

Artillery Carbine Model 1889/24

KRAG-JORGENSEN BREECH

FINLAND

7.62mm Sako TRG-21 Sniper's Rifle

Sako Ltd.	
7.62 × 51mm NATO	
Length overall	1,200mm (47.25in)
Weight empty	5.3kg (11.68lb) without sights
Barrel	660mm (25.98in), 4 grooves, rh
Magazine	10-shot double-row box
Muzzle velocity	840m/sec (2,756ft/sec)

This is a conventional bolt-action magazine rifle, since Sako are convinced that for first-shot accuracy the bolt action cannot be beaten. The barrel is fitted with a muzzle brake/flash hider which can be removed and replaced by a silencer. The bolt and receiver are rather larger than usual for the 7.62 calibre so that the rifle can be upgraded to heavier ammunition in the future. The bolt has three forward locking lugs and an indicator at the rear end showing whether the action is cocked. The safety catch, on the right side, is silent in operation.

The trigger is a two-stage type which can be adjusted for position and pressure without dismantling the rifle, and the trigger mechanism and trigger guard can be removed as a unit.

The stock is of wood or glass-fibre, and the action is bedded in special epoxy resin. The stock can be adjusted for height and length, and a sling can be fitted. The steel bipod is articulated so that the rifle has some degree of movement without requiring the bipod to be shifted. Folding iron sights are provided, but the receiver is shaped into a mount for optical or electro-optical sights which are normally used.

FRANCE

8mm Infantry Rifle Mle 1886 (Lebel)

Various state arsenals	
8 × 50R Lebel Mle 1886	
Length overall	1,295mm (50.98in)
Weight empty	4.28kg (9.44lb)
Barrel	800mm (31.5in), 4 grooves, lh
Magazine	8-shot under-barrel tube
Muzzle velocity	715m/sec (2,346ft/sec)

In 1886 the French Army replaced their single shot 'Gras' rifles (Infantry Rifle Mle 1874) with a weapon which, for a short time, put them ahead of the world. The new weapon, ultimately known as the Fusil d'Infanterie Modèle 1886, or the 'Lebel' after the senior officer on the Committee which selected it, was notable in that it introduced a smokeless cartridge firing a small-calibre jacketed bullet. The rifle itself was a strange combination of ideas and, in view of contemporary advances elsewhere it could well have been described as mechanically backward; indeed, improved weapons became widespread within a couple of years of the Lebel's appearance. It utilised the magazine system of the Austrian Kropatschek, a tube-fed mechanism dating back to the 1870s; and the bolt was a variation of that used on the 1874 Gras, which in turn was a modification of the even earlier Kropatschek.

The turnbolt action of the Lebel employed a magazine tube lying beneath the barrel, and as the bolt was withdrawn so a lifting mechanism extracted a round from this tube and brought it up into line with the chamber. When the bolt was closed the round was swept into the chamber and the lifter moved down to be supplied with a new cartridge, pushed backwards down the tube by a magazine spring. The result was a long and heavy weapon with a centre of gravity which changed at every shot and which retained its superiority for a very short time before being overtaken by the mechanically more perfect, and aesthetically more pleasing, patterns of Mauser and Mannlicher. The Mle 86, however, continued in service until the end of World War Two; many were shortened in 1935 but many more continued in Reserve service quite unmodified.

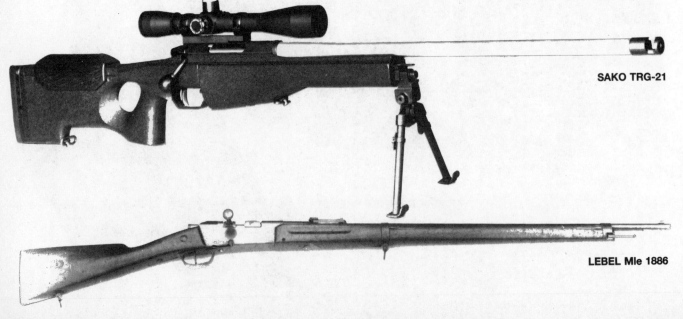

SAKO TRG-21

LEBEL Mle 1886

From time to time various minor improvements were incorporated; in 1898 the French replaced the round-nosed 'Ball M' bullet with the boat-tailed spitzer 'Balle D', but the day of the tubular-magazine rifle, in which there was always a danger of the pointed bullet firing the cap ahead of it in the magazine if the rifle was jarred violently, were numbered by the introduction of the Berthier clip-loading weapons.

The original production variant of the basic pattern could be easily recognised by the unusual receiver and the two-piece stock. The under-barrel tubular magazine held eight rounds and a long cruciform bayonet could be fixed beneath the protruding muzzle.

8mm Infantry Rifle Mle 1886/93

After the original rifles had seen some service, a number of deficiencies were discovered; the entire machining of the receiver was revised to eliminate weakness caused by insufficient rigidity, a gas escape hole was bored into the bolt head to act as a relief should a cartridge case fail, the rear sight was modified, and a piling prong was added to the muzzle cap.

8mm Rifle Mle 1886R35

This was a much-shortened version of either the Mle 86 or the Mle 86/93, intended to make them into handier weapons. The conversion was done by reducing the length of the barrel and the forestock, fitting a middle band, and replacing the original sight with the pattern developed for the 1916 Musket, modified to suit the contours of the Lebel barrel. Shortening the barrel, of course, also implied shortening the magazine.

Length overall	944mm (37.20in)
Weight empty	3.10kg (6.75lb)
Barrel	450mm (17.7in), 4 grooves, lh
Magazine	3-shot underbarrel tube
Muzzle velocity	610m/sec (2,000ft/sec)

Berthier Rifles

When the German Army adopted the Mauser and the Austro–Hungarians the Mannlicher, the French quickly realised that the Lebel was inferior to the rifles of their potential enemies. After some deliberation, therefore, they sanctioned the issue of a small number of a cavalry carbine designed by a committee headed by André Berthier, one of the most competent of French designers. The carbine continued to use the well-tried (but somewhat complicated) bolt action used on the 1886 rifle and its derivatives, but it adopted a magazine very similar to that of Mannlicher. The Carbine Mle 1890 was loaded through the action with a clip containing three cartridges, which were then forced up into the loading position by a spring-loaded follower, and after the last round had been chambered the clip fell through a slot in the magazine floor-plate.

Various state arsenals

8 × 50R Lebel Mle 1886
7.5 × 54 Mle 1929

A modified pattern of the carbine followed in 1892, in which a slight change was made to the design of the clip and a considerable change in the shape of the weapon's stock; apart from some detail changes in the action components, the Carbines manufactured to the system of 1892 were otherwise identical to those of 1890. Various rifles followed, similar in action to the carbines and differing only in dimensions, including the patterns of 1902 and 1907. Experience of World War One convinced the French that the three-round clip placed French troops at a disadvantage, as the German Mauser held five rounds and the British Lee-Enfield ten, so in 1915 it was decided to introduce a five-round clip (known as the Chargeur Mle 16). A modified

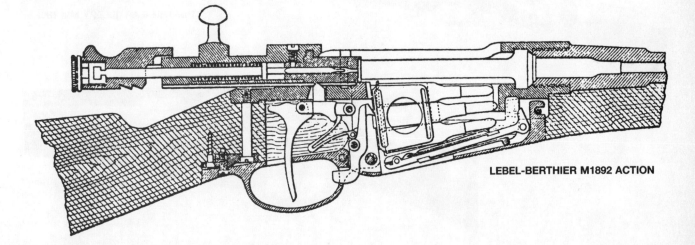

LEBEL-BERTHIER M1892 ACTION

rifle was introduced to make use of the increased magazine capacity, though it was structurally very little different from the 1907 pattern. At a later date many of the 1892 carbines were altered to accept the five-round clip, and in 1916 opportunity was taken to produce new carbines to the modified system.

Little then changed until 1934 when, as a result of trials involving modified ammunition, the French introduced a new rifle firing the 7.5mm Mle 1929 cartridge, although the rifle was still a Berthier pattern. The opportunity was also taken of replacing the Mannlicher-style magazine in which the clip was an integral part, with a staggered-row Mauser pattern magazine which was loaded from a five-round charger.

8mm Cavalry Carbine Mle 1890

Length overall	945mm (37.2in)
Weight empty	3.02kg (6.65lb)
Barrel	453mm (17.85in), 4 grooves, lh
Magazine	3-shot clip-loaded integral box
Muzzle velocity	610m/sec (2,000ft/sec)

A distinctive weapon with a combless stock, the Mle 1890 cavalry carbine had a turned-down bolt handle and a stock ring attached to the left side of the stock. There was neither handguard nor bayonet, but a cleaning rod was contained within the stock.

8mm Cuirassiers' Carbine Mle 1890

E ssentially similar to the cavalry carbine, the pattern adopted by the Cuirassiers had a leather butt-plate fixed to the butt by two screws.

8mm Gendarmerie Carbine Mle 1890

T his was similar to the other two 1890 weapons but was adapted for an épée bayonet, similar to that used with the Mle 1886 rifle, which required a special nosecap.

8mm Artillery Musketoon Mle 1892

Length overall	937mm (36.90in)
Weight empty	3.06kg (6.75lb)
Barrel	444mm (17.5in), 4 grooves, lh
Magazine	3-shot clip-loaded integral box
Muzzle velocity	610m/sec (2,000ft/sec)

T he 1892 system was very similar to that of 1890, though the weapons are instantly recognisable by their combed stock, giving them a more conventional appearance. The artillery 'musketoon' – in reality a carbine – carried a cleaning rod in a channel hollowed out in the left side of the forestock. A knife bayonet was provided, and the weapon's three-round magazine was concealed within the stock.

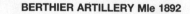

BERTHIER ARTILLERY Mle 1892

BERTHIER Mle 1892

This was identical with the artillery model of the same year except for the nose-cap, adapted to the Gendarmerie bayonet.

8mm Gendarmerie Musket Mle 1892

This was a conversion of the 1892 pattern weapons, applied to either the Artillery or Gendarmerie models – in which the action was modified to use the five-round charger. Apart from various detail alterations, mainly concerning the removal of the cleaning rod and the filling in of its groove, the Mle 92/27 was distinguishable from the Mle 16 or Mle 16/27 by the absence of a handguard above the barrel.

8mm Musket Mle 1892/27

This was the first rifle to be manufactured on the Berthier system and it was little more than a rifle-length version of the 1892 carbine. The rifle was only issued to native levies in Indo-China and served as a prototype for the succeeding designs of 1907 and 1915.

8mm Indo-China Rifle Mle 1902

Also known as the 'Colonial Model', this was the 1902 Indo-China rifle slightly modified and placed on general issue to French Colonial troops in 1907. The two patterns differed only in minor respects; the three-round clip of the 1892 Musketoon was used, and the rifle had a one-piece stock without a handguard.

8mm Senegal Rifle Mle 1907

After the start of World War One the French authorities soon realised that the Berthier rifles were superior to those of Lebel pattern then arming the line infantry; the Colonial Mle 1907 was seized on as a replacement and ordered into production, with only minor changes to the sights and action, as the Mle 07/15. As well as being manufactured in France, large numbers were made on contract in the USA by Remington Arms-Union Cartridge Company of Ilion, New York.

8mm Infantry Rifle Mle 1907/15

Length overall	1,303mm (51.3in)
Weight empty	3.79kg (8.35lb)
Barrel	798mm (31.42in), 4 grooves, lh
Magazine	3-shot clip-loaded integral box
Muzzle velocity	715m/sec (2,345ft/sec)

It was soon realised that the three-round magazine had insufficient capacity for the trenches, and so a modified pattern holding five rounds (Chargeur Mle 15) was issued in 1916. As a result the Rifle Mle 07/15 had to be redesigned to use the enlarged clip and thus became the Mle 16. This model is easily recognised by the full length one-piece stock, with handguard, and the protruding magazine box.

8mm Infantry Rifle Mle 1916

Length overall	1,303mm (51.3in)
Weight empty	4.15kg (9.15lb)
Barrel	798mm (31.42in), 4 grooves, rh
Magazine	5-shot clip-loaded integral box
Muzzle velocity	715m/sec (2,345ft/sec)

CARBINE 1907/15

LEBEL-BERTHIER ACTION

8mm Musket Mle 1916

A carbine version of the Mle 1916 rifle built around the five-shot clip. It can be distinguished from the earlier 1892 system by the adoption of a handguard and the protruding magazine. A cleaning rod was carried in a channel in the left side of the stock, and the butt had a sling bar.

8mm Musket Mle 1916/27

A conversion of the basic five-shot Mle 1916 to approximate to the Mle 92/27 conversion, done by removing the cleaning rod, filling the groove, and adding a piling prong to the nosecap.

7.5mm Infantry Rifle Mle 07/15M34 (Fusil Mle 34)

7.5 × 54 Mle 1929	
Length overall	1,084mm (42.68in)
Weight empty	3.53kg (7.78lb)
Barrel	575mm (22.64in), 4 grooves, lh
Magazine	5-shot integral box
Muzzle velocity	792m/sec (2,600ft/sec)

A much modified and shortened form of the basic Mle 07/15 in which the clip-loading magazine was abandoned and a charger-loaded pattern adopted. This became possible due to the adoption of a more modern design of rimless cartridge, the 7.5mm Model 1929 which was developed after the end of World War One to replace the awkwardly-shaped rimmed 8mm Lebel round.

7.5mm Cavalry Rifle 07/15M34

I dentical to the infantry rifle of the same pattern but with the bolt handle turned down.

7.5mm Rifle MAS36 and MAS36/CR39

Manufacture d'Armes de St Etienne	
7.5 × 54 Mle 1929	
Length	1,020mm (40.16in)
Weight empty	3.78kg (8.33lb)
Barrel	573mm (22.56in), 4 grooves, lh
Magazine	5-shot integral box
Muzzle velocity	823m/sec (2,700ft/sec)

F rench experience during World War One convinced them that the 8mm Lebel cartridge had outlived its usefulness; an awkward shape, with a wide rim and sharp tapering case, it was particularly inconvenient for automatic weapons, giving enormous feed problems, and could not stand comparison with the better-proportioned cartridges used elsewhere. Since one of the prime French needs in the post-war years was a good machine-gun, the logical place to start was by designing a new cartridge. After much trial, in 1924 a new 7.5mm rimless round, more or less based on the 7.92mm Mauser, appeared but this turned out less than successful and after more development a slightly shorter round appeared in 1929, the 7.5 × 54 Mle 29. The desired machine-gun followed, and after that thoughts turned to a magazine rifle.

The result was the MAS36, in general design a modified Mauser but with the bolt so altered as to lock into the receiver behind the magazine. This allows a shorter bolt stroke but is, of course, less strong than the original Mauser, and it was also found necessary to bend the bolt handle forward at an awkward angle so as to bring the handle closer to the firer's hand. Like all its predecessors in French service, the MAS36 had no safety catch. It was the last bolt-action rifle to be adopted for general service by any major military power, though a short-barrelled version for use by parachute troops was later made in small numbers; this, the MAS36/CR39, was basically the same weapon but with a folding hollow butt made of aluminium.

7.5mm INFANTRY RIFLE Mle 07/15

7.5mm MAS36

The Modèle F1 is a magazine rifle of modern design and considerable precision, offered in three versions; Modèle A for sniping, Modèle B for competition shooting, and Modèle C for big game hunting. The Modèle A entered service with the French Army in the 1960s, and the Modele B is also used by Army shooting teams. In design, the F1 is no great novelty, but is extremely carefully made and much effort goes into the manufacture of the components and the setting-up of the whole weapon. Butt length can be adjusted by a series of extension pieces, and the sniping rifle has a folding bipod which makes for steadier aiming. A night sight to aid shooting in poor light is available, and for daylight use the rifle is fitted with a telescope sight. The trigger pull can be adjusted by a micrometer screw, and a number of different foresights are available. The weapon is really a specialised competition rifle which has been adapted to the military role, which is probably a better approach than the more usual one of trying to improve the accuracy of a standard military rifle which was never designed for sniping in the first place. The first issues were chambered for the 7.5mm Mle 29 cartridge; later rifles were chambered for the 7.62mm NATO round, and the calibre is marked on the left side of the receiver.

7.5mm Sniping Rifle FR-F1

Manufacture d'Armes de St Etienne

7.5 × 54 Mle 1929 and 7.62 × 51mm NATO	
Length overall	1,138mm (44.80in)
Weight empty	5.20kg (11.46lb)
Barrel	552mm (21.73in), 4 grooves, rh
Magazine	10-shot integral box
Muzzle velocity	852m/sec (2,795ft/sec) (7.5mm)

Introduced in 1984 this is an improved version of the F1. The general characteristics are the same, though the F2 is only available chambered for the 7.62mm NATO cartridge, and the changes are entirely functional improvements. The forestock is of metal, covered in black plastic material; the bipod is stronger and has been moved back to a position just in front of the receiver, and the barrel is enclosed in a thermal sleeve. This keeps the barrel at an even temperature and reduces the chance of its bending due to differential heating effects, and it is also believed to reduce the infra-red signature of the weapon. Dimensions are exactly the same as for the FR-F1 rifle.

7.62mm Sniping Rifle FR-F2

7.62 × 51mm NATO

FR-FI SNIPING RIFLE

FR-F2 SNIPING RIFLE

GERMANY (PRE-1945)

7.92mm Commission Rifle M1888

Various manufacturers	
7.92 × 57mm Mauser M88	
Length overall	1,240mm (48.82in)
Weight empty	3.82kg (8.42lb)
Barrel	740mm (29.13in), 4 grooves, rh
Magazine	5-shot clip-loaded integral box
Muzzle velocity	640m/sec (2,100ft/sec)

The Commission Rifle was adopted by the German Army in 1888. Committees generally design poor weapons, as they tend to add too many desirable features, resulting in an over-complicated or inefficient weapon. In the case of this rifle, however, and the companion revolvers designed by the Commission, the result was a strong and workable design in no way inferior to the rifles of other countries (although, due to the speed of development in the latter part of the 19th century, it became obsolescent within a few years). Probably the best and longest-lasting work of the 1888 Committee was the development of the 7.92mm cartridge which has continued, with periodic improvements, to the present day and which has become so inseparably linked with the Mauser rifle that it is universally known as the 7.92mm Mauser.

The Commission Rifle had a short life. While mechanically sound (many thousands survive to this day, converted to various sporting calibres), its downfall was due to the limitations imposed by the clip loading system which prevented the rifle being used as a single loader and also prevented the firer topping-up the magazine with loose rounds. Other nations were content with the clip system, but the Germans, perhaps being more combat-oriented than most, turned to something better and evolved the Gewehr 98.

The original M1888 had a barrel jacket in the manner of the later Belgian Mauser, a straight stock, a protruding box magazine formed as a graceful continuation of the trigger-guard, and a split-bridge receiver in front of which the bolt handle locked down. A bar for the sword bayonet appeared on the right side of the nosecap. The various versions of the Gwehr 88 saw wide service during World War One, particularly in the hands of second-line and garrison troops of the German Army. A carbine version, the Kar 88, was also made in some quantity.

7.92mm Infantry Rifle M1898 (Gewehr 98)

Waffenfabrik Mauser AG	
7.92 × 57mm Mauser M98	
Length overall	1,255mm (49.40in)
Weight empty	4.14kg (9.13lb)
Barrel	740mm (29.14in), 4 grooves, rh
Magazine	5-shot integral box
Muzzle velocity	870m/sec (2,855ft/sec)

This version of the Mauser rifle was one of the most widely adopted versions. It shared the distinction of being the most extensively distributed Mauser rifle with the Spanish model, which also spread far and wide across the world. The Gewehr 98 introduced an improved bolt with a third locking lug behind the bolt handle engaging a recess in the receiver. Although not a particularly valuable addition in itself, it formed a useful and perhaps necessary safety factor. Other recognition features were the stock, with its pistol grip, its horizontal bolt handle, an ugly and clumsy arrangement, and the tangent backsight, a most elaborate affair of substantial ramps and slides. The magazine was wholly contained within the body, and the bottom plate was a continuation of the trigger guard. Loading was done by a five-round charger inserted into the action, from which the rounds were stripped down into the magazine.

The Gew 98 was among the most successful rifles ever produced, and it has only been rivalled in recent years by the phenomenal numbers of Soviet Kalashnikov weapons which are now in circulation. Literally millions of rifles based on the Gew 98 have been made, and many of them still survive. The German Army was still carrying substantial numbers of them in 1939, as were many other countries. They were reliable, robust and accurate. Their detractors would point to the forward-locking bolt lugs and claim that the locking recesses were difficult to keep clean and free from fouling, but this was never borne out in practice. Those who carried the Mauser in battle rarely complained of its performance. Only in one respect could it be faulted; the straight bolt handle did not lend itself to rapid manipulation, and the arm movement necessary to work it was awkward and slow.

COMMISSION RIFLE M1888

GEWEHR 98

The Kar 98 was no more than a short-stocked version of the original Mauser Gewehr 98 rifle. It was a rather clumsy little carbine and was only made for four years, from 1899 to 1903. After this there was a break in the issue of carbines while other designs were considered. In 1904 Mauser had startled the military world with his 'spitzer' pointed-nose bullets, and there was some consideration at Oberndorf as to the best pattern of carbine to fire it. Another factor was the British and American development of 'short' rifles which could serve both as infantry rifles and cavalry carbines and which were obviously as successful in both roles as had been their specialised predecessors. The 1904 pattern of the Kar 98 differed from the previous version in that the barrel stocking was removed on the upper surface, forward of the first barrel band. The bolt was turned down not only to make it easier to grasp but also to prevent it catching in clothing and equipment. At the same time a recess was cut into the wood of the stock to allow an easier grip. There was a prominent piling hook under the muzzle. The 1904 carbine was not issued until 1908 but it steadily replaced the rifle in general service and was the standard weapon of World War One. After 1920 the 1904 pattern was regularised by being re-named the Kar 98a, though no changes were made to the weapon itself. The Kar 98b was an aberration; it was the Gew 98 rifle given a turned-down bolt and simplified sights. It was not a carbine at all.

The Kar 98k was the standard German Army rifle of World War Two. The 'k' stands for 'kurz' and distinguishes it from the Kar 98a which was longer. The 98k appeared in 1935 and was little different from the 98a except that it was of new manufacture. No real attempt was made to bring it up to date, largely because at that time German industry was overloaded with other projects, particularly tanks and aircraft. Infantry weapons received scant attention in the excitement of re-arming and it was simpler to take existing drawings and continue to make the same design. Manufacture continued throughout the war, not only in the Mauser factory, but later models showed evidence of the material shortages in Germany towards the end, particularly in the use of inferior wood for the stocks. The 98k was the last Mauser bolt-action military rifle in general issue. It was in the best traditions of Mauser design, reliable and strong, and like its predecessors it served the German infantryman well.

This was the German service version of the Austrian-made Model 31 commercial rifle, manufactured in Steyr by the Oesterreichische Waffenfabrik; most were delivered to the Luftwaffe.

7.92mm Carbine M1898 (Kar 98)

Waffenfabrik Mauser AG

7.92 × 57mm Mauser M98

7.92mm Carbine M1898k (Kar 98k)

Waffenfabrik Mauser AG

	7.92 × 57mm Mauser M98
Length overall	1,110mm (43.70in)
Weight empty	3.9kg (8.60lb)
Barrel	600mm (23.62in), 4 grooves, rh
Magazine	5-shot integral box
Muzzle velocity	745m/sec (2,444ft/sec)

7.92mm Rifle M29/40(o)

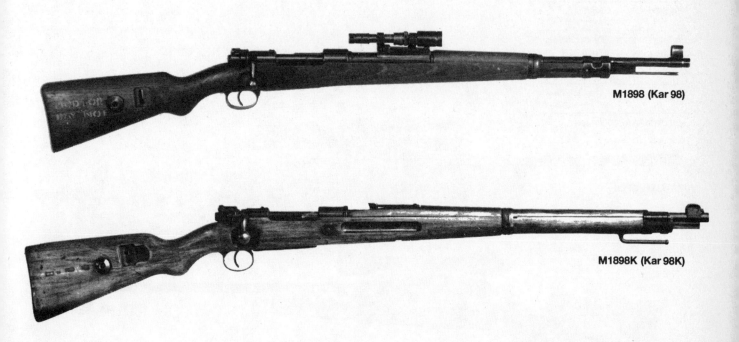

M1898 (Kar 98)

M1898K (Kar 98K)

7.92mm Rifle M33/40(t)

Length overall	1,000mm (39.37in)
Weight empty	3.65kg (8.05lb)
Barrel	490mm (19.29in), 4 grooves, rh
Magazine	5-shot integral box
Muzzle velocity	715m/sec (2,345ft/sec)

This was a German-adopted variant of a Czech carbine, the VZ/33, with modifications to shorten and lighten it. The result was a compact carbine which was issued to mountain troops. Like all such short weapons firing a full-power cartridge, the M33/40 had a violent recoil and excessive muzzle blast.

GERMANY: FEDERAL REPUBLIC

7.62mm Mauser SP66

Mauser-Werke Oberndorf GmbH	
7.62 × 51mm NATO	
Weight empty	6.12kg (13.5lb) with Zeiss telescope
Barrel	650mm (25.59in); (730mm with muzzle brake)
Magazine	3-shot integral box
Muzzle velocity	868m/sec (2,848ft/sec)

Although offered as a military sniping rifle, this is actually Mauser's commercial 'Model 66S Super Match', the 'S' indicating the use of their 'short action' bolt and receiver. The barrel is heavy gauge and made of a special rust-inhibiting steel, fitted with a combined muzzle brake and flash hider. The stock is fully adjustable and incorporates a thumb-hole to aid in maintaining a regular grip. Iron sights are available but the rifle is normally fitted with a Zeiss 'Diavari ZA' zoom telescope giving 1.5 to 6x magnification. It can also be fitted with more or less any type of telescope or image-intensifying sight to order, and the rifle can also be supplied to order in any chosen calibre. It is in use by the Federal German Army and several others.

7.62mm Mauser 86SR

Mauser-Werke Oberndorf GmbH	
7.62 × 51mm NATO	
Length overall	1,210mm (47.64in)
Weight empty	4.90kg (10.8lb) without sight
Barrel	730mm (28.74in) (with muzzle brake), 4 grooves, rh
Magazine	9-shot double-row integral box
Muzzle velocity	868m/sec (2,848ft/sec)

This is offered as a less expensive alternative to the SP66. It uses a newly developed bolt action, locking by forward lugs, and the stock is ventilated so as to allow the barrel maximum cooling. The trigger is adjustable and the barrel is fitted with a muzzle brake. The stock is of laminated wood and has an adjustable recoil pad. There is a rail let into the fore-end to which a sling or bipod can be attached. Iron sights are not fitted, but there is a mount which allows the use of most types of telescope and electro-optical sights.

MAUSER SP66

MAUSER 86SR

GREAT BRITAIN

During the 1880s the British Army busied itself with the study of various rifle systems, in an endeavour to determine which might best suit their requirements, and these deliberations ended with the adoption, in 1888, of the Lee-Metford rifle. This used the turnbolt action and magazine attributable to James Paris Lee, the Scots-born American inventor, together with the barrel and rifling designed by William Metford especially to combat the fouling inherent in the gunpowder propelling charges of the day. The Lee-Metford also marked the British Army's move to a small calibre weapon, using a jacketed compound bullet developed in accordance with the theories of Major Rubin of Switzerland. In retrospect, it can be considered unfortunate that the decisions were not delayed for a few more years until the rimless cartridge had been perfected; as it was the British adopted the rimmed .303in round, and in spite of its drawbacks – more theoretical than practical – retained it until the 1950s. It was, though, a well-proportioned cartridge, unlike the contemporary Lebel, Mauser and Mosin-Nagant rounds, and in the ensuing years various designers managed to make it function with a wide variety of weapons.

Introduced on 2 December 1888, this was a bolt-action rifle with dust-cover over the bolt and with a box magazine holding eight rounds in a single column. It was rifled on Metford's system, the grooves being .004in deep and the lands .023in wide. The left-hand twist was uniform, developing one complete turn in 10in (254mm). The foresight was a square block with a vertical slot in it, and the rear sight was a square notch fixed in its lowest place at 300 yards' range and graduated to 1,900 yards. On the side of the stock was an 'Extreme Range Sight' graduated from 1,800 yards to 3,500 yards. The Lee bolt locked at the rear and the striker had a half-cock notch which formed an additional safety device to the manual safety catch on the receiver. There was a cut-off plate on the right side of the receiver which, when pushed in, closed off the magazine and allowed the rifle to be used as a single-shot weapon; sliding the cut-off out allowed the rounds in the magazine to be loaded by the bolt. In August 1891 the designation was officially changed to 'Rifle, Magazine, Lee-Metford, Mark I'.

Introduced 19 January 1892. This design was sealed to govern future manufacture and also to govern the conversion of stocks of the Mark I rifle. The safety catch was removed, the handguard was modified and a brass disc for regimental numbering was let into the butt, the piling swivel was strengthened, the bolt mainspring and magazine spring changed, a blade front sight was fitted, and the rear sight graduation was changed to match a muzzle velocity of 2,000ft/sec. The long-range sight was also re-graduated from 1,600 to 2,900 yards.

Introduced on 30 January 1892. The principal difference in this new model was that the magazine was enlarged to accept 10 rounds, requiring slight modification to the receiver. The magazine spring was of 'C' shape instead of a coil, the barrel was lighter, and there were small changes in the construction of the bolt and the magazine cut-off. The weight fell to 4.25kg (9.25lb). A number of these rifles were re-barrelled with Enfield rifling in 1902 and had 'E' stamped on the Knox-form, though the nomenclature remained unchanged.

The Lee-Metford Rifles

Royal Small Arms Factory, Enfield;
Royal Small Arms Factory, Birmingham

.303in Rifle, Magazine, Mark I

Length overall	1,257mm (49.5in)
Weight empty	4.31kg (9.5lb)
Barrel	767mm (30.2in), 7 grooves, lh
Magazine	8-shot detachable box
Muzzle velocity	564m/sec (1,850ft/sec)

.303in Rifle, Magazine, Lee-Metford Mark I*

.303in Rifle, Magazine, Lee-Metford Mark II

LEE-METFORD Mk I

.303in Rifle, Magazine, Lee-Metford Mark II*

Introduced 22 April 1895. Differed from the Mark II in that the bolt was one inch longer and fitted with two grooves for a safety catch, and the cocking piece was also lengthened and carried the safety catch. In 1903 some rifles were Enfield barrelled and marked 'E' on the Knox-form, the designation being changed to 'Rifle, Magazine, Lee-Enfield Mark I' if fitted with the original pattern of nose-cap, or 'Mark I*' if fitted with the later pattern of solid fore-end and nose-cap.

.303in Rifle, Charger-Loading, Magazine, Lee-Metford Mark II

Introduced 1 July 1907. This was a conversion from Mark II, achieved by fitting a bridge charger guide across the bolt-way and a new magazine; the rifle also had an adjustable blade foresight with a fixed protector, and a new rearsight graduated for Cordite ammunition.

.303in Carbine, Magazine, Lee-Metford Mark I

Length overall	1,014mm (39.94in)
Weight empty	3.37kg (7.435lb)
Barrel	527mm (20.75in), 7 grooves, lh
Magazine	6-shot detachable box

Introduced 29 September 1894. This was based upon the Mark II rifle but differed in a number of small details as well as in its major dimensions. The bolt lever was bent closer to the body and had the top flattened, the magazine was shorter, and the sight was calibrated for Cordite cartridges. It was stocked almost to the muzzle.

The Lee-Enfield Rifles

Royal Small Arms Factory, Enfield;
Royal Small Arms Factory, Birmingham;
Birmingham Small Arms Company;
London Small Arms Company;
Lithgow Rifle Factory, Australia;
Ishapore Arsenal, India

With the adoption of Cordite as the standard military propellant, a change was made in the design of rifling. The Metford rifling had been designed to combat powder residues and function even when fouled; with the virtual absence of fouling from Cordite, it was possible to revert to a more efficient design of rifling which was better-suited to a high-velocity rifle. This was the Enfield rifling, so-called from its development at the Royal Small Arms Factory at Enfield Lock, north of London. The marriage of the new rifling to the Lee action produced the Lee-Enfield rifle. A carbine model was also produced, and there were several weapons derived from earlier patterns which were modernised by re-barrelling with Enfield barrels. One or two have already been mentioned, but in addition there were a number of older patterns of Martini-Henry rifles which changed to become Martini-Enfields. These were almost entirely adopted by Militia and other forces, for training purposes, and since they scarcely constitute 'Military Arms of the 20th Century' we do not consider them further.

.303in Rifle, Magazine, Lee-Enfield Mark I

Introduced on 11 November 1895, this was much the same as the Lee-Metford Mark II*, differing only in the rifling, which had five grooves, .005in deep, with a left-hand twist of one turn in 254mm (10in). The foresight was located .05in left of the axis of the bore so as to compensate for bullet drift due to the rifling. This rifle is sometimes called the 'Long Lee-Enfield'.

LEE-ENFIELD Mk I

LEE-ENFIELD Mk I
ACTION

Introduced 19 May 1899, this was simply the Mark I with the cleaning rod removed. It had been found that the rifles were easier to clean when firing Cordite, and the brute strength and ramrod technique was abandoned for the more easily carried cord pull-through.

.303in Rifle, Magazine, Lee-Enfield Mark I*

Introduced 1 July 1903. With the intention of developing one rifle which would serve the infantryman as a rifle and everybody else as a carbine, the 'Short Lee-Enfield' was designed. Universally execrated by every self-styled expert in the Western hemisphere when it was introduced, the rifle was held to be too short to be a target-shooter's arm and too long to be a cavalryman's companion, and that it was nothing but an abortion devised by unscrupulous government technicians by the simple expedient of robbing, whenever possible, every good feature from other rifles and then ruining them. In spite of this vicious onslaught, the 'SMLE' survived to become, in its later versions, probably the finest combat bolt-action rifle ever to see active service. Its most obvious feature was the all-enveloping furniture and the snub nose. The rear sight was half-way down the barrel, at a time when advanced thought was turning to aperture sights under the shooter's eyelids, and the familiar Lee magazine protruded through the bottom of the stock. This rifle also saw the introduction of charger-loading, a charger holding five rounds being adopted. The original introduction of the rifle was cancelled, and the design slightly altered by the addition of a wind-gauge to the rear sight and the substitution of screws for rivets in one or two minor places, after which it was re-introduced on 14 September 1903. An interesting but little-known feature of this rifle was that the rifling changed depth; it was .005in deep from the breech to a point 14in from the muzzle, after which it became .0065in deep for the remainder of the bore. This was done in order to achieve the desired muzzle velocity by reducing friction on the bullet for much of its travel.

.303in Rifle, Short, Magazine, Lee-Enfield Mark I

Length overall	1,132mm (44.57in)
Weight empty	3.71kg (8.18lb)
Barrel	640mm (25.19in), 5 grooves, lh
Magazine	10-shot detachable box
Muzzle velocity	617m/sec (2,025ft/sec)

Introduced 2 July 1906. This was a variant of the Mark I incorporating several small improvements suggested after the originals had been in the hands of troops. The sheet-steel buttplate was replaced by one of gunmetal and it incorporated a butt-trap for cleaning materials and an oil bottle. A new Number 2 magazine, slightly deeper at the front, was adopted, the striker was retained by a keeper screw with a slot large enough to be turned by a coin, and the sharp corners on various components were rounded.

.303in Rifle, Short, Magazine, Lee-Enfield Mark I*

Introduced 2 November 1903, this was a conversion of the Lee-Metford Mark I* by fitting new sights, shorter and lighter Enfield barrels, and adapting them for charger-loading. Although officially approved, no rifles other than the sealed pattern were ever made, and the design was declared obsolete on 2 July 1906.

.303in Rifle, Short, Magazine, Lee-Enfield, Converted Mark I

Introduced 6 November 1903. A conversion of Lee-Enfield Marks I and I* and Lee-Metford Marks II and II* by fitting new sights, shorter and lighter barrels, and modifying to permit charger-loading.

.303in Rifle, Short, Magazine, Lee-Enfield, Converted Mark II

LEE-ENFIELD Mk I

LEE-ENFIELD No 1 Mk III

.303in Rifle, Short, Magazine, Lee-Enfield, Converted Mark II*

Introduced 2 July 1906. Similar to the Converted Mark II above, but differing in having the butt recessed for a sling swivel, provision for a butt-trap, and the Number 2 magazine.

.303in Rifle, Short, Magazine, Lee-Enfield Mark III

Introduced 26 January 1907. The principal change in the Mark III lay in the sights; it was otherwise the same rifle as the Mark I or I*. The foresight was now a simple blade, instead of a barleycorn (an inverted V) and was supplied in five heights. The rear sight bed was wider, and the sight leaf, graduated to 2,000 yards, had a fine adjustment worm-wheel. A 'U' notch replaced the previous 'V' notch. The receiver was fitted with a bridge charger guide, shaped so that the closing stroke of the bolt would eject the charger, and the charger guide on the bolt head was abandoned. The weight now became 3.94kg (8.69lb).

In 1916 as a wartime concession to manufacturers, it was agreed that rifles might embody any of the following modifications: omission of the long-range sight, replacement of the rear sight wind gauge by a fixed cap, alteration of the contours of the striker, and omission of the piling swivel lugs.

.303in Rifle, Short, Magazine, Lee-Enfield, Converted Mark IV

Introduced 17 June 1907, this differed from the Converted Mark II* in that it embodied the various special features of the SMLE Mark III.

.303in Rifle, Charger Loading, Magazine, Lee-Enfield Mark I*

Introduced 1 July 1907, this was a conversion from Lee-Enfield Marks I and I* or Lee-Metford Mark II* by the addition of a bridge charger guide, Number 2 magazine and new rear sight.

.303in Rifle, Short, Magazine, Lee-Enfield Mark I**

Introduced on 22 October 1909, this was issued only to the Royal Navy. It was a conversion from SMLE Mark I rifles carried out in naval ordnance depots at Chatham, Portsmouth and Plymouth and consisted of fitting an SMLE Mark III foresight, and a backsight with wind gauge and U-notch.

.303in Rifle, Short, Magazine, Lee-Enfield, Converted Mark II**

Introduced 22 October 1909, this was another Naval conversion, the same as the Mark I** but performed on the SMLE Mark II rifle.

.303in Rifle, Short, Magazine, Lee-Enfield, Converted Mark II***

Introduced 22 October 1909, this was the third Naval conversion, the same as before but applied to the SMLE Converted Mark II*.

LEE-ENFIELD ACTION

Introduced 22 April 1914. This was a conversion from the SMLE Mark I* achieved by fitting a wind gauge and U-notch to the rear sight, and a new blade foresight to suit the Mark 7 ball cartridge. This marked the adoption of the Mark 7 pointed bullet, which superseded the Mark 6 blunt-nosed bullet.

.303in Rifle, Short, Magazine, Lee-Enfield Mark I*

Introduced 2 January 1916. This was a wartime model differing from the Mark III in having the magazine cut-off omitted, thus speeding-up manufacture.

.303in Rifle, Short, Magazine, Lee-Enfield Mark III*

Introduced 17 August 1896, this was basically the Lee-Metford Cavalry Carbine Mark I with Enfield rifling, improved sights, the sling fittings omitted, and with an attached leather cover to protect the rear sight. The weight and dimensions were the same as in the earlier weapon. On 19 May 1899 the Mark I* carbine appeared; like the rifle conversion, it marked the abolition of the cleaning rod.

.303in Carbine, Magazine, Lee-Enfield, Cavalry, Mark I

Introduced 1 August 1900, this differed from the Cavalry Marks I and I* in having a new barrel with an increased muzzle diameter so as to accept the 1888 sword bayonet, a V-notch backsight and barleycorn foresight, and protecting wings around the foresight. Confusion was brought into play on 13 January 1902 by the announcement that 'When Carbines, Magazine, Lee-Metford Mark I are fitted with Enfield barrels and have the wings of the nosecap drawn out to the same height as Lee-Enfield carbines, they will be described as Carbines, Magazine, Lee-Enfield Mark I. The barrels will be marked . . . on the Knox-form with the letter 'E'.

.303in Carbine, Magazine, Lee-Enfield Mark I

Between the wars the British Army decided to change the system of nomenclature used with rifles; the foregoing examples have shown how cumbersome the titles had become, and in the interests of brevity and accuracy rifles were now listed in a numbered series. Thus in May 1926 the 'Rifle, Short, Magazine, Lee-Enfield Mark III' now became the 'Rifle Number One Mark III', though nobody but quartermasters and armourers ever called it that. Since the last Mark number under the old system had been the Converted Mark IV, the first under the new system was the Rifle No 1 Mark 6. (Arabic numbers did not replace Roman numerals until 1944, but in the interest of simplicity we will make the change at this point.) This rifle was made in limited numbers in the early 1920s, but was never accepted for service; the principal difference between it and the SMLE Mark III was the moving of the rear sight back to the receiver bridge so as to extend the sight base and improve the accuracy of shooting. This model led to the Rifle No 1 Mark 6, which was a further simplification in the search for a design which was easier to mass produce in wartime than the SMLE Mark III. This, too, was never adopted for service. More work on simplifying the design eventually led to the Number 4 Rifle.

The Number 4 Rifle

Royal Small Arms Factory, Enfield;
Royal Ordnance Factory, Fazakerley;
Royal Ordnance Factory, Maltby;
Royal Ordnance Factory, Shirley (BSA);
Long Branch Arsenal, Canada;
Savage Arms Co, USA;
Lithgow Factory, Australia;
Ishapore Arsenal, India

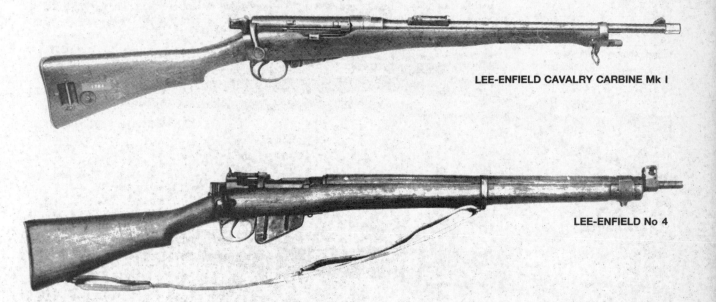

LEE-ENFIELD CAVALRY CARBINE Mk I

LEE-ENFIELD No 4

.303in Rifle Number 4 Marks 1 and 2

Length overall	1,128mm (44.43in)
Weight empty	4.11kg (9.06lb)
Barrel	640mm (25.2in), 2, 5 or 6 grooves, lh
Magazine	10-shot detachable box
Muzzle velocity	751m/sec (2,464ft/sec)

.303in Rifle Number 4 Mark 1 (T)

.303in Rifle Number 4 Mark 2

.303in Rifle Number 4 Mark 1/2

.303in Rifle Number 4 Mark 1/3

.303in Rifle Number 5 Mark 1

Royal Small Arms Factory, Enfield; Royal Ordnance Factory, Shirley (BSA)	
Length overall	1,000mm (39.37in)
Weight empty	3.24kg (7.14lb)
Barrel	478mm (18.7in), 5 grooves, lh
Magazine	10-shot detachable box
Muzzle velocity	610m/sec (2,000ft/sec)

The Number 4 Mark 1 was similar to the SMLE Mark III in most respects but had an aperture rear sight hinged at the rear of the receiver, the nosecap was done away with and the muzzle exposed for about two inches, with the sight and its protecting wings mounted on the barrel. The muzzle was also formed with lugs for a new 'spike' bayonet. This was introduced as the Number 4 Mark 1 in November 1939, after trials lasting almost ten years had perfected it.

In order to speed up manufacture by omitting some machining, and also to make operation slightly easier, the Mark 1* was approved some time in 1941. The difference between this and the Mark 1 lay in the receiver, which was modified to simplify manufacture and the removal of the bolt. Some two million of these rifles were made in Canada and the USA during the war years.

Introduced 12 February 1942, this was the Mark 1 fitted with a tangent rear sight and prepared for a telescope sight. The butt was fitted with a cheek rest.

Introduced 31 March 1949, the Mark 2 was similar to the Mark 1 but had a new design of trigger mechanism in which the trigger was hinged about a pin located in a bracket forged with the receiver, instead of being hinged to the trigger guard as in the earlier design.

Introduced 31 March 1949; as might be imagined, this was a Mark 1 modified to Mark 2 standard by having the trigger rebuilt.

Introduced 31 March 1949, this was the Mark 1* brought to Mark 2 standard by having the new trigger assembly fitted.

The operations in the Far East soon convinced the British Army that lightening the soldier's load would be a useful step; moreover, British troops were looking enviously at the neat and compact US M1 carbine and voicing questions about when they were going to have something comparable. As a result the 'Jungle Carbine' or Number 5 rifle was developed in 1943. It was broadly a Number 4 Mark 1 shortened, with a bell-mouthed flash hider on the muzzle, a single handguard, leaving much of the barrel exposed, and a rubber recoil pad on the stock. It was approved for issue on 12 September 1944, by which time it was already in production, and was issued widely to troops in the Far East. In post-war years it was seriously considered as the future standard rifle, but it suffered from two serious defects; the recoil was excessive, which the troops didn't much like, and it would not 'hold its zero' – in other words, the sighting wandered off and became inaccurate. Many modifications were tried to cure this, but it was finally realised that it was a defect inherent in the design and was incurable. As a result the Number 5 rifle was made obsolescent in July 1947.

LEE-ENFIELD No 4 SNIPER'S RIFLE

LEE-ENFIELD No 5

The Pattern 1914 Rifles

Various manufacturers (see text)

When the Short Magazine Lee-Enfield was introduced into service it met with a storm of criticism – though little of it came from the soldiers. A typical example, from *Arms and Explosives* magazine for November 1908, may suffice: 'The rifle was always bad, its defects always notorious . . . and the propagation of badness will doubtless continue for several more generations to come.' Whether or not this campaign of calumny had any effect, the War Office began developing a rifle more in keeping with what their critics thought a military weapon ought to be. The result was based upon the Mauser bolt action and was of .276in (7mm) calibre. After extensive experimentation, both in theory and practice, it was approved for issue on a trial basis as the **'Rifle Magazine, .276in Pattern 1914'** in 1913. The cartridge was roughly based on the .280in Ross and was exceptionally powerful. Loaded with Cordite the results included excessive muzzle flash and blast, severe erosive wear, barrel overheating, irregular chamber pressures and premature ignition due to barrel heat. Before these problems could be solved, the outbreak of war caused the entire project to be shelved indefinitely. In late 1914, though, the problems of mass production of the Lee-Enfield rifle led to the design being re-assessed. The Pattern 1914 has been designed with an eye to mass production, so it was rapidly converted to the standard .303 calibre and manufacturing contracts were placed in the USA, the rifles being brought into British service as the 'Pattern 1914'.

Formally introduced 21 June 1916. These rifles can be recognised by the long exposed muzzle and prominent wings protecting the foresight, by the distinctive shape of the rear sight housing, and by the fact that there is no exposed magazine. Although they may have been designed to the satisfaction of the target fraternity, they were not liked by the soldiers. The P'14 was too long, badly balanced, and cumbersome to handle in combat, especially when garlanded by a long bayonet. The number issued during World War One is not known, but most of them turned up in World War Two when they were principally used by the Home Guard. They were formally retitled 'Rifle No 3' in December 1941, finally being declared obsolete in July 1947. The 'E' models were manufactured in the USA by the Remington Arms-Union Metallic Cartridge Company at their factory in Eddystone, Pennsylvania and were distinctively marked. On the front top of the body appeared 'RE', on the right side of the stock 'IR', and on all the principal components 'e'.

Rifle, Magazine, .303in, Pattern 1914 Mark 1E

Length overall	1,176mm (46.3in)
Weight empty	3.94kg (8.69lb)
Barrel	660mm (26.0in), 5 grooves, lh
Magazine	5-shot integral box
Muzzle velocity	843m/sec (2,765ft/sec)

Introduced 21 June 1916. These were the same as the 1E but were made by Remington at their Bridgeport, Connecticut factory. They were marked 'ERA', 'IE' and 'r' in the places noted above.

Rifle, Magazine, .303in, Pattern 1914 Mark 1R

Introduced 21 June 1916. As for the previous models, but made by the Winchester Repeating Arms Company plant in New Haven, Connecticut and hence marked 'W', 'IW' and 'w' on the various parts.

This individual nomenclature and marking was necessary because the three manufacturers' output was not interchangeable.

Rifle, Magazine, .303in, Pattern 1914 Mark 1W

PATTERN 191

PATTERN 1914 ACTION

Rifle, Magazine, .303in, Pattern 1914 Marks 1E*, 1R* and 1W*

Rifle, Magazine, .303in, Pattern 1914 Mark 1*W(T)

.45in De Lisle Carbine

Sterling Armament Co	
.45 M1911	
Length overall	960mm (37.79in)
Weight empty	3.70kg (8.15lb)
Barrel	210mm (8.26in), 4 grooves, lh
Magazine	8-shot detachable box (Colt M1911A1)
Muzzle velocity	260m/sec (853ft/sec)

7.62mm Parker-Hale Model 82

Parker-Hale Ltd	
7.62 × 51mm NATO	
Length	1,213mm (47.75in)
Weight empty	4.80kg (10.58lb)
Barrel	660mm (25.98in), 4 grooves, rh
Magazine	4-shot internal box
Muzzle velocity	860m/sec (2,820ft/sec)

These three weapons were all introduced in February 1917 and were basically the same as the previous models but with a thicker fore-end and minor manufacturing changes.

Introduced 11 April 1918, this was the Mark 1W* with the addition of an Aldis sighting telescope and a cheekpiece on the butt.

The De Lisle carbine was an unusual weapon, produced in Britain in limited numbers during World War Two for use by Commandos and other clandestine forces. It was based on the standard Lee-Enfield action but was fitted with a .45in calibre barrel forming part of a large and extremely efficient silencer. It is undoubtedly one of the most silent weapons ever devised, the only noise audible on firing being the striker hitting the cap. Unfortunately this is somewhat spoiled by the clatter of the bolt action being operated to load the next round. It is also vastly superior to most silenced weapons in matters of range and accuracy; although the .45 ACP bullet is generally considered a short-range pistol load, this assumption is drawn from its use in short-barrelled pistols and submachine-guns. The barrel of the De Lisle was one of the longest in this calibre and, because of this, it shot with remarkable accuracy up to three or four hundred yards. In the 1980s one or two companies have begun manufacture of the De Lisle again, largely for the counter-insurgency market but also for sale to collectors.

The Model 82 is a sniping rifle developed with all the expertise of Parker-Hale, who have for decades dominated British target-shooting with their products. It uses a Mauser-type action, with all the components carefully selected and assembled. The one-piece body screws on to a heavy hammered barrel, and there are two bridge sections which are machined for the sight mounts. The fully floating barrel is the heaviest target type available, and it is carefully bedded into the one-piece wooden stock with epoxy resin. The foresight fits into a dovetailed base at the muzzle and the actual bore at the muzzle is recessed to prevent damage to the rifling. The bolt has the usual Mauser twin front-locking lugs and a smaller rear lug which rides on an inclined camway to give primary extraction. The trigger mechanism is a separate self-contained assembly located by axis pins in the body. The single-stage trigger is adjustable for pull, backlash and creep, but as set by the factory it gives a short pull with the minimum mechanical lock time. A useful military feature is that the safety is silent in operation and it works on trigger, bolt and sear at the same time, providing total safety against accidental discharge. The butt is adjustable for different firers and the forward sling swivel and hand stop can be moved over a wide range along the fore-end. The Parker-Hale 82 has been adopted by Australia and Canada as their official sniping rifle and may have been taken by other armies as well, though precise information is difficult to obtain.

DE LISLE CARBINE

PARKER-HALE MODEL 82

This was developed from the Model 82 (above) and the P-H 1200TX target rifle, and its appearance is almost identical with that of the Model 82. It is a single-shot weapon, the absence of a magazine and feedway stiffening the action and so improving accuracy. The rifling is matched to the standard 114 grain 7.62mm NATO ball bullet, and the entire length of the action is bedded in Devcon F metal compound. Accuracy is within a half-minute of arc over ten rounds, depending upon the quality of the ammunition. The target trigger is single-stage and fully adjustable for pull, creep and backlash. The length of stock is adjustable, the sights are fully adjustable, and a range of foresight inserts is provided to suit individuals. This rifle was adopted in 1983 as the British Army's 'Cadet Training Rifle L81A1'.

7.62mm Parker-Hale Model 83

(Cadet Training Rifle L81A1)
Parker-Hale Ltd

7.62 × 51mm NATO

Length overall	1,187mm (46.73in)
Weight empty	4.98kg (10.98lb)
Barrel	660mm (25.98in), 4 grooves, rh
Magazine	single shot
Muzzle velocity	860m/sec (2,820ft/sec)

The Model 85 is a sniping rifle intended to give 100 per cent first-round hit capability at ranges up to 600 metres, and it is sighted to 900 metres. The weapon uses a specially designed Mauser-type bolt action allied to a heavy barrel and fully adjustable stock. The receiver carries an aperture rear sight graduated to 900m for emergency use or when optical sights are not practical. The sight mount permits the removal and replacement of the optical sight without loss of zero.

7.62mm Parker-Hale Model 85

Parker-Hale Ltd

7.62 × 51mm NATO

Length overall	1,150mm (45.28in)
Weight empty	5.70kg (12.57lb) with telescope sight
Barrel	700mm (27.56in), 4 grooves, rh
Magazine	10-shot detachable box
Muzzle velocity	860m/sec (2,820ft/sec)

This is a conversion of the .303in Rifle No 4 Mark 1 or Mark 1*(T) sniping rifle to fire the 7.62mm NATO cartridge. It has a shortened 'sporterized' fore-end and is fitted with the Telescope, Straight, Sighting L1. Iron sights are also fitted, and modifications have been made to the extractor to suit the rimless cartridge. The same rifle, fitted with a zoom telescope sight, is offered as a police sniping rifle under the name 'Enfield Enforcer'.

7.62mm Rifle L42A1

RSAF, Enfield

7.62 × 51mm NATO

PARKER-HALE M.85

L42A1

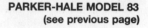

PARKER-HALE MODEL 83
(see previous page)

7.62mm Rifle L39A1

RSAF, Enfield	
7.62 × 51mm NATO	
Length overall	1,180mm (46.50in)
Weight empty	4.42kg (9.74lb)
Barrel	700mm (27.55in), 4 grooves, rh
Magazine	single-shot or 10/shot detachable box
Muzzle velocity	845m/sec (2,772ft/sec

The L39A1 was introduced to give the British forces a competitive target rifle for use by those units equipped with the L1A1 semi-automatic rifle. It was made by RSAF and is a modified .303in No 4; a new heavy barrel was fitted and the receiver and bolt modified to suit the rimless 7.62mm cartridge. The fore-end is cut down to the lower band. The butt is from the No. 4 rifle, but the handguard is a modification of the type used on the .22in No. 8 rifle. Unusually, the .303 magazine is retained, not for its normal use but merely as a loading platform, since the weapon is to be used in the single-shot mode. There is no positive ejection and the extracted round lies on the magazine platform until removed by hand. However, if required, a 10-round magazine designed for 7.62mm ammunition can be fitted, and this does give positive ejection. The Model 85 was approved for British Army service in 1987.

7.62mm Rifle L96A1

Accuracy International Ltd	
7.62 × 51mm NATO	
Length overall	1,124mm (44.25in)
Weight empty	6.50kg (14.32lb)
Barrel	655mm (25.79in), 4 grooves, rh
Magazine	10-shot detachable box
Muzzle velocity	840m/sec (2,830ft/sec)

This was designed as a sniping rifle to meet the specifications laid down by the British Army and was adopted as the service sniping weapon in 1986. The rifle uses an aluminium frame to which the components are firmly attached. This is then clad in a high-impact plastic stock, the stainless steel barrel floating freely. The bolt has three forward locking lugs with an additional safety lug at the handle. It is a short-throw bolt, allowing the firer to keep his cheek against the stock and continue observing the target while reloading. The stock is fitted with a fully adjustable light alloy bipod.

The rifle is fitted with fully adjustable iron sights for use out to 700 metres, but it is routinely fitted with a specially designed Schmidt & Bender 6 × 42 telescope sight designated the Sight L1A1.

L96A1

L39A1

GREECE

Towards the end of the 19th Century many inventors attempted to design and perfect rotary magazines in order to eliminate some of the less desirable feeding characteristics of rimmed cartridges in box magazines. Among the Austrians and Hungarians who produced designs were Antonin Spitalsky, Otto Schoenauer and Josef Schulhof; Mannlicher himself produced two rifles using rotary or 'spool' magazines, one in 1887 and one in 1888.

Few of these weapons met with any success and it was not until Schoenauer perfected his design in the 1890s that a chance arose of military adoption of such a magazine. Schoenauer's magazine was allied to a bolt action designed by Mannlicher, and in about 1900 the rifle was offered to the Austro-Hungarian authorities, who promptly rejected it, since they had just managed to get production of their Model 1895 rifle into operation and they were not prepared to change designs and involve themselves in expensive re-tooling. The design was then offered around Europe and was adopted by the Greeks in 1903 and extensively tested by Portugal in 1904, though they eventually adopted a modified Mauser design.

The Schoenauer magazine, also widely used in sporting rifles, used a spring-tensioned rotary spool into which five rounds were loaded from a Mauser-type charger. While ingenious and neat, the spool magazine conferred little advantage over the simpler and cheaper box when rimless cartridges were used, though the design did permit more sure feeding of rimmed rounds.

The Greek rifle was the only rotary magazine bolt-action rifle to achieve service issue, and was easily recognised by the absence of any protruding magazine. It was otherwise similar to the Roumanian Model 1893 rifle, with a split-bridge receiver in which the bolt handle locked down in front of the bridge to supplement the two locking lugs on the bolt head. Unlike many other Mannlichers, the Greek rifle could be cocked by simply raising and lowering the bolt handle, an idea taken from the Mauser system used on the Gewehr 98. Until 1914 the weapons were manufactured in Steyr, but the onset of World War One stopped deliveries as Greece declared for the Allies. The Greek Army continued with what it had until the 1920s when, owing to the rate of attrition, fresh supplies were obtained from Breda in Italy, deliveries commencing in 1927. Although these Breda rifles incorporated some minor manufacturing changes and improvements, they were still known as 'Model 1903'.

The 1903 carbine was simply a shortened full-stocked version of the rifle; it was not fitted for a bayonet.

This was another carbine version of the basic rifle, very similar to the 1903 model but with attachments for fitting a bayonet.

The Greek Mannlicher

6.5mm Rifle Model 1903

Osterreichische Waffenfabrik, Steyr;
Soc. Indust. Ernesto Breda

6.5 × 54mm Greek Mannlicher	
Length overall	1,225mm (48.25in)
Weight empty	3.78kg (8.33lb)
Barrel	725mm (28.55in), 4 grooves, rh
Magazine	5-shot rotary
Muzzle velocity	670m/sec (2,200ft/sec)

6.5mm Carbine Model 1903

6.5mm Carbine Model 1914

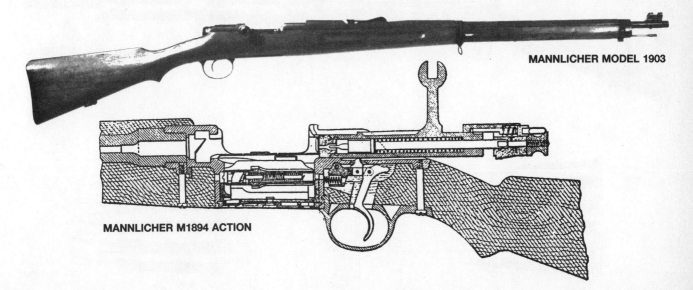

MANNLICHER MODEL 1903

MANNLICHER M1894 ACTION

HUNGARY

8mm Rifle Model 35M

Czepel Arsenal	
8 × 56R Hungarian Mannlicher	
Length overall	1,110mm (43.75in)
Weight empty	4.04kg (8.91lb)
Barrel	600mm (23.62in), 4 grooves, rh
Magazine	5-shot integral box
Muzzle velocity	730m/sec (2,400ft/sec)

After the dissolution of the Habsburg empire in 1918, Austria and Hungary went their separate ways. After developing a modified version of the standard 1895 model straight-pull short rifle, chambered for the Hungarian 8 × 56R M31 cartridge, an improved version of the old Austro–Hungarian M1893 round, the Hungarians developed their own turnbolt rifle based on the Mannlicher system. This was the last Mannlicher to be adopted as a service weapon, and was basically the Roumanian M1893 rifle redesigned to fire the rimmed M31 cartridge and shortened to more handy proportions. The result was a serviceable weapon using the protruding clip-loaded Mannlicher magazine, a two-piece stock and a bolt handle which locked down ahead of the receiver bridge.

7.92mm Rifle Model 98/40

This was not really a Hungarian service rifle, for it was manufactured in Hungarian factories under German supervision for supply to the German Army. The Germans found themselves in need of rifles and so, in 1940, they redesigned the 35M rifle to accept the standard 7.92mm Mauser cartridge. They also did away with the Mannlicher clip-loading system and adopted Mauser charger-loading. The resulting 'Gewehr 98/40' was stocked in German fashion and accepted the standard German bayonet.

7.92mm Rifle Model 43M

The Hungarians were so impressed by the German improvements to their rifle that after the German requirements had been satisfied they then adopted the design themselves, though changing the stock and fittings to standard Hungarian pattern. By this time all that was left of the original 1893 design was the Mannlicher bolt.

MODEL 98/40

MODEL 43

MAUSER-TYPE AMMUNITION CHARGERS

  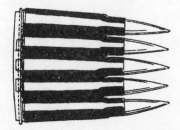

ITALY

The Italian rifle design was developed at Turin Arsenal between 1890 and 1891 and was formally adopted on 29 March 1892. The names of General Parravicino, president of the arms commission responsible for the rifle's adoption, and Salvatore Carcano, a technician at Turin who was instrumental in developing the design, are often linked to the result, which was little used outside Italy, though some examples, chambered for the Japanese 6.5mm cartridge, were supplied to Japan in 1904/5. The only Mannlicher feature to be retained by the design committee was the clip-loaded magazine; the turnbolt action came from the 1889 Belgian Mauser, with the addition of a bolt-sleeve safety mechanism designed by Carcano.

This was the original and standard pattern rifle, distinguishable by the full-length stock, box magazine, split-bridge receiver and tangent rear sight. A wooden handguard covered the barrel between the first barrel band and the rear sight.

The Mannlicher-Carcano Rifle

6.5mm Rifle Model 1891

State arsenals	
6.5 × 52mm Mannlicher-Carcano	
Length overall	1,290mm (50.79in)
Weight empty	3.80kg (8.38lb)
Barrel	780mm (30.71in), 4 grooves, rh
Magazine	6-shot integral box
Muzzle velocity	730m/sec (2,400ft/sec)

This was adopted during 1893 and was simply a shortened and half-stocked version of the rifle, with a permanently attached bayonet folded back under the barrel.

6.5mm Cavalry Carbine Model 1891

This is also known as the 'TS' model, for 'Truppo Speciale' and it existed in two forms. The first was provided with a peculiar bayonet which had a transverse fixing slot across the back of the pommel, mating with a transverse lug beneath the carbine's nosecap. It is generally believed that this was designed in order to prevent an opponent snatching the bayonet from the carbine in combat, though this seems an unlikely event. The second, and later, version reverted to a more usual method of bayonet attachment. A third version was simply the first model altered to approximate to the second by removing the special bayonet and its fittings; this version can be recognised by a barrel band behind the nosecap. These carbines are distinguished from the cavalry versions by being full-stocked.

6.5mm Special Carbine Model 1891

MANNLICHER CARCANO M1891

MANNLICHER CARCANO M1891 ACTION

6.5mm Carbine Model 91/24

This was a shortened version of the original rifle, numbers of which were cut down after World War One. The carbine, which was otherwise similar to the Model 1891 TS, could be recognised by the large rifle-pattern rear sight used, instead of the smaller carbine sight.

6.5mm Rifle Model 91/38

This was a shortened and modified version of the original 1891 rifle intended to approximate to the dimensions of the 7.35mm rifle of 1938.

7.35mm Rifle Model 1938

State arsenals

7.35 × 51mm Italian M38

In the course of their campaign in Abyssinia the Italians concluded that their 6.5mm cartridge was insufficiently lethal, and so a new 7.35mm cartridge was introduced in 1938, together with a 7.35mm version of the 1891 rifle. In addition to the change in calibre the new weapon had a fixed 300-metre rear sight in place of the earlier weapon's adjustable tangent sight.

7.35mm Cavalry Carbine Model 1938

This was a shortened, half-stocked version of the 1938 rifle, with a fixed rear sight and a folding bayonet beneath the muzzle.

7.35mm Special Carbine Model 1938

This carbine was full-stocked, with a protruding muzzle, and used the normal type of separate bayonet. At the close of World War Two somebody – perhaps the Germans – modified quantities of Italian rifles and carbines to take the 7.92mm Mauser cartridge. The result was somewhat dangerous, due to the higher chamber pressure, and although some appeared in Syria and Israel very few now exist.

7.62mm Beretta Sniper

Pietro Beretta SpA

7.62 × 51mm NATO

Length overall	1,165mm (45.87in)
Weight empty	5.55kg (12.23lb)
Barrel	586mm (23.07in), 4 grooves, rh
Magazine	5-shot detachable box
Muzzle velocity	840m/sec (2,755ft/sec)

This is a conventional rifle with heavy free-floating barrel fitted with a muzzle brake. There is a tube in the fore-end which carries the bipod and contains a harmonic balancer to smooth out barrel vibrations. The rifle is fitted with target-type iron sights, with hooded foresight, and the receiver carries a NATO-standard sight mount which will accept any telescope or electro-optical sight. The thumb-hole stock is of wood, with adjustable recoil pad and cheek-piece. An adjustable hand-stop is fitted on a rail in the fore-end, which also locates the firing sling when fitted.

7.35mm M1938

7.62mm BERETTA SNIPER

JAPAN

The Arisaka Rifle

During the Sino-Japanese War of 1894 the Japanese Army was principally armed with the 8mm Murata rifle of 1887, a turnbolt design with a tubular under-barrel magazine. This was generally considered out-dated and unsatisfactory, and since Western nations were re-arming with small-calibre magazine rifles the Imperial authorities followed suit and appointed a commission, headed by Colonel Arisaka, to devise a suitable replacement for the Murata. After reviewing various designs they settled on a 6.5mm rifle based, for the most part, on Mauser principles. This was adopted in 1897 as the 'Meiji 30th Year' and a carbine was introduced at the same time. Although the rifle used Mauser features, notably the magazine, the bolt was an odd combination of Mauser and Mannlicher ideas in that it was fitted with a separate bolt-head and a bolt-mounted ejector.

A word about the Japanese system of nomenclature might be in order; equipment was dated according to the year in which it was introduced, but in the case of the Japanese the year was that of the current Emperor's reign. This 'era' was given a distinctive name, and there are three eras relevant to our period, the Meiji (1868–1912), the Taisho (1912–1926) and the Showa (1926–1989). Thus the rifle introduced in 1897 became the 'Meiji 30th Year' model. This system was used until 1931 when it was changed, due to the danger of confusing certain Taisho and Showa designations. From 1931 onwards the last two figures of the calendar year were used, but this was complicated for Westerners by the use of the Japanese year notation. In Japanese form, 1939 was the year 2599, and thus any weapon introduced in 1939 became the 'Type 99', and in 1940 the 'Type 0'.

This 1897 rifle was the original pattern and is immediately recognisable by the unusual safety lever protruding from the cocking-piece – which earned for the rifle the sobriquet 'Hook Safety'. The Meiji 30 was fitted with a bolt-mounted ejector and extractor and the internal box magazine was loaded through the open action by a Mauser-type charger.

The 1897 carbine, introduced at the same time as the rifle, shared the rifle action and magazine but was otherwise much shorter.

This 1905 design was a considerable improvement upon the 1897, the result of experience gained in the Russo–Japanese War. It used a different bolt design based more closely on Mauser practice, and a receiver-mounted ejector. The hook safety device was replaced by a mushroom-headed cap at the rear of the bolt which was pressed in and turned to operate, and the bolt head was enlarged to make it easier to grasp.

6.5mm 30th Year Rifle

State arsenals

6.5 × 50SR Arisaka

6.5mm 30th Year Carbine

6.5mm 38th Year Rifle

Length overall	1,275mm (50.25in)
Weight empty	4.31kg (9.5lb)
Barrel	798mm (31.45in), 6 grooves, rh
Magazine	5-shot internal box
Muzzle velocity	730m/sec (2,400ft/sec)

30th YEAR RIFLE

38th YEAR RIFLE

6.5mm 38th Year Carbine

6.5mm Meiji 44th Year Carbine

Length overall	978mm (38.50in)
Weight empty	4.01kg (8.84lb)
Barrel	469mm (18.50in), 6 grooves, rh
Magazine	5-shot internal box
Muzzle velocity	685m/sec (2,250ft/sec)

6.5mm Type 97 Sniper's Rifle

7.7mm Type 99 Rifle

State arsenals	
7.7 × 57SR Type 99	
Length overall	1,115mm (43.90in)
Weight empty	4.19kg (9.23lb)
Barrel	654mm (25.75in), 4 grooves, rh
Magazine	5-shot internal box
Muzzle velocity	730m/sec (2,400ft/sec)

7.7mm Type 99 Parachutist's Rifle

This was the standard carbine version of the 38th Year Rifle, a much-shortened derivative using the same improved bolt mechanism. It could be fitted with the standard rifle bayonet which was a hangover from the 1897 rifle.

This 1911 carbine was intended for cavalry use and was generally similar to the 1905 carbine but fitted with an attached folding bayonet beneath the muzzle.

Introduced in 1937, this rifle featured a bipod and a telescope sight offset to the left so that the rifle could still be loaded by a charger. The bolt handle was turned down so as not to interfere with the sight when operated. It was otherwise similar to the 38th Year Rifle.

Experience in the Sino-Japanese war in Manchuria in the early 1930s convinced the Japanese (as the Italians) that the 6.5mm bullet was insufficiently lethal and that something heavier was needed. In 1932 a 7.7mm semi-rimmed cartridge had been developed and introduced into service with a new machine-gun; this was now redesigned into semi-rimmed form known as the Type 99 and a modified form of the 38th Year Rifle was developed to use it. The rifle, introduced in 1939, was little more than a re-chambered version of the 38th Year pattern, though the opportunity was taken to produce a 'short rifle' in line with the weapons of contemporary armies abroad, and to redesign the components to make mass production easier. The Type 99 Rifle was remarkable for being fitted with a flimsy wire monopod and a most optimistic sighting device (consisting of folding bars on the rear sight) intended for use against aircraft. This reflects the concern with air attack of the period, but it was more in the nature of a psychological crutch for the soldiers than a serious anti-aircraft threat.

The Type 99 Rifle was modified for use by parachute troops by the addition of a joint between the barrel and the action, which, in this pattern, took the form of an interrupted screw joint. This design of joint distinguishes the rifle from the later Type 2, and it was not a success.

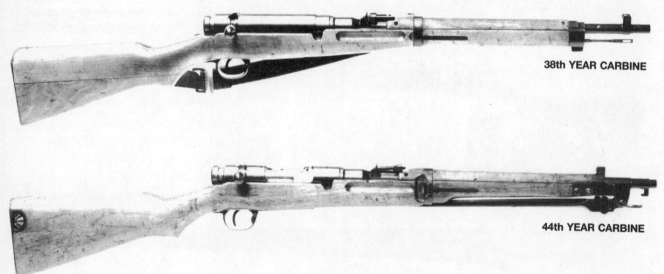

38th YEAR CARBINE

44th YEAR CARBINE

The Type 2 was introduced in 1942 in an attempt to improve upon the Type 99; the screw joint was replaced by a sliding horizontal wedge which mated with a cut-out in the top surface of the barrel. The result was quite serviceable, but relatively few were made.

It is as well to note that, towards the end of World War Two, the quality of Japanese rifles deteriorated sharply due to the shortage of raw materials and the lack of available machine time. Various production short-cuts were adopted; thus there are rifles in which the leaf rear sight was abandoned in favour of a simple aperture for 300 metres; monopods were discarded, and finish was gradually ignored until the last production was left covered in tool marks. Inferior substitute materials were used in 1944–45, which means that firing some of these weapons could be hazardous.

A little-known and unusual fact about the Arisaka rifle is that for a period of time it was an official British Army weapon. In 1914, faced with an enormous shortfall in rifles, the British Army needed weapons for training and arming its rapidly expanding army and a quantity of Arisaka rifles were purchased from Japan and used for training. They were given official British nomenclature as follows:

7.7mm Type 2 Parachutist's Rifle

Introduced on 24 February 1915, this was the 6.5mm Meiji 30th Year Rifle.

Rifle, Magazine, .256in Pattern 1900

Also introduced on the same date, this was the 6.5mm Meiji 38th Year Rifle.

Rifle, Magazine, .256in Pattern 1907

Also introduced on the same date, this was the 6.5mm Meiji 38th Year carbine. The terminology '1907' is of interest; the British 'Textbook of Small Arms 1909' quotes the Meiji 38th Year Rifle as having been introduced in 1907, and presumably this is where the date originated. All three .256in weapons were declared obsolete for British service on 25 October 1921.

Carbine, Magazine, .256in Pattern 1907

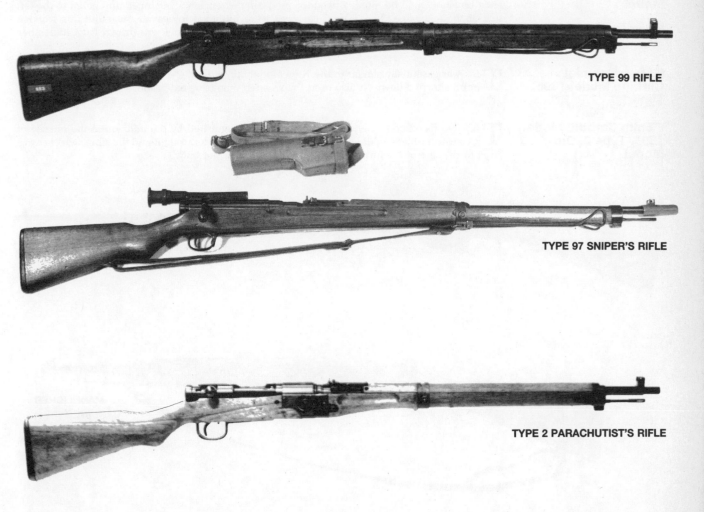

TYPE 99 RIFLE

TYPE 97 SNIPER'S RIFLE

TYPE 2 PARACHUTIST'S RIFLE

THE NETHERLANDS

6.5mm Rifle Model 1895

Osterreichische Waffenfabrik, Steyr	
6.5 × 54R Dutch Mannlicher	
Length overall	1,295mm (51.00in)
Weight empty	4.39kg (9.68lb)
Barrel	790mm (31.13in), 4 grooves, rh
Magazine	5-shot integral box
Muzzle velocity	730m/sec (2,400ft/sec)

This Dutch rifle was a slightly modified version of the Roumanian M1893 Mannlicher, firing an almost identical 6.5mm rimmed cartridge. The rear sight of the Dutch weapon was slightly different, a tangent sight similar to the contemporary Italian pattern instead of the Roumanian leaf sight. The Dutch rifle could be recognised by the location of the bayonet bar on the nosecap, since the Dutch used an unusual type of bayonet adapted from the British design used on the Lee-Metford and Lee-Enfield rifles; this meant that the bayonet bar protruded from the lower edge of the nosecap and slotted into the underside of the pommel.

6.5mm Carbine Model 1895, Type 1, Old Model

This was a short form of the rifle, with a short sporting-type stock, a straight bolt handle, and sling swivels on the left side of the butt and barrel band. A socket bayonet, taken from the old Beaumont rifle of 1871, was used with this carbine.

6.5mm Carbine Model 1895, Type 1, New Model

The New Model carbine was a modification of the Old Model, with similar sling swivels and bolt handle but with a more conventional stock and a nosecap to which a short-bladed knife bayonet could be fitted. A wooden magazine extension was pinned and glued to the left side of the magazine. The Type 1 carbines were intended for cavalry use and this wooden extension prevented the magazine from catching as the carbine was drawn from its leather saddle scabbard.

6.5mm Colonial Carbine Model 1895, Type 1

This was essentially similar to the New Model but without the handguard and with the bolt handle turned down. It also used the wooden magazine extension.

6.5mm Carbine Model 1895, Type 2, Old Model

This was for issue to Gendarmerie and was distinguished by the addition to the muzzle of a cruciform-blade folding bayonet. The bolt handle was straight and the sling swivels were fitted to the side of the forestock and the underside of the butt.

MANNLICHER MODEL 1895

MANNLICHER CARBINE TYPE 4

The New Model was similar to the preceding Old Model but with the addition of the wooden magazine extension first described under the Cavalry Carbine. The folding bayonet was retained.

6.5mm Carbine Model 1895, Type 2, New Model

The Type 3 was distinguished by an unusual handguard which protruded forward of the nosecap and forestock. The carbine was otherwise fitted with swivels on the underside of the nosecap and the butt, and had a straight bolt handle.

6.5mm Carbine Model 1895, Type 3, Old Model

The New Model was the same as the Old Model with the addition of the wooden magazine extension, not used on the previous model. Both Type 3 carbines made use of the long carbine bayonet which had a 483mm (919.0in) blade.

6.5mm Carbine Model 1895, Type 3, New Model

This was simply the Type 3 New Model modified by removal of the sling swivels to positions on the side of the forestock and butt.

6.5mm Carbine Model 1895, Type 3, modified

This could be distinguished by having a normal handguard and forestock assembly, differing from the Type 3's overhanging handguard. The sling swivels were on the side of the butt and forestock.

6.5mm Carbine Model 1895, Type 4, Old Model

The New Model was the same as the Old Model but with the addition of the wooden magazine extension.

6.5mm Carbine Model 1895, Type 4, New Model

This was a shortened and converted 1895 rifle and is said to have been designed for use by the Dutch Air Force. The bolt handle was straight, the magazine unprotected, and the sling swivels were placed beneath the butt and on the left of the forestock. The handguard and forestock assembly resembled that of the Type 4 carbines, and the standard infantry bayonet was used.

6.5mm Carbine Model 1895, Type 5

This rifle was developed during World War One to capitalise on the common ammunition supply used by Lewis and Schwarzlose machine-guns, then in Dutch service. The rifle was essentially the Model 1895 re-barrelled and re-sighted to use 7.92mm Mauser ammunition, though it appears that relatively few were ever made.

7.92mm Rifle Model 1917

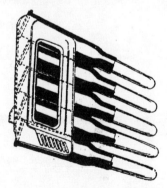

MANNLICHER-TYPE CLIPS

NORWAY

6.5mm Krag-Jorgensen Rifle M1894

State arsenals	
6.5 × 55mm Norwegian Krag	
Length overall	1,270mm (50.00in)
Weight empty	4.05kg (8.97lb)
Barrel	763mm (30.07in), 4 grooves, rh
Magazine	5-shot internal tray
Muzzle velocity	730m/sec (2,400ft/sec)

The original Norwegian Krag, the 1894 rifle, was quickly recognised by the semi-pistol grip stock and the wooden handguard which covered only the rear portion of the barrel between the breech and the rearmost barrel band. The loading gate, on the right side of the receiver below the bolt guideway, had a side-hinged trap. A tangent-leaf rear sight was fitted and a bayonet bar was positioned below the foresight.

6.5mm Cavalry Carbine M1895

A short version of the 1894 rifle was introduced in 1895 for cavalry use. It was distinguishable by the half-stock, which gave it a sporting appearance. A tangent sight was used, with a very small wooden handguard between the receiver ring and the rear sight; no bayonet was used.

6.5mm Artillery and Engineer Carbine M1897

This was issued for mountain artillery and engineers in 1897 and was no more than the cavalry carbine of 1895 with the butt sling swivel moved closer to the end of the butt.

6.5mm Engineer Carbine M1904

This was a variant of the 1895 cavalry carbine with a full stock and a full-length handguard over the barrel. No bayonet was used.

6.5mm Artillery Carbine M1907

This was issued for the field artillery and differed from the 1904 engineer carbine by having the sling swivels on the top band and on the underside of the butt.

6.5mm Carbine M1912

The final Norwegian carbine was somewhat longer than the preceding types and had a full-length stock with a handguard above the entire barrel. The bolt handle on early models was turned down, but later production had a straight handle. A bayonet bar was fitted under the top band/nosecap assembly.

KRAG-JORGENSEN M1894

KRAG-JORGENSEN CAVALRY CARBINE

A strengthening band was added to the forestock, immediately to the rear of the bayonet bar. Otherwise, this was the same as the 1912 carbine, and the modification was retrospectively applied to all 1912 weapons.

6.5mm Carbine M1912 M1916

This, the first of the Norwegian sniping rifles, had an aperture rear sight and a hooded foresight. The pistol grip was chequered and the barrel was covered with a handguard. Otherwise it was based upon the 1894 rifle.

6.5mm Sniper's Rifle M1923

This was a version of the M1923 sniping rifle which used the forestock – with a half-length handguard – of the 1894 rifle.

6.5mm Sniper's Rifle M1925

This was fitted with a half-length stock, giving it a sporting appearance. The heavy barrel was provided with a hooded foresight and an aperture rear sight and, unlike the previous sniping rifles, the M1930 had no provision for a bayonet.

6.5mm Sniper's Rifle M1930

This uses a Mauser M98 bolt action and was developed in close cooperation with the Norwegian Army. The stock is of laminated beech veneer and is adjustable for length by fitting spacers. The heavy barrel has no iron sights, a Schmidt & Bender telescope being fitted as standard, and a match trigger is also fitted. The weapon can be fitted with a bipod and a silencer if required. It was adopted in 1988 for the Norwegian Army and police forces.

7.62mm NM149S Sniper's Rifle

Vapensmia A/S	
7.62 × 51mm NATO	
Length overall	1,120mm (44.10in)
Weight empty	5.6kg (12.34lb) with telescope
Barrel	600mm (23.62in), 4 grooves, rh
Magazine	5-shot internal box
Muzzle velocity	838m/sec (2,750ft/sec)

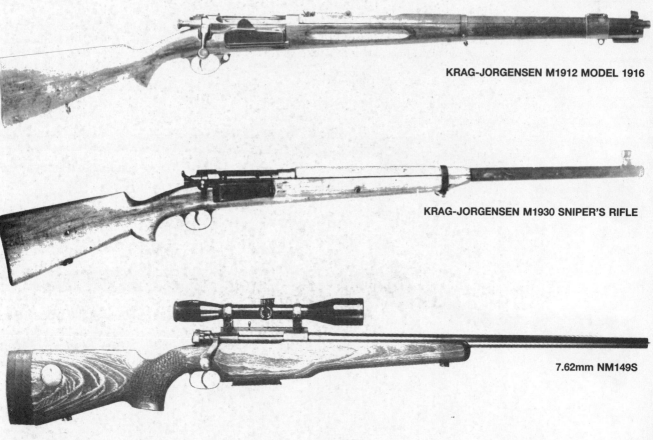

KRAG-JORGENSEN M1912 MODEL 1916

KRAG-JORGENSEN M1930 SNIPER'S RIFLE

7.62mm NM149S

ROUMANIA

The Roumanian Mannlicher

Mannlicher's perfected turnbolt action was developed in 1890 after some years of experimental work, and was of the split-bridge receiver type in which the bolt handle locked down in front of the bridge to form an additional safety feature, the bolt handle acting as an auxiliary locking lug. Mannlicher also incorporated a removable bolt head which allowed the bolt to be hollowed from the front and left only the firing pin hole at the rear. The result was a strong and simple rifle adopted in 1893 by Roumania and in 1895 by the Netherlands. The Austro–Hungarians were, however, quite satisfied with their straight-pull rifles, and Mannlicher's turnbolt met with little success in his native land.

6.5mm Rifle Model 1892

Osterreichische Waffenfabrik, Steyr

6.5 × 54R Roumanian Mannlicher

This was the first of the Roumanian rifles and served as the prototype for the definitive pattern of 1893 which followed. The ejector of the 1892 rifle was mounted on the bolt, and there was no piling hook on the top band, features which distinguish the two weapons. The rifle was clip-loaded, using a normal Mannlicher clip, and the magazine held five rimmed rounds.

6.5mm Rifle Model 1893

Length overall	1,232mm (48.50in)
Weight empty	4.00kg (8.82lb)
Barrel	725mm (28.56in), 4 grooves, rh
Magazine	5-shot integral box
Muzzle velocity	710m/sec (2,330ft/sec)

The rifle of 1893 was officially adopted as the service arm of the Roumanian Army. It differed little from the 1892 model, the extractor now being positioned at the rear of the receiver and a piling hook added to the muzzle. The action used a split receiver bridge, giving a third locking surface when the bolt handle was turned down in front of the bridge. In general appearance the rifle differed from most contemporary Mannlicher designs in having a smaller magazine, due to using a relatively small cartridge, an offset piling hook and a side-mounted bayonet bar.

6.5mm Carbine Model 1893

This was no more than a much-shortened version of the 1893 rifle, introduced for use by mounted troops. The bolt handle was turned down closer to the stock, and the bayonet bar and piling hook were dispensed with.

MANNLICHER MODEL 1892

MANNLICHER CARBINE MODEL 1893

SPAIN

The Spanish Mauser was one more example of the willingness of the 19th-century manu-facturers to produce whatever a customer required. The differences between this rifle and other contemporary Mausers were only minor, but are an interesting example of the varied approaches made by different nations to the same subject. The barrel was virtually the same as the German, being stepped in section and browned, the portions between steps being slightly tapered. The backsight on the Spanish model was a simple leaf, rather than the involved German tangent sight. The Spanish magazine was similar to that used in the Turkish M1890 model, protruding below the stock and holding five rounds in a straight line. The small of the butt was more straight, not unlike an English sporting gun. There were also changes in the handguard and the stocking bands, and the Spanish bayonet was smaller. Apart from these national preferences and a calibre of 7mm, the Spanish therefore carried a Mauser very similar to the Turkish model. There was also a carbine to accompany it, simply a shortened version of the rifle.

In 1893 the design was superseded by a slightly modified version which differed from the 1892 pattern in adopting a concealed magazine in the stock holding five rounds in staggered formation and a new bolt with a simplified safety and an improved bolt stop. It was this model which was ultimately manufactured under licence in Spain and in numbers it far exceeded the 1892 model.

The cavalry carbine version used the same action as the 1893 rifle but was, of course, shorter. It was stocked to the muzzle, but the handguard extended only as far as the barrel band, leaving the forward top half of the barrel exposed. The nosecap had wings to protect the sight, and no bayonet was used.

This was actually more of a 'short rifle' and was officially known as a 'musqueton'. It resembled the 1895 carbine but with a somewhat longer barrel, the exposed section being obviously longer. The nosecap was removed and the muzzle extended beyond the stock to allow the mounting of a sword bayonet. An improved gas escape system was incorporated into carbines made after 1925.

7mm Rifle Model 1892

Waffenfabrik Mauser AG; Industrias Nacional de Oviedo	
7 × 57mm Spanish Mauser	
Length overall	1,235mm (48.62in)
Weight empty	4.28kg (9.43lb)
Barrel	738mm (29.03in), 4 grooves, rh
Magazine	5-shot internal box
Muzzle velocity	700m/sec (2,295ft/sec)

7mm Cavalry Carbine Model 1895

Length overall	940mm (37.00in)
Weight empty	3.27kg (7.21lb)
Barrel	447mm (17.6in), 4 grooves, rh
Magazine	5-shot internal box
Muzzle velocity	610m/sec (2,000ft/sec)

7mm Artillery Carbine Model 1916

MODEL 1893

MODEL 1895 CARBINE

SWEDEN

6.5mm Mauser Rifle Model 1896

Carl Gustav Stads Gevarsfaktori; Husqvarna Vapenfabrik	
6.5 × 55mm Swedish Mauser	
Length overall	1,255mm (49.50in)
Weight empty	3.97kg (8.75lb)
Barrel	740mm (29.03in), 4 grooves, rh
Magazine	5-shot internal box
Muzzle velocity	730m/sec (2,400ft/sec)

In 1894 Sweden bought a few Mauser rifles and carbines for evaluation in comparison with their existing Jarmann bolt-action rifles and carbines. Finding that the Mausers were a considerable advance, the Swedish Army formally adopted a Mauser design in 1895, stipulating a calibre of 6.5mm. The first issues were made by Mauser in Oberndorf, but manufacture was quickly organised in Sweden by both Husqvarna and the state-owned Carl Gustav factory, where most were made.

Apart from the calibre the Swedish weapons were very similar to the German originals. The face of the bolt was rounded and a guide rib was added to the bolt body. An innovation later copied on other Mauser rifles was the use of a cut-out on the right side of the receiver to facilitate clip-loading. Another unusual detail, not found on other Mausers, was the addition of an upward projection on the cocking piece, which makes stripping the bolt much easier. The barrel was somewhat heavier than normal and these rifles had a high reputation for accuracy.

6.5mm Carbine Model 1894

Length overall	955mm (37.60in)
Weight empty	3.45kg (7.60lb)
Barrel	450mm (17.7in), 4 grooves, rh
Magazine	5-shot internal box
Muzzle velocity	705m/sec (2,313ft/sec)

Although dated earlier than the rifle, the carbine was issued at the same time and, in the same way, the early issues were made by Mauser, later being made in Sweden. The carbine closely resembles the Spanish M1895, being stocked to the muzzle and with a half-length handguard, and the bolt handle was turned down. The original models had a nosecap similar to the Spanish carbine; in 1917 this was modified so that a bayonet could be fitted.

6.5mm Mauser Rifle Model 1938

The 1896 rifle had been designed in the days when infantry had long rifles and cavalry had short carbines; by the 1930s the lesson of the short rifle had been assimilated, and the Swedes therefore began a programme of shortening numbers of the 1896 rifle, cutting the barrels to 610mm and thus reducing the rifle's overall length to 1,115mm (43.9in).

8mm Rifle Model 40

Length overall	1,250mm (49.20in)
Weight empty	4.00kg (8.82lb)
Barrel	740mm (29.13in), 4 grooves, rh
Magazine	4-shot internal box
Muzzle velocity	760m/sec (2,500ft/sec)

In 1939, in view of the world situation, the Swedes decided to increase their stock of rifles by purchasing some 2,500 7.92mm Kar 98k rifles from Germany. These were then re-worked by changing the calibre to 8mm in order to make use of the 8 × 63mm Swedish machine-gun cartridge. The magazine also had to be altered to cater for these larger cartridges and held only four rounds. The 8mm cartridge is probably the most powerful round ever used as an infantry rifle cartridge, and the rifles were fitted with muzzle brakes to try and reduce the recoil effects. This, of course, prevented the use of a bayonet. The rifles were issued to machine-gun troops, for commonality of ammunition supply, but they were not liked and in the late 1940s they were disposed of to Israel.

6.5mm Mauser Rifle Model 1941

This rifle is simply a carefully selected M1896 weapon fitted with a telescope sight. The bolt handle is bent down, and the telescope is mounted by a single-lever quick-release system.

MAUSER MODEL 1896

SWITZERLAND

This, the national rifle of Switzerland for the past hundred years, is a straight-pull bolt action weapon, one of the few such designs which prospered, although it is possible that its deficiencies would have shown up fairly rapidly had it ever been put to the test of war. The weapons are known as 'Schmidt-Rubin' from the two designers; Colonel Rudolf Schmidt, one of the foremost firearms experts of his day, was responsible for the rifle, while Colonel Rubin was responsible for the development of the jacketed small-calibre bullet and the general conception of the small-calibre high-velocity military rifle.

It is difficult to understand why a straight-pull design was selected, especially since Schmidt could draw upon the ideas of many of Europe's best designers, but it may be that there was in the design more than a hint of national pride, with an attendant desire to produce something different. It could also have been a way of avoiding existing patents, which could be costly to infringe or even license. The principal drawback to Schmidt's 1889 system lay in its inordinate length, something which was later resolved by the 1931 system, devised long after his death, and it can be seen from the illustrations that the early rifles have a considerable length of receiver behind the magazine.

The operation of the Schmidt action is relatively simple; but what appears to be the bolt handle is actually attached to an operating rod sliding in its own groove in the action body. This carries a lug which engages in a helical groove in the bolt carrier. When the rifle has been fired, pulling back on the 'bolt' handle causes the lug to travel down the helical groove, thus rotating the bolt assembly to unlock the lugs which are actually on the bolt carrier and lock into recesses in the receiver behind the magazine. Further movement of the handle then draws the bolt straight back. The return stroke forces the bolt forward to chamber a round, after which continued movement of the handle drives the lug forward in the helical groove and rotates the bolt carrier to lock it. The ring protruding from the rear is a combined safety device and re-cocking handle.

The complication of the Schmidt design is not favourably comparable to the more widespread turnbolt patterns. Straight-pull systems are usually more difficult to manufacture, and there are more moving and bearing surfaces involved; the action is therefore usually more difficult to operate and there is often difficulty in unseating a tight cartridge case, since there is no camming action to give a powerful primary extraction movement to unseat a sticky case. Most straight-pull enthusiasts claim that the speed of the action is superior to a manual turnbolt, but this depends upon which turnbolt is being considered; it is extremely doubtful whether the Schmidt action can be manipulated any faster than a Lee-Enfield. It is noteworthy that the only two other straight-pull systems adopted for military use, the Lee and the Ross, were both failures, and even Austria–Hungary, which championed the straight-pull system for several years, replaced her Mannlichers with Mausers before 1914. It is unlikely that the Schmidt would have been retained for so long had the Swiss had to fight a war with it, for its defects would have shown up quickly under field operational conditions.

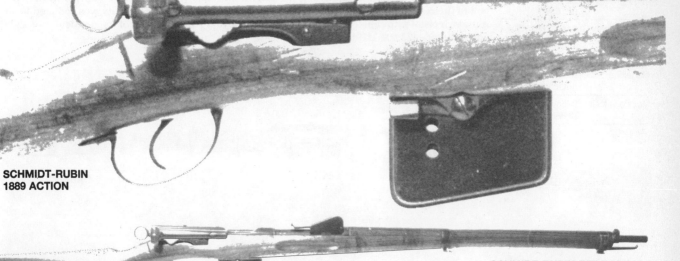

SCHMIDT-RUBIN 1889 ACTION

SCHMIDT-RUBIN RIFLE M1889

7.5mm Infantry Rifle M1889

Eidgenossische Waffenfabrik Berne;
Schweizerische Industrie Gesellschaft (SIG)

7.5 × 53.5 Schmidt-Rubin M90
7.5 × 54.5 Schmidt-Rubin M90/03

Length overall	1,302mm (51.25in)
Weight empty	4.44kg (9.79lb)
Barrel	780mm (30.75in), 4 grooves, rh
Magazine	12-shot detachable box
Muzzle velocity	610m/sec (2,000ft/sec)

This was the first of the Schmidt weapons, making use of Rubin's first perfected cartridge. The rifle used the original Schmidt bolt system and had an exceptionally long receiver to accommodate the bolt movement. The box magazine is abruptly rectangular and very prominent due to its large capacity. Some 212,000 of these rifles were made, most of which were later adapted to the M90/03 cartridge, slightly more powerful than the M90 and using a steel bullet instead of a lead one.

7.5mm Infantry Rifle M1889/96

This was a modified version of the 1889 weapon in which the receiver and bolt were modified to give a shorter action. The general system was the same but the bolt lugs were placed farther back on the bolt carrier and behind the helical groove, instead of in front as in Schmidt's original pattern. About 137,000 were manufactured.

7.5mm Cadet Rifle M1897

The cadet rifle was a much-lightened derivative of the M1889/96 rifle, intended for use by cadets whose stature was smaller than that of the regular infantry. The cadet rifle was equipped with an unusual spike bayonet, and about 7,000 were manufactured.

7.5mm Short Rifle M1889/00

This was for issue to cyclist battalions and machine-gunners, fortress artillery and other ancillary troops, and is really a hybrid derived from the M1889/96 rifle and the M1897 Cadet rifle. It had a 6-shot box magazine and weighed about 3.60kg (7.93lb). These were manufactured only by the Eidgenossische Waffenfabrik Berne, and 18,750 were made between 1900 and 1904.

7.5mm Cavalry Carbine M1905

The 1905 Cavalry Carbine was immediately recognisable by its full stock, six-shot magazine, and the short action of the M1889/96 rifle. No bayonet was used. The carbine was 1,070mm (42.12in) long and weighed 3.60kg (7.94lb); 7,900 were manufactured at the Berne arsenal.

7.5mm Infantry Rifle M1911

7.5 × 55mm Schmidt-Rubin M11

Length overall	1,312mm (51.65in)
Weight empty	4.59kg (10.12lb)
Barrel	780mm (30.75in), 4 grooves, rh
Magazine	6-shot detachable box
Muzzle velocity	805m/sec (2,650ft/sec)

In order to improve the ballistics of the 7.5mm M90 and M90/03 cartridges, a new round was designed using a pointed and streamlined bullet, a more powerful smokeless charge and a re-designed cartridge case. To accommodate the higher chamber pressure and lessen strain on the bolt, the Schmidt action was again modified, moving the locking lugs to the front of the bolt carrier, generally strengthening the action, and incorporating a bolt stop which held the bolt to the rear when the last round had been fired. The magazine capacity was reduced to six rounds, a pistol-grip replaced the straight-line butt, and a new pattern of tangent-leaf rear sight was adopted. 133,000 M1911 rifles were made.

CARBINE M1911

This is a shorter version of the 1911 rifle, using the same modified action. It was for issue to cavalry, fortress artillery, engineers and support troops. 185,000 were manufactured in the Berne arsenal.

7.5mm Carbine M1911

Length overall	1,100mm (43.30in)
Weight empty	3.93kg (8.66lb)
Barrel	590mm (23.30in), 4 grooves, rh
Magazine	6-shot detachable box
Muzzle velocity	760m/sec (2,500ft/sec)

This was a conversion of the original 1896 rifle to fire the M11 cartridge. The 12-round magazine was replaced by the 6-round version, a pistol-grip stock was fitted, and the old barrel was replaced by a modified one with a new rear sight. The original bolt action was retained.

7.5mm Infantry Rifle M1896/11

This was a modification of the M1889/00 Short Rifle to handle the M11 cartridge. Alterations included provision of a new barrel and the six-shot magazine.

7.5mm Carbine M1900/11

The opportunity was also taken to modify the remaining 1905 carbines to handle the M11 cartridge. The change was confined to re-barrelling and fitting the smaller magazine.

7.5mm Carbine M1905/11

INFANTRY RIFLE M1911

SCHMIDT-RUBIN M1911 ACTION

SCHMIDT-RUBIN M1931 ACTION

SCHMIDT-RUBIN M1931 ACTION

7.5mm Carbine M1931

Length overall	1,105mm (43.50in)
Weight empty	4.01kg (8.84lb)
Barrel	655mm (25.70in), 4 grooves, rh
Magazine	6-shot detachable box
Muzzle velocity	775m/sec (2,543ft/sec)

7.5mm Carbine M1931/42

7.5mm Carbine M1931/43

7.5mm Sniper's Rifle M1955

7.62mm SIG-Sauer Model SSG2000

Schweizerische Industrie Gesellschaft (SIG)	
7.62 × 51mm NATO	
Length overall	1,210mm (47.63in)
Weight empty	6.60kg (14.55lb) with sight
Barrel	610mm (24.01in), 4 grooves, rh
Magazine	4-shot detachable box
Muzzle velocity	750m/sec (2,460ft/sec)

The carbine, or short rifle, of 1931 was the first major change to be made to the Schmidt system. The principal objection to the earlier models was the long bolt throw and receiver length, so the unit was re-designed to operate in half the length, though still adhering to the basic system. The bolt and bolt carrier were now the same length, the bolt having been shortened, and the lugs on the front of the carrier now locked into the rear of the barrel giving a far stronger action. The 1931 rifle, issued to replace all previous rifles and carbines, was undoubtedly the best of the Schmidt-Rubin family and remained in first-line service until replaced by the StgW 57 in the late 1950s. Large numbers are still in use by reserve forces and are still used by these troops for their annual exercises and marksmanship training. A total of 528,180 were manufactured.

This was a variation on the standard M31 short rifle and was fitted with a low-power (1.8x) sighting telescope mounted on the left side of the receiver. The eyepiece of the sight could be folded down when not in use, when it lay alongside the stock.

This was a second telescope-sighted rifle, similar to the M31/42 but using a 2.8x sight, since it had been found that the lower-powered sight was inefficient.

This was the last Schmidt-Rubin design to be introduced into Swiss service. Based upon the M31 short rifle, it had a pistol-grip half-stock, a muzzle brake, a bipod, and a commercial sporting-pattern sighting telescope mounted above the receiver.

This rifle was adopted by Swiss forces in 1987 and has been purpose-built as a sniping rifle. It uses the Sauer 80/90 bolt action, a turnbolt which uses hinged lugs at the rear of the bolt to lock into the receiver, the lugs being driven outwards by cams as the bolt lever is turned down. The bolt body does not rotate during the opening and closing movements. This system reduces the angular movement of the handle and gives a fast and smooth action. The rifle has a heavy barrel, with combined muzzle brake and flash hider, and a double set trigger. There is also a signal pin indicating the presence of a round in the chamber. The thumb-hole stock is adjustable for length and has an adjustable cheek-piece, and the fore-end contains a mounting rail to which a sling or bipod can be attached. No iron sights are fitted, the rifle being normally provided with a Schmidt & Bender or Zeiss sighting telescope. The SSG2000 is available in 7.62 × 51mm, .300 Weatherby Magnum, 5.56 × 45mm NATO and 7.5 × 55 Swiss calibres as desired; the Swiss Army have adopted the 7.62mm version.

CARBINE M1931

SIG-SAUER MODEL SSG2000

TURKEY

The Turkish Mauser was one of a number of variations on the basic Belgian model. In fact there were several fundamental differences between them but the components of both are, in the main, the same. The Turkish model does not employ the peculiar Belgian barrel jacket, the Turkish barrel being thicker and stronger. Another change is the provision of a hold-open device on the magazine platform, in which a rib on the platform meets the bolt when the last round has been extracted. Finally, the Turks demanded a magazine cut-off, an unusual addition to a Mauser action, which is on the right side and operated by the thumb.

7.65mm Rifle M1890

Waffenfabrik Mauser AG	
7.65 × 53mm Turkish Mauser	
Length overall	1,235mm (48.62in)
Weight empty	4.11kg (9.06lb)
Barrel	740mm (29.13in), 4 grooves, rh
Magazine	5-shot integral box
Muzzle velocity	610m/sec (2,000ft/sec)

This is essentially the Spanish Model 1893 rifle with the calibre changed to 7.65mm and the Turkish cut-off fitted to the magazine. The principal change lay in the use of the usual staggered internal magazine instead of the single-row protruding box used on the 1890 rifle.

7.65mm Rifle Model 1893

Except for the adoption of 7.65mm calibre, these two rifles were the same as the German Gewehr 98 except for slight changes to the sights and furniture. There is also a full-stocked 1903 carbine with half-length handguard.

7.65mm Rifles Models 1903 and 1905

USA

James Paris Lee (1831–1904) was a talented inventor who worked in the second half of the 19th century. His greatest triumph was the box magazine which subsequently appeared in different forms in practically every military rifle in the world, but he also designed and patented many other projects. In the early 1890s he produced a design for a straight-pull bolt action that circumvented existing patents and offering what was hoped would be a faster action than the contemporary turnbolts. The United States Navy adopted the idea in 1895 in 6mm (.236in) calibre, and the manufacturing contract was awarded to Winchester, under licence from the Lee Arms Company who owned the rights.

The bolt in the 1895 Lee rifle does not rotate; it is locked by cam action into the receiver and is operated by a small movement of the cam lever, which lies downward along the right side of the receiver and looks very much like a conventional bolt handle. By pulling the handle to the rear the cams unlock from their recess in the receiver, allowing the rear end of the bolt to move upwards, after which further pulling on the handle draws the bolt back and opens the action; it sounds easy, but is, in fact, not quite so easy to operate on first acquaintance. Perhaps the US Navy found the same thing, for their original order for 20,000 was not completed, and of the 19,658 rifles which were made, 1,245 of them were never issued but were sold off as surplus. Winchester then tried the design as a sporting rifle but it made little impact.

6mm (.236in) Rifle, US Navy, M1895

Winchester Repeating Arms Co	
.236in US Navy Lee	
Length overall	1,194mm (47.00in)
Weight empty	3.63kg (8.00lb)
Barrel	692mm (27.25in), 5 grooves, lh
Magazine	5-shot integral box
Muzzle velocity	732m/sec (2,400ft/sec)

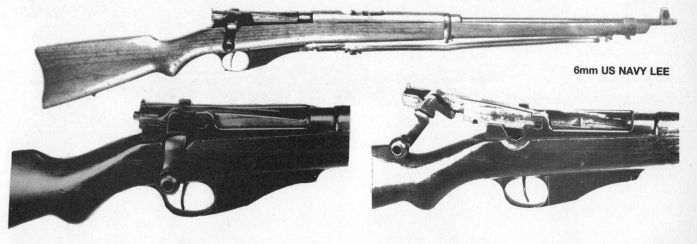

6mm US NAVY LEE

The Lee was a pleasant rifle to use, but the cartridge was against it; theoretically a good choice of calibre, the promise was let down by the available smokeless powder, which was not sufficiently powerful to develop good ballistics. This, coupled with the unusual bolt system, was enough to make the Lee obsolete within ten years of its introduction.

The Springfield Rifle

For reasons which no doubt seemed good at the time, the US Army had adopted the Krag-Jorgensen rifle in 1892, at the beginning of the smokeless powder era, but within a very short period the Krag's limitations were realised and the Ordnance Department had to begin looking into the matter of a replacement. Considering the large sums which had been sunk into the Krag-Jorgensen and its ammunition, this took some courage. After considering what designs were available at the time, together with some painful lessons from the Spanish–American War where the 7mm Mauser had impressed them mightily, the Ordnance Department decided that the Mauser system had the most to offer and entered into agreements with Mauser to build a modified Mauser rifle under licence in the USA.

Since it was first made at Springfield Arsenal, the rifle came to be known as the 'Springfield Rifle'. As originally designed it was built round a blunt-nosed bullet rimmed cartridge known as the .30in M1900, based on the Krag-Jorgensen rifle cartridge. This was soon abandoned when it became obvious that the Mauser magazine did not respond happily to rimmed cartridges, and the rimless .30in M1901 round, still using a Krag bullet, was developed. After more trials the case was lengthened from 60 to 63mm and a new blunt bullet developed, the result being the .30in M1903, and this became the first service issue cartridge. However, while the first issues of the rifle were still in progress the German Army developed the pointed or 'spitzer' bullet, and the M1903 round was rapidly converted, by developing a suitable pointed bullet, into the .30 M1906. Inevitably, this cartridge and the millions of rifles chambered for it, both military and commercial, came to be called the '.30-06'. At the time this new cartridge was developed, some 150,000 M1903 rifles had been issued and all were called back and re-chambered for the new round.

.30in Rifle, Magazine, M1903

Springfield Arsenal (1903–44);
Rock Island Arsenal (1903–19);
Remington Arms (1942–3);
L. C. Smith-Corona (1943)

.30in M1903
.30in M1906 (7.62 × 63)

Length	1,097mm (43.19in)
Weight empty	3.94kg (8.68lb)
Barrel	610mm (24.00in), 4 grooves, lh
Magazine	5-shot internal box
Muzzle velocity	853m/sec (2,800ft/sec)

This was the original version of the Springfield, first supplied with a rod bayonet and chambered for the M1903 cartridge. The introduction of the M1906 cartridge led to a change in chamber dimensions and re-graduation of the leaf rear sight. The M1903 is easily recognised among its contemporaries by the straight 'English' stock without a pistol-grip. The rod bayonet was abruptly discontinued when President Theodore Roosevelt raised objections and was replaced by a more conventional sword bayonet. The US authorities had also taken the step of adopting a short rifle, rather than the long rifle and short carbine favoured in the 19th century, parallel with the British adoption of the Short Lee-Enfield.

M1903

The Mark 1 was identical with the service M1903 except for modifications made to accept the ill-fated Pedersen Device (see the Automatic Rifles section for details of this). Changes were made to the sear mechanism, the cut-off was discarded, and a special ejection port was cut through the left wall of the receiver. It is recorded that 101,775 of these rifles were produced between 1918 and 1920, after which the devices were scrapped and the rifles reconverted to M1903 specification; they could, of course, still be recognised by the ejection port. And since the Pedersen Device had been classified 'secret', there were several thousand soldiers puzzled by the hole in their rifle for many years afterwards.

.30in Rifle, M1903 Mark 1

Introduced on 5 December 1929, this was no more than an M1903 fitted with a Type C semi-pistol-grip stock.

.30in Rifle, M1903A1

This was not a personal weapon but was the barrel and action of an M1903 rifle carried in mounting blocks which enabled it to be inserted into the chamber of an artillery piece and fired on the axis of the gun's bore. This allowed .30 bullets to be substituted for artillery shells for short-range training practice at low cost. Originally produced for the 3in Seacoast Guns, the M1903A2 was later adapted to a number of artillery weapons.

.30in Rifle, M1903A2

Introduced on 21 May 1942, this was a redesign of the M1903A1 in order to facilitate mass production. The principal and most obvious difference lay in the adoption of an aperture sight, adjustable for windage and elevation, mounted at the rear of the receiver and replacing the leaf sight on top of the barrel used on the earlier weapons. Various minor components were fabricated from sheet-metal stampings.

.30in Rifle, M1903A3

The standard sniping rifle derivative of the M1903, the M1903A4 was fitted with permanently mounted telescope sight blocks. The M1903A4 weighed 4.34kg (9.57lb) complete with telescope sight. No iron sights were fitted. This rifle remained in use well into the 1950s with the US Marine Corps.

.30in Rifle, M1903A4

When the USA entered World War One in April 1917, the rapid expansion of the armed forces immediately produced a shortage of rifles. At about the same time the Remington and Winchester companies were coming to the end of their contracts to make the .303 Pattern 1914 rifle for the British Army, and so as to make use of their facilities and expertise it was quickly decided to re-design the British rifle to take the American rimless cartridge, calling the result the M1917, commonly called the 'Enfield' as a tribute to its birthplace. A total of 2,193,429 M1917 rifles were made. The M1917 is identical in appearance to the British .303 Pattern 1914, so much so that during World War Two, when a million or more M1917 were supplied to Britain and issued to the Home Guard, they had to be marked round the butt with a two-inch stripe of red paint to remind people that they were only to be used with .30 rimless cartridges. Many Home Guard units were also issued Pattern 1914 rifles, and while attempting to load a .303 cartridge into an M1917 led to nothing more serious than a minor jam, the reverse usually demanded the services of an armourer to remove it. A large number of M1917 were also rebarrelled to 7.92mm Mauser calibre and supplied to Nationalist China during World War Two.

.30in Rifle, M1917 (Enfield)

Various manufacturers	
.30in M1906	
Length	1,175mm (46.25in)
Weight empty	4.36kg (9.61lb)
Barrel	660mm (26.00in), 5 grooves, lh
Magazine	5-shot internal box
Muzzle velocity	853m/sec (2,800ft/sec)

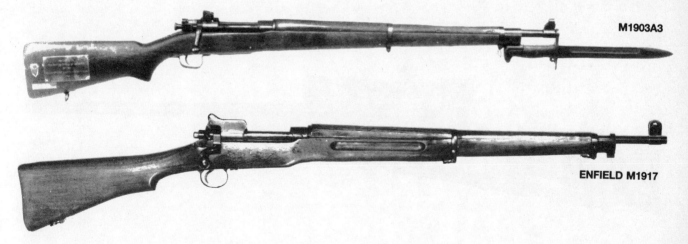

M1903A3

ENFIELD M1917

7.62mm Rifle, Sniping, M40A1

Remington Arms Co	
7.62 × 51mm NATO	
Length overall	1,117mm (43.98in)
Weight empty	6.57kg (14.48lb) with telescope
Barrel	610mm (24.0in), 4 grooves, rh
Magazine	5-shot internal box
Muzzle velocity	777m/sec (2,550ft/sec)

This was developed by Remington and based upon their commercial Model 700 rifle. It uses a heavy barrel with no iron sights, having a telescope sight permanently mounted. A special catch is provided in front of the trigger to permit the bolt to be removed without disturbing the telescope. A similar catch in front of the magazine floor plate allows the magazine spring and platform to be removed through the bottom of the stock for cleaning or unloading.

7.62mm Rifle, Sniping, M24

Remington Arms Co	
7.62 × 51mm NATO	

The Rifle M24 forms part of the US Army's M24 Sniper Weapon System and will eventually replace all other sniping rifles in US service. First issues took place in November 1987 and the system is to be issued to all infantry battalions, special forces and Ranger units. The rifle was developed by Remington, based upon their commercial M70 long bolt action and M40 custom trigger mechanism and was specifically designed around the M118 special sniper ball cartridge, though the possibility of future conversion to .300 Winchester Magnum has been kept in view. The stock is of synthetic material with an aluminium bedding block and an adjustable buttplate. Complete with its standard Leopold Ultra sighting telescope, the rifle weighs 6.35kg (14.0lb).

USSR/RUSSIA

The Mosin-Nagant Rifle

The Mosin-Nagant was the first small-calibre high-velocity Russian rifle and it replaced the earlier single-shot Berdan in the hands of the Tsar's troops. The first models were introduced in 1891, after a year of tests in which the Russians had sought to combine the best features of a series of rifles designed by the Belgians Emil and Leon Nagant with those of one designed by Captain S. I. Mosin of the Imperial Artillery. The resulting weapon was known as the '3-line Rifle Model 1891' and, contrary to common practice, the inventor's name was never included in the designation. The weapons were called '3-line' in reference to their calibre; the Russian 'line' was a now-obsolete measure approximating to 2.54mm (0.1in) so that the calibre was actually 7.62mm or .30in. When the Soviets adopted the metric system after the Revolution, the designation was changed to '7.62mm Rifle Model 1891'. In general appearance the Mosin-Nagant weapons were conventional turnbolt magazine rifles, loaded through the open action by means of a five-round charger. It was generally conceded that the bolt bore a strong resemblance to contemporary French designs and was unnecessarily complicated, but apart from that the rifle was serviceable enough. The magazine was unusual in having a control latch

M40A1

which secured the second and lower cartridges in the magazine and prevented them pressing against the underside of the bolt during reloading. Once the round was chambered, the latch was released and allowed the next round to move up against the bolt ready to be picked up on the next reloading stroke.

T his was the basic model, fully stocked except for a few inches at the muzzle, to which a socket bayonet could be fitted. Although obsolete elsewhere, the Russians still placed great reliance on the socket bayonet which was intended to be carried in a permanently fixed position; so much so that the calibration of the sights allowed for the change in point of impact due to the effect of the bayonet on barrel vibrations, and the individual soldiers were not generally issued with bayonet scabbards. The bayonet blade ended in a screwdriver point, with which the rifle could be dismantled for cleaning, and the cleaning rod, which protruded beneath the muzzle, acted as a piling hook. A leaf sight was fitted, graduated to 2,700 arshins, another now-obsolete measure, one arshin being about 711mm or 28in. After 1907 the sights were regraduated to allow for a new light bullet cartridge and after 1917 they were converted to metric measurements.

3-line Rifle M1891

Tula Arsenal;
Sestrorets Arsenal;
Izhev Arsenal

7.62 × 54R Mosin-Nagant

Length overall	1,304mm (51.25in)
Weight empty	4.43kg (9.77lb)
Barrel	802mm (31.60in), 4 grooves, rh
Magazine	5-shot integral box
Muzzle velocity	805m/sec (2,650ft/sec)

T his weapon, originally issued to the Russian Imperial Dragoons, was identical with the rifle except for having a shorter barrel. It was issued instead of a short carbine, due to a belief, common at that time, that the new smokeless powder cartridges would not develop useful power in a short-barrelled weapon. The argument had some reason, but the carbines of the day were, in fact, quite adequate for the rifle cartridges in use.

3-line Dragoon Rifle M1891

Length overall	1,240mm (48.75in)
Weight empty	3.95kg (8.75lb)
Barrel	730mm (28.75in), 4 grooves, rh
Magazine	5-shot integral box
Muzzle velocity	790m/sec (2,600ft/sec)

T his was almost the same as the Dragoon Rifle but was issued without a bayonet. It seems that few were actually manufactured, the Dragoon Rifle being adequate for all mounted troops.

3-line Cossack Rifle M1891

MODEL 1891

3-line Carbine M1910

Length overall	1,016mm (40.0in)
Weight empty	3.40kg (7.5lb)
Barrel	510mm (20.0in), 4 grooves, rh
Magazine	5-shot integral box
Muzzle velocity	760m/sec (2,500ft/sec)

Since the Dragoon and Cossack rifles were all but full-sized, they were not well adapted for mounted work, and once the ballistic problem was better understood, design of a proper carbine took place. The action was identical to that of the rifles, the barrel was shorter, but the stocking was virtually the same as that of the rifles. In the 1920s the sights of almost all rifles were re-graduated in metres, but for some unknown reason none of the 1910 carbines had their sights changed.

7.62mm Rifle M1891/1930

Length overall	1,230mm (48.43in)
Weight empty	4.00kg (8.82lb)
Barrel	730mm (28.75in), 4 grooves, rh
Magazine	5-shot integral box
Muzzle velocity	865m/sec (2,838ft/sec)

This was the first Soviet small arm development, a modified version of the M1891 rifle shortened to approximate to the Dragoon rifle and with the receiver body changed from hexagonal to cylindrical, a change which simplified manufacture. At the same time the opportunity was taken to change the sights from leaf to tangent type and to change the foresight from a barleycorn to a tapered post hooded by a cylindrical guard.

7.62mm Carbine M1938

Length overall	1,016mm (40.0in)
Weight empty	3.54kg (7.75lb)
Barrel	512mm (20.15in), 4 grooves, rh
Magazine	5-shot integral box
Muzzle velocity	820m/sec (2,690ft/sec)

This was a re-design of the 1910 carbine along the lines of the 1930 rifle; the receiver was made cylindrical and the sights were changed.

M1891/1930 SNIPER'S RIFLE

CARBINE M1938

These were issued in the late 1930s as snipers' weapons. The original was fitted with a telescope sight known as the PU, which was fitted to the rifle by a single block mount dovetailed to the left side of the receiver. The short length of the telescope meant that the firer had to stretch forward to adjust the sight whenever he fired, so the PU was replaced by the larger and heavier PE telescope fitted into two ring mounts. This placed the elevation and windage adjustment in a more convenient place. The rifles still carried their standard iron sights, and, indeed, except for the addition of the sight mounting blocks they were the standard M1891/30 weapons, though probably carefully selected specimens.

The 1944 carbine was no more than the 1938 type with the addition of a folding cruciform bayonet. One is at a loss to explain the adoption of such an archaic weapon as late as 1944, just as one is at a loss to understand why the Chinese decided to copy it as late as 1953.

7.62mm Sniper's Rifle M1891/30

7.62mm Carbine M1944

Length overall	1,020mm (40.16in)
Weight empty	3.90kg (8.60lb)
Barrel	517mm (20.35in), 4 grooves, rh
Magazine	5-shot integral box
Muzzle velocity	820m/sec (2,690ft/sec)

CARBINE 1944

Automatic Rifles

ARGENTINA

5.56mm Fara 83

Fabrica Militar de Armas Portatiles 'Domingo Matheu'	
5.56 × 45mm	
Length overall	1,000mm (39.34in) butt extended; 745mm (29.33in) butt folded
Weight empty	3.95kg (8.71lb)
Barrel	452mm (17.80in), 6 grooves, rh
Magazine	30-shot detachable box
Rate of fire	750rds/min
Muzzle velocity	965–1,005m/sec (3,166–3,297ft/sec)

The Fara 83 is a locally-designed gas operated, selective-fire assault rifle. The mechanism relies upon the conventional gas piston, bolt carrier and rotating bolt system similar to that of the M16 and other assault rifles. Manufacture is from steel castings and pressings, the receiver being of welded sheet steel to which components are attached by rivets. The butt is of plastic and folds alongside the receiver. The rear sight is a three-position drum, adjustable for windage. Two of the positions, for 200m and 400m, are for daylight firing, the third having a luminous insert and zeroed for 100m in poor light. There is an auxiliary foresight with luminous spot for use with the rear sight. A bipod is available as an optional fitting; when used, the rifle has a special fore-end with recesses for the bipod legs. Issues began in 1984 but at a low rate due to financial restrictions; the rifle will eventually become the standard Argentinian service rifle.

AUSTRIA

5.56mm Steyr AUG

Steyr-Mannlicher GmbH	
5.56 × 45mm NATO	
Length overall	790mm (31.10in)
Weight empty	3.6kg (7.93lb)
Barrel	508mm (20.00in), 6 grooves, rh
Magazine	30- or 42-shot detachable box
Rate of fire	650rds/min
Muzzle velocity	970m/sec (3,182ft/sec)

The Steyr 'Armee Universal Gewehr' is so-called because it has been designed in modular form so that it can be adapted as a rifle, carbine, assault rifle or light machine-gun by simply changing the barrel or lock mechanism or adding a bipod. In its standard rifle form it has a built-in 1.4x optical sight in the carrying handle; but by changing the receiver it can be adapted to any telescope or electro-optical sight.

The AUG is a bullpup of somewhat futuristic appearance and its construction is unusual. A basic structure of high-quality plastic supports the receiver, which is an aluminium casting with steel inserts for the barrel lugs and bolt guides. The sight bracket and carrying handle are an integral part of this casting. The steel barrel, with chromed chamber, locks into the receiver by an interrupted thread, and the barrel carries a short sleeve containing the gas port and cylinder and the front hand grip. A flash suppressor is attached to the muzzle and this is internally threaded to take a blank-firing attachment. The hand grip is used to rotate the barrel for locking and unlocking and to remove the barrel, and it is hinged so that it can be locked in the vertical position or folded beneath the barrel as desired. The magazine is transparent, allowing the contents to be checked instantly, and slots into the butt behind the handgrip. There is a cross-bolt safety catch above the grip, and a cross-bolt dismantling catch

STEYR AUG

ahead of it. No selector lever is fitted; single shots are fired by the first pressure on the trigger, and further pressure brings automatic fire. The rifle can be adjusted for left- or right-handed firers by changing the bolt and the ejection aperture cover. The rifle operates by gas tapped from the barrel driving back a piston in the conventional manner, though the piston is offset and acts as one of the bolt guide rods; this asymmetry does not affect the rifle's accuracy or reliability. The two guide rods hold a bolt carrier which contains a rotating bolt which locks into the chamber recess by multiple lugs. There is a plastic firing mechanism in the butt which contains a hammer; in standard form this unit provides for single shots and automatic fire, but it can be exchanged for one allowing single shots only, or one allowing single shots, automatic fire or three-round bursts, the latter two options being selectable by a lever on the mechanism. This lever can only be switched if the mechanism is removed; it is not possible to select between automatic and three-round bursts at will during firing.

The AUG is undoubtedly one of the classic designs; it was first adopted by the Austrian Army in 1977, since when it has been adopted by the Moroccan, Omani, Saudi Arabian, Australian, New Zealand and Irish armies. In spite of its appearance it is an extremely robust weapon and can withstand enormous abuse without failure. (Data table refers to the gun in its standard rifle form.)

This rifle was designed in 1987–9 as an entry for the US Army Advanced Combat Rifle (ACR) programme, a project intended to determine the likely shape of the US Army's rifle in the 21st century. Whether or not the US Army take to it, we gather it is likely to form the basis of Steyr's next generation of assault rifles and is therefore worth recording here. There is a definite family resemblance between this and the AUG rifle, both being bullpups and having similar plastic basic structures. There is a push-through firing selector giving single shots, three-round bursts or safe. A shotgun-style rib acts as a rough aiming guide and carrying handle, and mounts iron sights as well as a mount for an optical sight. The transparent magazine fits into the butt.

The weapon is gas operated, a sleeve around the barrel being driven backwards to actuate the mechanism. The breech unit is a vertically rising block with the chamber in it; to load, the cocking handle, beneath the rear sight block, is pulled back and returned. This cocks the mechanism. On pulling the trigger the mechanism is released and a rammer drives a cartridge into the chamber; the chamber then rises into alignment with the barrel and the cartridge is fired by a fixed firing pin mounted vertically above the chamber. The gas action now lowers the chamber again, into alignment with the rammer, and when the next shot is fired the new cartridge entering the chamber pushes the empty cartridge case out forward and ejects it below the rifle. The action will be more easily understood when the ammunition is explained: the cartridge is a plastic cylinder containing a flechette, a fin-stabilised dart about 1.6mm diameter and 41mm long, held in a plastic sabot. The propellant is behind the sabot, and a circular primer runs around the case near its rear end, also acting as a locator for the fins of the flechette. As the chamber rises into alignment with the barrel, a fixed firing pin above the chamber passes through a hole and stabs the circular primer, so firing the propelling charge. The flechette is ejected into the barrel, where it is held stable by its sabot until it leaves the muzzle, whereupon the sabot falls away and the flechette is left flying to the target. The sights have no form of adjustment, since the velocity of the flechette is so high that the trajectory is virtually flat out to the maximum operational range.

5.56mm Steyr ACR

Steyr-Mannlicher GmbH	
5.56mm special flechette	
Length overall	765mm (30.11in)
Weight empty	3.23kg (7.12lb)
Barrel	Smoothbore
Magazine	24-round detachable box
Muzzle velocity	1,495m/sec (4,9057ft/sec)

STEYR ACR

15mm Steyr AMR Anti-Material Rifle

Steyr-Mannlicher GmbH	
15mm flechette	
Length overall	approx. 2m (6.6ft)
Weight empty	approx. 20kg (44lb)
Barrel	1,200mm (47.25in) smoothbore
Magazine	5- or 8-shot detachable box
Muzzle velocity	1,500m/sec (4,920ft/sec)

This is a heavyweight precision rifle intended for the attack of vulnerable targets such as vehicles, aircraft, fuel and supply dumps, radar installations and communications centres. It can be dismantled into two parts for carriage by two men. The weapon is a semi-automatic of bullpup form, in which plastics and light alloys have been used to reduce the weight. The long recoil principle of operation is used, bolt and barrel recoiling locked together across the magazine; the bolt is then rotated and held while the barrel runs out to battery. The forward movement of the barrel leaves the empty case on the bolt face, and it is ejected clear. The bolt then runs forward to chamber a fresh round and lock. Recoil is reduced by a muzzle brake, and the barrel runs in a hydro-pneumatic recoil sleeve forming the front of the receiver. The rifle is supported by a bipod and an elevation-adjustable rear monopod. The level of recoil is approximately that of a .358 sporting rifle. The magazine is inserted obliquely from the right side; various sizes of magazine are under test. The cartridge is made partly of synthetic material and the projectile is a 36g (1.27oz) 5.5mm fin-stabilised flechette of tungsten. It has a probable effective range of 1,500/2,000m depending upon the type of target engaged. At 800m range the flechette can penetrate 40mm of armour steel. The AMR is currently under evaluation in several countries.

BELGIUM

Automatic Rifle M1930

Fabrique Nationale d'Armes de Guerre	
Various calibres	

The Belgian Model 1930 rifle is an FN-manufactured version of the American Browning Automatic Rifle (BAR) M1918. There are some small differences in the design of the magazine, the ejection port covers and the gas regulator, and the barrel is ribbed in a gesture towards solving the cooling problem. In addition to being a standard Belgian Army weapon, in 7.65mm calibre, it was also offered commercially and can be found in a variety of calibres. Some were provided with quick-change barrels. Weapons are known to have been supplied by FN to Chile, China, Poland and Sweden, all of whom received deliveries prior to 1939. Sweden also developed and manufactured the same design, having them made by the state-owned Carl Gustav factory.

7.92mm Browning Type D

Fabrique Nationale d'Armes de Guerre	
7.92 × 57mm and .30-06	
Length overall	1,143mm (45.00in)
Weight empty	9.18kg (20.25lb)
Barrel	508mm (20.00in), 4 grooves, rh
Magazine	20-shot detachable box
Muzzle velocity	730m/sec (2,400ft/sec)

The Type D automatic rifle is a modernised version of the BAR Model 30 described above. After World War Two FN saw a market for an improved model of this weapon as a light machine-gun, lighter than many available at that time. It was bought in small numbers by the Belgian and Egyptian Armies, by the latter after their defeat in the 1947 war with Israel. Two significant improvements over the original Browning design are incorporated in the Type D. The first is that the barrel can be quickly changed, so allowing the possibility of sustained fire provided spare barrels are available. The other was a simplification of the assembly of the receiver and trigger mechanism so that these components can be more easily stripped and cleaned. These changes made the Type D a much better machine-gun than the original BAR but the idea came too late and could not compete with more modern designs which began to appear in the early 1950s. One drawback was the bottom-mounted 20-round magazine which could not be easily enlarged. However, the Type D managed to serve the Egyptians for several years until it was replaced by Russian weapons.

STEYR AMR

The Model 49, offered in selective fire, automatic-only and sniper versions, was designed before World War Two, the design being shelved during the German occupation and brought out to catch the immediate post-war market for automatic rifles, one which became surprisingly large and lucrative. Available in a range of calibres to suit whatever the customer wanted, it was sold in large numbers in Egypt, Europe and South America. The bolt system is similar to the Russian Tokarev, the action being locked by the bolt tilting under the action of cams in the receiver sides. The action is gas operated, with a long cylinder and tappet above the barrel. The firing pin is struck by a hammer and the 10-round magazine can be charger-loaded or topped-up with individual rounds. The whole construction of the rifle was to a very high standard, making it expensive to produce, and it became the basis for a re-design which finished up as the FN-FAL. Among the users of the SAFN 49 were Colombia (.30-06), Venezuela (7mm), Egypt (7.92mm), and Indonesia (.30-06).

Probably the most successful of the many designs to emanate from Fabrique Nationale, the FAL (Fusil Automatique Léger) has been sold to more than 70 countries over the past forty years. It has been made under licence in many countries around the world and the weapon has equipped most of the NATO partners at one time or another. Such enormous success stems partly from political and economic causes, but these would have had little influence had the design not been sound and practical. It is doubtful if any future weapon will have the widespread application of the FN-FAL, since today many countries are manufacturing their own designs and the era of a few major manufacturers supplying most of the world is over. Developed from the Model 49 and using the same basic tilting bolt gas-actuated mechanism, the FAL appeared in 1950 and the first large orders were placed in 1953. Changes in the trigger mechanism allow the weapon to be used in automatic fire, but it is rather light and climbs excessively, even when fitted with a bipod. A version with a heavier barrel is intended to be used as a squad automatic and several armies have adopted it. All versions are outwardly similar, though there are some changes in furniture and such items as flash-hiders and bayonet mounts. The cocking handle is on the left side, so leaving the right hand for the trigger when cocking, and there is a folding carrying-handle. Robust, reliable, simple to maintain and use, the FAL set a new standard when it appeared and continued as a leading design until the gradual change to 5.56mm calibre began to make itself felt.

7.92mm SAFN Model 49

Fabrique Nationale d'Armes de Guerre

Various calibres

Length overall	1,116mm (43.93in)
Weight empty	4.31kg (9.5lb)
Barrel	590mm (23.25in), 4 grooves, rh
Magazine	10-shot detachable box
Muzzle velocity	730m/sec (2,400ft/sec)

7.62mm FN-FAL

Fabrique Nationale d'Armes de Guerre

7.62 × 51mm NATO

Length overall	1,053mm (41.46in)
Weight empty	4.31kg (9.5lb)
Barrel	533mm (21.00in), 4 grooves, rh
Magazine	20-shot detachable box
Muzzle velocity	853m/sec (2,800ft/sec)

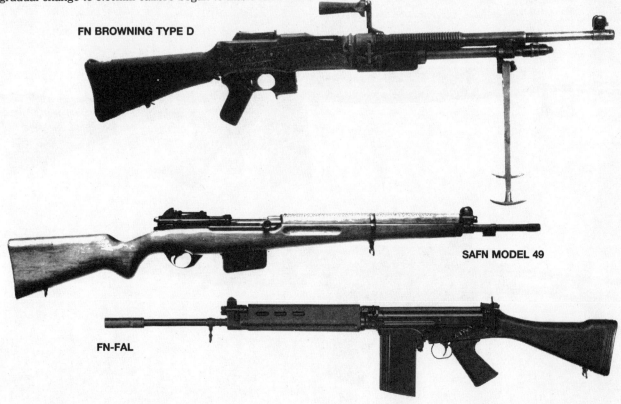

FN BROWNING TYPE D

SAFN MODEL 49

FN-FAL

5.56mm FN-CAL

Fabrique Nationale d'Armes de Guerre	
5.56 × 45mm	
Length overall	978mm (38.50in)
Weight empty	2.94kg (6.48lb)
Barrel	469mm (18.50in), 6 grooves, rh
Magazine	20-shot detachable box
Rate of fire	850rds/min
Muzzle velocity	975m/sec (3,200ft/sec)

5.56mm FN-FNC

FN Herstal SA	
5.56 × 45mm NATO	
Length (butt extended)	997mm (39.25in)
Length (butt folded)	766mm (30.15in)
Weight empty	3.8kg (8.38lb)
Barrel	449mm (17.68in), 6 grooves, rh
Magazine	30-shot detachable box
Rate of fire	600–750rds/min
Muzzle velocity	965m/sec (3,165ft/sec) with M193 bullet

The Vietnam war was the catalyst which ushered in the 5.56mm family of small arms and the success of this calibre prompted several manufacturers to develop 5.56mm weapons. FN produced the CAL (Carabine Automatique Légère), resembling a scaled-down FAL, though the system of operation was changed to use a rotating bolt. Early models had a three-round burst system as well as provision for full automatic fire or single shots. The barrel is attached to the receiver by a large threaded retaining nut and, once the handguard has been removed, changing the barrel was simple. The magazine held 20 rounds and the entire weapon was neat and workmanlike. However, it was somewhat ahead of its time, since most armies were well-stocked with 7.62mm weapons and were reluctant to make a major calibre change until the economic life of these existing rifles had expired. As a result the CAL failed to do very well in the market place and FN eventually withdrew it in 1975.

The FN-CAL attained minor success and was withdrawn, since it was considered to be too expensive to compete in the market-place and of doubtful reliability. FN then set to work to re-design it and produce an improved weapon to compete in the NATO trials of 1977–80. The development time, however, was too short and the FNC, though entered, was soon withdrawn to undergo further work. It eventually appeared in the early 1980s as a gas-operated weapon of conventional form, an improved and simplified CAL. The barrel is available rifled in various twists to suit either the American M193 bullet or the Belgian (now NATO standard) SS109 bullet, and for the Swedish Army a special slow rifling was developed so as to reduce the wounding effect of the bullet. The rifle was adopted, with some small modifications, by the Swedes in 1982 as their AK5 assault rifle and is also manufactured under licence in Indonesia. It is also the standard Belgian service rifle. As well as the standard FNC rifle there is a short-barrelled carbine variant. A further variant model, capable only of single shots, is sold as the Model 7030 Law Enforcement rifle for police forces. (Data table refers to the standard rifle.)

FN-CAL

FN-FNC

BRAZIL

The IMBEL Light Automatic Rifle (LAR) is simply the FN-FAL manufactured under licence for use by the Brazilian Army and for export into other South American countries. Some 150,000 had been produced to 1988, of which 40,000 were exported. Dimensions, weights, performance etc. are as for the Belgian FN-FAL.

7.62mm Imbel LAR

IMBEL: Industria Materiel Belico de Brasil

7.62 × 51mm NATO

This is a scaled-down version of the FN-FAL chambered for the 5.56mm cartridge. It differs mechanically from the standard FAL by having a tubular metal butt which folds alongside the receiver. The barrel is rifled one turn in 9 inches so as to perform equally well with either M193 or SS109 types of ammunition, and the rifle has been accepted for use by the Brazilian Army and has been exported to other South American countries.

5.56mm Imbel MD1

IMBEL: Industria Materiel Belico de Brasil

5.56 × 45mm NATO

CHINA

This is no more than a Chinese copy of the Soviet Simonov SKS carbine; the copy is so identical that in the first models it can only be identified by the Chinese characters stamped into the receiver. These early models used the same folding knife bayonet as the Soviet model, but this was later changed to a folding spike bayonet, making the weapon easier to distinguish.

7.62mm Type 56 Carbine

State arsenals

7.62 × 39mm Soviet

The Type 56 rifles are copies of the Soviet Kalashnikov AKM and are distinguishable only by the Chinese markings. After this weapon had been in production for some years the Chinese developed a modified version using a folding butt, also based on the Soviet original, calling this the Type 56-1. It was then followed by the Type 56-2 in which the folding butt was of a different design which folded sideways to lie alongside the receiver. All three weapons are in use by the Chinese forces and have also been exported to various South-east Asian countries. In addition, semi-automatic versions are offered in the commercial market.

7.62mm Type 56, 56-1 and 56-2 Rifles

State arsenals

7.62 × 39mm Soviet

IMBEL 7.62 LAR

IMBEL MD1

TYPE 56 RIFLE

7.62mm Type 68 Rifle

Sate arsenals	
7.62 × 39mm Soviet	
Length overall	1,030mm (40.50in)
Weight empty	3.49kg (7.69lb)
Barrel	521mm (20.50in), 4 grooves, rh
Magazine	15-shot detachable box
Rate of fire	750rds/min
Muzzle velocity	730m/sec (2,395ft/sec)

Although this rifle resembles the Soviet SKS it is, internally, quite different and is a native Chinese design. It uses a rotating bolt gas system derived from the Kalashnikov and has a gas regulator giving two positions but without a shut-off for grenade launching. The magazine resembles that of the AK weapons and can, if necessary, be charger-loaded while still in position on the rifle; the AK magazine can be used if the bolt stop is removed or ground down. The rifle is a curious mixture of old and new and almost an anomaly in modern times, but it is obviously simple to make and reliable in use, and for most armies that it sufficient.

7.62mm Type 79 Sniping Rifle

State arsenals	
7.62 × 54R Mosin-Nagant	

This is a direct copy of the Soviet SVD Dragunov sniping rifle, fitted with an optical sight which is a copy of the Soviet PS0-1 and has the same infra-red detecting ability.

CZECHOSLOVAKIA

7.92mm Rifle ZH 29

Ceskoslovenska Zbrojovka, Brno	
7.92 × 57mm Mauser	
Length overall	1,155mm (45.47in)
Weight empty	4.54kg (10.0lb)
Barrel	545mm (21.50in), 4 grooves, rh
Magazine	10- or 25-shot detachable box
Muzzle velocity	823m/sec (2,700ft/sec)

Designed by Emanuel Holek of the Brno factory in the middle 1920s, the ZH 29 was widely tested by many countries in the 1930s but few ever found their way into military service. Operation was by gas piston, using the principle which was later perfected in the various ZB machine-guns, though the ZH 29 made use of a tilting bolt which cammed into a recess in one side of the receiver. This design demanded a chamber which was eccentric to the axis of the barrel blank, an expensive item to machine accurately. Long and heavy, the ZH 29 was nevertheless reliable, and was obviously designed to provide a weapon capable of sustained fire, as shown by the unusual ribbed light alloy heat radiator, intended to dissipate barrel heat. The rifles were made in single-shot or selective-fire patterns, and they were available in virtually whatever calibre the customer desired.

TYPE 68 RIFLE

ZH29

This rifle is chambered for the Czech 7.62 × 45mm cartridge and is an unremarkable weapon which leaned heavily on other designs for its inspiration. The operating system was an adaptation of the German MKb42(W), an annular gas piston with a tipping bolt locking by frontal lugs, and the trigger mechanism owed much to the Garand rifle. The bolt lock system is unsatisfactory and has rarely been used elsewhere, though it is probably the only interesting thing about the rifle. The magazine was charger-loaded and the design incorporated a folding bayonet. The VZ 52 was not made in large numbers and did not stay in Czech service for very long. After the Czechs were incorporated into the Warsaw Pact, standardisation of ammunition led to the development of the VZ 52/57, the same weapon but chambered for the standard Soviet 7.62 × 39mm cartridge. This, too was not in service very long, and both models are now obsolete.

7.62mm Rifle VZ 52/57

Ceskoslovenska Zbrojowka, Brno

7.62 × 45mm Czech M52
7.62 × 39mm Soviet M43

Length overall	1,015mm (40.00in)
Weight empty	4.08kg (9.00lb)
Barrel	520mm (20.51in), 4 grooves, rh
Magazine	10-shot detachable box
Muzzle velocity	743m/sec (2,440ft/sec)

The VZ 58 is a Czech design, and although it bears some external resemblance to the Kalashnikov, the mechanism is totally different. Two versions exist: the VZ 58P with a conventional wooden stock, and the VZ 58V with a folding metal stock. Early models had wooden furniture, but this was soon replaced by resin-impregnated wood fibre compound and some may be found with plastic furniture. The rifle has been the standard Czech infantry arm since the late 1950s and has also been exported in limited numbers. The rifle has a tilting bolt and an axial hammer firing mechanism, and is gas operated. It is well made and finished, and has a notably simple trigger mechanism. There are several ancillaries which can be fitted to the weapon, including a light bipod which clamps to the barrel behind the foresight. Whether this is actually a better weapon than the Kalashnikov is hard to say, but it is certainly extremely workmanlike, robust and reliable. Original issues were chambered for the Czech M52 round but this was soon abandoned for the Soviet M43 cartridge.

7.62mm Rifle VZ 58

Ceszkoslovenska Zbrojowka, Uhersky Brod

7.62 × 45mm Czech M52
7.62 × 39mm Soviet M43

Length overall	843mm (33.20in)
Weight empty	3.11kg (6.86lb)
Barrel	400mm (15.80in), 4 grooves, rh
Magazine	30-shot detachable box
Rate of fire	800rds/min
Muzzle velocity	710m/sec (2,330ft/sec)

VZ 52

VZ 58

DENMARK

The Bang Rifle

Soren H. Bang, an inventive Dane, was greatly taken with the prospect of putting a neglected Maxim idea to some practical use. This, an idea which Maxim had patented in the 1880s and subsequently neglected, involved tapping the muzzle blast to make it actuate a loading mechanism. Bang developed a variety of rifles and machine-guns which used muzzle cones to trap the gas blast, the cones thus being driven forward to pull an operating rod. By various linkages this rod could be made to unlock and retract the bolt, the cycle then being completed by the usual spring. Bang's weapons were extensively tested by several nations prior to 1914 and again, in improved form, in the 1920s; none was ever adopted. Their principal drawback was a lack of robustness in their construction and high manufacturing cost. The principle was later revived by Walther and Mauser during World War Two in their Gew 41(W) and Gew 41(M) designs, equally without success. No dimensions can be given since virtually every Bang rifle was a one-off, the size and calibre depending upon his most recent idea and his prospective customer. Although never used in war, the design is recorded here as an example of the various systems which have been tried and discarded but which, one never knows, may be revived one day.

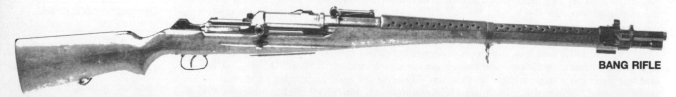

BANG RIFLE

DOMINICAN REPUBLIC

.30 Light Rifle Model 2

San Cristobal Arsenal	
.30 M1 Carbine	
Length overall	945mm (37.20in)
Weight empty	3.52kg (7.76lb)
Barrel	410mm (16.14in), 4 grooves, rh
Magazine	25- or 30-shot detachable box
Rate of fire	580rds/min
Muzzle velocity	572m/sec (1,876ft/sec)

In 1948 Dominica decided to develop its own weapons and set up a factory, with technical assistance from Beretta. The Hungarian designer Kiraly was employed, and he developed this interesting little rifle. Its appearance indicates the hand of Beretta, but the mechanism is pure Kiraly, using his two-part bolt delayed blowback system which is described under his Hungarian submachine-guns. The rifle fires from an open bolt and the double trigger provides for single shots or automatic fire. Kiraly later developed a heavier rifle for the 7.62 × 51mm NATO cartridge, using a similar breech mechanism, but few were made and it never saw service. The light rifle was adopted by the Dominican forces and sold to Cuba and other Central American countries in small numbers.

FINLAND

7.62mm Assault Rifle M62

Valtion Kivaarithedas	
7.62 × 39mm Soviet M43	
Length overall	914mm (36.00in)
Barrel	419mm (16.5in), 4 grooves, rh
Magazine	30-shot detachable box
Rate of fire	650rds/min
Muzzle velocity	730m/sec (2,400ft/sec)

The Finnish Army uses a number of rifles derived from the Soviet AK design, and the first of these to appear was the M60. It was no more than a copy of the AK47 with some minor modifications; the fore-end was of plastic-covered steel instead of wood, the fixed butt was a simple tubular design, and the rear sight was moved to the back of the receiver. The most remarkable feature was the absence of a trigger guard so that the rifle was easily used with heavy gloves. The M62 was a re-design to cater for various minor faults which appeared in use. The fore-end was now entirely plastic, with a different pattern of cooling holes, a removable trigger guard was fitted, the tubular pistol grip was slightly altered and the sights were given Tritium night aiming markers.

This is an improved model of the M62 which, in the course of improvement, has moved back closer to the original AK47 design. Much use has been made of stamped and pressed steel, the butt and fore-end are of plastic, the pistol grip is a more conventional flat-sided unit, and the rear sight has been moved back to its original place above the chamber. Several variant models of the M76 have been developed, mostly for export. The M76W has a fixed wooden buttstock; the M76P has a fixed plastic butt; the M76T has a folding tubular butt; and the M76F has a folding plastic butt. All are available in either 7.62 × 39mm or 5.56 × 45mm chambering, though the Finnish Army uses only the 7.62mm version. It has been sold to the army of Qatar and to Indonesian security troops in the 5.56mm version.

7.62mm Assault Rifle M76

Sako-Valmet AB

7.62 × 39mm Soviet M43

Length overall	914mm (35.98in)
Weight empty	3.60kg (7.94lb)
Barrel	420mm (16.53in), 4 grooves, rh
Magazine	15-, 20- or 30-shot detachable box
Rate of fire	650rds/min
Muzzle velocity	720m/sec (2,362ft/sec)

This is a variant of the M76 assault rifle, the principal differences being the use of a longer and heavier barrel fitted with a carrying handle, and the fitting of a bipod, from which it is apparent that this weapon is really intended to be a squad light automatic weapon. Normal rifle magazines are used, and the principal advantage of the design is that it is light in weight and offers portable firepower for troops operating on their feet in difficult country. The weapon is offered in three calibres, though the 7.62 × 51mm version is, strangely, offered only as a semi-automatic weapon, possibly due to the recoil load being excessive at automatic fire. Various armies are currently (1990) assessing the weapon.

7.62mm Rifle M78

Sako-Valmet AB

7.62 × 39mm Soviet M43
7.62 × 51mm NATO
5.56 × 45mm NATO

Length overall	1,060mm (41.73in)
Weight empty	4.70kg (10.36lb)
Barrel	550mm (21.65in),
Magazine	15- or 30-shot detachable box
Rate of fire	650rds/min
Muzzle velocity	720m/sec (2,362ft/sec) (7.62 × 39)

RIFLE M78

FRANCE

8mm R.S.C. Model 1917/1918

Manufacture d'Armes de St Etienne	
8 × 50R Lebel	
Length overall	1,331mm (52.40in)
Weight empty	5.25kg (11.57lb)
Barrel	798mm (31.40in), 4 grooves, rh
Magazine	5-shot internal box
Muzzle velocity	715m/sec (2,345ft/sec)

This semi-automatic rifle is variously known as the Modèle 1917 or as the R.S.C. from the names of the designers, Ribeyrolle, Sutter and Chauchat, or as the 'St Etienne' from the place of manufacture. It was the end product of a series of experimental designs developed during the early years of the century and was issued in great haste during World War One. Better designs were available, but the Model 1917 was the only one which used the standard 8mm Lebel cartridge, and it was thus selected in order not to disrupt ammunition production or complicate supply. It seems to have been beyond the power of early French firearms designers to produce an aesthetically acceptable weapon, and the RSC is no exception to this rule, an ugly and awkward-looking weapon whose length and weight go a long way to support this initial impression. It is gas operated by a piston and bolt carrier, and fed from a clip unique to the weapon and holding five rounds. The later Model 1918 was an attempt to improve matters by shortening and lightening the weapon and altering the feed system to take the standard rifle cartridge clip. The Model 1917 was used in limited numbers during the war, but the Model 1918 did not appear until after the Armistice. A transitional version of the Model 1917 is known; this is basically a shortened form of the 1917, probably a retrospective modification. In 1935 the surviving rifles were altered to a form of manual straight-pull bolt action, achieved simply by blocking off the gas port. It is believed that they were then issued to colonial troops in French Equatorial Africa. (Data table refers to the M1917.)

7.5mm MAS Models 49 and 49/56

Manufacture d'Armes de St Etienne	
7.5 × 54mm French Mle 29	
Length overall	1,010mm (39.76in)
Weight empty	3.90kg (8.60lb)
Barrel	521mm (20.51in), 4 grooves, rh
Magazine	10-shot detachable box
Muzzle velocity	817m/sec (2,680ft/sec)

France was among the first European nations to issue an automatic rifle to her infantry, and the MAS49 appeared in 1949, when most of Europe was still using bolt-action weapons. In many ways the MAS49 resembles the earlier MAS36 bolt-action rifle, using the same sort of two-piece stock, a slab-sided receiver and similar sights. It is, though, not an automatised version of the 36 but an entirely new design which incorporated some items from the 36 to

R.S.C. MODEL 1917

MAS MODEL 49

reduce cost. It is a rather heavy, very strong, and utterly reliable gas-operated weapon. The gas system uses no piston or cylinder, the gas being piped back to impinge directly on the face of the bolt and blow it backwards. This system has frequently led to problems in other weapons, largely due to fouling, but it seems to work well enough in this rifle, probably because the components are of ample size and there is clearance for fouling to accumulate without causing trouble. The muzzle was shaped to act as a launching spigot for hollow-tailed rifle grenades, one of the first weapons to incorporate this idea, and grenade-launching sights were provided. Unusually, there was no provision for a bayonet, though a small number were later modified to accept the small spike bayonet from the MAS36. Breech locking is done by tilting the breech-block in the same way as in the Tokarev and SAFN rifles, a simple and reliable system.

The MAS49/56 differs from the MAS49 in having the fore-end shortened so as to leave more barrel exposed, and the integral grenade-launcher has been replaced by a combined grenade-launcher and muzzle brake. Both these rifles were standard in the French Army until replaced by the 5.56mm FA-MAS in the middle 1980s, and many will still be found in use in former French colonies in Africa. Large numbers were converted from 7.5mm to 7.62mm NATO calibre in the 1970s. (Data table refers to the MAS 49/56.)

This rifle was developed in the 1970s and began issue to the French Army in the early 1980s. It has now completely replaced the earlier MAS49 model and has also been sold to Djibouti, Gabon, Lebanon, Senegal and the United Arab Emirates. The FA-MAS is a bullpup design; there are some disadvantages inherent in this layout, but this rifle appears to have managed to overcome all but the most minor difficulties. The barrel is only fractionally shorter than that of the M16 but the entire rifle is some 250mm shorter. It operates by a delayed blowback system based on a two-part bolt similar to the well-known Kiraly design. On firing, the case sets back against the light bolt head, and this force is transmitted to a lever which is engaged with a recess in the receiver. As the lever is turned, so it has to force the heavy bolt body back at a mechanical disadvantage, so slowing the opening of the bolt. There is the usual semi-automatic or full automatic option, and in addition the rifle can be set to fire a three-round burst for one pressure of the trigger. There is a bipod for steadier shooting, and a sling is also provided for off-hand firing and for use when launching grenades. The iron sights are concealed inside the channel section of the long carrying handle, beneath which is the cocking handle. A plastic cheek-piece clips on to the stock in front of the butt and covers one of two ejection openings; by removing the bolt and replacing the ejector claw on the other side, and by changing over the cheek-piece so as to expose one ejector slot and cover the other, the rifle can be converted for right- or left-handed firing in a few minutes without tools.

The muzzle is shaped to act as a grenade-launcher, and a small knife bayonet can be fitted. Despite its unconventional shape (which has led to its being nicknamed 'Le Clairon' ('The Bugle') by French troops, it is an effective and accurate weapon.

5.56mm Fusil Automatique MAS (FA-MAS)

Manufacture d'Armes de St Etienne

5.56 × 45mm NATO

Length overall	757mm (29.80in)
Weight empty	3.61kg (7.96lb)
Barrel	488mm (19.21in), 3 grooves, rh
Magazine	25-shot detachable box
Rate of fire	900–1,000rds/min
Muzzle velocity	960m/sec (3,150ft/sec)

FA-MAS

GERMANY (Pre-1945)

Mauser Automatic Rifles 1898–1914

The first self-loading rifle patents were granted to Mauser in February 1898, though it is probable that the actual design was due to the Federle brothers who had also invented the Mauser pistol; it was normal German practice to register employees' inventions in the proprietor's name. Mauser seems to have been fascinated by recoil action, as all of his rifle designs and most of his pistols relied upon recoil force for their actuation.

Rifle c/98. This was the first rifle, based on a block of patents granted late in February 1898 and operated by short recoil. The barrel and bolt were locked together by flaps, one on each side of the breech, which were positioned in a housing surrounding the chamber. When the rifle fired, recoil of the barrel cammed the flaps out of engagement with the bolt, which then continued rearwards; it was returned by a spring and the return of the barrel again forced the flaps into recesses cut in the bolt. The principal drawback was that the flaps protruded behind their housing during the reloading cycle and were thus prone to derangement from dust and dirt.

Rifle c/02. This was a long-recoil weapon based on a 1902 patent, in which locking was performed by a two-piece rotating bolt. On firing barrel and bolt recoiled across the magazine until the bolt reached the rear of the receiver and was stopped; further movement of the barrel forced the bolt head back and rotated it so that the barrel was unlocked from the bolt and could return by its own spring while the bolt was held to the rear. As the barrel reached its forward position it operated an ejector to knock the empty case from the bolt face, after which the bolt was released to run forward, chamber a fresh round, and lock to the barrel. Like most automatic rifles of the period it was possible to lock out the self-loading action and use it as a hand-operated repeater.

Rifle c/06/08. This designation covered three short-recoil designs with different locking systems. The first used a flap system similar to the Friberg-Kjellman system; two rear-pivoted locking flaps supported the rear of the bolt, and barrel recoil moved them in and out of recesses in the receiver. Two variants of this system discarded the flaps and substituted a block in the form of a saddle; the breech-block slid back in this saddle which was cammed in and out of a recess in the top of the receiver. Tests of this design continued until the outbreak of war in 1914 without the Army coming to any decision.

Aviator's Rifle Model 16. The principal use to which Mauser automatic rifles were ever put was the arming of aircraft observers and balloon crews before the arrival of the flexible machine-gun. Once production of machine-guns was sufficient for the aviation service, the rifles were abandoned, although a few managed to appear on the Western Front as infantry weapons, by which time they had managed to collect full-length stocks and bayonets. This Aviator's rifle was derived from the flap-locking version of the c/06/08.

In retrospect it is hard to say why the Mauser designs were such failures in view of the effort which went into their design and the care which went into their manufacture. The Model 1916 required oiled cartridges for reliable operation, and another drawback was the contemporary state of metallurgy, which ensured that the Mausers were all heavy weapons relying on the interaction of cam surfaces and various bearings, all of which wore rapidly. It is notable that some of his operating systems were to appear years later and some of these proved to be quite successful, with the benefit of better technology. Another interesting aspect is Mauser's single-minded pursuit of recoil-operated systems; he appears never to have attempted to develop a gas-actuated weapon.

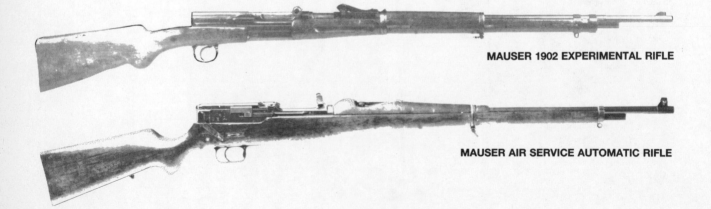

MAUSER 1902 EXPERIMENTAL RIFLE

MAUSER AIR SERVICE AUTOMATIC RIFLE

During the 1920–1939 period a number of automatic rifle designs were put forward in Germany but none was developed beyond prototype stage. In 1940 a military programme was begun to produce, as a matter of urgency, a semi-automatic rifle and the Gew 41 weapons were the result. Two designs, by Mauser and Walther, were developed but the Mauser was soon dropped and work concentrated on the Walther model. It was gas operated, using a rather crude adaptation of the Bang System in which the muzzle blast was deflected by a cup to turn back and strike an annular piston around the barrel and so drive an actuating rod. Locking was by hinged flaps similar to the Russian Degtyarev machine-gun. The magazine was integral and slow to load, and the weapon was expensive and slow to manufacture due to the complicated gas system. The rifle was not a great success as it was noticeably muzzle-heavy and badly balanced, though tens of thousands were made and issued to service units, principally on the Eastern Front. Once the Gew 43 appeared, all production of the Gew 41 was stopped, although it was never entirely withdrawn from service.

The FG42 was one of the outstanding small-arms designs of World War Two and came close to being a complete success. In the event, a combination of circumstances militated against it, and it is doubtful if as many as 7,000 were ever made. This remarkable weapon nearly achieved the impossible feat of being a serviceable selective-fire design firing an old-style full-power cartridge, and it was a notable forerunner of the now fashionable assault rifles, all of which use lower-powered ammunition and are thus more easily controllable. The FG42 was developed for Luftwaffe paratroops and was first used in the dramatic rescue of Mussolini; it later appeared in Italy and France. Many were captured by the Allies, giving the impression that it was on more common issue than was actually the case.

The rifle is gas operated, with many novel features. It fires from an open bolt in the automatic mode but from a closed bolt in single-shot mode, so allowing the barrel to cool during sustained fire and thus avoid cook-offs (premature firing due to the cartridge heating up in a hot chamber). It was one of the first military rifles to be made in the 'straight-line' configuration, and it had a light bipod and an integral bayonet. All this was contained in a package weighing less than ten pounds. The magazine, rather awkwardly, fed from the left side, a feature which is perhaps one of the few of this weapon not to have been copied, since it tends to unbalance the weapon. Unfortunately it was expensive and time-consuming to manufacture, as a result of which it was not favoured by the Army High Command; it was able to reach production largely because Hermann Goering, Marshal of the Luftwaffe, had the necessary political influence to get the weapon made for 'his' parachute troops. Once the importance of the German parachute forces declined, it became more difficult to justify production and the rifle was never properly developed.

7.92mm Gewehr 41 (Walther) (Gew 41(W))

Carl Walther Waffenfabrik

7.92 × 57mm Mauser

Length overall	1,130mm (44.50in)
Weight empty	4.98kg (11.00lb)
Barrel	545mm (21.50in), 4 grooves, rh
Magazine	10-shot integral box
Muzzle velocity	776m/sec (2,550ft/sec)

7.92mm Fallschirmgewehr 42 (FG42)

Rheinmetall-Borsig AG

7.92 × 57mm Mauser

Length overall	940mm (37.00in)
Weight empty	4.50kg (9.92lb)
Barrel	508mm (20.00in), 4 grooves, rh
Magazine	20-shot detachable box
Rate of fire	750rds/min
Muzzle velocity	760m/sec (2,495ft/sec)

GEWEHR 41

FG 42

7.92mm Machine Carbine 42 (Haenel) (MKb 42(H))

C. G. Haenel Waffen- und Fahrradfabrik	
7.92 × 33 Kurz	
Length overall	940mm (37.00in)
Weight empty	4.90kg (10.80lb)
Barrel	364mm (14.37in), 4 grooves, rh
Magazine	30-shot detachable box
Rate of fire	500rds/min
Muzzle velocity	700m/sec (2,300ft/sec)

This weapon was developed in response to a German Army requirement for an 'assault rifle' chambered for a new short-cased 7.92mm cartridge then under development by Polte of Magdeburg. It was designed by Louis Schmeisser in 1940–41 and fifty pre-production models had been made by mid-1942. A gas-operated, tipping-bolt type, it was more conventional in its mechanism than its Walther competitor (below), using a normal gas tube and piston. When the gas impinged on the piston, which was attached to the bolt carrier, it drove the carrier back to unlock the bolt by moving it back and down from its locking recesses. The piston, carrier and bolt continued to move back until stopped by the return spring, after which the assembly was sent forward to load a fresh round. The MKb 42(H) was externally similar to the later MP43 (for which it acted as a prototype) except for the visible gas tube above the barrel, the attachment of a bayonet lug and a different trigger and grip assembly. Approximately 8,000 of the MKb 42(H) were produced from November 1942 to April 1943, and after trials on the Eastern Front it was decided to place the weapon in full production after Schmeisser had attended to a few details; these detail changes turned it into the MP43.

7.92mm Machine Carbine 42 (Walther) (MKb 42(W))

Carl Walther Waffenfabrik	
7.92 × 33mm Kurz	
Length overall	931mm (36.68in)
Weight empty	4.40kg (9.70lb)
Barrel	406mm (16.00in), 4 grooves, rh
Magazine	30-shot detachable box
Rate of fire	600rds/min
Muzzle velocity	700m/sec (2,300ft/sec)

The MKb 42(W) was developed by Walther in response to the same demand which produced the Haenel design. Work began in 1940 and the first prototype was produced in July 1942. Like Haenel's design, the Walther was designed for simple reproduction using as little as possible of scarce materials and complex machining; much use was made of pressings and stampings which were riveted or welded together. It was a gas-operated locked-breech design using a tipping bolt locked by frontal lugs; an unusual gas assembly used an annular piston around the barrel which moved inside a cylindrical housing. Gas struck this piston and drove it backwards, and a sleeve attached to the piston unlocked the bolt. It was recognisable by the circular fore-stock and by the lack of a separate gas tube; a bayonet lug was fitted and there was a greater gap between the magazine and trigger asembly than on the Haenel weapon. The exact number of MKb 42(W) manufactured is unknown; estimates vary from 200 to 8,000, but it was certainly not a great number. After troop trials on the Eastern Front it was decided to abandon the Walther design and concentrate on the Haenel, and production was stopped.

7.92mm Rifle 43 or Carbine 42 (Gew 43 or Kar 43)

Carl Walther Waffenfabrik; Berliner-Lübecker Maschinenfabrik; Gustloff-Werke	
7.92 × 57mm Mauser	
Length overall	1,117mm (44.00in)
Weight empty	4.33kg (9.55lb)
Barrel	558mm (22.00in), 4 grooves, rh
Magazine	10-shot detachable box
Muzzle velocity	746m/sec (2,450ft/sec)

The Gew 43 was the logical development from the Gew 41, applying field experience to the earlier design. It used the same bolt locking system but radically altered the gas operating system, doing away with the muzzle cup and adopting a conventional gas cylinder and piston mounted above the barrel. The magazine was made detachable, and a dovetail was machined on the receiver to accept a telescope sight, the rifle being generally used for sniping. It was probably first used on the Eastern Front in late 1943, though it was later to be encountered on all fronts, always in small numbers and always as a specialist's weapon. A definite improvement on the Gew 41, the Gew 43 was much easier to manufacture; most were found with laminated wood furniture, but towards the end of the war plastic material was used. Owing to the economic situation there was ultimately a further simplification of manufacture which gives some of the remaining models a distinctly rough external appearance. The Gew 43 remained in production until the end of the war and, after 1945, it was briefly adopted by the Czech Army in small numbers as a sniper's rifle. The Kar 43 differed from the Gew 43 only in being some 50mm shorter and having a larger trigger-guard.

MKb 42

The MP43 was the developed version of the MKb 42(H) with certain modifications made in the light of combat experience on the Eastern Front. The first deliveries of the weapon were made in July 1943 and production continued until the first months of 1945. In late 1943 a variant model was made, under the designation MP43/1, in which the clamp-on grenade-launcher was replaced by one of screwed-on pattern; a short threaded section appeared on the muzzle to allow the launcher to be fitted. A mounting bracket for an optical sight was also fitted, something which never appeared on the original MP43. In April 1944 the nomenclature was advanced, for no accountable reason, to MP44, which was otherwise identical to the MP43 though some weapons were fitted with the sight bracket. Towards the end of 1944 a further name was given to the weapon, the 'Sturmgewehr' or 'assault rifle' 44; this is said to have been bestowed on the weapon by Hitler himself. At any rate, it adequately described the weapon's role.

7.92mm Machine Pistol 43 (MP43) or Machine Pistol 44 (MP44) or Assault Rifle 44 (StG44)

C. G. Haenel Waffen- und Fahrradfabrik;
Erfurter Maschinenfabrik ERMA;
Mauser-Werke AG

7.92 × 33mm Kurz	
Length overall	940mm (37.00in)
Weight empty	5.10kg (11.24lb)
Barrel	418mm (16.50in), 4 grooves, rh
Magazine	30-shot detachable box
Rate of fire	500rds/min
Muzzle velocity	700m/sec (2,300ft/sec)

The Krummlauf Attachment

This was a remarkable rifle accessory which goes far to illustrate the gusto with which the German High Command could lust after totally futile projects, promising relatively little return and diverting valuable technical and manufacturing resources away from more vital tasks. The Krummlauf device was a curved barrel attachment which was fitted to the MP44 and used in conjunction with a mirror sight mounted at the muzzle. It appears to have been the unexpected by-product of a test device invented to permit firing weapons into a sandpit at very short range in order to conduct tests without requiring a large firing area. During this work somebody suggested that the curved attachment might be useful to allow occupants of armoured vehicles to fire down, from firing ports, against attacking infantry close to the vehicle, so close that conventional firing port weapons could not depress far enough to reach them.

Three versions of the Krummlauf appeared; the MP44(P) which turned the bullet through a 30° angle; the MP44(K) which had a 90° angle; and the MP44(V) capable of a 40° deflection. Only the first type was ever developed fully, and 10,000 are reputed to have been

GEWEHR 43

MP44

ordered in 1944. The principle of operation was to have the curved extension perforated with holes on its outer side, through which gas would leak progressively to slow the bullet and so allow it to make the turn. This, however, substantially reduced the velocity to about 300m/sec (984ft/sec) and thus diminished the effectiveness of the weapon. Moreover the bullet was grossly unstable as it left the device and accuracy was only good over a short distance, though in view of its intended use, this was no great defect. It is doubtful if many were made, equally doubtful if any were ever used in their intended role, but some were certainly captured by Allied troops in the closing weeks of the war when they were being used as street-fighting weapons, to shoot round corners. The British appear to have thought enough of the device to develop a similar attachment and sight for the Sten gun, which was tested in the late 1940s and promptly abandoned.

7.92mm Volkssturm Rifle VG 1–5

Manufacturer unknown

7.92 × 33mm Kurz	
Length overall	885mm (34.84in)
Weight empty	4.52kg (9.96lb)
Barrel	378mm (14.88in), 4 grooves, rh
Magazine	30-shot detachable box
Muzzle velocity	655m/sec (2,150ft/sec)

The VG 1–5 was a self-loading assault rifle developed by the Suhl-based Gustloff-Werke as part of the Primitiv-Waffen-Programm of 1944; these weapons were intended to arm the Volkssturm (Home Guard) and sundry last-ditch organisations which were planned but which never came into being. The rifle was designed by Barnetzke, Gustloff's chief designer, who had developed the operating principle in 1943, using an MP43 as his base. The VG 1–5 is remarkable, as the mechanism incorporated a text-book example of delayed blowback operation; the barrel is surrounded by a hollow sleeve which can reciprocate and which carries with it the bolt, attached to the rear of the sleeve. Some 65mm from the muzzle are four gas ports, and when the gun was fired gas passed through these and into the annular space inside the sleeve. This gas pressure was sufficient to hold the sleeve forward, and hence hold the breech closed, until the bullet was clear of the muzzle and the chamber pressure had dropped to safe limits, whereupon the momentum of the bolt would drive it back, the gas inside the annular space being driven back through the ports to exhaust at the muzzle. A recoil spring then returned the bolt and sleeve to reload the weapon.

One drawback of the design was that the bearing surfaces of the sleeve, and the surface of the barrel upon which it moved, had to be machined to quite close tolerances; gas residue soon fouled the area unless the surfaces were carefully greased, and barrel expansion due to heat would eventually jam the weapon completely. The VG 1–5 was designed to fire the short 7.92mm cartridge, and the magazine of the MP44 was used to simplify supply. The principle was resurrected and refined by Steyr-Mannlicher in the 1970s for their GB pistol, in which application it worked very well.

KRUMMLAUF ATTACHMENT

VOLKSSTURM VG1-5

GERMANY, FEDERAL REPUBLIC

Although officially classified as a State-produced rifle that has had more than one maker in the past, the G3 (Gewehr 3) is firmly attached to the Heckler & Koch name, the firm which developed it and first put it into production and has continued to do so since 1959. In addition it is, or has been, made under licence in France, Greece, Norway, Portugal, Sweden, Turkey, Mexico, Iran, Saudi Arabia, Burma, Pakistan, the Philippines and Thailand. At the last count, in 1989, the rifle is in service in 50 countries. The G3 is a modification and improvement upon a design by CETME of Spain, and since the CETME rifle was itself founded upon a German wartime design, the wheel has turned full circle and the design has returned home, though it bears little resemblance to the original. Like the CETME, the G3 relies on delayed blowback action, the delay being obtained by a roller-locked breech-block in which the movement of the rollers is controlled by a large firing pin. This forces the rollers into recesses in the receiver as it runs forward, and the rearward movement of the bolt has to force the rollers out once again, against inclined faces on the firing pin which tend to resist the movement, so giving the desired delay. The rifle is made from sheet metal stampings with plastic furniture, the whole rifle demanding a minimum of expensive machining. The result may not be particularly pretty, but it is undeniably robust, reliable and effective. There are several variant models; data table refers to the G3A3.

7.62mm G3 is the basic G3 design and had a flip rearsight and a wooden butt.

7.62mm G3A1. In this version the butt was retractable, and the flip sight was retained.

7.62mm G3A2. This model introduced a rotary rear sight which has remained standard ever since.

7.62mm G3A3. This version used the rotary rear sight, a modified foresight, and a pronged flash-hider. It is the current production model and has a plastic butt and fore-end.

7.62mm G3A3ZF is fitted with a telescope sight, the 'ZF' standing for '*zielfernrohr*' – telescope.

7.62mm G3A4 is the folding stock variant of the G3A3, using a stock which telescopes into guides alongside the receiver.

7.62mm G3SG/1 is a police sniping rifle and is a specially selected G3 fitted with a precision set trigger unit and a Schmidt & Bender telescope sight.

The PSG-1 (*Präzisions Schützen Gewehr 1*) rifle has been developed for sniping use by military and police forces. It is a semi-automatic rifle based on the G3 and using the same roller-locked system but with a longer and heavier barrel. A 6 × 42 telescope sight with illuminated cross-hairs is an integral part of the weapon and the bolt has been specially designed and engineered to permit silent closure. An adjustable trigger shoe provides a variable-width trigger with approximately 1.5kg (3lb) pull. Length of stock, height of cheek-piece and drop of butt are all adjustable and a supporting tripod is available.

7.62mm Rifle G3

Heckler & Koch GmbH

7.62 × 51mm NATO

Length overall	1,025mm (40.35in)
Weight empty	4.40kg (9.70lb)
Barrel	450mm (17.71in), 4 grooves, rh
Magazine	20-shot detachable box
Rate of fire	500–600rds/min
Muzzle velocity	780–800m/sec (2,560–2,625ft/sec)

7.62mm Sniper's Rifle PSG-1

Heckler & Koch GmbH

7.62 × 51mm NATO

Length overall	1,208mm (47.56in)
Weight empty	8.1kg (17.86lb)
Barrel	650mm (25.60in), 4 grooves, rh
Magazine	5- or 20-shot detachable box
Muzzle velocity	815m/sec (2,675ft/sec)

7.62mm G3

7.62mm Sniper's Rifle MSG 90

Heckler & Koch GmbH

7.62 × 51mm NATO

Yet another sniping rifle based on the G3, this was introduced in 1987 and uses a cold-forged heavy barrel allied to the standard Heckler & Koch bolt mechanism. The special trigger unit has a shoe, the stock is fully adjustable, and there are no iron sights, the rifle being fitted with a NATO-standard telescope mount which will accept any standard optical or electro-optical sight.

Length overall	1,165mm (45.87in)
Weight empty	6.40kg (14.11lb)
Barrel	600mm (23.62in), 4 grooves, rh
Magazine	5- or 20-shot detachable box
Muzzle velocity	800m/sec (2,625ft/sec)

MSG 90

5.56mm Rifle HK33E

Heckler & Koch GmbH

5.56 × 45mm NATO

The HK33E (E for Export) is a scaled-down version of the G3, using exactly the same trigger, firing mechanism and bolt mechanism. It is available in five different models: a standard rifle with fixed butt, standard rifle with telescoping butt, standard rifle with fixed butt and bipod; carbine with short barrel and telescoping butt; and sniping rifle with telescope sight. The rifle models are capable of launching grenades from their muzzle without requiring any attachments.

HK 33E

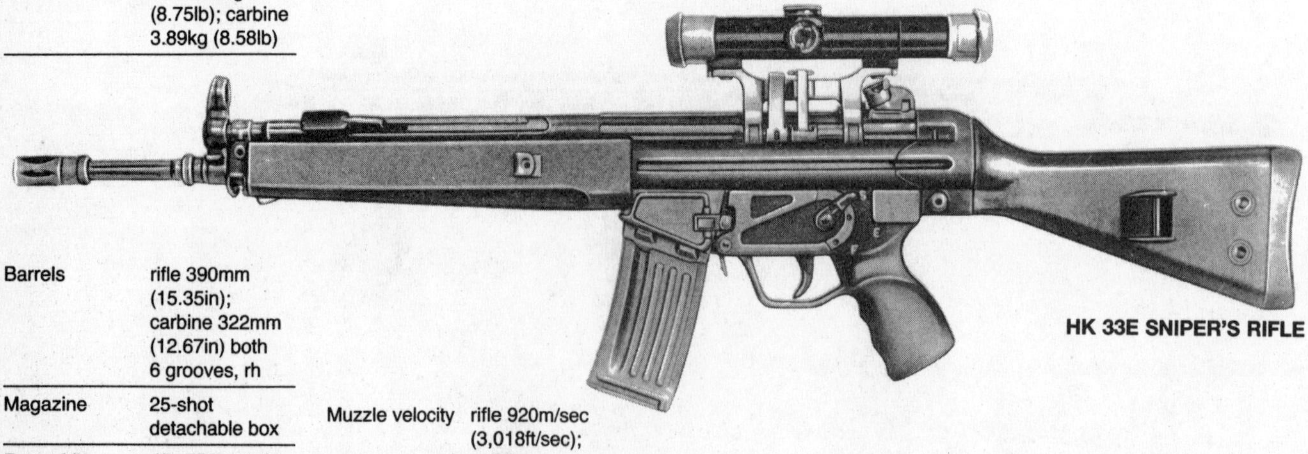

Length (rifle)	fixed butt 920mm (36.20in); extended butt 940mm (37.0in); telescoped butt 735mm (28.94in)
Length (carbine)	extended butt 865mm (34.0in); telescoped butt 675mm (26.57in)
Weights empty	fixed butt rifle 3.65kg (8.0lb); telescoping butt rifle 3.98kg (8.75lb); carbine 3.89kg (8.58lb)

Barrels	rifle 390mm (15.35in); carbine 322mm (12.67in) both 6 grooves, rh		
Magazine	25-shot detachable box		
Rate of fire	rifle 750rds/min; carbine 700rds/min	Muzzle velocity	rifle 920m/sec (3,018ft/sec); carbine 880m/sec (2,887ft/sec)

HK 33E SNIPER'S RIFLE

The G41 rifle is generally similar to the HK33E, the principal mechanical difference being the incorporation of a three-round burst facility in addition to normal automatic fire. However, in this design care has been taken to adhere to several NATO standards; thus the magazine aperture is to STANAG 4179 which means that it will accept M16 magazines and others built to the same specification – eg the British L85A1 rifle magazine. The chamber dimensions and contour conform to STANAG 4172 for the 5.56 × 45mm cartridge, and there is a STANAG 2324 sight mount. Other features include low-noise, positive-action bolt closure, a hold-open bolt catch and a dust-proof cover for the cartridge ejection port. Introduced in 1987, by 1989 this rifle was undergoing evaluation in several countries and it is possible that it may be adopted by the German Army to replace the G3 in second-line formations when first-line troops receive the G11. It is available in fixed butt, retracting butt or carbine (G41K) form.

5.56mm Rifle G41

Heckler & Koch GmbH

5.56 × 45mm NATO

Length (rifle)	fixed butt 997mm (39.25in); extended butt 996mm (39.21in); telescoped butt 806mm (31.73in)
Length (carbine)	extended butt 930mm (36.60in); telescoped butt 740mm (29.13in)
Weight empty	fixed butt 4.1kg (9.03lb); telescoping butt 4.35kg (9.59lb); carbine 4.25kg (9.37lb)
Barrel	rifle 450mm (17.71in); carbine 380mm (14.96in) both 6 grooves, rh
Magazine	30-shot detachable box
Rate of fire	850rds/min
Muzzle velocity	rifle 935m/sec (3,067ft/sec); carbine 910m/sec (2,985ft/sec)

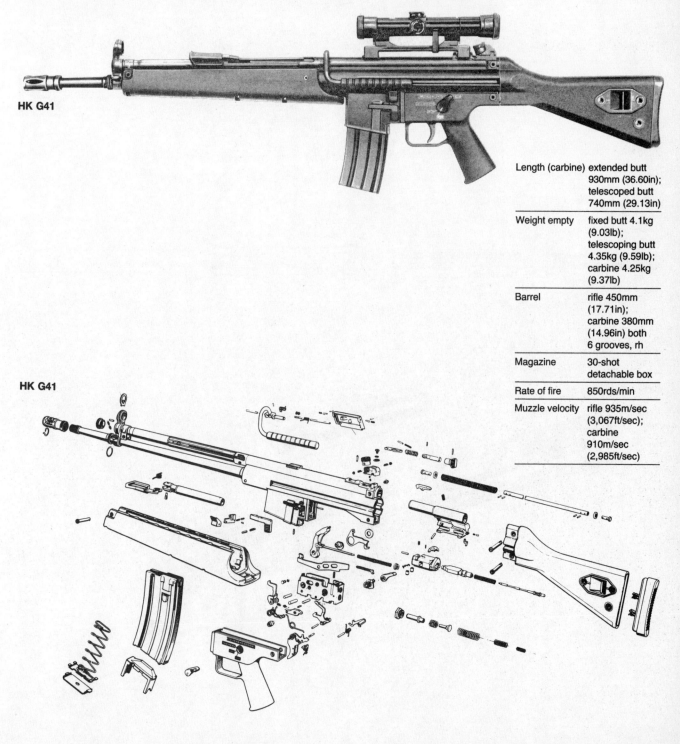

HK G41

HK G41

HK33

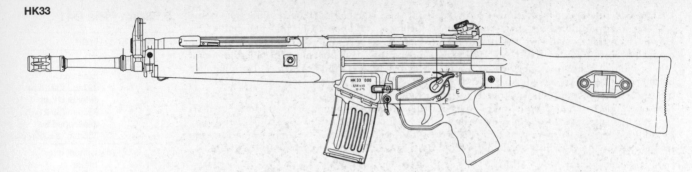

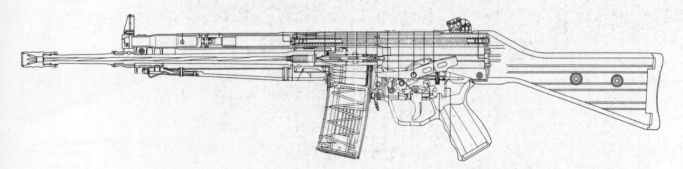

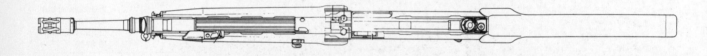

G11

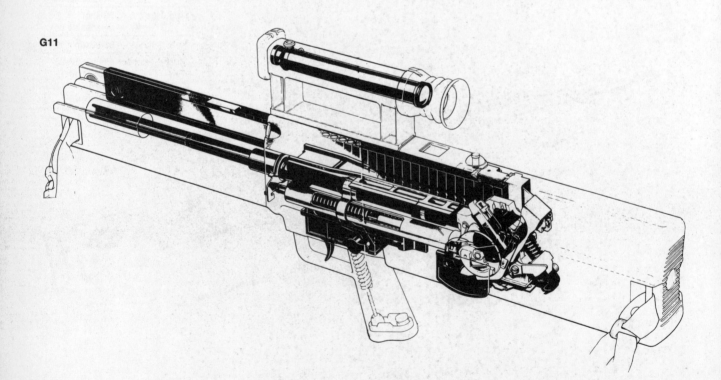

This is a revised version of a previous design, the HK11E, and has been specially designed as an exceptionally versatile arm for police and security forces. It uses the same roller-locked system as other H&K rifles and has the additional facility of a three-round burst. Feed is by a standard box magazine or from a special 50-shot drum, or by means of a conversion kit it can be belt fed. The barrel is heavier than normal, precisely rifled, and capable of being rapidly changed when the weapon is used in the machine-gun role. Iron sights are fitted, but the rifle is normally provided with a 4x telescope sight. The sight mount is NATO-standard, allowing the use of electro-optical sights.

7.62mm Rifle G8

Heckler & Koch GmbH	
7.62 × 51mm NATO	
Length overall	1,030mm (40.55in)
Weight empty	8.15kg (17.98lb) with sight & bipod
Barrel	450mm (17.71in) without muzzle brake
Magazine	20-shot detachable box; or 50-shot drum; or belt
Rate of fire	800rds/min
Muzzle velocity	800m/sec (2,625ft/sec)

G8

Development of this rifle, in response to a German Army requirement, began in 1969; the principal demand was for a very high first-round hit probability, and Heckler & Koch soon concluded that the only solution was an exceptionally fast three-round burst, one round of which would almost certainly strike the aiming point. Conventional rifles are poor in three-round burst performance since the rifle begins climbing after the first shot and spreads the other two far from the point of aim. This led them to examine ways of speeding up the action, which in turn led to the concept of caseless ammunition, since this removes the extraction and ejection phase from the operating cycle.

4.7mm Rifle G11

Heckler & Koch GmbH	
4.73 × 33 DM11 Caseless	
Length overall	752.5mm (29.625in)
Weight empty	3.80kg (8.38lb)
Barrel	537.5mm (21.16in), polygonal rifling, increasing twist, rh
Magazine	50-shot detachable box
Rate of fire	600rds/min
Muzzle velocity	930m/sec (3,050ft/sec)

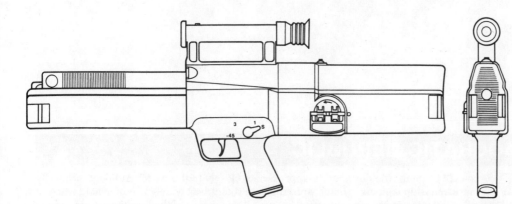

The G11 rifle uses an all-enclosing casing made of composite material, shaped to form a butt, pistol grip, and carrying handle with optical sight. Within this casing the rifle mechanism is free to move in recoil. The cartridge is a rectangular block of propellant with the bullet buried inside it and with a combustible cap at the rear end. Fifty such cartridges are carried in the weapon's magazine, which slides in horizontally, above the barrel. The cartridge is fed down from the magazine, into a chamber formed in a rotating metal breech-piece, and as soon as the cartridge is chambered this rotates through 90° and the chamber is aligned with the barrel. A percussion firing pin then strikes the cap and the cartridge is fired, leaving no residue of any kind in the chamber. The mechanism – barrel and breech unit – then recoil inside the rifle's casing, during which movement the breech-piece is rotated back so that the chamber is vertical and ready to receive another round to recommence the operating cycle. In automatic fire this sequence is continued so long as the trigger remains pressed. In the three-round burst sequence, however, the operation is entirely different. The first shot is fired as described; but as the mechanism begins its recoil stroke the second round is chambered and fired; recoil continues and the third round is chambered and fired. Only after the third round has been fired is the recoil stroke completed, and thus the firer does not feel any recoil blow until after all three shots have gone, so that the rifle does not begin to rise away from the target until it is too late to affect the flight of the bullets. As a result the three shots fall quite close together, much closer than can be achieved with any other weapon. The rate of fire in the three-round burst mode is about 2,200rds/min, the three shots sounding like one continuous explosion.

The precise details of the internal mechanism have not been made public, particularly the method of sealing the breech. The lack of a metallic cartridge case, which would tend to heat up the chamber very rapidly, has been countered by the adoption of a special propellant which has lifted the 'cook-off threshold' by about 100°C above that found with conventional propellants.

The G11 is scheduled to be issued to selected elements of the German Army in 1990, to be followed by a general issue to first-line formations by the middle of the decade. In 1987 the company announced that they have designed an experimental machine-gun using caseless ammunition, and this is still under development.

G11

GERMANY, DEMOCRATIC REPUBLIC

.22 Rifle KKMPi 69

State arsenals

.22 Rimfire

This is a .22 training rifle designed to approximate closely to the AKM. Although primarily for marksmanship training, photographs indicate that it was widely used for field training and that all initial weapon training is carried out with it. No details of the mechanism are known but it is no doubt a plain blowback weapon, using a special insert inside the magazine for the .22 cartridges.

GREAT BRITAIN

Although it had been realised for some years that the old-style full-power cartridges were far too powerful for what they were actually required to do, few countries had the resources or energy to make a change. In post-war Britain the time seemed right, for the old .303 Lee-Enfield rifles were obsolete, and in the late 1940s the EM2 appeared in small numbers. It was a bullpup rifle firing a 7mm bullet from a short-cased round, and was based on the assumption that 1,000 yards was the maximum likely fighting range. The rifle was a gas-operated selective-fire weapon of highly unconventional appearance for its day. The mechanism was very neat, though complicated, and it fired from a closed bolt. Locking was done by front-pivoted flaps and some trouble was taken to ensure that the design was resistant to dirt and dust. The balance was extremely good, due to the magazine lying behind the trigger grip, and the sight was an optical tube fitted into a fixed carrying handle.

The performance of this unusual rifle was extremely good and it was found to be highly reliable and easily learned. Although formally approved for service it was never put into manufacture, mainly because NATO was not ready for it and political opposition was widespread, particularly in the USA where the concept of a short-case short-range cartridge appeared to be incomprehensible. After much argument NATO chose the 7.62 × 51mm cartridge and the EM2, which could not be converted to this calibre without a major re-design, was abandoned. It should be noted that the L85 rifle (below), although a bullpup, has no relationship whatever with the EM2.

The L1A1 was the standard British service rifle from 1954 until its replacement by the L85A1 in the late 1980s; many are still in use since replacement has not yet been completed. It was adapted from the FN-FAL but there were some minor differences. The dimensions were all changed to Imperial measure to facilitate manufacture in Britain, and spring sizes and material specifications also had to be changed. The resulting rifle, though almost identical to the FAL, does not, therefore, have interchangeability of components. All dimensions and weights are the same as for the FAL.

7mm Rifle, Automatic, No 9 Mark 1 (EM2)

Royal Small Arms Factory, Enfield	
7 × 44mm (.280) British	
Length overall	889mm (35.00in)
Weight empty	3.41kg (7.52lb)
Barrel	623mm (24.50in), 4 grooves, rh
Magazine	20-shot detachable box
Muzzle velocity	771m/sec (2,530ft/sec)

7.62mm Rifle L1A1

Royal Small Arms Factory, Enfield;
Royal Ordnance Factory, Fazakerley

7.62 × 51mm NATO

EM2

L85A1

(see overleaf)

5.56mm Individual Weapon L85A1

Royal Small Arms Factory, Nottingham

5.56 × 45mm NATO

Length overall	785mm (30.90in)
Weight empty	4.98kg (10.98lb) with loaded magazine and sight
Barrel	518mm (20.39in), 6 grooves, rh
Magazine	3-shot detachable box
Rate of fire	650–800rds/min
Muzzle velocity	940m/sec (3,084ft/sec)

The Enfield Individual Weapon was first produced in 4.85mm calibre and submitted to the NATO trials in 1977–79. As a result of this trial the 5.56 × 45mm cartridge was selected as the future NATO standard, and therefore the 4.85mm cartridge is now obsolete. The rifle, however, had been designed with this possibility in mind and conversion to 5.56mm calibre was not difficult. Other changes resulting from the extended and searching NATO trial were incorporated into the design and it was formally issued for service with the British Army in October 1985.

The L85A1 is a completely new departure for RSAF and is a weapon designed from the outset as a battle rifle. The bullpup layout results in a short and handy overall length without losing barrel length, and it is a handy weapon to carry and shoot. It operates by a conventional gas piston system, acting upon a bolt carrier and rotating bolt. The bolt carrier rides on two rods which also carry the return springs. The body and many other parts are steel stampings, and welding and pinning is extensively employed for fastening. The cocking handle is on the right side and has a sliding cover to keep dirt from the interior. There are three positions for the gas regulator, two for firing in normal and adverse conditions and one for grenade-launching (although the British Army does not employ rifle grenades). A special feature of the IW is that it was designed from the start to use an optical sight, the SUSAT (Sight Unit, Small Arm, Trilux) with which excellent accuracy is easily attained. For emergencies, when the SUSAT sight has suffered damage, there is a set of iron sights which fold down for carriage. Infantry units are issued with SUSAT-sighted weapons; support units are issued with iron-sighted weapons. All furniture is of high-impact plastic and much attention was paid to ergonomics in positioning the grips and sights.

It must, however, be said that the first five years of this rifle's service have been disastrous. A number of manufacturing defects showed up in service conditions, and it was not until the closure of the RSAF at Enfield and the setting-up of an entirely new production line, with new computer-controlled machine tools, at the new RSAF Nottingham, that the quality of the production weapons began to improve. It will take some time for the poor reputation gained by the initial issue weapons to be overcome; the only consolation is that the same sort of thing has happened to other military rifles in the past, and they have managed to live down their early reputation and prove their innate reliability. It is to be hoped that the L85A1 will do as well.

5.56mm Cadet Rifle L98A1

Royal Small Arms Factory, Nottingham

5.56 × 45mm NATO

Length overall	775mm (29.72in)
Weight empty	4.10kg (9.04lb)
Barrel	495mm (19.49in), 6 grooves, rh
Magazine	10- or 30-shot detachable box
Muzzle velocity	900m/sec (2,952ft/sec)

This is a modified version of the Enfield Individual Weapon, resembling the L85A1 but with the interior redesigned so as to act as a single-shot repeating rifle. The gas system has been removed, and the weapon must be operated by manually pulling back the cocking handle so as to chamber a round for each shot. This re-design prevents it being converted to automatic operation, though by adapting components of the L85A1 it could be converted to semi-automatic. The SUSAT sight is not fitted, and a two-position aperture rear sight is set into the carrying handle, a blade foresight being fitted. It is normally fitted with a 10-round magazine, though the normal 30-round magazine can also be used. An adapter kit to convert the weapon to fire .22 Rimfire cartridge is available for marksmanship training at low cost.

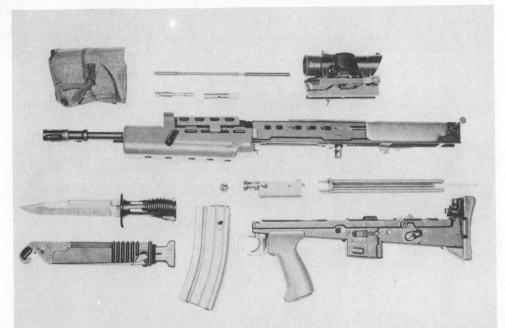

L85A1

HUNGARY

The NGM is more or less the Hungarian equivalent of the Soviet AK-74 assault rifle, but it is chambered for the Western 5.56 × 45mm cartridge and offered for export. The weapon is well-made of good quality materials and the barrel is cold forged and chromium-plated internally. The rifling is to a pitch of one turn in 200mm, a compromise which will deliver accurate shooting with either M193 or SS109 ammunition. The rifle is made only in standard form, with wooden butt and furniture and with selective-fire capability.

5.56mm NGM Assault Rifle

State arsenals	
5.56 × 45mm	
Length overall	935mm (36.81in)
Weight empty	3.18kg (7.01lb)
Barrel	412mm (16.22in), 4 grooves, rh
Magazine	30-shot detachable box
Rate of fire	600rds/min
Muzzle velocity	900m/sec (2,952ft/sec)

INDIA

This is a gas-operated selective-fire assault rifle which is an interesting mixture of features taken from other designs. The receiver and pistol grip show Kalashnikov influence, the fore-end resembles that of the M16, and the forward cocking handle is based on the Heckler & Koch rifles. Nevertheless, these various features have been well combined to produce a well-balanced and attractive weapon. The rifle uses the well-tried operating system of a gas piston driving a bolt carrier and rotating bolt, and the magazine housing has been standardised on the M16 dimensions. The fire selector permits single shots or three-round bursts, but there is no provision for automatic fire. There is also a heavy-barrelled version for use in the squad automatic role.

5.56mm INSAS Assault Rifle

Indian Small Arms Factory, Kanpur	
5.56 × 45mm NATO	
Length overall	990mm (38.97in)
Weight empty	3.20kg (7.05lb)
Barrel	464mm (18.26in)
Magazine	20- or 30-shot detachable box
Muzzle velocity	885m/sec (2,903ft/sec)

GALIL (see overleaf)

ISRAEL

5.6mm Galil Rifle

Israel Military Industries (IMI)	
5.56 × 45mm NATO	
Length, ARM	979mm (38.54in) overall, 742mm (29.21in) with butt folded
Length, SAR	840mm (33.07in) overall, 614mm (24.17in) with butt folded
Weight empty	ARM: 4.35kg (9.59lb); SAR 3.75kg (8.27lb)
Barrel	ARM: 460mm (18.11in); SAR 332mm (13.07in) both 6 grooves, rh
Magazine	35- or 50-shot detachable box
Rate of fire	650rds/min
Muzzle velocity	ARM: 950m/sec (3,117ft/sec); SAR 900m/sec (2.952ft/sec)

The idea for this rifle was born after the 1967 war, when the Israeli Army decided that it needed a lighter and handier rifle than the FN-FAL. The Arab armies had used the AK47 with great success, and IMI decided that the action of that rifle was worth copying. The operating system of the Galil, therefore, owes a lot to its principal military rival, and the first production batch actually used bodies made in Helsinki for the Finnish M62 assault rifle. They may also have used other parts, but the choice of the 5.56mm cartridge meant that most of the internal components had to be redesigned to suit the smaller dimensions.

The basic rifle can be fitted with a wide variety of accessories; a bipod allows steady and accurate shooting and permits automatic fire with reasonable consistency, and it also doubles as a wire-cutter. The flash-suppressor on the muzzle also acts as a grenade-launcher, and every rifle is fitted with luminous night sights. The Israeli Army uses a version with a folding metal butt; for other purchasers there are options of fixed wood or plastic butts. A shortened version of the ARM (the standard rifle) is the SAR (Short Assault Rifle) which differs only in the length of barrel. While the Israeli Galil is in 5.56mm calibre, a version in 7.62 × 51mm chambering is also made for export; this, too, comes in standard and carbine forms. (Data table refers to the 5.56mm model.)

7.62mm Galil Sniper's Rifle

Israel Military Industries (IMI)	
7.62 × 51mm NATO	
Length overall	Stock extended 1,115mm (43.89in); stock folded 840mm (33.0in)
Weight empty	6.4kg (14.11lb)
Barrel	508mm (20.00in) without brake; 4 grooves, rh

This has been developed in conjunction with the Israel Defence Forces to provide an extremely accurate sniping rifle. It begins with the basic Galil rifle mechanism in 7.62mm calibre but there are a number of special features. A bipod is mounted on the fore-end, close to the receiver where it can be easily adjusted by the firer; the barrel is heavier than standard; the telescope sight mount is on the side of the receiver and is particularly robust, and the sight can be mounted and dismounted without disturbing the zero. A Nimrod 6 × 40 telescope sight is provided as standard. The butt folds for convenience in storage and transport, and the cheek-piece and recoil pad are both adjustable. The barrel is fitted with a combined compensator and muzzle brake; this can be removed and replaced by a silencer, for which subsonic ammunition is provided. There is a two-stage trigger, and the rifle's mechanism has been altered so that only semi-automatic fire is possible.

GALIL SNIPER'S RIFLE

Magazine	20-shot detachable box
Muzzle velocity	815m/sec (2,675ft/sec) (FN Match ammunition)

GALIL

AR70/223

P. BERETTA Mod. 70/223 00000 MADE IN ITALY

ITALY

6.5mm Cei-Rigotti Rifle

Officine Glisenti	
6.5 × 52mm Mannlicher-Carcano	
Length overall	1,000mm (39.37in)
Weight empty	4.30kg (9.48lb)
Barrel	483mm (19.00in), 4 grooves, rh
Magazine	10-, 20- or 50-shot detachable box
Muzzle velocity	730m/sec (2,400ft/sec)

7.62mm Rifle BM59

Pietro Beretta SpA	
7.62 × 51mm NATO	
Length overall	1,095mm (43.11in)
Weight empty	4.6kg (10.14lb)
Barrel	490mm (19.29in), 4 grooves, rh
Magazine	20-shot detachable box
Rate of fire	750rds/min
Muzzle velocity	823m/sec (2,700ft/sec)

In 1900 Captain Cei-Rigotti of the Bersagliere invented and constructed a gas-operated selective-fire carbine which attracted considerable interest in European military circles. Gas was led into a cylinder about half-way down the barrel and operated a short-stroke piston from which a tappet curved up to the right-hand side of the barrel. This tappet struck a long operating rod connected to the bolt, and a lug on the rod ran in a cam track cut in the bolt; the reciprocal movement of the rod rotated the bolt, drew it to the rear, pulled it forward again and locked it by final rotation. Locking was achieved by two lugs on the bolt head engaging in recesses in the barrel. The system is very similar to that later adopted by the US M1 carbine and many other designs. A simple change lever gave single shots or automatic fire, and there were different sizes of magazine, up to 50 rounds. The few remaining examples show that the design had several failings, and contemporary reports speak of frequent jams and erratic shooting, although some of this may have been due to the ammunition. The Cei-Rigotti must be considered almost the earliest workable selective-fire rifle and it was unfortunate that no army could be found to take an interest in it for, with a little development work, it would probably have been quite successful. Eventually, despite efforts by the Glisenti firm to find buyers, the rifle had to be abandoned without hope of revival.

After World War Two the Italian Army adopted the US Garand rifle, which was made under licence by Beretta. When NATO adopted the 7.62mm cartridge it was decided to bring the Garand up to date rather than go to the expense of designing a new rifle, and Beretta took the basic Garand and from it developed a modern lightweight selective-fire rifle. The BM59 incorporates the basic mechanism of the Garand, a gas-operated weapon with rotating bolt, but did away with its greatest tactical defect, the eight-round clip loading system. A 20-round box magazine is fitted, which can be charger loaded on the rifle. The firing mechanism has been altered to permit automatic fire and a new trigger group is installed. The barrel is, of course, to 7.62mm calibre, and the gas operating system and return spring have been 'tuned' to the new cartridge. The standard BM59 has a full-length wooden stock, a rubber recoil pad and an optional light bipod. The BM59 Ital TA version, for mountain troops, has a cut-down stock, a pistol grip, a bipod, and a folding skeleton butt. The BM59 Ital Para, for airborne troops, is very similar except that the flash-hider can be removed. A more elaborate version of the standard model, the BM59 Mark 4, has a heavier bipod, a pistol grip, a plastic butt, and a hinged butt-plate, all intended to steady the weapon in automatic fire. (Data table refers to the BM59.)

CEI RIGOTTI

BM59

The Model 70 is a lightweight gas-operated magazine rifle for both full- and semi-automatic fire. It was offered in two forms, the assault rifle designated AR70 and the Special Troops Carbine SC70. The AR70 resembles many other similar rifles in this outline and is made from steel stampings and pressings, with plastic furniture. Extensive use was made of spot welding for the main components, and the removable parts were held by pins and spring catches. An optional light bipod could be fitted, and the muzzle had a combination flash-hider and grenade launcher. A special flip-up grenade sight was fitted which not only raised the sight line but also closed the gas regulator to ensure that the full force of the cartridge was available to drive the grenade. The whole standard of manufacture was very high, as with all Beretta products. The SC70 was very similar in all respects except that it had a folding metal butt-stock. A variant of this was the SC70 Short, which had a 320mm (12.60in) barrel instead of the standard 450mm length. The AR70 system was adopted by Italian Special Forces, Jordan, Malaysia and some other countries. Experience showed that there were some minor defects in the design and Beretta therefore set about developing the 70/90 model (below). (Data table refers to the AR70.)

The 70/90 system (rifle, carbine, short carbine and heavy-barrelled rifle) was developed primarily in response to an Italian Army demand for a new service rifle, but at the same time opportunity was taken to deal with the design defects which had shown up in the 70/223 rifle. In the earlier weapon, for example, the receiver was a pressed-steel rectangle in which the bolt moved on pressed-in rails; service life proved that under extreme conditions this would distort, jamming the bolt; in the 70/90, therefore, the receiver is of trapezoidal section and has steel bolt guide rails welded in place. Like the earlier weapon, the 70/90 uses a gas-operated rotating bolt system. The trigger mechanism allows single shots, three-round bursts or automatic fire, and the design is such that the mechanism can easily be adjusted to give any two of the three options. The receiver is topped by a carrying handle which can be removed to expose a NATO-standard sight mount; holes in the carrying handle allow for the sight line of the iron sights. One of the most unusual features is the retention of the barrel in the receiver by a barrel nut; this is not to facilitate changing the barrel so much as to allow for replacement of the barrel in forward echelons without the need to adjust bolt headspace.

The Carbine SC70/90 differs from the rifle only in having a folding tubular metal butt; the special carbine SCS70/90 had a folding butt and a shorter barrel and does not have any facility for grenade launching. All weapons have an ambidextrous magazine catch which means that with the butts folded, changing magazines is still easily accomplished. The heavy-barrel weapon is intended for use as a squad machine gun and is dealt with in the machine-guns section. The Italian Army stated its intention to run competitive trials in 1984; Beretta produced the 70/90 system in 1985; in July 1990 the rifle was approved for service with the Italian forces. Due to this, figures for the performance of the rifle have never been made public.

5.56mm AR70/223 Rifle

Pietro Beretta SpA

5.56 × 45mm NATO

Length overall	955mm (37.60in)
Weight empty	3.50kg (7.72lb)
Barrel	450mm (17.80in), 4 grooves, rh
Magazine	30-shot detachable box
Rate of fire	650rds/min
Muzzle velocity	950m/sec (3,117ft/sec)

5.56mm 70/90 Assault Rifle

Pietro Beretta SpA

5.56 × 45mm NATO

Length overall	998mm (39.29in)
Weight empty	3.99kg (8.80lb)
Barrel	450mm (17.72in), 6 grooves, rh
Magazine	30-shot detachable box

AR70/223

70/90 ASSAULT RIFLE

JAPAN

7.62mm Rifle Type 64

Howa Machinery Co	
7.62 × 51mm Type 64	
Length overall	990mm (38.97in)
Weight empty	4.40kg (9.70lb)
Barrel	450mm (17.72in), 4 grooves, rh
Magazine	20-shot detachable box
Rate of fire	500rds/min
Muzzle velocity	700m/sec (2,296ft/sec)

Although this rifle is a purely governmental undertaking, the design and manufacture was done by the Howa Machinery Company. The Japanese Defence Force decided that the 7.62 × 51mm NATO cartridge was too powerful for their needs and the Type 64 round uses the same bullet and case but with a reduced propelling charge. It is a perfectly adequate round for its purpose and compares well with the full-power version. The Type 64 rifle can also take the full-power round if necessary, the gas regulator being adjustable to allow for the greater gas pressure. The regulator can also be closed to permit the firing of rifle grenades, the muzzle being formed into a launcher spigot. The rifle is fitted with a bipod which folds under the fore-stock, and the Japanese soldier is taught to use it whenever possible; another aid to accurate shooting is a butt strap hinged to the top of the butt which lies on the shoulder and prevents the butt slipping down during firing. The bolt locking system uses a tipping bolt which rises to lock into the receiver and is lowered and driven back by a conventional gas piston.

KOREA, SOUTH

5.56mm Assault Rifle K2

Daewoo Precision Industries	
5.56 × 45mm NATO	
Length overall	
Weight empty	
Barrel	450mm (17.72in), 4 grooves, rh
Magazine	30-shot detachable box
Rate of fire	
Muzzle velocity	

This is a gas-operated, selective-fire rifle with a folding plastic butt. The gas system uses a long-stroke piston above the barrel, driving a bolt carrier with rotating bolt. The receiver is machined from aluminium alloy forgings, giving a very stiff and robust system. The weapon can fire single shots, three-round bursts or full automatic fire and the barrel is fitted with a muzzle brake and compensator dimensioned so as to function as a grenade-launcher. It is in use by the South Korean Army.

TYPE 64

K2 ASSAULT RIFLE

This resembles the K2 assault rifle, though smaller, but uses an entirely different method of operation. It has the usual bolt carrier and rotating bolt, but the gas is piped back from the barrel and strikes the bolt carrier directly, not through the agency of a piston; it is the same system as used with the M16 rifle. The fire selector gives the same options as the K2 rifle, and the muzzle brake/compensator is much larger so as to reduce the muzzle flash and blast otherwise to be expected with the short barrel.

5.56mm Carbine K1A1

Daewoo Precision Industries	
5.56 × 45mm NATO	
Length overall	
Weight empty	

K1A1 CARBINE

Barrel	250mm (9.84in), 6 grooves, rh
Magazine	30-shot detachable box
Muzzle velocity	

MEXICO

The Mexican-designed Mondragon, conceived in the early 1890s, was one of the earliest semi-automatic rifles to be taken into military service. Manuel Mondragon, granted a United States patent in 1907, was forced to seek a European manufacturer since there were no adequate facilities in Mexico and no US manufacturer was interested; as a result, the weapons were produced by SIG in Switzerland. The Mondragon utilises gas tapped from the barrel to drive an actuating piston to the rear and open the bolt, a now common-place method. Locking was achieved by lugs on the bolt, which was rotated by projections on the bolt operating handle engaging in cam tracks cut into the bolt body; there is a certain amount of resemblance between this and the Schmidt Rubin straight-pull bolt action. As with many automatic designs of the period, it is possible to disconnect the bolt from the gas mechanism and thus turn the rifle into a manually operated straight-pull bolt-action weapon, a proviso often insisted upon by military authorities with small faith in the survival of the automatic system.

As might be expected from SIG the rifles are beautifully made from the finest materials, and there are several separate models. Apart from the development models, which appear to have been made in a number of different calibres including 7mm Spanish and 7.5mm Swiss, the basic model, adopted by the Mexican Army in 1908 (as the 'Fusil Porfiro Diaz, Systema Mondragon, Modelo 1908') was in 7mm Spanish Mauser calibre and had a box magazine into which an eight-shot clip was loaded. At the same time, however, SIG marketed a version with a 20-shot box magazine and a rather spindly bipod, which was intended to serve as a rudimentary light machine-gun, though it seems that sales did not justify very large production. With the outbreak of war in 1914 some of the Mondragon rifles were still in SIG's hands and these were bought by Germany for issue to aviators as the 'Fliegerselbstladekarabine Modell 1915'. Most of these were fitted with a 30-shot helical 'snail' magazine, similar in principle to that used on the Luger pistol and Bergmann submachine-gun. Some of the rifles were sent for infantry use but the mud of the Western Front soon defeated them and the survivors were withdrawn.

7mm Mondragon Rifle

Schweizerische Industrie Gesellschaft	
7 × 57mm Spanish Mauser	
Length overall	1,105mm (43.50in)
Weight empty	4.18kg (9.25lb)
Barrel	577mm (22.75in), 4 grooves, rh
Magazine	8-shot clip-loaded integral box
Muzzle velocity	760m/sec (2,500ft/sec)

MONDRAGON

SINGAPORE

5.56mm Assault Rifle SAR80

Chartered Firearms Industries Pte Ltd	
5.56 × 45mm NATO	
Length overall	970mm (38.18in)
Weight empty	3.17kg (7.00lb)
Barrel	459mm (18.07in), 6 grooves, rh
Magazine	30-shot detachable box
Rate of fire	700rds/min
Muzzle velocity	970m/sec (3,182ft/sec)

5.56mm Assault Rifle SR 88

Chartered Firearms Industries Pte Ltd	
5.56 × 45mm NATO	
Length overall	970mm (38.18in)
Weight empty	3.66kg (8.07lb)
Barrel	459mm (18.07in), 6 grooves, rh
Magazine	20- or 30-shot detachable box
Rate of fire	750rds/min
Muzzle velocity	970m/sec (3,182ft/sec)

Originally known as 'Chartered Industries of Singapore', this company was set up to manufacture the M16 rifle under licence from Colt, and as a result of this experience decided to design and manufacture a locally developed weapon. The actual design was done by Sterling Armaments of England, and the prototypes were made in Singapore in 1978. After trials and modifications, production began in 1980. The SAR80 is a conventional gas-operated rotating bolt selective fire weapon. The barrel has a flash-suppressor which doubles as a grenade-launcher. Barrel, bolt and butt are almost in a straight line, reducing jump and making the rifle very controllable in automatic fire. It can be easily field-stripped by simply hinging down the lower part of the receiver and extracting the bolt carrier, bolt, return springs and guide rod assembly. The magazine is of the M16 pattern. A folding butt model is available for paratroops and armoured vehicle crews.

This is a lightweight gas-operated rifle which can be considered as an improved version of the SAR80. The same gas-operated rotating bolt system is used, housed in a cast aluminium alloy receiver. The gas system is chrome-plated throughout, giving high resistance to fouling and wear. The stock is of fibre-glass reinforced nylon and the tubular skeleton butt is fixed, though there is an optional folding butt which folds to the right side of the receiver. The butt can be adjusted for length by changing the butt pad, and it can be removed for greater compactness. The barrel is fitted to the receiver by a locknut system which simplified barrel replacement. Other features include luminous night sights, a carrying handle, an arctic trigger unit, and provision for mounting optical and electro-optical sights. A selector for full automatic or three-round bursts can be fitted, as desired, and the handguard is so designed that the US M203 grenade-launcher can be fitted without requiring any dismantling.

SAR 80

SR 88

SOUTH AFRICA

The R4 rifle is the standard South African infantry arm and is basically a copy of the Israeli Galil with some small modifications to better suit it to South African service. The butt is somewhat longer and made from fibre-glass filled nylon, since the average South African soldier is longer in the arms and in the climatic conditions a steel butt gets too hot to hold. The handguard has been strengthened and a bipod fitted, and there are some minor changes in the mechanical parts to facilitate manufacture. The magazine is of nylon/glass-fibre, which has little mechanical advantage but is cheaper to manufacture and this has reduced running costs due to the abandonment of magazines in combat. The R5 rifle is the same as the R4 but smaller, having a shorter barrel and no bipod. Semi-automatic versions of the R4 and R5 are also manufactured for commercial sale. (Data table refers to the R4.)

5.56mm Assault Rifles R4 and R5

Lyttleton Engineering Co	
5.56 × 45mm NATO	
Length overall	1,005mm (39.57in) butt extended; 740mm (29.13in) butt folded
Weight empty	4.30kg (9.48lb)
Barrel	460mm (18.11in), 6 grooves, rh
Magazine	35- or 50-shot detachable box
Rate of fire	650rds/min
Muzzle velocity	980m/sec (3,215ft/sec)

R4 ASSAULT RIFLE

SPAIN

This rifle originated in Germany during World War Two, as the Mauser StG45, a design which never got beyond prototype stage. The designers moved to Spain at the end of the war to work for CETME (Centro de Estudios Tecnicos de Materiales Especiales) and continued to develop the unique roller-locked delayed-action breech mechanism devised for the Mauser, eventually producing a 7.92mm rifle firing a special short cartridge with lightweight bullet.

7.62mm CETME Rifle Model 58 Series

Empresa Nacional 'Santa Barbara'	
7.92 × 51mm	
Length overall	1,015mm (39.96in)
Weight empty	4.5kg (9.92lb) with bipod and metal handguard
Barrel	450mm (17.72in), 4 grooves, rh
Magazine	20-shot detachable box
Rate of fire	600rds/min
Muzzle velocity	780m/sec (2,560ft/sec)

CETME MODEL 58

Through a Dutch licensee this rifle was offered to the German Army in the late 1950s, but they requested a 7.62mm calibre. After that the development passed to Heckler & Koch and resulted in the G3, but the design team in Spain also studied the 7.62mm conversion and eventually developed a rifle firing a reduced-charge 7.62 × 51mm round. This entered Spanish service as the CETME Model 58 in 1958. The Model 58 is made of stamped and formed metal in order to simplify manufacture, and uses the same delayed blowback system as the H&K rifles. In order to reduce problems due to cases sticking in the chamber, the walls of the chamber are fluted so as to float the case on a layer of gas and ease extraction. Automatic fire is from an open bolt, single shots from a closed bolt. A light bipod is permanently fitted and it folds back to form a handguard on the early model. Later models had tubular bipods or wooden handguards without bipods.

In 1974 the Spanish Army decided to adopt the full-power 7.62 × 51mm NATO cartridge; this necessitated some modification to the Model 58, turning it into the Model C. In general the rifle was the same but certain components needed to be strengthened to cope with the heavier charge. (Data table refers to the Model C.)

5.56mm CETME Rifle Models L and LC

This is a 5.56mm assault rifle which is basically a scaled-down CETME Model C, using the same roller-locked delayed blowback system. There are two versions, the Model L in standard length and the Model LC in carbine length. A 20-shot magazine was used at first but this was later changed and the magazine housing is to NATO standard and will accept any 30-shot M16-type magazine. Similarly, the sights were originally a four-position type but were soon changed to a simple flip-over graduated for 200m and 400m, which caters for most applications. First models had a three-round burst mechanism but this was soon removed, since it was found that it was easy to 'squeeze off' three rounds at automatic by trigger control instead of requiring an additional piece of mechanism. The Models L and LC entered service with selected Spanish Army units in 1988.

Empresa Nacional 'Santa Barbara'	
5.56 × 45mm NATO	
Model L:	
Length overall	925mm (36.40in)
Weight empty	3.40kg (7.49lb)
Barrel	400mm (15.75in), 6 grooves, rh
Magazine	30-shot detachable box
Rate of fire	700rds/min
Muzzle velocity	875m/sec (2,878ft/sec)

Model LC:			
Length overall	860mm (33.85in) butt extended, 665mm (26.18in) butt folded	Magazine	30-shot detachable box
		Rate of fire	750rds/min
Weight empty	3.22kg (7.10lb)	Muzzle velocity	832m/sec (2,730ft/sec)
Barrel	320mm (12.60in), 6 grooves, rh		

CETME MODEL L

SWEDEN

This is a modification of the Browning Automatic Rifle (BAR) developed in Sweden prior to World War Two. The differences are in the calibre and in the use of a quick-change barrel. The barrel is secured by a simple latch on the front of the receiver, and when this is unlocked the barrel can be lifted clear by the carrying handle. To permit this, the usual large forward hand grip of the BAR has been removed and the gun has to be carried by grasping the folded bipod legs. It is more of a mchine-gun than was its parent, although the limited magazine capacity still detracts from its use in this role. It has been phased out of first-line Swedish service but is still held by reserve units.

6.5mm Automatic Rifle Model 37

Carl Gustav Stads Gevarsfaktori	
6.5 × 55mm Swedish	
Length overall	1,168mm (46.00in)
Weight empty	9.53kg (21.00lb)
Barrel	610mm (24.00in), 6 grooves, rh
Magazine	20-shot detachable box
Rate of fire	500rds/min
Muzzle velocity	745m/sec (2,445ft/sec)

The AG42 was designed in Sweden by Erik Eklund and was introduced into the Swedish Army in less than a year after it left the drawing-board, an extraordinary feat by any standards. The basic feature of the Eklund-Ljungmann system was unusual when first introduced, though it has gained widespread acceptance since; the usual gas piston assembly was dispensed with in favour of a simple direct gas system in which the gas tapped from the barrel is allowed to strike the bolt, thus doing away with the usual piston and rod devices used to convert gas pressure into mechanical movement. The gas strikes the face of the bolt carrier which is thus blown back and rotates the bolt by suitably shaped cam tracks. The recoil spring them returns the bolt to load a fresh round and lock into the chamber. The direct gas system has since been used with success on the Stoner-designed AR10 and AR15/M16 rifles.

After adopting the AG42 the Swedes found deficiencies, which is not surprising considering the speed with which it went into production, and so a modified pattern, the AG42B, was introduced in 1953. The trigger mechanism and the extractor were modified, the foresight strengthened, the magazine modified, and stainless steel was used for the gas tube.

Apart from the Swedish patterns, the rifle was also manufactured in Denmark by Madsen; this version had a longer gas tube coiled around the barrel, and although this lessened the fouling of the bolt mechanism, the tube itself was difficult to clean. The Danish Army were not persuaded to adopt the rifle and Madsen soon ceased production. The AG42 pattern was also manufactured in Egypt, chambered for the 7.92mm Mauser cartridge, where it was known as the 'Hakim'. Some of these were later chambered for the 7.62 × 51mm cartridge, but all are now obsolete.

6.5mm Ljungmann Rifle Model AG42

Carl Gustav Stads Gevarsfaktori	
6.5 × 55mm Swedish	
Length overall	1,215mm (47.80in)
Weight empty	4.74kg (10.45lb)
Barrel	623mm (24.52in), 6 grooves, rh
Magazine	10-shot detachable box
Muzzle velocity	745m/sec (2,445ft/sec)

MODEL 37

LJUNGMANN AG42

5.56mm Assault Rifle AK5

FFV Ordnance	
5.56 × 45mm NATO	
Length overall	1,008mm (39.68in) butt extended; 753mm (29.65in) butt folded
Weight empty	3.90kg (8.60lb)
Barrel	450mm (17.72in), 6 grooves, rh
Magazine	30-shot detachable box
Rate of fire	650rds/min
Muzzle velocity	930m/sec (3,050ft/sec)

The AG42 was superseded by the H&K G3 rifle in 7.62mm calibre, and in the mid-1970s the Swedish Army began seeking a new 5.56mm assault rifle. All existing weapons were tested and the choice finally lay between a Galil made under licence or an FN-FNC, also under licence. The FNC was chosen in 1980 as it had 'developable characteristics', and various modifications to the original FN design were developed. Small changes were made to almost every part of the rifle, but the end result was still, mechanically, the FNC with such changes as a larger trigger and guard for gloved hands, a fatter and deeply-incised handguard for better grip, different sights, a larger cocking handle, removal of the three-round burst facility and a dark green baked enamel finish. The AK5 was introduced into Swedish Army service in 1984.

SWITZERLAND

7.5mm Assault Rifle Stgw 57

Schweizerische Industrie Gesellschaft	
7.5 × 54mm Swiss	
Length overall	1,105mm (43.50in)
Weight empty	5.55kg (12.24lb)
Barrel	583mm (23.00in), 4 grooves, rh
Magazine	24-shot detachable box
Rate of fire	450–500rds/min
Muzzle velocity	760m/sec (2,494ft/sec)

The early history of the Stgw57 is not entirely clear, though it appears that SIG were aware of the Mauser StG45 design and made their own version of the two-part bolt and roller-locked delayed blowback system which was adopted by CETME and by Heckler & Koch. In the Swiss version there is a unique variation; the rifle chamber is fluted to ease extraction of the empty case, and some of the flutes extend back to the mouth of the chamber. On firing gas passes down these flutes and passes through two holes in the bolt face, allowing the gas pressure to strike the bolt body and thus assist the rearward thrust of the cartridge in actuating the bolt mechanism. Another difference is that the Stgw57 fires from a closed bolt at all times. The Stgw57 has a permanently attached bipod, which can be located anywhere along the barrel jacket to suit the firer. There is an integral grenade-launcher on the muzzle, and the butt has a rubber recoil pad. The sights fold flat when not in use. It is heavy by modern standards but is exceptionally accurate and very reliable under extreme conditions.

AK5

Stgw57

The SIG 510 series of rifles was developed from the Stgw57 and can be considered as the commercial variant of the Swiss service weapon. The same system of delayed blowback action is used, the significant change being that of calibre, a change to 7.62mm NATO. With this change the opportunity was taken of improving the weapon in several minor aspects and the result was of a very high standard. From a technical standpoint the SG 510 was probably the best 7.62mm selective-fire rifle ever made, but such quality meant a high price. Moreover, it appeared in the market after other designs had made their mark, and thus its use has been limited to the Swiss Army and to a few African and South American states. There were a number of variant models; the 510-1 was almost identical to the Stgw57 except for the change of calibre; the 510-2 was to the same design but lighter; the 510-3 was among the first West European designs to be chambered for the 7.62 × 39mm Soviet round, in an attempt to attract sales from countries already committed to that cartridge; and the 510-4 was the final, perfected, design, using a wooden butt, a small wooden fore-end, and chambered for the 7.62mm NATO round. The 510-3 failed to attract many customers and few were made; the 510-4 is currently in use by the Swiss Army and by Chile and Bolivia. (Data table refers to the SG 510-4.)

The SG 530 started life as a scaled-down SG 510 chambered for the 5.56mm cartridge, but it was soon found that the 5.56 round was not happy with the SIG delayed blowback system and the weapon was redesigned to use a gas piston action. The piston acted upon the two-part breech-block to withdraw the rollers and then open the breech, which was an unnecessary complication but saved a total redesign. The rifles were neat and well-made but they failed to attract any sales since they appeared in the late 1960s when most European armies were waiting to see which way the wind blew before they committed themselves to any new calibre.

7.62mm Assault Rifle SG 510

Schweizerische Industrie Gesellschaft

7.62 × 51mm NATO

Length overall	1,016mm (40.00in)
Weight empty	4.25kg (9.37lb)
Barrel	505mm (19.80in), 4 grooves, rh
Magazine	20-shot detachable box
Rate of fire	500–650rds/min
Muzzle velocity	790m/sec (2,592ft/sec)

5.56mm Assault Rifle SG 530-1

Schweizerische Industrie Gesellschaft

5.56 × 45mm NATO

Length overall	953mm (37.52in)
Weight empty	3.27kg (7.21lb)
Barrel	391mm (15.39in),
Magazine	30-shot detachable box
Rate of fire	600rds/min
Muzzle velocity	877m/sec (2,877ft/sec)

SG 510-4

SG 530-1

5.56mm Assault Rifle SG 540

Schweizerische Industrie Gesellschaft Manurhin	
Length overall	950mm (37.40in)
Weight empty	3.26kg (7.19lb)
Barrel	460mm (18.11in), 6 grooves, rh
Magazine	20- or 30-shot detachable box
Rate of fire	650–800rds/min
Muzzle velocity	980m/sec (3,215ft/sec)

5.56mm Assault Rifle SG 550 and SG 551

SIG Swiss Industrial Company	
5.56 × 45mm NATO	
SG 550:	
Length overall	998mm (39.29in) butt extended; 772mm (30.39in) butt folded
Weight empty	4.1kg (9.04lb) with magazine & bipod
Barrel	528mm (20.79in), 6 grooves, rh
Magazine	20- or 30-shot detachable box
Rate of fire	700rds/min
Muzzle velocity	995m/sec (3,265ft/sec)
SG 551:	
Length overall	827mm (32.56in) butt extended; 601mm (23.66in) butt folded
Weight empty	3.5kg (7.71lb)
Barrel	372mm (14.64in), 6 grooves, rh
Magazine	20- or 30-shot detachable box
Rate of fire	700rds/min
Muzzle velocity	915m/sec (3,000ft/sec)

One of the faults of the SG 530 was its high price, and SIG set about designing a new 5.56mm rifle with a less complicated breech mechanism, adopting the familiar bolt carrier and rotating bolt system. Stampings and castings are used and the weapon is much easier and cheaper to make than its forerunners. It is a selective-fire weapon, with a three-round burst facility which is a separate unit and can be installed or removed without tools and without affecting the basic operation of the firing mechanism. Various accessories are supplied, including bipods, telescope sights and bayonets of tubular or conventional type. The muzzle has a combined flash-suppressor/compensator which doubles as a grenade-launcher, and a gas regulator on the front of the gas cylinder allows for two degrees of opening and a closed position for grenade-launching. The SG 540 was manufactured in Switzerland, and was also licensed to Manurhin of France, who supplied large numbers to the French Army to familiarise them with the 5.56mm calibre prior to the general issue of the FA-MAS rifle. It has been widely exported by both SIG and Manurhin and is in use in 17 countries in Africa, South America and the Middle East.

A variant model, the SG 542, was developed in 7.62 × 51mm calibre, but this appears never to have been produced in quantity, the 5.56mm weapon proving more attractive to purchasers. The SG 543 is a short, folding-butt version of the SG 540. (Data table refers to the SG 540.)

This rifle was developed in response to a Swiss Army requirement for a 5.56mm rifle to replace the 7.5mm Stgw57. Development took place in 1979–80 in competition with a design from the Swiss Federal Arms factory, and in 1983 the SG 550 was selected. Shortly afterwards it was announced that due to funds being required for the provision of tanks and other armoured vehicles, the issue of the new rifle would be delayed. Production eventually began in 1986 and it is now in service as the Stgw90. The design paid careful attention to weight saving, using plastics for the butt, handguard and magazine; the latter is transparent, so that the ammunition can be easily checked, and is provided with studs and lugs so that two or more magazines can be clipped together for rapid changing. The butt can be folded to one side and even when this is done the weapon is still well-balanced. There is a three-round burst mechanism, and the sights are provided with luminous dots for use in poor light. There is an integral sight mount which accepts Swiss telescope and electro-optical sights, though this mount can be provided to NATO standard if required. The SG 551 is a short carbine version of the rifle; it is mechanically identical except for its size.

SG 550

SG 540

TAIWAN

This rifle is similar to the M16 and is made in Taiwan, probably on machinery installed there for M16 manufacture. The lower receiver is a copy of that of the M16A1, while the bolt assembly and gas piston are those of the AR-18. The prototypes used stamped steel receivers, but production models have adopted machined aluminium construction. The principal missing feature of the M16 is the carrying handle, and the Type 65 uses a substantial rear sight bracket in the position occupied by the rear of the M16 handle. There is a very long plastic handguard, and a bipod can be fitted beneath the foresight. A later modified version of the Type 65 has adopted the gas tube system of the M16 in place of a piston and has also simplified the bolt assembly. This model uses a transparent plastic magazine and is understood to have a slightly higher rate of automatic fire. The final production model, the Type 65K2, has a harder buffer casing, better heat insulation under the handguard, and the twist of rifling is one turn in 12in to accommodate the SS109/NATO standard cartridge.

5.56mm Assault Rifle Type 65

Hsing-Hua Arsenal	
5.56 × 45mm NATO	
Length overall	990mm (38.97in)
Weight empty	3.17kg (6.99lb)
Barrel	508mm (20.00in), 4 grooves, rh
Magazine	20- or 30-shot detachable box
Rate of fire	750rds/min
Muzzle velocity	990m/sec (3,248ft/sec)

USA

After studying the actions in France during 1916/17, the US Army came to the conclusion that the most dangerous time for the infantryman was during his advance across No Man's Land, when the covering fire had stopped and the enemy was alert. With some urging from the French, the US authorities decided that the best solution would be to equip every man with an automatic rifle and have him fire from the hip as he advanced, so covering the area with bullets and making it most hazardous for any enemy to poke his head over the parapet of his trench. This was termed 'Walking Fire' and it is a theory which has re-appeared at various times since.

The prospect of producing an automatic rifle for every soldier was out of the question, and since the man would normally require a bolt-action rifle for other occasions the problem was a difficult one. It was eventually solved by John Pedersen, at that time working as a designer for Remington. He devised a method of removing the bolt from the standard M1903 Springfield rifle and replacing it with a simple blowback device fitted with its own magazine and a short barrel which, outwardly, resembled a .30 M1906 cartridge case. This fitted into the chamber of the rifle, after the bolt was removed, with the magazine protruding obliquely to one side and thus, in fifteen seconds, the soldier had transformed his manual rifle into a species of submachine-gun or automatic rifle. The cartridge was specially designed by Pedersen to suit the device and has never been used in any other weapon; it resembles a lengthened .32 ACP cartridge in appearance.

.30 Pedersen Device (.30 Self-loading Pistol M1918)

Remington Arms – Union Metallic Cartridge Co	
.30in M1918	

PEDERSEN DEVICE

The M1903 rifle, when altered to accept the device (principally by cutting an ejection hole in the receiver), became the 'Rifle, Magazine, Caliber .30, M1903 Mark 1' and some 65,000 of these devices (each with a special holster and two pouches of magazines sufficient to give each man 400 rounds, and the necessary converted rifles) were produced by Remington in conditions of the utmost secrecy in 1918 so as to be ready for the Allied 1919 spring offensive. The war then ended, and a more leisurely evaluation of the device concluded that it was not so desirable as first thought. Soldiers who used the device almost invariably lost the bolt, or, if using the rifle normally, lost or damaged the Pedersen device. Moreover the claimed 15-second changeover only held good in ideal conditions; in darkness, wet or cold the time increased enormously. In the middle 1920s the device was sentenced obsolete and almost the entire stock was broken up under military supervision. Although the Pedersen device was primarily made for the US M1903 rifle, a number were also made for the M1917 Enfield rifle for trial purposes. There is also evidence that a few were made for testing in the French M07/15 and Russian M1891 rifles, both of which were made by Remington under military contracts.

.30 Browning Automatic Rifle (BAR)

Colt's Patent Firearms Mfg Co; Winchester Repeating Arms Co; Marlin-Rockwell Corp

.30in M1906

The Browning Automatic Rifle (BAR) was another weapon which arose from the concept of 'Walking Fire', an idea urged upon the Americans by the French Army. The weapon never entirely lived up to the designer's hopes; neither a rifle nor a machine-gun, it fell between the two. As a rifle it was too heavy and could not be fired from the shoulder with any accuracy as it vibrated from the forward movement of the bolt. Set for automatic fire it was too light and moved excessively, and the small magazine demanded frequent reloading. For its day, though, it was a brilliant design produced in record time by John Browning, and it was bought and used by many countries around the world. It was the standard squad light automatic of the US infantry during World War Two and saw use in every theatre of war. It was also supplied in considerable numbers to the British Home Guard.

The BAR is a gas-operated weapon, using a piston moving in a cylinder below the barrel. This is linked to the bolt, which has a separate bolt lock which is cammed upwards as the bolt closes and wedges in front of a recess in the roof of the receiver; this is why the BAR had a characteristic 'hump' on the top of the receiver just in front of the rear sight, to allow space for the bolt to move up. The weapon fires from an open bolt, and the mechanism is extremely complicated; this, combined with the machined steel receiver, made the Browning slow and expensive to build but also made it virtually unbreakable and incapable of wearing out.

The World War One version had a selector allowing single shots or automatic fire; this was later modified so that there was no provision for single shots but two rates of automatic fire, 350 or 550rds/min. The US Marine Corps preferred to have single shots available and therefore modified many of their weapons back to the old standard. As a result of this and also of slight modifications made by other countries which adopted the weapon, the varieties and sub-varieties of the BAR are legion. The US forces abandoned the BAR in the middle 1950s, though it was retained in reserve stocks for several years; it survived in smaller countries until the late 1970s, but so far as we can determine it is no longer in use by any army.

BROWNING AUTOMATIC RIFLE

The M1918 BAR is fitted with a smooth tapered barrel, and the stock has a swivel between the pistol grip and the toe of the butt. No bipod was fitted.

US Automatic Rifle, Cal .30, M1918

Length overall	1,219mm (48.00in)
Weight empty	7.28kg (16.00lb)
Barrel	610mm (24.00in), 4 grooves, rh
Magazine	20-shot detachable box
Rate of fire	500rds/min
Muzzle velocity	807m/sec (2,650ft/sec)

The M1918A1 shares the barrel and stock design of the M1918, with a double butt plate, the upper section of which can be hinged up to lie on the firer's shoulder and prevent the butt slipping down during firing. A hinged bipod is attached to the gas cylinder just forward of the wooden fore-end. The M1918A1 weighed about 8.30kg (18.25lb).

US Automatic Rifle, Cal .30, M1918A1

The M1918A2 appeared shortly before World War Two and had a shorter fore-end with an internal metal plate to shield the recoil spring from barrel heat. The bipod, which had skids instead of spikes, was attached to the flash hider, though in later production it was moved back to the gas cylinder. As originally made it had a monopod or 'stock rest' attached to a hole in the butt, though this was soon abandoned. The single-shot mechanism was removed and replaced by the dual rate of fire mechanism.

US Automatic Rifle, Cal .30, M1918A2

A short-lived variant of the M1918 types with a finned barrel to improve cooling and a sling swivel on the left side of the stock. A bipod could be fitted and a wide groove around the butt was intended for the stock support or monopod. Intended for cavalry use, few were made and it was declared obsolete in 1940.

US Automatic Rifle, Cal .30, M1922

The M1 rifle has the distinction of being the first self-loading rifle to be adopted as a standard weapon; this took place in 1932 and the rifle actually began issue in 1936, and by 1941 a major proportion of the American regular army had it as their basic arm. Very large numbers had been made by 1945, and by the time manufacture ended in the 1950s, some 5.5 million had been made. Garands were still in regular service in Vietnam in 1963, and many are still no doubt in use in various parts of Asia. They were made under licence by Beretta for the Italian Army and also for Indonesia.

The rifle is simple and robust; it is not particularly light, and the forestock is somewhat bulky for a small hand, but by the standards of its day the weight was reasonable enough. It operates by gas action, using a piston beneath the barrel which terminates in an 'operating rod' with a cam groove interacting with a stud on the bolt. As the rod is driven back, so the groove rotates and then withdraws the bolt; a spring then returns the rod, drawing the bolt forward to chamber a fresh round and rotate to lock. Firing is performed by an ingenious and robust hammer mechanism which has been widely copied in subsequent years.

The magazine held only eight rounds and did not project beneath the stock; this had the advantage of smoothing the contours but restricted the magazine capacity. Another criticism of the Garand, the major one, was the loading system, by a clip of eight rounds. Single rounds could not be loaded, it was an eight-round clip or nothing. The spent clip was automatically ejected after the last round had been fired, making a distinctive sound which sometimes led to fatal results in close-quarter fighting. But these were small matters, and the main thing was

.30in US Rifle M1 (Garand)

Springfield Armory;
Winchester Repeating Arms Co;
Harrington & Richardson Arms Co;
International Harvester Corp

.30 M1906	
Length overall	1,103mm (43.50in)
Weight empty	4.37kg (9.5lb)
Barrel	610mm (24.00in), 4 grooves, rh
Magazine	8-shot internal box
Muzzle velocity	853m/sec (2,800ft/sec)

GARAND M1

that the US Army carried a self-loading rifle throughout World War Two.

US Rifle, Cal .30, M1E1. A slight variation of the standard M1, with modifications to the operating mechanism and with a more gradual cam angle in the operating rod. Few were made.

US Rifle, Cal .30, M1E2. The first version of the M1 rifle adapted for a telescope sight; an International Industries telescope was fitted by means of a mount. The M1E2 was strictly an experimental issue and was rapidly replaced by the M1E7.

US Rifle, Cal .30, M1E3. Another experimental weapon, intended to make the operation more smooth; a roller bearing was attached to the bolt cam lug and the operating angle of the cam path was changed.

US Rifle, Cal .30, M1E4. An experimental rifle which was designed to try and achieve a less violent operation by introducing a time-lag between the tapping of the gas and the opening of the bolt; an expansion chamber was introduced into the gas system.

US Rifle, Cal .30, M1E5. This was a shortened version of the M1 rifle, with a folding stock and with the barrel shortened to 457mm (18in); the accuracy was unimpaired but the flash and muzzle blast were excessive.

US Rifle, Cal .30, M1E6. An experimental sniping rifle in which the telescope was offset so that the iron sights could still be used in an emergency.

US Rifle, Cal .30, M1E7 (Sniper's Rifle M1C). One of the issue sniping rifles, the M1E6 was fitted either with the telescope Sight M73 (a Lyman Alaskan) or the Sight M73B1 (a Weaver 330). A detachable leather cheek-piece was fitted to the stock and a flash-suppressor was added in 1945. The M1E7 was re-named the M1C in June 1944.

US Rifle, Cal .30, M1E8 (Sniper's Rifle M1D). The second issue version of the M1 intended for sniping, the M1E8 was fitted with the Sight M73 in a block mount, in which guise it was known as the Sight M81 (with crosswires) or the Sight M82 (with a tapered post aiming mark). A Sight M84 was also issued. The M1E8 was re-named the M1D in June 1944.

US Rifle, Cal .30, M1E9. An experimental variant of the M1E4, with an alteration made to the gas expansion system in which the gas piston served as a tappet for the operating rod. It was hoped by this to avoid the overheating troubles experienced with the M1E4.

US Rifle, Cal .30, T26. This rifle combined the action of the M1E5 with a shortened M1 stock, and a quantity were ordered in 1945 for use in the Pacific Theatre; the order was later rescinded when the war ended.

.30in Johnson Rifle M1941

Cranston Arms Co	
.30 M1906	
Length overall	1,156mm (45.50in)
Weight empty	4.31kg (9.5lb)
Barrel	558mm (22.00in), 4 grooves, rh
Magazine	10-shot detachable rotary box
Muzzle velocity	807m/sec (2,650ft/sec)

The Johnson rifle was designed shortly before World War Two as a light military weapon and was tested extensively by the US Army and Marine Corps. Neither accepted it, which is hardly surprising since the Garand M1 had just been put into mass production, but in the difficult days of 1941, when rifles were in short supply, the Marine Corps bought several thousand for their Special Forces and especially for their parachutists. The Dutch also bought a quantity for their East Indies forces. With the Japanese occupation of the East Indies, and as Garand production hit its peak, the Johnson fought a losing battle for acceptance. It was retained only for the OSS and similar specialised forces. The Johnson was recoil-operated, one of the few such designs to be accepted by any army. It had several unusual features, including a rotary magazine with its lips machined as part of the receiver; this was less prone to damage than a removable magazine and could be loaded or emptied with the bolt closed and the weapon safe. The barrel was largely unsupported and thus rather vulnerable, but it could be easily dismounted and was thus easier for a parachutist to carry. In service use the Johnson proved to be less reliable than was acceptable, and throughout the war the design was continually modified, though never achieving perfection before production ended in 1945.

9mm Smith & Wesson Light Rifle M1940

Smith & Wesson Arms Co	
9 × 19mm Parabellum	
Length overall	845mm (33.25in)
Weight empty	3.92kg (8.64lb)

Smith & Wesson's self-loading carbine has a very clouded history. It was developed in 1939 as a possible police weapon and in 1940 was offered for trials to the British. The M1940 was a simple blowback weapon, and although of superior finish its only unusual feature lay in the magazine housing; this fixed and wide component not only accepted the magazine but also acted as a forward hand grip and the rear half contained a chute down which the empty cases were ejected. Britain rejected it on the grounds of fragility and expense, especially as lighter and cheaper submachine-guns had become available. The principal cause of trouble lay in the ammunition, for the service 9mm round was more powerful than the cartridge for which the

JOHNSON M1941

M1940 had been designed, and a string of breakages ensued. A modified version was developed as the Mark 2, and small numbers were taken by the Royal Navy in 1941–42; there is no record of the carbine's formal approval for British service, though it is recorded that in 1942 the Royal Small Arms Factory at Enfield Lock designed a 'Butt, Folding, Mark 2' for the 'Carbine, Self-loading, Smith & Wesson, 9mm'. It seems that a version in .45 ACP calibre was briefly mooted, but none was ever made. Fully automatic versions of the basic design were also considered, though none progressed beyond prototype stage.

The Reising Model 60 resembles the Model 50 submachine-gun and is virtually the same weapon with an extended barrel and with the mechanism modified to restrict operation to single shots; like the Model 50 it operated on a delayed blowback system, the bolt being delayed by an arm engaged in a recess in the receiver. The Model 60 was developed primarily as a police weapon; since it fired a pistol cartridge it found no application as a military weapon and spent its life in the hands of security guards and police in the USA during World War Two.

The Carbine, Caliber .30, M1, the most prolific American weapon of World War Two, began as a 1938 request for a light rifle suitable for arming clerks, cooks, bakers, drivers, mortarmen, machine-gunners and similar troops. The request was refused but, resubmitted in 1940, it met with a more favourable response. In October 1940 specifications were issued to 25 manufacturers, though their work was delayed until Winchester had produced a suitable cartridge. This was developed to another military specification, with a 110-grain bullet giving a muzzle velocity of 1,860ft/sec in an 18in barrel. Tests began in May 1941 after some 11 different makers had submitted designs, among them a Garand design from Springfield Armory. Some were rejected on the spot, others showed sufficient promise for their makers to be given the chance to modify them and remedy defects. A final trial took place in September 1941, resulting in the adoption of the Winchester design.

Contrary to accepted legend, 'Carbine' Williams had little or nothing to do with the design of this weapon. It had actually begun early in 1940 as a spare-time occupation by two employees in the Winchester tool-room; it had attracted the attention of Mr. Pugsley, the general manager, who permitted them to continue when nothing better was at hand. When the military request appeared in 1941, Pugsley recalled these two and their rifle, called them up and instructed them to modify their design in accordance with the specification as fast as possible. Since the Williams gas-tappet was used in the design, it was felt politic, and good propaganda, to attribute the whole design to Williams, from which the legend arose. It was this early in-house work which enabled Winchester to produce a tested and reliable weapon in the short time available.

The M1 carbine was a semi-automatic light rifle using a unique operating system for its day. A gas port in the barrel leads to a chamber containing a tappet, or short-stroke piston; when impelled by a rush of gas, this tappet is driven back violently for about 8mm, and the end outside the gas chamber, in contact with the weapon's operating rod, drives the rod backwards. This operates the bolt, through a cam and stud similar to the Garand, and rotates and opens it. A return spring then drives the slide back into contact with the tappet, so drawing the bolt forward to reload and close. A hammer mechanism is left cocked. (Data refers to Carbine M1.)

Barrel	247mm (9.72in), 6 grooves, rh
Magazine	20-shot detachable box
Muzzle velocity	378m/sec (1,240ft/sec)

.45 Reising Carbine M60

Harrington & Richardson Arms Co

.45 ACP

.30 US Carbines

Saginaw Steering Gear Div of General Motors;
Inland Manufacturing Div of General Motors;
International Business Machine Corp;
National Postal Meter Corp;
Quality Hardware & Machine Co;
Rochester Defense Corp;
Rock-Ola Manufacturing Corp;
Standard Products Co;
Underwood-Elliot-Fisher Co;
Winchester Repeating Arms Co

.30 M1 Carbine	
Length overall	905mm (35.65in)
Weight empty	2.48kg (5.47lb)
Barrel	457mm (18.00in), 4 grooves, rh
Magazine	15- or 30-shot detachable box
Muzzle velocity	593m/sec (1,950ft/sec)

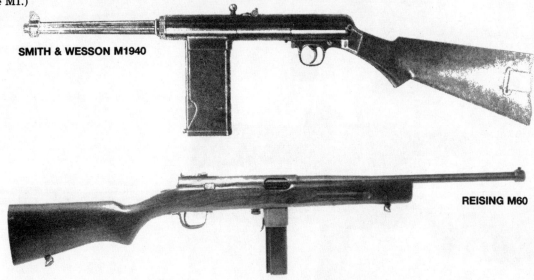

SMITH & WESSON M1940

REISING M60

US Carbine Cal .30, M1A1

US Carbine Cal .30, M2

US Carbine Cal .30, M3

7.62mm Armalite Rifle AR-10

Armalite Div of Fairchild Engine & Airplane Co

7.62 × 51mm NATO

Length overall	1,016mm (40.00in)
Weight empty	3.40kg (7.5lb)
Barrel	508mm (20.00in), 4 grooves, rh
Magazine	20-shot detachable box
Rate of fire	700rds/min
Muzzle velocity	760m/sec (2,500ft/sec)

This was the same basic weapon as the M1 but with a folding metal stock for the convenience of paratroops.

The original specification for the carbine required a selective-fire mechanism, but this was deleted during the development phase and the M1 was therefore capable of single shots only. After the M1 had been in service for some time a demand arose from users for automatic fire for use in emergencies, and the M2 was developed. It is simply the M1 with a selector switch added to the left side of the receiver, operating on the sear mechanism, plus a modified sear, hammer, operating slide and trigger housing.

The M3 was simply an M2 with various types of mounting to permit the use of different infra-red night sighting devices ('Snooper-scopes' as they were then called). No open or conventional sights were provided. The M3, sometimes known under its developmental number T3, was produced in limited numbers; only about 2,100 were made, compared to 5,510,000 M1, 150,000 M1A1 and 570,000 M2 carbines.

The AR-10 had a short and not particularly successful career as a military rifle. Prototypes appeared in 1955, production stopped in 1961, and few were made. Sudan is probably the only country to have bought it, and then only in small numbers. Events overtook the AR-10, which might otherwise have become more popular. The AR-10 was a good design; most of the metal parts were aluminium, steel being used for the bolt, bolt carrier and barrel, and many of these steel parts where chromium-plated. The weight was low, and because of this a muzzle compensator was fitted to reduce climb when fired in the automatic mode. The action was the same as that made famous by the M16, direct gas action through a tube impinging upon the face of the bolt carrier to blow it back. The M16 is, in fact, a smaller version of the AR-10 using nearly all its characteristics. Had the AR-10 started a little earlier in the race for a 7.62mm NATO rifle it might well have succeeded; as it was, it came too late and never made the grade with any country.

M1 CARBINE

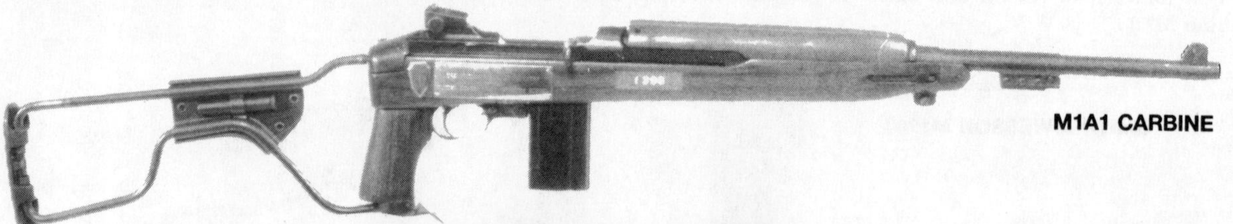

M1A1 CARBINE

M3 CARBINE

When the NATO nations decided to adopt a common cartridge in 1953 it was a matter of urgency for them all to find new weapons with which to fire it. Most of the Europeans opted for the FN-FAL rifle, but in the USA this did not compete sufficiently well with native designs to be adopted. The resulting American rifle was the M14, no more than a modernised and improved M1 Garand. There are many actual differences from the Garand, but the parentage is quite obvious. The M14 is, though, capable of selective fire and was the first American rifle to offer the option other than the early BAR. The 20-round magazine is a great improvement on the Garand's eight-shot clip, and there is a light bipod for use when in the squad automatic role. In spite of the selective fire option, it was, in fact, most usually found with the selector mechanism locked so as to permit semi-automatic fire only. It is a little light for sustained fire, and since the barrel cannot be changed there is a tendency to overheat. An M14A1 version, with some additions to make it rather more of a light machine-gun, was approved for issue but was cancelled due to financial restrictions. There have been several variations on the basic M14 design, including at least two with folding stocks and a special model for snipers known as the M21. This latter is most carefully finished and assembled and is fitted with a Leatherwood Redfield telescope sight with rangefinding reticle; it is an extremely accurate weapon which was used extensively in Vietnam. Mass production of the M14 ended some years ago, when roughly 1,380,000 had been made.

Eugene Stoner, a prolific and talented firearms inventor, produced the Armalite while he was employed by the Fairchild Engine & Airplane Company in the late 1950s. The rifle was developed in 1956 to an army specification, and Stoner chose to use the existing .222 Remington cartridge with an improved bullet; in many ways the rifle is a scaled-down AR-10, as already noted. In July 1959 production was licensed to Colt, and the AR-15 made its name by being adopted by some smaller countries in South-East Asia in the early 1960s, when Communist-inspired trouble flared in that area. The AR-15 was an ideal size for smaller men to carry; it was adopted by the US Air Force as a weapon for their South Vietnamese airfield guards, and from that spread to wider use in the US forces operating in that theatre. It eventually became the standard rifle of the US Army, first in the Far Eastern theatre and then in NATO, to the consternation of NATO standardisation agreements.

When the rifle was first adopted there were some problems. It operates on direct gas impingement on the bolt carrier, to drive the bolt carrier back and thus rotate and open the bolt. As originally designed it was 'tuned' to the then-standard military rifle powder, but the US Army then changed the rifle powder specification to a formulation which generated excessive fouling in the M16. This, together with some ill-advised instructions about minimal maintenance, led to the M16 (as it now was) gaining a reputation for jamming, but common-sense instruction on daily maintenance eventually cured the problem. The basic M16 was soon modified into the M16A1, the principal change being a positive bolt closure device which helped overcome any tendency for cartridges to stick as they were loaded. This was standardised in 1967 and remained the US Army's rifle until supplanted by the M16A2 in 1983.

7.62mm US Rifle M14

Springfield Armory;
Harrington & Richardson Arms Co;
Winchester-Western Arms;
Thompson-Ramo-Wooldridge

7.62 × 51mm NATO

Length overall	1,117mm (44.00in)
Weight empty	3.88kg (8.55lb)
Barrel	558mm (22.00in), 4 grooves, rh
Magazine	20-shot detachable box
Rate of fire	750rds/min
Muzzle velocity	853m/sec (2,800ft/sec)

5.56mm US Rifle M16 (Armalite AR-15)

Colt's Patent Firearms Mfg Co

5.56 × 45mm M193

Length overall	990mm (39.00in)
Weight empty	2.86kg (6.30lb)
Barrel	508mm (20.00in), 6 grooves, rh
Magazine	30-shot detachable box
Rate of fire	800rds/min
Muzzle velocity	1,000m/sec (3,280ft/sec)

M14 RIFLE

M16 RIFLE

5.56mm US Rifle M16A2

Colt Industries	
5.56 × 45mm NATO	
Length overall	1,006mm (39.63in)
Weight empty	3.58kg (7.89lb)
Barrel	508mm (20.00in), 6 grooves, rh
Magazine	30-shot detachable box
Rate of fire	600–940rds/min
Muzzle velocity	991m/sec (3,250ft/sec)

5.56mm Colt M4 Carbine

Colt Industries	
5.56 × 45mm NATO	
Length overall	840mm (33.07in) butt extended; 760mm (29.92in) butt retracted
Weight empty	2.54kg (5.60lb) without magazine
Barrel	368mm (14.49in), 6 grooves, rh
Magazine	20- or 30-shot detachable box
Rate of fire	700–1,000rds/min
Muzzle velocity	921m/sec (3,020ft/sec) M193; 906m/sec (2,972ft/sec) SS109

This is an improved version of the M16A1; the improvements consist of a three-round burst facility instead of automatic fire; a heavier barrel with the twist of rifling designed to suit the NATO bullet; a new rear sight incorporating adjustments for windage and elevation; the butt, handguard and pistol grip of improved material; and a new combined flash suppressor and muzzle compensator which has no aperture at the bottom so as to avoid kicking up dust when firing from the prone position. An unusual feature is a moulded excrescence on the right side of the receiver, behind the ejection port, which is a cartridge case deflector to prevent cases being flung into the face of left-handed firers. The M16A2 has also been adopted by the Canadian Army as the Rifle C7; this differs in having the full-automatic fire option instead of the three-round burst facility.

The Colt M4 Carbine (Model 723) is a lighter and shorter version of the M16A2 rifle, intended for use where lightness and speed of action are important. The action is precisely that of the M16A2 and all mechanical components are interchangeable. The sliding butt allows the firer to shoot from the shoulder or, when folded, from the hip. The M203 grenade-launcher can be fitted, and the muzzle is contoured to fire all US and NATO standard grenades. A new target-style rear sight is fitted, allowing effective fire to the maximum effective range of the ammunition.

M4 CARBINE

M16A2

This is a highly modified M16A1 rifle, designed solely for use in the firing ports of the M2 Bradley Infantry Fighting Vehicle. The mechanism is that of the M16A1 except that it fires from an open bolt, and most parts are interchangeable. It uses the standard M16 magazine. There is a quick-lock collar around the barrel which engages into the firing port, so that the firer is inside the protection of the vehicle's armour. There are no sights on the weapon, since sighting is done through a periscope or vision block in the vehicle, and fire is corrected using tracer ammunition. In an emergency the weapon can be removed from the port and used as a personal weapon, using the carrying handle as a rudimentary sight. Early models were fitted with a collapsible wire stock but these were soon deleted.

5.56mm Port Firing Weapon M231

Colt Industries	
5.56 × 45mm M193	
Length overall	710mm (27.95in)
Weight empty	3.90kg (8.5lb)
Barrel	368mm (14.5in), 6 grooves, rh
Magazine	30-shot detachable box
Rate of fire	1,100– 1,300rds/min
Muzzle velocity	914m/sec (3,000ft/sec)

5.56mm Armalite Rifle AR-18

Armalite Inc	
5.56 × 45mm M193	
Length overall	965mm (38.00in) butt extended; 730mm (28.74in) butt folded
Weight empty	3.04kg (6.70lb)
Barrel	463mm (18.25in), 4 grooves, rh
Magazine	20-shot detachable box
Rate of fire	750rds/min
Muzzle velocity	990m/sec (3,248ft/sec)

This rifle was developed as a result of the experience gained by the Armalite company in the production of other rifles in the series. There was a growing realisation that the then-new 5.56mm cartridge was a feasible military round and that the lighter weapons were attractive. But the AR-15 was not easy to make without modern plant and machinery, and Armalite realised there were many potential customers who would wish to make the rifle under licence but who did not have the necessary industrial capacity. The AR-18 was therefore designed to be easily manufactured on relatively simple machinery; it also incorporated improvements which offered the maximum simplicity in both manufacture and maintenance. In some respects the AR-18 was similar to the AR-15, though the systems are really very different, particularly in using a gas piston system instead of direct gas. The AR-18 uses steel stampings instead of the alloy forgings of the AR-15, thus considerably reducing the cost of manufacture. The design was simplified, leading to greater reliability and easier cleaning and handling. It was tested by the US Army who decided that it had military potential but, having settled on the M16, they did not adopt it. Production was subsequently licensed to Howa Machinery in Japan, NWM in Holland and Sterling Armaments in Britain. No military contracts were forthcoming, however, since countries which might, in the past, have bought the rifle were now more intent upon setting up their own facilities and making their own weapons. A commercial semi-automatic version, the AT-180, was made from 1967 to 1973 in Japan, and in the late 1970s by Sterling, but relatively few were sold and the licence eventually passed to a company in the Philippines, who have never got any further with it.

M231 PORT FIRING WEAPON

AR-18

5.56mm Ruger Mini-14 Rifle

Sturm, Ruger & Co	
5.56 × 45mm M193	
Length overall	946mm (37.24in)
Weight empty	2.90kg (6.39lb)
Barrel	470mm (18.50in), 6 grooves, rh
Magazine	5-, 10-, 20- or 30-shot detachable box
Rate of fire	750rds/min (AC-556 only)
Muzzle velocity	1,005m/sec (3,297ft/sec)

Introduced in 1973 this is mechanically much the same system as the Garand, a gas-actuated rifle with rotating bolt, though, due to ballistic considerations, it is by no means simply a scale-down exercise. One of the principal attractions of this rifle is that, due to the lower recoil forces derived from the 5.56mm bullet, it becomes possible to develop a light rifle which can be fired at full automatic and still have a reasonable chance of hitting the target. The gas system uses a cupped piston head surrounding the gas outlet from the barrel, so that the piston is given a brief impulse before the gas is exhausted to the atmosphere; the piston thereafter relies upon its own momentum to rotate and open the bolt. At the same time a hammer is cocked and held by the sear. A return spring closes the bolt and the hammer is released by the trigger. Variations of the Mini-14 include a stainless steel version; the Mini-14/20GB infantry rifle which had a flash hider and bayonet lug; and the AC-556 selective fire model which allows single shots, full-automatic or three-round burst fire.

.50mm Barrett Light Fifty M82A1

Barrett Firearms Mfg Co	
.50 Browning (12.7 × 99mm)	
Length overall	1,549mm (60.98in)
Weight empty	14.7kg (32.41lb)
Barrel	838mm (33.00in), 8 grooves, rh
Magazine	11-shot detachable box
Muzzle velocity	843m/sec (2,800ft/sec)

This is a semi-automatic sniping rifle firing the .50 Browning heavy machine-gun cartridge; it is intended as a long-range sniping and interdiction weapon, and as a suitable defensive weapon for light vessels. Its object is primarily the destruction of material, rather than anti-personnel sniping. The rifle operates on short recoil principles; on firing, a considerable amount of thrust is delivered through the base of the cartridge case to the face of the bolt, which is transferred through the bolt lugs and body to the rear of the bolt carrier. The barrel has recoiled about 13mm when the bullet leaves the barrel, and after about 25mm of movement the bolt carrier is unlocked and moves back to rotate the bolt and unlock it. An accelerator also transfers much of the barrel's momentum energy to the bolt. The barrel finally stops, and the bolt continues rearwards to extract the empty case and eject it, then return to load a fresh round. The barrel is fitted with a very efficient muzzle brake which reduces recoil by about 30 per cent. There is an adjustable bipod, and the rifle can also be fitted to the standard M82 tripod or any mount compatible with the M60 machine-gun. It is in use by US and other Special Forces.

RUGER MINI-14

BARRETT LIGHT FIFTY

The Colt ACR is a gas-operated weapon derived from the existing M16A2. The handguard, pistol grip and stock have been redesigned and the butt telescopes and incorporates a cheek-piece. The operating system is the same as that of the M16A2 but the barrel has an advanced muzzle brake/compensator to improve control and reduce recoil. There is an ambidextrous fire selector giving single shot and full automatic modes. There are iron sights and also a 3.5 power optical sight; this can be removed, leaving a mount which will accept other types of optical or electro-optical sight. For instinctive shooting, there is a long shotgun-type rib along the top of the weapon. The Colt ACR fires the NATO standard 5.56 × 45mm round, but is particularly designed for a new Duplex cartridge developed by Colt and Olin Industries (Winchester). Both rounds use the same cartridge case, but the Duplex round carries two projectiles, one behind the other, each using a hard steel core in a gilding metal jacket. The two bullets weigh 2.26g (front) and 2.14g (rear) and this round is specifically designed for use at ranges up to 325m. The leading bullet will go to the point of aim, while the other will have a slight random dispersion around the point of aim to compensate sighting errors.

5.56mm Colt Advanced Combat Rifle

Colt Industries	
5.56 × 45mm M855 or Duplex	
Length overall	1,031mm (40.60in) butt extended; 933mm (36.73in) butt retracted
Weight empty	3.31kg (7.30lb) less magazine and sight

ADVANCED COMBAT RIFLE

Barrel	Not known
Magazine	30-shot detachable box
Rate of fire	Not known
Muzzle velocity	948m/sec (3,110ft/sec) (NATO); 884m/sec (2,900ft/sec) (Duplex)

This is obviously based upon the G11 rifle, though there may be internal differences. It is a gas-operated bullpup with the options of single shots, three-round bursts and full automatic fire. For a general description of the system, reference should be made to the entry on the G11 rifle under 'Germany'. The US version is described as being 4.92mm calibre, but it should be pointed out that this notation is peculiar to this rifle and is arrived at by measuring the bore diameter from the bottom of the grooves; every other rifle measures diameter from the surface of the lands, and by this notation this is a 4.7mm rifle, using exactly the same ammunition as the German G11.

4.92mm Heckler & Koch Advanced Combat Rifle

Heckler & Koch Inc	
4.92 × 34mm Caseless	
Length overall	750mm (29.53in)
Weight empty	3.90kg (8.60lb)
Barrel	Not known
Magazine	50-shot detachable box
Rate of fire	600rds/min
Muzzle velocity	914m/sec (3,000ft/sec)

H&K ADVANCED COMBAT RIFLE

5.56mm AAI Advanced Combat Rifle

AAI Corporation	
5.56mm Flechette	
Length overall	1,016mm (40.00in)
Weight empty	3.53kg (7.78lb)
Barrel	Not known
Magazine	30-shot detachable box
Muzzle velocity	1,402m/sec (4,600ft/sec)

This is a gas-operated rifle firing a flechette cartridge. It is perhaps more conventional than the Steyr or H&K entrants, and has a long unobstructed top surface to act as an aid to quick alignment. It is a modified version of a 'serial bullet rifle' developed in the mid-1970s and it is believed to use a triple-chamber breech unit formed as a segment of a circle and pivoted so that the three chambers swing past the rear end of the barrel and fire in rapid succession. The closed-bolt mechanism has a two-position selector for single shots or three-round bursts; there is no provision for automatic fire. The flechette cartridge uses the standard 5.56 × 45mm case. The gas characteristics of this round demand that the gas tap for the rifle's action be closer to the chamber than is customary; a slight drawback is that the chamber will accept conventional 5.56mm rounds, but if these were to be fired the very different gas characteristics could cause dangerous malfunctions. For safety purposes, therefore, the magazine interface will not accept any conventional rifle magazine, and the dedicated magazine will not accept conventional bulleted cartridges. The rifle is provided with optical and iron sights, with a quick-release lever to permit the optical sight to be removed and another type of sight fitted to the mounting.

Note: For the fourth competing design, see under 'Steyr ACR' in the 'Austria' section.

AAI ADVANCED COMBAT RIFLE

USSR/RUSSIA

6.5mm Federov 'Avtomat'

Sestoretsk Arsenal	
6.5 × 50SR Arisaka	
Length overall	1,045mm (41.15in)
Weight empty	4.37kg (9.63lb)
Barrel	Not known
Magazine	25-shot detachable box
Rate of fire	600rds/min
Muzzle velocity	666m/sec (2,185ft/sec)

The Federov 'Avtomat' selective-fire rifle can fairly justly claim to be the ancestor of the modern assault rifle, though it achieved that post more by accident than design. Vladimir Federov was a prominent Tsarist arms designer who later continued in the service of the Soviets and became the author of many official textbooks. Prior to World War One he had developed a number of experimental rifles with some success, but his major problem was in the ammunition with which he was forced to work. The standard Russian 7.62 × 54R was a fat, awkward, rimmed round which did not lend itself easily to automation and much of the ammunition was of indifferent and inconsistent quality. It was also, typically of its day, a powerful cartridge which demanded a heavy and robust weapon. After the Russo-Japanese War, for reasons concealed in history, the Russians produced a number of rifle designs chambered for the 6.5mm Japanese cartridge, most of which remained paper exercises. In 1916, though, Federov developed a selective-fire rifle around this Japanese cartridge, using short recoil of the barrel to operate the mechanism. The rifle had a forward pistol-grip, a curved magazine, and weighed about 4.37kg (9.5lb). Although the October Revolution stopped production of the 'Avtomat' before it had fairly begun, it was re-started in 1919 and continued until finally halted in 1924, about 9,000 having been made. It was used by the Red Army during the Civil War, and Federov continued developing it and entered it in numerous trials until about 1928. Very few specimens are known to exist today.

SIMONOV MODEL 1936

The Simonov was the first automatic rifle to be adopted in quantity by the Soviet Army, who accepted it in 1936. It is a gas-operated weapon using a piston mounted above the barrel to unlock and retract the bolt; the locking system is rather unusual, relying on a vertically moving block to lock the bolt and its carrier securely to the receiver. The standard weapon is provided with a selective-fire device to permit its use as a light machine-gun. The AVS suffered from excessive muzzle blast and recoil, and to reduce these a two-port muzzle brake was fitted. The receiver is cut open to allow movement of the cocking handle and thus the interior of the weapon is exposed to mud and dirt. Whether it was this, or simply that the unusual locking system failed to live up to its promise, the fact remains that the AVS had a very short life. It was replaced in 1938 by the simpler Tokarev.

This Tokarev-designed weapon relied on gas operation with a locking block cammed downwards at the rear into a recess in the receiver floor. It had a two-piece wooden stock with a prominent magazine; there were two steel barrel bands and the forward portion of the wooden handguard was of sheet steel with circular cooling holes in each side. The principal distinguishing feature was the positioning of the cleaning rod, inserted along the right side of the stock rather than underneath the barrel, as is more usual. The rifle was originally fitted with a six-baffle muzzle brake, replaced in late 1940 or early 1941 by a simpler two-baffle design. Owing to its fragile construction manufacture of the 1938 pattern was stopped in 1940, but not before some selected weapons had been fitted with telescope sights for sniping.

A more robust version of the SVT38, the SVT40 was characterised by the removal of the earlier rifle's externally mounted cleaning rod and its replacement under the barrel. There was a single barrel band, beyond which a sheet metal handguard extended forward. Air circulation holes were cut in the guard and four rectangular slots appeared in the wooden continuation. Two variations in muzzle brake design existed; the first had six slender baffles, replaced in later production by a unit having only two large baffles. These self-loading rifles were issued principally to NCOs, although, as with the SVT38, a number were fitted with telescope sights for sniper use.

A fully automatic version, known as the AVT40, was outwardly identical to the SVT40, from which it was converted, except for alteration to the surround of the safety catch to allow the addition of an automatic fire setting. Only a few rifles were so converted. Carbine versions of the SVT40, some converted and some of new construction, are also known to exist.

7.62mm Simonov AVS36

State arsenals	
7.62 × 54R	
Length overall	1,260mm (49.60in)
Weight empty	4.40kg (9.70lb)
Barrel	627mm (24.69in), 4 grooves, rh
Magazine	15-shot detachable box
Muzzle velocity	835m/sec (2,740ft/sec)

7.62mm Tokarev SVT38

State arsenals	
7.62 × 54R	
Length overall	1,222mm (48.11in)
Weight empty	3.95kg (8.71lb)
Barrel	610mm (24.00in), 4 grooves, rh
Magazine	10-shot detachable box
Muzzle velocity	840m/sec (2,755ft/sec)

7.62mm Tokarev SVT40

State arsenals	
7.62 × 54R	
Length overall	1,226mm (48.27in)
Weight empty	3.90kg (8.60lb)
Barrel	610mm (25.00in), 4 grooves, rh
Magazine	10-shot detachable box
Muzzle velocity	840m/sec (2,755ft/sec)

TOKAREV SVT 38

7.62mm Simonov Carbine SKS

State arsenals	
7.62 × 39mm M1943	
Length overall	1,022mm (40.20in)
Weight empty	3.86kg (8.51lb)
Barrel	520mm (20.47in), 4 grooves, rh
Magazine	10-shot detachable box
Muzzle velocity	735m/sec (2,410ft/sec)

7.62mm Kalashnikov AK47 and AKM

State arsenals	
7.62 × 39mm m1943	
Length overall	880mm (34.65in)
Weight empty	4.30kg (9.48lb)
Barrel	415mm (16.34in), 4 grooves, rh
Magazine	30-shot detachable box
Rate of fire	600rds/min
Muzzle velocity	600m/sec (2,350ft/sec)

The SKS carbine was the first Soviet weapon developed to make use of the M1943 'intermediate' cartridge. The history of this cartridge is in some doubt; it is known that the Soviets were experimenting with short cartridges in various calibres prior to the war, but it is generally accepted that it was the appearance of the German MP44 and its short 7.92mm round which led them to capitalise on their previous work and develop the 7.62 × 39mm round. Although the SKS is important for its introduction of this round, it is otherwise a fairly uninspired design. It was simple, easy to operate and robust, but a little heavy for the cartridge it fired; all of which is understandable, since it was developed under the stress of war. The system of operation and locking appears to have been taken from the PTRS anti-tank rifle, locking being done by the same type of tipping bolt. Stripping and maintenance is easy, and the hinged bayonet and one-piece wooden stock are also prominent features of the weapon. Loading can be done by chargers or by pushing single rounds into the magazine. Unloading can be quickly done by releasing the pivoting magazine cover, swinging it away from the receiver and spilling out the rounds. Enormous numbers of this carbine have been made, and although it is no longer in use in the Soviet forces it has appeared in almost every Communist country in the world. It has also been made, with slight variations, in several countries; in Yugoslavia it is known as the M59, while in China it is the Type 56. North Korea calls it the Type 63, and the East German version is the 'Karabiner-S'.

The Kalashnikov is the standard Soviet assault rifle. After seeing the German MP44 and its intermediate cartridge the Soviets rapidly appreciated the logic behind it and set about developing their own version, which evolved into the Kalashnikov. It is probably one of the best automatic rifles in existence and certainly the most widely distributed, having been supplied to every satellite nation, many of which evolved their own variations. More than 35 million are reputed to have been produced and the design lives on on the AK74 pattern. In addition to its service in regular forces, the Kalashnikov will always be found where Communist-inspired Nationalist movements are pressing their cause.

The AK is gas operated, and is rather unusual in having the gas piston rod permanently attached to the bolt carrier. A cam track in the carrier rotates the bolt to lock and unlock, and during the rearward stroke a hammer is cocked. The barrel, like that of many Soviet weapons, is chromium plated internally. In spite of its popularity and efficiency the AK is not without its defects. There is, surprisingly, no hold-open device on the bolt to indicate an empty magazine nor, indeed, any method of retaining the bolt in the open position. Its accuracy over 300m is relatively poor.

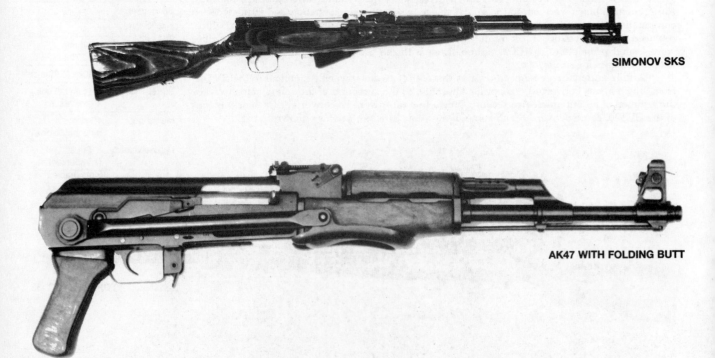

SIMONOV SKS

AK47 WITH FOLDING BUTT

After contemplating the inferior finish of Soviet wartime weapons, it is a pleasant surprise to find that the AK reverted to more traditional methods of construction and finish, the receiver being machined from solid steel. This state of affairs was not conducive to cheapness and mass production and the design which followed the AK47, the AKM ('M' for 'modernised'), reverted to a stamped steel construction. The bolt is Parkerised instead of the polished steel of the AK47, and the bayonet is an ingenious design with a slot in the blade which, when engaged with a stud on the scabbard, converts the assembly to a wire-cutter – an innovation widely copied since. The muzzle is formed into a spoon-like lower extension which acts as a simple compensator to reduce climb during automatic fire. There were other, minor modifications in the AKM but they were an entirely logical development from the AK47 with the intention of reducing manufacturing time and cost and improving combat efficiency. Variant models are the *AKS-47* and *AKMS*, which have folding skeleton butts and are generally found in use by parachute troops and armoured units.

AKM

The Dragunov is the standard sniper's rifle of the Soviet and Warsaw Pact armies, and although it uses the basic mechanism of the Kalashnikov it is a completely fresh rifle, designed from the start with sniping in mind. It is an excellent and accurate weapon, firing the old, powerful, rimmed 7.62mm rifle cartridge. All parts are most carefully made and assembled, and a telescope sight known as the PSO-1 is part of the outfit of each rifle, though iron sights are also fitted. The PSO-1 is also capable of detecting infra-red emissions, though it has no pretensions to being a night sight. The rifle is easy and pleasant to fire, the trigger mechanism, although that of the AK series, having been carefully refined to give a smooth and consistent pull-off. It has been copied in China as the 'Type 79', and a commercial version, known as the *Medved* ('Bear') is available chambered for the 9 × 54R sporting cartridge.

7.62mm Dragunov SVD

State arsenals	
7.62 × 54R	
Length overall	1,225mm (48.20in)
Weight empty	4.31kg (9.5lb)
Barrel	610mm (24.00in), 4 grooves, rh
Magazine	10-shot detachable box
Muzzle velocity	828m/sec (2,720ft/sec)

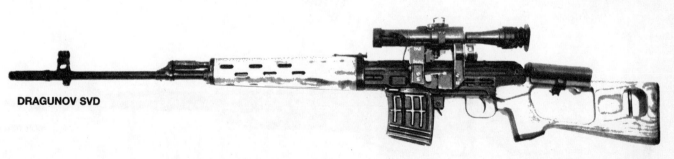

DRAGUNOV SVD

5.45mm Kalashnikov AK74 and AKS74

State arsenals	
5.45 × 39mm M74	
Length overall	930mm (36.60in)
Weight empty	3.60kg (7.94lb)
Barrel	400mm (15.80in), 4 grooves, rh
Magazine	30-shot detachable box
Rate of fire	650rds/min
Muzzle velocity	900m/sec (2,952ft/sec)

The Soviet Army began experiments with small-calibre weapons in the 1970s and there had been persistent rumours of such weapons for several years before, in November 1977, the AK74 rifle was seen for the first time in the annual Red Square parade, carried by parachute troops. Since that time it has become the standard Soviet infantry rifle, gradually replacing the 7.62mm AKs in the hands of regular troops. It has also begun to appear in other Warsaw Pact armies and is known to be manufactured in Poland and Bulgaria. The general design has also been copied in China and Yugoslavia but chambered the Western 5.56mm cartridge and intended for export. In general terms the AK74 is a small-calibre version of the AKM, and it uses the same receiver, furniture and system of operation. Indeed, it is quite likely that apart from a new barrel and bolt little else needed to be changed. The 5.45mm round is almost the same length as the 7.62 × 39mm round and the magazine thus fits into the same opening in the receiver. A noticeable feature of this rifle is the laminated plastic and steel magazine, the design of which has subtly changed since its introduction as stiffening fillets have been added. Another feature is the muzzle brake and compensator, designed to reduce the recoil and compensate for the upward climb always present in automatic weapons. It is highly efficient, reducing the felt recoil to a low level and keeping the weapon steady during automatic fire, though it is said to be somewhat harsh on bystanders since the muzzle gases are diverted sideways. The AKS74 version has a folding steel butt which swings to lie along the left side of the receiver.

YUGOSLAVIA

7.62mm Rifle M59/66A1

Zavodi Crvena Zastava	
7.62 × 39mm Soviet M43	
Length overall	1,120mm (44.09in)
Weight empty	4.1kg (9.04lb)
Barrel	620mm (24.39in) with grenade-launcher
Magazine	10-shot integral box
Muzzle velocity	735m/sec (2,410ft/sec)

This closely resembles the Soviet SKS from which it was derived, by way of the earlier M59 rifle, a direct SKS copy. The principal change lies in the forming of the muzzle into a spigot-type grenade-launcher and a ladder-type grenade-firing sight, behind the launcher, which folds down flat behind the foresight when not required. As with the SKS there is a folding bayonet beneath the barrel, but due to the length of the grenade-launcher there is less free blade in front of the muzzle when the bayonet is fixed.

AK74

M59/66A1

This is the most recent in a series of Kalashnikov copies, beginning with the M64 and M70. The M70B1 is based on the Soviet AKM, while the M70AB2 is a folding stock model based on the AKMS. The only significant difference is that these weapons are provided with a grenade-launcher unit which can be readily attached to the muzzle when required, and have a ladder-type grenade sight attached to the front end of the gas cylinder and coupled to the gas regulator. The sight normally lies flat on the gas tube, and when required is lifted to the vertical position; this movement automatically shuts off the gas supply to the gas cylinder, so ensuring that all the power of the cartridge is used in propelling the grenade. A variant model, the M77B1, is available for export; this is chambered for the 7.62 × 51mm NATO cartridge and has a closed prong flash hider on the muzzle. An accessory grenade-launcher and sight are provided, both of which need to be attached to the rifle when required for use. (Data refers to the M70B1).

7.62mm Rifle M70B1 and M70AB2

Zavodi Crvena Zastava

7.62 × 39mm Soviet M43

Length overall	900mm (35.43in)
Weight empty	3.70kg (8.15lb)
Barrel	415mm (16.33in), 4 grooves, rh
Magazine	30-shot detachable box
Rate of fire	640rds/min
Muzzle velocity	720m/sec (2,362ft/sec)

This uses the same basic Kalashnikov mechanism as the M70 rifles but is more robust and larger, as required by the more powerful 7.92mm Mauser cartridge. It is standard issue to snipers of the Yugoslav Army and variant models chambered for the 7.62 × 51mm NATO and 7.62 × 54R Soviet cartridges have been developed for export. The rifle is fitted with the usual type of iron sights associated with the Kalashnikov family of weapons, but in addition has a mount on the receiver top to accept a telescope sight which appears to be closely modelled on the Soviet PSO-1. It has also been seen with electro-optical image-intensifying sights attached to the same mount.

7.92mm Sniper's Rifle M76

Zavodi Crvena Zastava

7.92 × 57mm Mauser

Length overall	1,135mm (44.68in)
Weight empty	4.20kg (9.26lb)
Barrel	550mm (21.65in), 4 grooves, rh

M76 SNIPER'S RIFLE

Magazine	10-shot detachable box
Muzzle velocity	720m/sec (2,362ft/sec)

These rifles resemble the M70 series in being Kalashnikov copies but they are chambered for the 5.56 × 45mm cartridge and may be rifled either one turn in 178mm for use with the US M193 cartridge or one turn in 305mm for use with the NATO-standard SS109 bullet. The gas regulator has been redesigned so as to give consistent performance with ammunition of varying energy levels, and the muzzles carry closed-prong flash hiders. Accessory grenade-launchers and sights are available. These weapons are not issued to Yugoslav forces but have been developed solely for export. The M80 has a fixed wooden butt; the M80A has a folding steel butt which hinges down and forward to fold beneath the receiver. (Data table refers to the M80.)

5.56mm Assault Rifle M80 and M80A

Zavodi Crvena Zastava

5.56 × 45mm M193 or SS109

Length overall	990mm (38.97in)
Weight empty	3.60kg (7.94lb)
Barrel	460mm (18.11in), 6 grooves, rh
Magazine	30-shot detachable box
Rate of fire	600rds/min
Muzzle velocity	970m/sec (3,182ft/sec)

M80 ASSAULT RIFLE

Submachine-Guns

ARGENTINA

9mm Halcon M1943, M1946 and M1949

Fabrica de Armas Halcon	
.45 ACP and 9 × 19mm Parabellum	

M1943:

Operation	Blowback
Length overall	848mm (33.4in)
Weight empty	4.76kg (10.5lb)
Barrel	292mm (11.5in), 6 grooves, rh
Magazine	17- or 30-shot detachable box
Cyclic rate	700rds/min
Muzzle velocity	277m/sec (910ft/sec)

M1949:

Operation	Blowback
Length, stock extended	790mm (31.1in)
Length, stock folded	610mm (24.01in)
Weight empty	4.08kg (9lb)

The Halcon M1943 was developed in the early 1940s and issued to the Argentine Gendarmeria Nacional. It was in .45 calibre, and the curious shape and considerable weight are evidence of pre-war design concepts. Nevertheless the design was ingeniously simple and the weapon could be made in two hours by a skilled workman using simple machine tools. It was a blowback weapon, and the muzzle compensator and weight helped to make it quite steady in automatic fire. The M1946 was also in .45 ACP and had a folding stock; it was issued to the Air Force and was known as the 'Modelo Aeronautica'. Like the M1943 it used 17- or 30-shot straight magazines. The M1949 was made in 9mm Parabellum calibre, used a curved 36-shot magazine, and was adopted by the Army, being called the 'Modelo Ejercito Argentino'. The total production of all three models was in the region of 6,000. They were replaced in production, in 1957, by a lightweight model but few of these were ever made.

Barrel	292mm (11.5in), 6 grooves, rh
Magazine	36-shot detachable box
Cyclic rate	700rds/min
Muzzle velocity	365m/sec (1,197ft/sec)

HALCON M1946

9mm PAM1 and PAM2

Fabrica Militar de Armas Portatiles 'Domingo Matheu'	
9 × 19mm Parabellum	
Operation	Blowback
Length, stock extended	725mm (28.5in)
Length, stock folded	535mm (21.06in)
Weight empty	2.99kg (6.59lb)
Barrel	200mm (7.87in), 6 grooves, rh

The PAM1 and PAM2 are almost identical to the US M3A1 from which they were derived; the only major differences are that the Argentine weapons are slightly shorter and lighter and chamber the 9mm cartridge. The guns were issued to Argentine military and police forces in the 1950–66 period and numbers may still be in use and in reserve stocks. The PAM2 differs in having an additional left-hand grip safety, intended to reduce the number of accidents due to inertial firing, ie, dropping a weapon hard enough to cause the bolt to fly back and chamber and fire a round. This safety locks the bolt in the forward position except when released by the firer gripping it, together with the magazine, when in the firing position.

Magazine	30-shot detachable box
Cyclic rate	450rds/min
Muzzle velocity	365m/sec (1,197ft/sec)

9mm PA-3DM

Fabrica Militar de Armas Portatiles 'Domingo Matheu'	
9 × 19mm Parabellum	
Operation	Blowback
Length, stock extended	693mm (27.28in)
Length, stock folded	523mm (20.50in)
Weight empty	3.40kg (7.49lb)

This is a complete re-design of the PAM1, developed in the late 1960s and put into production in 1970. It was heavily influenced by the Uzi, adopting the use of the grip as the magazine housing and a wrap-around bolt used in the Israeli weapon, but the body and sliding wire butt are much the same as the PAM1. Some models were produced with a fixed wood or plastic butt, and all have a plastic fore-end. Manufacture ceased in 1978 after about 15,000 weapons had been made.

Barrel	290mm (11.42in), 6 grooves, rh	Muzzle velocity	375m/sec (1,230ft/sec)
Magazine	25-shot detachable box		
Cyclic rate	650rds/min		

This is an updated version of the PA-3DM and is the weapon currently manufactured for the Argentine forces. It uses only the sliding butt form and, like the PAM series, has a grip safety in the rear of the pistol grip. The magazine capacity has been increased.

9mm FMK-3 Mod 2

Fabrica Militar de Armas Portatiles 'Domingo Matheu'

9 × 19mm Parabellum

Operation	Blowback
Length, stock extended	690mm (27.16in)
Length, stock folded	520mm (20.47in)
Weight empty	3.76kg (8.29lb)
Barrel	290mm (11.42in), 6 grooves, rh
Magazine	40-shot detachable box
Cyclic rate	600rds/min
Muzzle velocity	400m/sec (1,312ft/sec)

PA-3DM

AUSTRALIA

In 1941 Australia was without submachine-guns; arrangements were made to put the Owen into production (see below) as a stopgap, but the main reliance was placed on receiving supplies of the Sten from Britain. However, when the first samples of the Sten arrived, the Australians were not impressed by the quality, and set about re-designing it, resulting in the Austen (AUSTralian StEN) gun. The receiver, barrel and trigger mechanism were still those of the Sten, but the mainspring, bolt, folding butt and foregrip were inspired by the German MP40. The Mark I Austen went into production in mid-1942 and about 20,000 were made before production ended in March 1945. It was, though, never as reliable as the Owen and was not particularly liked by the Army, and there is something of a mystery about why it remained in production long after the Owen was a proven success. A Mark II Austen was developed in 1944; this had a unique two-piece aluminium receiver, but only prototypes were made.

9mm Austen

Diecasters Ltd;
W. J. Carmichael & Co

9 × 19mm Parabellum

Operation	Blowback
Length, stock extended	845mm (33.25in)
Length, stock folded	552mm (21.75in)
Weight empty	3.98kg (8.75lb)
Barrel	196mm (7.75in), 6 grooves, rh
Magazine	28-shot detachable box
Cyclic rate	500rds/min
Muzzle velocity	380m/sec (1,246ft/sec)

AUSTEN Mk1

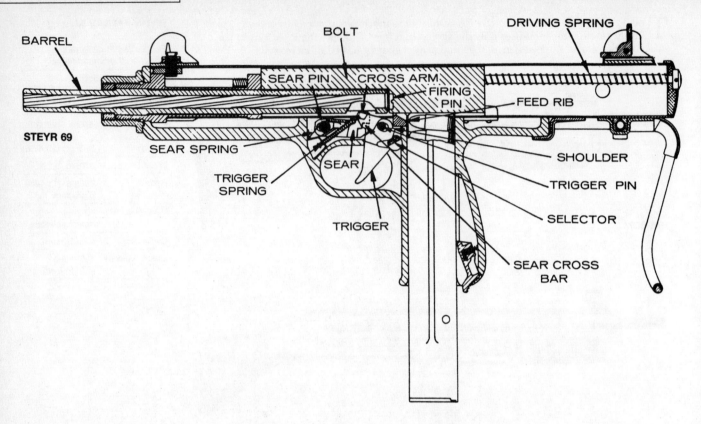

STEYR 69

BARREL

BOLT

DRIVING SPRING

SEAR PIN

CROSS ARM

FIRING PIN

FEED RIB

SEAR SPRING

SHOULDER

TRIGGER SPRING

SEAR

TRIGGER PIN

SELECTOR

TRIGGER

SEAR CROSS BAR

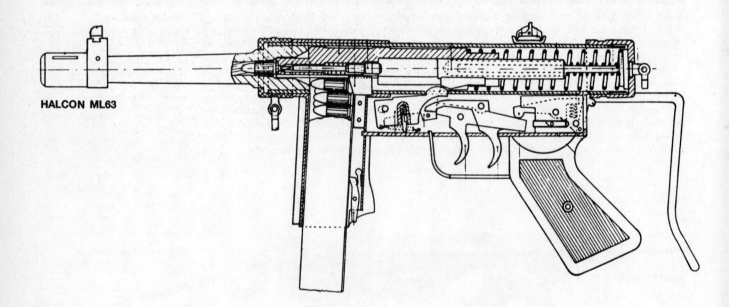

HALCON ML63

This weapon was developed by Evelyn Owen in .22 calibre in 1939, and he offered it to the army without raising much interest. On the outbreak of war he was called up into the Army and left the gun and details with a friend, who managed to interest Lysaghts in manufacturing a prototype in .32 ACP calibre. The Australian Army were awaiting supplies of the Sten, but after some delay decided to purchase 100 Owen guns in .38 calibre, the necessary design work being done by G. S. Wardell, chief engineer of Lysaghts. The first of these were made in August 1941 but merely proved that the .38 revolver round was useless as a submachine-gun cartridge, and Lysaghts, on their own responsibility, changed the design to 9mm Parabellum. The prototype was tested against the Thompson and Sten and proved superior to both, and went into production. Due to a shortage of machine tools it was not until mid-1942 that full production of 2,000 per month was achieved, and thereafter production was held at this rate solely by the availability of tooling. Although the US Army in Australia wanted to purchase 60,000 Owen guns, the proposal was refused by the Australian authorities since they could not find the necessary materials and machine tools. The Owen was a simple blowback weapon with two odd features: the overhead feeding magazine, and a separate bolt compartment inside the receiver, so that the bolt was isolated from its cocking handle by a small bulkhead. This ensured that the bolt could not be jammed by dirt or mud, though it was expensive in terms of space. Two other unusual features were that the ejector was built into the magazine, rather than into the gun, and the barrel could be removed quickly by pulling up on a spring-loaded plunger, necessary since the gun could only be stripped by removing the barrel and then taking the bolt out forwards. Three models of Owen were made; the Mark I (or I/42), which went through several minor modifications; the Mark I Wood Butt (or I/43), and the Mark II which was a simplified model and only produced in prototype. Total production amounted to about 45,000 before Lysaghts ended manufacture in September 1945. The guns remained in use until the 1960s and numbers are still held in reserve stocks.

9mm Owen

Lysaghts Newcastle Works	
9 × 19mm Parabellum	
Operation	Blowback
Length overall	813mm (32in)
Weight empty	4.21kg (9.28lb)
Barrel	247mm (9.75in), 7 grooves, rh
Magazine	33-shot detachable box
Cyclic rate	700rds/min
Muzzle velocity	380m/sec (1,247ft/sec)

OWEN

The Owen was feeling its age by the 1960s, and although it was still extremely popular with the troops it had features such as the non-interchangeable barrel and the high rate of fire which could be eliminated in a more modern design. Another gun, the X3, was therefore designed by the Australian Ordnance Department which might be said to combine the best features of the Owen with those of the Sterling. The bayonet, pistol grip and buttplate came from the L1A1 (FN-FAL) rifle, to simplify production, and the butt fits into the end of the receiver to give a straight line layout which helps accuracy. The bolt has a modified Owen

9mm F1

Australian Defence Industries, Lithgow Facility	
9 × 19mm Parabellum	
Operation	Blowback

Length overall	715mm (28.15in)
Weight empty	3.26kg (7.18lb)
Barrel	203mm (8in), 6 grooves, rh
Magazine	34-shot detachable box
Cyclic rate	600rds/min
Muzzle velocity	380m/sec (1,247ft/sec)

seal, giving it good protection against dirt, and the top-feed magazine was retained, largely because the troops trusted it and were used to it. The British and Canadian Sterling magazines will also fit. The X3 gave a good account of itself in Vietnam and was standardised as the F1.

9mm F1

AUSTRIA

9mm Steyr MPi 69

Steyr-Mannlicher GmbH	
9 × 19mm Parabellum	
Operation	Blowback
Length, stock extended	670mm (26.38in)
Length, stock folded	465mm (18.30in)
Weight empty	3.13kg (6.9lb)
Barrel	260mm (10.23in), 6 grooves, rh
Magazine	25- or 32-shot detachable box
Cyclic rate	550rds/min
Muzzle velocity	380m/sec (1,247ft/sec)

This is a simple and robust weapon, designed by Engineer Stowasser of Steyr-Mannlicher with the objects of reliability and simple manufacture. The receiver is a steel pressing with a moulded nylon cover and much of the assembly of components is by welding and brazing. The barrel is cold-hammered, a system which gives a cleaner rifling contour and a tougher barrel at less expense than the traditional system of boring and rifling. The bolt is of the wrap-round type, the bolt face being about half-way along the length of the bolt body, permitting the use of a barrel rather longer than usual while keeping the overall length within reasonable bounds. Selection of single shots or automatic fire is made by trigger pressure; a light pressure produces single shots, while a heavier pressure brings in a locking device which holds down the sear and permits automatic fire. An additional control is provided in the cross-bolt safety catch; pushed to the right it makes the weapon safe, pushed to the left the weapon is freed for automatic fire; pushed half-way the weapon is freed for single shots. The gun is cocked by pulling back on the carrying sling, the front end being attached to the cocking handle. A telescoping wire stock is fitted and mounts for various types of optical sight are available.

The MPi 69, as noted above, has an unusual cocking system in which the sling is pulled back to withdraw the cocking handle. Some users do not like this method, particularly those who prefer to wrap the sling around their arm to act as a brace – in this situation the tight sling prevents the cocking handle going fully forward and prevents the bolt closing. To satisfy these users, Steyr modified the design by fitting a conventional cocking handle. This version is known as the MPi 81.

This is a submachine-gun version of the well-known Steyr AUG rifle. It uses the rifle stock and receiver but is fitted with a new 9mm barrel, a special blowback bolt unit, a magazine adapter and a magazine. These components may also be ordered in kit form and used to convert an existing AUG rifle into submachine-gun form. The bolt is a one-piece unit, instead of the bolt and carrier system used with the rifle, and the weapon fires from a closed bolt. The long barrel gives good velocity to the bullet, and makes the AUG Para an exceptionally accurate weapon in this class.

9mm Steyr MPi 81

Steyr-Mannlicher GmbH

9 × 19mm Parabellum

9mm AUG Para

Steyr-Mannlicher GmbH

9 × 19mm Parabellum

Operation	Blowback
Length overall	665mm (26.18in)
Weight empty	3.30kg (7.27lb)
Barrel	420mm (16.53in), 6 grooves, rh
Magazine	25- or 32-shot detachable box
Cyclic rate	650–750rds/min
Muzzle velocity	400m/sec (1,312ft/sec)

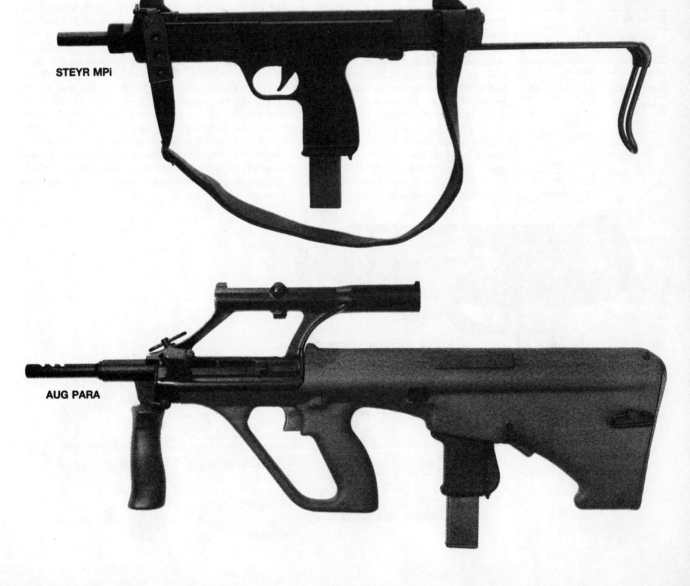

STEYR MPi

AUG PARA

9mm Tactical Machine Pistol

Steyr-Mannlicher GmbH	
9 × 19mm Parabellum	
Operation	Delayed blowback
Length overall	270mm (10.63in)
Weight empty	1.40kg (3.08lb)
Barrel	150mm (5.9in), 6 grooves, rh
Magazine	15-, 20- or 25-shot detachable box
Cyclic rate	450rds/min
Muzzle velocity	370m/sec (1,214ft/sec)

This new weapon, introduced in 1989, consists of a synthetic butt and frame, synthetic receiver top, and a steel barrel and breech-block combination. It is hammer-fired, the firing mechanism being modified from that of the AUG rifle. The weapon works on the delayed blowback principle, the delay being performed by a rotating barrel which owes a good deal to the Steyr 1912 pistol. The barrel lies inside a casing which fits into the top cover and acts as a guide for the bolt. On firing, bolt and barrel recoil 10–12mm or so and then a lug on the barrel, having moved down a slot, hits a cam surface and rotates the barrel about 45° clockwise. This unlocks the bolt; the barrel stops and the bolt goes rearwards. A spring drives the bolt back to collect a fresh round and chamber it and then drives the bolt into lock with the barrel and the barrel forward again, rotating it so as to lock the bolt before it goes into battery. Semi-auto or auto fire can be selected by a cross-bolt safety or by trigger pressure, as in the MPi 69. There are 52 parts, and only one screw, the lateral adjustment for the rear sight. There is no stock, but a grip in front of the trigger-guard can be folded down to give a two-handed hold.

BELGIUM

5.7mm FN P90 Personal Weapon

FN Herstal SA	
5.7 × 28mm FN	
Operation	Blowback
Length overall	400mm (15.75in)
Weight empty	2.80kg (6.17lb)
Barrel	
Magazine	50-shot detachable box
Cyclic rate	800–1,000rds/min
Muzzle velocity	850m/sec (2,800ft/sec)

This unusual weapon was announced in 1988 by FN Herstal and is intended to arm that two-thirds of an army whose principal activity is something other than firing a weapon – cooks, drivers, clerks, storemen and similar personnel. In addition, FN felt that the 9mm Parabellum cartridge is outmoded and so developed a new cartridge with powerful ballistic capabilities. The P90 is a blowback weapon firing from a closed bolt. The pistol grip is well forward so that when held at the hip most of the weight lies on the forearm giving good balance and support. When fired from the shoulder the rear of the receiver acts as the stock and the curved front of the trigger guard acts as a fore grip. The receiver is largely plastic, and the magazine lies on top, above the barrel, with the cartridges at 90° to the axis of the barrel. A turntable device in the magazine aligns the cartridges with the bore as it feeds them down in front of the bolt. The magazine is translucent so that the ammunition content can be easily checked. Ejection is downwards, through the hollow pistol grip. All controls are fully ambidextrous; a cocking handle is fitted on both sides and the selector/safety catch is a rotary switch beneath the trigger. There are open sights on both sides of the main collimating optical sight, so that should the optical sight be damaged one set of sights can be used by either left- or right-handed firers. The P90 is still in course of advanced development and is currently being evaluated by a number of military forces.

STEYR TACTICAL MACHINE PISTOL

FN P90

The Vigneron was designed in the 1950s and adopted by the Belgian Army in 1953. It has now been replaced by the Uzi and MP5 and the weapons were disposed of to Algeria, Burundi, Congo, Portugal and Rwanda. The Vigneron is similar to many designs of the period, a light weapon made from steel stampings and uncomplicated components. The barrel is longer than normal but it incorporates a compensator and muzzle brake. The pistol grip has an integral grip safety which locks the bolt to the rear when free. The change lever also has a safety position, and when the lever is set for automatic fire a slight pressure on the trigger will produce single shots; heavier pressure produces automatic fire. A wire stock telescopes into tubes alongside the receiver, and the stock length can be adjusted to suit the individual.

9mm Vigneron M2

Soc Anon Précision Liégeoise

9 × 19mm Parabellum

Operation	Blowback
Length, stock extended	890mm (35.0in)
Length, stock folded	705mm (27.75in)
Weight empty	3.29kg (7.25lb)
Barrel	305mm (12in), 6 grooves, rh

VIGNERON M2

Magazine	32-shot detachable box
Cyclic rate	625rds/min
Muzzle velocity	365m/sec (1,200ft/sec)

BRAZIL

The INA MB50 is a copy of the Danish Madsen made in Brazil under licence by Industria Nacional de Armas who acquired all manufacturing rights. The M953 is a modified version, with an elongated magazine housing and with the cocking handle moved from the top of the receiver to the right side. The extractor, ejector and some other small components were also improved. Both models are in use by military and para-military forces. (Data table refers to the M953.)

.45 INA MB50 and M953

Industria Nacional de Armas

.45 ACP

Operation	Blowback
Length, stock extended	794mm (31.26in)
Length, stock folded	546mm (21.50in)

INA MB50

Weight empty	3.40kg (7.49lb)
Barrel	213mm (8.39in), 4 grooves, rh
Magazine	30-shot detachable box
Cyclic rate	650rds/min
Muzzle velocity	280m/sec (918ft/sec)

9mm Madsen CEL

Industria Materiel Belico de Brasil	
9 × 19mm Parabellum	
Operation	Blowback
Length, stock extended	794mm (31.26in)
Length, stock folded	546mm (21.50in)
Weight empty	3.74kg (8.25lb)
Barrel	213mm (8.39in), 6 grooves, rh

This is a conversion of the INA M953 (above) to 9mm Parabellum chambering, developed in the middle 1980s. The weapon remains the same except that the barrel is now fitted with a very efficient muzzle compensator. The CEL is in process of issue to military and paramilitary forces and will, within the next few years, replace the .45 INA models.

Magazine	30-shot detachable box
Cyclic rate	600rds/min
Muzzle velocity	392m/sec (1,286ft/sec)

9mm Mekanika Uru

Mekanika Industria e Comercio Lda	
9 × 19mm Parabellum	
Operation	Blowback
Length overall	671mm (26.4in)
Weight empty	3.01kg (6.63lb)
Barrel	175mm (6.89in), 6 grooves, rh
Magazine	30-shot detachable box
Cyclic rate	750rds/min
Muzzle velocity	390m/sec (1,280ft/sec)

This was designed in 1974 and first produced in 1975. After testing, production for the Brazilian police began in 1981. It has also been adopted in small numbers by the Brazilian Army. The Uru is of conventional type, using the blowback system of operation. It is largely made from tubular elements and stampings, spot-welded together; no pins or screws are used and there are only 17 component parts. A silenced version has been developed but has not been put into production.

MEKANIKA URU

CANADA

The C1 submachine-gun is the Canadian version of the British Sterling, manufactured in Canada. All weapons are marked 'CAL' with the date of manufacture on the magazine housing. A few modifications have been made from the original Sterling design, particularly in the magazine and the trigger mechanism. The magazine capacity has been reduced from 34 to 30 rounds, and an alternative magazine holding 10 rounds can be provided for special operations. The other obvious difference lies in the bayonet, which is that of the Canadian version of the FN-FAL rifle. Apart from these external changes, there are some small internal modifications which are solely for ease of manufacture and do not affect operation or dimensions.

9mm C1 (Sterling)

Canadian Arsenals Ltd	
9 × 19mm Parabellum	
Operation	Blowback
Length, stock extended	686mm (27.0in)
Length, stock folded	493mm (19.4in)
Weight empty	2.95kg (6.5lb)
Barrel	198mm (7.80in), 6 grooves, rh
Magazine	30-shot detachable box
Cyclic rate	550rds/min
Muzzle velocity	366m/sec (1,200ft/sec)

CHILE

This is a simple blowback weapon which appears to have been influenced by the Sterling. The pistol grip has the same steep rake, the curved magazine fits into the left side of the cylindrical receiver, and the bolt has deep dirt-clearing grooves. Other features have been adopted from other designs, such as the telescoping wire stock of the M3A1 and the spoon shaped muzzle compensator. The FAMAE is in use by Chilean military and police forces.

9mm Famae

Fabricacions Militares FAMAE	
9 × 19mm Parabellum	
Operation	Blowback
Length, stock extended	
Lenght, stock folded	
Weight empty	2.44kg (5.38lb)
Barrel	175mm (6.89in), 4 grooves, rh
Magazine	43-shot detachable box
Cyclic rate	800–875rds/min
Muzzle velocity	400m/sec (1,312ft/sec)

9mm FAMAE

CHINA

7.62mm Type 64

State arsenals	
7.62 × 25mm Type 64	
Operation	Blowback, silenced
Length, stock extended	840mm (32.8in)
Length, stock folded	635mm (25.0in)
Weight empty	3.40kg (7.5lb)
Barrel	244mm (9.5in), 4 grooves, rh
Magazine	30-shot detachable box
Cyclic rate	1,000rds/min
Muzzle velocity	330m/sec (1,082ft/sec)

This is a silenced weapon firing a special subsonic version of the standard 7.62mm Soviet pistol cartridge. It is a selective-fire weapon, operating by blowback, and looking very much as if the inspiration for the mechanism came from the Soviet PPS-43. The trigger mechanism may have been taken from the ZB 26 machine-gun, though it has been simplified and is made from steel stampings. Unlike all Western silenced submachine-guns, the Type 64 is not a standard weapon with a silencer added; the silencer is an integral part of the design. The barrel is drilled for most of its length and fits into the Maxim-type silencer, the sleeve of which locks to the receiver by a threaded ring. The top of the sheet steel body is an unstressed light metal cover which lifts off to reveal the bolt and return spring and a plastic buffer block. There are two manual safeties; the first is a pivoting plate on the right side which swings up to close part of the ejection opening and hold the bolt forward, much like the safety catch on the Kalashnikov rifles; the second is a more usual button which locks the trigger when the bolt is cocked. A change-lever allows single shots or automatic fire, an unusual feature in a silenced weapon where automatic fire usually wears out the barrel and silencer very rapidly. The butt folds beneath the body and the sights have two settings, marked '10' and '20' which relate to 100m and 200m ranges.

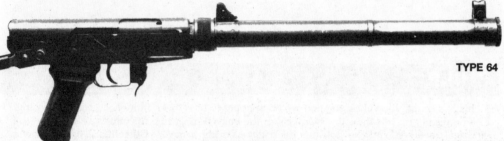

TYPE 64

7.62mm Type 79

State arsenals	
7.62 × 25mm Soviet	
Operation	Blowback
Length, stock extended	740mm (29.13in)
Length, stock folded	470mm (18.5in)

This is an extremely lightweight weapon made from steel stampings and firing the standard 7.62mm pistol cartridge. The receiver is rectangular and has a safety lever and fire selector on the right side which is modelled after that of the Kalashnikov rifles. Operation is simple blowback, and the steel stock can be folded over the top of the receiver.

Weight empty	1.90kg (4.19lb)	Magazine	20-shot detachable box
Barrel	275mm (10.82in, 4 grooves, rh	Cyclic rate	650rds/min
		Muzzle velocity	500m/sec (1,640ft/sec)

7.62mm Type 85

State arsenals	
7.62 × 25mm Soviet	
Operation	Blowback

This is a modified and simplified version of the Type 79. It is a plain blowback weapon with a cylindrical receiver carrying the bolt and return spring. The magazine is a curved box, but the straight magazine of the Type 79 can also be fitted if desired. It is notable that the manufacturers claim that this weapon will fire the subsonic Type 64 cartridge with equal facility.

TYPE 85

Length, stock extended	628mm (24.7in)
Length, stock folded	444mm (17.5in)
Weight empty	1.90kg (4.19lb)
Barrel	210mm (8.27in), 4 grooves, rh

Magazine	30-shot detachable box
Cyclic rate	780rds/min
Muzzle velocity	500m/sec (1,640ft/sec)

As the title implies, this is a silenced version of the Type 85 and is, broadly, a simplified and cheaper version of the Type 64 silenced weapon, produced principally for export. It uses the same silencing arrangements as the Type 64 and fires the same subsonic cartridge. It is also possible to fire the standard Type 51 pistol cartridge though in such cases the silencing effect will be less and will be confined to the gun blast.

7.62mm Type 85 Silenced

State arsenals	
7.62 × 25mm Type 64	
Operation	Blowback, silenced

TYPE 85 SILENCED

Length, stock extended	869mm (34.2in)
Length, stock folded	631mm (24.84in)
Weight empty	2.50kg (5.51lb)
Barrel	240mm (9.45in), 4 grooves, rh
Magazine	30-shot detachable box
Cyclic rate	800rds/min
Muzzle velocity	300m/sec (985ft/sec)

CZECHOSLOVAKIA

The ZK 383 was first produced in the late 1930s and although production ended in about 1947, it remained in use in odd places until the early 1960s. A large and heavy weapon, a design typical of its period, it is an exceptionally robust weapon which has been used as a squad light machine-gun on occasions. During World War Two it was issued to the Bulgarian Army and to some German units. It is generally similar to contemporary designs of submachine-gun but has a few features which are peculiar to it; the first is a bipod which obviously helps accurate shooting, the second is a quick-change barrel, and the third is a removable weight in the bolt. This allows the gun to fire either at 500 or 700 rounds per minute, although it is difficult to see what benefit was supposed to accrue from this, since the bipod and the gun's weight were enough to ensure steadiness even at the higher rate of fire. Early versions had a rigidly fixed barrel, a bayonet lug on the barrel jacket, and a front pistol grip. One variation, the ZK 383H, had a folding magazine which stowed under the barrel by pivoting on a pin, and the police version, the ZK 383P, did away with the bipod and had a more simple rear sight. Despite this variety and the apparent complication of the design, the ZK 383 sold in small numbers to the Bulgarian Army and to Venezuela, Bolivia and other South American states; it is believed that some may still be held in reserve in some South American police and para-military formations.

9mm ZK 383, 383H, 383P

Ceskoslovenska Zbrojovka	
9 × 19mm Parabellum	
Operation	Blowback
Length	902mm (35.5in)
Weight empty	4.25kg (9.37lb)
Barrel	325mm (12.80in), 6 grooves, rh
Magazine	30-shot detachable box
Cyclic rate	500 or 700 rds/min
Muzzle velocity	380m/sec (1,247ft/sec)

ZK383

9mm CZ 23 and 25

Ceskoslovenska Zbrojovka	
9 × 19mm Parabellum	
Operation	Blowback
Length overall	686mm (27.0in)
Weight empty	3.06kg (6.75lb)
Barrel	285mm (11.22in), 6 grooves, rh
Magazine	24- or 40-shot detachable box
Cyclic rate	600rds/min
Muzzle velocity	380m/sec (1,247ft/sec)

7.62mm CZ 24 and 26

Ceskoslovenska Zbrojovka	
7.62 × 25mm Soviet	
Operation	Blowback
Length, stock extended	686mm (27.0in)
Length, stock folded	445mm (17.52in)
Weight empty	3.29kg (7.25lb)
Barrel	285mm (11.22in), 4 grooves, rh
Magazine	32-shot detachable box
Cyclic rate	600rds/min
Muzzle velocity	550m/sec (1,805ft/sec)

The CZ 23 was designed in the late 1940s and went into production in 1948 as the M48A; the designation was changed to CZ 23 in 1950. It was issued to the Czech Army in considerable numbers in the early 1950s but manufacture ceased in about 1954, largely because of the demand for standardisation of calibres in the Warsaw Pact armies. Most of the 100,000 or so which had been made were exported to various Middle Eastern countries and to Cuba. Since then, they have appeared in all parts of the world. The principal mechanical feature of the CZ 23 is that it was probably the first submachine-gun made in any quantity to use the wrap-around bolt; the bolt is partly tubular and encloses the rear end of the barrel at the moment of firing. Slots in the tubular portion allow for feed and ejection, and the design gives the necessary mass but allows the overall length to be reduced. The technique is now quite common, but in 1948 it was quite unusual and made the CZ 23 a pioneer. Another innovation was the placing of the magazine in the pistol grip, which can only be done when the breech is set well back in the receiver, as is the case with the wrap-around bolt design. The magazine was another step forward, since it was of near-triangular section and was later taken up and extensively promoted by the Swedish Carl Gustav company. The CZ 25 was similar except that it had a folding metal stock instead of a fixed wooden stock. (Data table refers to the CZ 23.)

The CZ 24 and 26 are much the same as the 23 and 25 except for their calibre; they replaced the 23 and 25 in Czech Army service in 1951 when a general conversion to Soviet standard calibres and ammunition was made. However, the Czechs managed to retain their individuality to the extent that their version of the Soviet 7.62mm pistol cartridge, loaded in Czechoslovakia, carries a more powerful charge and has a somewhat higher velocity. There are some minor differences in the sights and the slope of the pistol grip, but the basic operating characteristics remain the same. The weapons were in first-line use by the Czech Army until the middle 1960s and are now relegated to the reserve. (Data table refers to the CZ 26.)

MODEL 24

MODEL 26

This is variously classed as either a submachine-gun or a machine pistol; it fires a bullet which is marginally useful as a combat round, and it is small enough to be carried in a holster and fired from one hand. It was designed in order to provide armoured vehicle crews with a weapon which they could carry at all times and which would provide some element of self-defence in an emergency. The Skorpion is a blowback weapon, and with its light reciprocating parts a high rate of fire might be expected. However, it contains an ingenious rate-reducing mechanism inside the pistol grip. As the bolt recoils, it drives a weight down into the grip against a spring, and as the bolt reaches the end of its travel it is held by a catch. As the weight rebounds from the spring and returns to the top of the grip, so it trips the catch and releases the bolt to go forward and chamber the next round. The pause is very brief but sufficient to bring the rate of fire down to manageable proportions. One might expect that this mechanism would make itself felt to the firer in the form of unwelcome vibrations, but it is masked by the general recoil and is not noticeable. Since the original introduction in 1963, some variant models have appeared, the differences lying principally in the calibre. The Model 64 is chambered for 9mm Short, and the 65 for 9mm Makarov, but are otherwise identical with the 62. The 68 is chambered for the 9mm Parabellum cartridge and is therefore somewhat larger and more robust. In fact, very few of these variants have ever been seen and it is suspected that they never went past prototype models.

7.65mm Skorpion vz/62

Ceskoslovenska Zbrojovka	
7.65 × 17mm (.32 ACP)	
Operation	Blowback
Length, stock extended	520mm (20.47in)
Length, stock folded	270mm (10.63in)
Weight empty	1.31kg (2.89lb)
Barrel	115mm (4.52in), 6 grooves, rh
Magazine	10- or 20-shot detachable box
Cyclic rate	700rds/min
Muzzle velocity	295m/sec (968ft/sec)

vz/62 SKORPION

DENMARK

One of the last traditional wood-stocked submachine-guns to be developed, this Madsen design had some unusual features. The breech-block was attached to the slide cover (instead of a cocking handle) which extended forward over the barrel and was formed, at the front, into a serrated grip. The recoil spring was wrapped around the barrel and contained within the slide. In order to cock the weapon the slide was grasped and pulled to the rear; in other words, the basic mechanism was that of a giant automatic pistol. An advantage of this design is that the mass of the slide unit helps to resist the breech opening force and thus keeps the rate of fire down, but the drawback is that the slide oscillates back and forth during firing, and the spring around the hot barrel soon overheats and weakens. It met with little success, a small number being sold to Central American states. A version with a folding wire stock was also made in limited numbers.

9mm Madsen M/45

Dansk Industri Syndikat AS Madsen	
9 × 19mm Parabellum	
Operation	Blowback
Length overall	800mm (31.5in)
Weight empty	3.22kg (7.10lb)
Barrel	315mm (12.4in), 4 grooves, rh
Magazine	50-shot detachable box
Cyclic rate	850rds/min
Muzzle velocity	400m/sec (1,312ft/sec)

After the lukewarm reception of the M/45, Madsen set about designing a totally new weapon, applying those manufacturing lessons which the war had taught but aiming to produce a more reliable and attractive weapon than some of the wartime designs. The result was a weapon which was completely conventional in its operation, apart from a rather unusual safety system, but which offered remarkable accessibility and ease of manufacture. The gun is a blowback, firing from the open bolt, and is capable only of automatic fire. A grip safety behind the magazine housing has to be squeezed forward to allow the gun to fire, and a safety catch

9mm Madsen M/46

Dansk Industri Syndikat AS Madsen	
9 × 19mm Parabellum	
Operation	Blowback

Length, stock extended	800mm (31.5in)
Length, stock folded	545mm (21.45in)
Weight empty	3.17kg (6.99lb)
Barrel	196mm (7.72in), 4 grooves, rh
Magazine	32-shot detachable box
Cyclic rate	500rds/min
Muzzle velocity	380m/sec (1,247ft/sec)

on the rear of the receiver locks the bolt in the open position. The receiver is formed from two metal pressings which comprise two halves of the receiver, pistol grip, magazine housing and barrel bearing. The two halves are hinged together at the rear of the body and the heel of the pistol grip, and are held together by a massive barrel nut which encloses the rear of the barrel and engages in a screw thread formed in the two halves. The left half can be hinged open, leaving all the working parts in place, giving unrivalled access to the mechanism for cleaning and maintenance. The only difficulty lay in the cocking handle, which was a flat plate on top of the receiver which extended down the sides to provide finger grips; this had to be unscrewed from the bolt to allow the gun to be stripped. The weapon was well made and reliable, but it sold in relatively small numbers to South American countries and to Thailand.

MADSEN M46

9mm Madsen M/50 and M/53

Dansk Industri Syndikat AS Madsen	
9 × 19mm Parabellum	
Operation	Blowback
Length, stock extended	800mm (31.5in)
Length, stock folded	530mm (20.85in)
Weight empty	3.17kg (6.99lb)
Barrel	197mm (7.75in), 4 grooves, rh
Magazine	32-shot detachable box
Cyclic rate	550rds/min
Muzzle velocity	380m/sec (1,247ft/sec)

The Madsen M/50 was a minor modification of the M/46; the cocking handle was changed to be a small knob attached to the top of the bolt, acting in a slot between the two halves of the receiver. This meant that it was no longer necessary to remove the cocking handle before stripping. It was a moderately successful design, selling to Indonesia and several South and Central American countries. The M/53 is a further advance on the same general design; the principal change is the adoption of a curved magazine, giving more reliable feeding, and a change in the barrel securing nut. The M/53 nut screws on to a thread on the barrel itself, the portion surrounding the forward end of the receiver being a plain ring which simply holds the two halves tightly together. First models of the M/53 were like the M/46 and M/50 in firing automatic only, but a Mark 2 version had a selector switch above the pistol grip and could fire single shots. Sales of the M/53 were fairly substantial, again mainly to South America. The Madsen company went out of the weapons business in the early 1960s and the submachine-gun design was not taken further, but the INA of Brazil is derived from it.

MADSEN M50

Although this has a superficial resemblance to the Carl Gustav, it is a different weapon and was originally developed by Husqvarna of Sweden during World War Two as a contender for the Swedish Army requirement. The Swedes chose the Carl Gustav and in 1947, when the Danes wanted a submachine-gun, Husqvarna sold them the production rights to the Hovea. There is nothing unusual about the design which, so far as the internals go, is more or less based upon the Sten gun. The external appearance is only noteworthy for the peculiar magazine housing, which was designed to take the Suomi drum magazine, though in the end the Carl Gustav box magazine was selected for service use.

9mm Hovea

Haerens Vabenarsenalet	
9 × 19mm Parabellum	
Operation	Blowback
Length, stock extended	806mm (31.72in)
Length, stock folded	550mm (21.65in)

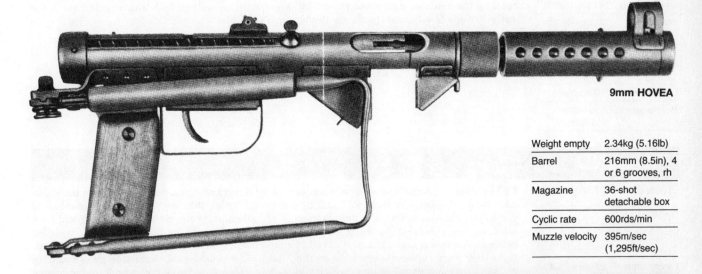

9mm HOVEA

Weight empty	2.34kg (5.16lb)
Barrel	216mm (8.5in), 4 or 6 grooves, rh
Magazine	36-shot detachable box
Cyclic rate	600rds/min
Muzzle velocity	395m/sec (1,295ft/sec)

DOMINICAN REPUBLIC

The Cristobal Model 2 was manufactured in San Cristobal in a factory originally organised with the assistance of technicians who had worked with Beretta and with the Hungarian 'Danuvia' plant in Budapest. Although, in appearance, the Cristobal resembles the early Berettas, it uses a different operating system, relying upon a delayed blowback two-piece bolt patented by Kiraly, a Hungarian designer, who worked in San Cristobal in the post-World War Two years. A pendant lever attached to the bolt engages with the receiver, and as the lighter front section of the bolt recoils, it is forced to rotate the lever against the fulcrum formed by a recess in the receiver, so that the upper end of the lever pushes the heavier rear section of the bolt backwards. This causes sufficient delay in the opening to allow the bullet to leave the barrel before case extraction begins. The Modelo 62 is a more modern version, using the same mechanism but with a perforated barrel jacket instead of the full-length wooden stock of the Modelo 2. It may also be found with a folding skeleton butt. Both models use double triggers, the front trigger giving single shots, the rear trigger for automatic fire. Perhaps the most unusual feature is the use of the .30in Carbine cartridge; the light bullet, deficient in stopping power, is, to some extent, balanced by the velocity, which is higher than usual for this class of weapon.

.30in Cristobal Modelo 2 and Model 62

Armeria Fabrica de Armas	
.30in M1 Carbine	
Operation	Delayed blowback
Length overall	945mm (37.2in)
Weight empty	3.51kg (7.74lb)
Barrel	410mm (16.14in), 4 grooves, rh
Magazine	25- or 30-shot detachable box
Cyclic rate	575rds/min
Muzzle velocity	564m/sec (1,850ft/sec)

CRISTOBAL MODEL 2

ESTONIA

9mm Tallinn M1923 Submachine-gun

Tallinn Arsenal, Estonia	
9 × 19mm Parabellum	
Operation	Blowback
Length overall	809mm (31.85in)
Weight empty	4.28kg (9.44lb)
Barrel	210mm (8.27in), 4 grooves, rh twist
Magazine	40-shot detachable box
Cyclic rate	600rds/min
Muzzle velocity	390m/sec (1,280ft/sec)

An early and little-known weapon, and probably the only weapon designed and manufactured in Estonia, the Tallinn is broadly compiled from the Bergmann MP18/1. It was a blowback weapon with wooden stock and a slot-perforated jacket around the barrel. The magazine fits into the side, and there is the usual optimistic tangent sight of the period, marked up to 600m, on top of the receiver. The magazine is remarkably slender, and the bolt does not follow the massive Bergmann pattern but has a reduced-diameter front end similar to the Thompson. The barrel is unusual in having longitudinal cooling fins machined in its surface, concealed by the jacket except for the last few millimetres around the muzzle. The Tallinn was used by the Estonian Army and police, but appears to have been withdrawn some time in the early 1930s; a few turned up during the Spanish Civil War.

FINLAND

9mm Suomi Model 31

Oy Tikkakoski AB	
9 × 19mm Parabellum	
Operation	Blowback
Length overall	875mm (34.45in)
Weight empty	4.87kg (10.74lb)
Barrel	318mm (12.52in), 6 grooves, rh

The Suomi submachine-guns were designed by Aimo Lahti and manufactured in the state-owned Tikkakoski factory. Lahti began designing in 1922 and produced a number of varying prototypes before the first Finnish Army adoption of the m/26. This was chambered for the 7.63mm Mauser cartridge and was distinguished by a long buffer housing extending behind the receiver and a sharply curved 36-round box magazine. Few of these were produced, since they were replaced very soon by the Model 31, a considerably improved design and an outstandingly successful weapon which was widely adopted and which was built under licence in Sweden, Denmark and Switzerland. Until 1939 the Suomi was generally accepted as the standard by which to measure other designs. Although heavy by today's standards the M31 is capable of surprising accuracy from its long barrel and it is, of course, made in the 'old-

SUOMI M31

SWEDISH-MADE MODEL 37/39

fashioned' way with all the parts either machined from solid steel or forged from heavy gauge material. The bolt handle is at the rear of the receiver and works in much the same manner as a rifle bolt, being pulled to the rear to retract the bolt and then pushed forward and turned down, to remain stationary while the bolt moves within the receiver. The barrel dismounts from the jacket fairly easily and the bolt has a fixed firing pin. Perhaps the most significant feature of the Suomi was the magazine; box magazines for 20 and 50 shots were provided and so, too, was a 71-shot drum which was later copied by the Russians for their PPSh41. It seems probable that Lahti drew upon the Thompson drum for his inspiration, and he made a very good job of copying it for, despite the loaded weight of 2.49kg, the magazine is remarkably robust. A smaller drum for 40 shots was later developed, and in the middle 1950s all the M31 guns were converted to take the Swedish Carl Gustav 36-shot magazine.

Magazine	20-, 36-, 40- or 50-shot detachable boxes or 40- or 71-shot drums
Cyclic rate	900rds/min
Muzzle velocity	395m/sec (1,295ft/sec)

The M44 is a copy of the Soviet PPS43, modified so as to permit the use of 9mm ammunition. The weapon is a simple blowback, capable only of automatic fire, and made from simple stampings and pressings welded together. The modified feed system, however, allows the use of the 71-shot Suomi drum, as well as the other box magazines. In common with the M31, the M44 was modified in the mid-1950s to use the 36-shot Carl Gustav magazine. The M44 remained in use until the late 1960s but has now been replaced by the 7.62mm Valmet assault rifle.

9mm Model 44

Oy Tikkakoski AB	
9 × 19mm Parabellum	
Operation	Blowback
Length, stock extended	825mm (32.48in)
Length, stock folded	623mm (24.53in)
Weight empty	2.80kg (6.17lb)
Barrel	247mm (9.72in), 4 or 6 grooves, rh
Magazine	71-shot drum or 50-shot detachable box
Cyclic rate	650rds/min
Muzzle velocity	380m/sec (1,247ft/sec)

This is simply an improved model of the M44, produced after the end of the war and thus given more time and a better finish. The only major change is that the feed arrangements are again changed so that the 71-shot drum can no longer be used and the only magazine which would fit was the 36-shot Carl Gustav pattern. There are very small changes in some dimensions due to changed manufacturing techniques, but for all practical purposes the M44 and M44/46 can be considered the same.

9mm Model 44/46

Oy Tikkakoski AB	
9 × 19mm Parabellum	

FRANCE

Derived from the SE-MAS of 1935, the MAS 38 was first made in 1938 and continued in production until 1949, a limited number being made for police use during the German occupation. It was a good and workmanlike design, well made and somewhat in advance of contemporary thinking. It was reasonably light and diverged from the usual pattern of full-length wooden stock and complicated mechanisms. Although primarily made from machined steel stock, the MAS 38 contained nothing that was not necessary and so managed to avoid the weight penalty. A slide on the right side engages with the bolt and, on being pulled to the rear, cocks the weapon and opens the ejection port at the same time. The slide then stays to the rear. A spring plate covers the magazine housing aperture when the weapon is not loaded. The bolt moves in a tube which contains a long return spring and which is not in line with the barrel. The bolt therefore meets the breech at an angle and the bolt face is machined to allow for this. The stock is almost in a straight line with the barrel and this, combined with the low-powered cartridge, gives the gun good accuracy and low recoil movement.

7.65mm MAS 38

Manufacture d'Armes de St Etienne	
7.65 × 19.5mm Longue	
Operation	Blowback
Length overall	734mm (28.90in)
Weight empty	2.87kg (6.33lb)
Barrel	224mm (8.82in), 4 grooves, rh
Magazine	32-shot detachable box
Cyclic rate	600rds/min
Muzzle velocity	351m/sec (1,152ft/sec)

The MAS 38 was never produced in any other calibre than 7.65mm Longue and was consequently of no interest to any other European power; a 9mm version might well have enjoyed commercial success. It saw use in French Indo-China and from there passed into Vietnamese hands, and a number were subsequently modified to accept the Soviet 7.62mm pistol cartridge. They are likely to be met in any former French colony.

MAS 38

9mm MAT 49

Manufacture d'Armes de Tulle

9 × 19mm Parabellum

Operation	Blowback
Length, stock extended	720mm (28.35in)
Length, stock folded	460mm (18.11in)
Weight empty	3.50kg (7.72lb)

MAT 49

Barrel	228mm (8.98in), 4 grooves, rh
Magazine	20- or 32-shot detachable box
Cyclic rate	600rds/min
Muzzle velocity	390m/sec (1,280ft/sec)

This was adopted by the French Army in 1949 and is still in limited use by them; it is also widely used by Gendarmerie and police units, and by the military forces of former French colonies. As with the MAS 38, a number which fell into Vietnamese hands can be found modified to fire the Soviet 7.62mm pistol cartridge. Like the MAS 38, the MAT 49 is a simple and effective design; it is made from heavy steel stampings and a minimum of machined parts, and this effort to reduce manufacturing costs has resulted in a somewhat 'square' appearance. The sliding wire stock resembles that of the US M3 gun, and the pistol grip has plastic furniture and a grip safety. The magazine housing is unusual in pivoting forward to lie under the barrel when it is necessary to carry the weapon compactly; the housing also serves as a forward hand grip, and the magazine being folded forward acts as a very positive safety device. The magazine itself is a single-column design which is prone to misfeed stoppages.

5.7mm GIAT Personal Weapon

Groupement Industrial des Armements Terrestres

5.7 × 25mm GIAT

This is currently in the prototype stage but is said to form part of a new family of weapons known as the 'Armes de Défense Rapprochée' or ADR. The family will consist of a pistol, a small assault rifle and this 'Personal Defence Weapon'. All will be chambered for a new 5.7 × 25mm cartridge which has been developed by GIAT, which is the French government bureau controlling the various armament factories. GIAT claim that this round had an effective range four times that of the 9mm Parabellum bullet, and one-third less recoil. The weapon shown here is the first prototype and is only one of several ideas being explored. The intention is to develop a compact and easily used weapon which can be carried comfortably and which will be easy to use in confined spaces. It will weigh under 2kg and will be less than 300mm long. The magazine is inserted into the rear pistol grip; the rear grip and trigger are used to fire from the hip. For more deliberate fire the rear grip is placed against the shoulder as a butt and the front grip and trigger used to fire the weapon. No dimensions or details of the mechanism have yet been made public.

GERMANY (Pre-1945)

The MP18/I is an historic weapon and a landmark in the history of submachine-guns and of military weapons in general. Although pre-empted by the Italian Vilar Perosa (qv), the MP18 is undoubtedly the first true submachine-gun, designed around a tactical concept of infiltration, fire and movement. Development began in 1916 and over 30,000 had been made by November 1918, most of which were in use on the Western Front. Designed by Hugo Schmeisser, whose name is so well-known in the small arms field, it was the first true blowback submachine-gun, it set the pattern for subsequent development for some 20 years, and its influence can be seen in almost every design of the 1920s and early 1930s. Although forbidden to the German Army of the 1920s by the Versailles Treaty, they were allowed to be used by the German police in some numbers. The gun was originally designed to use the Parabellum 'snail' magazine developed for the Artillery Model pistol, and an adapter slipped over the mouth of the magazine located it at the correct feeding distance. This proved unsatisfactory and during the police use of the weapon most were modified to accept a conventional straight box magazine of 20- or 32-shot sizes. The MP18/I was simple, strong, not too difficult to manufacture, and, except for initial feed troubles which were eventually shown to be due to the bullet shape, very reliable. It was a success from its inception, and later designers who departed from its basic principles frequently found themselves in trouble.

The MP28/II was the direct descendant of the MP18/I and was substantially similar, though there are several minor modifications and improvements. The principal changes were the inclusion of a selector mechanism to allow single-shot firing as well as automatic, and the adoption of a side-feeding box magazine instead of the original 'snail'. A separate firing pin and an improved mainspring were the chief internal changes and, apart from a new rearsight, the external appearance was little changed. The gun was intended purely as a commercial proposition and was entirely successful, large numbers being made in Germany and under licence in Belgium and Spain. It was used by the Belgian Army and widely sold to South America. As well as being made in 9mm Parabellum, it was supplied to Portugal in 7.65mm Parabellum calibre in 1929.

9mm MP18/I

Theodor Bergmann Waffenbau AG

9 × 19mm Parabellum

Operation	Blowback
Length overall	812mm (31.97in)
Weight empty	4.19kg (9.25lb)
Barrel	196mm (7.75in), 6 grooves, rh
Magazine	32-shot helical drum
Cyclic rate	400rds/min
Muzzle velocity	380m/sec (1,247ft/sec)

9mm MP28/II

C. G. Haenel Waffen- und Fahrradfabrik AG

9 × 19mm Parabellum

Operation	Blowback
Length overall	812mm (32.0in)
Weight empty	3.97kg (8.75lb)
Barrel	196mm (7.75in), 6 grooves, rh
Magazine	20- 32- or 50-shot detachable box
Cyclic rate	500rds/min
Muzzle velocity	380m/sec (1,247ft/sec)

MP18/1

MP28/II

9mm Bergmann MP34/I and 35/I

Carl Walther Waffenfabrik AG; Junker & Ruh AG	
9 × 19mm Parabellum	
Operation	Blowback
Length overall	840mm (33.1in)
Weight empty	4.05kg (8.93lb)
Barrel	196mm (7.75in), 6 grooves, rh
Magazine	24- or 32-shot detachable box
Cyclic rate	650rds/min
Muzzle velocity	380m/sec (1,247ft/sec)

This is the only submachine to be actually designed by a Bergmann brother, other so-called Bergmanns being actually due to Schmeisser. The prototypes were made in Denmark by Schutz & Larsen in 1932, due to the restrictions of the Versailles Treaty, after which Bergmann licensed production to Carl Walther. About 2,000 MP34/I were made for the German police and for export to Bolivia. The Bergmann was very well made and finished and had few unusual features, the most obvious of which was the right-hand side-feeding magazine. The bolt handle was also peculiar to this design, as it projected from the rear of the receiver and had to be rotated and pulled back to retract the bolt. The advantage claimed for this was a stationary handle when firing and no bolt slot through which dirt could enter the mechanism. Another feature was the 'double-acting' trigger; the gun fired semi-automatically when the trigger was pulled half-way back, and full automatic when pulled further back. The MP34/I was offered in various calibres and with long and short barrels, but so far as is known only 9mm versions were ever produced. In 1935 some modifications were applied; these were almost entirely internal and designed to simplify production and improve reliability, and the resulting design became the MP35/I, quantities being sold to Ethiopia, Denmark and Sweden. In 1940 the Waffen SS arranged licensed production by Junker & Ruh AG, and this company produced some 40,000 weapons before 1945, entirely for the Waffen SS.

9mm Erma MPE

Erfurter Maschinenfabrik B. Geipel GmbH (Erma-Werke)	
9 × 19mm Parabellum	
Operation	Blowback
Length overall	902mm (35.5in)
Weight empty	4.14kg (9.13lb)
Barrel	254mm (10.0in), 6 grooves, rh
Magazine	25- or 32-shot detachable box
Cyclic rate	500rds/min
Muzzle velocity	380m/sec (1,247ft/sec)

The MPE (Maschinen Pistole Erma) was designed by Vollmer, an Erma employee, and is frequently referred to by that name. Vollmer developed it in the late 1920s and the design was manufactured as a commercial venture from 1930 until 1938, when production of the MP38 swept all else aside in the Erma factory. During the early 1930s numbers were sold to France, Mexico and South American countries, and it appeared in the Gran Chaco War of 1932–35. It also saw a little use in the Spanish Civil War. The German Army began taking deliveries in about 1933 and it remained in use until about 1942, when it was eventually withdrawn and replaced by the MP40. The design was a simple tubular receiver with a jacketed barrel and a side-feed magazine; the most obvious recognition feature is the vertical wooden fore-grip located just behind the magazine area. Internally, the MPE used Vollmer's telescoping mainspring casing which later appeared on the MP38, and the bolt handle locked into a safety slot. Minor variants include one with a conventional wooden fore-end, and one which has a bayonet attachment, though these are rare.

ERMA MPE

9mm MP38

Erfurter Maschinenfabrik B. Geipel GmbH (Erma-Werke)	
9 × 19mm Parabellum	
Operation	Blowback
Length, stock extended	832mm (32.75in)
Length, stock folded	630mm (24.75in)
Weight empty	4.14kg (9.13lb)
Barrel	247mm (9.75in), 6 grooves, rh

This is probably the most famous and well-recognised military submachine-gun of all time, and it has gone into history under an entirely incorrect name; frequently called the 'Schmeisser', in fact Hugo Schmeisser had nothing at all to do with its design or manufacture. It was designed by Vollmer and produced by the Erma-Werke, the first development being a private venture which was offered to the German Army and turned down. But in 1938 the infant Panzer Corps required a weapon for their tank crews and mechanised infantry, turned to Erma and were rewarded with the MP38. From the very first, it was a leader in its field. It was the first submachine-gun to be without wood in its furniture, the first to use a successful folding metal stock and the first to have been designed for a modern, fast-moving mechanised army. Like its predecessor the MP18/1 it set a fashion which was followed by others, and even today its influence can still be discerned. A simple enough blowback weapon, the MP38 suffered from two drawbacks; the first, shared by others, was the single-column magazine, which was inefficient and led to jams, and the second was that the gun was made in the traditional manner, machined from steel stock, and was therefore slow and expensive to make. Not long after the

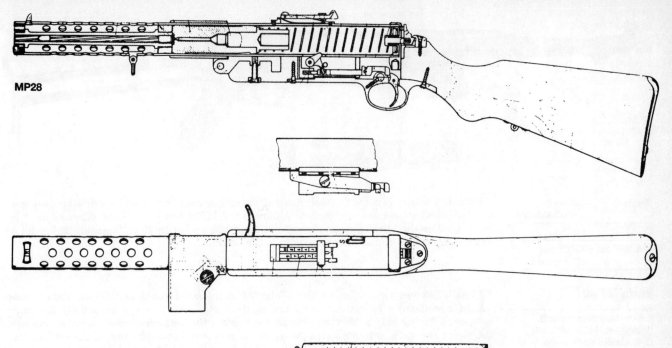

MP28

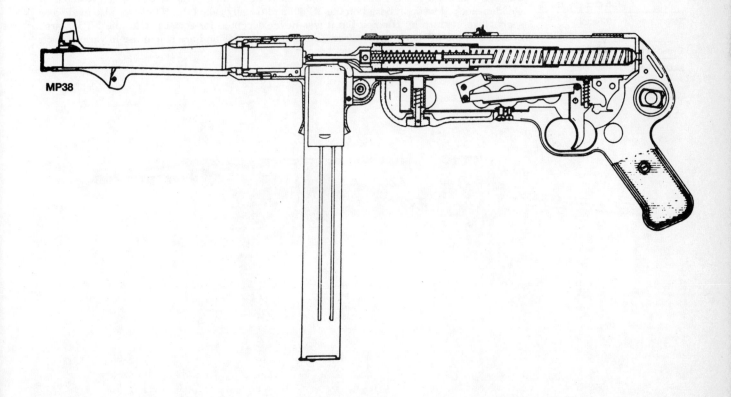

MP38

MP38

MP40

Magazine	32-shot detachable box
Cyclic rate	500rds/min
Muzzle velocity	380m/sec (1,247ft/sec)

outbreak of war in 1939 the German Army realised they could not afford the time and expense involved, and sought another design. Although the MP38 has never been officially used by anyone other than the German Army, and their use ended in 1945, there are still a lot in existence and they can appear anywhere in the world.

9mm MP40

Erfurter Maschinenfabrik B. Geipel GmbH (Erma-Werke); C. G. Haenel Waffen- und Fahrradfabrik AG; Steyr-Daimler-Puch AG

9 × 19mm Parabellum	
Operation	Blowback
Length, stock extended	832mm (32.75in)
Length, stock folded	629mm (24.75in)
Weight empty	3.97kg (8.75lb)
Barrel	248mm (9.75in), 6 grooves, rh
Magazine	32-shot detachable box
Cyclic rate	500rds/min
Muzzle velocity	380m/sec (1,247ft/sec)

The MP40 was a simplified version of the MP38, intended to reduce the time and expense of manufacture by introducing more modern methods. It was substantially the same weapon, differing only in such matters as the ejector, the magazine catch, and the receiver; the major and most important change lay in the method of manufacture, designed for mass production using pressings and simple sub-assemblies which could be made by small subcontractors spread throughout Germany. As far as possible the use of high-grade steel was avoided, and spot welding was used for joints. The result was a highly practical and effective weapon, the manufacturing techniques of which were soon copied by almost every other nation, and the idea of building basic sub-assemblies for limited life has been followed by every military firearms manufacturer. The MP40 went through several minor variants, but the external differences are few. The most interesting version was the MP40/II, produced in late 1943 in an effort to match the firepower of the Soviet PPSH41. This used a 71-shot drum magazine, and in order to try and compete with this the 38/II had a dual magazine housing which held two magazines. One was aligned with the feedway; after this was emptied, the other magazine could be pushed across into alignment and the first one changed. In practice the idea was not a success because of the excess weight and poor balance which resulted. A wooden-stocked weapon based on the MP40, and usually called the MP41 was also made as a speculative venture by Haenel, but it was never accepted for service. Like the MP38, large numbers of the MP40 emigrated from Germany after 1945 and are still in use in various parts of the world.

Although not an outstanding weapon, the 'Gerät Potsdam' is one of the most interesting and unusual weapons of the World War Two period. It was a careful and deliberate attempt to produce an identical copy of another design – a forgery, in fact – in this case of the British Sten Mark II, and a great deal of work went into ensuring that the copy was indistinguishable from the original, even the British markings being reproduced. Although it is possible for the expert to detect differences, at the time these guns were made very few people would have known what to look for, and the ordinary soldier would have taken it at face value. The object behind this was to provide weapons for German guerrilla and 'stay-behind' parties behind Allied lines. Between 25,000 and 28,000 of these guns were made by Mauser over the winter of 1944/45, but although a few reached the hands of German regular troops, none were ever used for their intended purpose, since the German guerrilla forces never came into existence. The entire expensive exercise was to no purpose and remains one more example of the extraordinary way in which the German High Command would follow some impulsive scheme which bore no relation to reality.

Any gunmaker, given a new design to study, will tell you how he could have done it better, and Mauser were no exception. In studying the Sten gun for the development of the Gerät Potsdam, they saw various ways of altering the design to better suit their own predilections and methods of manufacture, and when the German Army demanded a cheap and simple submachine-gun in early 1945 the MP3008 was the result. The Army, faced with massive losses on the Eastern Front and demands for weapons from the Volkssturm and the putative guerrilla movement, ordered several firms into production and each made slight changes in the design, so that some had pistol grips, some had wooden butts, while most were similar to the Sten. The principal two changes are firstly the use of a vertical magazine in the usual German manner, and secondly the exposed barrel without the perforated jacket of the Sten. Methods of welding and assembly differed according to the ideas of the factory which made the weapon, and some of the makers have never been identified. In general, the finish was crude in the extreme, but the weapons worked. Figures for production are not available, but it is doubtful if more than one or two thousand were ever made since production did not begin until early in 1945 and was soon disrupted.

9mm Gerät Potsdam

Mauser-Werke AG

9 × 19mm Parabellum

Operation	Blowback
Length overall	762mm (30.0in)
Weight empty	2.98kg (6.57lb)
Barrel	196mm (7.75in), 2 or 6 grooves, rh
Magazine	32-shot detachable box
Cyclic rate	550rds/min
Muzzle velocity	380m/sec (1,247ft/sec)

9mm MP3008

Mauser-Werke AG;
Erfurter Maschinenfabrik B.
Geipel GmbH (Erma-Werke);
C. G. Haenel Waffen- und
Fahrradfabrik AG;
Walter Steiner Eisenkonstruction

9 × 19mm Parabellum

Operation	Blowback
Length overall	800mm (31.50in)
Weight empty	2.95kg (6.5lb)
Barrel	196mm (7.75in), 6 or 8 grooves, rh
Magazine	32-shot detachable box
Cyclic rate	500rds/min
Muzzle velocity	380m/sec (1,247ft/sec)

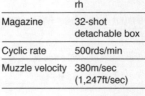

MP3008

GERMANY (Post-1945)

9mm DUX M53

Fabrica de Arms de Oviedo	
9 × 19mm Parabellum	
Operation	Blowback
Length, stock extended	825mm (32.5in)
Length, stock folded	615mm (24.25in)
Weight empty	3.49kg (7.69lb)

It will be recalled that the Finnish M44 was a redesign of the Soviet PPS43 submachine-gun. In 1944, Willi Daugs, one of the M44 design team, fled from Finland, taking with him the drawings of the M44. After a spell in Germany, he ended up in Spain where he obtained employment at the Oviedo Arsenal. There, in collaboration with Ludwig Vorgrimmler, another refugee, another weapon was designed, based upon the M44 drawings. Ten prototypes were made, known as the DUX M51, and one was given to the German Border Police for test. They were sufficiently impressed to order 1,000, which were made at Oviedo in 1954 as the DUX M53. The design was later studied by the Bundeswehr, who contracted with Anschutz to develop a number of improved prototypes, but none was taken into use. The DUX M53 was, quite simply, the Soviet PPS43/Finn M44 but of better quality and finish. The only major change is the use of a Swiss-made 50-shot magazine based on that of the Suomi. Although a somewhat ugly weapon, there is no argument that it was effective and robust, and it remained in use by the Border Police until the late 1960s.

DUX M59

Barrel	248mm (9.75in), 6 grooves, rh
Magazine	50-shot detachable box
Cyclic rate	500rds/min
Muzzle velocity	390m/sec (1,280ft/sec)

9mm Walther MPL and MPK

Carl Walther Waffenfabrik	
9 × 19mm Parabellum	
MPL:	
Operation	Blowback
Length, stock extended	746mm (29.4in)
Length, stock folded	462mm (18,20in)
Weight empty	3.0kg (6.61lb)
Barrel	250mm (10.25in), 6 grooves, rh
Magazine	32-shot detachable box
Cyclic rate	500rds/min
Muzzle velocity	390m/sec (1,280ft/sec)
MPK where different from above:	
Length, stock extended	660mm (25.6in)
Length, stock folded	380mm (15.0in)
Weight empty	2.83kg (6.24lb)
Barrel	173mm (6.81in), 6 grooves, rh
Muzzle velocity	360m/sec (1,180ft/sec)

The Walther MP is a blowback weapon using steel stampings for most of the basic structure. The bolt is overhung, the bulk of it being above the axis of the barrel and overlapping the breech in the closed position, and it is located on a guide rod which carries the return spring. The sights are an ingenious combination of open sights for snap shooting and an aperture and barleycorn for more accurate work when time allows. The folding stock is unusual in that it can be folded to either side of the weapon. Production began in 1963 and two models were produced, the MPL with a long barrel and MPK with short barrel. The only differences are in the length of barrel and associated handguard. It was not widely adopted for military service but several police forces took it and are still using it. Manufacture ceased in 1987.

MPL & MPK

This is derived from the highly successful H&K series of rifles insofar as it uses the same roller-locked delayed blowback system of operation and shares a number of components – such as the pistol grip and trigger unit – with the rifles. Because of its system of operation it fires from a closed bolt and is thus a good deal more accurate than the average submachine-gun. Constructed largely of stampings, with plastic furniture, the MP5 is a well-built and reliable weapon which is in service with the Bundeswehr and Bundes Grenz-Schutz (Border Police) as well as by many military and security forces around the world, including Special Forces such as the British Special Air Service. There are two variants of the MP5; the MP5A2 with rigid plastic butt and the MP5A3 with a telescoping metal stock. The stocks can be exchanged by removing a single locking pin in the rear of the receiver. The standard weapons are provided with single shot or automatic fire, but a three-round burst facility is available as an optional addition and most production weapons now incorporate it. (Data table refers to the MP5A2.)

This is a special short version of the MP5 intended for use by police and anti-terrorist squads who require very compact firepower. The weapon can be carried concealed under clothing or in the glove compartment of a car, and it can also be concealed in, and fired from, a specially fitted briefcase. Mechanically it is the same as the MP5 but with a shorter barrel and smaller magazines. Four versions are made; the MP5K is fitted with adjustable iron sights or a telescope if desired; the MP5KA1 has a smooth upper surface with very small iron sights so that there is little to catch in clothing or a holster in a quick draw; the MP5KA4 is similar to the MP5K but has an additional three-round burst facility; and the MP5KA5 is similar to the A1 with the addition of the three-round burst fitment. No butt is fitted, but there is a robust front grip which gives good control when firing.

9mm Heckler & Koch MP5

Heckler & Koch GmbH	
9 × 19mm Parabellum	
Operation	Delayed blowback
Length overall	680mm (26.77in)
Weight empty	2.55kg (5.62lb)
Barrel	225mm (8.85in), 6 grooves, rh
Magazine	15- or 30-shot detachable box
Cyclic rate	800rds/min
Muzzle velocity	400m/sec (1,312ft/sec)

9mm Heckler & Koch MP5K

Heckler & Koch GmbH	
9 × 19mm Parabellum	
Operation	Delayed blowback
Length overall	325mm (12.80in)
Weight empty	2.1kg (4.63lb)
Barrel	115mm (4.53in), 6 grooves, rh
Magazine	15- or 30-shot detachable box
Cyclic rate	900rds/min
Muzzle velocity	375m/sec (1,230ft/sec)

MP5A5E

MP5K

9mm Heckler & Koch MP5SD

Heckler & Koch GmbH

9 × 19mm Parabellum

Operation	Delayed blowback
Length overall	550mm (21.65in)
Weight empty	2.90kg (6.39lb)
Barrel	146mm (5.75in), 6 grooves, rh
Magazine	15- or 30-shot detachable box
Cyclic rate	800rds/min
Muzzle velocity	285m/sec (935ft/sec)

5.56mm Heckler & Koch MP53

Heckler & Koch GmbH

5.56 × 45mm

Operation	Delayed blowback
Length, stock extended	755mm (29.72in)
Length, stock folded	563mm (22.17in)
Weight empty	3.05kg (6.72lb)
Barrel	211mm (8.30in), 6 grooves, rh
Magazine	25-shot detachable box
Cyclic rate	700rds/min
Muzzle velocity	750m/sec (2,460ft/sec)

This is another variation on the MP5, this one having an integral silencer. The barrel is drilled with 30 holes and is surrounded by the silencer which is divided into two chambers. One chamber surrounds the holes in the barrel and acts as an expansion chamber, from which the gases bleed into the front chamber which further slows them and eventually vents them at the muzzle. The result is that the bullet is rendered subsonic and both bullet crack and muzzle blast are greatly reduced. The MP5K is probably the most quiet 'off the shelf' silenced weapon now available. There are six versions; the MP5SD1 has no butt; the SD2 has a fixed butt and the SD3 a retractable butt. The SD4, 5 and 6 are the same as the SD1, 2 and 3 but with the addition of the three-round burst fitment. All are fitted with standard iron sights and are prepared for the addition of telescopes, night vision equipment or laser aiming spots. (Data table refers to the MP5SD1.)

This is virtually the same weapon as the MP5 but chambered for the 5.56mm assault rifle cartridge. The idea of a submachine-gun in this calibre may seem a little strange since, until now, pistol ammunition has been almost the only type used in this class of weapon. The 5.56mm bullet has, however, a lethality and stopping power disproportionate to its size, and the idea also has logistic attractions for forces already using the cartridge in rifles and light machine-guns. One drawback of this cartridge in short weapons is excessive muzzle flash, but the MP53 is fitted with a special flash suppressor which totally eliminates muzzle flash. The normal MP53 is provided with selective single shot or automatic fire; optionally, a special grip with an additional three-round burst facility and an ambidextrous safety catch can be provided. The MP53 is in use by a number of special military and police forces in various countries.

MP5SD4

HK MP53

GREAT BRITAIN

In 1940 the British forces desperately needed a submachine-gun, and the easiest and quickest solution appeared to be to make a direct copy of an existing and simple design. The MP28/II was selected and, slightly redesigned to suit British manufacturing techniques, was adopted as the Lanchester. Production was organised at the Sterling Armaments Company, but at the proverbial eleventh hour the Sten gun appeared; this, being easier and cheaper to make, was immediately approved for the Army, and to take advantage of the tooling which had been set up, and also to avoid interference with the Army's requirements, the Lanchester was allocated to the Royal Navy, where it remained until replaced by the Sterling in the early 1960s. The only changes from the Bergmann specification lie in the butt, which was the standard Lee-Enfield rifle butt, and the addition of a bayonet lug for the Long 1907 bayonet. The magazine housing was machined from brass, enabling it to be highly polished in the best Naval tradition but of doubtful utility in time of war. The magazine held 50 rounds, though the standard Sten magazine could also be used. Two versions were made. The Mark 1 had the rear sight of the No 1 rifle and a selector switch on the front of the trigger guard; the Mark 1* had a much simpler rear sight and no selector switch, being capable of automatic fire only. Most Mark 1 weapons were eventually converted to Mark 1* standard and original Mark 1s are rare.

This was designed at the Royal Small Arms Factory, Enfield, by Major Shepherd and Mr Turpin as the 'Machine Carbine N.O.T.40/1' and it was first fired on 10 January 1941. A full-scale trial was completed by the end of the month and it was adopted as the submachine-gun for the British Army and RAF, now called the 'Sten' for Shepherd, Turpin and Enfield. First supplies were issued in June 1941 and by 1945 nearly four million of the different marks had been made. The basic Sten was very simple both in mechanism and in manufacture; early versions cost about £2.50 to make, later versions slightly more. It was never entirely popular with British troops, largely because it looked cheap and nasty in comparison with the traditional pattern weapons they were used to and because the single-column magazine frequently caused stoppages. But it armed troops and resistance fighters across Europe and many survive to this day. The Sten Mark 1 consisted of a tubular receiver with a bolt and return spring. At the front end of the receiver was a side-feeding magazine housing, a barrel surrounded by a perforated jacket, and a spoon-like muzzle compensator which resisted the usual tendency to climb on automatic firing. There was a metal skeleton butt and a small folding wooden foregrip. About 100,000 of the Mark 1 weapons were made.

9mm Lanchester

Sterling Armament Co

9 × 19mm Parabellum

Operation	Blowback
Length overall	850mm (33.5in)
Weight empty	4.34kg (9.56lb)
Barrel	203mm (8.0in), 6 grooves, rh
Magazine	50-shot detachable box
Cyclic rate	600rds/min
Muzzle velocity	380m/sec (1,247ft/sec)

9mm Sten Mark 1

Birmingham Small Arms Co; Royal Ordnance Factory, Fazakerley

9 × 19mm Parabellum

Operation	Blowback
Length overall	895mm (25.25in)
Weight empty	3.26kg (7.18lb)
Barrel	196mm (7.75in), 6 grooves, rh
Magazine	32-shot detachable box
Cyclic rate	550rds/min
Muzzle velocity	380m/sec (1,247ft/sec)

LANCHESTER

STEN Mk2

9mm Sten Mark 2

See Sten Mark 1	
9 × 19mm Parabellum	
Data as for Mark 1 except: Length overall	762mm (30.0in)
Weight empty	2.95kg (6.50lb)
Barrel	196mm (7.75in), 2 or 6 grooves, rh

9mm Sten Mark 2S

See Sten Mark 1	
9 × 19mm Parabellum	
Data as for Mark 1 except: Length overall	908mm (35.75in)
Weight empty	3.52kg (7.76lb)
Barrel	89mm (3.5in), 6 grooves, rh
Cyclic rate	450rds/min
Muzzle velocity	305m/sec (1,000ft/sec)

9mm Sten Mark 3

See Sten Mark 1	
9 × 19mm Parabellum	
Data as Mark 1 except: Length overall	762mm (30.0in)
Weight empty	3.18kg (7.0lb)

The Mark 2 was the work-horse of the Stens, more of this type being made than of any other, over two million in three years. It was smaller and simpler than the Mark 1, though the basic mechanism remained the same. Instead of the long barrel jacket and muzzle compensator there was a short perforated sleeve acting as a barrel retaining nut and leaving about half the barrel exposed. There was no front grip or wooden fore-end and the stock was merely a single strut with a shoulder-piece welded on the end. The magazine housing was rotatable through 90° so that it could be positioned beneath the weapon for packing and to close the feed and ejection openings against dirt. The sights were fixed for 100 yards and non-adjustable.

The Mark 2S was one of the few submachine-guns produced with an integral silencer as a separate variant, rather than being a standard weapon with a silencer screwed on the muzzle. The basic weapon was the same as the Mark 2 Sten but the barrel was part of the silencer unit which screwed into the front of the receiver in place of the usual barrel nut. The integral barrel was very short and the bullet emerged at subsonic speed; the remainder of the silencer casing contained baffles which trapped and slowed the gases until they emerged from the muzzle silently. The loudest noise on firing was that of the bolt moving back and forth. The only drawback was that the Mark 2S had to be fired only as single shots, except in grave emergencies, since automatic fire soon wore out the baffles and was also inclined to build up pressure inside the silencer and blow off the end cap. The gun was designed to meet requirements of Commando and other special forces, and remained in use until the Korean War.

The Mark 3 was the second of the series to be made in large numbers and, together with the Mark 2, was the one most often seen in British service. It was really a variant of the Mark 1 designed for easier manufacture. The receiver and barrel jacket were in one piece, made from a sheet-steel tube which extended almost to the muzzle. The barrel was fixed, and could not be removed, and the magazine housing was also fixed. A feature of the Mark 3 which did not appear on any other model was a small guard in front of the ejection opening to prevent the firer's little finger straying into the opening as he gripped the weapon; it is worth noting here that the approved method of gripping the Sten was to hold the barrel jacket with the left hand so that the magazine lay across the left forearm – *not* to hold the magazine as a front grip, since this frequently caused stoppages. The Mark 3 appeared in 1943 and was made until 1944 both in the UK and in Canada.

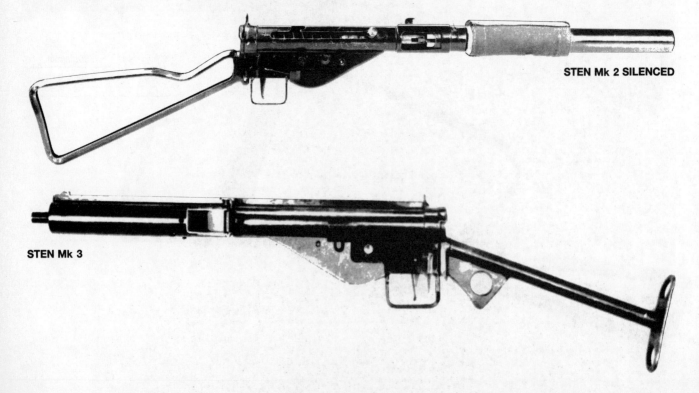

STEN Mk 2 SILENCED

STEN Mk 3

The Mark 4 Sten was a compact model for paratroops, but it was never taken beyond prototype stage. The Mark 5 was developed in 1944 in an attempt to produce a rather more attractive and better-finished weapon. The basic mechanism remained the same as the Mark 2 but more care was taken during manufacture and assembly, the finish was better, and a wooden rifle butt and pistol grip were fitted, while the muzzle carried the foresight of the No 4 rifle and could accept the No 4 rifle's bayonet. The first models even had a forward vertical grip, but this was found to break easily and was removed. But the one really serious defect, the magazine, was left unchanged and the troops were not fooled by the cosmetic exercise; it was still the same old 'Woolworth Gun' as before. It remained in service until replaced by the Sterling in the early 1950s. A silenced version, the Mark 6, was also produced in very small numbers; this had a similar-appearing silencer to the Mark 2S though the internal arrangements were slightly different.

This design began life as the Patchett gun and was developed in 1942/43. Prototypes were taken on the airborne assault on Arnhem in 1944 but the end of the war reduced the urgency of replacing the Sten and it was not until 1953 that it was finally approved for service as the Sterling L2A1, named for the manufacturers. The L2A2 appeared in 1955 and the L2A3 in 1956; it has been adopted in over 90 countries and manufactured under licence in India. The Sterling company closed down in 1988 and its assets were purchased by Royal Ordnance plc, who maintain a spares and repair service from ROF Nottingham; whether the Sterling will ever be manufactured again remains to be seen. The Sterling is made entirely from steel and plastic, with a side-feeding box magazine and a folding stock. There is rather more machining in the design than appears in other submachine-guns and this leads to a higher cost than many contemporaries. It is, however, extremely robust and reliable and performs well in adverse conditions. The bolt has four special clearance ribs machined on its body and these push any dirt or fouling into special vent holes. There is an integral firing pin and a means of ensuring that it only aligns with the primer at the moment of firing, which is a useful safety measure. The curved magazine holds 34 rounds and has rollers instead of the more usual platform follower. A bayonet can be attached, the foresight can be adjusted for zero, and the rear sight has a flip setting for 100 and 200 metres. The differences between the L2A1, 2 and 3 were relatively minor and concerned with improving manufacture and robustness. The basic appearance and functioning was not affected.

This is the silenced version of the Sterling L2A3 submachine-gun. The basic mechanism is the same as the plain Sterling, but the barrel has 72 radial holes drilled through it allowing some of the propellant gas to enter a diffuser tube. This has holes bored in which allow the gas to pass through into an expanded metal wrapper. The gases are contained in this and eventually seep forward and return to the barrel mouth. The silencer casing forward of the barrel contains a spiral diffuser, and the bullet passes through the centre of this but the gases following it are given a swirling motion by the diffuser; some gas is reflected off the end cap so as to mingle with the gas still moving, and the nett result is to ensure that the gas leaves the end of the silencer at a low speed. Since the effective gas pressure in the breech is reduced, the bolt is lighter and has a single return spring. An advantage of this design is that the weapon can be fired in automatic mode without danger.

STERLING L2

STEN Mk 6

9mm Sten Mark 5 and Mark 6

See Sten Mark 1	
9 × 19mm Parabellum	
Data as for Mark 1 except: Length overall	762mm (30.0in)
Weight empty	3.86kg (8.51lb)
Cyclic rate	600rds/min

9mm Sterling L2

Sterling Armament Co.; Royal Ordnance Factory, Fazakerley	
9 × 19mm Parabellum	
Operation	Blowback
Length, stock extended	690mm (27.16in)
Length, stock folded	483mm (19.0in)
Weight empty	2.72kg (6.0lb)
Barrel	198mm (7.79in), 6 grooves, rh
Magazine	34-shot detachable box
Cyclic rate	550rds/min
Muzzle velocity	390m/sec (1,280ft/sec)

9mm Sterling L34A1

Sterling Armament Co	
9 × 19mm Parabellum	
Operation	Blowback
Length, stock extended	864mm (34.0in)
Length, stock folded	660mm (26.0in)
Weight empty	3.60kg (7.94lb)
Barrel	198mm (7.80in), 6 grooves, rh
Magazine	34-shot detachable box
Cyclic rate	515rds/min
Muzzle velocity	300m/sec (984ft/sec)

HUNGARY

9mm Models 39M and 43M

Danuvia Ipari- Es Kereskedelmi RT, Budapest

9 × 25mm Mauser

39M:

Operation	Delayed blowback
Length overall	1,041mm (41.0in)
Weight empty	4.08kg (9.0lb)
Barrel	450mm (17.72in), 6 grooves, rh
Magazine	20- or 40-shot detachable box
Cyclic rate	750rds/min
Muzzle velocity	450m/sec (1,475ft/sec)

The Danuvia 39M was designed by Pal Kiraly and incorporated his patented two-part bolt giving delayed blowback operation. The bolt had a light head and heavier body, the two separated by a lever which abutted against a transom in the receiver. The result was that the light bolt head had to lever the heavy bolt body back against considerable mechanical disadvantage, so delaying the opening of the breech. This measure was necessary because of the unusually powerful round used, perhaps the most potent 9mm cartridge of the period. The 39M was a fully stocked weapon resembling a rifle and was a very reliable and accurate weapon. The magazine fitted beneath the weapon and could be folded forward into a recess in the wooden fore-end, whereupon a spring plate snapped into place over the aperture in the receiver. The Model 43M used the same mechanism but had a folding metal shoulder stock and pistol grip; it was designed for use by paratroops. Approximately 8,000 Model 39M and a considerably greater number of Model 43M were made between 1939 and 1944 and were issued to the Hungarian Army, who retained them into the post-war years until they were replaced by Soviet weapons.

MODEL 39

43M:

Length, stock extended	953mm (37.5in)
Length, stock folded	750mm (29.5in)
Weight empty	3.64kg (8.02lb)
Barrel	425mm (16.73in), 6 grooves, rh
Magazine	40-shot detachable box
Cyclic rate	750rds/min
Muzzle velocity	445m/sec (1,460ft/sec)

MODEL 43

ISRAEL

9mm Uzi

Israel Military Industries	
9 × 19mm Parabellum	
Operation	Blowback
Length, stock extended	650mm (25.60in)
Length, stock folded	470mm (18.50in)
Weight empty	3.70kg (8.15lb)
Barrel	260mm (10.23in), 4 grooves, rh
Magazine	25- or 32-shot detachable box
Cyclic rate	600rds/min
Muzzle velocity	400m/sec (1,312ft/sec)

First designed in the early 1950s and based loosely on the Czech CZ23 series, the Uzi is one of the most widely used submachine-guns in existence today. In 1948 when Israel became independent, urgent steps were taken to foster a national arms industry, and the Uzi was one of the first products. It is an extremely compact weapon, achieving its short length by having a wrap-around bolt which encloses much of the barrel at the instant of firing. The idea was not entirely novel when the Uzi was designed, but it was among the first weapons to use the principle and brought it to the attention of many who would not otherwise have heard of it. The magazine housing forms the pistol grip and the whole gun balances so well that single-handed firing is perfectly possible. Early models had a wooden butt, but for many years the standard design has been a folding metal butt. The weapon is, of course, used by the Israel Defence Force, and it has been adopted by West Germany and some 26 other countries for military use, as well as use by security and police forces in scores of countries. It was manufactured under licence by Fabrique National Herstal for many years.

9mm Mini-Uzi

Israel Military Industries	
9 × 19mm Parabellum	
Operation	Blowback
Length, stock extended	600mm (23.62in)
Length, stock folded	360mm (14.17in)
Weight empty	2.70kg (5.95lb)
Barrel	197mm (7.76in), 4 grooves, rh
Magazine	20-, 25- or 32-shot
Cyclic rate	950rds/min
Muzzle velocity	352m/sec (1,155ft/sec)

This has been developed in response to demands for a more compact weapon, and as the name implies is merely a smaller version of the standard Uzi. Due to the changed weight and ballistic characteristics the muzzle has compensating slots cut in its upper surface in order to assist control of the weapon. A special 20-shot magazine is available, but it will also accept the standard Uzi magazines.

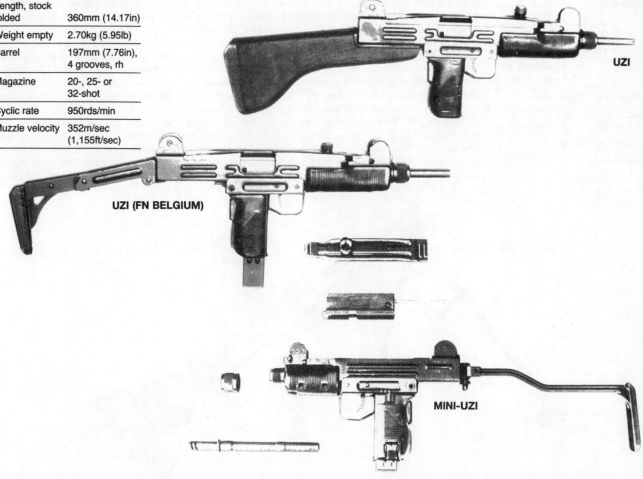

UZI

UZI (FN BELGIUM)

MINI-UZI

9mm Micro-Uzi

Israel Military Industries	
9 × 19mm Parabellum	
Operation	Blowback
Length, stock extended	460mm (18.11in)
Length, stock folded	250mm (9.84in)
Weight empty	1.95kg (4.29lb)
Barrel	117mm (4.60in), 4 grooves, rh
Magazine	20-shot detachable box
Cyclic rate	1,250rds/min
Muzzle velocity	350m/sec (1,150ft/sec)

This is an even smaller version of the Uzi, the basic design reduced to its absolute minimum. It is marginally larger than a heavy pistol and in an attempt to keep the rate of fire at a practical figure the bolt has been given a tungsten insert to increase the mass. The folding stock is a much simpler design than in the larger weapons and folds sideways so that the shoulder-piece can act as a front grip when firing from the hip. This model is also available in .45 ACP calibre, with a special 16-shot magazine.

MICRO-UZI

ITALY

9mm Vilar-Perosa

Officina Vilar Perosa; Fiat SpA; Canadian General Electric Co	
9 × 19mm Glisenti	
Operation	Delayed blowback
Length overall	533mm (21.0in)
Weight empty	6.52kg (14.37lb)
Barrel	318mm (12.5in), 6 grooves, rh
Magazine	25-shot detachable box
Cyclic rate	1,200rds/min
Muzzle velocity	365m/sec (1,200ft/sec)

This venerable weapon perhaps has the distinction of being the very first submachine-gun ever made; it may not look like a submachine-gun, but it meets all the criteria and incorporates most of the features found in more modern weapons. It was always made as a double gun, and it was originally intended to be used in the same manner as any other machine-gun, but to be a lightweight weapon particularly for use by mountain troops. The first models appeared in 1915 and went into use with the Italian Army as a light machine-gun, complete with a tripod and shield. After two years of war its proper potential was realised and it became a short-range fire support weapon for the infantry, the two guns being mounted on a tray suspended from a man's shoulders by straps. He marched forward with his comrades, firing the two guns as he walked. The gun was made by a number of Italian factories, and also in Canada, and is sometimes known by the name of the inventor, Revelli, or as the Fiat gun after one of the makers, adding a certain amount of confusion. The mechanism is a form of retarded blowback, though there is some doubt as to whether the inventor actually meant it that way; the bolt has a lug which moves in a spiral groove in the receiver, making it rotate about 15° as it closes. At the same time the striker, which also has a cam riding in a groove in the bolt, was driven by this rotation on to the cartridge cap, firing the round just before closure was completed. The recoil force then had to 'unwind' the bolt and striker in their cam paths and this imposes a slight delay. The overhead magazine fed by a combination of gravity and spring power and, because the bolt was light, the rate of fire was very high. Although the Vilar Perosa did not have a very long or distinguished career, it pointed the way for those which followed, and it was a significant milestone in firearms history.

VILAR-PEROSA

The OVP was derived from the Vilar Perosa and was produced in small numbers, in the 1920s, for the Italian Army. It was simply one half of the twin Vilar Perosa removed from its mounting, given a wooden stock and a conventional sort of trigger, and a different cocking mechanism so as to make it a shoulder arm. It still used the top-mounted magazine, and cocking was done by drawing back a knurled sleeve around the receiver to pull back the bolt. The return spring was stiffened so as to slow down the rate of fire. There were two triggers, the front one giving automatic fire and the rear one single shots. A handful of these weapons survived in use until the early 1940s.

OVP

9mm OVP

Officina Vilar Perosa

9 × 19mm Glisenti

Operation	Delayed blowback
Length overall	901mm (35.47in)
Weight empty	3.67kg (8.09lb)
Barrel	280mm (11.02in), 6 grooves, rh
Magazine	25-shot detachable box
Cyclic rate	900rds/min
Muzzle velocity	355m/sec (1,165ft/sec)

Like the OVP the Beretta 1918 was another improved version of the original Vilar Perosa mechanism to turn it into a more convenient weapon. The receiver, action and barrel of the VP were fitted to a wooden stock and a folding bayonet was added; the result looked more like a rifle, until the magazine was fitted, and was a very successful design, so much so that almost all the existing Vilar Perosa guns were converted and original VPs are now uncommon. Two versions of the Model 1918 are known, one using two triggers and one with a single trigger. The double-trigger system allowed either automatic or semi-automatic fire, depending upon which trigger was used, while the single trigger model had the full-auto facility removed. The delayed blowback system was modified, using two inclined planes in the receiver walls whose resistance had to be overcome before the bolt could open. This slowed the rate of fire to more manageable proportions. Numbers of Model 1918 were still in Italian Army use during World War Two.

9mm Beretta Model 1918

Pietro Beretta SpA

9 × 19mm Glisenti

Operation	Delayed blowback
Length overall	850mm (33.5in)
Weight empty	3.26kg (7.19lb)
Barrel	305mm (12.0in), 6 grooves, rh
Magazine	25-shot top-mounted detachable box
Cyclic rate	900rds/min
Muzzle velocity	380m/sec (1,247ft/sec)

This was a modification of the Model 1918, converting it first to fire semi-automatically in 9mm Parabellum calibre and secondly using a bottom-mounted magazine instead of the former top-mounted pattern. The more powerful cartridge required stronger return springs to control the bolt and keep the rate of fire down. The Model 1918/30 was used by the Italian Milizia Forestale and was also sold to South American countries.

9mm Beretta Model 1918/30

Pietro Beretta SpA

9 × 19mm Parabellum

BERETTA M1918

BERETTA MODEL 1918/30

9mm Beretta Model 38A

Pietro Beretta SpA	
9 × 19mm Parabellum	
Operation	Blowback
Length overall	953mm (37.5in)
Weight empty	4.19kg (9.25lb)
Barrel	318mm (12.5in), 6 grooves, rh
Magazine	10-, 20-, 30- or 40-shot detachable box
Cyclic rate	600rds/min
Muzzle velocity	417m/sec (1,370ft/sec)

This was a further development from the Model 1918, and proved to be an excellent design. The complicated bolt and delayed blowback system of the Vilar Perosa was abandoned and a simple blowback mechanism adopted. It was chambered for the 9mm Parabellum cartridge and also for a new Italian 9mm M1938A round of equal power. Early models were machined from solid steel, but wartime models saw more sheet metal and some other small modifications to speed up production. It was used extensively by the Italian Army and numbers were also adopted by the German and Roumanian armies. All models used twin triggers, the front trigger giving semi-automatic fire and the rear one full automatic operation.

9mm Beretta Model 38/42

Pietro Beretta SpA	
9 × 19mm Parabellum	
Operation	Blowback
Length overall	800mm (31.5in)
Weight empty	3.26kg (7.19lb)
Barrel	216mm (8.5in), 6 grooves, rh
Magazine	20- or 40-shot detachable box
Cyclic rate	550rds/min
Muzzle velocity	380m/sec (1,250ft/sec)

While the Model 38A was an excellent weapon, it proved too difficult to mass produce in wartime, and the Model 38/42 was a modification in which a number of changes were incorporated. The barrel was shorter and no longer had a perforated jacket, the receiver and other parts were of sheet steel, the wooden stock stopped at the magazine, and the sights, trigger-guard and other metal components were simplified. The bolt handle incorporated a dust cover, as a result of desert warfare experience, and the gun was regulated for use with standard 9mm Parabellum ammunition only. Once more, the German and Roumanian armies took large numbers of this design.

9mm Beretta Model 38/44

Pietro Beretta SpA

9 × 19mm Parabellum

This was a minor variation on the Model 38/42, in which the bolt was simplified and a large-diameter return spring was adopted. This resulted in a changed design of receiver end cap, no longer showing the central spring housing common to the earlier models. Although designed in 1944, production did not begin until late 1945 and sales continued until 1949.

BERETTA MODEL 38A

BERETTA MODEL 38/42

The 38/49 was a further development from the original Model 38A, being more or less a 38/44 with the addition of a cross-bolt safety catch in the stock, just forward of the trigger. In addition, various modifications could be added to suit the customer – folding or removable bayonet, wooden stock or folding metal stock, optional grip safety and various types of sling. Large numbers were sold to several countries between 1949 and the end of production in 1961. In its latter years the designation was changed to 'Model 4'.

The Model 38A and its derivatives were designed by Tullio Marengoni; after his death, design became the responsibility of Domenico Salza and his first effort was this Model 5, developed in 1957. This was simply the existing Model 4 (38/39) with a change in the safety system. Instead of a cross-bolt positive safety catch, a spring-loaded catch was fitted which had to be gripped by the forward hand when firing and pushed in against its spring to free the bolt. So long as this catch was held down, the weapon functioned, but as soon as it was released the bolt was locked, either in the forward or rearward position.

By the middle 1950s, the Model 38 derivatives were beginning to look old-fashioned and, moreover, they were slow manufacturing propositions. Domenico Salza set about a complete redesign and ran through the prototype Models 6 to 11 before settling on the Model 12 as the production standard. Production began in 1959 and the Italian Army adopted it in 1961. It has since been widely adopted in other countries and manufactured under licence in Brazil. The Model 12 is a modern design, compact and well-made, and was among the first commercial designs to adopt the telescoping bolt, in which the barrel is recessed into the bolt head. This allows the overall length of the weapon to be much reduced without sacrificing either barrel length or bolt mass. The weapon is designed for simple mass production and is largely made of steel stampings and pressings welded together. It is generally seen with a folding metal stock, though it was originally offered with an optional wooden stock.

9mm Beretta Model 38/49 (Model 4)

Pietro Beretta SpA

9 × 19mm Parabellum

9mm Beretta Model 5

Pietro Beretta SpA

9 × 19mm Parabellum

9mm Beretta Model 12

Pietro Beretta SpA

9 × 19mm Parabellum

Operation	Blowback
Length, wooden stock	660mm (26.0in)
Length, stock extended	645mm (25.4in)
Length, stock folded	416mm (16.4in)
Weight empty	2.95kg (6.5lb)
Barrel	203mm (8.0in), 6 grooves, rh
Magazine	20-, 30- or 40-shot detachable box
Cyclic rate	550rds/min
Muzzle velocity c.	380m/sec (1,247ft/sec)

BERETTA MODEL 5

BERETTA MODEL 12

9mm Beretta Model 12S

Pietro Beretta SpA

9 × 19mm Parabellum

This is an improved Model 12, the principal differences being a new design of manual safety and fire selector, and modifications to the sights. In addition the rear cap retaining catch has been modified, there is a new butt-plate, and the weapon is coated in a corrosion-proof epoxy resin finish. Dimensions, etc., are as for the Model 12. The Model 12S is currently in use by Italian and several other armies and is made under licence by Taurus SA of Brazil.

BERETTA MODEL 12S

9mm FNAB Model 1943

Fabrica Nazionale d'Armi, Brescia	
9 × 19mm Parabellum	
Operation	Delayed blowback
Length, stock extended	790mm (31.10in)
Length, stock folded	527mm (20.75in)
Weight empty	3.25kg (7.16lb)
Barrel	198mm (7.79in), 6 grooves, rh
Magazine	20- or 40-shot detachable box
Cyclic rate	400rds/min
Muzzle velocity	380m/sec (1,247ft/sec)

9mm TZ45

Manufacturer unknown	
9 × 19mm Parabellum	
Operation	Blowback
Length, stock extended	850mm (33.46in)
Length, stock folded	545mm (21.45in)
Weight empty	3.26kg (7.19lb)
Barrel	230mm (9.05in), 6 grooves, rh
Magazine	40-shot detachable box
Cyclic rate	550rds/min
Muzzle velocity	380m/sec (1,247ft/sec)

This interesting and unusual weapon was designed and built in 1943/44 in small numbers and was used by both German and Italian troops. Expensively produced by traditional milling and machining methods, it employed a two-piece lever-retarded bolt to give a delayed blowback action. On firing the front portion of the bolt pressed back and had to rotate a lever which, in turn, drove the rear section back at a mechanical disadvantage. On closing the forward portion chambered the round, then the delay lever turned forward and finally the heavy rear portion of the bolt closed up to drive in the firing pin. There are obvious affinities with the Swiss MKMO and the Hungarian M39. Another unusual feature for the period was a simple one-strut folding stock.

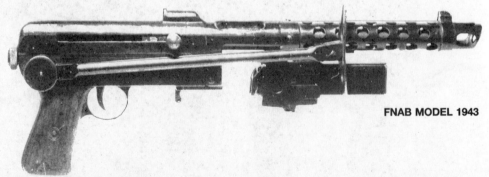

FNAB MODEL 1943

This weapon was developed in Italy in 1944 and less than a thousand were ever made. It was a simple blowback design typical of the period, with the addition of a grip safety on the magazine housing which locked the bolt in a similar manner to the grip safety on the Madsen weapon. The telescoping butt was held in the closed position by an index plate beneath the barrel casing. The weapon was briefly evaluated by various Allied agencies after the war but the general opinion seems to have been unfavourable; most reports speak of the TZ45 as being unreliable in prolonged use and having a generally poor standard of manufacture. In spite of this the designers managed to sell it to the Burmese Army in 1950, and it was manufactured there as the BA52 for several years.

The Franchi was first produced in 1956 and was modified in the following year to become the LF57. It was the first complete gun to be produced by the Luigi Franchi company, and although interesting and well made it was not a commercial success. A small number were purchased by the Italian Navy in the early 1960s. The LF57 used the principle of the telescoping bolt so as to reduce the length of the weapon, in much the same way as the Beretta 12. The difference lay in the fact that the Franchi carried the mass of the bolt above the barrel, rather than around it as in the Beretta, thus simplifying manufacture to some extent. The weapon dismantles very easily, the barrel being secured by a single nut. There is no furniture in the accepted sense, the pistol grip being entirely of steel, and the sights are rather crude. The tubular stock folds sideways, to the right side of the receiver. The Franchi was a neat weapon, but not significantly better than others being produced at the same time, and it failed to make an impact.

FRANCHI LF57

9mm Franchi LF57

Luigi Franchi SpA

9 × 19mm Parabellum

Operation	Blowback
Length, stock extended	686mm (27.0in)
Length, stock folded	419mm (16.5in)
Weight empty	3.17kg (7.0lb)
Barrel	203mm (8.0in), 6 grooves, rh
Magazine	20- or 40-shot detachable box
Cyclic rate	500rds/min
Muzzle velocity	365m/sec (1,200ft/sec)

9mm Socimi Type 821

Societa Construzioni Industriali Milano SpA

9 × 19mm Parabellum

Operation	Blowback
Length, stock extended	600mm (23.6in)
Length, stock folded	400mm (15.7in)
Weight empty	2.45kg (5.40lb)
Barrel	200mm (7.87in), 6 grooves, rh
Magazine	32-shot detachable box
Cyclic rate	550–600rds/min
Muzzle velocity	380m/sec (1,245ft/sec)

This was announced in 1983 and is based broadly on the Uzi design. It has a similar type of telescoping bolt, has a similar safety mechanism and uses the hand grip as the magazine housing. There are, though, significant differences in construction; the Socimi has a solid rectangular receiver into which the bolt is inserted from the rear end, and the barrel from the front, secured by a nut. The receiver, barrel housing and pistol grip are all of light alloy, and the stock folds forward by pivoting underneath the receiver and lying alongside the weapon. The Type 821 is in series production but purchases appear to have been confined to police and security units in various countries.

SOCIMI TYPE 821

9mm Spectre M-4

SITES SpA	
9 × 19mm Parabellum	
Operation	Blowback
Length, stock extended	580mm (22.83in)
Length, stock folded	350mm (13.78in)
Weight empty	2.90kg (6.39lb)
Barrel	130mm (5.12in), 6 grooves, rh
Magazine	30- or 50-shot detachable box
Cyclic rate	850rds/min
Muzzle velocity	400m/sec (1,312ft/sec)

Introduced in 1984, this unusual weapon is the only 'double-action' submachine-gun in existence. It was designed primarily for security and anti-terrorist forces, to provide them with a weapon which can be carried safely and brought into action instantly without requiring any safeties to be released or cocking handles to be pulled. The weapon is loaded and prepared in the usual way by inserting a magazine, pulling back the cocking lever and releasing it; this loads a cartridge and closes the bolt, but leaves the separate hammer unit cocked. Pressing a release lever now allows the hammer to run forward and be held a short distance behind the bolt. The weapon can now be carried in perfect safety; when required, a pull on the trigger will cock the hammer and release it to fire the round in the chamber, after which the weapon acts in the normal blowback manner. Firing from a closed bolt suggests a hot barrel, and a forced draught system controlled by the bolt ensures that cooling air is pumped through and round the barrel during firing. The magazines are an ingenious four-column design which enables a 50-round capacity in the length normally associated with 30 rounds. The Spectre has been well received and is in use by numerous security agencies.

SPECTRE M-4

JAPAN

8mm Type 100

Kokura Arsenal; Nagoya Arsenal	
8 × 21.5mm Nambu	
Operation	Blowback
Length overall	890mm (35.0in)
Weight empty	3.83kg (8.44lb)
Barrel	228mm (9.0in), 6 grooves, rh
Magazine	30-shot detachable box
Cyclic rate	450rds/min (1940); 800rds/min (1944)
Muzzle velocity	335m/sec (1,100ft/sec)

Although the submachine-gun might be thought the ideal weapon for jungle warfare, the Japanese were surprisingly slow to adopt one. Apart from a few MP28 and Bergmann weapons bought in the 1930s, it was 1940 before a Japanese design appeared. The Type 100 was robustly made, and of conventional pattern, though it lacked effectiveness due to firing the weak 8mm Nambu cartridge. About 10,000 of the standard model and perhaps another 7,500 of the folding-butt parachutist's model were produced before production ceased in 1943. The former were produced at Kokura Army Arsenal, the latter at Nagoya. The weapon was not really successful, first because little factory space could be spared for a continuous development programme, and secondly because the ammunition gave frequent stoppages. In 1944 an improved model was introduced, a slight improvement on the original, but only about 8,000 were produced by a Nagoya sub-factory before the war ended. The 1944 design was simplified in order to eliminate as much time-consuming machining as possible, which led to the adoption of welding and such simplifications as fixed sights. The 1944 model had a considerably greater rate of fire than did the 1940 model.

TYPE 100

This design is an amalgam of features found in other submachine-guns and represents a sound attempt to produce a reliable but cheap weapon. In appearance it resembles the Carl Gustav; the grip safety is of Madsen type; there is an ejection port cover which acts as a safety catch, as in the US M3A1; and the side-folding stock resembles that of the Madsen. The result is a somewhat heavy but robust and easily controlled weapon using the normal blowback system of operation. Only a small number were produced, in 1966–67, and its use was confined to the Japanese Self-Defence Force. The Type 66 resembles the Type 65, but the bolt and return spring were modified so as to give a slower rate of fire.

9mm SCK Models 65 and 66

Shin Chuo Kogyo	
9 × 19mm Parabellum	
Operation	Blowback
Length, stock extended	762mm (30.0in)
Length, stock folded	500m (19.7in)
Weight empty	4.08kg (9.0lb)
Barrel	140mm (5.5in)
Magazine	30-shot detachable box
Cyclic rate	550rds/min (Type 65); 450rds/min (Type 66)
Muzzle velocity	360m/sec (1,180ft/sec)

LUXEMBOURG

The rise of the submachine-gun during World War Two coupled with the inferior quality of many wartime models, led to a profusion of designs being put on the market in the post-war years in the hope of landing a military contract to replace the wartime weapons. The Sola Super was one of these, made in small numbers in 1954–57, and sold with some success in North Africa and South America. It was evaluated by several other countries but was never adopted by a major army. The Sola was a conventional blowback selective-fire weapon, obviously designed with an eye to cheap and simple production. There was considerable use of stamped components and the design was pared to the point of having no more than 38 parts. For its class it was a long and cumbersome weapon, though the long barrel with integral compensator gave a reasonable degree of accuracy and an above-average velocity. There was, though, nothing in the design which had not been done as well, or better, elsewhere, which is probably why the Sola failed to prosper. In an attempt to make it a commercial success, the makers redesigned it, doing away with the bulky trigger mechanism housing and shortening the barrel. The resulting 'Sola Light Model' went on the market in 1957 but met with no success whatever, and with that the company decided to quit the armaments field.

9mm Sola Super

Société Luxembourgoise d'Armes SA	
9 × 19mm Parabellum	
Operation	Blowback
Length, stock extended	890mm (35.0in)
Length, stock folded	610mm (24.0in)
Weight empty	2.90kg (6.4lb)
Barrel	305mm (12.0in), 6 grooves, rh
Magazine	32-shot detachable box
Cyclic rate	550rds/min
Muzzle velocity	425m/sec (1,395ft/sec)

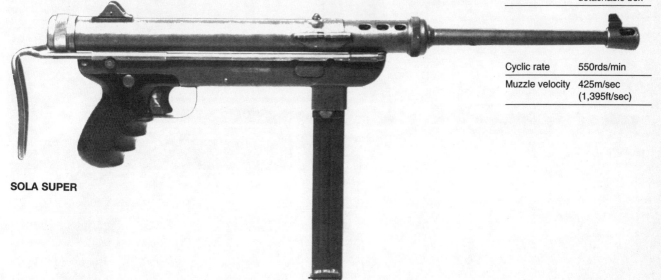

SOLA SUPER

MEXICO

9mm Mendoza HM-3

Productos Mendoza SA	
9 × 19mm Parabellum	
Operation	Blowback
Length overall	635mm (25.0in)
Weight empty	2.69kg (5.93lb)
Barrel	255mm (10.04in)
Magazine	32-shot detachable box
Cyclic rate	600rds/min
Muzzle velocity c.	350m/sec (1,148ft/sec)

This weapon was developed in the early 1970s by Hector Mendoza, son of Rafael Mendoza, the designer of machine-guns. It went into production in about 1976 and is the standard submachine-gun of the Mexican armed forces. The mechanism of the Mendoza is rather unusual, in that the bolt is very large, recessed so as to surround much of the barrel when closed, and much of it is exposed. In one sense the system could be described as resembling the slide of an automatic pistol, enclosed in a much cut away receiver. The wings surrounding the foresight act as a cocking handle and allow the bolt to be pulled back, and the receiver really consists of little more than a platform with pistol grip and two tunnels, one supporting the foresight and the other supporting the rear sight; between the two the entire bolt is exposed. This method of construction was chosen so as to permit the bolt to be easily wiped clean of dust without having to dismantle the weapon. There is a grip safety which locks the bolt in either the cocked or forward position, and a selector switch allowing single shots or automatic fire. A small but interesting detail is the fact that the firing pin is double-ended and can be reversed should the point break.

PERU

9mm MGP-79A

Sima-Cefar	
9 × 19mm Parabellum	
Operation	Blowback
Length, stock extended	809mm (31.85in)
Length, stock folded	544mm (21.52in)
Weight empty	3.08kg (6.79lb)
Barrel	237mm (9.33in), 12 grooves, rh
Magazine	20- or 32-shot detachable box
Cyclic rate	600–850rds/min
Muzzle velocity	410m/sec (1,345ft/sec)

This weapon was developed by Sima-Cefar, the manufacturing arm of the Peruvian Naval Base at Callao, and is a conventional blowback weapon. The barrel is enclosed in a perforated jacket, and both barrel and jacket can be easily removed and replaced with a silencer assembly if required. The shoulder stock folds round the right side of the receiver and the butt pad lies alongside the magazine housing where it helps to form a forward hand grip. The safety catch is above the pistol grip, while the fire selector is positioned close to the magazine housing, so that the two controls can be operated by different hands. The MGP-79A is the standard submachine-gun of the Peruvian armed forces.

MENDOZA HM-3

MGP-79A

This is a very small weapon designed for use by special forces and security guards. It is a blowback weapon, the basic mechanism of which is based on that of the MGP-79A described above. In this case, though, the barrel is considerably shortened and set back in the receiver, and the bolt is of the telescoping type, allowing the magazine to be placed into the pistol grip. The safety catch and fire selector switch is a single unit, placed ahead of the trigger guard where it can be conveniently operated by the forward hand. The stock folds sideways and the buttplate acts as a forward grip. As with all Sima-Cefar weapons, the magazine uses the Uzi interface so that Uzi magazines can be used in an emergency.

9mm MGP-84

Sima-Cefar

9 × 19mm Parabellum

Operation	Blowback
Length, stock extended	503mm (19.8in)
Length, stock folded	284mm (11.18in)
Weight empty	2.31kg (5.09lb)
Barrel	166mm (6.53in), 12 grooves, rh
Magazine	20- or 32-shot detachable box
Cyclic rate	650–700rds/min
Muzzle velocity	390m/sec (1,280ft/sec)

MGP-84

The MGP-87 is to the same basic design as the MGP-79A described above, but is a simplified design. There is no barrel jacket and the barrel and the folding stock are both shorter. The cocking handle is turned up into the vertical position and made larger so that it can be readily grasped and operated. The weapon has been designed for use by counter-insurgency forces who require a more compact gun and one which can be brought into action quickly.

9mm MGP-87

Sima-Cefar

9 × 19mm Parabellum

Operation	Blowback
Length, stock extended	702mm (27.64in)
Length, stock folded	500mm (19.68in)
Weight empty	2.89kg (6.37lb)
Barrel	194mm (7.64in), 12 grooves, rh
Magazine	20- or 32-shot detachable box
Cyclic rate	600–850rds/min
Muzzle velocity	400m/sec (1,312ft/sec)

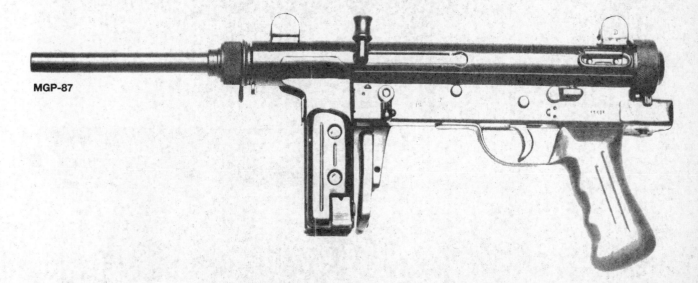

MGP-87

POLAND

9mm PM-63

State arsenals	
9 × 18mm Makarov	
Operation	Blowback
Length, stock extended	583mm (22.95in)
Length, stock folded	333mm (13.11in)
Weight empty	1.8kg (3.97lb)
Barrel	152mm (5.98in), 6 grooves, rh
Magazine	25- or 40-shot detachable box
Cyclic rate	600rds/min
Muzzle velocity	323m/sec (1,060ft/sec)

7.62mm wz/43/52

State arsenals	
7.62 × 25mm Soviet	

This is really an enlarged automatic pistol in its construction. It was designed as a light and handy weapon for self-defence use by drivers and vehicle crews and similar groups whose primary job is not operating small arms. The weapon is built up from a frame, a slide and a barrel, just like a pistol, and even the barrel fits into the frame by interrupted lugs in the same way as the Browning 1903 and similar pistols. The magazine fits into the butt, and there is a small front grip which folds down. The butt is formed from two metal strips which slide alongside the frame so that the shoulder pad lies under the rear end; when extended it drops slightly and locks so as to position the weapon in front of the eye. The PM-63 is cocked by pulling back the slide until it locks; pulling the trigger then releases it to fly forward and chamber and fire a round. The slide is then blown back and is again held, ready for the next round. Pulling the trigger harder withdraws the sear and allows automatic fire. In this case, the lightness of the slide would result in a very high rate of fire, and therefore a rate reducer is used. This is a loose inertia pellet in the rear of the slide. When the slide runs back it is held, not by the sear but by a special catch; the slide stops moving but the inertia pellet continues backward, compressing a spring, and then rebounds forward. As it comes back, so it trips the catch and releases the slide to fire the next shot. This device reduces the rate of fire to manageable proportions. The weapon can be fired single-handed, like a pistol, or two-handed, but in either case accuracy is doubtful since the slide is moving backwards and forwards, and since it carries the sights it is impossible to aim once fire has been opened. Nevertheless, the PM-63 is a practical weapon for the purpose for which it was designed.

The Polish Army was provided with the usual armoury of Soviet weapons in post-war years, and among them was the PPS-43 submachine-gun. In this they were fortunate, since there were few other instances of this weapon being supplied to a Warsaw Pact army, and a variant of the PPS-43 was developed and made in Poland as the wz/43/52. Basically it was the same gun fitted with a wooden stock and a few small production alterations to suit the Polish manufacturing system. It employed the same stamped steel construction, and the only significant mechanical difference was that the Polish weapon was capable of firing single shots as well as automatic fire. It is no longer in first-line service and its use appears to be confined to factory guards and some police forces.

PM-63

PM-63

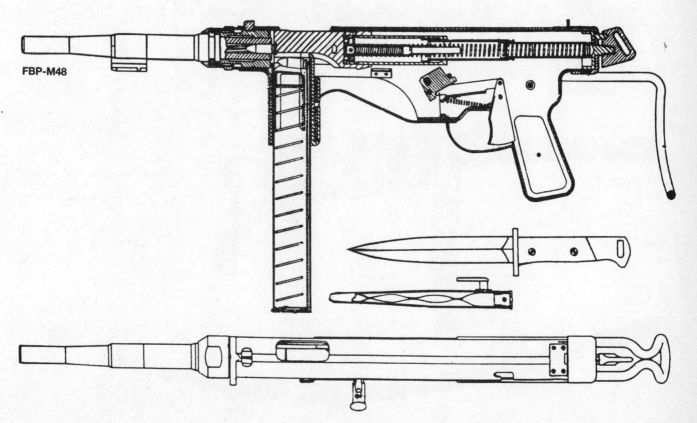

FBP-M48

PORTUGAL

9mm FBP M/948

Fabrica do Braco de Prata	
9 × 19mm Parabellum	
Operation	Blowback
Length, stock extended	812mm (32.0in)
Length, stock folded	635mm (25.0in)
Weight empty	3.74kg (7.65lb)
Barrel	250mm (9.84in), 6 grooves, rh
Magazine	32-shot detachable box
Cyclic rate	500rds/min
Muzzle velocity	380m/sec (1,247ft/sec)

The FBP M/948 is a combination of features of the German MP40 and the American M3 and was designed by Major Goncalves Cardoso of the Portuguese Army. The receiver, with telescoping return spring casing and barrel attached by a screwed collar, is taken from the MP40, while the pistol grip, wire sliding stock and trigger mechanism are from the M3. Extensive use was made of steel pressings and the result was a reliable and inexpensive weapon, though, according to report, its accuracy left something to be desired.

9mm FBP M/976

Fabrica do Braco de Prata	
9 × 19mm Parabellum	
Operation	Blowback
Length, stock extended	850mm (33.45in)
Length, stock folded	657m (25.87in)
Weight empty	3.12kg (6.88lb)
Barrel	250mm (9.84in), 6 grooves, rh
Magazine	32- or 36-shot detachable box
Cyclic rate	650rds/min
Muzzle velocity	395m/sec (1,295ft/sec)

The M/976 is an improved version of the M/948 and uses the same mechanical components, though with some modifications to improve reliability and simplify production. Two versions were made, one with a plain barrel and one with a perforated barrel jacket. It is probable that the jacketed model gave better accuracy, due to fuller support for the barrel, thus removing one of the principal complaints against the M/948. Construction is still from metal pressings and stampings, though the barrel is cold-forged from high quality steel, another factor in improving the accuracy.

FBP M/948

FBP M/976

This weapon appeared in 1987 and is a compact and robust design which owes nothing to the previous models. The receiver is in the form of a double cylinder, with the barrel and bolt in the lower section, and the overhung mass of the bolt in the upper section, very similar to the Italian Franchi design. The sliding stock, of steel rod, retracts into the 'waist' between the two sections of the receiver. The pistol grip and trigger unit attach below the receiver and there is a prominent safety/selector switch convenient to the firer's thumb. Two versions are made, one with a detachable barrel secured by a nut, the other with a fixed barrel surrounded by a perforated jacket.

INDEP LUSA

9mm Indep Lusa

Fabrica do Braco de Prata	
9 × 19mm Parabellum	
Operation	Blowback
Length, stock extended	600mm (23.6in)
Length, stock folded	445mm (17.5in)
Weight empty	2.5kg (5.5lb)
Barrel	160mm (6.30in), 6 grooves, rh
Magazine	30-shot detachable box
Cyclic rate	900rds/min
Muzzle velocity	390m/sec (1,280ft/sec)

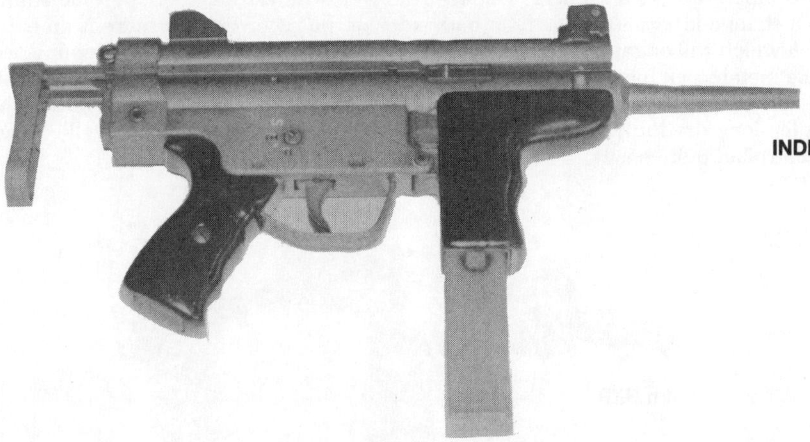

ROUMANIA

This appears to have been the only locally designed submachine-gun to appear from Roumania, and though few have been seen outside the country the production was fairly extensive and was certainly sufficient to equip the Roumanian Army in time to oppose the German invasion. The designer was Leopold Jasek, who probably chose the German MP38 as his source of inspiration, since there are several similarities, though the Orita was better finished and hence more expensive to manufacture. A unique firing pin was incorporated into the bolt, the reason being unknown. Most of the production models had a wooden one-piece stock, though a folding metal stock has also been seen. An unusual tangent rear sight was mounted well forward on the body, offering ranges up to 500m. A substantial change-lever on the right side allowed single shot or automatic fire, and the safety was a button on the front of the trigger guard which moved from side to side. In general terms the Orita was a good weapon for its day and probably gave good service. It remained in use by factory guards and reservists until the early 1970s.

9mm Orita M1941

Cugir Arsenal	
9 × 19mm Parabellum	
Operation	Blowback
Length overall	894mm (35.2in)
Weight empty	3.45kg (7.6lb)
Barrel	278mm (10.94in), 6 grooves, rh
Magazine	25-shot detachable box
Cyclic rate	600rds/min
Muzzle velocity	400m/sec (1,312ft/sec)

ORITA M1941

SOUTH AFRICA

9mm BXP

Armscor	
9 × 19mm Parabellum	
Operation	Blowback
Length, stock extended	607mm (23.9in)
Length, stock folded	387mm (15.2in)
Weight empty	2.5kg (5.5lb)
Barrel	208mm (8.2in), 6 grooves, rh
Magazine	22- or 32-shot detachable box
Cyclic rate	1,000–1,200rds/min
Muzzle velocity	370m/sec (1,214ft/sec)

Developed in the early 1980s, this is a simple but effective weapon, built from stainless steel pressings and precision castings. It is very compact and with the butt folded can be fired one-handed like a pistol. The bolt is of the telescoped type, surrounding the rear end of the barrel when closed, and when forward it effectively seals all the apertures in the body, so preventing ingress of dirt and dust. The perforated barrel nut carries a screw-thread which will accept a compensator or a silencer which works well with standard or subsonic ammunition. There is a change-lever/safety catch on both sides of the receiver, and there is an extra notch on the bolt which will engage the sear should the weapon be dropped, so preventing accidental firing. The metal stock folds beneath the body with the shoulder pad acting as a forward hand grip and heat deflector. The exterior surfaces are coated with a rust-resistant finish which also acts as a life-long dry lubricant. The rate of fire is high, but the weapon is well-balanced and can be controlled quite easily.

9mm BXP

SPAIN

9mm Labora

Industrio de Guerra de Cataluna	
9 × 23mm Largo	
Operation	Blowback
Length overall	806mm (31.75in)
Weight empty	4.25kg (9.37lb)
Barrel	260mm (10.25in), 4 grooves, rh
Magazine	36-shot detachable box
Cyclic rate	750rds/min
Muzzle velocity	396m/sec (1,300ft/sec)

This was manufactured for a short time in 1938–9, during the closing stages of the Spanish Civil War, and was in many ways a remarkable weapon. Produced by a small factory in the middle of a war, it was carefully machined from steel stock and to a high quality. This was probably due to the ready availability of trained gunmakers with no commercial market to serve and who were thus able to devote all their time and energy to making this weapon. The design was fairly simple, with no obvious affinities to any existing weapon. The bolt was unusually light and the return spring unusually heavy, since the cartridge was rather more powerful than the usual 9mm Parabellum.

Few examples of the Labora remain; most were used up during the Civil War and the design was never revived.

LABORA

The Echeverria company, whose tradename is 'Star', spent much of the 1930s experimenting with submachine-gun designs, and the SI35 is representative of their efforts – perhaps the most involved of their models. The series began with a semi-automatic carbine and continued building upon this basic design until about 1942 when the company changed to more simple designs, broadly copying contemporary German models. The SI35 operated on delayed blowback principles, delay being achieved by a cam plate engaging in the receiver body. A hold-open device indicated when the magazine was empty, and, most unusual of all, a switch was provided to change the rate of fire to 300 or 700 rounds per minute. While the weapon worked well, it was unnecessarily complicated and difficult to manufacture. A slightly altered version was offered to the USA in 1942 as the 'Atlantic', and the SI35 was also tested by the British Army at the same time, but neither country considered the design suitable for wartime production and the gun was rejected. The gun was made in small numbers and saw service with the Spanish Army in the closing months of the Civil War.

This was a Spanish adaptation of the German MP40. The Star company acquired the original German drawings in 1942, made some modifications to the design, and began production in 1944. It was adopted in quantity by the Spanish armed forces and police and was also sold to Portugal and some Middle Eastern countries. The modifications included a bolt lock to prevent accidental discharges and a two-stage trigger which gave single shots for the first pressure and automatic fire when pressed further. The barrel was enclosed in a perforated jacket and retained by a muzzle compensator; by twisting the compensator it was possible to remove the barrel. The Z45 was the first submachine-gun to use a fluted chamber to ease extraction, doubtless necessary due to the higher pressure of the special 9 × 23mm submachine-gun cartridge which was adopted with this weapon, more powerful than the standard pistol round. The military version of the Z45 used a folding stock similar to that of the MP40, but another version was made with a fixed wooden stock.

9mm Star SI35

Star-Bonifacio Echeverria SA

9 × 23mm Largo

Operation	Delayed blowback
Length overall	900mm (35.45in)
Weight empty	3.74kg (8.25lb)
Barrel	269mm (10.6in), 6 grooves, rh
Magazine	10-, 30- or 40-shot detachable box
Cyclic rate	300 or 700rds/min
Muzzle velocity	410m/sec (1,345ft/sec)

9mm Star Z45

Star-Bonifacio Echeverria SA

9 × 23mm Largo

Operation	Blowback
Length, stock extended	841mm (33.1in)
Length, stock folded	580mm (22.85in)
Weight empty	3.87kg (8.5lb)
Barrel	192mm (7.75in), 6 grooves, rh
Magazine	10- or 30-shot detachable box
Cyclic rate	450rds/min
Muzzle velocity	415m/sec (1,362ft/sec)

STAR SI35

STAR Z-45

9mm Star Z70/B

Star-Bonifacio Echeverria SA	
9 × 19mm Parabellum	
Operation	Blowback
Length, stock extended	700mm (27.56in)
Length, stock folded	480mm (18.90in)
Weight empty	2.87kg (6.33lb)
Barrel	200mm (7.87in), 6 grooves, rh
Magazine	20-, 30- or 40-shot detachable box
Cyclic rate	550rds/min
Muzzle velocity	380m/sec (1,247ft/sec)

This weapon was designed to replace the Z45 in the middle 1960s; it originally appeared as the Z62 and incorporated two unusual features; first a hammer firing system, which was locked by the bolt except when the bolt was forward and the trigger pressed, and secondly a double trigger unit which gave automatic fire when the upper section was pulled and single shots when the lower section was used. Otherwise it was a simple blowback weapon which used metal pressings and plastics in its construction. Experience showed that the complicated trigger mechanism was prone to malfunction, and the design was changed to a conventional trigger with an external change lever. The lateral push-through safety catch was also changed to a simple lever catch below the trigger guard. This became the Z70/B and was introduced in 1971 for Spanish Army service. Note also that this weapon introduced the 9mm Parabellum cartridge as the service standard. The Z62 had used the Largo round; a modification, in 9mm Parabellum, became the Z63. The Z70/B was also in 9mm Parabellum, and the Z63 had its name changed to Z70.

9mm Star Z84

Star-Bonifacio Echeverria SA	
9 × 19mm Parabellum	
Operation	Blowback
Length, stock extended	615mm (24.21in)
Length, stock folded	410mm (16.14in)
Weight empty	3.00kg (6.6lb)
Barrel	215mm (8.46in), 6 grooves, rh
Magazine	25- or 30-shot detachable box
Cyclic rate	600rds/min
Muzzle velocity	400m/sec (1,312ft/sec)

With this design Star abandoned all that had gone before and started afresh. The result is a light, compact and efficient weapon which entered Spanish service in 1985 and has since been sold to several other countries. The design uses steel stampings and precision castings, and special attention has been paid to the feed system which will feed soft-point and semi-jacketed bullets as well as normal full-jacketed military ammunition. The Z84 fires from an open bolt, using the blowback system of operation, and the bolt is telescoped around the rear end of the barrel. The centre of gravity is above the pistol grip, which contains the magazine, so allowing the gun to be fired single-handed with remarkable accuracy. The bolt travels on two rails and there is ample clearance all round so that any dirt is unlikely to interfere with the action. There is a sliding fire selector on the left side and the safety is a sliding button inside the trigger guard. The bolt has three bents which hold it securely in any position, and there is also an automatic inertia safety unit which locks the bolt in the closed position. This is over-ridden by the cocking handle and is disconnected while the weapon is being fired.

STAR Z84

SWEDEN

9mm Carl Gustav M45

Carl Gustavs Stadsgevarfaktori	
9 × 19mm Parabellum	
Operation	Blowback
Length, stock extended	808mm (31.81in)
Length, stock folded	552mm (21.73in)
Weight empty	3.9kg (8.6lb)
Barrel	213mm (8.38in), 6 grooves, rh
Magazine	36-shot detachable box
Cyclic rate	600rds/min
Muzzle velocity	410m/sec (1,345ft/sec)

World War Two awakened Sweden to the realisation that her own weapons were somewhat lacking, and the state arms factory 'Carl Gustav' set about remedying this as quickly as possible. As a stop-gap some Finnish Suomi submachine-guns were made under licence by Husqvarna Vapenfabrik, but by 1945 the Carl Gustav team had produced a design which was cheap and simple to manufacture. The M45, as it became, is still manufactured in the 1990s, still used by the Swedish and other armies, and although it has passed through several minor variations in its long life, it retains its essential original characteristics. The M45 is a well-made gun of conventional blowback type, capable of automatic fire only. The tubular receiver resembles that of the Sten, but the barrel is concealed in a perforated jacket, and the stock is rigid but hinges forward to fold along the right side of the weapon. The design was originally intended to use the 50-round Suomi magazine, but an excellent two-column 36-round magazine was also developed and the magazine housing was made detachable so that the correct housing could be quickly fitted. In due course the 36-round magazine became standard, and, indeed, proved so reliable that it has been widely adopted for other designs in other countries, and the magazine housing became a fixed pattern changing the nomenclature to M45/B. The M45/C has a bayonet lug, and the M45/E has the option of single-shot fire. The M45 was built under licence in Egypt as the 'Port Said' and also in Indonesia.

SWITZERLAND

9mm Steyr-Solothurn SI-100

Waffenfabrik Solothurn AG	
9 × 23mm Steyr	
Operation	Blowback
Length overall	851mm (33.5in)
Weight empty	3.87kg (8.53lb)
Barrel	196mm (7.72in), 6 grooves, rh
Magazine	32-shot detachable box
Cyclic rate	500rds/min
Muzzle velocity	380m/sec (1,247ft/sec)

The history of this weapon shows the shifts to which German companies went to in order to get round the restrictions of the Versailles Treaty in the 1920–34 period. Manufacture of submachine-guns was forbidden to German firms; design, however, was not. Rheinmetall designed the weapon, then passed the designs to a Swiss subsidiary, the Waffenfabrik Solothurn AG who made the prototypes, carried out the testing and made whatever modifications were necessary. But they were not equipped for mass production, and Switzerland, even then, had restrictions on weapon export. So the prototype and manufacturing drawings now went to the Waffenfabrik Steyr in Austria where the actual manufacture was done. The weapon was adopted by the Austrian and Hungarian Armies and sold widely in South America and the Far East. It was also bought by Portugal in 1935, and the Portuguese Guarda Fiscal were still using them into the mid-1970s. Manufacture ceased in 1940. The Steyr-Solothurn is the Rolls-Royce of submachine-guns; machined from solid steel throughout, the quality and finish is perhaps the highest ever seen in this class of weapon. Its design is quite conventional, a blowback firing from an open bolt, with a jacketed barrel, and it closely resembles the Bergmann MP28. One unique feature is the formation of a quick-loading device for the magazine in the magazine housing. The ammunition was supplied in chargers, and a suitable charger slot is cut in the upper surface of the side magazine housing. The empty magazine slides into a secondary housing beneath this slot, the charger is placed in the top, and a sweep of the thumb loads the rounds into the magazine. Once loaded, the magazine can be quickly removed from its bottom position and replaced into the housing.

CARL GUSTAV M45

9mm MP41/44

Federal Arms Factory Berne	
9 × 19mm Parabellum	
Operation	Recoil, toggle lock
Length overall	775mm (30.5in)
Weight empty	5.19kg (11.44lb)
Barrel	247mm (9.72in), 6 grooves, rh
Magazine	40-shot detachable box
Cyclic rate	900rds/min
Muzzle velocity	395m/sec (1,295ft/sec)

9mm MP43/44

SA Suisse Hispano-Suiza	
9 × 19mm Parabellum	
Operation	Blowback
Length overall	863mm (33.98in)
Weight empty	4.76kg (10.49lb)
Barrel	318mm (12.5in), 6 grooves, rh
Magazine	50-shot detachable box
Cyclic rate	800rds/min
Muzzle velocity	395m/sec (1,295ft/sec)

The MP41/44 was probably the most complicated and over-designed submachine-gun ever made, undoubtedly the most expensive, and should never have been allowed into military service. The design was by Colonel Furrer, Superintendent of the Federal Arms Factory; this factory had machinery for making Parabellum pistols, and Furrer became obsessed with the toggle action, designing an enormous variety of impractical ways of using this action on weapons of every sort, including heavy anti-aircraft and anti-tank guns. In 1940, when invasion by the German Army seemed highly probable, the Swiss Army was panicked into making the decision to adopt this design; this was doubtless a political decision, since better designs were available within Switzerland. Indeed, a promising SIG design was turned down in favour of the Furrer model. It took almost three years to get the MP41/44 into production and in the following two years only about 4,000 were made, manufacture being slow and difficult. The difficulty lay in the mechanism. The weapon used a Parabellum-style toggle lock, but laid on its side, and with an addition link to the toggle to act as a form of accelerator. This, of course, all had to be concealed within a casing, which made the weapon extremely clumsy to handle. The design was so complex that soldiers were forbidden to field strip them, and only armourers were allowed that luxury.

As might be expected, the Swiss Army were soon disillusioned about the MP41/44, particularly with its slow supply, and in 1943 they began looking about for something 'off the shelf'. The Finnish Suomi design appeared practical, and they therefore obtained a licence from the Finns and set the Hispano-Suiza factory to make it. The weapon was scarcely changed other than to fit Swiss sling swivels and simplify the sights. The drum magazine was not adopted, a 50-round double-row box being used instead. With this the Swiss finally had a serviceable and inexpensive submachine-gun which remained in service until the 1960s and is still held in reserve stocks.

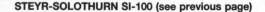

STEYR-SOLOTHURN SI-100 (see previous page)

MP41/44

SIG had built a number of submachine-guns in pre-1939 days, but they were complex and expensive and failed to prosper in the market-place. In 1944 they set about designing a new weapon which would adopt a more modern system of manufacture, and the MP48 was the production model which resulted. It was unusual in using precision castings instead of machined or stamped parts, a method adopted in order to reduce cost. One previous SIG idea was continued, and this was the folding magazine, which could be swung forward beneath the barrel. This obviously removed any danger of accidental firing, and there was no other type of safety device fitted. A retractable tubular steel butt was fitted. However, the only country that ever purchased any significant number was Chile.

9mm MP48

Schweizerische Industrie-Gesellschaft (SIG)

9 × 19mm Parabellum

Operation	Blowback
Length, stock extended	711mm (28.0in)
Length, stock folded	570mm (22.4in)
Weight empty	2.92kg (6.43lb)
Barrel	196mm (7.72in), 6 grooves, rh
Magazine	40-shot folding detachable box
Cyclic rate	700rds/min
Muzzle velocity	380m/sec (1,247ft/sec)

This was developed by SIG in the early 1950s, and was little more than an improved MP48. It retained the unusual forward-folding magazine, together with a sprung flap which closed the feed aperture when the magazine was folded. It also had a two-stage trigger, giving single shots for a short pull and automatic fire for a long pull. A drum-type rear sight was used with settings for 50, 100, 200 and 400 metres. Many of the expensive machined components of the earlier design were replaced by precision castings, and there was a good deal of plastic used, but the MP310 failed to make much of an impression in the market, probably because at that time there was a surplus of wartime weapons to be had cheaply. It was adopted by the Swiss police, and a few were sold overseas, but the lack of success appears to have decided SIG to abandon this type of weapon, and they have never made a submachine-gun since then.

9mm SIG MP310

Schweizerische Industrie-Gesellschaft (SIG)

9 × 19mm Parabellum

Operation	Blowback
Length, stock extended	735mm (28.93in)
Length, stock folded	610mm (24.0in)
Weight empty	3.15kg (6.94lb)
Barrel	200mm (7.87in), 6 grooves, rh
Magazine	40-shot detachable box
Cyclic rate	900rds/min
Muzzle velocity	365m/sec (1,198ft/sec)

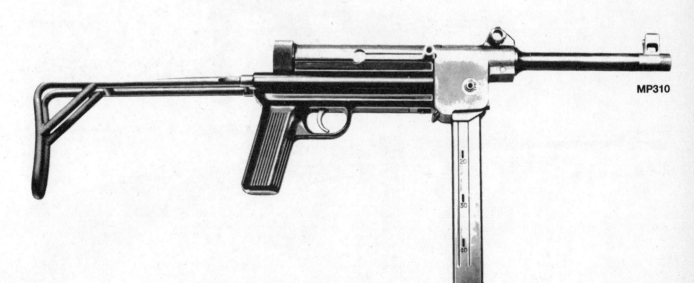

MP310

9mm Rexim-Favor

SA Suisse Rexim Geneva	
9 × 19mm Parabellum	
Operation	Blowback
Length, stock extended	873mm (34.37in)
Length, stock folded	617mm (24.3in)
Weight empty	4.67kg (10.29lb)
Barrel	340mm (13.38in), 6 grooves, rh
Magazine	32-shot detachable box (MP40 pattern)
Cyclic rate	600rds/min
Muzzle velocity	425m/sec (1,395ft/sec)

The Rexim company entered the arms business in the 1950s with a design which, some aver, was stolen from the French; though whether there is anything in that tale is of little consequence. The subsequent development of the weapon, however, was just as involved; although Rexim were set up in Switzerland the weapons were made for them in Spain, and samples were hawked around the world with little success until the company failed in 1957. After this the Spanish manufacturers marketed the gun under their own name, La Coruna, with equally little success. The version shown here is the 'Favor', the first model to be offered. It was later slightly modified and the production model, which had a perforated barrel jacket, was known as the 'FV Mark IV'. A variety of stock patterns and barrel lengths were produced as alternatives during prototype development, and offered in the company's optimistic brochures, but the basic configuration of the weapon remained the same. The mechanism was unnecessarily complicated, firing from a closed bolt by allowing an independent annular hammer to be released by the trigger to operate the firing pin. So far as can be ascertained, the only service use of the Rexim was in Turkey, where a number were issued as the 'Model 68' and are still in use.

USA

.45in Thompson M1928A1

Colt's Patent Firearms Corp; Auto-Ordnance Corporation; Savage Arms Co	
.45in M1911	
Operation	Delayed blowback
Length overall	857mm (33.75in)
Weight empty	4.88kg (10.75lb)
Barrel	266mm (10.5in), 6 grooves, rh
Magazine	18-, 20- or 30-shot box or 50- or 100-shot drum
Cyclic rate	700rds/min
Muzzle velocity	280m/sec (920ft/sec)

This was the first model of the Thompson submachine-gun to be definitely used by the military, even though several models had been offered in the 1920s as 'Military Models'. The 1928 version was used by the US Marine Corps in Nicaragua and also by the US Coast Guard. It was directly derived from the 1921 model, which it closely resembled, and some 1928 models appear to be 1921 models modified and overstamped with the new date. The so-called 'Navy' model has the horizontal fore-grip, sling swivels and muzzle compensator, whereas the commercial model of the same year has the more familiar vertical fore-grip with finger notches. Less than 400 were purchased and taken into service in the 1928–34 period, and serious manufacture did not begin until 1939, to meet orders from France and Britain. The genuine Thompson weapons made use of the much-argued Blish system, a method of delaying the opening of the breech by the friction created by two blocks of metal sliding obliquely across each other. Under high pressure the two blocks will freeze, but as the pressure drops they are free to move. The efficiency of this device is questionable, but if it did nothing else it kept the rate of fire down to a reasonable figure.

REXIM-FAVOR

THOMPSON M1928A1

When the demand for the Thompson soared in the 1939–41 period it was soon realised that the mechanism was not well-suited to mass production, and by 1942 it was imperative to simplify the design. The Savage Arms Co, which was making M1928A1 guns on contract, redesigned the mechanism to do away with the Blish system and turn it into a simple blowback. Auto-Ordnance, patentees and owners of the Thompson design, objected bitterly, saying that this entirely removed any Thompson features from the weapon, but the US Army over-rode their objections and insisted on the design, since it was easier and quicker to supply. In addition to removing the locking system, the M1 design moved the bolt handle to the right-hand side, did away with the barrel fins and muzzle compensator and made the butt a fixed item instead of removable. The drum magazine was dropped in favour of boxes, and the sights were simplified. Later the hammer mechanism was dropped and a fixed firing pin formed in the bolt face, turning the weapon into the M1A1. The Thompson, in its various forms, was a popular gun; although heavy in comparison to many contemporaries it was utterly reliable and became a favourite of Commando and Ranger forces. It continued in production until 1945, re-appeared in the Korean War and was still being offered to Asian countries under the Offshore Programme as late as 1960. Although no longer in official use by any army, it will be many years yet before the last one wears out.

This weapon was designed just before World War Two and about 100,000 of this and the later model 55 were made between 1941 and 1945. Most of those produced went to the US Marine Corps, though a few were sold to Allied countries and some were given to the USSR. The Reising was an ingenious design which fired from a closed bolt. The internal mechanism was complicated and the pressing of the trigger set off a series of inter-related movements which culminated in the striking of the primer, a far remove from the simplicity of most open-bolt blowback mechanisms. Automatic fire was really a series of semi-automatic shots in sequence, since the mechanism always operates in the same way. Another unusual feature was the 'semi-locking' of the bolt on firing, by being cammed upwards into a recess in the receiver. Cocking was performed by pulling back a lever concealed inside a slot under the fore-end. The Reising proved entirely unsuitable for combat use; the complicated mechanism made no allowance for the presence of dirt or grit, which promptly jammed it, and the breech-locking recess soon attracted fouling or dirt which prevented the block rising and thus prevented the weapon firing at all. These shortcomings were discovered in the Guadalcanal operation, where most Marines jettisoned their Reisings in favour of anything else they could find. The weapons which remained were withdrawn and issued to police and security forces in the USA where, in the absence of combat conditions, they performed quite adequately.

.45in Thompson M1 and M1A1

Auto-Ordnance Corporation; Savage Arms Corporation

.45in M1911

Operation	Blowback
Length overall	813mm (32.0in)
Weight empty	4.82kg (10.62lb)
Barrel	266mm (10.5in), 6 grooves, rh
Magazine	20- or 30-shot detachable box
Cyclic rate	700rds/min
Muzzle velocity	280m/sec (920ft/sec)

.45in Reising Model 50

Harrington & Richardson Arms Co

.45in M1911

Operation	Delayed blowback
Length overall	907mm (35.75in)
Weight empty	3.10kg (6.75lb)
Barrel	279mm (11.0in), 6 grooves, rh
Magazine	12- or 20-shot detachable box
Cyclic rate	550rds/min
Muzzle velocity	280m/sec (918ft/sec)

THOMPSON M1A1

REISING MODEL 50

.45in Reising Model 55

Harrington & Richardson Arms Co	
.45in M1911	
Operation	Delayed blowback
Length, stock extended	787mm (31.0in)
Length, stock folded	570mm (22.5in)
Weight empty	2.89kg (6.37lb)
Barrel	266mm (10.5in), 6 grooves, rh
Magazine	12- or 20-shot detachable box
Cyclic rate	550rds/min
Muzzle velocity	280m/sec (918ft/sec)

The Reising 55 was an attempt to produce a slightly lighter version of the Model 50 by removing the compensator and the butt and adopting a wire butt and a pistol grip. The mechanism of the Model 50 was retained, and thus all the mechanical disadvantages with it. The wire stock proved far too weak in combat conditions, and the Model 55 was retired from military service together with the Model 50.

9mm UD M42

High Standards Mfg. Co; Marlin Firearms Co	
9 × 19mm Parabellum	
Operation	Blowback
Length overall	820mm (32.25in)
Weight empty	4.11kg (9.06lb)
Barrel	279mm (11.0in), 6 grooves, rh
Magazine	20-shot detachable box
Cyclic rate	700rds/min
Muzzle velocity	400m/sec (1,312ft/sec)

This was designed by High Standard in the late 1930s, patented in 1940, and after testing was put into production in early 1942. The development models and prototypes were made by High Standard, but the production (of about 15,000) was by Marlin. A few early models were made in .45 calibre, but the production models were all in 9mm Parabellum and were principally made to fill an order from the Dutch, most of them being shipped to the Dutch East Indies. The remainder were taken by the OSS, though a few appear to have crept into regular military units. The UD (United Defense) M42 was rather more complicated than the normal run of submachine-guns, but it was very well made from good material and it performed well in adverse conditions. It was unfortunate in appearing just after the Thompson had gained official approval, and so it never achieved a major contract. The gun fired from an open bolt and the firing pin was operated by a hammer as the bolt closed. The bolt handle was unusual in being a slide which did not move with the bolt and acted as a shutter to seal the boltway against dirt. A .45 version was made, in an attempt to interest the US Army, but with the Thompson M1 in ample supply the army reported 'no requirement' and the design lapsed.

UD M42

REISING MODEL 55

Often called the 'Hyde' after its designer, this was another of the many weapons tested in the USA in the early years of World War Two when there was an urgent need for submachine-guns and no fixed notions of how best to make them. Although the M2 was a relatively simple and straightforward design, it was not easy to make, and when the Marlin company received a contract in mid-1942, the first production models did not appear until May 1943. By that time the M3 (below) had been approved for service and was in production, and manufacture of the M2 was stopped after no more than 400 had been made. The M2 performed well on test and appears to have been reliable and accurate. It was a simple blowback design, though the bolt was of peculiar shape with the rear end being quite large in diameter and the front half long and slender. The receiver was built up from a seamless tubular section and a steel forging, and it appears that the machining and finishing of this element was the Achilles' heel of the design. It was a pity, because the M2 shoots quite well, feels good, and would probably have been a good deal more popular than was the M3.

In the early years of World War Two the US government tested a large number of privately developed submachine-guns, few of which showed any signs of fulfilling the army's requirements. Eventually a design team was formed at the Aberdeen Proving Ground, charged with developing a suitable weapon, and within two years it was in production. This was the M3, a simple, cheap and entirely adequate gun which met the specification in every way, though after some practical experience it was found to have certain defects, particularly in the magazine. As a first try at designing a submachine-gun, though, it was a remarkable effort. It was approved for service in December 1942, remained in first line use until 1960, and numbers are still in service with the US Army and other countries. The simple cylindrical shape and thin protruding barrel gave rise to its nickname 'The Grease Gun'. The M3 was designed for mass production, and construction is mainly of stampings and pressings; few machining operations are required. The barrel was swaged in a single process. The rate of fire is unusually low, but this allows single shots to be touched off without requiring a selector mechanism and it also makes the weapon quite steady when firing bursts. Inevitably, some small mistakes were made; one such was in the magazine design, a single-column affair which gave feed troubles throughout the gun's life. Another lay in the choice of materials for some of the first production models, whose component broke too easily. But for all this the M3 was cheap and effective and did all that was asked of it. It had one interesting feature designed in; the ability to change the calibre to 9mm Parabellum by simply changing the bolt and barrel, and inserting an adaptor into the magazine housing to allow the Sten magazine to be used. All this could be done quickly and without tools, but in fact very few were ever modified and almost all remained in .45 calibre.

.45in US M2

Marlin Firearms Co

.45in M1911

Operation	Blowback
Length overall	813mm (32.0in)
Weight empty	4.19kg (9.25lb)
Barrel	305mm (12.0in), 6 grooves, rh
Magazine	20- or 30-shot detachable box
Cyclic rate	500rds/min
Muzzle velocity	293m/sec (960ft/sec)

.45in US M3

Guide Lamp, Div of General Motors

.45in M1911

Operation	Blowback
Length, stock extended	762mm (30.0in)
Length, stock folded	577mm (22.75in)
Weight empty	3.70kg (8.15lb)
Barrel	203mm (8.0in), 4 grooves, rh
Magazine	30-shot detachable box
Cyclic rate	450rds/min
Muzzle velocity	275m/sec (900ft/sec)

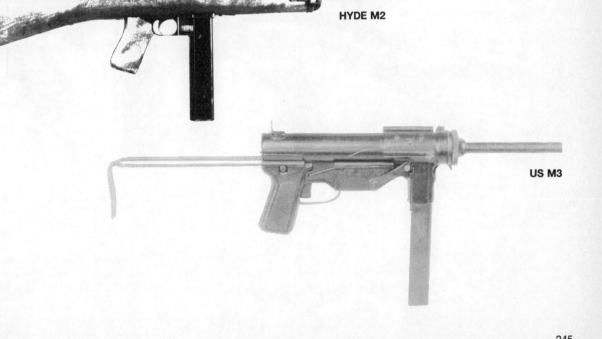

HYDE M2

US M3

.45in US M3A1

Guide Lamp, Div of General Motors; Ithaca Gun Co	
.45in M1911	
Operation	Blowback
Length, stock extended	756mm (29.75in)
Length, stock folded	577mm (22.75in)
Weight empty	3.71kg (8.18lb)
Barrel	203mm (8.0in), 4 grooves, rh
Magazine	30-shot detachable box
Cyclic rate	400rds/min
Muzzle velocity	275m/sec (900ft/sec)

Although the M3 appeared to be simple enough, it was found that still further improvements could be made and some of the original defects cured. In December 1944 the M3A1 was standardised and eventually supplanted the M3 as the standard weapon. It differed from the M3 by eliminating the bolt retracting mechanism altogether, so that the firer pulled back the bolt by the unusual, but supremely basic, method of inserting his finger into a hole in the bolt and pulling it back. For this to be possible the ejection opening was enlarged and fitted with a hinged cover; this had a protrusion on the inside which, when the cover closed, entered the hole in the bolt and securely locked it against movement. Other minor improvements were made, including the redesign of some parts so that they could be used as tools to strip other parts. The troublesome magazine remained, though the tendency to jam was reduced by giving it a plastic dust cap. For all that, the M3 was never very popular, since it lacked visual appeal; most soldiers preferred to obtain an M1 carbine, even though it had far less combat utility than did an M3. About 700,000 M3 and M3A1 were made, and many more have been produced in other countries, either under licence or as copies.

9mm Ingram Model 6

Police Ordnance Co	
9 × 19mm Parabellum	
Operation	Blowback
Length overall	762mm (30.0in)
Weight empty	3.29kg (7.25lb)
Barrel	228mm (9.0in), 6 grooves, rh
Magazine	30-shot detachable box
Cyclic rate	600rds/min
Muzzle velocity	275m/sec (902ft/sec)

The Ingram is not a very inspired design, but it is one of the few American commercial designs to have been successful since the end of World War Two. The Model 6 appeared in the early 1950s and was sold in limited numbers to various police forces, the Cuban Navy, the Peruvian Army and the Thai forces. It was a simple design and its principal talking point was the adoption of a two-stage trigger. Single shots were produced by a short pull, automatic fire by a longer pull; the system is, today, fairly commonplace, but at the time of the Ingram's introduction was still something of a novelty. Care was taken during the design stage to ensure that the Ingram could be made with the minimum of special and expensive tools, and the receiver, barrel and magazine were all made from steel tubing. There was little machining, and no need for expensive stamping machinery. It was generally made in 9mm calibre, though .38 Super and .45in versions were also available. The Ingram failed because no real market existed for it on the American continent, and in Europe the market was flooded with cheap weapons left over from the war. Ingram was probably lucky to sell as many as he did.

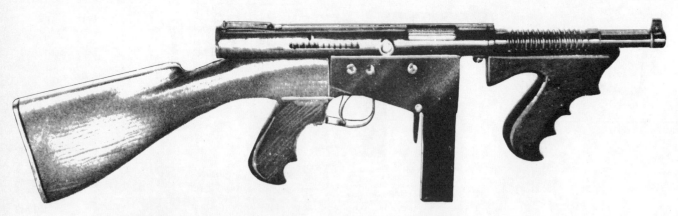

INGRAM MODEL 6

Ingram left the Police Ordnance Corporation and in 1970 developed this weapon for the Military Armament Corporation. The Model 10 is extremely compact and built of steel pressings. The bolt is of the telescoping type, enclosing the rear of the barrel when closed, and the magazine feeds through the pistol grip; these two features ensure that the point of balance is over the grip, which makes the gun very steady and even allows single-handed firing. A cocking handle protrudes through the top of the receiver and is notched to allow the sight line to pass. To lock the bolt the handle is rotated, and this then obstructs the sight line and acts as an indication that the weapon is safe. The barrel is threaded to accept a 'sound suppressor', which is similar to a silencer but only muffles the noise of discharge and does nothing to reduce the bullet's velocity. A Model 11 was also made; this was of the same appearance as the Model 10 but smaller in all dimensions, since it was chambered for the 9mm Short cartridge and was put forward as a possible police weapon. The Model 10 could also be had in .45 calibre. Small numbers of M10 and M11 were bought by several South American countries, Portugal and Israel, and limited numbers were taken by US and UK special forces. In 1975 the Military Armaments Corporation went bankrupt, and, after passing through various hands, the rights to the weapon are now owned by the SWD Corporation, who market it as the 'Cobray M11' in two versions, the M11 in 9mm Short and the M11/9 in 9mm Parabellum. (Data table refers to the 9mm M10.)

At some time or other most manufacturers of 5.56mm assault rifles try making a short-barrelled version as a submachine-gun; but the 5.56mm cartridge is not well-suited to that role and few of them have ever prospered. So they then do the obvious thing and convert the weapon into 9mm calibre, which makes a good deal more sense. The Colt came by this route, after various short assault rifle designs, and was introduced in 1987. It uses the basic body and configuration of the M16 rifle, but with a short, telescoping butt which is exceptionally rigid when extended. As with the rifle, the submachine-gun fires from a closed bolt, and the action remains open after the last shot. The magazine housing of the original M16 remains, though modified internally to take a narrow 9mm magazine. Operation and controls are the same as the M16 rifle, so that troops trained on the rifle can easily adapt to using the submachine-gun. The Colt submachine-gun has been adopted by the US Drug Enforcement Agency, other US armed forces and law enforcement agencies, and is under evaluation by several other armies.

9mm Ingram Model 10

Military Armament Corp S.W.D. Inc	
9 × 19mm Parabellum	
Operation	Blowback
Length, stock extended	548mm (21.57in)
Length, stock folded	269mm (10.59in)
Weight empty	2.84kg (6.25lb)
Barrel	146mm (5.75in), 6 grooves, rh
Magazine	32-shot detachable box
Cyclic rate	1,090rds/min
Muzzle velocity	366m/sec (1,200ft/sec)

9mm Colt

Colt Firearms	
9 × 19mm Parabellum	
Operation	Blowback
Length, stock extended	730mm (28.74in)
Length, stock folded	650mm (25.6in)
Weight empty	2.59kg (5.71lb)
Barrel	260mm (10.23in), 6 grooves, rh
Magazine	20- or 32-shot detachable box
Cyclic rate	800–1,000rds/min
Muzzle velocity	397m/sec (1,302ft/sec)

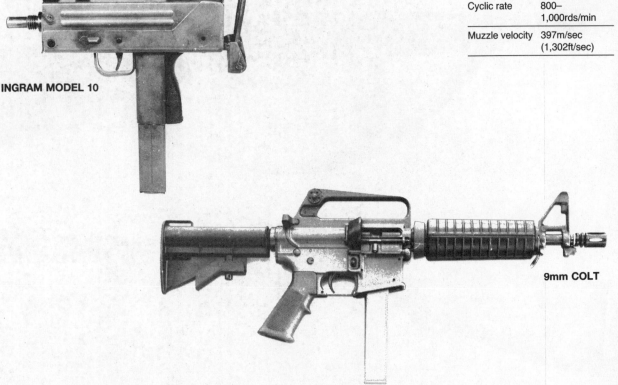

INGRAM MODEL 10

9mm COLT

247

USSR

7.62mm PPD-34/38

State arsenals	
7.62 × 25mm Soviet	
Operation	Blowback
Length overall	775mm (30.5in)
Weight empty	3.76kg (8.25lb)
Barrel	272mm (10.75in), 4 grooves, rh
Magazine	25-shot box or 71-shot drum
Cyclic rate	800rds/min
Muzzle velocity	500m/sec (1,640ft/sec)

7.62mm PPD-40

State arsenals	
7.62 × 25mm Soviet	
Operation	Blowback
Length overall	777mm (30.6in)
Weight empty	3.70kg (8.16lb)
Barrel	269mm (10.6in), 4 grooves, rh
Magazine	71-shot drum
Cyclic rate	800rds/min
Muzzle velocity	500m/sec (1,640ft/sec)

The PPD is really a series of weapons developed by Degtyarev in the Soviet Union during the period 1934–40. The model illustrated was standard issue (in small numbers only) to the army until 1940, when it was supplemented by the PPD-40 and then replaced by the PPSh-41. It was a fairly conventional gun for its time, although it looks as if much of its inspiration came from the German MP28 and the Finnish Suomi. The mechanism is quite straightforward but it must have been somewhat expensive to manufacture as the component parts are all machined from high-quality steel; there are no stampings. The box magazine feeds from below, and an unusual pattern of drum magazine could also be used. This was the first Soviet weapon to utilise the drum magazine which later became a regular feature of all but two of the entire series of Soviet submachine-guns. The 7.62mm cartridge was, of course, the standard Soviet pistol round, firing a comparatively light bullet at a high velocity; this increased velocity, though, did not give it any greater effectiveness than the 9mm Parabellum, nor any better range. One feature of this gun, and all those that followed it, was that the barrel was internally chromium plated, an expensive process but popular with Soviet designers as it considerably extended barrel life.

The early Soviet submachine-guns, from 1926 onwards, were only made in token numbers, and it was not until the middle 1930s that a serviceable weapon, the PPD-34/38, appeared. This was replaced in 1940 by the PPD-40, a better weapon in most respects. It was designed with more of an eye to ease of manufacture, and the peculiar drum magazine was replaced by a model copied from the Finnish Suomi drum, an open-topped pattern which slid into a recess below the breech. The PPD-40 was well-made of good material and was obviously a peace-time design; once the war ensnared the Russians, the PPD was abandoned for weapons which were even simpler and quicker to make.

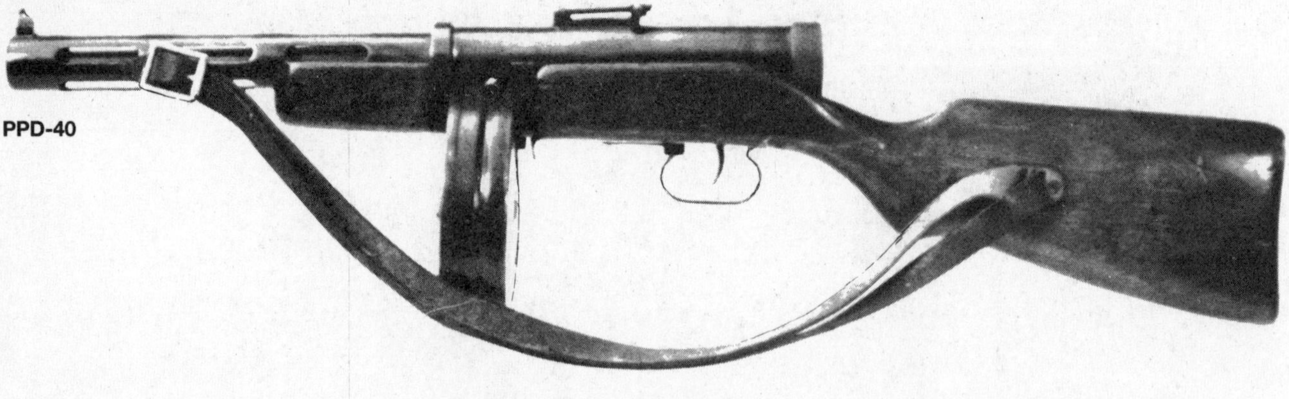

PPD-40

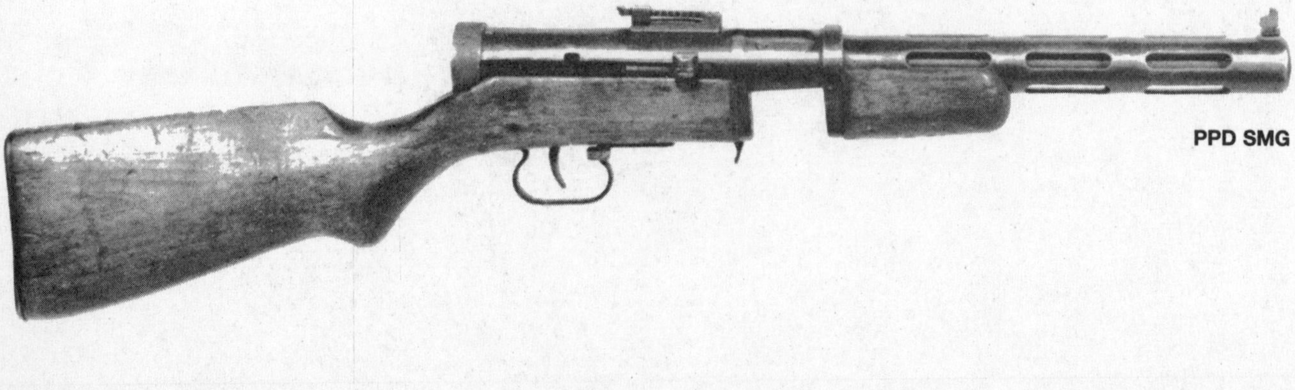

PPD SMG

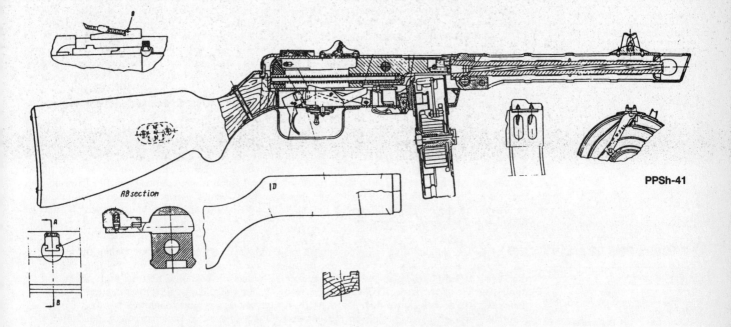

AB section

PPSh-41

PPS-43

7.62mm PPSh-41

State arsenals	
7.62 × 25mm Soviet	
Operation	Blowback
Length overall	838mm (33.0in)
Weight empty	3.64kg (8.0lb)
Barrel	266mm (10.5in), 4 grooves, rh
Magazine	35-shot box or 71-shot drum
Cyclic rate	900rds/min
Muzzle velocity	500m/sec (1,640ft/sec)

Two national catastrophes contributed to the Soviet enthusiasm for submachine-guns. The first was the Winter War with Finland in 1939–40, when the Finns used submachine-guns with devastating effect during close combat in the forests, and the second was the German invasion of 1941, when the Soviets lost, in the retreat, both huge quantities of small arms and much of their engineering capability. There then arose an urgent demand for a light and simple weapon capable of a high volume of fire, and the answer to this was Georgi Shpagin's PPSh-41. This new design was much cheaper and quicker to make than the preceding models, and was roughly finished; the barrel was still chromed, however, and there was never any doubt about the weapon's effectiveness. Stripping was simplicity itself, as the receiver hinged open to reveal the bolt and its spring. Early models had a selector lever, but this was soon abandoned and most were capable of only automatic fire, and the magazine was the tried and trusted 71-round Suomi drum. The rate of fire was high, but a rudimentary compensator built into the barrel jacket helped to counteract the muzzle climb.

About five million PPSh guns had been made by 1945 and the Soviets adapted their infantry tactics to take full advantage of such huge numbers; often complete units were armed with nothing else. In Russia the PPSh went out of service in the late 1950s, but it was supplied in enormous quantities to satellite and pro-Communist countries and is still likely to turn up for several years to come. It has been made in several Communist countries and in Iran, and there are several variants and copies. At one time the German Army converted numbers of captured guns by changing the barrel to 9mm and alerting the magazine housing, which must have been a policy of desperation.

7.62mm PPS 42 and 43

State arsenals	
7.62 × 25mm Soviet	
PPS-42:	
Operation	Blowback
Length, stock extended	889mm (35.0in)
Length, stock folded	635mm (25.0in)
Weight empty	2.99kg (6.5lb)
Barrel	272mm (10.75in), 4 grooves, rh
Magazine	35-shot detachable box
Cyclic rate	700rds/min
Muzzle velocity	488m/sec (1,600ft/sec)
PPS-43:	
Operation	Blowback
Length, stock extended	820mm (32.28in)
Length, stock folded	615mm (24.21in)
Weight empty	3.36kg (7.40lb)
Barrel	254mm (10.0in), 4 grooves, rh
Magazine	35-shot detachable box
Cyclic rate	650rds/min
Muzzle velocity	500m/sec (1,640ft/sec)

The PPS weapons are, to some extent, an oddity in the Soviet armoury since the policy during the war was one of rigid concentration on one proven model of any weapon. During the siege of Leningrad, however, the supply of weapons was intermittent and stocks fell dangerously low, and the PPS-42 was hurriedly designed and put into manufacture in local factories, the design being developed around what materials and machines were available. Naturally enough it was simple in the extreme, but it proved to be surprisingly good and it continued in production after the siege was raised. It was then replaced by the PPS-43, which differed only in the design of the folding stock, the form of the safety catch, and in the barrel jacket (which in the PPS-42 had a vertical joint in front of the magazine housing). In all about one million PPS were made and they stayed in service for a few years after the war. Unusually, for a Soviet weapon, it was designed to take a 35-shot box magazine and was never adapted to the standard 71-shot drum. Despite its crudity, the PPS was surprisingly effective. It did not survive in Soviet service but was disposed of entirely to other Communist countries and turned up in large numbers in North Korean hands during the Korean War. It is generally believed that this was a political decision by Stalin; the siege of Leningrad became something of a national saga, and the leaders of the siege were gaining too much political influence; they were all replaced, and the gun that reminded everyone of the siege was removed from public view.

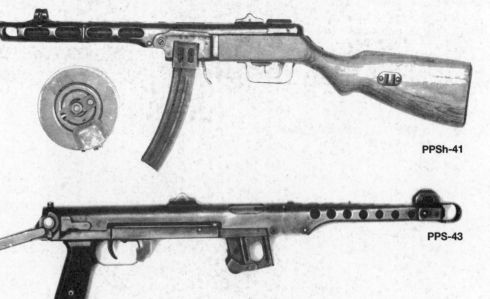

PPSh-41

PPS-43

This weapon was first reported in Afghanistan late in 1983 and is a shortened version of the AKS 5.45mm assault rifle. The barrel and gas tube are much shorter, and in order to reduce the violence of the gas action there is a cylindrical expansion chamber attached to the muzzle and fitted with a bell-shaped flash hider. The receiver top is slightly different from that of the normal AK series in that it is hinged at the front end and lifts forward on opening. There is a steel butt which folds sideways and forwards to lie alongside the receiver. Some of the plastic magazines have stiffening ribs along the front rebate, suggesting that the original AKS design may not have been strong enough. Some reports suggest that this weapon was originally developed as a firing port weapon for use in armoured personnel carriers; this is possible, but it does now seem to be on more general issue. Other reports state that there is a similar weapon in 7.62mm calibre, known as the AKMSU, but samples have not yet been seen in the West.

5.45mm AKSU-74

State arsenals

5.45 × 39.5mm Soviet

Operation	Gas, selective fire
Length, stock extended	675mm (26.6in)
Length, stock folded	420mm (16.5in)
Weight empty	Not known
Barrel	200mm (7.87in), 6 grooves, rh
Magazine	30-shot detachable box
Cyclic rate	800rds/min
Muzzle velocity	800m/sec (2,625ft/sec)

VIETNAM

Although it may not be readily apparent, this design was derived from the Soviet PPSh-41. The Soviet weapon was copied by the Chinese as their Type 50, and this was then copied by the Vietcong, though with considerable cosmetic modification. The wooden stock of the PPSh has been replaced by a sliding wire stock copied from the French MAT-38; the barrel jacket has been shortened and faired-in, the muzzle compensator removed and a front sight fitted to the barrel. A pistol grip has been fitted and the lower contours of the receiver cleaned up. Nevertheless, under all this the mechanism is still that of a PPSh-41, a simple and robust blowback weapon, and the magazine is that of the parent gun.

7.62mm Model K-50M

State arsenals

7.62 × 25mm Soviet

Operation	Blowback
Length, stock extended	750mm (29.5in)
Length, stock folded	572mm (22.5in)
Weight empty	3.40kg (7.5lb)
Barrel	269mm (10.6in), 4 grooves, rh
Magazine	35-shot detachable box
Cyclic rate	700rds/min
Muzzle velocity	488m/sec (1,600ft/sec)

AKSU-74

TYPE K-50M

YUGOSLAVIA

7.62mm Model 49

Zavodi Crvena Zastava	
7.62 × 25mm Soviet	
Operation	Blowback
Length overall	847mm (34.4in)
Weight empty	3.80kg (8.38lb)
Barrel	267mm (10.5in), 4 grooves, rh
Magazine	35-shot detachable box
Cyclic rate	750rds/min
Muzzle velocity	500m/sec (1,640ft/sec)

As with all Communist countries of Eastern Europe, Yugoslavia was equipped with generous quantities of Soviet weapons after World War Two, but in keeping with their intransigent attitude to the political parent, the Yugoslavs elected to make indigenous versions of some of them. The PPSh-41 was modified for Yugoslav manufacture and was adopted as the Model 49 in the early months of 1949. The ancestry was quite apparent, except for the box magazine; the Yugoslavs chose to abandon the 71-shot drum. The box magazine they selected was almost the same as that made for the PPSh-41 and was said to be interchangeable with it. The general outline of the M49 was similar to that of the PPSh, and it looked to be little more than a neater and better-finished version. In fact it was more than that, as it had an improved bolt and spring apparently taken from the Beretta M38A, and there was also a better buffer. The furniture was well finished, in common with most of the construction. It was still made from steel stampings, but more care appears to have been taken in the final assembly.

7.62mm Model 56

Zavodi Crvena Zastava	
7.62 × 25mm Soviet	
Operation	Blowback
Length, stock extended	870mm (34.25in)
Length, stock folded	591mm (23.27in)

The Model 56 replaced the elderly Model 49 and was a simpler design to manufacture. It is broadly similar in outline to the German MP40 and follows some of that weapon's internal design layout. The folding butt is a direct copy of the MP40, as is the pistol grip. The bolt has been simplified and the return spring is a single large coil. A bayonet can be fitted, and the overall effect is that of a well-designed and modern weapon. In fact, it suffers from using the 7.62mm Soviet pistol round, and something with more stopping power would make it more effective.

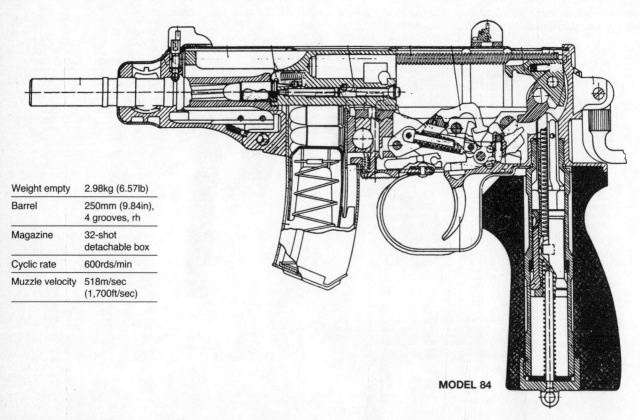

MODEL 84

Weight empty	2.98kg (6.57lb)
Barrel	250mm (9.84in), 4 grooves, rh
Magazine	32-shot detachable box
Cyclic rate	600rds/min
Muzzle velocity	518m/sec (1,700ft/sec)

7.65mm Model 84

Zavodi Crvena Zastava	
7.65 × 17mm (.32 ACP)	

This is the Czech 'Skorpion' (see page 203) manufactured under licence in Yugoslavia. It is identical to the Czech model.

This appears to be a conversion from the M80 assault rifle in a similar vein to the Soviet AKSU-74. It uses the normal rotating bolt mechanism of the M80 rifle but has a short barrel to which is fitted a tubular muzzle attachment which acts as a flash hider and as an expansion chamber to reduce the muzzle blast; it also balances the ballistics of the 5.56mm cartridge when fired in such a short barrel. Without some form of compensation the gas action would be badly out of balance due to the different gas performance in the barrel.

The weapon has a two-strut folding stock similar to those used on the assault rifles. It is intended for use from APCs and helicopters, and by aircrew, special forces and internal security troops.

5.56mm Zastava M85

Zavodi Crvena Zastava	
5.56 × 45mm	
Length overall	790mm (31.10in) butt extended; 570mm (22.44in) butt folded
Weight empty	3.20kg (7.05lb)
Barrel	315mm (12.40in), 6 grooves, rh
Magazine	20- or 30-shot detachable box
Muzzle velocity	790m/sec (2,592ft/sec)
Cyclic rate	700rds/min

ZASTOVA M85

Machine-Guns

AUSTRIA–HUNGARY/AUSTRIA

The Skoda Machine-Gun

Waffenwerke Skoda

8 × 50R Austrian Mannlicher

The Skoda machine-gun was based on patents granted in 1888 to Archduke Karl Salvator and George Ritter von Dormus, then a major in the Austro–Hungarian army. The weapon relied upon an unusual system of delayed blowback operation in which the delay was provided by a system of pivoting blocks and a large coil spring housed in a tube at the rear of the receiver; the principal locking member was, in fact, reminiscent of the Martini dropping block, a device which had a considerable vogue in the years 1870–90 and which had seen much military application. A special feature of the early Skoda models was a 'rate regulator' in the form of a pendulum with adjustable weight. This hung below the receiver and oscillated as the gun fired; it was coupled to the breech mechanism and by adjusting the position of the weight, and thus the speed of the pendulum, the rate of fire could be varied between 180 and 250 rounds per minute.

8mm Skoda M1893

The M1893 was the first machine-gun to be adopted by the Austro–Hungarian forces, being principally used as a naval weapon and in fixed fortifications; in these roles it usually appeared on a pedestal mounting. The external appearance was rather strange; in addition to the pendant rate regulator and the coil spring housing (to which a shoulder stock was usually attached) the weapon was fed by an open-sided gravity-feed magazine clamped to the left side of the receiver. In service for about ten years, the M1893 saw little use except for employment in the Boxer Rebellion of 1900, when they were used in the defence of the Austro–Hungarian Legation in Peking. The gun's principal advantage was its few working parts and hence, for its time, good reliability. But the design precluded the use of any but the weakest service cartridges and the top-mounted magazine was prone to damage and malfunction.

8mm Skoda M1902

The water-cooled M1902 was a modification of the M1893, intended for field use and hence mounted upon a shielded tripod; the shield was almost essential since, due to the rate reducer pendulum, the weapon's axis was quite high off the ground. The feed and rate reducing mechanisms were extensively redesigned in order to try and obtain a better rate of fire without the attendant feed problems, but the gravity-fed magazine was no help in this respect and was eventually replaced by an equally strange belt-feed system. Few M1902 guns ever saw service, for in their time the Schwarzlose machine-gun was adopted and put an end to Skoda's aspirations in this field.

8mm Skoda M1909

To compete with the Schwarzlose guns, which Austro–Hungary had adopted in 1905, Skoda completely re-designed their gun, resulting in the M1909. The rate reducer was discarded and the breech mechanism was re-designed, although its principle remained the same. A lubricator was added to oil the cartridges before they were chambered, and the nett result was an increase in the rate of fire to about 425 rounds per minute. The gravity feed was replaced by a belt system using a 250-round fabric belt which entered the left underside of the receiver and exited through the left top, which probably did little to solve the feed problems.

8mm Skoda M1913

The M1913 was the last spasm of the long-obsolete Salvator-Dormus design, though it managed to see active service during World War One – with unspectacular results – in the hands of reserve troops. It was similar to the M1909 with more alterations to the feed system, and a new and lower tripod, still with an armoured shield. As soon as wartime production of better machine-guns got into its stride the M1913 was abandoned, and with it Skoda's involvement in the machine-gun business. Except for some experimental designs produced in the inter-war years – more from a sense of duty, one feels, than with any enthusiasm – they have never re-entered it.

8mm Schwarzlose M/05 and M/07

Osterreichische Waffenfabrik, Steyr

8 × 56R Austrian Mannlicher

Length overall	1,066mm (42.0in)
Weight empty	19.9kg (43.87lb)

The Schwarzlose machine-gun was the only unlocked breech (or 'blowback') design ever to see widespread military adoption. It relied entirely upon an exceptionally heavy breech-block and a toggle lever which worked at a considerable mechanical disadvantage when the block first began to open. The barrel was short, to ensure that the bullet cleared the muzzle and the chamber pressure dropped to a safe value before the block began opening, and this, of course, affected the muzzle velocity and maximum range. The first models, of 1905 and 1907, used an oil pump to lubricate the cartridges as they were fed into the breech, but by 1912 (Model 07/12) this had been abandoned and more weight was added to the breech-block in order to force dry rounds into the chamber. There are disadvantages in using the blowback system with powerful bottle-necked cartridges, but the Schwarzlose was popular for its simplicity and strength. It was sold commercially throughout Europe until 1918 and was adopted by several mid-European armies. It was used by the German Army in World War One in 7.92mm Mauser calibre, and by the Greek and Dutch Armies in 6.5mm calibre. It was still in use by Hungary and Italy, in the 8mm calibre, as late as 1945 as a second-line weapon. A lighter version of the basic design, sometimes called the Model 07/16, was manufactured for aircraft use during World War One; this was air-cooled, doing away with the water-jacket, and was frequently modified by the use of a muzzle booster or heavier return spring to give higher-than-standard rates of fire.

Barrel	526mm (20.70in), 4 grooves, rh
Feed system	250-shot fabric belt
Rate of fire	400rds/min
Muzzle velocity	625m/sec (2,050ft/sec)

SCHWARZLOSE

This is basically the Steyr AUG rifle (described in the Automatic Rifles section) but fitted with a heavy barrel and a bipod to act in the light automatic role. The barrel can be supplied with either 178mm, 228mm or 305mm pitch of rifling to suit various types of ammunition, and a muzzle attachment acts as a flash hider and reduces recoil and muzzle climb during automatic fire. There are two different versions, the HBAR and the HBAR/T; the former has a carrying handle with built-in optical sight, as the AUG rifle, the latter has a receiver with a mounting bar in place of the handle and sight upon which any type of telescope or electro-optical sight can be mounted. Both the HBAR and the HBAR/T can, if required, be further modified to fire from an open bolt; a new hammer assembly is inserted into the butt and a new cocking piece is fitted to the bolt assembly. This modification can also be made retrospectively to weapons already issued to military forces. Changing to open-bolt firing does not change any of the firing characteristics.

5.56mm Steyr AUG/HBAR

Steyr-Mannlicher GmbH	
5.56 × 45mm NATO	
Length overall	900mm (35.43in)
Weight empty	4.90kg (10.75lb)
Barrel	621mm (24.45in), 6 grooves, rh
Feed system	30- or 42-shot detachable box
Rate of fire	680rds/min
Muzzle velocity	1,000m/sec (3,280ft/sec)

STEYR AUG/HBAR

BELGIUM

7.62mm FN MAG

Fabrique Nationale Herstal	
7.62mm × 51mm NATO	
Length overall	1,250mm (49.20in)
Weight empty	10.15kg (22.25lb)
Barrel	546mm (21.50in), 4 grooves, rh
Feed system	metal link belt, infinite length
Rate of fire	850rds/min
Muzzle velocity	853m/sec (2,800ft/sec)

5.56mm FN Minimi

FN Herstall SA	
5.56 × 45mm NATO	
Length overall	1,040mm (40.56in)
Weight empty	6.83kg (15.05lb)
Barrel	466mm (18.34in), 6 grooves, rh
Feed system	30-shot box magazine or 200-shot belt
Rate of fire	750–1,000 rds/min
Muzzle velocity	915m/sec (3,000ft/sec)

The MAG (Mitrailleur à Gaz), like most FN products, is a sound, well-engineered and reliable weapon which has been widely adopted throughout the world. In common with many other manufacturers FN had looked at the many designs which World War Two had brought into prominence and, also like many others, was impressed by the simple and effective feed mechanism which had been developed for the German MG42. Since FN had been involved with John Browning for many years, it is hardly surprising to find that the breech mechanism of the MAG is basically the same as that of the Browning Automatic Rifle, the principal difference being the inversion of the bolt so that the bolt lock moves downwards. This allowed a lug to be placed on the top of the bolt which engages in a cam track in the receiver cover plate to drive the belt feed mechanism.

There are minor variations in the various models of the MAG adopted by different armies – finned barrels, smooth barrels, shoulder stocks, spade grips and so forth – which largely reflect the national preferences of the customers. The weapons are all basically the same.

The Minimi is a gas-operated weapon with a variable gas supply and a rotating bolt breech system. It is simple and robust, with a remarkably low incidence of stoppages during many military trials. The barrel is heavy and easily changed, features which permit sustained fire without a reduction in accuracy due to wear. The feed system is unusual in being able to fire from a belt or from an M16-type magazine without the need for adjustment. On top of the receiver is the usual belt feed which draws the belt through from the left side and strips the rounds out, feeding them into the chamber by two horns on top of the bolt. There are also two more horns on the lower left side of the bolt and these line up with a magazine housing below the belt aperture. When a magazine is inserted the lower horns load the cartridge into the chamber. There is a difference in the rate of fire, since when a belt is used the gun mechanism needs to lift the weight of the free portion of the belt; with a magazine there is no such load and thus the gun fires rather faster. There is a magazine cover which closes the magazine housing when a belt is being used, and closes off the belt aperture when opened to permit insertion of a magazine. The Minimi has been adopted by the US Army as their M249 machine-gun; it is also used by the Belgian, Australian, Canadian, Italian and other armies. A 'Paratroop' model with shorter barrel and telescoping butt is also made, for those requiring a more compact weapon.

FN MAG

FN MINIMI

This heavy machine-gun was announced in October 1983 and is intended to replace the elderly .50 Browning. It is gas-operated, using a tappet above the barrel which drives back an operating rod to move the bolt carrier and rotating bolt. The receiver is of pressed steel and incorporates recoil buffers which help to reduce the recoil blow on the gun mounting. The weapon has a dual feed system, an ammunition belt entering the gun on each side of the receiver, and a selector lever allows the gunner to select either belt for firing. There is also a single-shot selector for use when firing specialised ammunition, such as discarding-sabot armour-piercing rounds. Four safety systems are present; a manual bolt lock is incorporated in the rotary feed selector; a neutral position of the feed selector throws both belts out of engagement; a safety catch beneath the bolt carrier automatically functions if the working parts do not recoil completely to the rear; and a mechanism prevents the firing pin striking the cartridge cap unless the bolt is closed and locked. A quick-change barrel is fitted, and the gas port, cylinder and tappet are part of the barrel and are changed with it. After the initial introduction of the BRG15 (which was then in 15mm calibre) it was found that prolonged burst fire rapidly wore out the barrel. It was discovered that this was due to the ammunition, which was simply a large small-arms bullet. The projectile was therefore redesigned to use a plastic driving band and a solid projectile which did not set up or engage in the rifling; a consequence of this was the change to 15.5mm calibre. A longer barrel was also developed and changes made in the feed mechanism, and the gun was re-introduced in early 1989. It is currently under test by various armies but no decisions are yet forthcoming.

One of the drawbacks of the standard .50 Browning machine-gun is the lack of an easily changed barrel and the need to adjust the cartridge headspace whenever the barrel has been changed or removed. In the late 1970s FN decided to remedy this and designed a quick-change barrel (QCB) system for the .50 Browning which also does away with the need to adjust headspace. The system is built as a new gun or it is available as a conversion kit for existing guns; the conversion involves a new barrel, barrel extension, breech locks and accelerator, though it is also possible to machine the existing barrel to fit the QCB system. The QCB gun has the same dimensions, etc., as the standard M2 heavy-barrel gun, which is more fully described in the USA section.

15.5mm FN BRG15

FN Herstall SA

15.5 × 106mm BRG	
Length overall	2,150mm (83.85in)
Weight empty	60.0kg (132.2lb)
Barrel	not known
Feed system	dual disintegrating-link belt
Rate of fire	600rds/min
Muzzle velocity	1,055m/sec (3,460ft/sec)

.50in FN M2HB/QCB

FN Herstal SA

.50 Browning (12.7 × 99mm)

FN M2HB/QCB

FN BRG15

BRAZIL

7.62mm Uirapuru Mekanika

Mekanika Industria Comercio Lda	
7.62 × 51mm NATO	
Length overall	1,300mm (51.18in)
Weight empty	13.0kg (28.66lb)
Barrel	600mm (23.62in), 6 grooves, rh
Feed system	disintegrating link belt,
Rate of fire	700rds/min
Muzzle velocity	850m/sec (2,788ft/sec)

This weapon began as a Brazilian Army research project in 1969; some prototypes were built but did not work very well, and in 1972 the Army, with other things to worry about, handed it over to private enterprise. This produced no results, and the project was given to a member of the original design team who produced a highly modified but successful weapon in 1976. After extensive trials it was approved for the Brazilian Army in 1979 and manufacture has continued since then. The Uirapuru is a general-purpose machine-gun capable of operating in the light, medium, or vehicle-mounted roles. It is gas-operated, the gas piston lying in the barrel cradle to the right side of the barrel and controlling the movement of a bolt with a dropping lever locking system. There is a quick-change barrel with carrying handle, and feed is by means of a disintegrating-link belt. The barrel has a very efficient muzzle brake.

CHINA, PEOPLE'S REPUBLIC

7.62mm Type 67

State arsenals	
7.62 × 54R	
Length overall	1,143mm (45.01in)
Weight empty	9.90kg (21.75lb)
Barrel	597mm (23.50in), 4 grooves, rh
Feed system	100-round metal belt
Rate of fire	650rds/min
Muzzle velocity	835m/sec (2,740ft/sec)

This is of local design and has replaced earlier copies of Soviet weapons in first-line formations. It was developed in the early 1970s and was used in Vietnam. It is gas operated and belt fed and can be fired from bipod or tripod. The design is an amalgam of features; the bolt tilts to lock in the manner of the Czech ZB26 guns, the belt-feed mechanism is basically Maxim, and the quick-change barrel is taken from the Soviet SG43. The gas regulator is based on that of the Soviet RPD and allows three settings to compensate for fouling or lack of lubrication.

UIRAPURU MEKANIKA

This weapon was first seen in 1988 and full details are not yet known. It is a gas-operated light machine-gun, bipod mounted, and is fed from a drum magazine, though it is also possible to use the Type 56 rifle magazine in place of the drum. It appears to be an entirely new design and not a copy of any Soviet weapon.

7.62mm Type 74

State arsenals	
7.62 × 39mm M43	
Length overall	1,070mm (42.12in)
Weight empty	6.20kg (13.67lb)
Barrel	
Feed system	101-shot drum magazine
Rate of fire	
Muzzle velocity	735m/sec (2,410ft/sec)

This is another gas-operated light machine-gun which has probably been produced for export and has not been formally adopted by the Chinese Army. It is believed to use an adaptation of the rotating bolt breech mechanism used in the Type 68 rifle. Feed is from a drum magazine, but one of a different pattern to that used with the Type 74 machine-gun, and it is also said to accept the box magazine from the Type 81 rifle, though the Type 81 rifle is a mystery which has not been publicly acknowledged.

7.62mm Type 81

State arsenals	
7.62 × 39mm M43	
Length overall	1,024mm (40.31in)
Weight empty	5.30kg (11.68lb)
Barrel	
Feed system	75-shot drum
Rate of fire	
Muzzle velocity	735m/sec (2,410ft/sec)

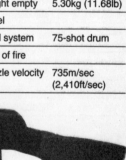

TYPE 74

TYPE 81

12.7mm Type 77

State arsenals

12.7 × 107mm Type 54

Length overall

Weight empty	56.1kg (123.6lb) with tripod

Barrel

Feed system	60-shot belt
Rate of fire	700rds/min
Muzzle velocity	800m/sec (2,625ft/sec)

This is a new weapon designed principally for air defence purposes, though it is also capable of operating as a ground gun. Full details are not available, but it is believed to be recoil operated and is of light construction for this calibre. The weapon is fed by belt, from a box carried on the left side. An optical anti-aircraft sight is standard and there is also a somewhat complex tripod air defence mount.

12.7mm Type W–85

State arsenals

12.7 × 107mm Type 54

Length overall	1,995mm (78.54in)
Weight empty	18.5kg (40.78lb) gun only

Barrel

Feed system	60-shot belt
Rate of fire	
Muzzle velocity	800m/sec (2,625ft/sec)

This is another new design, for use as a general support ground weapon or in the air defence role. It is gas operated and belt fed and is exceptionally light for its calibre. It is provided with an optical sight, and also with a tripod which can be configured for ground or air firing.

14.5mm Type 75–1

State arsenals

14.5 × 114mm Type 56

Length overall	2,390mm (94.10in)
Weight empty	165kg (364lb) with mount

Barrel

Feed system	80-shot link belt
Rate of fire	550rds/min
Muzzle velocity	995m/sec (3,264ft/sec)

This is a Chinese copy of the Soviet KPV machine-gun, differing from it in details of the belt feed and in the provision of cooling fins on the barrel. The standard mounting is an air defence tripod which also has two small wheels allowing the tripod to convert to a lightweight carriage which can be towed behind a vehicle. The tripod has mechanical elevating and traverse controls and a parallelogram-mounted optical air defence sight. Photographs of this gun have been seen showing an electro-optical sight in use, which is believed to be for ground firing.

TYPE W-85

CZECHOSLOVAKIA

The Czech armament firm generally called ZB (for Zbrojovka Brno or Brno Arms Factory) was formed after World War One and the ZB26 was its first successful machine-gun design. Together with its later variants it sold widely throughout the world. The ZB26 was similar in concept to many other light machine-guns being produced at that time, mostly in response to lessons perceived in the Great War, but it was far better than most. The gas cylinder was unusually long, tapping the gas close to the muzzle, and this led to a slower rate of fire and smoother action with less strain on the working parts. The piston and cylinder were made from stainless steel to prevent corrosion, and the barrel could be quickly and easily changed by rotating a collar and releasing interrupted lugs on the barrel breech end. A carrying handle was positioned at the gun's centre of balance and it also acted as a handle to remove a hot barrel. A tripod mounting was available as an extra, a device which gave the gun some measure of stability in sustained fire. Many ZB26 guns served the German Army during World War Two, by whom they were known as the MG26(t).

As the name suggests, the ZB30 was a descendant of the ZB26 incorporating certain internal improvements, so that the guns are difficult to tell apart. The changes were in the cam surfaces which controlled the breech-block and in a different method of striking the firing pin. A few changes in design were made so as to reduce machining time during manufacture, so that the gun was slightly easier to make and more reliable in use. In fact, both the ZB26 and ZB30 were expensive and slow to make, since they relied on machining large blocks of steel into intricate components; this gave great dimensional accuracy and could be done with moderately inexpensive machines, but it demanded skilled workmen and diligent inspectors. China liked the gun, whatever its manufacturing difficulties, and made it under licence in substantial numbers in the 1930s. Britain was also impressed and adopted a variant which became the Bren gun (below). Production continued in Czechoslovakia throughout World War Two, the Germans using the gun under the title MG30(t). It was also made in Iran, and in Spain as the 'FAO' from the name of the factory, the Fabrica de Armas de Oviedo. The Spanish even developed an improved, belt-fed version in 7.62mm NATO calibre but never produced it in quantity.

7.92mm Light Machine-Gun ZB26

Ceskoslovenska Zbrojovka, Brno	
7.92 × 57mm Mauser	
Length overall	1,161mm (45.75in)
Weight empty	9.60kg (21.16lb)
Barrel	672mm (26.50in), 4 grooves, rh
Feed system	30-shot detachable box
Rate of fire	500rds/min
Muzzle velocity	762m/sec (2,500ft/sec)

7.92mm Light Machine-Gun ZB30

Ceskoslovensaka Zbrojovka, Brno	
Various calibres	
Length overall	1,161mm (45.75in)
Weight empty	9.60kg (21.16lb)
Barrel	672mm (26.5in), 4 grooves, rh
Feed system	30-shot detachable box
Rate of fire	500rds/min
Muzzle velocity	762m/sec (2,500ft/sec)

ZB26

ZB30

.303mm Light Machine-Gun ZB33

Ceskoslovensaka Zbrojovka, Brno

.303 British Service

This is among the most rare machine-guns; the exact number made is not known but is unlikely to have exceeded ten or a dozen. It came about as a result of Britain's interest in the ZB30. In the early 1930s the British Army was searching for a light machine-gun and was impressed with the ZB30; it asked ZB if a .303 version was possible. There were difficulties due to the rimmed .303 round, but within a very short time the test batch of ZB33 guns was delivered. In accordance with what the British had requested it was converted to .303 calibre, had a shorter barrel, had the gas port re-positioned closer to the breech because of the ballistic characteristics of the British cordite charge, and had the sights re-graduated in yards. The magazine adopted the curved shape characteristic of magazines for rimmed cartridges. The weapon was then tested in Britain and from it the specification for the Bren gun was drawn up and the pattern sealed. The ZB33 never saw service; it was merely a salesman's sample. But it is worth recording as being the father of the Bren, and also as an example of how attention to detail and the customer's wants was fundamental to the Czech manufacturers' policy.

7.92mm Heavy Machine-Gun ZB53 or vz/37

Ceskoslovenska Zbrojovka, Brno	
7.92 × 57mm Mauser	
Length overall	1,104mm (43.50in)
Weight empty	18.6kg (41lb)
Barrel	678mm (26.70in), 4 grooves, rh
Feed system	100-shot belt
Rate of fire	500 or 700rds/min, adjustable
Muzzle velocity	792m/sec (2,600ft/sec)

The ZB53 was introduced into Czech service in 1937; ZB53 being the factory designation, vz/37 the army nomenclature, and it is variously known under both titles. It was an air-cooled, gas-operated machine-gun of robust and simple design, belt-fed and with two rates of fire. It was made in large numbers by ZB and widely exported and it was made under licence in Britain as the Besa tank machine-gun. In many respects the action resembles that of the ZB light guns, though the forward motion of the piston lifts the rear of the breech-block and engages it into lugs on the barrel extension rather than into the receiver. As a result the bolt and barrel are locked together, and after firing they recoil together until the piston unlocks the block. The action is a curious combination of gas and short recoil; the piston and bolt, being lighter than the barrel, move quickly and complete the extracting and reloading cycle before the barrel has returned to its firing position, and the actual firing of the cartridge, performed by the piston's forward movement, takes place while the entire action is still moving forward. As a result the recoil force must first stop the moving parts and then reverse their motion, which absorbs a large proportion of the recoil energy and reduces the recoil load on the gun mounting. Another unusual feature is that there is no cocking handle; the pistol grip is pushed forward until a catch engages the bolt, and is then drawn back to cock the action. It remains stationary, of course, while the gun is firing. Despite the apparent complication the action is extremely reliable and the gun very accurate. Although obsolete in most armies by the early 1950s, it remained in use with several African armies until the late 1960s.

VZ37

7.62mm Light Machine-Gun vz/52/57

Ceskoslovenska Zbrojovka, Brno	
7.62 × 45mm Czech	
7.62 × 39mm Soviet	
Length overall	1,041mm (41.00in)
Weight empty	7.96kg (17.54lb)

Although classed as a light gun and bearing obvious affinities with the ZB26 and 30 weapons, the vz/52 leans more to the general-purpose machine-gun concept in its ability to fire from magazine or belt, on bipod or tripod, without requiring any adjustment. Chambered for the Czech 7.62mm intermediate cartridge, selection of single shots or automatic fire was done by a dual trigger system; pressure at the top of the trigger gave single shots, at the bottom of the trigger automatic fire. The operating system uses a piston and breech-block unit very similar to the ZB30 but using a bolt carrier; this moves back under piston pressure and, by cam surfaces, pulls down the rear of the bolt from an abutment in the receiver. The barrel is easily changed, using the magazine port cover as the unlocking lever. The gun body is mainly of stamped steel, with a machined receiver inserted in the appropriate space, an interesting essay in production engineering and cheaper to produce, but otherwise of doubtful value. A later version of this weapon was the vz/52/57, which was the same weapon but chambered for the Soviet 7.62 × 39mm cartridge. Both models are now obsolete in Czech service but can be found in use in some smaller African countries.

The dual feed (magazine or belt) capability of the vz/52 appears not to have been found as useful as expected by the Czechs, and the gun was therefore replaced by a new model, the vz/59. In most respects it is no more than an improved vz/52 but without the magazine feed, being belt-fed only. However, the general-purpose concept was not only retained but improved; the weapon is provided with two alternative barrels, a light one with attached bipod for use in the light squad automatic role, and a heavy barrel, some four inches longer, for use in the sustained fire role, in which the gun is mounted on a tripod of unusual appearance and design. There is also an unusual ballistic reversion; instead of using the 7.62 × 39 Soviet intermediate cartridge, the vz/59 adopted the old, rimmed 7.62 × 54R Soviet round. It seems that the Czechs are willing to encumber the squad light machine-gun with a non-universal cartridge (for the remainder of the squad weapons use the intermediate round) so that in the medium machine-gun role it can be provided with a cartridge having a heavier bullet and long range. A light-barrel-only version of the vz/59 is manufactured for export as the CZ vz/59L, and a variant of this, in 7.62 × 51mm NATO chambering, is also made for export, though so far as is known neither has been sold in any numbers.

Barrel	686mm (27.00in), 4 grooves, rh
Feed system	25-shot box or 100-shot belt
Rate of fire	900rds/min (magazine) or 1,150rds/min (belt)
Muzzle velocity	745m/sec (2,445ft/sec)

7.62mm Machine-Gun vz/59

	Ceskorslovenska Zbrojovka Brno
	7.62 × 54R
Length overall	1,220mm (48.0in)
Weight empty	8.60kg (18.95lb) with heavy barrel
Barrel	694mm (27.3in) (heavy), 4 grooves, rh
Feed system	50-shot belt
Rate of fire	750rds/min
Muzzle velocity	823m/sec (2,700ft/sec)

DENMARK

The Madsen is a remarkable gun in almost every way. It was undoubtedly the first light machine-gun ever to be produced in quantity – it was used by the Russian cavalry during the Russo–Japanese war in 1904; the same basic model continued to be manufactured, with only minor variations, for over fifty years; it featured in innumerable wars, both large and small; and yet it was never officially and universally adopted by any country. Special models were fitted in tanks, cars and aeroplanes. And finally it possessed a mechanism which, although compact and light, exceeded most others in complexity and ingenuity. The Madsen was really an automatic form of the Peabody/Martini block-action rifle, and as such it had several peculiarities. With no bolt to move the cartridge in and out of the breech, it was provided with a separate rammer and a powerful extractor. The action worked by recoil, part long and part short, and the movement of the hinged breech-block was controlled by a system of cams and lugs on the block and on a plate set into the side of the receiver. The top-mounted box magazine was another innovation and was the model for the innumerable weapons which have used the idea since then.

The Madsen Machine-Guns

	Dansk Rekylriffel Syndikat A/S 'Madsen'
	Various calibres
Length overall	1,143mm (45.00in)
Weight empty	9.07kg (20.00lb)
Barrel	584mm (23.00in), 4 grooves, rh
Feed system	25-, 30- or 40-shot detachable box
Rate of fire	450rds/min
Muzzle velocity	c.700m/sec (2,300ft/sec) depending upon calibre

VZ52/57

Despite its complexity, which might appear to be a drawback, the Madsen was remarkably successful and sold to no less than 34 countries, remaining in production until the late 1950s. Its manufacturers were quick to appreciate that the experience of World War One indicated that it was sometimes desirable to have a machine-gun which combined the characteristics of a light weapon when mounted on a bipod with those of a medium gun when on a tripod. The Madsen was therefore offered with these possibilities and the necessary associated equipment. In British service it was first used as a tank machine-gun during World War One, after which its use as a light machine-gun was explored. But it gained a reputation for frequent jamming, doubtless due to the rimmed .303 cartridge. With rimless ammunition, however, the gun's performance was excellent, and it was offered in virtually any calibre the customer desired.

7.62mm Madsen-Saetter

Dansk Industrie Syndikat A/S 'Madsen'	
7.62 × 51mm NATO	
Length overall	1,165mm (45.90in)
Weight empty	10.65kg (23.48lb)
Barrel	565mm (22.20in), 4 grooves, rh
Feed system	49-shot belt
Rate of fire	650-1000rds/min adjustable
Muzzle velocity	853m/sec (2,800ft/sec)

This was the last Madsen machine-gun to be developed and was a general-purpose gun capable of being used on a bipod as the squad automatic or on a tripod for sustained supporting fire. It was made in a variety of calibres, though principally in 7.62mm NATO, and could be easily changed to a different calibre by changing barrel and bolt. The rate of fire was adjustable to any speed between 650 and 1,000 rounds per minute. The gun was gas operated, the bolt being locked by lugs forced into recesses in the receiver wall, and it fired from an open bolt. Manufacture was simple, much pressed and punched metal being used together with precision castings. The bore was internally chrome-plated to prolong barrel life. The gun was adopted and manufactured by Indonesia as a light machine-gun in the late 1950s, and in 1958 was tested by the British Army in its search for a general-purpose weapon and rejected. Madsen thereafter tried to market a light automatic rifle in the early 1960s, but this, too, failed to attract a market and with that they left the firearms field.

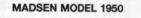

MADSEN MODEL 1950

MADSEN/SAETTER

EGYPT

The Egyptian model of the Alfa Model 44 differed slightly from the original Spanish version. It was a medium machine-gun, using the same operating system, but certain modifications were introduced, either as a result of experience with the original gun or to suit the requirements of the Egyptians. The most obvious difference was the addition of cooling fins to the barrel. These were of aluminium and covered the entire length of the barrel, with a cut-away section in the middle to take the carrying handle. The other difference, a less noticeable one, was in the holes for the escape of gas from the operating cylinder. These were enlarged and slotted, which was probably done to prevent fouling building up in the holes during prolonged firing. Apart from these two features, and the Arabic markings, the Egyptian pattern was the same as the standard Alfa; dimensions, etc., can be found in the Alfa entry in the Spanish section.

7.92mm Alfa Model 44

Fabrica de Armas de Oviedo

7.92mm × 57mm Mauser

ALFA MODEL 1944

FINLAND

Designed in 1926 by Aimo Lahti, the M26 is a good example of the type of machine-guns produced in the 1920s. It is simple, strong, and not too heavy. It was hoped to offset some of the development costs by selling the gun in Europe, but the Depression years were no time to try selling machine guns and only the Finnish Army ever employed it. It was used extensively in the Russo–Finnish 'Winter War' of 1939/40 and did not pass out of service until the late 1940s when Soviet equipment was introduced. The M26 was a recoil-operated gun which fired from an open bolt. Barrel and bolt recoil, locked together, until the bolt is unlocked by a cam on the receiver wall striking a stud on the bolt and lifting it out of engagement with the cam groove. An accelerator then flings the bolt back while the barrel is halted; on the return stroke the bolt chambers a round and then engages with the cam groove which forces the lug down to lock, after which bolt and barrel run back into the firing position, the cartridge firing just before the barrel comes to rest. Thus the recoil has to halt the forward movement before reversing it, so absorbing a proportion of the recoil force. The feed system could use either a box magazine or a drum, both of which fitted below the receiver. The barrel could be quickly removed, but the bolt had to come out with it, which was not always practicable in the field. Single shot or automatic fire could be selected, and the rate of fire was reasonably low, giving good control.

This gas-operated light machine-gun entered service with the Finnish Army in 1966, replacing the Lahti-Saloranta. It has affinities with the Czech ZB26 series, using the same type of vertically-cammed bolt which locks into the roof of the receiver. It uses a belt feeding into the right side from a clip-on belt box and has a quick-change barrel fitted with a flash hider. In addition to its use in Finland, numbers were sold to the armed forces of Qatar.

7.62mm Lahti-Saloranta M26

Valtion Kivaarithedas

7.62mm × 54R Soviet

Length overall	1,180mm (46.50in)
Weight empty	8.60kg (19.0lb)
Barrel	566mm (22.3in), 4 grooves, rh
Feed system	20-shot detachable box or 70-shot drum
Rate of fire	500rds/min
Muzzle velocity	800m/sec (2,630ft/sec)

7.62mm Valmet M62

Sako-Valmet

7.62 × 39mm Soviet

Length overall	1,085mm (42.70in)
Weight empty	8.30kg (18.30lb)
Barrel	470mm (18.5in), 4 grooves, rh
Feed system	100-shot belt
Rate of fire	1,000rds/min
Muzzle velocity	730m/sec (2,395ft/sec)

FRANCE

The Hotchkiss Machine-Guns

Hotchkiss & Co

The Hotchkiss machine-gun was a significant advance in the design of automatic arms at a time when most of the possible operating systems were carefully covered by patents which almost totally precluded evasion. By 1893 only Maxim and Browning had produced truly workable machine-guns (though others had tried) and both had used recoil to power the mechanism. In the same year, however, an Austrian aristocrat named Odkolek brought to Hotchkiss & Co a prototype of a gas-operated machine-gun; seeing the potential of the weapon, though it still required considerable development, the Hotchkiss organisation promptly acquired the sole rights, in a manner none too satisfactory from the viewpoint of the luckless inventor. Hotchkiss & Co would countenance only a straight cash payment, with the exclusion of any consideration of royalties from the contract. As a result Odkolek scarcely benefited from the transaction. The chief engineer of Hotchkiss at that time was an American, Laurence Benet, to whom fell the responsibility of the redesign and perfection of the mechanism. The Hotchkiss Gun first appeared in 1895, a gas-operated weapon locking the bolt by means of a pivoted locking flap which secured the bolt to the barrel until a stream of gas struck the flap and removed it from alignment. The gun was given a smooth barrel to facilitate air-cooling, since it was thought too difficult to adapt a water-cooling system to a gas-operated gun. It was adopted by the French Army in 1897 and a number of subsequent improvements were made to the basic design, which saw hard use throughout World War One. (Data table refers to Mle 1914.)

8mm Hotchkiss Mle 1897

The first of the official patterns, the Mle 1897 was closely based on the experimental Mle 1895; brass cooling fins were added to the barrel in an attempt to cure the overheating problems found in the experimental weapons, but although this helped, the guns were soon notorious for the rapidity with which the barrel absorbed heat. The Mle 1897 used the standard Hotchkiss feed system, probably the greatest single failing of the design, using a metallic (originally brass but later steel) strip holding 24 or 30 8mm cartridges and fed into the gun from one side; the cartridges were stripped out and the empty strip fed out of the gun on the other side, ready to be reloaded. A second failing was the mounting, a spindly tripod which had no provision for elevation or traverse. The gun weighed 25.5kg (56lb) and the mount added another 16.5kg (36.5lb).

HOTCHKISS 1914

This was a modified pattern of the Mle 1897, the principal recognition feature being the steel-finned barrel, yet another attempt to cure the overheating. A new type of mount – the Affut-Trépied Mle 00 – was provided with elevation and traverse controls, and either of the two patterns of gun could be mounted upon it. The latter Affut Mle 07 could also be adapted to the gun. After the Hotchkiss had seen service for several years, the French designers attempted to improve it by adding such things as a variable rate of fire device and returning once more to brass cooling fins. The results of these changes were the Mle 05 'Puteaux' and the Mle 07 'Saint-Etienne' which are described separately. Both were failures and the army turned back to the Hotchkiss.

8mm Hotchkiss Mle 1900

The Mle 1909 was originally designed in an attempt to provide a light automatic weapon which would fit the French theories of 'assaulting at the walk', but it ultimately proved too heavy and was therefore relegated to tanks, aircraft and fortification work. It deviated from the normal Hotchkiss design in the locking mechanism; the new pattern was, therefore, often called the 'Hotchkiss-Mercié' or 'Bénét-Mercié' and it replaced the flap locking by using a 'fermeture nut'. This was a collar around the rear of the barrel with interrupted threads; the bolt had interrupted lugs, and the nut, rotated by the gas piston, thus locked the bolt to the barrel and then unlocked it when rotated in the opposite direction. At the same time the opportunity was taken of reversing the feed unit so that the cartridges were now on the underside of the feed strip, greatly complicating the problem of feeding ammunition to the weapon. These strictures apart, the mechanism was relatively simple, though not as uncomplicated as some competing designs. The Mle 1909 was actually adopted by the US Army as the 'Machine Rifle, Benet-Mercie, Cal .30 M1909' and was used in the Mexican war of 1916. The British Army also adopted it for cavalry use as the 'Gun, Machine, Hotchkiss, Mark 1', further described on a later page.

8mm Hotchkiss Mle 1909

The Mle 1914 was no more than a slightly re-designed version of the Mle 1900, with the elimination of the safety system and the revision of certain mechanical components. It was provided with a variety of tripod mounts, some better than others. Although rather heavy, the Hotchkiss was reliable, which meant a lot to those whose lives depended upon it, and it survived in French service until World War Two. The principal drawback lay in the feed system, although in the Mle 1914 the authorities tried to improve this by developing a 'metallic strip belt' holding 249 rounds; it was simply a long series of three-round strips with a hinge at each joint. Hotchkiss heavy machine-guns were exported in 7mm calibre to Brazil, Mexico and Spain, where they were extensively used by their armies. The 8mm French version was also used by Greece and other Balkan states, and the American Expeditionary Force in 1917 used Hotchkiss guns on a divisional basis.

8mm Hotchkiss Mle 1914

Length overall	1,270mm (50.00in)
Weight empty	23.58kg (51.98lb)
Barrel	775mm (30.5in), 4 grooves, lh
Feed system	24- or 30-shot metallic strip
Rate of fire	600rds/min
Muzzle velocity	725m/sec (2,380ft/sec)

The Hotchkiss 'Balloon Gun' was employed to deal with German observation balloons which were an important part of the German artillery fire-direction system on the Western Front, although the design actually began as a heavy infantry machine-gun. It used similar mechanical principles to the lighter Hotchkiss but was chambered for a special 11mm round developed from the old 11mm Gras rifle cartridge and carrying an incendiary bullet to ignite the hydrogen-filled balloons. The gun was relatively heavy and immobile and its use did not continue into the post-war years, though the Americans adapted the cartridge to a special version of the Vickers gun for use in a similar role and continued the development into the 1920s, eventually abandoning it when the .50 Browning began to show promise.

11mm Hotchkiss Mle 1917 'Balloon Gun'

The Puteaux machine-gun was an abject failure and survived in service for just two years before it was relegated to static and reserve use. The design began as an attempt to provide the French Army with a gun superior to the service Hotchkiss. It proved to be no improvement and, when compared to work being done elsewhere in Europe in the same period, merely exposed the ineptitude of the French ordnance personnel of the time. The Puteaux worked in similar fashion to the gas-operated Hotchkiss to which it bore several affinities, and with which it shared the strip-feed system – the first thing which any sensible designer would have discarded. The normal rate of fire was 500 rounds per minute, but this was complicated by the addition of a variable rate of fire regulator which could be adjusted from 8 to 650 rounds per minute. The device was a poor copy of that designed by Maxim in 1884 and was all but useless.

8mm Puteaux Modèle 1905

Manufacture d'Armes de Puteaux

8 × 50R Lebel

The external appearance foreshadowed the Saint-Etienne gun, for which the Puteaux served as a prototype, but the barrel was covered entirely in brass cooling fins which, in real life, rapidly overheated. Due to the many deficiencies uncovered in service the Puteaux was withdrawn and supplied to fortresses as a defensive gun, the 'Mitrailleuse de la Fortification Mle 07'.

8mm Saint-Etienne Modèle 1907

Manufacture d'Armes de St Etienne	
8 × 50R Lebel	
Length overall	1,180mm (46.50in)
Weight empty	25.73kg (56.72lb)
Barrel	710mm (28.0in), 4 grooves, rh
Feed system	24- or 30-shot metallic strip
Rate of fire	500rds/min
Muzzle velocity	700m/sec (2,300ft/sec)

This represents a hopelessly unsuccessful attempt to improve on the Puteaux machine-gun. It was designed by a small team working in the government arsenal at Saint-Etienne, none of whom appear to have had much idea of how automatic weapons worked. They began with the Puteaux and promptly reversed the gas piston operation, so that instead of moving backwards, it moved forwards, and hence a rack-and-pinion mechanism had to be introduced in order to get the bolt moving in the proper direction. The bolt was locked by an over-centre cam lever instead of the Hotchkiss flap, and the gas cylinder could be varied in volume so as to vary the rate of fire; it was hardly worth the trouble since it merely over-complicated the mechanism and provided new methods of going wrong. The return spring was placed in a tube below the barrel so that the barrel heat rapidly drew the temper from the steel, so the tube was removed and the spring left exposed to the elements. In the trenches of the Western Front the faults of the Saint-Etienne were quickly exposed and it was retired and replaced by the Hotchkiss.

Modifications were made to the gun in an attempt to improve it, including a new gas regulator, firing pin and foresight, and a form of drum rear sight replaced the earlier leaf pattern. The result was called the 'Modèle 1907 Transformée 1916' but after prolonged testing the Army decided that the gun was best suited to arid regions – another way of getting rid of the thing without actually having to embarrass the staff of Saint-Etienne – and it was shipped off to the African colonies.

SAINT-ETIENNE MODELE 1907

Known also as the 'CSRG' after the names of the four-man commission who accepted it for service prior to 1914, this, like most commission-designed weapons, was nothing to be admired. It has been described as the world's worst machine-gun, and it was universally execrated by everyone who ever used it. To begin with, it was a long-recoil weapon in which barrel and bolt recoil, locked together, for the full stroke; the bolt was then unlocked and held while the barrel returned to battery. Once the barrel had come to rest the bolt was released and went forward to chamber a round and lock. It is not a system which lends itself readily to a light weapon where steadiness is important, and the long movement generates rapid wear and attracts grit and dust. To compound the mischief the Chauchat was badly made of poor material, even though it foreshadowed future production techniques in its use of steel stampings. Its service career was an unending tale of malfunctions and jams.

The peculiar semi-circular magazine was forced on the designers by the wide rim and sharp taper of the 8mm Lebel cartridge. When the US Army arrived in France in 1917 the French smartly unloaded 16,000 Chauchats on to them; in order to rationalise the ammunition supply the gun was re-designed to accept the standard American .30–06 cartridge, and the resulting weapon, over 19,000 of which were provided to the luckless Doughboys, was called the M1918. The principal change was the adoption of a straight magazine, possible because of the slender and rimless .30–06 cartridge. Although this rechambering was theoretically an improvement, in fact the more powerful round merely shook the gun to pieces quicker. In spite of its dismal performance the Chauchat was adopted by the Belgians and Greeks, both in 8mm calibre, the Greeks calling it the 'Gladiator' and terming it 7.8mm. Sufficient survived World War One to turn up in the Spanish Civil War to harass a second generation of soldiers, but very few survived this second exposure.

The Darne company, long renowned for their sporting weapons, became interested in machine-guns as a result of a World War One contract to make Lewis Guns for the French Army. However, unlike most manufacturers they saw no point in spending large amounts of time and money to produce a military weapon to commercial standards of finish, and they succeeded in producing one of the cheapest machine-guns ever marketed. Although their name is attached to the weapon by virtue of their having designed it, the majority of Darne guns were made by Unceta in Spain at an even lower price than the French could have turned them out. For all its cheapness, the gun was undeniably efficient, serving the French and several other nations as an aircraft gun during the 1930s. It was among several guns tested by the Royal Air Force prior to World War Two, but was turned down in favour of the Browning. Gas operated and belt fed, it had the high rate of fire desirable in an aircraft weapon, though this was one of the features which prevented its gaining a wide following as an infantry gun. Nevertheless it was marketed as a ground gun from 1920 onwards, and small quantities were purchased by several armies.

8mm Chauchat Modèle 1915

Manufacturers unknown	
8 × 50R Lebel .30 M1906	
Length overall	1,143mm (45.00in)
Weight empty	9.07kg (20.0lb)
Barrel	469mm (18.5in), 4 grooves, rh
Feed system	20-shot detachable box
Rate of fire	250rds/min
Muzzle velocity	700m/sec (2,300ft/sec)

8mm Darne Modèle 1918

Unceta y Cia, Guernica, for R & P Darne et Cie	
8 × 50R Lebel	

CHAUCHAT MODELE 1915

DARNE MODELE 1918

269

Hotchkiss Light Machine-Guns 1922–26

Length overall	1,214mm (47.75in)
Weight empty	9.52kg (20.98lb)
Barrel	577mm (21.75in), 4 grooves, rh
Feed system	25-shot metallic strip
Rate of fire	450rds/min
Muzzle velocity	745m/sec (2,450ft/sec)

7.5mm Châtellerault Mle 1924, 1924/29 and 1931

Manufacture d'Armes de Châtellerault Manufacture d'Armes de St Etienne	
7.5 × 54mm M1924 and M1929	
Length overall	1,082mm (42.60in)
Weight empty	9.24kg (20.37lb)
Barrel	500mm (19.7in), 4 grooves, rh
Feed system	25-shot detachable box
Rate of fire	500rds/min
Muzzle velocity	823m/sec (2,700ft/sec)

The Hotchkiss light machine-gun was offered in the immediate post-war years to several armies. The gun was the standard gas-operated, flap-locked weapon which had served throughout World War One, though it now added a rate-reducing mechanism in a housing in front of the trigger-guard. The feed mechanism was altered so that top-mounted box magazines, side-feeding strips or the metallic hinged-strip belt could be used on different models. Other features of the 1920s gun were the rocker feet on the bipod and the flash hider/compensator, cut obliquely so as to direct gas upwards to counteract climb. The guns saw little use apart from some .303 weapons purchased by the British in 1922–23 for trials, when it was found wanting in many respects. Trials in other countries also took place, and some 5,000 guns in 6.5mm calibre were bought by the Greeks – perhaps to replace their Chauchats – and examples in 7mm Spanish calibre were supplied to Central and South America, which suggests that Hotchkiss found the market sufficiently lucrative to keep the gun in production (as the Modèle 1924) well into the 1930s. (Data table refers to the Greek M/1926.)

The French light machine-gun at the end of World War One was the infamous Chauchat, and it was patently obvious that something better was needed. Since the 8mm Lebel cartridge was an awkward shape and size for use in machine guns, the French began by developing a new 7.5mm round, broadly based upon the 7.92mm Mauser. With this in hand, work began on a suitable machine-gun and in due course a limited number, known as the Mle 24, were produced for trials. It was a gas-operated weapon with a tilting breech-block, based upon the American BAR. The gun was a considerable improvement on its predecessor, even though it was a long way from perfection, but the cartridge had several defects which led to damaged guns, and it was re-designed with a shorter case. The gun was modified to suit, and various other minor improvements made, and was tested in about 1928 with the new cartridge. The results were successful and the weapon was standardised as the Mle 24/29.

In 1931 a slightly modified version was issued for use in fixed defences – notably along the Maginot Line – and this was later adopted as a tank gun. This, the Mle 31, was distinguished by its peculiar butt and handgrip and a 150-shot drum magazine mounted on the right side. The Châtellerault guns remained in French Army service until the early 1950s; during World War Two large numbers were taken over by the German Army and used, principally in anti-invasion defences on the Channel Islands and the French coast.

HOTCHKISS 1922

CHATELLERAULT 1924/29

The AAT-52 is the French Army's general-purpose machine-gun. It is a considerable improvement on earlier French designs but still manages to exhibit that flair for 'la différence' which characterises most French weapons. Used with a light barrel and bipod as a light squad automatic, it can be fitted with a heavy barrel and mounted on a tripod to act in the sustained fire role. In the light role it also exhibits that favourite and useless European appendage, the butt monopod. The belt-feed system owes a great deal to the German MG42, and the general operating system has some elements in common with the CETME and G3 rifles. Like them, the AAT-52 operates on delayed blowback, using a two-part bolt unit which is separated by a delay lever rather than by rollers. On firing the case tries to set back in the fluted chamber and succeeds in pushing the light bolt head, but must then overcome the mechanical braking effect of the delay lever before the heavy rear portion of the bolt can be made to move and thus complete the bolt opening. Like all blowback weapons using bottle-necked cases, extraction is critical and is eased by the fluted chamber, which allows high-pressure gas to pass to the outside of the cartridge case and thus equalize the pressure to prevent sticking. In spite of this the system is working close to the safe limits and the ejected cases are always marked by the gases in the chamber flutes and are frequently expanded ahead of the base or even split. The AAT-52 works, but only just. The AAT-52 was originally produced, in the early 1950s, in 7.5mm calibre. With the adoption of NATO standardisation most of these guns were converted to 7.62mm NATO calibre, and subsequent production has all been in this calibre. In this guise the gun is known as the AA 7.62 NF-1; the dimensions of the two types are the same but their ballistic performance differs, as might be expected. (Data table refers to the light-barrel version).

7.5mm Arme Automatique Transformable (AAT–52)

Manufacture d'Armes de St Etienne
Manufacture d'Armes de Tulle

7.5 × 54mm M1929
7.62 × 51mm NATO

Length overall	1,145mm (45.08in) butt extended; 980mm (38.58in) butt retracted
Weight empty	9.97kg (21.98lb) with bipod
Barrel	500mm (19.68in), 4 grooves, rh. Heavy barrel 600mm (23.62in)
Feed system	disintegrating link belt
Rate of fire	700rds/min (7.62mm - 900rds/min)
Muzzle velocity	840m/sec (2,755ft/sec). (7.62mm - 830m/sec (2,723ft/sec))

CHATELLERAULT 1931

AAT-52

GERMANY (PRE–1945)

7.92mm Maxim MG08, 08/15, 08/18

Spandau Arsenal
Deutsche Waffen- und
Munitionsfabrik AG

7.92mm × 57mm Mauser and
others

Length overall	1,175mm (46.25in)
Weight empty	26.44kg (58.29lb)
Barrel	719mm (28.30in), 4 grooves, rh
Feed system	250-shot fabric belt
Rate of fire	300rds/min; 450rds/min with booster
Muzzle velocity	892m/sec (2,925ft/sec)

German involvement with the machine-gun began in 1887 with Hiram Maxim's demonstration of his automatic gun; as a result of this demonstration extensive field trials were carried out from 1890 to 1894. By 1895 limited numbers of Maxim guns had been acquired by the Army and the Navy followed in 1896. Widespread troop trials in 1899 were followed by the official adoption of the Maxim in 1901. In the following years minor changes were made until the design was perfected, and the result was the MG08. In 1914 the German Army was well aware of the value of machine-guns, largely due to the reports of their observers in the Russo–Japanese War, and each infantry regiment was issued with six MG08, the total number of guns in the armed services being about 12,500.

The MG08 (sometimes referred to as the 'sMG08' or 'schweres Maschinengewehr – heavy machine-gun – 08') was of typical Maxim pattern, working on short recoil in which the barrel and breech-block moved approximately 18mm rearwards securely locked together. The barrel was then halted and the toggle, locking the breech-block, broke to allow the block to continue rearward. The recoil spring then halted the movement and propelled the breech-block back towards the barrel, having stripped a fresh round from the belt. The toggle then snapped down into its rigid strut form once more and the weapon was ready to fire. In 1915 many were fitted with muzzle boosters to increase the recoil force, drive the working parts back quicker and thus increase the rate of fire by about 45 per cent. The MG08 was originally issued with a heavy sledge carriage called the 'Schlitten 08' but this made the combination far too heavy – the basic gun weighed 26.5kg and the sledge another 32kg. Together with two spare barrels and two spare locks which made up the complete weapon system, this meant a total weight for the team of 62kg (137lb). As a result, the German authorities issued a lighter pattern of the weapon, the MG08/15, which was fitted with a pistol grip, shoulder stock and light bipod. The weapon now weighed about 18kg without the 4 litres of cooling water required, which was still too heavy for a light machine-gun. At the same time a lightened version, the lMG08/15 (the 'l' for 'luftgekuhlt' – air-cooled, and not for 'light') was supplied as an aircraft gun; it was fitted with a skeleton jacket which allowed air to pass across the barrel and it could also be adapted for the German interruptor gear for firing between the blades of a rotating propeller. In 1916 a new tripod, the 'Dreifuss 16' was introduced to replace the sledge mount; assorted Maxim-system weapons captured from Belgium and Russia were also adapted to the tripod mounting.

The last of the wartime guns, the MG08/18, was introduced as a last attempt to make a light machine-gun from the MG08. In this version the water jacket was discarded and a light casing substituted. The result was only 1kg lighter than the MG08/15 and it was not fitted with a removable barrel, so that sustained fire soon led to overheating. In an attempt to overcome this, the German Army often grouped the guns in threes and advised alternate use of them.

In addition to its use by Germany, the MG08 was exported to many countries in various calibres. It continued in use with the German Army well into the 1930s and was seen on manoeuvres as late as 1938. By 1939, though, it had been replaced in first-line service with more modern weapons but it remained in reserve formations until 1945. (Data refers to the MG08.)

MAXIM MG08

These guns are generally called 'Bergmann' but it is more probable that they were designed by Louis Schmeisser. The first of these designs was patented in 1900, and the first, limited, production was of the 1902 Model. A slight modification appeared in the following year, but the first model to achieve reasonable success was the MG10, after extensive testing by the German Army. The MG10, and its wartime successor the MG15, were water-cooled guns, belt fed, and using short recoil actions. The recoiling parts moved about 13mm rearwards before a locking block was cammed down from the underside of the breech-block, allowing the block to continue in its travel. A recoil spring then returned the block and cammed the locking piece back into place. A notable feature of the MG10 and MG15 was the provision of a quick-change barrel, remarkable in weapons of this class.

A much lightened version on the basic design, the MG15nA (nA = neuer Art – new pattern) was issued, in 1916, to German troops on the Italian front. This discarded the water jacket of the MG10 and MG15 and instead adopted a perforated jacket for air cooling. A bipod, pistol grip and shoulder pad – hardly a stock in the conventional sense – were added and the weapon fed from a drum-like belt container on the right side of the receiver.

The Bergmann designs never gained the acceptance they appear to have deserved, particularly as they incorporated some quite advanced features – such as an aluminium flexible-link belt which was a considerable advance over the canvas belts of its contemporaries. It is probable that the success of the MG08 blinded the German authorities to the many good features of the Bergmann which was, after all, an indigenous product. On the other hand, there is a good argument for sticking to a successful design and not veering from the MG08 at a time when such a change might have caused considerable logistic problems. (Data table refers to the MG15nA.)

The Parabellum light machine-gun was the standard aircraft flexible gun and was mounted singly, or in parts, in many German aircraft. It was also used as a Zeppelin gun and occasionally appeared in the ground role; this was particularly the case in 1918 when the Germans experienced a severe shortage of weapons.

The Parabellum arose from a 1909 specification for a weapon suited to aircraft use and much lighter than the service MG08; at that time no service arsenal was capable of designing and manufacturing such a weapon and so the authorities turned to a commercial firm, the Deutsche Waffen- und Munitionsfabrik (DWM) of Berlin, who were then producing Mauser rifles under contract. The project was assigned to Karl Heinemann who, after two years of work, produced the Parabellum in 1911, having taken the Maxim as his starting point. The Parabellum was a much-lightened Maxim in which the toggle broke upwards – in the manner of the Parabellum pistol and the British Vickers machine-gun – rather than downwards as in the original Maxim design. Feed was controlled by a pawl on the lock, rather than by the lock itself, and an accelerator speeded up the return of the barrel, thus increasing the rate of fire to 700 rounds per minute without recourse to a muzzle booster.

The most common use of the Parabellum was as an aircraft flexible gun (the MG14) with a pistol-grip and shoulder stock; it was fed from a belt drum on the right side of the receiver. Some of these appeared with a large barrel jacket and others (the so-called MG17 or 14/17) with a more slender jacket. Most of the heavy Zeppelin MG14s were provided with full water

7.92mm Bergmann MG10, MG15, MG15nA

Theodor Bergmann Waffenbau AG	
7.92 × 57mm	
Length overall	1,121mm (44.13in)
Weight empty	12.92kg (28.5lb)
Barrel	726mm (28.50in), 4 grooves, rh
Feed system	200-shot metal link belt
Rate of fire	500rds/min
Muzzle velocity	892m/sec (2,925ft/sec)

7.92mm Parabellum MG14, LMG14, MG17

Deutsche Waffen- und Munitionsfabrik AG	
7.92 × 57mm Mauser	
Length overall	1,223mm (48.13mm)
Weight empty	9.80kg (21.60lb)
Barrel	705mm (27.75in) 4 grooves, rh
Feed system	250-shot belt
Rate of fire	650–750rds/min
Muzzle velocity	892m/sec (2,925ft/sec)

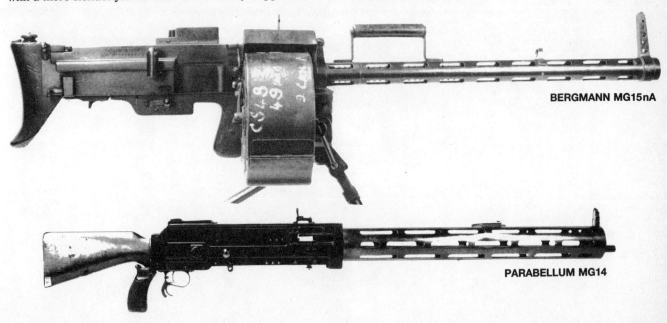

BERGMANN MG15nA

PARABELLUM MG14

jackets, a precaution taken in view of the hydrogen content of the airships. Optical sights were sometimes used on the aircraft weapons, and in ground applications the gun was fitted with a simple bipod, with which they weighed about 23kg.

The Parabellum was an efficient gun, perhaps the best of the many flexible guns developed during World War One, and lacked only a readily changeable barrel. Rather than bother converting the MG08 to the MG08/15 it might have paid the Germans to have produced more of the Parabellum, but as it was most were taken for air use.

7.92mm Dreyse Model 10, Model 15

Rheinische Metallwaren und Mashinenfabrik AG

7.92 × 57mm Mauser

The Dreyse machine-guns were based on 1907 patents granted to Louis Schmeisser and they were manufactured by RM&M of Sommerda, inheritors of the Dreyse company in 1901. Like the Bergmann designs the Dreyse weapons, though possessing advanced features, found little success in view of the firmly-established MG08. Both the Dreyse Model 10 and Model 15 were watercooled weapons; the former was mounted on a tripod for use in the sustained fire role and the latter had a small bipod fixed to the rear end of the water-jacket. The Model 15 was also provided, on occasion, with a crude monopod which, fixed beneath the receiver, was sometimes needed in order to prevent the gun resting on its spade grips, since no shoulder stock was provided. The Model 15 was a reworked version of the Model 10 intended to provide a somewhat rudimentary light machine-gun for service in Palestine, Turkey and Mesopotamia, but the improvements were, at best, marginal.

Both types operated by short recoil, with a hinged breech-block camming upwards at the rear by tracks in the receiver and consequently lowering the front, or locking portion, of the block. Further rearward travel of the block allowed the novel three-claw feed unit to remove a cartridge from the belt; the recoil spring then returned the breech-block and cammed the lock upwards. The weapons were hammer-fired, and an accelerator augmented the recoil impulse, which was then checked by a buffer, resulting in a rate of fire higher than most contemporary weapons in this class. Although placed in service in some numbers during World War One, most of the surviving Dreyse weapons were converted in 1933–34 into the MG13 (qv) and ultimately sold to Spain and Portugal.

7.92mm Gast Machine-Gun

Vorwerk & Cie

7.92 × 57mm Mauser

Length overall	1,390mm (54.72in)
Weight empty	18.5kg (40.78lb)
Barrel	720mm (28.34in), 4 grooves, rh
Feed system	2 × 192-shot drums
Rate of fire	1,300rds/min
Muzzle velocity	895m/sec (2,935ft/sec)

The Gast machine-gun has generally been described as an oddity thrown up by the exigencies of World War One, but this view ought to be modified in the light of the development of a similar gun in the USA in the middle 1980s. Odd it may have been, but there is a good deal of sense and logic in the design. It was designed in response to a 1917 demand for an aircraft gun capable of a high rate of fire; the flexible gun then in use was incapable of much more then 700rds/min, and this, it was felt, was not sufficient to guarantee a damaging number of bullets striking an enemy machine in the few seconds available in aerial combat. (The same problem has exercised air ordnance engineers ever since, it may be said.) The Gast gun was designed by Carl Gast, and his solution was to provide two barrels and breech mechanisms in a single mounting, controlled by a single trigger. The units were recoil-operated and cross-connected so that the recoil of one barrel provides the impulse to feed and load the other unit. Large spring-operated drum magazines were placed vertically on each side of the gun.

The Gast gun was secretly developed and tested in the autumn of 1917. It was a success and orders for 3,000 were placed, delivery beginning by the end of 1917. It appears that some

MAXIM 08/15

GAST MG

guns were installed in aircraft for operational tests, and some were installed as anti-aircraft weapons. Development of 11mm and 13mm versions was also studied. Nevertheless, the secret was so well kept that it was not until 1921, when inspectors of the Allied Control Commission found 25 guns in Königsberg fortress, that the Allies became aware of its existence; apparently the fact that Gast had applied for a US patent in 1920 had been overlooked. The Allies tested the weapon and were astonished at the performance and reliability. The guns were then destroyed, except for a handful kept in museums, and the Gast was virtually forgotten. It remained that way until 1974 when the General Electric company in the USA obtained one, refurbished it, fired it, and then went on to develop a 25mm cannon using the same principle.

The MG13 was a light machine-gun constructed by rebuilding the old Dreyse guns left over after World War One. The only significant change was the adoption of air-cooling, done by using a perforated barrel jacket, mounting a bipod close to the muzzle, and fitting a tubular butt. When sufficient supplies of the much better MG34 became available, the MG13s were sold, in 1938, to Portugal where they were adopted as the M38 and remained in service until the late 1940s.

7.92mm MG13

Rheinische Metallwaren und Maschinenfabrik

7.92 × 57mm Mauser

Length overall	1,466mm (57.75in)
Weight empty	10.89kg (24.00lb)
Barrel	717mm (28.25in), 4 grooves, rh
Feed system	25-shot detachable box or 75-shot saddle drum
Rate of fire	650rds/min
Muzzle velocity	823m/sec (2,700ft/sec)

MG13

The MG15 was an aircraft gun which was pressed into ground service when Germany began to run short of weapons and replacements in the late stages of World War Two. The background of the MG15 is of interest, because from it evolved another and more widely used weapon, the MG34. During the inter-war years Rheinmetall – then still known as the Rheinische Metallwaren und Maschinenfabrik – acquired control of the Solothurn company in Switzerland, using it as a development engineering agency and also as an outlet for weapons unrestricted by the provisions of the Treaty of Versailles. The Rheinmetall design staff, working through Solothurn, developed a variety of machine-guns and other weapons, and in 1930 they produced the Model 30 machine-gun for aircraft use. In 1932 Rheinmetall produced in Germany an improved version firing from an open bolt, known as the MG15. The design had been lightened, the locking system was new, it was capable only of automatic fire, and it used a 75-shot saddle drum magazine which fed rounds from each side alternately so that the balance of the weapon did not change as the ammunition was expended. The MG30 was a recoil-operated gun; the barrel recoil drove back the bolt which was then rotated to unlock by two rollers riding in cam tracks in the receiver. It was slender, the butt being in prolongation of the body and giving a 'straight-line' configuration. There was also an ingenious barrel-change facility in which the butt was rotated through 90° and pulled off; bolt and barrel could then be withdrawn through the receiver and a fresh barrel slid into place.

The first experimental version was known as the T6-200 and was for fixed installation. It was soon followed by the T6-220 for flexible use, but this terminology was dropped upon military acceptance of the weapons and both versions became known as the MG15. An open bolt weapon is, however, inconvenient for synchronisation with a revolving propeller, and a new model, firing from a closed bolt – the MG17 – superseded the MG15 in fixed installations. When adapted into the ground role a stock was clamped to the receiver, a bipod was pinned to the barrel, and simple sights were fitted to the barrel casing. The resulting gun was long, heavy and clumsy; it was not issued in any quantity.

7.92mm MG15

Rheinmetall AG

7.92 × 57mm Mauser

MG15

7.92mm MG34

Mauser-Werke AG	
7.92 × 57mm Mauser	
Length overall	1,219mm (48.00in)
Weight empty	12.10kg (26.67lb)
Barrel	627mm (24.75in), 4 grooves, rh
Feed system	250-shot belt or 75-shot saddle drum
Rate of fire	800–900rds/min
Muzzle velocity	762m/sec (2,500ft/sec)

7.92mm MG42

Mauser-Werke AG	
7.92 × 57mm Mauser	
Length overall	1,219mm (48.00mm)
Weight empty	11.50kg (25.35lb)
Barrel	533mm (21.0in), 4 grooves, rh
Feed system	50-shot belt
Rate of fire	1,200rds/min
Muzzle velocity	755m/sec (2,480ft/sec)

The MG34 was derived from the MG30 (above); the German Army felt that the MG30 had promise and gave it to Mauser to improve. When Mauser had finished with it, the result bore little resemblance to what they had started with. The magazine feed was replaced by belt feed which, by quick substitution of the top cover could be changed back to the 75-shot saddle drum magazine feed. The bolt locking system was modified so that only the bolt head revolved, locking by interrupted threads. A muzzle booster was added to increase the recoil impulse. The quick-change barrel system was altered by hinging the receiver to the rear of the barrel casing, allowing the receiver to be swung sideways to allow the barrel to be pulled straight out of the casing. And finally the trigger was designed as a double unit so that pressure on the top half gave single shots, while pressure on the lower half gave automatic fire. The MG34 was introduced in 1934, and although officially superseded in 1943 by the MG42 it was never withdrawn and served until 1945. The gun introduced two radical concepts: the idea of a general or multi-purpose machine-gun, and the use of belt feed in a 'light' gun. The saddle drum magazine was almost exclusively used for anti-aircraft work, since the absence of belt lift meant a somewhat higher rate of fire, desirable in that role, and field units found it preferable to stay with the belt option. The MG34 was built to a high standard – a factor which was largely responsible for its supersession by the cheaper MG42 – but it was an excellent weapon. On the infantry tripod the gun was steady and effective to a maximum range of 3,800 yards, but on the bipod it was not so steady and tended to be less accurate. It suffered from a tendency to jam in dusty or dirty conditions, but for all this it served in first-line formations throughout the war.

Faced, in 1941, with a critical shortage of infantry weapons, Germany looked for a machine-gun that could be produced more easily and quickly than the MG34 and yet retain its better features. Mauser saw the production aspect was the most vital and consulted an expert in stamping and forming metal, and his advice, coupled with Mauser's expertise in weapon design, resulted in a gun which adopted stamping, pressing and welding for much of its manufacture and yet managed to be an even better field weapon than the MG34, most popular with its users even though the finish was not to the standard of the earlier gun.

The action was changed to use a non-rotating bolt locking into a barrel extension by two rollers which were cammed outwards into recesses. Unless these rollers were out and the bolt securely locked, the firing pin could not pass through the bolt to fire the weapon. On firing, barrel and bolt recoiled until cam tracks in the gun body moved the rollers inwards to release the bolt. Movement of the bolt drove a feed arm mounted in the top cover which operated pawls to feed in the ammunition belt. The rate of fire, at 1,200rds/min, was higher than any other machine-gun, and as a result the barrel change system was simplified; by unlatching the breech end of the barrel it could be swung outwards through a wide slot in the jacket and slipped out to the rear; the new barrel could be slipped in just as easily and a barrel change took no more than five seconds. Like the MG34, the MG42 was a general-purpose weapon, provided with a bipod and also with a tripod for sustained fire. The high rate of fire made the gun difficult to control on its bipod, but the Germans felt that any loss of accuracy was compensated for by the high rate of fire. More reliable than the MG34 and better able to resist dirt and rough conditions, the MG42 soon made a name for itself. By the end of the war over 750,000 had been made and many were later sold by the Allies to countries in need of small arms. It was keenly studied by post-war designers and, in particular, the feed system was widely copied. In 1957 the design was revived in 7.62mm NATO calibre for the new Bundeswehr, and in similar form it has also been used by Italy and Yugoslavia among others (see below).

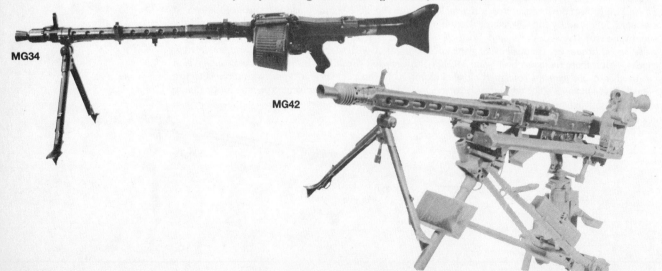

MG34

MG42

GERMANY, FEDERAL REPUBLIC

The MG1 series of weapons used by the Federal German Army all stem from the MG42; when the Bundeswehr looked at the available machine-guns in the 1950s, they saw nothing that they considered as good as their MG42 and therefore asked for the MG42 to go back into production. Unfortunately all the engineering drawings had vanished in the aftermath of World War Two, and it was necessary to 'reverse engineer' the design, using a wartime MG42 as the specimen. There are, therefore, a few deviations from the original pattern, and more modifications have been made in the light of experience. The basic operation of the weapon remains the same, however, although in some patterns the rate of fire can be altered by changing the bolt and buffer. The Type N buffer and V550 bolt give a rate of 1,150–1,350rds/min, while the Type R buffer and V950 bolt drops the rate to 750–950rds/min. The variations on the basic design are as follows; data table refers to the MG3.

7.62mm MG1 is the initial design, reconstructed from the MG42. It is virtually identical with the wartime gun, even to the 7.92mm calibre; the bolt and feed system have been very slightly changed for production convenience, but the two weapons are practically indistinguishable externally. The old pattern of muzzle booster, with gas ports and fins, was retained.

7.62mm MG1A1, 1A2. Both these were experimental patterns which did not enter service; the MG1A1 had a slightly modified trigger mechanism, a chromed bore and modified sights. The MG1A2 had the feed system modified to accept the American M13 disintegrating link belt. Both were in 7.62mm NATO calibre.

7.62mm MG1A3. A developed form of the MG1, though with the calibre changed to 7.62mm, alterations were made to the bolt, trigger, bipod and feed mechanism. A new type of muzzle booster was fitted which was integral with the flash hider. The feed mechanism only accepts the German DM1 continuous link belt.

7.62mm MG1A4 was a version designed for use in mountings on tanks and APCs. The bipod and carrying strap are removed, together with the AA sight, and a rubber shoulder pad is fitted in place of the normal stock. A fresh (third) pattern of muzzle booster was used.

7.62mm MG1A5 was a conversion of the MG1A3 to MG1A4 pattern.

7.62mm MG2 is a conversion of wartime MG42s to 7.62mm NATO calibre. They can be recognised by the pre-1945 dates on the receiver. It is unlikely that any now survive.

7.62mm MG3 was developed from the MG1A2 and is now the accepted standard version, in service use. The feed system is modified so as to accept the German DM1 continuous or German DM13 or US M13 disintegrating link belts with equal facility. Provision is made for the attachment of a 100-round belt case to the receiver, and the ejection port is enlarged. The barrel is externally tapered and chrome-lined. The MG3 is currently made under licence in Greece and Turkey.

7.62mm MG1, MG3A1, MG42/59

Rheinmetall GmbH	
7.62 × 51mm NATO	
Length overall	1,225mm (48.23in)
Weight empty	11.05kg (24.36lb) with bipod
Barrel	531mm (20.90in), 4 grooves, rh
Feed system	Belt (see text)
Rate of fire	700–1,300rds/min (see text)
Muzzle velocity	820m/sec (2,690ft/sec)

MG3A1

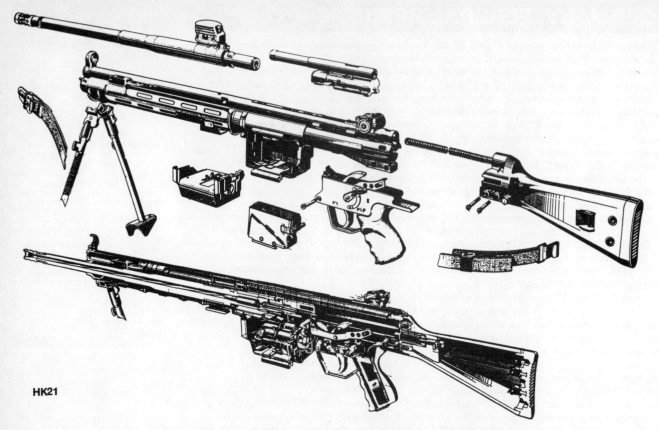

HK21

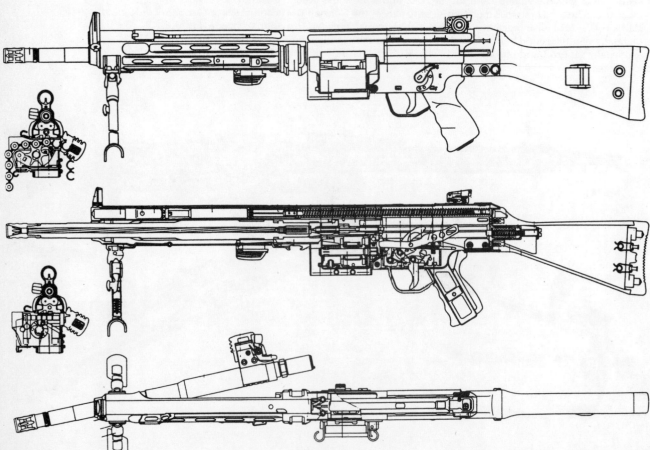

This is the fixed version of the MG3, for use on tanks and APCs; it has been modified in the same manner as the MG1A4.

7.62mm MG3A1

The MG42/59 is essentially the commercial version of the German Army's MG3. It is the standard machine-gun of the Italian Army, being made under licence by three Italian firms. This Italian version was also supplied to the Austrian Army, since they were forbidden to purchase armaments from Germany under the terms of their Neutrality Agreement. The weapon operates in the same way as the MG3 but there are some dimensional differences due to different manufacturing techniques and Italian military requirements.

7.62mm MG42/59

Rheinmetall GmbH;
Pietro Beretta SpA;
Luigi Franchi SpA;
Whitehead Motofides SpA

7.62 × 51mm NATO	
Length overall	1,220mm (48.03in)
Weight empty	12.00kg (26.45lb) with bipod
Barrel	531mm (20.90in), 6 grooves, rh
Feed system	Belt
Rate of fire	800rds/min
Muzzle velocity	820m/sec (2,690ft/sec)

MG42/59

The HK13 is a light machine-gun which is largely derived from the HK33 rifle, using the usual Heckler & Koch roller-locked delayed blowback system of operation. Magazine-fed and fitted with a bipod, it was a handy weapon but experience showed the need for several modifications and it was discontinued in favour of the HK13E (below).

5.56mm Heckler & Koch HK13

Heckler & Koch GmbH

5.56 × 45mm	
Length overall	980mm (38.58in)
Weight empty	5.4kg (11.9lb)
Barrel	450mm (17.72in), 4 grooves, rh
Feed system	25-shot detachable box
Rate of fire	750rds/min
Muzzle velocity	950m/sec (3,115ft/sec)

HK13

5.56mm Heckler & Koch HK13E

Heckler & Koch GmbH	
5.56 × 45mm NATO	
Length overall	1,030mm (40.55in)
Weight empty	8.0kg (17.64lb) with bipod
Barrel	450mm (17.72in), 6 grooves, rh
Feed system	20- or 30-shot detachable box, or belt
Rate of fire	750rds/min
Muzzle velocity	925m/sec (3,035ft/sec)

This is an improved model of the HK13 and incorporates a lengthened receiver, giving a greater sight radius and softer recoil; an improved trigger mechanism with a three-round burst facility in addition to normal single shot and automatic fire; a forward grip for the quick-change barrel; an assault firing forward grip; and an improved drum-type rear sight. It is basically magazine fed, but can be quickly converted to belt feed by exchanging the bolt assembly with magazine adapter for a bolt assembly with belt feed adapter. The magazine housing is to NATO STANAG 4179 so that it will accept any magazine with an M16-type interface.

HK13

This was derived from the HK13, which it closely resembles, and the principal difference is that the HK23 is belt-fed. The feed is operated by a stud working in a channel in the bolt. The channel is angled, and as the bolt moves back and forth the stud moves from side to side. This motion is transferred to two star wheels which engage with the rounds in the belt. There is adequate power to drive the feed mechanism, even in adverse conditions; lack of power is frequently a defect of blowback-operated automatic weapons. The HK23 was highly regarded, but the manufacturers decided to subject it to the same modernisation programme as the HK13E and production was ended in the late 1970s.

This is the HK23 improved in the same way as the HK13E, with extended receiver, three-round burst facility, drum rear sight and front grip. In addition the belt feed mechanism is improved so that half the feed action is performed during the rearward stroke of the bolt and half on the forward stroke.

HK23

The HK21 is a very versatile general-purpose machine-gun which uses the normal H&K delayed blowback system of operation. It is a belt-fed weapon, capable of digesting DM13 and M13 disintegrating link belts or DM1 continuous link belts. It can also be converted by removing the belt feed mechanism and fitting a magazine adaptor, to take any of the H&K magazines used by the G3 and other 7.62mm rifles. There is a quick-change barrel, and by changing the barrel, belt feed plate and bolt the weapon can be converted to fire 5.56 × 45mm or 7.62 × 39mm cartridges. A bipod can be fitted either to the front or rear of the barrel jacket, so giving the user a degree of flexibility in mounting the weapon. A selector lever permits firing single shots or automatic fire. The HK21 is no longer in production in Germany but is still manufactured under licence in Portugal.

5.56mm Heckler & Koch HK23

Heckler & Koch GmbH	
5.56 × 45mm	
Length overall	1,016mm (40.00in)
Weight empty	7.99kg (17.6lb)
Barrel	558mm (22.0in), 6 grooves, rh
Feed system	50-shot belt
Rate of fire	600rds/min
Muzzle velocity	990m/sec (3,250ft/sec)

5.56mm Heckler & Koch HK23E

Heckler & Koch GmbH	
5.56 × 45mm NATO	
Length overall	1,030mm (40.55in))
Weight empty	8.75kg (19.29lb)
Barrel	450mm (17.72in), 6 grooves, rh
Feed system	Metal link belt, infinite length
Rate of fire	750rds/min
Muzzle velocity	925m/sec (3,035ft/sec)

7.62mm Heckler & Koch HK21

Heckler & Koch GmbH	
7.62 × 51mm NATO	
Length overall	1,021mm (40.20in)
Weight empty	7.92kg (17.46lb) with bipod
Barrel	450mm (17.72in), 4 grooves, rh
Feed system	belt or magazine (see text)
Rate of fire	900rds/min
Muzzle velocity	800m/sec (2,625ft/sec)

7.62mm Heckler & Koch HK21A1

Heckler & Koch GmbH	
7.62 × 51mm NATO	
Length overall	1,030mm (40.55in)
Weight empty	8.30kg (18.30lb) with bipod
Barrel	450mm (17.72in), 4 grooves, rh
Feed system	metallic link belt
Rate of fire	900rds/min
Muzzle velocity	800m/sec (2,625ft/sec)

It appears that many customers were not keen on the alternative feed system of the HK21 and H&K therefore modified the weapon to become the HK21A1. This had the magazine facility removed entirely, and the receiver and feed mechanism were slightly modified so that the belt feed unit can be hinged down to afford faster reloading of a fresh belt. The design was also changed to fire from a closed bolt, instead of the open-bolt of the HK21, in the interests of accuracy. The HK21A1 was tested by the US Army for possible adoption as their Squad Automatic Weapon but was not adopted; it has, though, been taken into use by several other armies around the world.

7.62mm Heckler & Koch HK21E

Heckler & Koch GmbH	
7.62 × 51mm NATO	
Length overall	1,140mm (44.88in))
Weight empty	9.30kg (20.50lb) with bipod
Barrel	560mm (22.04in), 4 grooves, rh
Feed system	Metal link belts
Rate of fire	800rds/min
Muzzle velocity	840m/sec (2,755ft/sec)

This is the latest in the HK21 series and the modifications are as described above for the 13E and 23E weapons; lengthened receiver, three-round burst, front grips, drum sight and two-stage belt feed. The bipod has three height settings and allows the gun to be swung 30° to either side before repositioning the bipod is required. It is in service with the Mexican Army (manufactured in that country under licence) and undergoing evaluation elsewhere.

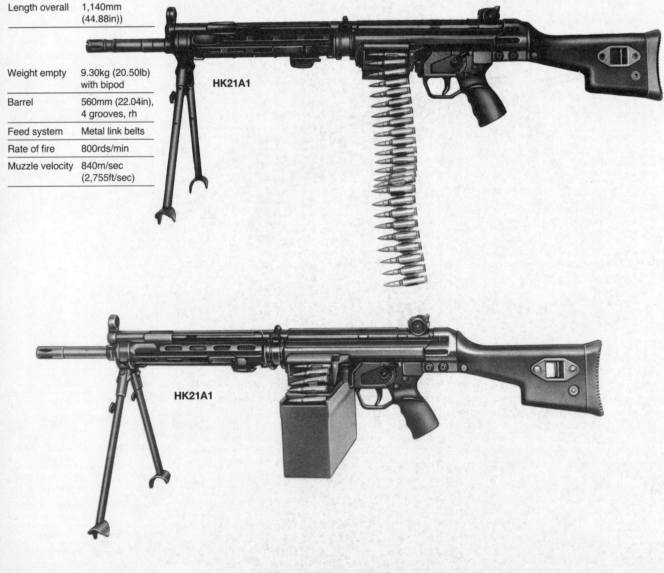

HK21A1

HK21A1

GREAT BRITAIN

Hiram Maxim was one of the geniuses of the 19th century; his inventions, an astonishing list, covered many fields. The one for which he is most remembered, however, is the Maxim machine-gun, the first practical firearm to utilise the power of the cartridge to generate automatic action. First demonstrated in 1884 it was eventually adopted by many nations; Britain (first trials 1887), Austria–Hungary (1887–88), Italy (1887), Germany (1887), Russia (1887), Switzerland (1887) and the USA (1888). Most of the trials were successful, though few of the countries which tried the Maxim adopted it before 1900, largely due to the innate conservatism of the contemporary military authorities. The first recorded use in action was by a small British force in Sierra Leone in November 1887, and it was formally adopted by the British Army in February 1889. Adoption by Switzerland followed in 1894 and the US Navy took a limited number in 1896. Most of the early guns were made in Britain by Vickers, who held most of the patents; they later developed a modified design known as the Vickers-Maxim, or, more commonly, the Vickers, which ultimately replaced the Maxim in many armies. Other nations, including Germany and Russia, produced Maxim guns in their own factories. Most of these guns are covered separately in these pages; see also *Germany pre-1945* for the MG08, its derivatives and the Parabellum; *USSR* for the 1905 and 1910 Maxims. Apart from the rifle-calibre weapons, assorted Maxim-system guns were made in calibres up to 37mm. The Maxim guns employed in British service were as follows:

Gun, Maxim, 0.45in Mark 1. Introduced on 4 February 1889, mounted on a parapet carriage. It used the Martini-Henry .455 rifle cartridge in a 250-round fabric belt. Weight of gun 60lb (27.22kg). Obsolete 1903.

Gun, Maxim, 0.45in Mark 1/N/, Gardner-Gatling Chamber. Introduced in September 1892, this was similar to the Mark 1 gun above but chambered for the Gardner-Gatling .45 cartridge, already in use in Naval service. It used either a 140-round or a 334-round fabric belt and was pedestal-mounted with a small shield. Obsolete 1917.

Gun, Maxim, .303in. Introduced June 1889, this was generally similar to the 0.45in Mark 1 but chambered for the .303in cartridge. The price, in 1912, was £64.15s. It was declared obsolete in 1928.

Gun, Maxim, .303in Converted Mark 1. Introduced November 1897 this was a conversion of the 0.45in guns to .303in calibre by substitution of the barrel and lock mechanism. Obsolete 1928.

Gun, Maxim, .303in Converted Mark 2. Introduced in 1901, this was a similar conversion of old 0.45in guns but differed from the Converted Mark 1 in using a different pattern of barrel and muzzle attachment and the introduction of some new parts instead of conversions. Obsolete 1928.

Gun, Maxim, 'G', Pattern A, B or C, .303in. No formal date of approval for this pattern is known, but the designation covers the conversion of captured German Maxim guns to .303in calibre. The official announcement said 'a small number are in use' and the model was declared obsolescent in June 1917. The difference between the patterns was not recorded and has been lost in history.

The Maxim Machine-Gun

Albert Vickers Ltd;
Vickers, Son, & Maxim Ltd;
Vickers Ltd

.303in British

MAXIM .45in

.303in Hotchkiss Marks 1 and 1*

Royal Small Arms Factory, Enfield Lock	
.303in British	
Length overall	1,187mm (46.73in)
Weight empty	12.25kg (27.0lb)
Barrel	596mm (23.50in), 4 grooves, rh
Feed system	30-shot metal strip
Rate of fire	500rds/min
Muzzle velocity	739m/sec (2,425ft/sec)

The Lewis Machine-Gun

Birmingham Small Arms (BSA) Ltd	
.303in British	
(Mark I) Length overall	50.50in (1,283mm)
Weight unloaded	26lb 0oz (11.80kg)
Barrel	26.25in (666mm), 4 grooves, left-hand twist
Magazine	47-round pan
Cyclic rate	550rpm
Muzzle velocity	c 2,450fps (745mps)

During World War One the supply of machine-guns for the British Army was augmented by purchasing manufacturing rights to the Hotchkiss gun and making it in Britain in .303 calibre. The gun was basically the French Mle 1909 and was introduced as the Mark 1 in March 1916. Fitted with a butt and bipod it became a useful light machine-gun. The basic design was then altered so that the gun could be loaded either from the standard metal strips or from the (belt) feed which consisted of three-round metal strips joined with hinges. This was based on a French design and was adopted principally for those guns used in tanks. This revised gun became the Mark 1* and was introduced in June 1917. Although superseded by the Lewis gun and later by the Bren gun, the Hotchkiss survived to be used in World War Two as a Home Defence and reserve weapon, and was not formally declared obsolete until June 1946. In about 1926, though, its nomenclature changed to 'Gun, Machine, Hotchkiss, Number 2 Marks 1 and 1*.

The Lewis gun was the first light machine-gun to be extensively used in war. It had been adopted by the Belgian Army in 1913 and soon afterwards the British Army expressed interest and BSA obtained the manufacturing rights. The first combat use of the gun occurred during the Belgian retreat in 1914, by which time a few were in the hands of the British Army. It was made in large numbers during the war, the principal attraction being that six Lewis guns could be made for the time and expense involved in making one Vickers gun. Moreover, it could be carried and operated by one man, fast enough to keep up with an infantry advance. And, of course, it was widely used as an aircraft gun in both fixed and flexible modes. The original design is due to Samuel MacLean of the USA, considerably modified by Colonel Isaac Lewis, US Army and, as originally patented, was intended as a medium or heavy gun, air or water cooled and mounted on a tripod. It had the distinctive Lewis action and drum feed, but was without the unique air cooling system later added when the design was transformed into a light gun.

The action is based on a turning bolt with rear locking lugs and is very similar to the Swiss Schmidt-Rubin rifle action, whence MacLean might have obtained his inspiration. A vertical post on the gas piston extension engages in a helical slot cut in the bolt body, and also carries the striker, riding within the bolt. With the gun cocked, and working parts to the rear, pressing the trigger releases the gas piston which is driven forward by a helical return spring, another distinctive Lewis feature. As the piston moves, so the post carries the bolt forward, stripping a round from the overhead magazine and chambering it, rotating the bolt by the movement of the post through the helical slot until the lugs engage in the receiver, and finally driving the striker into the cartridge cap. After firing gas pressure drives the piston back, withdrawing the striker, revolving the bolt and withdrawing it, extracting the case and rewinding the helical return spring. Cooling of the barrel was accomplished by forced draught, the barrel being enclosed in a longitudinally-finned radiator unit surrounded by a light metal

HOTCHKISS Mk 1

tubular cover which is open at the rear but projects a short distance ahead of the muzzle. The expansion of propellant gases at the muzzle induced a flow of air into the rear of the radiator tube, along the radiator and out at the front, so cooling the barrel. When the gun was adapted to aircraft installation this device was obviously redundant and was removed, leaving the barrel and gas piston tube exposed to the airflow. During World War Two many of these aircraft guns were pressed into ground service and found to work just as well as the forced-cooling pattern, though prolonged firing might have displayed some difference. The general opinion, however, was that it seemed that the soldiers had been carrying a few pounds of excess weight around for several years.

Although Lewis energetically promoted his weapon to various US authorities, it was not until the gun has been produced in tens of thousands in Europe and proved in war that it was finally adopted in the land of its inception. In spite of subsequent combat experience, though, the US Army were quick to get rid of it after 1918, retaining only a small number for training purposes, though the Army Air Corps adopted it as a standard weapon. The truth of the matter will probably never be known, but it seems to have been a personality clash between Lewis and some of the higher elements of the US Ordnance Corps. The Lewis gun continued in service with many countries around the world until World War Two. By that time it had been replaced as the standard squad weapon in British service by the Bren gun, but after Dunkirk the many weapons held in reserve were issued until the stock of Bren guns could be built up once more. The Lewis continued to be used throughout the war by the Home Guard and Merchant Navy.

The Lewis gun's principal virtue was that it was the first in the field; its defects lay in the excessive weight and in the astonishing variety of stoppages to which its complicated mechanism was liable.

.303in Lewis Mark 1 (introduced 15 October 1915) was the original model, sighted for 2,000 yards and provided with a 47-round drum magazine. It was officially declared obsolete in August 1946, though none had been seen for years.

.303in Lewis Mark 1*. A conversion of Mark 1 guns to Mark 4 pattern, it is doubtful if any were ever made; it was introduced for service on 16 August 1946 and declared obsolete on the same day.

.303in Lewis Mark 2. Introduced 10 November 1915, this differed from Mark 1 in having the cooling radiator removed, for aircraft use. A spade grip was fitted in place of the butt and the 97-round magazine was introduced for this gun in November 1916.

.303in Lewis Mark 2*. Introduced on 13 May 1918, this differed from Mark 2 in having a larger gas port and certain other parts modified to produce a faster rate of fire. Mark 2* guns were modified from existing weapons.

.303in Lewis Mark 3. Also introduced on 13 May 1918, this was exactly the same as the Mark 2* but of new manufacture instead of a conversion.

.303in Lewis Mark 4. Introduced on 16 August 1946, this was a conversion of the Mark 3 in order to make it more simple to manufacture. As with the Mark 1* it was introduced and declared obsolete on the same day, a day so late in the gun's career as to make it fairly obvious that this was a 'paper transaction' to regularise a design which, though never produced, had got into the accounting system during the previous thirty years and had to be formally disposed of.

.303in Lewis SS was introduced in August 1942 for naval use, 'to guide modification of existing guns for Shoulder Shooting' as the official announcement said, leaving one to wonder how the Navy had been holding them until now. The modification consisted of removing the radiator assembly and fitting a new short butt and a muzzle compensator, and adding a cylinder guard and fore-grip. It could be applied to any Mark of gun, whereupon the existing Mark had a 'star'

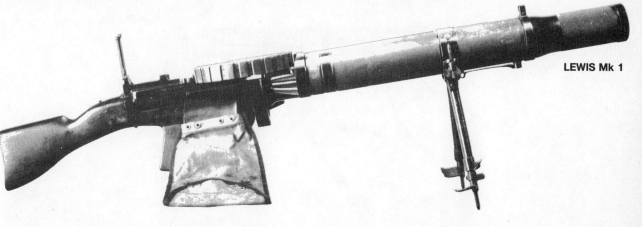

LEWIS Mk 1

added; these guns were, though, also referred to, rather indiscriminately, as 'Mark XI SS', which did nothing to clarify matters.

.30in Savage-Lewis was the American .30in Lewis gun made by the Savage Arms Corporation and purchased via Lease-Lend some time in 1940 for Naval use (though it was later taken into service by the Home Guard). Originally aircraft guns, as supplied they had no adjustable sights but they were later provided with simple battle sights zeroed for 400 yards; the spade grip was extended into a skeleton butt by welding metal strip and adding wooden shoulders and cheek-pieces. Some of the first guns supplied had spare standard wooden butts from store, but when this supply ran out the welded model was developed. The name 'Savage-Lewis' was adopted by the Naval authorities in order to distinguish the American .30 guns from the British .303 weapons. In addition a two-inch red stripe was painted around the receiver in front of the magazine post, and the rear half of the magazine centre was painted red to remind users of the non-standard calibre.

The Vickers Machine-Gun

Vickers, Son and Maxim Ltd; Vickers-Armstrongs Ltd; Royal Ordnance Factories	
.303in British	
Length overall	1,155mm (45.50in)
Weight empty	18.10kg (40.0lb)
Barrel	723mm (28.50in), 4 grooves, rh
Feed system	250-shot fabric belt
Rate of fire	450rds/min
Muzzle velocity	745m/sec (2,450ft/sec

The Vickers machine-gun was an improvement upon the Maxim; the main difference lies in the inversion of the mechanism so that the toggle breaks upwards, instead of downwards, making the receiver more compact – a similar modification as that which led to the German Parabellum. In addition the weight was considerably reduced by careful stress calculations and the use of high grade steel and aluminium. The gun was adopted by the British Army in November 1912 and remained as the standard support-fire machine-gun until the middle 1960s, when it was replaced by the L7A1 GPMG. In its time, the Vickers pattern went through twelve or more modifications, mostly minor, and was substantially the same gun after fifty years of service; indeed, so far as the infantry were concerned it remained the Mark 1 for the entire time, since all the variant models were for other branches of the services. It was heavy, fairly slow-firing, prone to a number of stoppages from ammunition, but totally reliable in itself and loved by all. It continued to work in the most adverse conditions and its water-cooled barrel ensured a long barrel life by helping to maintain a low temperature. It was used in aircraft (for which it was air-cooled), ships, tanks, as a ground AA gun, on armoured trains and armoured cars, and in a host of other roles. It remained in use as a first line gun with smaller armies well into the 1980s and doubtless many are still held by reserve forces around the world. While it fired all the standard types of .303in ammunition, a special round, the streamlined Mark 8z, was developed for the Vickers and this added another 1,000 yards to the maximum range.

.303in Vickers Mark 1. Introduced 26 November 1912, this was the standard water-cooled gun described above. It remained in service until 1965 and was finally declared obsolete in April 1968.

.303in Vickers Mark 1* (1916). An air-cooled aircraft gun, introduced as the armament of the Sopwith 1½-strutter. The barrel jacket was louvred for the passage of air and the receiver was prepared for the fitting of interruptor gear to permit firing through the propeller. The gun weighed 12.47kg (27.5lb).

.303in Vickers Mark 2 (1917). A minor variant of the Mark 1*, and also intended for air service, this had a smaller-diameter barrel jacket perforated with small holes, and weighed 10kg (22lb). The Marks 1* and 2 also came in 'SU' (Speed Up) versions which had a special muzzle booster and buffer spring to increase the rate of fire.

.303in Vickers Mark 2* (1927). Another air service gun, this had revised loading arrangements and came in two versions: the 'A' gun had right-hand feed, the 'B' gun left-hand feed.

.303in Vickers Mark 3 (1928). Another aircraft gun, this was a Mark 2* with an elongated flash hider to protect the engine cowling of the aircraft.

VICKERS Mk 1

.303in Vickers Mark 4A (1933). This was developed for use in armoured vehicles; it was a converted Mark 1 with new cooling arrangements and various other changes, but after trials showed that the Mark 4B was better, the design was abandoned and in spite of being formally approved it was never put into manufacture.

.303in Vickers Mark 4B (1933). This became the standard AFV weapon and, again, as a Mark 1 but with a cooling system which was connected to reservoirs inside the tank and allowed a constant stream of water to be circulated. It appears not to have been very successful since it was made obsolescent in 1934.

.303in Vickers Mark 5 (1932). An aircraft gun similar to the Mark 3 but with a modified method of opening the receiver.

.303in Vickers Mark 6 (1934). An armoured vehicle gun, similar to the Mark 4B but with a better barrel-removal system and a corrugated self-contained water-jacket. Versions with right- or left-hand feed were made.

.303in Vickers Mark 6* (1938). Similar to the Mark 6 but with external cooling connections like the Mark 4B.

.303in Vickers Mark 7 (1938). The last of the tank versions, the mounting was strengthened, the barrel casing stronger and smooth, and details of the cooling system were changed. Marks 4 to 7 were declared obsolete in August 1944, and none of the aircraft guns saw service in World War Two. Vickers-system machine-guns were also used by the US Army under the designation '*U.S. Machine Gun, Cal .30in, M1915*'. They were manufactured by Colt under licence from Vickers and were chambered for the .30-06 cartridge. Some were commercially marketed after 1918 in various military calibres, and some in .30 were purchased by Mexico in 1922. Vickers also exported the gun in various calibres, including 7.92mm Mauser; guns in this calibre were supplied to Bolivia and Paraguay, and possibly to Argentina.

Vickers-Berthier Machine-Guns

The French designer Adolph Berthier, who had developed the French Army's rifle, also designed a machine-gun in the early 1920s. He found no takers in France since the Army were pursuing their own design, the Châtellerault, and Vickers obtained the rights in 1925. They made some modifications and placed it on the market as the Vickers-Berthier. A small number were made in Britain and a few sales were made to minor powers, including Bolivia, in the early 1930s. In 1933 the Indian Government (who were always, to some degree, independent of Britain when it came to the selection of armaments) adopted the Vickers-Berthier as their army's standard light machine-gun, replacing the Lewis and Hotchkiss. It was also highly regarded as the possible next British light machine-gun, but in the event it was beaten to the post by the Bren gun. The Vickers-Berthier was a gas-operated gun with remarkably few moving parts, a smooth action, and the ability to be completely dismantled without tools. The action locked by tilting the bolt into a recess in the top of the receiver, and it fed from a curved overhead magazine similar to that used on the Bren; indeed, the two guns are remarkably similar and frequently confused. There is no doubt that many Indian Army actions reported in the press as having been performed by Bren guns were done by VBs. The variants of the Vickers-Berthier were as follows; data table refers to Mark 3.

Mark 1. Introduced in 1928, this was the original model and could be recognised by a slab-sided fore-end under the receiver. The barrel was finned for cooling.

Vickers-Armstrongs Ltd	
.303in British	
Length overall	1,180mm (46.50in)
Weight empty	9.40kg (20.72lb)
Barrel	607mm (23.90in), 5 grooves, rh
Feed system	30-shot detachable box
Rate of fire	450–500rds/min
Muzzle velocity	745m/sec (2,450ft/sec)

VICKERS BERTHIER Mk 2

Mark 2 (1929/30). Similar to the Mark 1, this had a rounded fore-end which extended forward of the receiver. A bipod and a butt monopod were fitted, similar to those used on the Mark 1.
Light Mark 2. Produced in 1931 as an experiment for the Indian Army, this had a smooth barrel, a light fore-end, no monopod and a cutaway butt.
Marks 3 and 3B. The Mark 3 was adopted by the Indian Army in 1933 as their standard weapon and was simply a heavier version of the Light Mark 2. The Mark 3B was a minor variant in which alterations were made to the gas system to improve reliability. Both were manufactured at the Indian Small Arms Factory at Ishapore.

.303in Vickers 'K' or VGO

Vickers-Armstrongs Ltd	
.303in British	
Length overall	1,016mm (40.00in)
Weight empty	8.86kg (19.5lb)
Barrel	508mm (20.0in), 5 grooves, rh
Feed system	100-shot non-rotating flat drum
Rate of fire	1,050rds/min; later modified to 950
Muzzle velocity	745m/sec (2,450ft/sec)

The Vickers 'K' was an aircraft gun derived from the Vickers-Berthier in 1935. Although it was a re-designed Berthier, the 'K' used the same principles but was more robust and therefore heavier. This had been done in order to increase the rate of fire. To distinguish it from other Vickers guns in air service it was generally called the 'VGO' for 'Vickers Gas Operated' and it served with the RAF as an observers' gun until the general introduction of power-operated turrets in 1941, when the remaining VGOs were offered to the Army. There were not sufficient for a general issue, so the guns were used by various special service units such as the Long Range Desert Group and the Special Air Service, who mounted them in vehicles in the desert. It was found that the VGO stood up to desert conditions exceptionally well, and their high rate of fire was ideally suited to the hit-and-run raids carried out by these forces. A few remained in use with this type of force until the mid-1960s.

VICKERS-BERTHIER 3B

BREN Mk 1

The Bren Light Machine-Gun

Royal Small Arms Factory, Enfield Lock	
.303in British	
Length overall	1,150mm (42.50in)
Weight empty	10.15kg (22.38lb)
Barrel	635mm (25.00in), 6 grooves, rh
Feed system	30-shot detachable box

During the early 1930s the British Army was searching for a light machine-gun to replace the Lewis. The Vickers-Berthier was the strongest contender, but before any decision had been taken the British Military Attaché in Prague called attention to the Czech ZB26 gun. Specimens of the gun were obtained and tested, and it performed so well that it was adopted forthwith. The only difficulty was that it had been designed around the 7.92mm Mauser cartridge, and had to be re-designed to suit both the different rimmed shape and the different internal ballistics of the British .303 round. This accounts for the characteristic curved magazine and also for the altered position of the gas port in the barrel, much further back than is seen on the Czech guns. Once the necessary modifications had been made the gun went into production at Enfield Lock in 1937. In subsequent years large numbers were made in Canada, including a quantity redesigned back to 7.92mm Mauser calibre for the Chinese Nationalist Army. Without doubt, the Bren is one of the finest light machine-guns ever made. Gas-operated, its mechanical components are simple and easily understood; it can be stripped and assembled by a trained soldier in seconds. There are only a few possible stoppages, and the

| Rate of fire | 500rds/min |
| Muzzle velocity | 731m/sec (2,400ft/sec |

Bren built up an enviable reputation for accuracy and reliability during World War Two.

.303in Bren Mark 1. Introduced August 1938, this was a direct copy of the original design and was equipped with a rather luxurious drum-pattern rear sight. The butt was fitted with a strap to go over the firer's shoulder, and a pistol grip beneath it for his non-firing hand; this particular style of grip did not commend itself to the British soldier, and when modification and simplification was called for the butt fittings were the first to go. The gas piston drove the bolt, which locked by being cammed up into a recess in the top of the receiver, and there was a four-position gas regulator at the front of the cylinder. The front sight was offset on a bracket to the left of the flash hider, the rear sight being on the side of the receiver; this offset was required by the overhead magazine.

.303in Bren Mark 2. In June 1941 the Mark 2 was introduced. This changed the rearsight to a more conventional folding leaf type, replaced the telescoping bipod by a fixed-height model, simplified the butt by doing away with the fittings, simplified the cocking handle by making it rigid instead of folding, and did away with various lightening grooves in the receiver, all in the interest of making the gun simpler and quicker to manufacture in wartime.

.303in Bren Marks 3 and 4. Both these were introduced in July 1944. The Mark 3 was similar to the Mark 1 but lighter and with a shorter barrel; the Mark 4 was a similar conversion of the Mark 2. The object behind this was to produce a somewhat handier weapon for use in jungle warfare, but in fact they eventually became common issue in all theatres of war.

.303in Bren Mark 2/1. Introduced in 1948, this was similar to the Mark 2 but had a new and simplified cocking handle assembly.

7.62mm Machine-Guns L4. When the 7.62mm NATO cartridge was adopted by the British Army the Bren L4 series was introduced. By and large this consists of conversions of earlier .303in Brens to 7.62mm calibre, but there are a number of distinct models. The L4A1 was a conversion of the Mark 3 by fitting a new barrel, flash eliminator, ejector assembly, a Canadian 7.92mm Bren extractor and a Canadian 7.92mm breech-block suitably modified. The body and magazine cover were modified to suit a new 29- or 30-round straight magazine. The L4A2 was the L4A1 with some minor design improvements. The L4A3 was a conversion of Mark 2 models by modification of the body and fitting a new barrel, butt slide and gas deflector. Obsolete for Army use, it is still in service with the Royal Navy. The L4A4 was similar to the L4A2 except that the bore of the barrel was chrome-plated, a step which so extended the life of the barrel that the provision of a spare barrel with each gun was no longer necessary. The L4A5 was never produced, the number being allotted to a development model, and the L4A6 was a conversion of the L4A1 by replacing the barrel with a chrome-lined one.

A fter purchasing the ZB26 machine-gun from Czechoslovakia the British were offered another weapon, the ZB53, from the same source. At the time the British Army was seeking a new machine-gun for mounting in tanks and armoured cars, and since the supply of ammunition for this specialised role could be fairly easily regulated, it was decided to accept the gun in its original 7.92mm calibre and manufacture a suitable supply of ammunition in Britain. Time was pressing, and this was a quicker and easier solution than converting the

The Besa Machine-Guns

Birmingham Small Arms (BSA) Co

7.92 × 57mm Mauser

BREN Mk 3

Length overall	1,105mm (43.50in)
Weight empty	21.46kg (47.0lb)
Barrel	736mm (29.0in), 4 grooves, rh
Feed system	225-shot belt
Rate of fire	See below
Muzzle velocity	823m/sec (2,700ft/sec

design to .303 calibre. After some slight modification to suit production techniques, and after being put into production by the BSA company, the gun went into service as the 'Besa', the name taken from the manufacturer. It is gas-operated but unusual in having a recoiling barrel, the movement of which provides it with a system called 'differential recoil'. The essence of the system is that the cartridge is chambered and fired while the moving parts are still going forward in the counter-recoil stroke, so that the recoil impulse has first to stop these parts and then reverse them. This enforced change of direction absorbs a good deal of the recoil impulse and reduces the stresses on the rest of the gun and on its mounting. Whether or not this system was responsible for it, the fact remains that the Besa was renowned in the British Army for its accuracy.

7.92mm Besa Mark 1 was officially introduced in June 1940, though numbers were in use well before then. It was declared obsolete on the day of its introduction.

7.92mm Besa Mark 2 was introduced at the same time as the Mark 1 and the differences are relatively minor. In the Mark 2 the accelerator is cranked to the rear instead of forward, the barrel sleeve is shorter, the flash guard has no vent holes, and there are minor changes in the receiver and cover to facilitate production. Both the Mark 1 and Mark 2 had a selection device allowing two different rates of fire. With the accelerator set at 'H' (for high) the guns fired at 750–850rds/min. Set at 'L' (for low) the rate dropped to 450–550rds/min. The idea was to have a low rate for routine covering fire and a high rate for repelling attacks.

7.92mm Besa Marks 2*, 3 and 3*. These were all introduced in August 1943. The Mark 2* is a transitional model between the Mark 2 and the Mark 3. Some components are simplified but all are interchangeable with Mark 2. The Mark 3 was a simplified design with components which were not interchangeable with any earlier guns. The greatest change was the removal of the rate selector, leaving only the high rate of fire available. The Mark 3*, on the other hand, had the regulator removed but the rate set at the low figure. Except for this there was no difference between the two guns. The idea seems not to have been favoured, since all Mark 3 guns were later converted to Mark 3*.

7.92mm Besa Marks 3/2 and 3/3. The design of the Besa remained stationary until 1952, when the Mark 3/2 was introduced. This was simply a conversion of the Mark 3* to accept a new bracket and body cover. Then in 1954, came the Mark 3/3 which differed from the 3/2 in having a new pattern of barrel and sleeve and a new gas cylinder with larger gas vents. It was introduced to ensure that guns using belts of mixed natures of ammunition would function reliably. A number of existing Mark 3/2 guns were converted to 3/3 pattern, but no manufacture to this standard ever took place. All the earlier Marks of gun were declared obsolete in 1951, and the Marks 3/2 and 3/3 survived until the late 1960s.

15mm Besa Mark 1

Birmingham Small Arms (BSA) Co	
15 × 104mm Besa	
Length overall	2,050mm (80.70in)
Weight empty	56.9kg (125.5lb)
Barrel	1,462mm (57.60in), 8 grooves, rh
Feed system	25-shot belt
Rate of fire	450rds/min
Muzzle velocity	823m/sec (2,700ft/sec

The Besa 15mm Mark 1, introduced in June 1940, was another Czech design, a modification of the ZB60. Basically it was an enlargement of the 7.92mm weapon and, like it, was destined solely for the armament of light tanks and armoured cars. It had, however, one additional feature in that it was possible to fire single shots from it. Only the one Mark was ever introduced, and the 15mm Besa appears not to have been very popular; in 1942 there was an abortive attempt to re-design it into 20mm calibre so as to use Hispano-Suiza ammunition. The 15mm gun was declared obsolescent in 1944 and obsolete in 1949. The design's principal drawback was said to be its weight and size, but it is of interest to see that similar heavy machine-guns now form the armament of armoured personnel carriers and infantry fighting vehicles of several armies, and it has been said that the 15mm Besa would have been well suited to this role had it still been in service, though in the British Army this role has been taken over by the 30mm Rarden cannon.

7.92mm BESA

During World War Two the Bren gun was manufactured in Britain exclusively by the Royal Small Arms Factory at Enfield Lock. This was relatively close to London and in the early days of the war it became patently obvious that one large air raid on Enfield would put an end to Bren gun production for some considerable time. BSA was consequently asked to prepare an alternative design capable of rapid and uncomplicated production by almost any engineering factory in the event of such a disaster. The resulting design was known as the Besal, though it was later known as the Faulkner, from the name of the designer. In many ways it was a highly simplified Bren gun, designed with production limitations in mind. The body and the gas cylinder were simple pressings, the trigger mechanism basic in the extreme, and the piston and breech-block, devoid of any frills, were of square section. The block locks by two lugs which are forced by a ramp into recesses cut in the receiver, and the return spring is contained in the piston and retained by a removable pin pushed up from underneath. Cocking the Mark 2 is achieved by pulling the pistol grip to the rear, like the Besa design. The gas plug is a finned cylinder offering four sizes of port which can be changed by turning the unit with a bullet. A handle projects from the left side and is used as a hand grip when changing the barrel; it does not rotate and is of little value as a carrying handle. The rearsight has two positions only, and the bipod is not adjustable for height. Nevertheless the Besal is an impressive weapon and on trials it worked well, with few stoppages. Only a few pilot models were made, since production at Enfield was never interrupted and the occasion for the Besal's production never arose.

The Hefah machine-gun was developed as a private venture by the Ductile Steel Company of Short Heath, Staffordshire in 1940 and was first submitted for trial in June of that year. It was basically a modified Lewis action, simplified to facilitate rapid manufacture. The breech-block used only one locking lug, a slightly altered Bren drum magazine was fitted beneath the gun, and the return spring was contained within a tube projecting from the rear of the receiver. On trial it was noted that this casing tended to bruise the cheek of the firer, and with the gun resting on bipod and butt there was only a bare half-inch clearance between the magazine and the ground. Although these faults weighed against it when considered as an infantry weapon, the Director of Naval Ordnance, who was desperate for anti-aircraft machine-guns for light coastal vessels, felt that the simple design was of value in view of the production capacity available at that time. The Director General of Munitions Production, however, suspended all work on the gun for several months because there was no factory available to make and rifle the barrels. Capacity was eventually found and the gun, by this time the property of the Hefah Company of Wednesfield, went into production for the Royal Navy, approved in May 1942. Why it came to be called the 'Hefah V' is unexplained. The gun's subsequent employment is not entirely clear, although it seems that only a limited number were made; it was declared obsolete in November 1944.

.303in Besal Marks 1 and 2

Birmingham Small Arms (BSA) Co

.303in British

Length overall	1,185mm (46.63in)
Weight empty	9.74kg (21.5lb)
Barrel	558mm (22.0in), 4 grooves, rh
Feed system	30-shot detachable box (Bren)
Rate of fire	600rds/min
Muzzle velocity	745m/sec (2,450ft/sec

.303in Hefah V Mk 1

Ductile Steel Co (originally); Hefah & Co (finally)

.303in British

BESAL

The General Purpose Machine-Gun, L7 Series

Royal Small Arms Factory, Enfield Lock

7.62 × 51mm NATO

The L7 series of machine-guns is derived from the Fabrique National MAG (see Belgium) with several minor changes made at Enfield to suit British production methods. The operation remains unchanged; a gas-operated tipping bolt design. Among the British variants are the following:

7.62mm GPMG L7A1 is the basic model with pistol grip, butt and stamped-steel bipod. The action is fed from the right side by means of a disintegrating-link belt of 250 rounds. Dimensions, etc., are as for the Belgian MAG.

7.62mm GPMG L7A2. The L7A2 differs from its predecessor only in the provision of mounting points for a box containing a 50-round belt, and the provision of double feed pawls in the mechanism.

7.62mm Tank MG L8A1. Intended for use in the Chieftain tank, this weapon is fitted with a bore evacuator to keep the interior of the tank free from fumes. It is also fitted with a variable-aperture gas regulator and there is provision for a firing solenoid.

7.62mm GPMG L19A1. The L19 is a version of the L7 fitted with a heavier barrel to reduce the number of barrel changes necessary when the gun is used for sustained fire. It is not a general-issue weapon.

7.62mm GPMG L20A1. The L20 is intended for post-mounting in helicopters and aircraft. It is fitted with the L8 gas regulator and an L7 barrel and can be adjusted for right or left side feed.

7.62mm Tank MG L37A2 is intended for use in tanks other than Chieftain and in sundry other armoured vehicles. It is basically an L8 gun with an L7 barrel, and can sometimes be found with a folding pistol grip unit which, together with the bipod, butt and trigger assembly carried on the vehicle, enables the gun to be dismounted in an emergency and used as a ground gun.

7.62mm Ranging MG L43A1. Until recently it was not possible to use the standard tank coaxial machine-gun as a ranging gun, to determine range to a target for application to the main armament. The L43 was therefore produced to fill this role, and differs in having special barrel bearings between the gas block and the muzzle to support the barrel in the armour. This reduces the shift of the bullet's mean point of impact between hot and cold conditions and gives consistent ranging. It is principally used on the Scorpion tracked reconnaissance vehicle.

5.56mm Light Support Weapon L86A1

Royal Small Arms Factory, Nottingham

5.56 × 45mm NATO

This is a heavy-barrel version of the L85A1 Individual Weapon, described in the automatic rifles section. A high proportion of components are interchangeable and both work in the same way, using a gas piston to drive a bolt carrier and rotating bolt, but the bolt is held open when the trigger is released so as to allow the barrel to cool. The L86 has a much heavier barrel than the rifle and a long, perforated barrel support with a bipod on the front end, beneath the muzzle. The original version had a short plastic fore-end with bipod and a long

GPMG L7

L86A1

exposed barrel, but this design was found to give 'split groups' – a different point of impact between single shots and automatic fire – and the barrel support and new bipod location were adopted to cure this. The weapon also has a butt strap and hand grip similar to that used on the original Bren gun. It has a greater effective range than the rifle and is extremely accurate in the single-shot mode.

Length overall	900mm (35.43in)
Weight empty	5.4kg (11.90lb)
Barrel	646mm (25.43in), 6 grooves, rh
Feed system	30-shot detachable box
Rate of fire	700–850rds/min
Muzzle velocity	970m/sec (3,182ft/sec)

ISRAEL

This weapon, resembling the Johnson designs, particularly the Johnson M1944 machine-gun, was developed for the Israeli Defence Force in the early 1950s. Only a small quantity was produced and it seems likely that it was found cheaper to purchase a foreign design of proven worth than to go to considerable expense to set up a mass-production facility to produce the relatively small numbers which were required. Moreover the design is a recoil-operated weapon, an unusual feature in a light machine-gun, and the sliding surfaces were not the best sort of feature to have in a gun expected to work reliably in a dusty and sandy environment. For further details of the design see under Johnson, in the USA section.

7.92mm Dror Machine-Gun

Israel Military Industries

7.92 × 57mm Mauser

The Negev is a multi-purpose weapon which can feed from standard belts, drums or box magzines and can be fired from a bipod, tripod or vehicle mounts. The standard barrel is rifled for SS109 ammunition; an alternative barrel is rifled for US M193 ammunition. The weapon is gas operated with a rotating bolt which locks into the barrel extension. It fires from an open bolt. The gas regulator has three positions, allowing the rate of fire to be changed from 650–800rds/min to 800–950rds/min or the gas supply cut off to permit launching grenades from the muzzle. The weapon will fire in semi- or full-automatic modes, and by removing the bipod and attaching a normal fore-end it can be used as an assault rifle. The Negev was introduced in 1988 and has been adopted by the Israel Defence Force.

5.56mm Negev

Israel Military Industries

5.56 × 45mm NATO

Length overall	1,020mm (40.15in) long barrel, stock extended; 780mm (30.7in) stock folded. 890mm (35.03in) short barrel, stock extended; 650mm (25.6in) stock folded
Weight empty	7.2kg (15.87lb) long barrel
Barrel	460mm (18.11in) long; 330mm (13.0in) short; 6 grooves, rh
Feed system	30-shot box, or belts or drums
Rate of fire	650–950rds/min (see text)
Muzzle velocity	950m/sec (3,115ft/sec)

NEGEV

ITALY

6.5mm SIA Light Machine-Gun

SIA G. Ansaldo, Armstrong & Co

6.5 × 52mm Mannlicher-Carcano

The SIA machine-gun – the initials stand for an abbreviated form of 'Societa Anonima Italiana G. Ansaldo, Armstrong & Co' – was a relatively simple light machine-gun of dubious value. There is no evidence to suggest that it was ever taken into military service in appreciable numbers, though it was used as a training weapon by the Italian Army in the 1930s. The design is a questionable form of delayed blowback based upon patents of Giovanni Agnelli which relate to a system of locking the rotating bolt by using a positively located firing pin with a lug riding in helical grooves in the bolt. Thus, as the pin went home under the pressure of the return spring the bolt was revolved to lock the breech, but the pin was kept clear of the cartridge cap by an auxiliary spring which was overcome by an additional blow from a hammer. There are some similarities with the Vilar Perosa machine-gun breech mechanism here.

Like every other inventor of a blowback mechanism using bottle-necked cartridges, Agnelli had his share of trouble due to the case sticking in the chamber instead of extracting cleanly, and he must be credited as the first patentee of the idea of machining flutes in the chamber walls so as to allow gas to flow along the outside of the case and so 'float' the case on a layer of high pressure gas and thus overcome the extraction problem. The Ansaldo-Armstrong combine took over his patents and produced a gun shortly before World War One, but it was not developed into a workable proposition until the 1920s, by which time there were many other and better ideas available. Perhaps the worst feature of the SIA was the open-sided magazine which allowed the dust and dirt raised by firing to thoroughly coat the cartridges waiting to be fed into the chamber; which may account for some of Agnelli's extraction problems.

6.5mm Fiat-Revelli Model 14

Fiat SpA

6.5 × 52mm Mannlicher-Carcano

Length overall	1,180mm (46.50in)
Weight empty	17.0kg (37.5lb)
Barrel	654mm (25.75in), 4 grooves, rh
Feed system	50-shot strip-feed box
Rate of fire	400rds/min
Muzzle velocity	640m/sec (2,100ft/sec)

The Model 1914 Revelli was the first Italian-designed machine-gun to appear in any quantity. It was chambered for the under-powered 6.5mm M95 rifle cartridge but was as heavy as any of the more powerful Maxims, to which it bore considerable resemblance. The action was novel, for it worked by a delayed blowback system in which the barrel recoiled for a short distance before the bolt moved away from the breech. The arrangement did not allow for any primary extraction, and, to ensure that the cartridge cases did not rupture and were easily extracted, each round was oiled as it was fed into the breech, the oil being drawn from a reservoir on top of the receiver. Another curiosity was a buffer rod attached to the top of the bolt and working outside the receiver, along the top surface. The rod buffered against a stop immediately in front of the firing spade grip, in which position it was a constant source of danger while the gun was firing, and where it also picked up its fair share of dust and grit and fed it into the mechanism. In any case the oiled cartridges attracted any loose dust and the gun was notorious for stoppages.

The Model 14 was fitted with an extraordinary pattern of magazine containing ten compartments, each holding five rounds. It was loaded from the left side and fired the first stack of five rounds; then a projection at the rear of the compartment raised a pawl, allowing an arm to push the magazine to the right and align the next compartment with the feed mechanism. This peculiar feed system constitutes a good example of the needless mechanical complexity which was frequently to be found in Italian machine-gun designs but, even so, the Model 14 survived in first-line use throughout World Wars One and Two, though many were modernised in 1935.

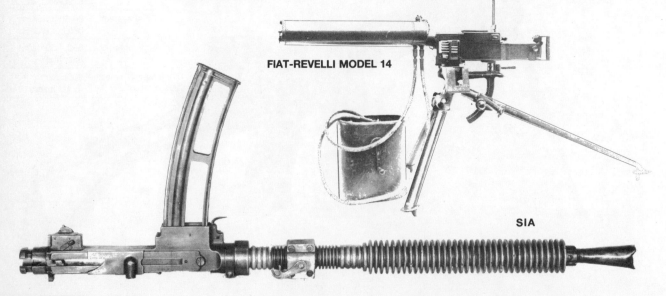

FIAT-REVELLI MODEL 14

SIA

The Breda Company got into the machine-gun business almost by accident; they were a heavy engineering company who were contracted by Fiat, during World War One, to make some of the Model 14 guns. Fiat set up a subsidiary firm called Safat solely to make armaments, and after the War Breda, having acquired a lot of machinery, decided to start making their own machine-guns. Both Fiat and Breda sold their weapons to the Italian Air Force, after which it came down to a contest over who would get the lucrative Army light machine-gun contract. Breda won, and Fiat decided to quit the arms business, selling their Safat plant to Breda; which is why some Breda designs are sometimes referred to as 'Breda-Safat'. Breda produced a number of machine-guns for the Italian Army which, for the sake of convenience, might be considered together. Their first design was the Model 24 which was little different from the succeeding Model 30, adopted by the Army on a large scale.

6.5mm Breda Model 30. The Model 30 was an ungainly looking weapon which must have been difficult to clean and maintain in field conditions. It was blowback operated and, like most blowback weapons, was disposed to difficult extraction; it therefore carried an oil pump which squirted lubricant on to each cartridge as it was being loaded. The magazine, on the right side of the receiver, hinged forward, in which position it could be loaded from rifle chargers. This design offered a theoretical advantage in that the feed lips could be machined into the receiver and were therefore less liable to damage than the lips of a detachable magazine. But there were disadvantages, principally that the practical rate of fire was considerably reduced by the delay inherent in loading the magazine in position on the gun, and the danger that should the magazine become damaged in any way, the gun was out of action. The barrels of these guns could be changed quite rapidly, but there was no form of handle with which to grasp the hot barrel; nor, indeed, was there any carrying handle: the unfortunate gunner had to carry the gun on his shoulder or cradle it in his arms. The Model 30 differed from the earlier Model 24 in having a bipod instead of a tripod and a pistol grip and shoulder stock in place of spade grips and a thumb trigger.

13.2mm Breda RM Model 31. In 1931 the Italians introduced a 13.2mm heavy machine-gun intended for the armament of light tanks, although it could also be tripod-mounted for use as an infantry support weapon. It has few unusual features except for some exceptionally sensitive explosive bullets, though from the aspect of gun design it appears to have been an intermediate step towards the development of the Model 37.

This became the standard Italian Army medium machine-gun throughout World War Two and was a fairly conventional gas-operated weapon, though with some features which put it in a class of its own. The design of the breech mechanism failed to provide for a slow initial extraction of the spent case, and it was therefore still necessary to lubricate the rounds before they were loaded. The second unusual feature stemmed from the fact that the gun was first designed as a tank weapon; the army objected to the ejection of spent cases on to the tank floor, where they might well jam vital machinery or roll under a crewman's foot and unbalance him at a critical moment. The feed mechanism was therefore designed to feed the cartridges in a metal strip into the right side of the gun, fire each round, replace the empty case into the strip and eject the strip full of empties on the left side. This may have been good housekeeping inside a tank, but it meant that the gunner's assistant had to empty the cases out of the strip before he could reload, and in field operations this was an unnecessary complication. Nevertheless, the Model 37 managed to remain in first-line service throughout the war and emerged from it with a reputation for reliability.

Breda Machine-Guns

Soc. Anon. Ernesto Breda

6.5 × 52mm Mannlicher-Carcano
7.35 × 51mm Breda
8 × 59RB Breda
13.2 × 99mm Breda

Length overall	1,230mm (48.40in)
Weight empty	10.20kg (22.5lb)
Barrel	520mm (20.50in), 4 grooves, rh
Feed system	20-shot integral box
Rate of fire	475rds/min
Muzzle velocity	610m/sec (2,000ft/sec)

8mm Breda Model 37

Length overall	1,270mm (50.00in)
Weight empty	19.5kg (43.0lb)
Barrel	679mm (26.75in), 4 grooves, rh
Feed system	20-shot metal strip
Rate of fire	450rds/min
Muzzle velocity	791m/sec (2,600ft/sec)

BREDA MODEL 30

8mm Breda Model 38 was the basic rifle-calibre tank and armoured car machine-gun and was a far more sensible design than most of its contemporaries, using a top-mounted box magazine and supplied with a heavy barrel which made it capable of sustained fire. It was a gas-operated locked-breech weapon.

7.35mm Breda Model 38. In 1938 the Italians decided to increase their rifle calibre from 6.5mm to 7.35mm in an attempt to improve the efficiency of the rifles; at the same time they took the opportunity of re-barrelling some of the Model 30 machine-guns for the larger round, and the Model 38 was the result. The cartridge was carefully designed to have the same rim diameter as the 6.5mm round, so that apart from changing the barrel there was little more work needed to make the conversion.

7.7mm Scotti Model 28

Isotta-Fraschini SpA

7.7 × 56R Italian

The Scotti light machine-gun was one of a range of weapons designed by Alfredo Scotti of Brescia. He was a freelance designer associated, for the most part, with Italian aircraft firms, and most of his successful weapons were for use in aircraft, though at one time or another he designed pistols, submachine-guns, automatic rifles and machine-guns for army use. The Model 28 was the best of his light infantry guns, using his patent principle of operation which used a gas piston arrangement to unlock the breech and then allowed residual chamber pressure to blow the bolt back. Both belt and drum feed were offered, but the design was not taken up by anyone and few were made. The gun is included here since it shows a different approach to the breech locking problem; in larger form, in a 20mm cannon, the system was used by the Italian Air Force during World War Two.

8mm Fiat-Revelli Model 35

Fiat SpA

8 × 59RB

Length overall	1,270mm (50.00in)
Weight empty	18.10kg (40.0lb)
Barrel	653mm (25.75in), 4 grooves, rh

The Model 35 is simply the old Fiat Model 1914 brought up to date. The water-cooled barrel gave way to an air-cooled one, the feed was changed to a belt, the oiler was discarded and a fluted chamber substituted, and the calibre was changed to 8mm. This ought to have ensured success, but, sadly, it did not. There was too much of the old Revelli left to allow the gun to work well. Despite the fluted chamber the cartridge cases still stuck, and in the end either the oiler had to be replaced or the cartridges had to be lubricated by hand before being loaded into the belt. The gun fired from a closed bolt, overheating the barrel and giving rise to 'cook-off' problems when chamber heat prematurely fired the cartridge. In fact the Model 35 succeeded in being a worse weapon than the one that it supposedly improved upon. It survived the war but was scrapped immediately afterwards.

Feed system	50-shot belt
Rate of fire	500rds/min
Muzzle velocity	792m/sec (2,600ft/sec)

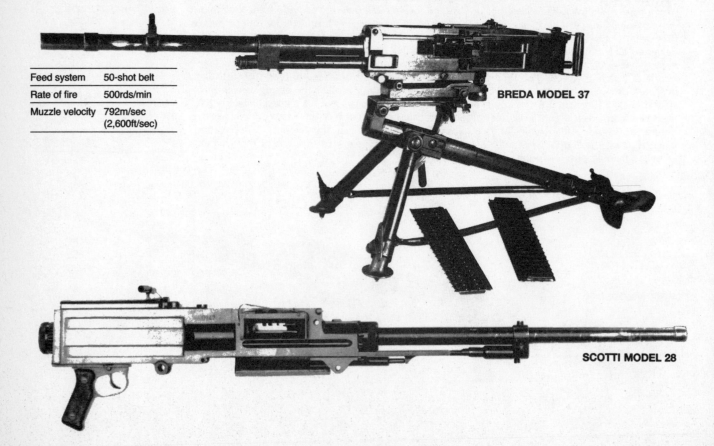

BREDA MODEL 37

SCOTTI MODEL 28

This light machine-gun is derived from the Beretta AR70 rifle and many of the components are interchangeable. The principal difference lies in the adoption of a heavy barrel with quick-change facility. A bipod, capable of adjustment for height, is fitted and the muzzle is shaped to form a combination muzzle brake and grenade-launcher. Each barrel carries its own sight, so that each barrel can be zeroed-in separately. There is a long, perforated barrel jacket and handguard, and the butt has been shaped so as to afford a better grip. The weapon uses the same rotating bolt system as the rifles but fires from an open bolt. It is believed that some have been sold to Middle and Far Eastern countries.

This is the squad automatic version of the 5.56mm AR70-90 assault rifle. It uses the same gas-operated rotating bolt system as the rifle but fires from an open bolt, and has a heavy barrel which cannot be quick-changed. The butt is cut away to provide a firm grip and has an over-shoulder strap, and there is a long, perforated barrel jacket. The bipod is articulated and can be adjusted for height. A carrying handle is fitted and, like that of the rifle, it can be easily removed to expose a mount for optical sights. The AR70-90 is currently undergoing trials by the Italian Army.

5.56mm Beretta AR70-84

Pietro Beretta SpA

5.56 × 45mm NATO

Length overall	955mm (37.60in)
Weight empty	5.3kg (11.68lb)
Barrel	450mm (17.72in), 4 grooves, rh
Feed system	30-shot detachable box
Rate of fire	670rds/min
Muzzle velocity	970m/sec (3,182ft/sec)

5.56mm Beretta AR70-90

Pietro Beretta SpA

5.56 × 45mm NATO

Length overall	1,000mm (39.37in)
Weight empty	5.34kg (11.77lb) without magazine or bipod
Barrel	465mm (18.30in), 6 grooves, rh
Feed system	30-shot detachable box (M16 standard)
Rate of fire	800rds/min
Muzzle velocity	980m/sec (3,215ft/sec)

BERETTA AR70-84

BERETTA AR70-90

JAPAN

6.5mm Taisho 3rd Year (1914)

State arsenals	
6.5 × 50mm Arisaka	
Length overall	1,156mm (45.5in)
Weight empty	28.10kg (61.95lb)
Barrel	749mm (29.5in), 4 grooves, lh
Feed system	30-shot metal strip
Rate of fire	400rds/min
Muzzle velocity	731m/sec (2,400ft/sec)

6.5mm Taisho 11th Year (1922)

State arsenals	
6.5 × 50mm Arisaka	
Length overall	1,104mm (43.5in)
Weight empty	10.19kg (22.5lb)
Barrel	482mm (19.0in), 4 grooves, rh
Feed system	30-shot hopper
Rate of fire	500rds/min
Muzzle velocity	700m/sec (2,300ft/sec)

6.5mm Type 91 (1931)

State arsenals	
6.5 × 50mm Arisaka	
Length overall	1,066mm (42.0in)
Weight empty	11.0kg (24.25lb)
Barrel	488mm (19.21in), 4 grooves, rh
Feed system	50-shot hopper
Rate of fire	500rds/min
Muzzle velocity	700m/sec (2,300ft/sec)

The Third Year machine-gun is really a Japanese version of the Hotchkiss Model 1900. During the Russo-Japanese War of 1904–5, the first in which machine-guns were employed in significant numbers, the Japanese used the Hotchkiss to great effect. Kirijo Nambu used the gun as his point of departure to design a weapon suitable for Japanese manufacture and the resulting close copy of the original is chambered for the 6.5mm Arisaka rifle cartridge. The only obvious external differences are in the barrel finning and the fittings on the tripod. It was adopted in 1914 and some of the original weapons continued in service throughout World War Two. The Third Year inherited from its French ancestor the merits of reliability and strength, though the need to oil the cartridges was always a potential source of trouble in dusty conditions. Like the models which followed, the tripod feet had holes through which the crew passed bearer poles so that the gun and tripod could be carried in one lift, something unique to the Japanese Army.

The 11th Year model was the first light machine-gun the Japanese had designed themselves; it was unusual in several ways and was probably never entirely satisfactory, but it survived until 1945 and gave a good account of itself. Apart from its ungainly outline and angular shape, it possessed some features seldom found in other machine-guns. The chief of these was the feed system, in which a hopper on the left of the gun accepted chargers for the 38th Year rifle, stripped out the rounds and fed them into the breech. Thus any rifleman could provide the gun with ammunition without having to load a magazine or belt. However, the system was complicated and led to stoppages. Another feature of the feed was that the rounds were oiled as they passed into the breech, for the mechanism gave no primary extraction and without lubrication the empty case was difficult to extract. A specially loaded cartridge, somewhat less powerful than the standard infantry rifle round, was generally used to prevent case rupture. The gun was only capable of automatic fire.

The Type 91 was the tank version of the 11th Year ground gun; it differed very little, except for the feed; it was found necessary to give the gunner more than the 30 rounds held by the hopper feed system, so it was enlarged to almost twice the original size. This can hardly have been advantageous for the gunner still had to refill it with clips in the confined space of the tank's turret. It does not appear that the Type 91 remained in service for very long, although some were converted to infantry use by fitting a bipod and also, in many cases, a telescope sight. It can hardly have been popular with the infantry since it was heavier than any other 'light' machine-gun and no more effective.

TAISHO 3rd YEAR

The Type 99 was no more than an improved Taisho Third Year gun, and in all respects except the barrel, breech and ammunition it is the same gun. It was recognised in the late 1920s that the 6.5mm Arisaka round was inadequate for machine-gun use and the more powerful 7.7mm round was introduced in 1932; hence the Type 92 designation. Strangely no effort was made to improve the extraction, and thus the 7.7mm cartridges still had to be oiled. The Type 92 round was semi-rimless and was one of three similar cartridges introduced at the same time; the others were the Type 89 rimmed and the Type 99 rimless, and all were identical except for the rims. There has never been an adequate explanation of why the Japanese chose to adopt three similar but different cartridges, which must have given their supply services some headaches during the war. The rimmed round was, fortunately, only used by the Navy and Air Force; even more fortunately the Type 92 gun could fire either the semi-rimmed or the rimless round equally well, and it became one of the most-used Japanese guns of World War Two. The rate of fire was slow by comparison to other wartime weapons and its peculiar stuttering sound caused it to be nicknamed the 'Woodpecker' by Allied troops. A modified version was introduced in 1941, and is rather confusingly known as the Type 1. It was a little lighter than the Type 92, the barrel could be removed more easily, and it could only fire Type 99 rimless ammunition.

The Type 96 was introduced in 1936 as an improvement on the 11th Year model. The cartridge hopper was replaced by a box magazine holding 30 rounds and the cartridge oiler was abolished. The rounds were still oiled, with all the drawbacks that accrued from doing it, but in the Type 96 the oiler was introduced into the magazine loading machine instead of being part of the gun. The barrel was easier to change, which was a distinct advantage in action, but apart from these small advances the gun was little better than the one it set out to replace. In fact it never did replace the 11th Year gun because Japanese arms manufacture could not possibly satisfy the demands being made upon it, and the two guns therefore existed side by side throughout the war. One feature of the Type 96 rarely found on other machine-guns is the sight, for in many cases a low-power telescope sight was fitted. The exact reason for this is not clear, since the inherent lack of consistent accuracy in the gun makes a telescope largely unnecessary. The standard ammunition for the Type 96 was a reduced-charge 6.5mm round, adopted in order to reduce the likelihood of case ruptures and head separations.

The Type 97 is the successor to the Type 91, and not to the Type 96 as might be thought from the numbering. A tank machine-gun, it was used throughout World War Two alongside the Type 91, though it never replaced it as it was obviously meant to do. It is a straightforward copy of the Czech ZB26, firing the Japanese 7.7mm semi-rimmed round and it retains almost all the characteristics of the Czech weapon. It can hardly have been a success in a tank since the feed is by a top-mounted box magazine, though that was undeniably better than the old hopper. The barrel is too light for the sort of fire demanded of a tank gun, and this meant that the gunner was restricted in the rate at which he could fire, or the barrel would rapidly overheat. In fact this became apparent to the Japanese and a Browning-pattern gun, the Type 4, was designed; but no more than a few prototypes were completed before the war ended.

7.7mm Type 92 (1932)

State arsenals

7.7 × 58SR Type 92
7.7 × 58 Type 99

Length overall	1,156mm (45.50in)
Weight empty	55.30kg (122lb) with tripod
Barrel	698mm (27.5in), 4 grooves, rh
Feed system	30-shot metal strip
Rate of fire	450rds/min
Muzzle velocity	732m/sec (2,400ft/sec)

6.5mm Type 96 (1936)

State arsenals

6.5 × 50mm Arisaka

Length overall	1,054mm (41.5in)
Weight empty	9.07kg (20.0lb)
Barrel	552mm (21.7in), 4 grooves, rh
Feed system	30-shot detachable box
Rate of fire	550rds/min
Muzzle velocity	732m/sec (2,400ft/sec)

7.7mm Type 97 (1937)

State arsenals

7.7 × 58SR Type 92

Length overall	864mm (34.00in)
Weight empty	10.88kg (24.0lb)
Barrel	711mm (28.0in), 4 grooves, rh
Feed system	30-shot detachable box
Rate of fire	500rds/min
Muzzle velocity	732m/sec (2,400ft/sec)

11th YEAR 1922

TYPE 96

7.7mm Type 99 (1939)

State arsenals	
7.7 × 58SR Type 92	
Length overall	1,181mm (46.50in)
Weight empty	10.43kg (23.0lb)
Barrel	545mm (21.5in), 4 grooves, rh
Feed system	30-shot detachable box
Rate of fire	850rds/min
Muzzle velocity	715m/sec (2,350ft/sec)

7.62mm Type 62 (1962)

Sumitomo Heavy Industries	
7.62 × 51mm NATO	
Length overall	1,200mm (47.24in)
Weight empty	10.7kg (23.59lb)
Barrel	524mm (20.63in), 6 grooves, rh
Feed system	Metal link belt
Rate of fire	600rds/min
Muzzle velocity	855m/sec (2,805ft/sec)

When the decision was taken, in 1939, to adopt the 7.7mm rimless Type 99 cartridge, the Japanese Army had no gun specifically designed to use it and the Type 99 was therefore developed. Since time was short, the design team worked from existing service designs and the Type 99 was thus a development from the Type 96, itself a new weapon at that time. The Type 99 was a considerable improvement upon its predecessors and more clearly resembled the light machine-guns which were then in use in Europe. The new rimless round did not require oiling, there was adequate primary extraction which reduced stoppages, tolerances were held to fine limits, and a new pattern of barrel change was used. It was a good weapon but came too late to be effective and never appeared in large numbers; Japan's war industries were already overloaded when it was developed and the arsenals never caught up with demand. There was more than a hint of ZB26 ancestry in its outline, though the Type 96 ancestry was also clear. A small monopod was fitted to the toe of the butt to allow the gun to be fired on fixed lines, somewhat after the manner of a tripod-mounted gun; this idea has been adopted on other guns, but is neither stable nor accurate enough to be of much value. The principal advantages of the Type 99 lay in its more powerful ammunition and its magazine feed. As with most Japanese machine-guns, it was only capable of automatic fire.

The Type 62 is a general-purpose machine-gun similar in outline and performance to many others. The specification which led to the Type 62 was developed in the 1950s and the gun was adopted in 1962. In appearance it resembles the FN-MAG, though the mechanism is not the same; the Type 62 is a gas-operated gun which has a tilting bolt, the front end of which is forced up by cams in the piston extension to lock. The final closing movement of the piston carries the firing pin into the cap; until the block has risen there is no passage for the firing pin. The design is good, the finish is excellent. The gun is capable of firing the full-charge NATO cartridge and also a reduced-charge version used in the Japanese service rifle. It can be fitted to the standard American M2 buffered tripod for use as a sustained-fire gun. There is no selector lever, and the gun can only fire in the automatic mode.

TYPE 97 (see previous page)

TYPE 99

KOREA, SOUTH

This new weapon is a gas-operated, air-cooled, belt-fed light machine-gun with quick-change barrel. The operating system is similar to, and probably derived from, the company's assault rifles, using the usual gas piston, bolt carrier and rotating bolt based upon the M16 system. The gas regulator is adjustable to provide additional power when the weapon is dirty or operating in adverse conditions.

5.56mm K3

Daewoo Precision Industries	
5.56 × 45mm	
Length overall	1,000mm (39.37in) butt extended; 830mm (32.67in) butt folded
Weight	6.1kg (13.45lb) with bipod
Barrel	6 grooves, rh
Feed system	100-shot link belt
Rate of fire	700–900rds/min
Muzzle velocity	1,000m/sec (3,280ft/sec)

MEXICO

Mexico has been fortunate in having a talented arms designer, Rafael Mendoza, as the driving force behind small-arms production, which has enabled Mexico to develop a range of inexpensive weapons suited to her needs. The Model B-1933 machine-gun was an original design, though it owed something to both the Hotchkiss and the Lewis. The bolt locking action is an improved Lewis type, with some of the locking friction diminished by the use of two cam slots. The gas cylinder is broadly of Hotchkiss form, though with improvements. The overall layout, the feed system and the quick-change barrel are purely of Mendoza's conception. The operating stroke of the piston is short and the gas is quickly released to the atmosphere; the bolt then continues under its own momentum. The gun was much lighter than its contemporaries, provision was made for selective fire and the magazine was small and easily handled. At the time of its inception it represented an advance on most other similar guns in the world. It went into service with the Mexican Army and remained in first-line use until 1945.

7mm Mendoza B-1933

Fabrica de Armas Nacional	
7 × 57mm Spanish Mauser	
Length overall	1,168mm (46.0in)
Weight	8.39kg (18.5lb)
Barrel	635mm (25.0in), 4 grooves, rh
Feed system	20-shot detachable box
Rate of fire	450rds/min
Muzzle velocity	822m/sec (2,700ft/sec)

MENDOZA B-1933

.30in Mendoza M45

Fabrica de Armas Nacional	
.30 M1906	
Length overall	1,142mm (45.0in)
Weight	8.15kg (18.0lb)
Barrel	622mm (24.5in), 4 grooves, rh
Feed system	20-shot detachable box
Rate of fire	500rds/min
Muzzle velocity	837m/sec (2,750ft/sec)

By 1945 it seemed that the 7mm Spanish cartridge was becoming outdated, and at the same time large quantities of US .30-06 ammunition existed. Mexico had long enjoyed a close relationship with the USA and it was expedient, as well as good sense, to develop weapons which could take advantage of common calibres. Mendoza took the opportunity to improve his 1933 design while retaining its main features, and changing the calibre to .30. The M45 has a slightly shorter barrel, a perforated muzzle brake and a simplified receiver. There is also a slight cleaning-up of the outline, but otherwise the gun is still the M1933.

.30in Mendoza RM-2

Productos Mendoza SA	
.30 M1906	
Length overall	1,092mm (43.0in)
Weight	6.30kg (14.0lb)
Barrel	609mm (24.0in), 4 grooves, rh
Feed system	20-shot detachable box
Rate of fire	600rds/min
Muzzle velocity	837m/sec (2,750ft/sec)

The RM-2 was the last of the Mendoza designs and its main features were low cost and simplicity of manufacture. It is also remarkably light, so light that it can almost be considered as an automatic rifle. It does not have a readily detachable barrel, a drawback in a light machine-gun since it restricts the gunner's capability for sustained fire before he has to stop and allow the barrel to cool. One feature of the weapon which is an advance on others is its method of stripping; the rear of the receiver is hinged so that it folds down to allow the working parts to be removed easily and quickly. The method is reminiscent of the FN series of rifles, which may have been the source of inspiration. The RM-2 has now been replaced in first-line service by foreign designs such as the Ameli, FN-MAG and HK21, but it remains in reserve stocks.

MENDOZA RM-2

SINGAPORE

Design of this weapon began in 1978 with the intention of providing a one-man weapon with high reliability, ample firepower and ease of handling. It was announced in 1982 and was adopted by the Singapore armed forces; it is also offered for export and has been evaluated by several armies. The Ultimax 100 is a gas-operated weapon using a rotating bolt. It fires only in the automatic mode, from an open bolt, and feeds from a special 100-shot drum or from box magazines. The bolt group has an exceptionally long recoil travel and is entirely cushioned by its return spring, never making contact with the back plate or any buffer; this gives what the makers call 'soft recoil' and it is remarkably comfortable to shoot. The barrel has a quick-change ability, and the flash hider also functions as a grenade-launching spigot. The rear sight is fully adjustable to 1,200m range and the front sight is adjustable for windage and elevation, so that all barrels can be zeroed to the weapon. The butt can be removed and a short 'para-barrel' fitted when required.

In view of the age of the .50 Browning and its known drawbacks – lack of a quick-change barrel and need for frequent headspace adjustment – CIS began development of a new .50 weapon in 1983. In addition they aimed at a simpler and lighter weapon so as to improve portability and reduce maintenance demands. The CIS .50 is modular in construction, with five basic groups. It is gas operated and fires from the open bolt position. The locking system is the now-familiar bolt carrier and rotating bolt, the firing pin being part of the carrier assembly and driven on to the cap by the final forward movement of the gas piston assembly; there are actually two gas pistons and cylinders, disposed below the barrel so as to obviate any torque twisting. The barrel is a quick-change pattern and is fitted with an efficient muzzle brake. Feed is by two belts, entering one on each side of the receiver, and the gunner can select either belt instantly as required. The gun can be provided with either a tripod mount or a pintle mount for fitting into APCs. It is believed that the CIS .50 has been taken into use by the Singapore armed forces; it is also being evaluated elsewhere.

5.56mm Ultimax 100

Chartered Industries of Singapore

5.56 × 45mm

Length overall	1,024mm (40.31in)
Weight empty	4.9kg (10.80lb) with bipod
Barrel	508mm (20.0in), 6 grooves, rh
Feed system	100-shot drum, 20- or 30-shot detachable box
Rate of fire	540rds/min
Muzzle velocity	970m/sec (3,182ft/sec)

.50 CIS

Chartered Industries of Singapore

.50 Browning (12.7 × 99mm)

Length overall	1,660mm (65.35in)
Weight	33.0kg (72.75lb)
Barrel	1,275mm (50.19in), 8 grooves, rh
Feed system	dual disintegrating link belt
Rate of fire	450–600rds/min
Muzzle velocity	887m/sec (2,910ft/sec) (M8 Ball)

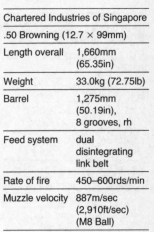

.50 CIS

ULTIMAX 100

SOUTH AFRICA

7.62mm SS-77

Lyttleton Engineering Works	
7.62 × 51mm NATO	
Length overall	940mm (37.0in) butt folded; 1,155mm (45.47in) butt extended
Weight empty	9.60kg (21.16lb) with bipod
Barrel	550mm (21.65in), 4 grooves, rh
Feed system	disintegrating link belt
Rate of fire	600–900rds/min
Muzzle velocity	840m/sec (2,756ft/sec)

Development of this weapon became necessary due to the UN embargo upon the export of weapons to South Africa which cut off the hitherto normal supply of weapons such as the FN-FAL rifle and FN-MAG machine-gun. Work began in 1977 and first issues were made in 1986. The SS-77 is gas operated and uses a breech-block which swings sideways into a recess in the receiver wall to lock, a method very similar to that used by the Soviet Goryunov. After firing gas drives the piston back and a post in the piston extension rides in a cam groove in the block and swings it out of engagement, then withdraws it to extract the empty case. During this movement a post on top of the block engages with a belt feed arm in the top cover, and this moves the ammunition belt a half-step inwards. On the return stroke the belt is moved a further half-step and the block strips out the fresh cartridge and chambers it. The final forward movement of the piston forces the block back into engagement with the receiver recess; the piston post then strikes the firing pin to fire the next round. The barrel has a quick-change facility and is externally fluted to save weight and also increase the cooling surface. The gas regulator is adjustable and also has a position which closes the exhaust to give minimal emission of gas, allowing the gun to be safely fired in enclosed spaces. There is an adjustable bipod and a carrying handle.

SPAIN

7.92mm Alfa M44 and M55

Fabrica de Armas de Oviedo	
7.92 × 57mm Mauser (M44) 7.62 × 51mm NATO (M55)	
Length overall	1,447mm (57.00in)
Weight empty	12.92kg (28.5lb)
Barrel	750mm (29.5in), 6 grooves, rh
Feed system	100-shot metal link belt
Rate of fire	800rds/min
Muzzle velocity	845m/sec (2,772ft/sec)

The Alfa Model 44 is a medium machine-gun, usually found mounted on a tripod. It is gas-operated and belt fed, the belt usually being carried in a fixed box on the side of the receiver. The operation is conventional; a gas piston in a cylinder below the barrel drives back the bolt while also operates the belt feed mechanism and cocks the action. A return spring then sends the bolt back to load the fresh round. A selector mechanism permits the firing of single shots. The original 1944 model was chambered for the 7.92mm Mauser round; a later model, the M55, is simply the same gun but chambered for the 7.62mm NATO cartridge. The Alfa is no longer used in Spain; the weapons were disposed of in various ways and many have appeared in various smaller African armies and from there have found their way into the hands of terrorist groups.

SS-77

This design appeared in 1982 and is a light 'assault' machine-gun using delayed blowback action relying upon the same roller system as the CETME rifles. There is some interchangeability of components between the Ameli machine-gun and the CETME Model L rifle. As can be seen, the design resembles a scaled-down MG42, which was manufactured under licence in Spain for many years, and it incorporates a similar method of barrel changing. Feed is by disintegrating metal link belt, and a small internal alteration allows the rate of fire to be set at either 850 or 1,200rds/min. A tripod is available, though a bipod is normally provided and seems the more logical form of mounting. A lightweight version has also been developed; this has a different form of muzzle flash hider and incorporates light alloy components where possible, saving about 1.15kg in weight. The Ameli has been adopted by the Spanish and Mexican Armies and is under evaluation by others.

5.56mm Cetme Ameli

Empresa Nacional Santa Barbara

5.56 × 45mm NATO

Length overall	970mm (38.19in)
Weight empty	6.35kg (14.0lb) standard; 5.20kg (11.46lb) lightweight
Barrel	400mm (15.75in), 6 grooves, rh
Feed system	100- or 200-shot boxed belt
Rate of fire	850 or 1,200rds/min
Muzzle velocity	875m/sec (2,870ft/sec)

CETME AMELI

SWEDEN

The Kjellmann machine-gun was never adopted for service but it deserves mention because it pioneered a breech locking system which has since become widely used. The original idea was conceived by a Swedish officer named Friberg, but it lay dormant for over 20 years until put into a gun designed in 1907 by Rudolf Kjellmann. The locking system uses two pivoting locking lugs which are forced into recesses in the receiver as the firing pin moves forward. The moving masses are thus kept light and can move quickly. At the same time, the gun cannot fire until the breech is locked, since the firing pin cannot reach the cartridge until the locking flaps are in their locked position. The system was subsequently used in the Russian Degtyarev machine-gun and, in modified form, in the German MG42 machine-gun and the British EM2 rifle. The Kjellmann was offered both as a light gun on a bipod with box magazine, and as a heavy water-cooled gun on a tripod with belt feed. Although it appears to have been a sound design it found no takers.

6.5mm Kjellmann

Husqvarna Vapenfabrik

6.5 × 55 Swedish Mauser

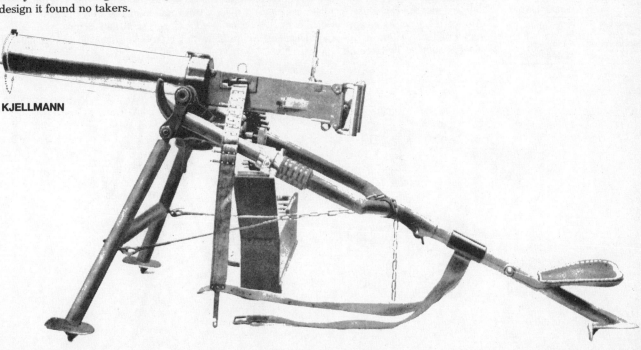

KJELLMANN

6.5mm Knorr-Bremse LH33

Knorr-Bremse AG	
6.5 × 55 Swedish Mauser (Sweden)	
7.92 × 57mm Mauser (Germany)	
Length overall	1,308mm (51.08in)
Weight empty	10.0kg (22.04lb)
Barrel	691mm (27.25in), 4 grooves, rh
Feed system	20-shot detachable box
Rate of fire	490rds/min
Muzzle velocity	792m/sec (2,600ft/sec) (7.92mm)

This weapon first appeared in the early 1930s as a Swedish design called the LH33, in 6.5mm calibre. It was intended as a simple and cheap light machine-gun, and after the Swedish Army bought a few for evaluation the inventor made a few small improvements and looked around for an export market. He tried the Norwegians, but they declined the weapon, and he then sold his patents to the German Knorr-Bremse company who, as their name implies, were in the automobile brake business. They appear to have rushed blindly into the arms business in the hopes of a lucrative contract from the German Army and in 1935 they began manufacture of a slightly simplified version of the LH33 under their own name. This version was capable of automatic fire only and so discarded the double trigger of the original LH33. Feeding from a horizontal box magazine on the left side, the Knorr-Bremse had some odd features. The barrel was retained by a quick-release nut, and for no apparent reason the rifling ended three inches from the muzzle. The safety catch was a trap for the unwary since, if wrongly applied, it could hold the bolt three-quarters cocked without engaging the sear; subsequent release of the safety thus released the bolt and fired the gun. The butt was secured by a metal clip plate which vibrated loose so that the butt dropped off during firing, which must have been a trifle disconcerting, to say the least.

Although the gun worked, the general standard of design and manufacture was poor, even allowing for the intention to keep it cheap. The Waffen-SS purchased a number which were soon relegated to the training role and were then unloaded on to the various 'Legions' formed during the war, among them the Latvian Legion. Apart from this the only major sales were in early 1940 to the hard-pressed Finns, who were glad to get anything, and a few more to Sweden where it was adopted as the m/40. Thereafter manufacture ceased and Knorr, sadder but wiser, went back to the brake business.

SWITZERLAND

7.5mm Model 25 (Furrer)

Swiss Federal Arms Factory	
7.5 × 54mm Schmidt-Rubin	
Length overall	1,163mm (45.79in)
Weight empty	10.59kg (23.35lb)
Barrel	585mm (23.03in), 4 grooves, rh
Feed system	30-shot detachable box
Rate of fire	450rds/min
Muzzle velocity	745m/sec (2,444ft/sec)

As we observed when discussing Swiss submachine-guns, Colonel Furrer, the Chief Designer at the Swiss state arsenal, had something of a fixation on toggle mechanisms. Thus his MG25 was typical of its origin: exceptionally well conceived, beautifully made, and far too expensive to ever be considered a mass-production weapon. It is a recoil-operated gun which, not to put too fine a point on it, is simply a Parabellum pistol toggle mechanism laid on its side, since the locking system is exactly the same. However, Furrer took a leaf from submachine-gun design and used the differential recoil theory to produce a weapon with a very light recoil. The system is arranged so that the cartridge is actually fired while a substantial portion of the recoiling mass is still moving forward, so that the recoil force is largely absorbed in bringing the parts to rest and then reversing its direction of motion. Most applications of this system are in blowback weapons where the mass of the bolt has to be reversed. In the Furrer MG25, however, the breech is closed and locked while the entire barrel and action unit are moving forward. The sear is released during this movement, so that the entire mass of barrel, barrel extension and bolt has to be stopped before recoil can begin. Although a very efficient system it demanded careful manufacture, which is one reason for its lack of success outside Switzerland.

KNORR-BREMSE

MODEL 25

The Solothurn company was originally a watchmaking concern, but was bought and converted to arms manufacture in the 1920s. In 1929 Rheinmetall gained control and used the plant as a design engineering shop for their own designs in order to evade the provisions of the Versailles Treaty. The first such design was the M29 machine-gun which was soon modified into the MG30 and sold in Austria and Hungary. The MG30 had a quick-change barrel which was removed by rotating the butt and pulling it off, so allowing the bolt and barrel to be removed from the receiver. Another feature was a rocking double trigger; pressure on the top section gave single shots, pressure on the lower section automatic fire. The gun was recoil operated; on firing the barrel and bolt recoiled for a short distance, after which the bolt was rotated by lugs riding in cam grooves in the gun body and allowed to continue its rearward movement. It was a simple and rapid action with a high rate of fire. The weapon fed from a horizontally mounted box magazine on the left side of the receiver, a system which has the drawback of shifting the weapon's balance as the magazine empties. Whatever the theoretical drawbacks, though, some 5,000 were made between 1930 and 1935 and of these a large proportion must have seen service during World War Two. But the real significance of the MG30 is that it was the starting point for the later MG34 and MG42 designs.

The KE7 was developed as a private venture by SIG in the early 1930s; the gun was designed by Kiraly and Ende (hence KE) and represented an attempt to produce a practical light machine-gun at a realistic price. However the Swiss Army could not raise any interest and it had only limited success in overseas sales, principally to China in 7.92mm calibre. The KE7 was an interesting recoil-operated design which used a most unusual locking system. A pivoted arm attached to the barrel extension carried a hook at its rear end which engaged with the bolt and kept it locked to the breech; the front end locked into a recess in the receiver, preventing any movement of the arm until the barrel extension had recoiled some distance. As the barrel, extension and bolt recoiled, the front end of the arm kept the bolt locked until the front end had left its recess, after which the arm could be forced down by cam action to free the bolt. A stud on the arm dropped into a recess, so holding the barrel in the recoiled position. As the bolt returned, a cam surface picked up the hook and re-engaged it with the bolt, at the same time lifting the stud clear so that the bolt and barrel assembly could run forward to the firing position. The KE7 was very light for a full-power light machine-gun, and was probably difficult to hold in continuous fire. It fired from an open bolt at all times and had very few moving parts. A light bipod was attached to the fore-end, and there was an optional tripod which improved stability in sustained fire.

The MG51 was developed from the German MG42 in the immediate post-war years. It was only used in Switzerland in small numbers and the only export sale of significance was to Denmark, who equipped her army with it. The interesting point was that while the MG42 had been deliberately engineered to be made cheaply from stamped metal, the Swiss re-engineered it to be made from machined solid steel, which rather negated the original idea. It was therefore a heavy gun but of superlative quality and utmost reliability. Another minor change was the adoption of locking flaps for the bolt instead of the rollers used on the MG42, a change which did not affect the performance. It was usually mounted on a robust tripod provided with straps and back-pads for man carrying. It was replaced, in both armies, in the mid-1960s.

SIG MG51

KIRALY KE7

7.5mm Model 30 (Solothurn)

Waffenfabrik Solothurn AG	
7.5 × 54mm Schmidt-Rubin	
Length overall	1,174mm (46.25in)
Weight empty	7.80kg (17.25lb)
Barrel	595mm (23.42in), 4 grooves, rh
Feed system	25-shot detachable box
Rate of fire	800rds/min
Muzzle velocity	760m/sec (2,493ft/sec)

7.92mm SIG Model KE7

Schweizerische Industrie-Gesellschaft (SIG)	
7.92 × 57mm Mauser & others	
Length overall	1,190mm (46.87in)
Weight empty	7.80kg (17.20lb)
Barrel	600mm (23.62in), 4 grooves, rh
Feed system	20-shot detachable box
Rate of fire	550rds/min
Muzzle velocity	745m/sec (2,444ft/sec)

7.5mm SIG MG51

Schweizerische Industrie-Gesellschaft (SIG)	
7.5 × 54mm Schmidt-Rubin (Swiss) .30 M1906 (Denmark)	
Length overall	1,270mm (50.00in)
Weight empty	16.0kg (35.27lb)
Barrel	565mm (22.24in), 4 grooves, rh
Feed system	250-shot belt
Rate of fire	1,000rds/min
Muzzle velocity	795m/sec (2,608ft/sec) (7.92mm)

7.62mm SIG MG710-1, -2

Schweizerische Industrie-Gesellschaft (SIG)	
7.62 × 51mm NATO; 7.92 × 57mm Mauser	
Length overall	1,189mm (46.85in)
Weight empty	11.3kg (25.0lb)
Barrel	500mm (19.75in), 4 grooves, rh
Feed system	200-shot belt
Rate of fire	750 or 1,400rds/min
Muzzle velocity	792m/sec (2,600ft/sec)

The SIG 710 series of machine-guns was developed in the 1960s, not only for service in the Swiss Army but also for export sale. They bear some resemblance to the MG42 and are direct derivations from the StuG57 assault rifle (qv). The machine-gun uses the same delayed blowback locking system as the rifle, and despite its apparent complication the guns are most reliable. The 710-1 and 710-2 differ in respect of their barrel-changing system; the 710-1 has a perforated barrel jacket like the MG42, with a long slot in the right side, and the rear end of the barrel can be unlatched and swung out through the slot. The 710-2 barrel has a vertical carrying handle and this is also used to turn and push forward the barrel to remove it forwards from the receiver. The guns were offered with a wide range of accessories, including tripod, drum magazines and carrying attachments. Although offered in various calibres they appear not to have sold in large numbers, and they were eventually replaced in production by the 710-3 (below). (Data table refers to the 710-1.)

7.62mm SIG MG710-3

Swiss Industrial Company (SIG)	
7.62 × 51mm NATO	
Length overall	1,143mm (45.0in)
Weight empty	9.25kg (20.39lb)
Barrel	559mm (22.0in), 4 grooves, rh
Feed system	200-shot disintegrating link belt
Rate of fire	800–950rds/min
Muzzle velocity	790m/sec (2,592ft/sec)

The 710-3, which replaced the earlier 710 models, uses the same method of operation but with a less expensive form of manufacture. Steel stampings and pressings are used instead of heavy machined parts wherever possible, and this has saved weight and also resulted in some changes in the outline. The barrel change is the same system as used on the 710-1, sliding breech-first out of a slot in the jacket, and the barrel has a large plastic handle attached on its right side so that a hot barrel can be removed more easily. The feed system is adapted from the MG42, a lever in the top cover being driven by the movement of the bolt, and the feed mechanism will work equally well with a variety of belt types. A variety of accessories are offered and, as with the others in the series, it is meant to be used as a general-purpose weapon from bipod or tripod. Although expensive it has been sold to a number of South American armies and to Brunei.

7.5mm Model 87

Swiss Federal Arms Factory	
7.5 × 54mm Schmidt-Rubin	
Length overall	1,175mm (46.26in)
Weight empty	30.0kg (66.14lb) including mount
Barrel	475mm (18.7in), 4 grooves, rh
Feed system	250-shot belt
Rate of fire	700 or 1,000rds/min
Muzzle velocity	790m/sec (2,590ft/sec)

This weapon was developed for use in fixed fortifications and armoured vehicles and is based on the Model 51. Its principal feature is that it has been designed with the receiver virtually sealed and with a gas extraction sleeve which surrounds the barrel and terminates outside the armour or shield. Thus there is no escape of dangerous fumes into the tank or pillbox and special ventilation arrangements to remove gun fumes are no longer required. It is normally produced in 7.5mm calibre for purely Swiss use, but it can be converted to 7.62mm NATO by merely changing four component parts. The gun is supplied with a suitable port mounting for its particular role; it has no butt or pistol grip and has an electric firing solenoid attached to the sear.

SIG MG 710-3

USA

The original Colt machine-gun of 1895 was developed by John Browning from an action based on a rifle he had produced while experimenting to see whether the muzzle blast of a weapon could be put to any practical use. The unique feature of the Colt was a swinging arm beneath the barrel. Gas was tapped off at a point just short of the muzzle to drive the end of this arm down and back through an arc of about 170°. The arm was connected to a linkage which opened the breech, extracted the spent case and loaded the new one into the chamber. The breech was locked by camming the rear end of the breech-block downwards to wedge into a recess in the receiver. The action of the driving arm led to the gun being nicknamed the 'Colt Potato Digger', and, of course, prevented the gun being mounted too close to the ground without first digging a pit. The action may seem clumsy and odd, but it had the great advantage of producing a progressive and gentle bolt movement which gave particularly effective and reliable extraction and kept the rate of fire down to a practical figure. Numbers of these guns were bought by the US Navy, in both .30 Krag and 6mm Lee calibres, in the 1890s and Colt sold them in large numbers to many other countries in a variety of calibres, notably in Spain and Italy. The guns were first used in action with the US Marine Corps at Guantanamo Bay, Cuba, in 1898. It was later used by the US Army in both .30 Krag and .30-06 calibres, but was largely relegated to use as a training weapon. Very few were used in action during World War One.

The Marlin gun was a variation on the Colt M1895 'Potato Digger'. In 1915 Marlin were given a contract to produce Colt guns for the Russian Government, and having set up a production line their chief engineer Carl Swebilius decided to take a closer look at the Colt and see if it could be improved. He did away with the swinging arm system and replaced it with a simple gas cylinder and piston beneath the barrel; various other minor improvements were made resulting in a lighter gun which was extremely reliable. It had the advantage of firing from a closed bolt, about the only gas-operated gun of the period which did, and it could thus be synchronised for air use, to fire through a rotating propeller. The Marlin gun, as the conversion was known, reached perfection just about the time of the US entering the war, and by August 1917 it was in use in aircraft in France. It was then modified for use as a tank gun; 38,000 aircraft guns and 1,470 tank guns were made by the end of 1918, and there was also a projected version for infantry use but this was not pursued. In 1941, when Britain was desperately short of all types of weapons, several thousand Marlins were supplied by the USA and were used for anti-aircraft defence on small merchant ships. In this role the gun was valuable, though inconspicuous; it was not used to any extent elsewhere.

The Colt-Browning Machine-Guns

Colt's Patent Firearms Co

.30 M1906 and others

.30 Marlin M1918

Marlin-Rockwell Corp

.30 M1906

Length overall	1,016mm (40.0in)
Weight empty	10.2kg (22.5lb)
Barrel	711mm (28.0in), 4 grooves, rh
Feed system	250-shot cloth belt
Rate of fire	600rds/min
Muzzle velocity	853m/sec (2,800ft/sec)

COLT BROWNING M1895

MARLIN M1918

The Browning Machine-Guns

Various manufacturers

.30 M1906
.50 (12.7 × 99mm)

Length overall	978mm (38.5in)
Weight empty	14.97kg (33.0lb) without water
Barrel	610mm (24.0in), 4 grooves, rh
Feed system	250-shot fabric belt
Rate of fire	500rds/min
Muzzle velocity	853m/sec (2,800ft/sec)

After his experiments with gas operation, Browning came to the conclusion that recoil operation offered the greater possibilities and as early as 1900 began taking out patents which covered the operating system he later perfected for his machine-guns. The Browning gun utilised the force of the expanding powder gases to push the barrel and bolt to the rear; after a short recoil the bolt is unlocked by camming down a lock plate holding the bolt to the barrel extension and the barrel is halted. An accelerator then throws the bolt to the rear and the movement of the bolt, by cam surfaces, operates the belt feed mechanism. The bolt is then returned by a spring, chambering a fresh round, until it closes up against the breech, the lock plate is lifted and the complete barrel and bolt assembly returns to the firing position. Although the design was fully perfected by about 1910 it was not until the US entered World War One in April 1917 that Browning was able to raise any interest in the US authorities. Once interest was roused, however, and he had demonstrated a successful working weapon, the gun was promptly accepted as the M1917.

.30in Browning M1917. In appearance the M1917 is very similar to the contemporary Vickers or Maxim, with a rectangular receiver and a round water jacket, though the pistol grip at the rear readily identifies it. Slightly more than 68,000 M1917 were manufactured before the end of World War One by Remington, Colt and Westinghouse. As a result of combat experience, some small modifications were made after the war, and in 1936 the opportunity was taken of a complete revision of the design, resulting in the M1917A1.

.30in Browning M1917A1. Introduced in 1936, this is almost identical in appearance to the M1917, from which it was modified. Changes were made in the feed mechanism, the sights were re-graduated, and the tripod was altered. Service weapons were reworked by Rock Island Arsenal in 1936–37, and further small changes were made between 1942 and 1944, again as a result of combat experience.

.30in Browning M1918, M1918M1. The M1917 was a water-cooled gun and, consequently, unsuited to use in aircraft. Modified patterns were therefore developed by discarding the water jacket and substituting light pierced casings and by lightening components wherever possible. These 1918 designs led to the introduction of the M1919 models.

.30in Browning M1919 was intended to be the definitive Browning tank gun of World War One, but it appeared too late. It was fitted with a heavier barrel than the M1917 ground gun, the water jacket was discarded, and a slim jacket with long slots was adopted.

.30in Browning M1919A1. A variant of the M1919 intended solely for the Mark VIII tank, suitable modifications being made to the mounting.

.30in Browning M1919A2 was a version of the M1919 for use by mounted cavalry; it was fitted with a special small tripod and could be placed on a special saddle for transportation.

.30in Browning M1919A3. A general-purpose derivative of the M1919, this served as a prototype for the M1919A4.

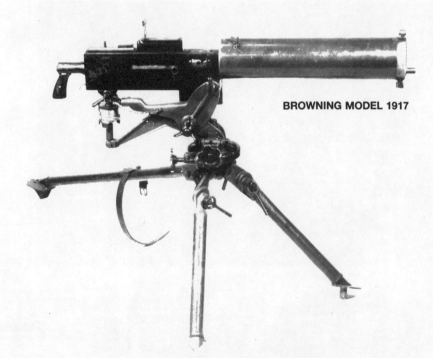

BROWNING MODEL 1917

This was issued in fixed and flexible forms; the fixed gun was intended for use in tanks and multiple anti-aircraft gun installations, while the flexible gun was for use in combat vehicles, or, on a tripod, for infantry use. It became virtually the standard US medium ground gun during World War Two.

.30 in Browning M1919A4E1. A post-World War Two version of the M1919A4, it has the slide retracting mechanism of the M1919A5.

.30in Browning M1919A5 was a special gun intended for mounting in the Light Tank M3; it was provided with a special bolt-retracting slide instead of the usual crank handle.

.30in Browning M1919A4

Length overall	1,041mm (41.0in)
Weight empty	14.05kg (31.0lb)
Barrel	610mm (24.0in), 4 grooves, rh
Feed system	250-shot fabric belt
Rate of fire	500rds/min
Muzzle velocity	853m/sec (2,800ft/sec)

Adopted in April 1943, the A6 is essentially similar to the A4 with the addition of a shoulder stock, a bipod, carrying handle, lighter barrel and flash suppressor. It was an attempt to provide the infantry with a light machine-gun; in the event it ended up heavier than the standard gun and was a dismal failure, though it stayed in service until the early 1960s.

.30in Browning M37 A tank version of the M1919 series, the feed mechanism was changed to permit either left- or right-hand feed. An ejection chute was also added for the links of the disintegrating link belt.

.30in Browning M2 This variety was designated specifically as an aircraft weapon. The principal difference between the M2 and the earlier M1918 lay in the provision of a special bolt-retracting and cocking mechanism. Internal adjustments were made to speed up the rate of fire to 1,200rds/min. A solenoid release was provided for fixed aircraft guns, and spade grips were provided for the flexible guns.

7.62mm Browning Mark 21 Mod 0 As the nomenclature indicates, this is a US Navy weapon; it is, in fact, no more than an M1919A4 altered to fire 7.62mm NATO ammunition.

.30in Browning M1919A6.

Length overall	1,346mm (53.0in)
Weight empty	14.73kg (32.5lb)
Barrel	610mm (24.0in), 4 grooves, rh
Feed system	250-shot fabric belt
Rate of fire	500rds/min
Muzzle velocity	853m/sec (2,800ft/sec)

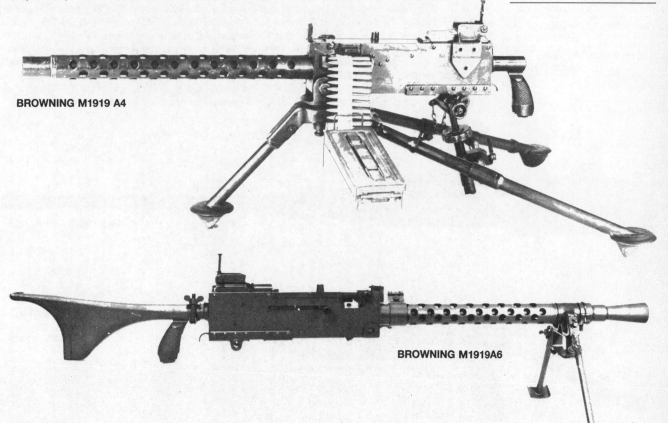

BROWNING M1919 A4

BROWNING M1919A6

.50in Browning M1921, M1921A1, M2, M2HB

Length overall	1,653mm (65.10in)
Weight empty	38.22kg (84.0lb)
Barrel	1,143mm (45.0in), 8 grooves, rh
Feed system	110-shot metallic link belt
Rate of fire	500rds/min
Muzzle velocity	898m/sec (2,950ft/sec)

.30in Johnson M1941, M1944

Cranston Arms Co	
.30 M1906	
Length overall	1,066mm (42.0in)
Weight empty	6.48kg (14.28lb)
Barrel	558mm (22.0in), 4 grooves, rh
Feed system	20-shot detachable box
Rate of fire	variable, 300 to 900rds/min
Muzzle velocity	853m/sec (2,800ft/sec)

In the latter days of World War One General Pershing requested a more powerful machine-gun, comparable with the 11mm Hotchkiss and capable of attacking observation balloons and aircraft. After some experimenting, a Browning-system gun was developed in .50in (12.7mm) calibre and eventually introduced into service as the M1921, a modified form of which later appeared as the M1921A1. During the 1930s the M2 version appeared, in which provision was made for the constant circulation of water through the water jacket, which greatly helped to dissipate the heat built up in the barrel during continuous firing. After this version had entered service an air-cooled version, which was still called the M2, also appeared, having been developed for aircraft use. Like the .30 M2 it came in fixed and flexible forms. The cooling of the M2 barrel was soon overtaxed by the power of the cartridge and no more than a 75-round burst could be fired without stopping to allow the barrel to cool. Such a restriction was impractical, and so a special heavy barrel with better heat-resisting qualities, was developed, and the gun became the M2HB (Heavy Barrel). This was again made available in fixed, flexible and anti-aircraft forms; the fixed gun was mounted in the bow of the Heavy Tank M6 and in multiple-gun anti-aircraft equipments, as well as in fighter aircraft, while the flexible gun was used on tank turret cupolas and as a heavy ground-support gun.

The Johnson light machine-gun was developed between 1936 and 1938 from the rifle of the same designer. The US Marine Corps tried it without adoption, and the only sizeable order the company ever received was from the Dutch Army in the Dutch East Indies. Before this could be completed the Japanese invaded and the supply stopped, although use by the US Army Rangers and Special Services ensured that a small continuous production was kept up for the rest of World War Two. The Johnson was one of the few light machine-guns to operate on recoil principles, and, although an elegant design manufactured to a high standard, it was too flimsy and too prone to jamming for prolonged field use. An interesting milestone in the history of firearms development, it perhaps deserved a better fate, but it appeared at a time when the US Army had made up its mind regarding light machine-gun policy and had settled on the BAR and the Browning M1919A4.

The Johnson possessed a number of unusual features, including firing from an open bolt in the automatic mode and from a closed bolt in single-shot mode. The box magazine was on the left side of the receiver, but it was possible to reload the magazine with rifle chargers through the right side without removing the magazine; this was Melvin Johnson's way of overcoming the Army's demand for a belt-fed gun. The cyclic rate could be altered by changing the tension in the buffer spring and was theoretically variable between 300 and 900rds/min. Two basic models were made by the Cranston Arms Company, the M1941 and the M1944. The earlier pattern was provided with a bipod and a wooden butt, while the M1944 had a light tubular monopod and a butt made from two parallel pieces of tubing closed by a butt-plate.

BROWNING M2HB .50in

JOHNSON M1941

The M60, with its modified successor the M60E1, is the standard general-purpose machine-gun of the US Army. It was designed in the late 1950s and has been in service since the early 1960s. It is interesting in that it uses the feed system of the German MG42 and the bolt and locking systems of the German FG42, an impressive example of imitation being the most sincere form of flattery. Much expense and effort went into producing the gun which in its original form barely justified the work. Despite its illustrious forebears the M60 had some serious defects, the most noticeable of which was the barrel change. Each barrel had its own gas cylinder and bipod, but no handle. It was, therefore, not only an expensive item but also unnecessarily heavy and dangerous to handle when hot. An asbestos glove formed part of the gun's equipment. Furthermore, when the barrel was removed there was nothing under the gun to keep it out of the mud, and the gunner had to cradle it awkwardly while his assistant performed the change. The later M60E1 has a simple barrel with the gas cylinder and bipod fixed to the gun, and it also has a handle for barrel changing. There are other changes which bring the M60E1 into line with current practice and give it better reliability. A feature of both models has been the very good Stellite lining to the barrels, which prolongs their lives well beyond that normally experienced with unprotected steel, and both models have a constant-energy gas system to work the piston.

This is a modification of the M60 machine-gun for use as a coaxial weapon in armoured vehicles. It is used by the US Marine Corps in M60A1 tanks. The principal difference is the addition of an extension tube and flash suppressor to the barrel and an evacuator tube on the gas cylinder which extends forward beneath the barrel. A collar on the operating rod and reduced clearance in the gas cylinder ensure that virtually all the gas from the system is vented forward, outside the tank, and so prevents any build-up of fumes inside the vehicle. A short back cap is fitted in place of the butt and there is a chain-operated cocking system. There is a solenoid trigger with an additional manual trigger for emergency use.

This was designed by Saco Defense to provide a light and more versatile version of the M60 while maintaining all the capabilities of the original weapon. A lightweight bipod is mounted on the receiver; the fore-end carries a forward pistol grip; the feed system has been modified to allow charging the weapon with the feed cover closed; and the gas system has been simplified. All the operating parts are common to and interchangeable with the M60 gun. The M60E3 has been adopted by the US Navy and US Marine Corps and is under consideration by the US Army.

7.62mm M60

Bridge Tool & Die Mfg Co;
Inland Div General Motors;
Saco Defense Inc

7.62 × 51mm NATO

Length overall	1,100mm (43.5in)
Weight empty	10.5kg (23.15lb)
Barrel	560mm (22.05in), 4 grooves, rh
Feed system	disintegrating link belt
Rate of fire	550rds/min
Muzzle velocity	855m/sec (2,805ft/sec)

7.62mm M60E2

Saco Defense Inc

7.62 × 51mm NATO

7.62mm M60E3

Saco Defense Inc

7.62 × 51mm NATO

Length overall	1,067mm (42.00in)
Weight empty	8.61kg (18.98lb)
Barrel	560mm (22.04in), 4 grooves, rh
Feed system	disintegrating link belt
Rate of fire	550rds/min
Muzzle velocity	860m/sec (2,821ft/sec)

M60E3

5.56mm M249 SAW

FN (USA) Inc

5.56 × 45mm NATO

The M249 is the American nomenclature for the FN Minimi light machine-gun, which was adopted into US service in the mid-1980s. For further details see under 'Belgium'.

5.56mm Colt M16A2 Light Machine-Gun

Colt Industries

5.56 × 45mm NATO

Length overall	1,000mm (39.37in)
Weight empty	5.78kg (12.74lb) without magazine
Barrel	510mm (20.07in), 6 grooves, rh
Feed system	30-shot detachable box (M16 type)
Rate of fire	600–750rds/min
Muzzle velocity	991m/sec (3,250ft/sec) (M193); 948m/sec (3,110ft/sec) (SS109)

This is a heavy-barrel version of the M16A2 rifle intended for use as a light squad automatic. It has been developed by Colt in co-operation with Diemaco of Canada, and it is used by the Canadian Army as the C7 machine-gun. The gun shares many common features with the M16A2 rifle. It has wider handguards and a forward grip below the handguard, and it uses a heavy-duty bipod which can be rapidly adjusted with one hand. The feed is by magazine, using the standard M16 interface and the weapon will accept the numerous accessory drum and snail magazines now being produced by accessory manufacturers. The Colt light machine-gun is in use with the US Marine Corps and the armies of Brazil and El Salvador among others.

.50 Saco 'Fifty/.50'

Saco Defense Inc

.50 Browning (12.7 × 99mm)

Length overall	1,560mm (61.42in)
Weight empty	25.0kg (55.11lb)
Barrel	1,143mm (45.0in), 8 grooves, rh
Feed system	disintegrating link belt
Rate of fire	variable 500 to 750rds/min
Muzzle velocity	850m/sec (2,788ft/sec)

This is a 'product-improved' version of the .50 Browning M2HB which has been developed by Saco as a private venture. It was announced in 1985 and is currently undergoing evaluation. The new design offers fixed headspace with quickly interchangeable barrels, an adjustable rate of fire capability, welded receiver construction, new charging system and a new backplate assembly. It retains the standard Browning mechanism but weighs some 35 per cent less than the M2HB. Although many new parts are used, in most cases standard M2HB spares can be used, though this carries a weight penalty.

COLT M16A2

M60E3

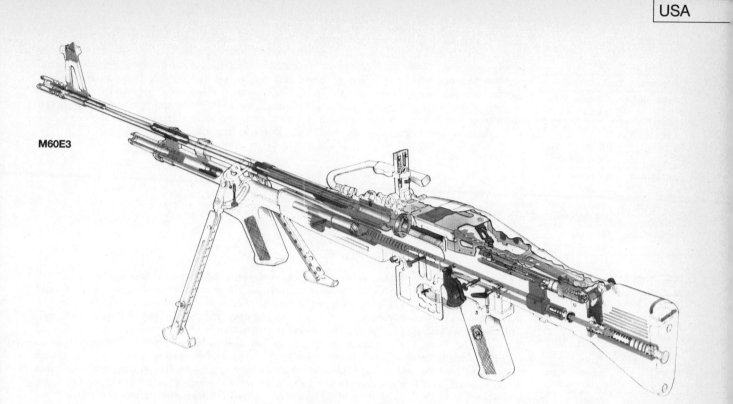

CHAIN GUN

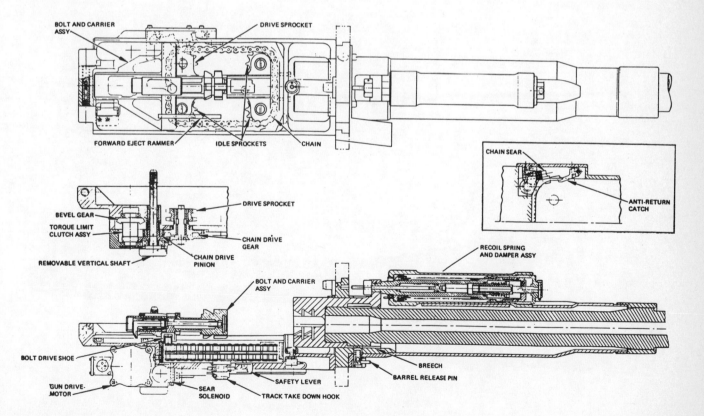

.50 M85

General Electric (USA) Co	
.50 Browning (12.7 × 99mm)	
Length overall	1,384mm (54.50in)
Weight empty	27.90kg (61.5lb)
Barrel	914mm (34.0in), 8 grooves, rh
Feed system	disintegrating link belt
Rate of fire	variable, 1,050 or 400rds/min
Muzzle velocity	866m/sec (2,841ft/sec)

7.62mm M73

General Electric (USA) Co	
7.62 × 51mm NATO	
Length overall	883mm (34.75in)
Weight empty	12.7kg (28.0lb)
Barrel	558mm (22.0in), 4 grooves, rh
Feed system	250-shot disintegrating link belt
Rate of fire	500rds/min
Muzzle velocity	853m/sec (2,800ft/sec)

Designed by the Aircraft Armament Corporation, this was intended to replace the .50 Browning as a tank coaxial or cupola-mounted machine-gun. It is recoil-operated, using a bolt carrier and bolt; the movement of the carrier cams locking lugs into recesses in the receiver to lock the bolt. On firing, barrel and bolt recoil into the receiver; an accelerator throws the bolt carrier back, and this movement cams in the locking lugs and then retracts the bolt. Feed is by a disintegrating link belt and, due to the lightness of the recoiling parts, the rate of fire is high. A rate regulator can be switched in to reduce this to a slower rate when desired. The M85 is used by the US Air Force and by other countries.

The M73 was designed as a tank weapon, with the specific aim of producing a gun with a short inboard length and one in which all the necessary immediate actions and maintenance, including barrel changes, could be done from inside the vehicle. Another important design consideration was the necessity of avoiding powder fumes inside the turret. The design is attributed to Russell Robinson, an Australian who had worked in Britain during the post-war years, and it uses a horizontal sliding breech-block instead of the more usual axially moving block. It is this feature which gives the gun its desired shortness of body. Other advantages for tank use include the side-hinging of the top cover, demanding less headroom when opened, and the entire receiver can be swung to one side to allow the barrel to be withdrawn from the jacket. The M73, however, turned out to be prone to jams which were difficult to clear; it went through several modifications during its short life but none appear to have cured the basic trouble and it was redesigned to become the M219; the redesign involved a new rammer, extractor and feed tray and a complete re-timing of the firing cycle to obviate feed jams. In spite of all this the M219 was still not satisfactory and in 1978 it was withdrawn from service. It was replaced by the FN-MAG machine-gun in a special mounting for tanks.

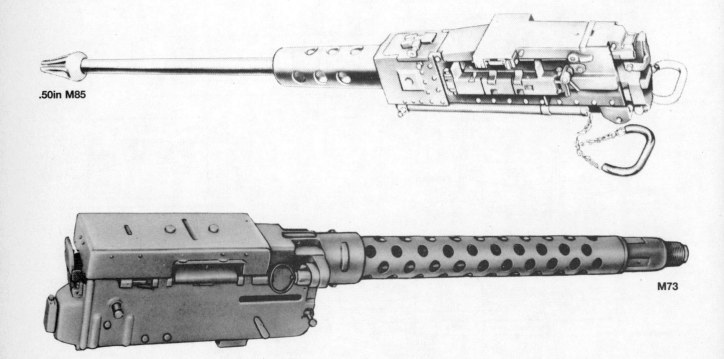

.50in M85

M73

This multiple-barrelled 'Gatling' pattern machine-gun is based on the 20mm Vulcan development and was specifically designed for use in helicopters in Vietnam. Due to its demands for power and ammunition its application is restricted to helicopters or vehicles which provide the necessary space and electrical source. The six barrels are revolved by an electric motor; they are normally parallel but can be clamped into various degrees of convergence as required. The action body, behind the barrels, carries six bolts in a rotating unit; these bolts lock into the barrels by rotation of their heads, controlled by studs moving in a cam groove inside the receiver. The ammunition is belt fed into the action body, the rounds are stripped out and positioned in front of the bolts, and as the bolt unit revolves so each round is chambered. At the uppermost position of the barrel the firing pin is released and the round fired, after which the empty case is extracted and the bolt makes a complete circuit to pick up another round. When the trigger is released the ammunition feed is isolated so that there is no danger of a cook-off during the short time the barrel and bolt assembly is coming to rest.

7.62mm GE Minigun M134

General Electric (USA) Co

7.62 × 51mm NATO

Length overall	800mm (31.50in)
Weight empty	15.90kg (35.0lb)
Barrels	559mm (22.0in), 4 grooves, rh
Feed system	4,000-shot link belt
Rate of fire	6,000rds/min
Muzzle velocity	869m/sec (2,850ft/sec)

This weapon was originally developed by Hughes as an aircraft weapon in 25mm and 30mm calibres and it was later adapted to rifle calibres for use in armoured vehicles. Hughes were absorbed by McDonnell Douglas, who now make the weapon, and it is also made under licence in Britain for the Warrior MICV and the Challenger tank. The Chain Gun derives its name from the use of a conventional roller chain in an endless loop which drives the bolt. The chain is driven by an electric motor and a shoe on the chain engages in the bolt, carries it forward to chamber the round, holds it closed while the round is fired, then retracts it to extract the spent case. Cams rotate the bolt head to lock into the barrel and also to actuate the firing pin. A dynamic brake on the motor ensures that when the trigger is released the bolt stops in the open position, so that there is no danger of cook-off. The belt feed is also driven by the motor, independently of the bolt mechanism but in synchrony with it, so that there is ample power to handle long belts, particularly in a vehicle bounding over rough country. The Chain Gun is particularly well suited to tank installation, since case ejection is forward, under control, and the relatively long bolt closure dwell time reduces the amount of fumes entering the turret. The Hughes chain gun is one of the relatively few new operating principles which have appeared in recent years and it has achieved considerable success.

7.62mm Hughes Chain Gun Ex-34

Hughes Helicopter Co (originally); McDonnell Douglas Helicopter Co. (present); Royal Ordnance Factory, Nottingham

7.62 × 51mm NATO

Length overall	889mm (35.0in)
Weight empty	13.16kg (29.0lb)
Barrel	558mm (22.0in), 4 grooves, rh
Feed system	link belt
Rate of fire	variable from 1 to 600rds/min
Muzzle velocity	870m/sec (2,850ft/sec)

HUGHES CHAIN GUN EX-34

USSR/RUSSIA

7.62mm Maxim M1910

State arsenals	
7.62 × 54R Soviet	
Length overall	1,107mm (43.60in)
Weight empty	23.80kg (52.5lb)
Barrel	721mm (28.4in), 4 grooves, rh
Feed system	250-shot fabric belt
Rate of fire	520–580rds/min
Muzzle velocity	863m/sec (2,830ft/sec)

The first machine-guns adopted by the Russians were Gatlings, some of which stayed in service long enough to be used in the Port Arthur defences during the Russo-Japanese War of 1904–5. The first automatic machine-guns were Maxims supplied by Vickers of Britain, but by 1905 the Russian armaments factories were capable of producing their own weapons and manufacture of a Maxim began at Tula Arsenal, the first model being that of 1905. This had a bronze water jacket. The next model was the M1910, and on this the water jacket reverted to the sheet steel used by every other army, and the opportunity was taken to make a slight alteration to the feed system. A later variant of this model had a fluted water jacket, and the final version had a distinctively large water filling port on top of the jacket to facilitate rapid refilling or topping-up in action. The last version of the M1910 was produced in vast numbers and remained in first-line service with the Soviet Army until replaced by the Goryunov SG43. It can still be seen in the hands of various smaller Asian and African armies and is in second-line and reserve stocks with many others in the Eastern bloc. It is probably the longest-lived of all the Maxim variants.

In the late 1920s the Red Army attempted to lighten and improve the design in the hope of producing a light machine-gun for infantry use, which could be manufactured on the same machinery. There were two trial types, one designed by Tokarev and called the 'Maxim-Tokarev' and one by Kolesnikov, the 'Maxim-Kolesnikov'. Neither was a success and the idea was abandoned as impractical; the guns found their way to Spain and were used up in the Civil War. Eventually Degtyarev produced a light machine-gun design which was adopted in 1928.

Most Soviet Maxims are seen with the 'Sokolov' mounting, a pair of wheels supporting a large turntable (to allow traversing) and a U-shaped trail. Early models had two extra legs which folded underneath when the gun was being moved but could be put to the front for extra stability or to raise the gun well clear of the ground to shoot over high cover. Sometimes a steel shield was fitted, but this was unpopular because of its weight and the marginal protection it offered. For winter warfare there was a sledge adaptation, and all models could be fitted with drag-ropes.

7.62mm Degtyarev DP

State arsenals	
7.62 × 54R Soviet	
Length overall	1,290mm (50.80in)
Weight empty	9.12kg (20.10lb)
Barrel	605mm (23.80in), 4 grooves, rh
Feed system	47-shot drum
Rate of fire	500–600rds/min
Muzzle velocity	840m/sec (2,760ft/sec)

The DP was adopted by the Red Army in 1928 after two years of trials, and it was the first truly original development in Russia. It is extremely simple, yet remarkably reliable and robust. It remained the standard light gun until the 1950s and huge numbers were made, many of which survive today in Eastern Bloc countries and Asia. The secret of the DP was the simple locking system, a modification of the Friberg-Kjellman locking flaps pushed outwards by the forward movement of the firing pin. The DP proved to be resistant to dust and dirt and free from any serious vices. Its weak point was its ammunition, as the long rimmed 7.62mm cartridge was difficult to load into an automatic weapon without jamming. The distinctive flat pan magazine almost overcame this fault, but was itself liable to damage and distortion. The operating spring was housed beneath the barrel in the gas piston tube and tended to lose its tempering when the barrel became hot. The gun was capable of automatic fire only and the bolt remained open between bursts to allow the barrel and chamber to cool.

MAXIM M1910

The DT is a variant of the DP and was designed for the armament of tanks and armoured cars. The stock is of metal and can be telescoped to reduce the inboard length, and there is an added pistol grip for greater control when the stock is not in use. The barrel is a little heavier than that of the DP and cannot be quickly replaced. The drum magazine remained, which is an undesirable feature in an armoured vehicle, but was of smaller diameter and greater depth and held more ammunition in two tiers. The gun was intended to be available as a ground weapon in emergency, and so it had a detachable bipod, carried in the vehicle, and a removable foresight. As with the DP, the return spring gave trouble when overheated. There was also an aircraft version which appeared in two forms, as a single machine-gun and as a twin-coupled gun. The first was designated DA, and the second DA-2.

There were four models in the ShKAS series: KM33, KM35, KM36 and KM41. They began in 1933 and ended in 1941. The gun was designed by Shpitalny and Komaritsky, from whose names the designation is derived; the 'AS' was added to show that the gun was for aircraft and capable of a high rate of fire. It was a complicated and expensive gun, but had the desirable high rate of fire and a good reputation for reliability. It may be that the early guns were all hand-made, and it is distinctly possible that mass production in the accepted sense was never achieved with the ShKAS designs. The gun is gas operated and belt fed, the belt being picked up by a rotating mechanism sometimes called a 'squirrel cage', and the rounds are then taken out and fed to the breech. The same mechanism takes the empty cases and ejects them in two stages forward out of the gun in order to keep the aircraft cockpit clear of spent cases, and the design is unusual in going to such lengths to achieve this. Breech locking was based on the Berthier system of using the gas piston to lift and lower the breech-block into and out of engagement with a recess in the receiver. Numerous variations of the basic guns were made, for fixed or free mountings, and the various numbered models represent modifications due to experience. The ShKAS was permuted into the ShVAK 12.7mm machine-gun and 20mm cannon, but these were little more than scale-ups from the basic ShKAS design. The ShKAS remained in use until the middle 1950s, specimens being captured from North Korean aircraft during the Korean War.

7.62mm Degtyarev DT

State arsenals	
7.62 × 54R Soviet	
Length overall	1,193mm (47.0in)
Weight empty	12.70kg (28.0lb)
Barrel	605mm (23.80in), 4 grooves, rh
Feed system	60-shot drum
Rate of fire	650rds/min
Muzzle velocity	840m/sec (2,750ft/sec)

7.62mm ShKAS

State arsenals	
7.62 × 54R Soviet	
Length overall	935mm (36.80in)
Weight empty	10.66kg (23.5lb)
Barrel	675mm (26.5in), 4 grooves, rh
Feed system	250-shot belt
Rate of fire	1,800rds/min
Muzzle velocity	850m/sec (2,788ft/sec)

DEGTYAREV DP

ShKAS

12.7mm DShK M1938 and DShKM M1938/46

State arsenals	
12.7 × 107mm Soviet	
Length overall	1,586mm (62.50in)
Weight empty	35.50kg (78.5lb)
Barrel	1,066mm (42.0in), 4 grooves, rh
Feed system	50-shot belt
Rate of fire	550rds/min
Muzzle velocity	860m/sec (2,825ft/sec)

7.62mm Goryunov SG43

State arsenals	
7.62 × 54R Soviet	
Length overall	1,120mm (44.10in)
Weight empty	13.60kg (29.98lb)
Barrel	719mm (28.30in), 4 grooves, rh
Feed system	250-shot belt
Rate of fire	650rds/min
Muzzle velocity	850m/sec (2,788ft/sec)

The DShK heavy machine-gun originated in 1938 as a design by Degtyarev and Shpagin, using Degtyarev's gas operation and flap locking system and Shpagin's rotating feed. It was the standard Soviet heavy gun throughout World War Two and was also widely used by the Communists forces during the Korean War, particularly as an anti-aircraft weapon. It is still in service with Warsaw Pact armies, though in a modified form, and can be found all over the world in places where Communist weapons have been supplied. The rotating feed system, although effective, appears to have been considered rather too complicated to manufacture and immediately after the war there was a redesign, simplifying the feed mechanism to a lever system which extracts the round from the belt and positions it in front of the bolt; this version became the DShKM and began entering service in 1946; it entirely replaced the DShK in Warsaw Pact armies but the earlier weapon can still be found elsewhere. The guns were provided with a wheeled mount which converted to an anti-aircraft tripod mount or a ground mount. The performance is comparable to that of the .50 Browning and the gun is carried on almost all Soviet armoured vehicles, particularly as air defence weapons. In the 1980s they began to be replaced on new production vehicles with the NSK (below) but the DShKM will be around for many years to come.

The Goryunov was developed during World War Two as a replacement for the Maxim M1910. An earlier replacement, the DS of 1939, designed by Degtyarev, had failed to meet specifications, and by 1942 a modern medium machine-gun, capable of easy manufacture, was desperately needed. Goryunov adopted some of the features of the failed DS gun in order to save himself time, but the locking system was radically changed. A tilting breech-block is used, similar to that of the Bren and other designs, but moving sideways instead of vertically and locking into the side of the receiver. The feed is not simple, since the gun uses the old rimmed cartridge and thus the round has to be withdrawn from the belt backwards before being chambered forwards. The reciprocation is obtained by using two claws to pull the round from the belt, after which an arm pushes the round into the cartridge guide ready for the bolt to carry it forward into the breech; despite this complication the Goryunov is remarkably reliable and feed jams are apparently uncommon. The barrel is air-cooled and massive in construction, thereby contributing to the fairly high overall weight, but the thickness does absorb and dissipate heat efficiently. The bore is chromium-plated and capable of standing continuous fire for quite long periods, though the barrel can be easily changed by releasing a simple barrel lock and lifting the hot barrel out by its handle. The wartime version of the gun had a smooth barrel, and the cocking handle was beneath the receiver. In post-war years minor variants were developed; the basic gun became the SGM, with a fluted barrel and cocking handle on the side of the receiver. The SGMT was the tank version, with a solenoid firing trigger; and the SGMB was similar to the SGM but fitted with dust covers over the feed and ejection ports.

It should be noted that several Communist countries have manufactured their own versions of the SG43 series; most are virtually identical, but the Hungarian version has a pistol grip, a butt and a bipod. (Data table refers to the SGM.)

DShK M1938

GORYUNOV SG43

The Degtyarev DP was not without certain faults; the return spring weakened from the heat of the barrel and the bipod legs broke or bent from heavy handling. Hard use during the German invasion of Russia in 1941 turned these minor defects into major problems and a modified gun was developed. This was the DPM, the 'M' indicating 'Modernised', and delivery to the troops began early in 1945. The return spring was moved to behind the bolt and protruded over the small of the butt in a cylindrical housing, where it prevented the gunner grasping the gun in the usual way and so induced the fitting of a pistol grip. The bipod was replaced by a stronger version attached to the barrel casing. This raised the roll centre of the gun and made it easier to hold upright. The grip safety device was replaced by a conventional safety catch, but apart from these changes the basic gun remained the same. The DPM appears to have been popular with the troops and was said to be more accurate and easier to hold and shoot than the original 1928 design.

7.62mm Degtyarev DPM

State arsenals	
7.62 × 54R Soviet	
Length overall	1,265mm (49.8in)
Weight empty	12.20kg (26.89lb)
Barrel	605mm (23.80in), 4 grooves, rh
Feed system	47-shot drum
Rate of fire	520–580rds/min
Muzzle velocity	845m/sec (2,772ft/sec)

The DTM is simply the tank version of the DPM and the same conversions were applied to it. Apart from the position of the return spring it is almost exactly the same gun as the original DT of 1929 and it used the same 60-shot drum magazine.

7.62mm Degtyarev DTM

State arsenals	
7.62 × 54R Soviet	

The RP46 is a second modernisation of the DP, intended for use as a company-level sustained fire support weapon. It is capable of delivering a high volume of fire but is not so portable as the original DP and DPM guns. It has a heavier barrel and a belt feed system. There is also a carrying handle, which was conspicuously absent from the earlier designs, and an improved barrel change. In addition to the belt feed it is still possible to fit the 47-round drum of the DPM if required. The gun seems to have failed to live up to expectations and was fairly quickly replaced in first-line service in Warsaw Pact armies and is relatively uncommon in other Communist-aligned countries.

7.62mm RP46

State arsenals	
7.62 × 54R Soviet	
Length overall	1,270mm (50.0in)
Weight empty	13.0kg (28.75lb)
Barrel	605mm (23.80in), 4 grooves, rh
Feed system	50-shot belt or 47-shot drum
Rate of fire	650rds/min
Muzzle velocity	840m/sec (2,755ft/sec)

DEGTYAREV DTM

RP46

7.62mm RPD

State arsenals	
7.62 × 39mm M1943	
Length overall	1,041mm (41.0in)
Weight empty	7.0kg (15.43lb)
Barrel	520mm (20.5in), 4 grooves, rh
Feed system	100-shot belt
Rate of fire	700rds/min
Muzzle velocity	735m/sec (2,410ft/sec)

This appeared in 1953 and the 'D' in the title indicates a design by Degtyarev, his last design as it turned out, since the Kalashnikov family of weapons has dominated Soviet infantry arms since the middle 1950s. It is the logical development of the DP and DPM and was progressively improved during its life. The original model used a cup-type piston head, had a straight cocking handle which oscillated back and forth during firing, and was without a dust cover. The piston was then modified to the more usual plunger pattern and the dust cover added, and then came a change in the cocking handle to a folding type which remained still as the gun fired. The fourth modification had a longer gas cylinder, and a recoil buffer incorporated in the butt, measures intended to improve stability which has always been a problem with this somewhat light weapon, and also to try and improve the reserve of power available to lift the feed belt. The final version was very slightly changed, having a combined magazine bracket/dust cover and a sectional cleaning rod housed inside the butt.

The RPD fires the M1943 intermediate cartridge and is belt fed from a drum container clipped beneath the gun at the centre of gravity. The mechanism therefore has to lift the belt up to the breech, and there is evidence that the power available to do that is barely sufficient even after the fourth modification, giving rise to malfunctions under adverse conditions. The replaceable barrel of the DP was abandoned in this design, and it became a matter of drill and training for the gunner to avoid firing more than 100 rounds in one minute to prevent overheating of the barrel. The remainder of the mechanism is similar to the DP, merely scaled-down to suit the smaller ammunition, and, like most Soviet machine-guns, it is capable of only automatic fire.

12.7mm NSV

State arsenals	
12.7 × 107mm Soviet	
Length overall	1,560mm (61.42in)
Weight empty	25.0kg (55.11lb)
Barrel	Not known
Feed system	disintegrating link belt
Rate of fire	700–800rds/min
Muzzle velocity	845m/sec (2,770ft/sec)

This weapon was developed from 1969 onwards by Nikitin, Sokolov and Volkov. As a ground gun it is known as the 'NSV-12,7' and is fired from a tripod. It has a skeleton shoulder-stock which probably folds, a pistol grip, optical and iron sights. When used on armoured vehicles it is known as the 'NSVT-12,7' and the pistol grip is replaced by a solenoid-controlled firing unit. The gun is gas operated, using a rotating bolt, and is belt-fed from the right side. The barrel is interchangeable and it is recommended that it be changed after every 1,000 rounds. The gun is also manufactured under licence in Yugoslavia.

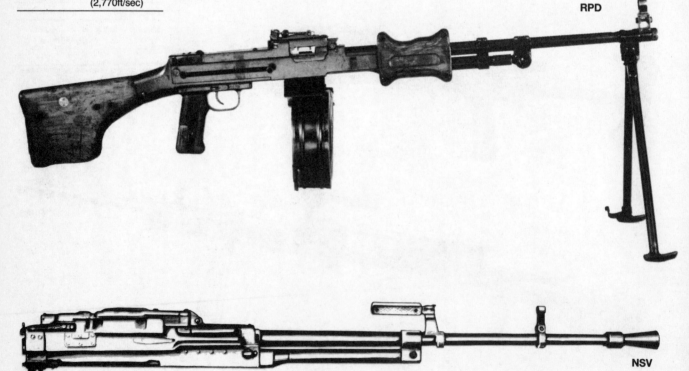

RPD

NSV

The KPV is an anti-aircraft machine-gun of advanced design which entered service in the 1950s. It has appeared on a number of wheeled mountings in single (ZPU-1), twin (ZPU-2) and quadruple (ZPU-4) form. It has also been mounted in Soviet armoured personnel carriers and some other vehicles. It is widely distributed through the Warsaw Pact armies and the anti-aircraft mounts will be found with several African and Far Eastern forces. The KPV is unusual among Soviet machine-guns in operating by recoil and the bolt is locked by rotation, to engage two projections on the outer surface of the breech. The chromium-lined barrel can be quickly and easily changed, and the number of parts in the mechanism is small. The ammunition was originally developed for use in wartime anti-tank rifles and is exceptionally powerful, with good penetrative capabilities.

14.5mm KPV

State arsenals

14.5 × 114mm Soviet	
Length overall	2,002mm (78.80in)
Weight empty	48.97kg (107.95lb)
Barrel	1,349mm (53.10in), 8 grooves, rh
Feed system	100-shot belt
Rate of fire	600rds/min
Muzzle velocity	988m/sec (3,250ft/sec)

The RPK entered service in the early 1960s and replaced the RPD as the standard light gun of the Soviet infantry squad. It can really be thought of as an enlarged Kalashnikov AK rifle, since it uses the same action and many of the same parts and spares in its manufacture. The gun accepts the magazine of the AK as well as its own. Like the RPD the barrel is fixed, so that the tactical use is to some extent restricted, but since the rest of the squad carry AK rifles capable of automatic fire the restriction is not serious, since the overall volume of fire is high. The finish on the RPK is good, and, like the AK, the bolt and bore are chromium-plated to reduce wear.

7.62mm RPK, RPKS

State arsenals

7.62 × 39mm M1943	
Length overall	1,041mm (41.0in)
Weight empty	4.76kg (10.5lb)
Barrel	589mm (23.20in), 4 grooves, rh
Feed system	30- or 40-shot box or 75-shot drum
Rate of fire	600rds/min
Muzzle velocity	732m/sec (2,400ft/sec)

RPK

KPV

YUGOSLAVIA

During World War Two and afterwards the Yugoslav Army acquired numbers of German MG42 machine-guns. They were so satisfied with them that when they began to wear out they simply copied them, calling the result the M53, and have continued to use them ever since. As with the German weapon, the M53 can be used on a bipod as the squad automatic or on a tripod as a sustained-fire weapon. Over the years some small changes have crept in, probably better to suit the design to manufacture in Yugoslavia, and therefore the dimensions differ somewhat from the original.

7.92mm Model M53

Zavodi Crvena Zastava	
7.92 × 57mm Mauser	
Length overall	1,210mm (47.64in)
Weight empty	11.5kg (25.35lb)
Barrel	560mm (22.04in), 4 grooves, rh
Feed system	50-shot drum or 50-shot continuous belt
Rate of fire	800–1,050rds/min
Muzzle velocity	715m/sec (2,345ft/sec)

The Models 64A and 64B were the Yugoslav standard light guns which introduced the 7.62 × 39mm cartridge and they were the equivalents of the Soviet RPD and RPK weapons. Both were designed to use as many parts as possible of the Yugoslav M64 assault rifles, assuring uncomplicated production. Both were fitted with light bipods and heavier barrels than the assault rifles, though, since the barrels were non-changeable the utility of this was questionable. The barrels were finned as far as the gas port in order to dissipate heat but, as is usual with finned barrels, they tended to trap dirt and oil and generate a heat haze in the sight line once the barrels got hot. Both weapons have now been replaced in first-line service by the M72 (below) but are probably retained in reserve stocks. (Data table refers to the M64A.)

7.62mm Model 64A, 65B

Zavodi Crvena Zastva	
7.62 × 39mm Soviet	
Length overall	1,095mm (43.11in)
Weight empty	5.5kg (12.12lb)
Barrel	470mm (18.5in), 4 grooves, rh
Feed system	30-shot detachable box
Rate of fire	600rds/min
Muzzle velocity	745m/sec (2,445ft/sec)

M53

7.62mm Model M72B1, M72AB1

Zavodi Crvena Zastava	
7.62 × 39mm Soviet	
Length overall	1,025mm (40.35in)
Weight empty	5.0kg (11.02lb)
Barrel	540mm (21.25in), 4 grooves, rh
Feed system	30-shot box or 75-shot drum
Rate of fire	600rds/min
Muzzle velocity	745m/sec (2,444ft/sec)

7.62mm Model M77B1

Zavodi Crvena Zastava	
7.62 × 51mm NATO	
Length overall	1,025mm (40.35in)
Weight empty	5.1kg (11.24lb)
Barrel	535mm (21.06in), 6 grooves, rh
Feed system	20-shot detachable box
Rate of fire	600rds/min
Muzzle velocity	840m/sec (2,756ft/sec)

These have replaced the M64 series as the standard squad light machine-guns in the Yugoslav Army and form part of the FAZ family of weapons which are based on the M70B1 rifle. Broadly, the M70B1 is an AKM clone, and thus the M72 machine-guns are simply heavy-barrelled rifles. The two models differ only in the butt; the M72B1 has a fixed wooden butt, while the M72AB1 has a folding metal butt which swings down and lies beneath the receiver when folded. The normal feed is from the standard rifle-type box magazine but there is also a 75-round drum which will fit into the magazine housing and is probably a more practical system for normal use. There is, of course, no provision for changing the barrel.

This has been developed for export and is simply the M72B1 light machine-gun (above) in NATO calibre. The only significant difference is that it feeds from a straight 20-round box magazine instead of the usual curved Kalashnikov pattern.

M72AB1

M77

These have been developed as part of the 5.56mm family, the other members of which are the M80 and M80A rifles. Since 5.56mm is not a standard Yugoslav calibre it is apparent that they have been developed for export sales, though there is no information about where they may have been sold. In appearance they are simply variants of the M72 machine-gun described above, with a change of calibre, though the manufacturers claim that they are equipped with a new type of gas regulator which ensures a constant action even though ammunition of varying energy levels may be used. The M82 has a fixed wooden butt, the M82A has the folding metal butt described for the M72AB1.

This is the Yugoslav Army's general-purpose machine-gun, introduced in 1985. It is a gas-operated, rotating-bolt weapon chambered for the powerful 7.62mm rimmed cartridge and appears to be a slight modification of the Soviet PKM machine-gun. It is provided with a bipod and feeds from a belt box clipped beneath the receiver. It can also be used with a tripod for sustained fire and is claimed to have an effective range of up to 1,000m against ground or air targets.

5.56mm Model M82, M82A

Zavodi Crvena Zastava

5.56 × 45mm

Length overall	1,020mm (40.15in)
Weight empty	4.0kg (8.82lb)
Barrel	542mm (21.34in), 6 grooves, rh
Feed system	30-shot detachable box
Rate of fire	650–rds/min
Muzzle velocity	1,000m/sec (3,280ft/sec)

7.62mm Model M84

Zavodi Crvena Zastava

7.62 × 54R Soviet

Length overall	1,175mm (46.26in)
Weight empty	10.0kg (22.04lb)
Barrel	658mm (25.9in), 4 grooves, rh
Feed system	100- or 250-shot belt
Rate of fire	700rds/min
Muzzle velocity	825m/sec (2,706ft/sec)

M82

M84

Anti-tank Rifles

FINLAND

20mm Lahti Model 39

State arsenals	
20 × 138B Long Solothurn	
Length overall	2,232mm (87.75in)
Weight empty	42.19kg (93.0lb)
Barrel	1,393mm (54.84in), 12 grooves, rh
Magazine	10-shot vertical box
Muzzle velocity	900m/sec (2,952ft/sec)
Armour penetration	20mm/250m/0°

The Lahti anti-tank rifle was derived directly from the Lahti aircraft cannon of 1937, and as little modification as possible was done to develop the ground weapon. A pistol grip and trigger mechanism were provided, a muzzle brake, a shoulder pad, sights and a dual-purpose bipod. The chambering was changed for a more powerful cartridge. A rack-and-pinion cocking handle was fitted on the outside of the receiver and a wooden sleeve was put on the fore-end of the barrel. Most of the weapons were single shot, but some were made to give automatic fire only. The only buffering provided was in the shoulder pad, and the effect on the gunner of firing a burst must have been traumatic. The bipod always attracts interest since it was the only one ever to have been provided with alternative feet. One set is the usual spiked variety for use in firm ground; the other set has short plywood skis for use in snow and mud. The legs of the bipod contain small spring dampers to balance the muzzle-heavy gun. It seems that few of these guns were ready in time for the 1939–40 Winter War, and there are no records of their performance. Production started again after the war and continued from 1941 to 1944, a total of 1,906 weapons being made. By 1944 it was realised that the weapon was no longer efficient against tanks and many were converted to full automatic fire and use as light anti-aircraft guns. Most were scrapped in the late 1940s except for a handful which were sent to the USA for sale to collectors.

GERMANY

13mm Mauser Tank-Gewehr M1918

Waffenfabrik Mauser AG	
13 × 92SR Mauser	
Length overall	1,680mm (66.13in)
Weight empty	17.69kg (39.0lb)
Barrel	983mm (38.69in), 4 grooves, rh

This, the first anti-tank rifle ever introduced, was developed by Mauser; it was little more than an enlarged Mauser bolt-action rifle action fitted to a long barrel with a heavy butt and furniture. Supported on a light bipod, it was a one-man weapon firing a 13mm jacketed bullet with an armour-piercing steel core. While the Allied tanks of the time were immune to rifle bullets, they were certainly vulnerable to this missile, delivered at a very high velocity. The Mauser was to set the pattern for almost everything which followed.

Magazine	None; single-shot
Muzzle velocity	913m/sec (3,000ft/sec)
Armour penetration	25mm/200m/0°

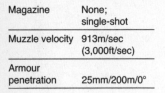

LAHTI MODEL 39

MAUSER TANK-GEWEHR M1918

The SS41 is something of a mystery weapon; very few survived World War Two and it seems highly likely that only a limited number were ever made. There is little written record of them and the design is unusual and intriguing. The SS41 is a single-shot 'bullpup' which fired the standard German anti-tank rifle round, a 7.92mm armour-piercing bullet in a necked-down 13mm case. The magazine fits behind the pistol grip, and this grip is attached to a long sleeve which forms the breech and chamber. The sleeve slides on the barrel, and when at its rearmost position is locked to the barrel by lugs. At the same time it also locks to the face of the breech by lugs. The breech face is on the front surface of the shoulder rest. Thus the barrel and breech remain stationary at all times and the chamber slides back and forwards to open and close the breech.

The sequence of operations is as follows: after firing, the pistol-grip is rotated to the right, unlocking it from the barrel and breech, and pushed briskly forward. It slides up the barrel, carrying the sleeve with it, leaving the empty case attached to the breech face by the extractor. As the sleeve reaches the end of its stroke an ejector knocks the empty case out of the feedway and a fresh round feeds up from the magazine, to be held by the magazine lips. The pistol grip is then pulled back, drawing the chamber over the fresh round and closing the breech; turning the pistol grip back to the vertical locks the breech, cocks the action, and the rifle is ready to fire. This complicated and unusual action was obviously adopted to save weight and reduce the inordinate length normally associated with anti-tank rifles, but its manufacture must have been difficult. Furthermore the sleeve slides forward on the unprotected outer surface of the barrel, so that it would be highly vulnerable to dust and dirt. Finally, the 7.92mm bullet was known to be ineffective by 1939, so its introduction at this late date was an anachronism. The magazine fed into the left side at an angle of 45°, thereby keeping it clear of the firer's wrist and hand. A light Bren (or CZ) bipod was pinned to the long, unsupported barrel, and a small muzzle brake was fitted to the muzzle. The well-padded stock had a small shoulder-strap.

It is of interest that a German report dated 1943 speaks of a 15mm PzB41 developed by the Brno factory; the brief description given is very similar to this weapon, the dimensions are, of course, greater, but nothing further is known. It was probably an attempt to produce a heavier rifle, perhaps based on the 15mm machine-gun cartridge, using the same operating system but by that time the futility of anti-tank rifles was recognised and the project was probably abandoned.

The PzB38 was a considerable improvement over the Mauser 1918 rifle, giving greater velocity and penetrative effect by combining a 7.92mm bullet with a 13mm cartridge based on the Mauser design. The bullet contained a core of armour-piercing steel together with a capsule of lachrymatory gas which (it was hoped) would contaminate the air inside the tank and either disrupt the crew's effectiveness or force them to leave the tank. It was entirely useless in this respect; the bullet had a satisfactory penetrative capability but none of the victims ever complained of sneezing and the lachrymatory capsule was not discovered until captured ammunition was examined. The PzB38 was a single-shot rifle using a vertical sliding-wedge breech-block, almost a scaled-down artillery piece in its operation. On firing the barrel recoiled in the stock, and on return a cam opened the breech and ejected the spent case, the block then remaining open for reloading. The block was held, by the extractors, against a spring and as a new round was inserted and forced the extractor forward, so the block automatically closed, leaving the firing mechanism cocked. During the Polish campaign of 1939 the Germans captured numbers of the Polish anti-tank rifle and stocks of ammunition. This was also of 7.92mm calibre but the bullet carried a tungsten core of much better penetrative power than the German bullet; the Polish design was soon copied.

7.92mm SS41

Waffenwerk Brunn (Zbrojowka Brno)	
7.92 × 94mm	
Length overall	1,195mm (47.05in)
Weight empty	18.14kg (40.0lb)
Barrel	840mm (33.07in)
Magazine	10-shot detachable box
Muzzle velocity	1,219m/sec (4,000ft/sec)
Armour penetration	Not known

7.92mm PzB38

Rheinmetall-Borsig AG	
7.92 × 94mm	
Length overall	1,295mm (51.0in)
Weight empty	15.88kg (35.0lb)
Barrel	1,092mm (43.0in), 4 grooves, rh
Magazine	None; single-shot
Muzzle velocity	1,210m/sec (3,970ft/sec)
Armour penetration	30mm/100m/30°

PzB38

7.92mm PzB39

Rheinmetall-Borsig AG; Steyr-Daimler-Puch AG	
7.92 × 94mm	
Length overall	1,581mm (62.25in)
Weight empty	12.35kg (27.25lb)
Barrel	1,086mm (42.75in), 4 grooves, rh
Magazine	None; single-shot
Muzzle velocity	1,265m/sec (4,150ft/sec)
Armour penetration	30mm/100m/30°

While the PzB was an effective weapon it was also expensive and slow to manufacture and it was replaced by a simpler design, the PzB39. While of the same general appearance the mechanism was changed by discarding the recoiling barrel and semi-automatic breech mechanism and, instead, operating the vertical block manually by the pistol grip, which swung down below the receiver to open the breech and cock the action. Some small modifications were also made in the interest of simplifying manufacture. The principal difference to the user was that since the barrel no longer recoiled in the stock and absorbed some of the recoil, it was a more punishing weapon to fire.

20mm PzB41

Rheinmetall-Borsig AG	
20 × 138B Long Solothurn	
Length overall	2,108mm (83.0in)
Weight empty	44kg (97.0lb)
Barrel	1,360mm (53.54in), 8 grooves, rh
Magazine	5- or 10-shot box
Muzzle velocity	900m/sec (2,952ft/sec)
Armour penetration	30mm/250m/0°

The origins of this enormous rifle lie in a design for a ground-strafing aircraft cannon of 1918. The drawings lay in Holland and Switzerland until resurrected in the 1930s and modernised. From this sprang the idea for a semi-automatic anti-tank rifle, and the automatic principle was altered by the two Solothurn designers, Herlach and Rakale. As early as 1938, just as the PzB38 was coming into service, it was realised that it could have an effective life of only a year or two before the improvement in tanks outdistanced it, and a design for a successor was suggested. A very general specification was issued and it was taken up by Rheinmetall, who then passed it to Herlach and Rakale to refine. The resulting rifle was a derivative of an existing Solothurn design which had originated in 1930 and had been sold as the S-18/100 (see below under Switzerland). There is some evidence to show that Solothurn were inspired to begin development of anti-tank rifles by Rheinmetall, who owned the major part of the company at that time.

The PzB41 was one of the largest anti-tank rifles ever made, and certainly the most complicated. Operation was by recoil, the bolt being locked to the barrel extension by a locking collar, the Stange system; the locking ring carried interrupted lugs which engaged with similar lugs on the bolt, and as the unit recoiled so a post on the ring travelled in a cam groove in the receiver and partly rotated the ring until the lugs were out of engagement, after which the bolt could move back under its own momentum as the barrel came to a stop. Initial cocking was done by winding back the recoiling parts by rotating a crank on the right side of the receiver, turning a sprocket to pull on a chain attached to the barrel assembly. Once cocked, the system recocked after each shot. The recoil must have been considerable, and to minimise it, a highly efficient muzzle brake was fitted. A rear monopod also took some of the shock.

The magazine fed from the left, to reduce the overall height of the weapon. A very few PzB41s were tried on the Eastern Front and were immediately discarded since they had no effect on the Soviet T34 tank. The Italian Army took delivery of a quantity and used them in the 1943 campaign, and it was from here that the few existing specimens were captured. Like most anti-tank rifles, the PzB41 was enormously expensive to make and ineffective in use.

PzB39

PzB41

GREAT BRITAIN

This weapon was developed in the mid-1930s by the British Small Arms Committee and one of the principal designers was Captain Boys. The gun was originally code-named 'Stanchion', but Boys died after the development had been completed and while the gun was being prepared for production; as a mark of respect, the Small Arms Committee decided that the weapon should be named after him. The Boys rifle was an enlarged bolt-action weapon feeding from a top-mounted magazine and equipped with a muzzle brake and a monopod firing support. The barrel was permitted to recoil in the stock and the butt was heavily padded, both measures to reduce the powerful recoil impulse. The bullet was steel-cored and was carried in a belted cartridge case. In 1940 a tungsten-cored bullet in a plastic and alloy body was approved and issued, but shortly afterwards the Boys was withdrawn and replaced by the PIAT projector. In 1942 the gun had a brief return to popularity when a short-barrelled Mark 2 version was approved for use by airborne troops, but it was eventually admitted that the weapon stood no chance against tanks by that time and the requirement was dropped. Another attempt to revive it, also in 1942, was the development of a taper-bore version; this was a success in trials, so far as its penetrative performance went, but it was singularly unpleasant to fire (as was the airborne model) and it was not accepted for service. (Data table refers to Mark 1.)

.55in Boys Marks 1 and 2

Royal Small Arms Factory, Enfield Lock	
.55in Boys	
Length overall	1,614mm (63.50in)
Weight empty	16.32kg (36.0lb)
Barrel	915mm (36.0in), 7 grooves, rh
Magazine	5-shot detachable box
Muzzle velocity	990m/sec (3,250ft/sec)
Armour penetration	21mm/300m/0°

JAPAN

The Type 97 was the apotheosis of the anti-tank rifle. It was a gas-operated, fully automatic 20mm weapon, sometimes referred to as an anti-tank machine-gun. It was by far the heaviest of its breed and probably the most unpleasant to fire. It fired from a closed bolt, the bolt being unlocked by a gas piston and the remaining movement of the bolt being due to simple blowback forces. This system made no allowance for absorbing recoil, so the entire barrel and receiver recoiled along a slide in the stock for about 150mm. Even so, this must have been more than the average lightly built Japanese soldier could manage, and the weapon was given a rear monopod support under the butt which was inclined rearwards and had to be dug into the ground. This absorbed a large amount of recoil, but it meant that the rifle could not be easily swung to engage crossing targets, since it had to be firmly dug in on one line. In the hands of a large and determined man the accuracy was quite good for the first shot, but any attempt at burst fire resulted in the bipod moving off the aiming line. The Type 97 was far heavier than any other anti-tank rifle and needed a four-man crew to manhandle it. Two carrying handles were provided, which looked like oversized bicycle handlebars and plugged into the bipod and monopod. With one man on each handle the crew could then move it fairly easily. There was also a shield provided, but this was rarely used as it was merely excess weight. A muzzle brake was fitted, another step to reduce the recoil blow. The ammunition came in two types, a solid armour-piercing shot and a high-explosive shell, and was also used by a Japanese Navy aircraft gun. A small number of Type 97s were used in the Pacific theatre, where they had some slight success against light armour used by the US Marines, and some are said to have been used in China in 1939–40. Apart from these actions, the gun saw little service.

20mm Model 97

State arsenals	
20 × 124mm Type 97	
Length overall	2,035mm (80.12in)
Weight empty	68.95kg (152lb)
Barrel	1,195mm (47.0in),
Magazine	7-shot detachable box
Muzzle velocity	765m/sec (2,510ft/sec)
Armour penetration	Not known

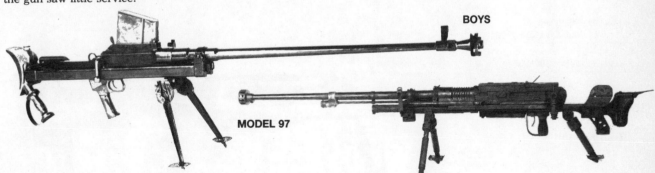

BOYS

MODEL 97

POLAND

7.92mm Marosczek wz35

Fabryka Karabinow Warsaw	
7.92 × 107mm	
Length overall	1,760mm (69.30in)
Weight empty	9.10kg (20.06lb)
Barrel	1,200mm (47.24in), 4 grooves, rh
Magazine	10-shot detachable box
Muzzle velocity	1,280m/sec (4,200ft/sec)
Armour penetration	20mm/300m/0°

Towards the end of 1935 the Polish Army began taking delivery of this anti-tank rifle. It was of conventional bolt-action pattern resembling the Mauser of 1918, but stripped of every unnecessary ounce to provide the lightest weapon of the class ever made. The tungsten-cored bullet was fired from an oversized case, and it has been claimed that it was examination of this ammunition which led the Germans and Russians to develop tungsten bullets for their own rifles. It was certainly responsible for a British development in which a tungsten-cored .303 bullet was married to a necked-down .55 Boys case for a modified Boys rifle. Loaded from five-round chargers, and with a muzzle brake to cut down the recoil, it was ahead of the field for ease of handling and, owing to the cored bullet, had a slight supremacy in penetrative power. Unfortunately, such virtue had to be paid for somehow, and in this case it was a barrel life of only about 200 rounds, after which the muzzle velocity and penetration figures began to fall rapidly.

In 1939 work began on a coned-bore weapon on the Gerlich principle, using a bullet having a tungsten core surrounded by a soft lead jacket and a cupro-nickel envelope, formed with a raised band around the centre. The breech calibre was 11mm and the emergent calibre 7.92mm, the squeeze action of the bore deforming the raised portion of the bullet and reducing the diameter. This gave a velocity of almost 1,545m/sec (5,000ft/sec) and almost doubled the penetration. When Poland was overrun the rifle and drawings were smuggled to France, where development continued. At the time of the French collapse in 1940 the weapon was undergoing its final tests at Satory and had been scheduled to go into production later in the year. In the confusion following the German advance the rifle was lost; neither it nor the drawings have ever been seen since and no specimen is known to exist.

SWITZERLAND

20mm Solothurn S-18/100

Waffenfabrik Solothurn AG	
20 × 105B Short Solothurn AG	
Length overall	1,760mm (69.24in)
Weight empty	45.0kg (99.21lb)
Barrel	900mm (35.43in),
Magazine	5- or 10-shot detachable box

The Solothurn company began work on anti-tank rifles in the early 1930s, their design being derived from an Erhardt 20mm cannon of World War One. In 1934 the S-18/100 appeared and was adopted by Italy, Hungary and Switzerland in small numbers. The gun was recoil-operated to provide semi-automatic fire and had a well-padded shoulder stock above a rear monopod, a combination which helped to absorb much of the recoil. It fired a base-fuzed piercing shell which gave quite effective results for the period, and it was one of the more powerful pre-war anti-tank weapons. Solothurn then developed a more powerful cartridge and a heavier weapon; this became the S-18/1000 and is dealt with in these pages under its German nomenclature, the PzB41.

MAROSCZEK WZ35

Muzzle velocity	762m/sec (2,500ft/sec)
Armour penetration	27mm/300m/0°

SOLOTHURN S-18/100

USSR

This rifle, which appeared in 1941, was designed by Degtyarev and fired a heavy 14.5mm bullet from a massive cartridge case which was the heaviest 'small arms' round in service for many years; after becoming redundant in its anti-tank role it has survived as a heavy machine-gun round for the KPV machine-gun. The rifle itself, while appearing simple, was actually a very ingenious design and probably owed something to the German PzB38. The barrel was allowed to recoil in the stock, and during this movement the bolt rode on a cam which rotated and unlocked it. At the end of the recoil stroke the bolt was held and the barrel moved back into battery, moving away from the bolt to open the breech and eject the spent case. A fresh round was then inserted and the bolt closed by hand; in some respects this could perhaps be called a 'long recoil' system.

The bullet was originally a steel-cored, streamlined, armour-piercing type but it was eventually replaced by a non-streamlined tungsten-cored armour-piercing-incendiary type.

This design of Simonov's was a contemporary of the PTRD and it fired the same ammunition, although the weapon was a more complex self-loading design. A gas piston acted on a bolt carrier to open the bolt, eject the spent case, and re-load in the usual manner, and the gas regulator could be adjusted to give sufficient power to overcome dirt or freezing conditions. Moreover, the moving parts probably absorbed some of the recoil and made the PTRS more pleasant to fire than the PTRD. Despite its theoretical superiority the PTRS was less robust, much heavier and considerably longer than the PTRD, and few of them were issued. Both rifles remained in Soviet service to the end of World War Two, long after they had been abandoned by other nations, probably because no suitable replacement was forthcoming.

14.5mm PTRD

State arsenals	
14.5 × 114mm Soviet	
Length overall	2,000mm (78.70in)
Weight empty	17.30kg (38.14lb)
Barrel	1,227mm (48.3in), 8 grooves, rh
Magazine	None; single-shot
Muzzle velocity	1,010m/sec (3,320ft/sec)
Armour penetration	25mm/500m/0°

14.5mm PTRS

State arsenals	
14.5 × 114mm Soviet	
Length overall	2,134mm (84.0in)
Weight empty	20.86kg (45.98lb)
Barrel	1,220mm (48.03in), 8 grooves, rh
Magazine	5-shot clip-loaded box
Muzzle velocity	1,010m/sec (3,315ft/sec)
Armour penetration	25mm/500m/0°

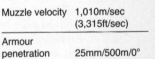

PTRD

PTRS

Ammunition

By the start of the 20th century smokeless powder and the jacketed bullet had become the standard military rifle ammunition components; lead bullets survived only in revolver ammunition and black powder survived only in the cartridges for obsolescent weapons. All the ammunition of the period was more or less the same in concept, if not in calibre and appearance; rifle ammunition was powerful and designed to retain its accuracy and lethality to ranges well in excess of 1,000 yards, while pistol ammunition was generally of low velocity, firing a heavy bullet with ample stopping power. There were exceptions to this generalisation, but they were few and, for the most part, regarded with suspicion by the military establishment.

The first major improvement was the adoption of pointed bullets for rifle ammunition. In fact the French were the pioneers in this, as in so many other fields, though nobody seems to have taken very much notice. The French introduced their 'Balle D' bullet (named for the inventor, Captain Desaleux) in 1898; this was a pointed and boat-tailed bullet, lathe-turned from 90/100 brass which, like most French innovations, was kept a military secret for some years. The general acceptance of pointed bullets came in 1905 when the Germans introduced the 'Spitzer' bullet for the 7.92mm Mauser, the shape having been determined from the study of spark photographs of bullets in flight which allowed the air flow over the bullet to be seen for the first time. The German lead was rapidly followed by other countries, as with the USA in 1906 and Britain in 1911, though a surprising number of countries ignored it and continued to use round-nosed rifle bullets for many years, largely because of the belief that they had a better knock-down power than did a pointed bullet.

During World War One the increased use of medium machine-guns at long ranges led to the discovery that much of their fire was wasted, since the bullets did not fall where they were intended when the range was in excess of 2,000 metres or so. Further research revealed that the shape of the bullet had considerable bearing upon long-range performance. A pointed bullet with square-cut base – which was the norm, in the wake of the German Spitzer – was satisfactory at short ranges, less so at long ranges. The reason was that at short ranges it was supersonic, and in that speed range head shape was important; the sharper the point, the more the Mach wave was bent back and there was less drag on the bullet. But once velocity fell into the subsonic region, as it did at long ranges as the drag gradually whittled down the velocity, the nose compression wave vanished and base drag suddenly became the dominating factor, upsetting accuracy and reducing the maximum range below the value arrived at by theoretical calculations based on supersonic performance. To counter this the 'boat-tailed' or 'streamlined' bullet was developed, in which the rear portion of the bullet had its diameter decreased in a taper so that the air flowing over the bullet merged behind it with less turbulence, and this increased the regularity and maximum range to a remarkable degree; in the case of the American .30-06 bullet, for example, boat-tailing lifted the maximum range from 3,500 to 5,000 yards.

This type of bullet was developed during the 1920s and was generally in service before World War Two. But most countries that developed boat-tailed bullets found that the shape gave rise to gas swirl and to heavy erosive wear of the weapons. While this was a stiff price to pay, it was thought to be acceptable in machine-guns in order to gain the benefit of long-range accuracy; and in any case, regular barrel-changing was already an accepted fact of life in the machine-gun world. But in rifles it was unacceptable, and so the streamlined bullet was usually restricted to use in machine-guns.

The obsession with long-range performance from rifles had been founded in the early days of the 20th century by a strong lobby of long-range target shooters who, having seen their speciality put to use occasionally in the South African War, managed to give it the status of a minor religion and foist it on the military. One example of this attitude was the abortive .276in Pattern 1913 rifle proposed for the British Army. In an endeavour to produce a weapon capable of accurate fire at 2,000 yards and a practically flat trajectory out to 500 yards or more, the designers came up with a 165-grain (10.69gm) bullet propelled by 49.5 grains (3.20gm) of a particularly 'hot' cordite, a combination which produced a muzzle velocity in the region of 3,000ft/sec (985m/sec) and, with it, objectionable muzzle blast, flash and recoil, excessive erosion of the barrel, irregular ballistics, poor accuracy and severe overheating. Fortunately the outbreak of World War One gave the soldiers an excellent excuse to scrap the whole project and, of course, the war demonstrated that the service .303in rifle and its cartridge were more than adequate for the practicalities of combat.

Indeed, the war showed that the normal type of service rifle was more than enough; with the exception of snipers it was rare for a front-line soldier to fire at any range greater than 300 yards, and the ballistic potential of the cartridge was largely wasted at that range. Few people, though, appear to have assimilated this lesson, probably because it was widely held that trench warfare was an aberrant form of warfare which had been thrown up by the peculiar conditions of Flanders and northern France, and future wars would probably revert to the open combat found in South Africa, where the ability to shoot accurately to 1,000 yards had been of some value. In the case of the British, whose experience in the 1920s and 1930s was restricted to the North-West frontier of India, long-range rifle shooting still had its points.

But more than pure ballistics came into this question;

there was also the problem of hastily training wartime conscripts to handle these powerful cartridges and shoot accurately with them. The 'old' British Army prided itself on its musketry, and rightly so, but it overlooked the fact that this immaculate marksmanship was the product of long peace-time hours spent on rifle ranges (at a time when a round of rifle ammunition cost fourpence – less than 2p in today's coinage), time which could not be found under the pressures of wartime trainng.

Another problem which was never mentioned was that of actually seeing and identifying targets at extreme ranges; it was one thing to lie comfortably on a firing range and take a leisurely aim at a white six-foot square two-thirds of a mile away, but it was a far different thing to throw oneself down into a shell-hole of mud, burdened with sixty pounds of equipment and panting with exertion, to take aim at the slender figure of a man, clothed in khaki or field-grey, merging into his background and flitting among the shadows at even half that distance.

During the 1930s a group of German Army officers began to look more closely at these aspects of combat rifle shooting, and they arrived at the conclusion that the service rifle cartridge could be halved in size and power if a more realistic view were taken of the tactical requirements. Provided the rifle was accurate and lethal to about 500 yards' range, no more need to be looked for; this was all that was needed for 95 per cent of the time, and the balance could be taken care of by machine-guns or snipers using the old-style cartridge. To achieve their ends they called for a cartridge in which the bullet retained its size and lethality but in which the case and propelling charge were smaller. Over and above the tactical advantages, others would then accrue: the soldier could carry more ammunition (there was small chance of his being allowed to keep the same number of smaller rounds and thus reduce his burden), and since the cartridge would be shorter the weapons designed to use it would be more compact, since a shorter operating stroke would be neccessary for re-loading. Moreover, the smaller impulse arising from the smaller propelling charge would allow lighter weapons to be made, and would reduce the recoil and jump, and this, in turn, would make the training of recruits easier and quicker.

The Polte company of Magdeburg were given the task of designing a new cartridge to suit these requirements and they produced a totally new round with a short cartridge case and a 7mm bullet. While this gave admirable ballistics, the imminence of war argued against tooling-up for something completely new, and a modified design, using the service 7.92mm bullet, was prepared, allowing much of the manufacture to be done on existing machinery. To suit this new cartridge a new rifle, known at first as the MP43 and later as the 'Sturmgewehr or Assault Rifle, was developed (see p. 149 for further details of these weapons) and the short cartridge was off to a flying start. The Soviets followed the example, developing the short round called the 7.62mm M1943 (though the grounds for this terminology have never been publicly substantiated) and which is now known and used throughout the world as the 7.62 x 39mm cartridge.

In post-war years much development on similar lines was carried out in several countries, but old ideas die hard, especially among victors, and the British 7mm round proposed for NATO was resisted by the Americans on the ground, among others, that its long-range performance (the one feature consciously designed out of it) was insufficient. The inevitable compromise was no more than the old .30in M2 bullet in a slightly shorter case, a compromise which was neither flesh, fowl nor good red herring. But because of its NATO acceptance the 7.62 x 51mm round is another which has encompassed the world.

The next move was the reduction of calibre. This was impelled by a need to improve the 'first round hit probability', as the current catch-phrase has it. More honestly it came about because the speed of modern training, and the increasing diversity of subjects the soldier had to know, meant less time was available for instruction in rifle shooting and hence the combat results were poor. Reducing the calibre brought less recoil and less shift of the weapon on firing, so that it was hoped that hastily trained soldiers would have less trouble in keeping the rifle at its point of aim; always assuming they aimed at all. Allied with this came a variety of mechanical solutions such as multiple bullets and flechettes, all meant to spread the effect of a single shot so that should the aimed round miss, the unaimed accompaniment might save the day.

A descriptive list of the micro-calibre cartridges developed in the course of this hunt would fill a fair-sized book, but the practical result was the adoption, first by the USA and later by other armies, of the 5.56 x 45mm cartridge. The terminal effect of this small bullet was quite astonishing and many legends sprang up about its terrible wounding effect, which led, among other things, to some emotional outbursts from various humanitarian organisations which had remained silent so long as soldiers were being killed by shell fragments, grenades and full-calibre bullets, but who were somehow enraged by a small bullet doing the damage. If nothing else, this has resulted in some serious studies being made of 'wound ballistics', the nature and mechanism of the effects of the bullet upon the human body, and the past few years have seen some of the more outrageous myths put to rest. The belief that the original 5.56mm bullet was under-spun and thus became unstable on impact now seems to be discounted, and it appears that most of the damage is more attributable to bullet fragmentation than simple tumbling.

The great NATO trial of 1977–80 resulted, as most people had foreseen, in the adoption of the 5.56mm round as the new standard, though with a heavier and longer bullet than the original American round. This demanded a tighter twist of rifling to stabilise it, leading to the belief that the wounding effects would be reduced; that these effects did not appear is one reason for the sudden interest in wound ballistics and the discovery that rifling twist had less effect than had hitherto been thought.

The Soviets entered the field in the early 1970s with a 5.45mm round and weapons to suit. Early examination of a bullet showed that it had a two-part steel and lead core with a vacant space inside the point, and it was generally assumed that this empty tip would deform and turn to one side on impact, so destabilising the bullet and causing severe wounding. However, practical tests have shown that, in fact, the tip rarely deforms and the bullet, due to its balance and spin, takes a curved path through tissue, slowly turning end-over-end as it progresses. The result is a fearsome wound cavity but one usually devoid of fragmentation, which is more than can be said for the 5.56mm bullet.

Rifle and Machine-gun Ammunition

Type	Round length (mm)	Case length (mm)	Rim diameter (mm)	Bullet weight (g)	Muzzle velocity (m/sec)	Remarks
4.7 x 33 DM1 Caseless	32.80	–	7.90	3.2	930	For G11 rifle
5.45 x 39.5 Soviet	56.50	39.50	10.00	3.44	900	AK-74 rifle
5.56 x 45mm M193	57.30	44.45	9.50	3.56	975	For M16; rifling 1/178mm
5.56 x 45mm SS109	57.30	44.45	9.50	3.95	930	NATO standard; rifling 1/305mm
6mm Lee	79.00	59.69	11.38	7.25	780	
6.5 x 54mm Greek	77.50	53.60	11.43	10.32	680	Mannlicher
6.5 x 54R Dutch	77.50	53.60	13.33	10.30	740	Mannlicher
6.5 x 50SR Arisaka	75.70	50.80	12.14	9.0	762	Japanese service
6.5 x 52 Italian	76.20	52.32	11.43	10.50	700	Mannlicher-Carcano
6.5 x 55 Swedish	80.00	54.90	12.20	10.10	793	Mauser
6.5 x 58 Portuguese	81.79	57.91	11.81	10.04	610	Mauser-Verguero
7 x 43mm British	64.26	43.18	11.99	8.42	730	EM2 rifle
7.35 x 51mm Breda	75.69	51.05	11.40	8.42	760	Italian service
7.5 x 54mm French	75.95	53.59	12.24	9.07	793	Ball M1929
7.5 x 54mm Swiss	77.50	55.40	12.60	11.34	780	Schmidt-Rubin
.30 M1 Carbine	42.50	32.80	9.10	7.0	579	US service
.30 M1906	84.80	63.20	12.00	9.85	837	Ball M2
7.62 x 39mm M1943	55.80	38.65	11.30	7.97	710	Ball Type PS
7.62 x 45mm Czech	70.50	44.92	11.20	8.40	744	Ball M1952
7.62 x 51mm NATO	69.85	51.05	11.94	9.33	838	UK Ball L2A2
7.62 x 54R Soviet	76.70	53.60	14.30	9.65	870	Light Ball LPS
7.65 x 53mm Belgian	77.72	53.59	12.04	13.93	620	Ball M1889
7.65 x 53 Turkish	77.72	53.09	12.04	10.04	829	Ball M1890
.303in British	77.47	54.61	13.46	11.27	731	Ball Mk 7
7.7 x 56R Italian	76.96	56.10	13.50	11.25	620	Breda Ball
7.7 x 58 Japanese	79.50	57.60	12.11	11.73	728	Type 99 ball rimless
7.7 x 58SR Japanese	80.00	57.66	12.95	10.37	716	Japanese semi-rimmed
7.7 x 58R Japanese	77.98	56.13	13.72	11.34	716	Japanese rimmed
7.92 x 33mm German	47.75	33.00	11.94	8.10	700	'Kurz' for assault rifle
7.92 x 57 Mauser	80.50	56.80	12.00	11.53	837	German Ball SmE Lang
7.92 x 95 German	117.86	95.25	20.93	14.58	1158	PzB38, etc., anti-tank rifles
8 x 50R Lebel	74.98	48.69	15.97	12.90	732	Balle N
8 x 50R Mannlicher	76.20	50.29	14.07	15.81	620	Austrian service
8 x 56R Mannlicher	76.71	56.13	13.97	13.48	730	Hungarian M1931
8 x 58R Danish	81.28	57.91	14.55	12.70	770	Krag-Jorgensen
10.15 x 63R Serbian	79.50	62.48	15.04	22.03	488	Mauser M1878
11.15 x 60R Mauser	76.20	56.82	14.88	23.98	436	Mauser M1871
12.7 x 77 Spotting Rifle	116.50	77.00	20.30	53.60	532	Tracer M48A1
12.7 x 80SR Vickers	109.47	80.26	18.16	37.58	774	Vickers .50in machine-gun
12.7 x 99mm Browning	137.80	99.10	20.30	46.0	854	Ball M2
12.7 x 107mm Soviet	146.80	105.90	21.60	44.13	840	AP/I/T BZT44
13.2 x 99mm Breda	136.52	98.80	20.15	51.25	674	
.55in Boys	134.87	100.33	20.24	47.63	884	
13 x 92SR Mauser	133.10	91.69	23.11	51.65	792	M1918 anti-tank rifle
14.5 x 114mm Soviet	155.80	114.30	26.90	63.44	976	AP/I Type B-32
15 x 104mm Besa	147.80	103.75	24.76	75.20	884	AP W Mk 1
15.5 x 106mm BRG	175.90	106.00	26.80	78.00	1055	AP

The American Advanced Combat Rifle program has brought some old ideas back into play; the flechette was discredited in the 1970s because of its lack of accuracy, but this was principally due to defective sabot design. The thin flechette has to be supported in the barrel by a full-calibre sabot, and the early patterns were inefficient, largely due to the choice of materials. Developments in plastic materials have now produced far better substances and Steyr-Mannlicher and AAI have been able to develop flechette rounds which are far superior to earlier designs. The multiple-bullet cartridge, another child of the 1960s, has also reappeared and can be assumed to have been improved in the interval. Above all, the caseless cartridge stands upon the threshold of its military career, with its adoption in Germany and the high probability of its adoption in the USA some time in the 1990s.

Through the century the number of different cartridges which have actually been manufactured, and had weapons produced to match, runs well into four figures, and it is probable that a fair proportion of them have been fired in combat at some time or other, even if they never appeared in an official inventory. To make a complete list of all the possible cartridges would, we feel, be a waste of effort and of limited interest. There are a number of specialised books on cartridges which can be studied if details of the less common rounds are required or if more detail on service ammunition is necessary. We have, therefore, confined our attention to those cartridges in general use by the principal armies and those which were used with the weapons described in the body of the book. We have ignored the innumerable variants of the basic cartridge; there were, for example, scores of variations on the British .303in or the German 7.92mm Mauser –

Pistol and submachine-gun ammunition

Type	Round length (mm)	Case length (mm)	Rim diameter (mm)	Bullet weight (g)	Muzzle velocity (m/sec)	Remarks
5.45mm Soviet	24.9	17.8	7.55	2.6	315	For PSM pistol only
7mm Nambu	26.92	19.81	9.12	3.56	320	
7.62mm Soviet Auto	34.55	25.14	9.91	5.57	455	Type 'P'
7.62mm Soviet Revolver	38.86	38.86	9.85	7.0	285	Type 'R'
7.63mm Mauser	34.55	25.14	9.91	5.57	455	German service
7.63mm Mannlicher M1900	28.45	21.33	8.48	5.5	312	Austrian service
7.65mm Auto Colt (.32)	26.16	17.27	8.99	4.7	300	Commercial
7.65mm French Longue	30.23	19.81	8.56	5.5	365	Balle Type L
7.65mm Parabellum	29.21	21.60	9.93	6.02	368	
8mm Nambu	31.75	21.84	10.49	6.67	335	
8mm French M1e 92	36.70	27.30	10.16	7.75	265	Lebel revolver
8mm Roth-Steyr M07	28.95	18.79	9.04	7.52	332	Austrian service
8mm Rast & Gasser	36.07	26.92	9.53	7.78	240	
9mm Glisenti	29.21	19.05	9.98	7.97	320	Italian service
9mm Parabellum	29.28	19.35	9.94	7.45	396	NATO standard
9mm Bergmann-Bayard	33.53	23.11	9.95	8.75	340	
9mm Steyr	33.00	22.86	9.65	7.58	360	
9mm Browning Long	27.94	20.30	10.16	7.25	335	
9mm Browning Short	24.98	17.27	9.50	6.15	270	
9mm Makarov	24.79	17.98	9.98	6.02	340	
9mm Police	25.15	17.98	9.52	6.10	330	
9mm Japanese Revolver	30.73	21.84	10.97	9.65	228	
9mm Mauser Export	35.00	24.90	9.90	8.15	415	
.380in Revolver Mk 1	31.62	19.38	11.00	12.96	168	Lead bullet
.380in Revolver Mk 2	31.11	19.38	11.00	11.53	180	Jacketed bullet
.38in Long Colt	33.53	26.16	11.00	9.59	239	US Government
.38in Special	38.86	29.46	11.00	10.23	260	
10.4mm Bodeo	29.75	19.80	13.25	11.25	255	
10.6mm German	30.73	24.38	12.92	16.20	205	'Reichsrevolver'
.45 Auto Colt Pistol	32.19	22.79	11.86	15.16	250	
.45 Colt M1909	40.64	32.77	13.66	16.20	225	US Government
.455 Webley Revolver	31.24	19.05	13.46	15.23	176	Mk 2 lead bullet
	31.24	19.05	13.46	15.23	189	Mk 6 jacketed bullet
.455 Webley Automatic	30.99	23.11	12.70	14.51	216	Service Mk 1

incendiary, tracer, armour-piercing and many other types of bullet, changes in propellant and cap, and so on – but we do not think such fine detail is necessary here.

Propelling charges have not been quoted; these tend to vary from lot to lot because cartridges are usually loaded to produce a particular velocity and chamber pressure, and as the characteristics of the propellant change from lot to lot, so the weight will vary slightly. The muzzle velocities quoted are those of the country of origin and, where possible, from the official specification, and they are usually related to the standard weapon which fired the round and to a specific length of barrel. Different countries have different specifications and different ways of specifying their velocities, so a certain amount of variation can be found. To quote but one example, the US .30in Carbine Ball M1 in US service carries a 13-grain (0.84gm) charge, a 108-grain (7gm) bullet and has a specification velocity of 1,900ft/sec (579m/sec). The same cartridge manufactured in Britain, to the British service specification 'Cartridge, SA, .30in Carbine Ball Mk 1' carries a 15-grain (0.97gm) charge, a 111-grain (7.19gm) bullet, and is specified to achieve 1,970ft/sec (600m/sec). For all practical purposes they are interchangeable; indeed, it is doubtful if a firer, given a clip of the two types mixed together, would notice any difference. But it goes to show that differences between 'identical' cartridges do exist – and that not too much should be made of the fact.

Glossary

Before beginning any study of small arms it is as well to examine a few definitions and technical terms, so that the explanations and discussions in later sections can be more easily understood. This Glossary is concerned solely with presenting an outline of the standard concepts in small arms design and explaining how various mechanisms function. It does not purport to treat the subject in exhaustive detail, and those who wish to take their study further are advised to refer to the varous advanced texts available.

AAT Arme Automatique Transformable; French term analogous to General Purpose Machine-Gun.

Accelerator *(1)* A component of a recoil-operated weapon which delivers additional velocity to the recoiling bolt or breech-block. It is generally driven by the movement of the recoiling barrel and has a leverage advantage which enables it to deliver a higher impulse speed than it receives. *(2)* A trade name for discarding sabot small-arms ammunition manufactured by Remington.

ACP Automatic Colt Pistol. A descriptive abbreviation added after the calibre notation of certain cartridges originally devel-oped for use in Colt designs of pistol; used to distin-guish these cartridges from others of the same calibre but different dimen-sions.

ACR Advanced Combat Rifle; a US program initiated in 1982 to determine the infantry rifle/ammunition combination to be adopted in the late 1990s.

Advanced Primer Ignition A system of operation, found principally in submachine-guns, wherein the primer is struck and the cartridge fired while the bolt is still moving forward on the loading stroke. The explosion must arrest the bolt before causing it to return, thus giving a slight delay between firing and breech opening.

AUG Armee Universal Gewehr; Austrian assault rifle made by Steyr-Mannlicher which is of modular construction and can thus be configured in various barrel lengths, firing modes and tactical applications.

Automatic A weapon which will continue to load and fire so long as the trigger is pressed and there is ammunition available in the feed system.

Ball Term used to describe the standard inert bullet used with small-arms ammunition.

Ballistite A propellant formerly used for launching rifle grenades, due to its fast-burning characteristic; now obsolete, but the term 'Ballistite Cartridge' is still used occasionally to indicate a grenade-launching cartridge.

BAR Browning Automatic Rifle. A light machine rifle used as a squad automatic weapon by the US and other armies; now obsolete.

Barrel That part of a weapon through which the projectile is discharged, giving it direction.

Barrel Extension A frame attached to the barrel of a weapon, carrying the bolt and usually carrying the means of locking bolt and barrel together.

Battery The position of the barrel of a weapon when it is ready to fire; in some weapons the barrel recoils and then returns 'to battery'.

Beaten Zone That part of a bullet's flight between 'first catch' and 'first graze' *(qv)* in which it is close enough to the ground to strike a human target.

Belt Feed Method of supplying ammunition to a weapon by means of cartridges held in a flexible belt. May be of canvas or metal; may retain its form after the cartridges have been removed or may be of the 'disintegrating link' type in which the cartridges hold the belt together and it falls apart into individual links as the cartridges are removed.

Bent A notch cut in the weapon's firing pin, striker or other component, into which the sear engages to hold the component ready to fire.

Blowback System of operation in which the bolt is not locked to the barrel at the moment of firing, the cartridge being held in place solely by the inertia of the bolt. Breech pressure eventu-ally overcomes this inertia and forces the bolt back.

Blow-forward System of operation analogous to blow-back but in which the bolt is fixed and the inertia of the barrel holds the cartridge in place. Breech pressure then forces the barrel forward to open the breech.

Bolt That part of a weapon which closes the breech; it may also perform the functions of loading and extracting, and often carries the firing pin or striker.

Bolt Action Breech closure of a small arm by means of a hand-operated bolt moving in prolongation of the weapon's axis. May be a 'turnbolt' in which the bolt is pushed forward and then turned down to lock, by means of a handle; or a 'straight pull' in which the manual action is a simple to-and-fro movement and the bolt is turned and locked by cam action.

Bolt Carrier A component which supports the bolt in its movement and generally contains the means of rotating or otherwise locking it.

Bore The interior of a weapon's barrel, from the face of the bolt to the muzzle, including both the chamber and the rifled portion.

Box Magazine A method of ammunition supply in the form of a metal or plastic box, either detachable from the weapon or integral with it, below, above, or to one side of the weapon. The cartridges are held inside the box and impelled to the magazine mouth by a spring.

Breech The rear end of a gun barrel; the entrance to the chamber through which the ammunition is loaded.

Breech-block Analogous to 'bolt' in that it is a component which closes the breech; there is no rigorous rule of definition, but, in general, a bolt implies a cylindrical component which is revolved to lock, while a breech-block is generally rectangular, more massive, and locks without rotation.

Buffer A resilient component at the rear of an automatic weapon against which the bolt or breech-block comes to rest after recoil. It absorbs some of the recoil energy and assists in controlling the rate of fire. The resilience may be due to springs, rubber, oil or pneumatic media.

Bullet General term used to describe the projectiles fired by small arms.

Bullpup Colloquial term for a rifle in which the mechanism is set well back in the stock so that the end of the receiver is against the firer's shoulder. This design permits the use of a full-length barrel in a weapon which is shorter overall than one of conventional stocked shape.

Butt That part of a shoulder arm which rests against the firer's shoulder and transfers the recoil force to his body.

Calibre The diameter of the interior of a gun barrel, defined as the diameter of a cylinder which will fit inside the lands of the rifling. More commonly, the diameter as measured from the top of one land to the top of the opposite land.

Carbine A short rifle; traditionally the arm of cavalry, engineers, etc., whose primary battlefield role is not that of using a rifle but who required a self-defence weapon. More recently it implies a shorter type of assault rifle for airborne and special forces.

Cartridge A unit of ammunition, consisting of a cap, cartridge case, propelling charge and bullet. Also called a 'round' of ammunition.

Cartridge brass A mixture of 70% copper and 30% zinc from which cartridge cases are traditionally made.

Cartridge case Metal or plastic container which holds the propellant charge and the means of ignition. Can be various shapes and incorporates a design feature which enables it to be removed from the chamber.

Cartridge headspace Distance between the face of the bolt and the rear of the chamber when the breech is closed. A critical dimension, since if it is insufficient the bolt will not close and if it is too great the cartridge may set back on firing and burst.

Caseless cartridge A small-arm cartridge which dispenses with the conventional type of case and has the propellant formed into a solid mass attached to the bullet. It may or may not incorporate the means of ignition. It has the advantage of weight-saving and of removing the extraction requirement

from the operating cycle, but demands that the chamber be effectively sealed by the breech mechanism.

Chamber Enlarged-diameter section at the rear of the barrel in which the cartridge is positioned for firing.

Change lever A lever or switch which allows the firer to select single shots or automatic fire in certain types of weapon. Also called a 'selector'; may be combined with the safety catch.

Charger A metal or plastic frame in which cartridges are held and from which they can be loaded into the magazine of a weapon. The loaded charger is positioned opposite the magazine and the cartridges are swept from the charger into the magazine by thumb pressure. Common on bolt-action rifles, occasionally found on automatic pistols and rifles.

Clip A metal frame in which cartridges are held and from which they are loaded into the weapon's breech. Differs from a *charger* in that the loaded clip is inserted into the magazine, the cartridges are removed from it one at a time as they are loaded, and the empty clip is usually ejected as the last cartridge is removed. The clip forms an integral part of the feed system; without it, the weapon cannot be used. Found on bolt-action rifles, notably the Mannlicher, and on some automatic rifles, notably the Garand.

Closed bolt A weapon is said to 'fire from a closed bolt' when the bolt is closed up to the breech (but not necessarily locked) before the trigger is pulled. It has the advantage over the 'open bolt' system *(qv)* that there is no shift of mass after the trigger is pulled and the weapon is therefore generally more accurate.

Coaxial A machine-gun in a tank or other armoured vehicle turret which is parallel to the main armament and traverses and elevates in sympathy with it.

Compensator Device attached to, or forming part of, the muzzle of a weapon and which diverts some of the escaping gas upwards or to one side so as to counter the tendency of the gun muzzle to rise or swing during automatic fire.

Compound bullet A bullet built up from a heavy core surrounded by a jacket of lighter metal. The core provides the necessary density and mass, while the lighter jacket is ductile and engraves in the weapon's rifling.

Cook-off Premature ignition of the propelling charge by heat absorbed from a chamber made hot by prolonged firing.

Cycle of Operation The series of operations necessary to cause a weapon to fire one round and return to a state of readiness. May be performed by hand or by an automtic mechanism. It consists of:

  1 Chambering the round
  2 Closing and possibly locking the breech
  3 Firing
  4 Unlocking and opening the breech
  5 Extracting the spent case
  6 Ejecting the spent case
  7 Cocking the firing mechanism
  8 Feeding the next cartridge into place.

Not all these functions may be present; e.g., a blowback weapon does not perform unlocking and locking, a caseless weapon does not perform extraction and ejection, and they may not be in the order given – e.g., cocking can take place before extraction – but the entire cycle must be followed by any small arm.

Cyclic rate The theoretical rate of fire of an automatic weapon assuming a continuous and infinite supply of ammunition – i.e., disregarding the need to change magazines or belts.

Cylinder Component of a revolver which carries the individual chambers. It is held behind the barrel on an axis pin or 'arbor' and is revolved by a mechanical link to the hammer or trigger so as to present successive chambers to be fired.

Delayed Blowback A blowback (qv) weapon in which the rearward movement of the bolt is mechanically delayed for a brief period to allow the chamber pressure to drop to a level at which it is safe to open the breech.

Differential recoil In small arms, an operating system in which the recoiling mass of the weapon – the barrel and breech mechanism – is still moving forward in the counter-recoil stroke when the gun fires. The recoil force of the explosion must then arrest the forward movement and reverse it, so absorbing much of the force. It is similar to 'Advanced Primer Ignition' (qv) in effect, but is used with locked-breech weapons.

Disconnector A mechanism in self-loading weapons which disconnects the trigger from the firing mechanism after each shot. It can only be reconnected by the firer releasing the trigger. It prevents a semi-automatic weapon firing in the automatic mode. In selective-fire weapons it is thrown out of action by the selector or change-lever.

Double action A pistol firing mechanism which permits firing in either of two ways; either by manually cocking the hammer and then releasing it by trigger pressure, or by pulling through on the trigger so as to cock and release the hammer.

Double pull A trigger mechanism on selective-fire weapons in which pressing the trigger a short distance gives single shots, pressing it further, usually against an additional spring, gives automatic fire.

Double trigger Trigger mechanism on some selective-fire weapons in which two triggers are provided, one giving single shots and the other giving automatic fire.

Drum magazine A circular magazine into which cartridges are loaded axially or radially and propelled to the weapon's feed system by spring pressure or by mechanical rotation driven by the gun. The spring system is more usual, e.g., Thompson, Lahti and other submachine-guns; the mechanical system is uncommon, but was used on the Lewis machine-gun.

Dum-Dum A bullet with a soft nose which deforms easily on striking and thus causes severe wounding. So-called from the manufacture of such bullets for the British Army at Dum-Dum Arsenal in India in the 1880s. Shortly afterwards outlawed for military use. In common usage, any bullet which has been modified, as by cutting or incising the nose, so as to make it deform more easily on striking.

Duplex A cartridge containing more than one bullet.

Ejector Component of a weapon which throws the spent cartridge case clear after it has been extracted.

Explosive Bullet (1) A small-arms bullet containing a charge of explosive and intended to detonate on striking; intended for observation and range-finding purposes. Frequently called a 'Spotter' bullet. (2) By definition of the Hague Convention, 'Any bullet which expands or flattens easily in the human body.' Such bullets are proscribed for military use.

Extractor A claw-like device which removes the empty cartridge case from the chamber of a weapon and presents it to the ejector.

Feed That portion of the operating cycle of a weapon in which the cartridge is removed from the ammunition supply and loaded into the chamber.

Feedway The area of a weapon mechanism in which the cartridge is removed from the ammunition supply and aligned before loading into the chamber.

Fermeture nut System of breech locking used with some automatic weapons which has a collar around the weapon chamber with interrupted lugs. Operated by a gas piston, which gives a part-turn to the collar, this movement engages or disengages the lugs from mating lugs on the breech bolt, allowing it to be withdrawn or locked to the barrel.

Fin stabilisation A method of stabilising a projectile in flight by fins at the rear end, as with an arrow. Used with flechettes.

First Catch The point on the trajectory of a bullet when it falls close enough to the ground to strike the head of a standing man; the start of the 'Beaten Zone'.

First Graze The point on the trajectory of a bullet where it will strike the ground or a prone man; the end of the 'Beaten Zone'.

Flash eliminator Attachment to the muzzle of a weapon which cools the emergent propellant gas so that it does not cause flash or flame when meeting the outside air.

Flash Hider Muzzle attachment intended to conceal the muzzle flash from the firer so as to prevent his being dazzled when firing in poor light. It can also act as a flash eliminator but is not so efficient in this role.

Flashless Term used to classify propellant powders and signifies that firing will not produce flash, or at least not sufficient flash to be readily detected by an enemy. Flashlessness depends upon the weapon; a powder which is flashless on one weapon might not be flashless in another of different type, and each gun/cartridge combination has to be determined by trial.

Flechette A thin, fin-stabilised projectile resembling an arrow and much smaller than the bore of the weapon in which it is fired, and therefore needs to be supported in the bore by some form of sabot (qv).

Flip rearsight A rear sight consisting of two notches or apertures mounted at right-angles to each other, pivoted so that either can be upright, providing two alternative range settings.

Fluted chamber *(1)* Chamber of a small arm which has longitudinal grooves cut into most of its length and beyond the mouth of the cartridge case. On firing, a proportion of gas flows down these flutes and equalises the pressure inside the case, so preventing the case expanding and sticking tightly to the chamber walls. Usually found in blowback weapons using bottle-necked cartridge cases. *(2)* Chamber of a small arm which has a number of shallow grooves either axial or radial, which do not extend to the cartridge mouth. On firing, the case expands and these flutes offer an increased amount of friction to the rearward movement of the case which is tending to open the breech, so giving a degree of delay. *(3)* Similar to 1, but with one or two flutes extending to the mouth of the chamber so as to deliver gas to the face of the bolt and assist in bolt unlocking.

Follower *(1)* The spring-driven platform in a weapon magazine upon which the cartridges rest. *(2)* A spring or mechanically driven arm in the magazine of a clip-loaded weapon which forces the rounds up in the clip and presents them to the loading mechanism.

Furniture The parts of a weapon which are there to facilitate handling – e.g., the stock, butt, pistol grip, handguard. Traditionally of wood, but today often of plastic material.

Gas Operation Weapon in which the cycle of operation is performed by gas pressure. The gas is part of the propellant gas, tapped from the barrel through a port or regulator, and directed either against a piston or against the bolt or bolt carrier. The gas pressure causes the bolt to be unlocked and driven rearward to commence the cycle for the next shot.

GPMG General Purpose Machine-Gun. A machine-gun capable of being employed either as a bipod-mounted squad automatic weapon or as a tripod-mounted sustained-fire weapon.

Grip Safety A lever or plunger set into the grip of a weapon and which must be depressed by the firer's hand before the firing mechanism can operate. Used as an automatic safety device, preventing the weapon firing unless it is correctly held.

Grooves Spiral cuts in the bore of a weapon which form the rifling and so impart spin to the bullet. The uncut portion between the grooves are the 'lands'. The number and form of the grooves, and the degree of curvature, depend on the weapon, the ammunition, and the designer's preferences.

Hangfire An ignition failure in a cartridge which results in a delay before the charge fires. Invariably due to faulty ammunition.

Hinged frame A revolver, or occasionally an automatic pistol, in which the barrel can be hinged down about an axis pin in the frame so as to expose the cylinder or chamber for loading.

HMG Heavy Machine-Gun; implies a calibre of 12.7mm or greater.

Hold-open device A catch, usually operated by the maga-zine platform, which prevents the bolt of the weapon closing on an empty chamber after the last round in the magazine has been fired. Indicates to the firer that the weapon requires reloading.

Interchangeable barrel Barrel of a machine-gun which can be quickly removed from the gun when hot and a cold barrel substituted. The object is to reduce wear, since a hot barrel wears more quickly than a cool one, and by changing the barrel at frequent intervals overheating is avoided.

Jump The vertical movement of a gun barrel at the instant of firing. It is related to the rigidity and mounting of the barrel and is not generated by recoil; it is a constant value for any given charge and projectile combination and can be compensated for in the sights.

Knoxform That part of the barrel of a small arm (principally a rifle) which is formed externally with flat surfaces so that a spanner can be used to screw the barrel into the receiver, and so proportioned that by matching one flat with an index mark on the receiver, the gun sight is vertical. A corruption from 'Nock's Form', after Nock, the English gunsmith who invented the idea.

Lands The interior surface of a gun barrel between the grooves.

Lead (pronounced 'leed'). The conical front end of the chamber of a small arm which directs the bullet into the rifling.

Lead (pronounced 'led'). Metal used in the manufacture of small arms bullets and bullet cores. Usually mixed with a small amount of antimony to give the correct hardness.

Lead fouling A deposit of lead left in the rifling grooves of a firearm after prolonged firing of lead bullets. Eventually has a deleterious effect upon accuracy if not removed and is the reason for the adoption of jacketed compound bullets.

Lead shaving Term referring to a condition arising when the chamber of a revolver is not perfectly aligned behind the barrel. As the bullet passes from the chamber to the barrel, one side will strike the edge of the barrel which will 'shave' a thin layer of metal from the bullet. This affects balance and therefore accuracy; the metal shaving also tends to jam the revolver mechanism.

LMG Light Machine-Gun; abbreviation generally used to describe the infantry squad automatic weapon. A machine-gun capable of being carried and operated by one man.

Locked Breech Blowback Weapon operating system in which the breech is unlocked by gas or recoil action but the rearward movement of the bolt is caused by blowback action of the spent case. Uncommon; used in some Fiat and Breda machine-guns and some 20mm cannon.

Locking flaps Method of breech locking in which metal plates or flaps are forced outwards from the bolt to engage in recesses in the receiver.

Lock Time The interval between applying the firing impulse –e.g., pulling the trigger – and the ejection of the bullet from the muzzle. Is shortest in closed bolt weapons where the firing pin or hammer is cocked and merely needs to be released, longest in open bolt weapons where the bolt must move forward and chamber the cartridge before firing can take place.

Long Recoil System of operating an automatic weapon in which barrel and bolt recoil, locked together, for a distance greater than the length of a complete cartridge. The bolt is then unlocked and held, while the barrel runs forward again, so opening the breech. During this movement the empty case is extracted and ejected. After the barrel has stopped moving the bolt is released, to run forward, load a round and lock to the barrel ready for firing. The long movement tends to absorb much of the recoil force.

LSW Light Support Weapon. Contemporary term for a squad automatic weapon or light machine-gun.

Machine-gun An automatic firearm capable of delivering continuous fire.

Machine Pistol Ambiguous term which can mean either a self-loading pistol modified to deliver automatic fire, or a submachine-gun.

Machine Rifle Obsolescent term used to describe a heavy-barrelled automatic rifle capable of being used as a light machine-gun. It differs from a 'true' machine-gun in not having an interchangeable barrel and being based directly upon an existing automatic rifle design.

Magazine A feed system for a firearm in which cartridges are stored in an integral or attachable carrier, from which they are fed into the weapon by spring or other agency.

Magazine Safety A safety device used in pistols which interrupts the firing mechanism when the magazine is removed. Prevents the accidental firing of a round inadvertently left in the chamber.

Misfire Total failure of a propelling charge to ignite. Often due to defective ammunition but can also be due to mechanical defects in the weapon.

MMG Medium Machine-Gun; a machine-gun of rifle calibre, capable of sustained fire for long periods; usually water-cooled.

MRBF Mean Rounds Between Failures. The average number of rounds a weapon can be expected to fire before a major defect occurs.

Muzzle The front end of the gun barrel, from which the projectile emerges.

Muzzle brake A device fitted to the muzzle of a weapon and designed to deflect some of the emergent gas and direct it against surfaces so as to produce a pull on the muzzle and thus reduce the recoil force. Not widely used on small arms, since the gas diverts sideways and increases the blast and noise level to the firer and his companions.

Muzzle velocity The speed at which the bullet leaves the muzzle of the gun. Also referred to as 'Vo', the Velocity at zero distance from the weapon.

Non-ramming Breech-block Term used to describe breech closing systems which do not reciprocate and therefore cannot load the cartridge into the chamber. Rarely found today, but the most common examples were the Martini rifle action and the Madsen machine-gun. Most recently used with the US M73 tank machine-gun, which had a horizontal sliding breech-block.

Open bolt A weapon is said to fire 'from an open bolt' when the bolt is held back until released by the trigger. This means that the barrel and chamber are empty when the trigger is engaged, and allows the weapon to cool down between shots. The disadvantage is that the balance of the weapon changes as the bolt moves forward, leading to a possible lack of accuracy. For this reason some selective-fire weapons are designed to fire from a closed bolt in single-shot fire, from an open bolt in automatic fire.

Parabellum Descriptive term used for weapons and ammunition developed by the Deutsche Waffen-und Munitionsfabrik, Berlin; derives from their telegraphic address 'Parabellum Berlin'.

Primary Extraction The first movement of extracting the spent cartridge case which takes place as the bolt is being unlocked. It is usually slow and powerful and moves the case a very small amount, freeing it for the much faster secondary extraction stroke which removes it from the chamber. When primary extraction is not incorporated in a weapon's design (as on some blowback weapons) its absence can lead to ruptured cases unless lubrication or a fluted chamber are used.

Primer Or 'primer cap'. The sensitive component in the base of the cartridge which, when struck by the firing pin, explodes and ignites the propellant charge inside the cartridge case. Can also be electrically initiated, though this is rare in small arms.

Propellant Explosive used to generate gas and so drive the bullet from the weapon. Usually based on nitro-cellulose, though nitro-glycerin and nitro-guanidine are often incorporated. Found in a wide variety of shapes and sizes, selected to control the rate of burning to suit different weapons.

Rebated rimless Type of cartridge case in which the extraction rim is considerably smaller than the base of the cartridge case. Used in weapons where it is necessary completely to enclose the case in the chamber but still have it held by the bolt, and also in order to allow a large case to be manipulated by a standard-size bolt face.

Receiver The body of a weapon; the casing inside which the bolt operates and to which the magazine and barrel are attached.

Recoil Rearward movement of the barrel or weapon due to reaction against the forward ejection of the bullet.

Recoil Intensifier A device attached to the muzzle of a recoil-operated weapon which resists the emergent gas and thus makes the rearward movement more positive and provides a reserve of power to overcome friction due to dirt or lack of lubrication.

GLOSSARY

Recoil Operated A weapon in which the cycle of operation is performed by power derived from the recoil movement of the barrel. The barrel and bolt recoil locked together long enough to allow the chamber pressure to drop. The barrel is then halted and the bolt unlocked and allowed to continue rearwards to complete the cycle. When the bolt has returned and chambered the cartridge, barrel and bolt then run forward into battery, locked together as they do so.

Regulator Device on a gas-operated weapon which controls the amount of gas fed to the gas piston; generally adjustable to permit more gas to flow so as to overcome friction due to dirt or fouling during long actions. Can also be shut off to permit all the propellant gas to be directed up the barrel for launching grenades from the muzzle.

Return spring Spring in an automatic or self-loading weapon which cushions the rearward movement of the bolt and returns it to the foward position.

Revolver Weapon in which the supply of ammunition is carried in a rotating cylinder behind the barrel, the cylinder being moved round so as to present the cartridges in succession to the barrel. Also used to describe a machine-gun in which a cylindrical mechanism removes cartridges from the belt and rotates to align them with the breech.

Rifling Spiral grooves cut into the interior of a gun barrel so as to spin the bullet and thus impart gyroscopic stabilisation to it. The degree of curvature depends upon the weight and length of the bullet fired from the weapon.

Rimless Type of cartridge case in which there is an extraction groove cut in the head, so that the rim upon which the extractor grips is of the same diameter as the head of the case.

Rimmed Type of cartridge case in which the head is shaped into an upstanding rim which can be gripped by the extractor, and which butts against the chamber face so as to position the cartridge correctly in the chamber.

Sear Part of the firing mechanism of a weapon, linked to the trigger, which engages in the *bent* on the striker, firing pin, hammer or bolt, and which is withdrawn from engagement to fire the weapon.

Selective fire Descriptive of a weapon which, at the firer's choice, can be set to fire single shots, automatic fire or specific-length burst, according to its mechanism.

Self-cooking A firing mechanism on pistols in which the striker or hammer is cocked and then released by the operation of the trigger.

Self-loading A firearm which, for a single pressure of the trigger, fires a round and then reloads. The trigger must be released and pressed again to fire another round.

Semi-automatic Weapon which fires one round, re-loads, and requires another pressure on the trigger to fire again. Synonymous with 'self-loading.'

Short recoil Another term for recoil operation, sometimes used to distinguish it from 'long recoil' operation.

Silencer Device attached to the barrel of a weapon and which traps the emergent gas and forces it to pass round a series of baffles, cooling it and thus reducing its volume, so that it emerges at low speed and does not, therefore, make much noise. The silencer also has holes bored in the gun barrel so as to bleed off propellant gas behind the bullet and reduce its speed to below that of sound, so avoiding a sonic crack due to the bullet's fight.

Sound suppressor Similar to a silencer insofar as it baffles the emergent gas, but does not bleed gas from behind the bullet. Therefore it only silences the muzzle discharge and not the bullet's sonic wave. If used with subsonic ammunition is effectively a silencer.

Submachine-gun Pistol-calibre selective-fire or automatic weapon, magazine fed, fired from the shoulder or hip, used for close-range combat.

Tilting block Method of breech locking in which the breech-block is raised, dropped or slewed so as to lock into a recess in the top, bottom or side of the receiver.

Toggle lock Method of breech locking which uses a hinged arm, the hinge moving past the dead centre position to form a rigid strut. It is then moved back, so as to become a flexible member, by recoil action. Most common use was in the Maxim machine-gun and the Parabellum (Luger) pistol.

Vertex The highest point of the bullet's trajectory.

Windage Adjustment of a weapon sight to right or left to compensate the effect of a cross-wind on the bullet.

Zeroing The adjustment of a weapon sight so that the bullet will strike the point of aim at some specified distance. Once this has been achieved the sight's adjusting mechanism will automatically provide the compensation required to make the bullet and sight line coincide at other ranges.

Index

7.62mm PK Family

7.62 × 39mm M1943	
Length overall	1,160mm (45.67in)
Weight empty	9.0kg (19.84lb)
Barrel	658mm (25.90in), 4 grooves, rh
Feed system	100-, 200- or 250-shot belt
Rate of fire	710rds/min
Muzzle velocity	825m/sec (2,706ft/sec)

The PK family introduced the first truly general-purpose Soviet machine-gun. It replaced the RP46 and uses the same rimmed 7.62mm full-power cartridge; in this respect it is remarkably old-fashioned since the round dates back to 1891 and the rim gives rise to feed complications. Presumably there is a quantity of manufacturing capacity devoted to this cartridge, making it an economic proposition, and the additional power of this round certainly gives it a greater battlefield range than the intermediate M1943 round, a useful property for a company support weapon. The mechanism is a clever combination of the AK rifle's rotating bolt, the Goryunov's cartridge feed and quick-change barrel, the belt drive mechanism of the Czech vz52 and the trigger from the DP. The gas regulator can be adjusted without tools and the weight is low. There are a number of versions in existence; data table refers to the PK.

PK is the basic gun, with a heavy fluted barrel, feed cover from both stamped and machined components, and a plain butt plate.

PKS is the basic gun tripod-mounted.

PKT. The PK altered for coaxial installation in armoured vehicles. The sights, butt, bipod and trigger mechanism are removed, a longer and heavier barrel fitted, and a solenoid trigger unit attached to the backplate.

PKM. An improved PK with a lighter, unfluted, barrel, the feed cover wholly made from stampings, and a hinged shoulder strap fitted to the buttplate. The weight is reduced to about 8.4kg.

PKMS. The PKM mounted on a tripod.

PKMB. The PKM with the bipod, butt and trigger mechanism removed and spade grips and a thumb-trigger fitted to the backplate.

5.45mm RPK74

5.45 × 39mm M1974	

Just as the RPK was the light squad automatic version of the AK, so the RPK74 is the squad automatic version of the AK74 rifle. It took longer to be recognised in the West and it was not until the middle of 1980 that identification was certain. It follows exactly the same line of development as with the RPK and is simply a heavy-barrelled AK74 fitted with a light bipod. All indications are that the furniture is the same and quite probably most of the parts are interchangeable with the rifle. The unusual muzzle brake/compensator of the rifle is not fitted, though there is a very short open-prong flash hider. No dimensions are available but it appears that the barrel is about 60 per cent longer than that of the rifle.

PKT

PKM